UNLAWFUL INTERFERENCE WITH LAND

AUSTRALIA
Law Book Co.
Sydney

CANADA and USA
Carswell
Toronto

HONG KONG
Sweet & Maxwell Asia

NEW ZEALAND
Brookers
Wellington

SINGAPORE and MALAYSIA
Sweet & Maxwell Asia
Singapore and Kuala Lumpur

UNLAWFUL INTERFERENCE WITH LAND

by

DAVID ELVIN, Q.C.
B.A. (Oxon), BCL, Barrister

and

JONATHAN KARAS
M.A. (Oxon), Barrister

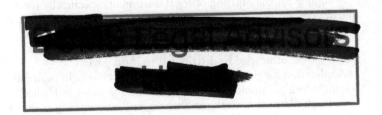

LONDON
SWEET & MAXWELL
2002

First edition 1995

Published in 2002 by
Sweet & Maxwell Limited
100 Avenue Road
London NW3 3PF
Typeset by J&L Composition Ltd, Filey, North Yorkshire
Printed in Great Britain by MPG Books Ltd, Bodmin

No natural forests were destroyed to make this product:
only farmed timber was used and replanted

A CIP catalogue record for this book is
available from the British Library

ISBN 0421 727306

TO OUR WIVES AND FAMILIES

FOREWORD
by the Right Honourable Lord Justice Carnwath, CVO

I am delighted to be able to welcome a new edition of this important work. As I wrote in the Foreword to the first edition, some seven years ago –

> "In modern times, the interaction of public and private law has become of increasing importance ... the traditional law of trespass and nuisance must now be seen as part of a comprehensive framework, embracing common law and statute, civil and criminal remedies, and public and private enforcement agencies. This interaction may take the form of the strenghtening or emasculation of private law remedies by statute in the interest of some public policy objective ... or the creation of new remedies enforceable by public authorities, alongside those in private law ..."

That interation between public and private law has continued to develop. The Human Rights Act 1998 has been at the forefront of the changes. The difficult questions which it raises in terms of its interaction with traditional concepts of property rights, and the effect on the exercise of the courts' own powers, is the subject of frequent reference to the courts. I am pleased to see that the book's treatment of public law defences has been expanded to encompass Convention issues.

There have been other important developments. For example, the Land Registration Act 2002, the product of a major study by the Law Commission in collaboration with the Land Registry, will transform the law of limitation and adverse possession, meeting the criticisms in *J. A. Pye (Oxford) Ltd v. Graham*, that the old law had outlived its purpose and was out of step with a modern, rights-based approach. The Countryside and Rights of Way Act 2000 creates important new rights for those wishing to have access to roam the countryside and new remedies which may be used by those wishing to protect their occupation of property by the Protection from Harassment Act 1997. These new developments, and many others, receive detailed and authoritative discussion in this new edition, which will be of interest and assistance to practitioners and students alike.

Robert Carnwath
RCJ
August, 2002

PREFACE TO SECOND EDITION

The text of the first edition of this book was completed in August 1995, since then there have been numerous developments of importance in the law relating to interference with real property rights. These include not only significant cases and statutes, such as *Manchester Airport Plc. v. Dutton, Lloyds Bank v. Carrick, D.P.P. v. Jones, J A Pye (Oxford) Ltd v. Graham, Trustees of Dennis Rye Pension Fund v. Sheffield City Council, Poplar Housing & Regeneration Community Association Ltd v. Donoghue, London Borough of Lambeth v. Howard, London Borough of Wandsworth v. Michalak, Southwark LBC v. Mills, Pemberton v. Southwark LBC* and *Holbeck Hall Hotel v. Scarborough BC*, the Countryside and Rights of Way Act 2000 and the Land Registration Act 2002, but also procedural reforms initiated by Lord Woolf with the newly minted CPR Part 55 being of prime importance. The public law aspects of property have continued to develop, with the Human Rights Act 1998 standing as the single most important advance, bringing with it interesting (and as yet unresolved) questions as to the limits of the effects of that Act given that the Court is itself a "public authority" within section 6 of the Act. At a late stage in the production of this edition, the Land Registration Act 2002 received the Royal Assent introducing important reforms including a major revision to the law relating to adverse possession and limitation of actions. The text assumes the 2002 Act is in force although much of the delegated legislation is not yet available.

As with the first edition, we are indebted to a number of people for their support and assistance, not least to our families who have had to endure our undergoing the writing process again. More particularly, we would like to thank the staff at Sweet and Maxwell for their patience, and, more specifically, Tim Buley, Alex Cooke, Andrew Walklate, and Tiffany Scott for assistance with research and proof reading. We also wish to thank Lord Justice Carnwath for undertaking the Foreword for a second time.

The law is stated as at April 2, 2002, although we have included, where possible, later developments, including the judgment of the House of Lords in *J.A. Pye (Oxford) Ltd. v. Graham* delivered on July 4, 2002.

David Elvin, Q.C.
4 Bream's Buildings

Jonathan Karas
Wilberforce Chambers

Contents

Table of Cases

(References are to paragraph numbers)

Table of Statutes

(References are to paragraph numbers)

Table of Statutory Instruments

Table of Civil Procedure Rules

Table of Practice Directions

Table of European Legislation

Introduction

There is no single principle in English law by which it can be decided when a person may and when he may not interfere with land occupied by another or that other's enjoyment of his land. This is perhaps not surprising when one considers the diversity of behaviour which may result in an interference with land and the different modes of enjoyment of land.

The principles by which the private law of England and Wales gives remedies to those who have suffered an interference with their enjoyment of land have as much to do with the old forms of action and more recent piecemeal attempts by Parliament to protect residential occupiers than with any all-embracing system of categorising interferences and deciding whether the private citizen whose enjoyment of land has been interrupted should have a remedy.

As with other areas of the Common Law, however, the legacy of the old forms of action and the absence of an apparent scheme has not hampered the law developing in such a way that most unreasonable interferences with private occupation of land can now be remedied by action by the private citizen if that citizen has a legal interest in the land in question.[1]

Private law has developed a number of means of protecting interests in land. There are the torts of trespass and private nuisance as well as remedies for breaches of agreements and covenants relating to land: these topics are considered in the first four chapters of this book. Additionally, there are now many statutes which give remedies for interference with occupation and rights in land which are closely connected with the common law causes of action considered in Chapters One to Three: the principal statutory provisions amongst these are discussed in the final chapter.

The purpose of this book is to provide a guide to the multiplicity of causes of action, both at common law and under statute, which may be available to an occupier of land, or the owner of some interest in land, as a result of the principles which have evolved for his protection. These causes of action generally depend upon the claimant who has suffered an interference with his enjoyment of land having some interest in the land or at least a better interest than the defendant responsible for the interference.

---

[1] See, for instance, *Manchester Airport plc v. Dutton* [2000] 1 Q.B. 133; and see 1–013 below.

Historically, the majority of the legal remedies considered in the first four chapters are closely tied in with the development of the old action of trespass and the related actions on the case. These provide not only the forbears of modern trespass itself but also much of modern tort law and contract law. None of the modern remedies for interference with possession of land or interests in land stems directly from the oldest common law actions for the protection of title, such as the writ of right and the later possessory assizes (*e.g.* novel disseisin) introduced during the reign of Henry II. In time these became so bogged down in arcane and ancient machinery and procedure that litigants gradually turned to the more flexible actions on the case.[2] The principle remedy for unlawful occupation of land, the modern action for the recovery of land, now given effect to by the procedures found mainly in CPR. Part 55, is the current version of the old action for ejectment which was developed as a remedy for tenants who were unable to use the old common law actions.[3]

This book, however, is not intended to be an historically-based work (although historical matters inevitably raise their heads from time to time) but one which is unified only in the practical sense by our aim of providing a reasonably comprehensive guide to the principal forms of interference with land and interests in land, and the remedies for such interference.

It has long been recognised that private law is not necessarily the most effective way of providing controls for the environment and a system of planning for the country as a whole. The crime of public nuisance, the Public Health and Control of Pollution Acts, the Building Acts, the Town and Country Planning Acts, Housing Acts, and the Environmental Protection Act have all provided methods by which the public interest may be protected by regulating the use and enjoyment of land and penalising abuses.

Public law, however, does not necessarily provide an adequate mechanism for redressing commercial disputes or all disputes between neighbours or landlords and tenants and it is inevitable the private law will remain an important, if not the most important, method by which individuals and commercial entities vindicate or protect their rights to enjoy property. For example, although the planning system regulates, in the public interest, the use and development of land, it generally does so by considering only the broader public interest and does not consider the specific position, or the presence or absence of legal rights, of the particular occupiers[4] — such as any diminution which they would suffer in the value of their property as the result of a particular development.

---

[2] See, *e.g.* Maitland, *The Forms of Action at Common Law*; Sutherland, *The Assize of Novel Disseisin* (1973), especially Chap. V ("Trespass Takes Over"); Simpson, *The History of the Land Law* (2nd ed.) pp. 144–151; Milsom, *Historical Foundations of the Common Law* (2nd ed.) Chap. 6, 7, 11 & 13; and Baker, *An Introduction to English Legal History* (3rd ed.) pp. 262–271, 341–343 and Chap. 23.

[3] *Manchester Airport plc v. Dutton* [2000] 1 Q.B. 133.

[4] See, *e.g. Stringer v. Ministry of Housing and Local Government* [1970] 1 W.L.R. 1281 and *Brewer v. Secretary of State for the Environment* [1988] 2 P.L.R. 13 (absence of rights of light held to be an irrelevant consideration in determining a planning appeal).

Apart from public law regulation, it has been a sign of legal development in the last hundred years or so that much of what has been developed by the courts in the evolution of common law remedies has been increasingly altered by the intervention of Parliament. One of the more controversial provisions of recent years was provided by the Criminal Justice and Public Order Act 1994 which provided far-reaching incursions into areas which are principally the preserve of trepass. As a result of that Act it finally became correct to state that "trespassers will be prosecuted."

Statutory intervention aimed at protecting the environment, which overlaps with the subject-matter of the private law of nuisance, is far less controversial — as in the case of the Environmental Protection Act 1990. Part III of the Act carries forward, and strengthens, a variety of controls over nuisances (referred to as "statutory nuisances")[5] and has the benefit of public law enforcement and criminal sanctions — even though, in a number of cases, what is an actionable statutory nuisance may also be the subject of a private law nuisance action.

A more recent and potentially far-reaching development has been the Human Rights Act 1998. However, despite many predictions to the contrary, it has not heralded a state of widespread revisionism but has seen the Courts adopt a measured approach to considering the effect of the European Convention on Human Rights on existing law. Of interest in the areas covered by this book is the extent to which the duties imposed on public authorities not to act incompatibly with Convention Rights[6] apply in the wider context of private property rights where the public authority in question, namely the Court[7] is being asked to exercise its own powers and those powers in turn may impact on Convention Rights. Where one of the parties is a public authority, there is clear authority that the 1998 Act applies.[8] However, the question of the Act's application to wholly private parties remains an open one for the present,[9] although the words of Sedley L.J. in *London Borough of Lambeth v. Howard*[10] (albeit in the context of a local authority landlord) suggest the potential for a wider approach:

> ". . . any attempt to evict a person, whether directly or by process of law, from his or her home would on the face of it be a derogation from the respect, that is the integrity, to which the home is prima facie entitled."

Whilst we have had to draw a line somewhere, we have included within the Appendices what we hope will be most useful statutory extracts and rules.

---

[5] See Chapter 5.

[6] See section 6(1) of the 1998 Act.

[7] See section 6(3) of the 1998 Act.

[8] *Poplar Housing & Regeneration Community Association Ltd v. Donoghue* [2001] 3 W.L.R. 183, CA, *London Borough of Lambeth v. Howard* (2001) 33 H.L.R. 458, CA, and *McLellan v. Bracknell R (on the application of McLellan) v. Bracknell Forest B.C.* [2002] 1 All E.R. 899, CA.

[9] See Chapter 1 at 1–127 to 1–135 and Chapter 4 at 4–104 and 4–113, below.

[10] Above, at paras 30–32.

Chapter One

Trespass

Abstulerat totam temerarius institor urbem
inque suo nullum limine limen erat
[Martial, Epigrams, LXI]

Introduction and definitions

In Blackstone's words:[1]

> "Every unwarrantable entry on another's soil the law entitles a
> trespass by breaking his close; the words of the writ of trespass
> commanding the defendant to show cause *quare clausum* querentis
> *fregit*. For every man's land is in the eye of the law inclosed and set
> apart from his neighbour's; and that either by a visible and material
> fence, as one field is divided from another by a hedge; or by an ideal
> invisible boundary, existing only in the contemplation of the law, as
> when one man's land adjoins another's in the same field."

Trespass is one of the oldest of the causes of action to provide civil remedies
for (amongst other wrongs) the unlawful interference with land.[2] The early
forms of trespass *vi et armis*, and the related action on the case,[3] form the
basis of much of the modern law of contract and tort in addition to providing the foundation of the narrower topic of trespass to land.[4] In its modern
form, trespass to land is the unwarranted intrusion upon land and interference with certain interests in land in the possession of, or belonging to,
another. That intrusion may take the form of entry onto the land itself by
foot or by vehicle or other means,[5] or by the depositing, throwing or

---

[1] *Bl.Com.*, Vol. 3, pp. 209–210.
[2] On the introduction of criminal remedies into this traditionally civil area of the law, see
below, para. 5–058.
[3] See Milsom (1958) 74 L.Q.R. 195, 407 and 561 and *Historical Foundations of the Common Law*
(2nd ed.), pp. 283–313.
[4] Maitland, *The Forms of Action at Common Law*, esp. Lectures V, VI and VII; *Milsom, op. cit.*
and Sutherland, *The Assize of Novel Disseisin*, Ch. V. See also the discussion in *Manchester
Airport Plc. v. Dutton* [2000] 1 Q.B. 133, CA, below.
[5] *Blundell v. Catterall* (1821) 5 B. & Ald. 268.

discharging on the land of material or water.[6] Trespass may also consist in the erecting of structures[7] without permission, failing to remove items originally lawfully on the land once the authority to remain has ended,[8] entering the airspace above property[9] taking possession,[10] or removing or taking possession of minerals from beneath the land.[11] Although trespass is not available to remedy the infringement of easements[12] it does lie to protect many varieties of interest in land, including structures placed on land, materials in the soil, fishing rights and other *profits à prendre*.[13]

1–002   The historical antecedents of trespass provide the source not only for one of the action's main limitations, namely that it lies only to remedy cases of direct interference, but also for one of its advantages, in that the action lies without proof of damage, *i.e.* it is actionable *per se*.[14] The principle remedy for dispossession by trespass is the action for the recovery of land (the modern equivalent of the older action of ejectment).[15] Other lesser forms of trespass to land, and to interests in and on land, can be remedied by injunction and (where loss is shown) damages. In exceptional cases, exemplary or aggravated damages may be awarded.[16] Self-help also has a role to play, although its survival may be seen as anachronistic and increasingly inconsistent with modern legal procedure and may conflict with fundamental rights under the European Convention on Human Rights protected by the Human Rights Act 1998.[17]

Who may sue

The general position — protection of possession

1–003   Trespass is, in essence, a remedy for the infringement of possession and, accordingly, to sue in trespass a claimant must have been in actual

---

[6] *Hurdman v. North Eastern Railway Co.* (1878) 3 C.P.D. 168, *Whalley v. Lancashire & Yorkshire Railway Co.* (1884) 13 Q.B.D. 131, *Ponting v. Noakes* [1894] 2 Q.B. 281 and *Rigby v. Chief Constable of Northamptonshire* [1985] 1 W.L.R. 1242.

[7] *e.g. Holmes v. Wilson* (1839) 10 A. & E. 503 and *Sussex Investments Ltd v. Jackson, The Times*, July 29, 1993, CA (the placing of gangplanks from houseboats on the Thames onto a towpath on the river bank).

[8] *Konskier v. B. Goodman Ltd* [1928] 1 K.B. 421, CA.

[9] *Bernstein (Baron) v. Skyviews & General Ltd* [1978] 1 Q.B. 485 and *Anchor Brewhouse Developments Ltd v. Berkley House (Docklands Developments) Ltd* [1987] 2 E.G.L.R. 173.

[10] *Murray v. Hall* (1849) 7 C.B. 441 (eviction by tenant in common); *Watson v. Gray* (1880) 14 Ch.D. 192; *Watson v. Murray & Co.* [1955] 2 Q.B. 1 (exclusion of debtor by sheriff's officer); *McPhail v. Persons Unknown* [1973] Ch. 447 (squatters). This category includes an unlawful eviction of a tenant by a landlord: see, *e.g. Guppys (Bridport) v. Brookling & James* (1983) 269 E.G. 846 and 942 and below, para. 4–026.

[11] *Dartmouth v. Spittle* (1871) 19 W.R. 444, *Low Moor Co. v. Stanley Coal Co. Ltd* (1875) 33 L.T. 436 and (1876) 34 L.T. 186, *Eardley v. Granville* (1876) 3 Ch.D. 826.

[12] See below, para. 1–033.

[13] See below, paras. 1–017 to 1–034.

[14] *Woollerton & Wilson Ltd v. Richard Costain Ltd* [1970] 1 W.L.R. 411 and *Stoke-on-Trent City Council v. W. & J. Wass Ltd* [1988] 1 W.L.R. 1406 at 1410–1411.

[15] See below, paras. 4–057 to 4–083.

[16] See below, paras. 4–023 to 4–030.

[17] See, further, below at 1–139 to 1–147 and 4–105 to 4–122.

possession at the time of the infringement (or be deemed to have been in possession by relation back — see paragraph 1–004 below). For example, whilst a freeholder in possession may bring an action in trespass, if he lets the land to a tenant he thereby parts with possession of it and, other than in exceptional cases,[18] loses the entitlement to sue in trespass. In general, trespass does not protect real property interests *per se* except where they are supported by possession. Conversely, possession itself carries the right to bring an action in trespass even where no better right to the land exists and may arise now even in the case of non-exclusive licenses.[19]

In *J. A. Pye (Oxford) Ltd. v. Graham*, Lord Hope explained the common law concept of possession as follows[19A]:

> "The general rule, which English law has derived from the Roman law, is that only one person can be in possession at any one time. Exclusivity is of the essence of possession. The same rule applies in cases where two or more persons are entitled to the enjoyment of property simultaneously. As between themselves they have separate rights, but as against everyone else they are in the position of a single owner. Once possession has begun, as in the case of the owner of land with a paper title who has entered into occupation of it, his possession is presumed to continue. But it can be transferred from one person to another, and it can also be lost when it is given up or discontinued. When that happens, possession can be acquired by someone else."

It appears that a plaintiff need prove only that he was in possession prior to the defendant in order to demonstrate title against the defendant,[20] *i.e.* prove relative title, more recent than the defendant's. In these circumstances, it is said that the fact that a third party has better title than the plaintiff (*ius tertii*) is no defence to the trespassing defendant.[21] However, a trespasser who has ousted another from possession may not take advantage of the general rule against setting up a *ius tertii*: in that case the trespasser is not considered as having entered into possession at all. The person who was originally ousted is the person lawfully entitled to possession.

Persons immediately entitled to possession

Introduction and relation back

Since, historically, trespass has been concerned with the protection of actual possession and not of real property interests themselves (unless **1–004**

---

[18] See below, paras. 1–009 to 1–010.
[19] *Manchester Airport Plc. v. Dutton* [2000] 1 Q.B. 133, C.A. See 1–013, below.
[19A] [2002] 3 W.L.R. 221, HL, at para. 70. See, further, in connection with adverse possession at paras 1–096 to 1–100 below.
[20] *Asher v. Whitlock* (1865) L.R. 1 Q.B. 1.
[21] See below, paras. 1–094 and 1–095.

coupled with possession), a person who is entitled to possession appears to be in a difficult position where he does not have actual possession to enable him to bring an action in trespass. However, the development of the principle of trespass by relation has, in practice, removed this problem by treating the immediate entitlement to possession as actual possession. Accordingly, the modern law protects not only actual possession but the immediate entitlement to possession.

Where a person who is entitled to possession of land enters (whether actually or by acts deemed to be entry) upon that land, he thereby acquires lawful possession of it and may, thereafter, sue in trespass against any persons unlawfully in possession. The courts have treated the actual entry as relating back to the date when the owner became entitled to possession, thus allowing a landowner to sue in respect of trespasses which have occurred before the actual entry into possession but after his entitlement to it arose. A person who wrongfully enters after such entitlement has arisen becomes, on the landowner's entry, a trespasser by relation.[22] Similarly, the vesting of possession in a mortgagee relates back to the date when the right to possession arose (generally the date of execution of the mortgage deed)[23] and such mortgagee may bring trespass against any person who has unlawfully occupied the mortgaged premises since his entitlement commenced.[24]

What amounts to entry

(1) Actual entry

1–005 In practice it is not difficult for a person entitled to possession to prove actual entry onto land. Indeed, the act constituting entry need be so slight[25] that its execution may be little more than symbolic. Any crossing of the boundary to the land (even the presence of a part of the body will suffice), whether by the person entitled to possession or his agent,[26] is a sufficient act of entry to vest possession in the person entitled. Prior to that entry, the person in actual possession may have been able to maintain trespass against strangers based on nothing more that the fact of his possession.[27] However, the entry of the person entitled to possession vests possession in that person and puts an end to the precarious possession of the occupier, notwithstanding that he remains in occupation after entry by the lawful owner.[28]

---

[22] *Barnet v. Earl of Guildford* (1855) 11 Exch. 19.
[23] *Four-Maids Ltd v. Dudley Marshall (Properties) Ltd* [1957] Ch. 317 at 320 and *Fisher and Lightwood's Law of Mortgage* (10th ed.), pp. 331–334.
[24] *Ocean Accident & Guarantee Corporation v. Ilford Gas Co.* [1905] 2 K.B. 493, HL.
[25] *Ocean Estates Ltd v. Norman Pinder* [1969] 2 A.C. 19, H.L., at 25 (*per* Lord Diplock).
[26] See *Ocean Accident*, above.
[27] See above, para. 1–003.
[28] *Jones v. Chapman* (1847) 2 Exch. 803, 821 and *Lows v. Telford* (1876) 1 App.Cas. 414, 416.

Under section 149(2) of the Law of Property Act 1925 all terms of years absolute shall "be capable of taking effect in law or in equity from the date fixed for commencement of the term, without actual entry."[29] In accordance with the decision in *Walsh v. Lonsdale*,[30] an agreement for a lease is regarded in equity as equivalent to the grant of a lease provided that specific performance of the agreement would be available. The tenant under such an agreement may accordingly bring an action for trespass after the date specified in the agreement for the commencement of the term or tenancy since, from that date, he is regarded in equity as the tenant and entitled to possession. In *Lowther v. Heaver*,[31] Cotton L.J. stated:

> "... a tenant holding under an agreement for a lease of which specific performance would be decreed stands now in the same position as if the lease had been granted. He is entitled only in equity it is true to a lease, but being entitled in equity to have a lease granted, his rights ought, in my opinion, to be dealt with in the same way as if a lease had been granted to him and do not depend upon its actually having been granted."

(2) Deemed entry

The making of a claim to possession of land is equivalent to an actual entry in that it entitles an owner to sue in trespass.[32] In order to bring an action to recover land, a person who is entitled to possession of that land need only claim an entitlement to possession in the proceedings and need not first effect actual entry.

1–006

(3) Re-entry and forfeiture

The right of a landlord to re-enter premises and to forfeit a lease of those premises, for specified breaches of that lease (which are breaches of condition and therefore give the landlord an opportunity to terminate the lease),[33] may also be effected either by actual entry onto the land or by a claim for possession made in proceedings which are deemed to amount to entry. Although it is the breach of condition which entitles the landlord to forfeit,[34] the entitlement to possession does not arise until forfeiture is

1–007

---

[29] See *Hill & Redman's Law of Landlord and Tenant*, paras. A[906]–A[909].

[30] (1882) 21 Ch.D. 9 at 14–15.

[31] (1889) 41 Ch.D. 248 at 264.

[32] See *Ocean Accident* [1905] 2 K.B. 493, and *Wuta-Ofei v. Danquah* [1961] 1 W.L.R. 1238.

[33] Although a proviso for re-entry (or forfeiture clause) is normal, and preferable from the landlord's point of view, it is possible to forfeit in the absence of such a provision if the landlord can prove breach of a condition: *Doe d. Lockwood v. Clarke* (1807) 8 East 185. In the absence of a forfeiture clause, it is necessary for the landlord to prove that the provision was intended to be a condition, breach of which would entitled him to terminate the tenancy, and that it was not merely an ordinary covenant: *Doe d. Wilson v. Phillips* (1824) 2 Bing. 13.

[34] Subject to the requirements of the Law of Property Act 1925, s. 146 and the Leasehold Property (Repairs) Act 1938.

effected by re-entry or service of the proceedings.[35] The landlord's re-entry has the dual effect of terminating the tenancy and perfecting his claim to possession. Where a claim is made in proceedings for forfeiture and possession, re-entry is effected in law when the proceedings are served upon the tenant[36] or by peaceable re-entry[37] onto the premises.[38] Following such forfeiture, the tenant ceases to occupy the premises lawfully and the landlord may sue for mesne profits[39] which claim for mesne profits relates back to the date on which the entitlement to possession arises (*i.e.* the date of forfeiture). Where a landlord has re-entered, he may sue in respect of any trespasses committed after the lease was terminated by that re-entry, *e.g.* such a trespass may be committed by the tenant remaining in possession.[40]

Particular cases

Landlord and tenant

1–008   This sub-heading is used in a broad sense to encompass the various rights of reversioners/landlords, tenants, lodgers, licensees and invitees to bring an action for trespass. In drawing a distinction between the categories of tenant, lodger and licensee, care must be taken in the light of the considerable bulk of recent case law on this topic and the re-affirmation by the House of Lords in *Street v. Mountford*[41] that the primary test (or "hallmark") of the existence of a tenancy is the grant of exclusive possession.[42]

---

[35] *Elliot v. Boynton* [1924] 1 Ch. 236.

[36] *Canas Property Co. Ltd v. K.L. Television Services Ltd* [1970] 2 Q.B. 433, CA.

[37] For example, actual entry without violence.

[38] *Hill & Redman's Law of Landlord and Tenant*, paras A[8989]–A[9002] and *Billson & Others v. Residential Apartments Ltd* [1992] 1 A.C. 494, H.L.

[39] See below, paras. 4–005, 4–017 to 4–022.

[40] Unless the tenant obtains relief against forfeiture, in which case the forfeited lease is reinstated.

[41] [1985] A.C. 809. See also, for example, *Heslop v. Burns* [1974] 1 W.L.R. 1241, CA, *London & Associated Investment Trust plc v. Calow* [1986] 2 E.G.L.R. 80, *Crancour v. Da Silvaesa* (1986) 52 P. & C.R. 204, CA, *A G Securities v. Vaughan* [1990] 1 A.C. 417, HL, *Norris v. Checksfield* [1991] 1 W.L.R. 1241, CA, *Westminster City Council v. Clarke* [1992] 2 A.C. 288, HL, *Tower Hamlets London Borough Council v. Miah* [1992] Q.B. 622, CA, *Bruton v. London & Quadrant Housing Trust* [2000] 1 A.C. 406, H.L. and, generally, *Megarry & Wade* (6th ed.) pp. 758–769.

[42] Lord Templeman's leading judgment in *Street v. Mountford* also refers to the importance of the grant of exclusive possession at a rent for a term (including a periodic term), see [1985] 1 A.C. at 826 E-F, but it appears that the reservation of a rent is not essential: *Ashburn Anstalt v. Arnold* [1989] Ch. 1 (overruled by the House of Lords in *Prudential Assurance Co. Ltd v. London Residuary Body* [1992] 2 A.C. 386 on the question of uncertainty of duration of the tenancy but still applied as good law on the reservation of rent point by the Court of Appeal in *Wrexham Maelor Borough Council v. MacDougall,* [1993] 2 E.G.L.R. 23) — although see *Bostock v. Bryant* (1991) 61 P. & C.R. 23. "Exclusive possession" is not simply defined but means essentially the right to exclude all others from possession of the demised premises (including the landlord) save where the lease otherwise permits: see *Heslop v. Burns* [1974] 1 W.L.R. 1241, CA. It is not clear whether there is any sensible distinction to be drawn between exclusive possession and exclusive occupation although in *Wrexham Maelor Borough Council v. MacDougall,* [1993] 2 E.G.L.R. 23, CA. at 28K, Ralph Gibson L.J. (giving the judgment of the Court) held in the circumstances of that case that exclusive occupation conferred possession but not exclusive possession sufficient to create a tenancy.

Earlier cases[43] which broadly indicated that a landlord might stipulate that an agreement conferred merely a licence were overruled[44] and the test now is whether, on a true analysis of the substance of the agreement, a tenancy has been created[45] provided that, in the circumstances, the landlord has the appropriate power to create a tenancy.[46]

(1) Reversioner

In general, a landlord who has parted with possession (or the right to possession)[47] of land by the creation of some inferior interest cannot bring trespass since he has parted with possession for the duration of that interest.[48] It is often the case that the freeholder will stand at some distance from the right to possession if there has been created a series of inferior interests, e.g. lease, sub-lease and sub-underlease.　　1–009

It is not always necessary for the reversioner to await the expiry of the tenant's interest by effluxion of time in order to maintain trespass since upon forfeiture of a tenancy, the reversioner becomes entitled to possession and may bring an action in trespass. The creation of other interests will not defeat the reversioner's entitlement to bring trespass since upon the forfeiture of a lease all inferior interests created out of that lease are simultaneously determined.[49] However, forfeiture may be avoided by the grant of relief from forfeiture[50] in which case the status of the reversioner will be restored and the right to bring an action in trespass lost.

There are other means by which a tenancy can come to an end other than by effluxion of time and forfeiture: for example, a tenancy may be surrendered or a tenant may exercise a contractual option to determine the tenancy prior to expiry of the term.[51] A periodic tenancy is typically　　1–010

---

[43] Including *Somma v. Hazlehurst* [1978] 1 W.L.R. 1014, CA and *Aldrington Garages Ltd v. Fielder* (1978) 37 P. & C.R. 461, CA.

[44] Although it is still possible to create a licence (apart from Lord Templeman's specific exceptions): see, for example, *Crancour v. Da Silvaesa* (1986) 52 P. & C.R. 204, CA, especially at 229–230, *Essex Plan Ltd v. Broadminster Ltd* [1988] 2 E.G.L.R. 73, *Esso Petroleum Co. Ltd v. Fumegrange* [1994] 2 E.G.L.R. 90, CA and *National Car Parks Ltd. v. The Trinity Development Company (Banbury) Ltd* (2001) 81 P. & C.R. 21.

[45] Subject to certain exceptions, *e.g.* family arrangements, acts of generosity, service occupiers and where the occupation is attributable to the relationship of vendor and purchaser see *Street v. Mountford* [1985] A.C. 809, at 818 and 821–822.

[46] See *e.g. Minister of Agriculture and Fisheries v. Matthews* [1949] 2 All E.R. 725, *Family Housing Association v. Jones* [1990] 1 W.L.R. 779, *Camden L.B.C. v. Shortlife Community Housing Ltd.* (1992) 90 L.G.R. 358 and *Bruton v. London & Quadrant Housing Trust* [2000] 1 A.C. 406, HL.

[47] See paras. 1–004 to 1–006, on the question of trespass by relation.

[48] Subject to any statutory restrictions on possession and security of tenure: see below, paras. 4–059 to 4–061.

[49] *Great Western Railway Co. v. Smith* (1876) Ch.D. 235, CA, and *Official Custodian for Charities v. Mackey* [1985] Ch. 168.

[50] See *Hill & Redman*, paras A[9068]–A[9389], the Common Law Procedure Act 1852, the Law of Property Act 1925, s. 146, the Supreme Court Act 1981, s. 38, the County Courts Act 1984, ss. 138–139 and *Billson v. Residential Apartments Ltd* [1992] 1 A.C. 494, HL. Applications for relief against forfeiture may also be made by sub-tenants and mortgagees; see, *e.g. Escalus Properties Ltd v. Robinson* [1996] Q.B. 231, CA.

[51] See, *e.g. Hankey v. Clavering* [1942] 2 K.B. 326, CA, and *Bass Holdings Ltd v. Morton Music Ltd* [1987] 2 All E.R. 1001, CA.

brought to an end by service of a notice to quit but also may be surrendered.

In all cases of determination or expiry, the landlord's right to bring an action in trespass does not arise until the tenant's interest has come to an end and the landlord's entitlement to possession has arisen.

A reversioner has a limited right of action in cases where a trespass has a permanent injurious effect on his interest, but such an action lies in nuisance not in trespass since the reversioner has not been dispossessed: where such an injury is caused to the reversion the proper allegation is not one of unlawful entry but of unlawful injury to the reversion.[52] However, where a reversioner proves damage he may obtain an injunction without joining the tenant as a party to the proceedings.[53]

(2) Tenant

1–011 If the tenant is a tenant in possession then he will be entitled to bring an action in trespass and is the proper plaintiff if there is an unlawful entry onto the land demised. The entitlement to bring an action in trespass exists in the case of all species of tenancy in possession including tenancies at sufferance notwithstanding that these are highly precarious and terminable by the landlord without notice at any time.[54]

The tenant may bring an action in trespass even against his landlord, for example if the landlord enters the property demised without the authority of the lease[55] or the tenant. Whilst a lease may be forfeited in certain circumstances by *peaceable re-entry* — *i.e.* by an act of entry evincing an intention to determine the lease[56] — if the entry is made without meeting any necessary preconditions for forfeiture[57] then the entry will be unlawful and a trespass.

The entitlement of a tenant to maintain trespass ceases with the determination of his tenancy and, if a tenant remains in occupation of premises formerly demised without due authority, then he may himself be subject to proceedings in trespass by the person then entitled to immediate possession.

---

[52] For example, *Battishill v. Reed* (1856) 18 C.B. 696, *Rust v. Victoria Graving Dock Co.* and *London and St Katherine Dock Co.* (1887) 36 Ch.D. 113, CA, *Shelfer v. City of London Electric Lighting Co.* [1895] 1 Ch. 287, CA., *Mayfair Property Co. v. Johnston* [1894] 1 Ch. 508, *Jones v. Llanrwst U.D.C.* [1911] 1 Ch. 393. See further *Harris v. Hall, The Independent*, August 8, 1992, CA, where damages were apparently recovered in negligence and assessed by reference to loss of rent.

[53] *Jones v. Llanrwst*, [1911] 1 Ch. 393, *i.e.* as a co-plaintiff.

[54] See *Hill & Redman*, paras. A[150]–A[163], *Woodfall's Landlord and Tenant* Vol. 1, paras. 6.075 to 6.077, *Graham v. Peat* (1801) 1 East 244, *Asher v. Whitlock* (1865) L.R. 1 Q.B. 1 and *Perry v. Clissold* [1907] A.C. 73, PC.

[55] Many leases contain powers of entry by the landlord, although these are generally restricted to very particular circumstances, *e.g.* in order to carry out an inspection of the state of repair of the premises.

[56] *Hill & Redman*, paras A[8989]–A[9002], and *Woodfall* Vol. 1, para. 17.089.

[57] Such as the due service of a notice under the Law of Property Act 1925, s. 146 (not required in the case of arrears of rent — s. 146(11)) and the meeting of the requirements of the proviso for re-entry contained in the lease.

As in the case of a freehold reversioner, a leasehold reversioner may not bring an action in trespass since he has himself granted the entitlement to possession to another, *e.g.* to a subtenant who is the proper person to bring an action in trespass.[58]

(3) Lodger

Although a lodger has the exclusive right to the enjoyment of the room he occupies, he does not enjoy exclusive possession of that room and established authority supports the proposition that he may not bring an action in trespass.[59] In *Allan v. Liverpool*,[60] Blackburn J. stated that:

> "A lodger in a house, although he has the exclusive use of rooms in the house, in the sense that nobody else is to be there, and though his goods are stowed there, yet he is not in exclusive occupation, because the landlord is there for the purpose of being able, as landlords commonly do in the case of lodgings, to have his own servants to look after the house and furniture, and has retained to himself the occupation, though he has agreed to give exclusive enjoyment of the occupation to the lodger. Such a lodger could not bring ejectment, or *trespass quare clausum fregit*, the maintenance of the action depending on the possession."

However, the orthodox position which required exclusive possession to bring proceedings in trespass appears to have been exploded by a reassessment of the circumstances in which trespass proceedings may be brought by the majority of the Court of Appeal in *Manchester Airport Plc. v. Dutton*.[61] If the reasoning in *Dutton*, based on the conferring of a contractual right to occupy (whether exclusively or not) applies to the lodger (and there seems no reason in principle why it should not at least in some cases), then earlier authority is likely to require reconsideration.

(4) Licensee/invitee

Since a simple licence to occupy or enter premises does not grant possession to the licensee but merely some form of personal right, then the licensee is not able to bring proceedings in trespass. The application of the approach in *Street v. Mountford*[62] leads to the conclusion that if the substance of a purported licence in fact confers exclusive possession then a tenancy is created since a licence is, by definition, an agreement which

1–012

1–013

---

[58] *Lane v. Dixon* (1847) 3 C.B. 776.
[59] Otherwise, on the basis of *Street v. Mountford*, above, he would be a tenant. See also *R. v. St George's Union* (1871) L.R. 7 Q.B. 90 at 97, *Cory v. Bristow* (1877) 2 App. Cas. 262 at 267, *Allan v. Liverpool Overseers*, above, and *Marchant v. Charters* [1977] 1 W.L.R. 1181, CA.
[60] (1874) L.R. 9 Q.B. 180, 191.
[61] [2000] 1 Q.B. 133, CA, and see further below.
[62] See above, para. 1–008.

does not confer exclusive possession on the grantee. It does not follow that a licensee cannot be dispossessed and cannot bring an action in trespass as against others having no title to the land since he enjoys *de facto* possession (as opposed to exclusive possession against his landlord/licensor) and the law recognises that he has grounds to maintain an action. *De facto* possession will generally suffice provided that the defendant cannot set up some better title in himself. On the other hand, a licensee may not maintain trespass against his licensor or those deriving title under him.[63]

In some cases what seems to have been a licence has been held to confer, or to be coupled with, some more enduring right, which right would confer an entitlement to possession.[64] Prior to 1999, it appeared unlikely that such a licence would of itself be sufficient to enable a licensee to bring trespass unless the court gave effect to the right by declaring the existence, or ordering the transfer, of some right which did confer possession.[65] However, the entitlement to sue in trespass no longer appears to require fine lines to be drawn between exclusive and non-exclusive possession[66] and a contractual entitlement to possession, even if non-exclusive and not supported by prior occupation, will suffice to entitle a claimant to bring possession proceedings against trespassers.[67] In *Manchester Airport Plc. v. Dutton,*[68] a majority of the Court of Appeal[69] held that a licensee was entitled to bring summary possession proceedings even though it had not been in actual occupation before the trespasses occurred. Laws L.J. having heard "the rattle of mediaeval chains"[70] held.[71]

> "I think there is a logical mistake in the notion that because ejectment was only available to estate owners, possession cannot be available to licensees who do not enjoy de facto occupation. The mistake inheres in this: if the action for ejectment was by definition concerned *only* with the rights of estate owners, it is necessarily silent upon the question, what relief might be available to a licensee. The limited and

---

[63] Note that a licensee is estopped from denying his licensor's title: *Meeruppe Sumanatissa v. Warakaptiye Pangnananda Terunnanse* [1968] A.C. 1086, P.C.

[64] See *Megarry & Wade* (6th ed.), pp. 1046–1063 and, *e.g. Binions v. Evans* [1972] Ch. 359, CA, *Crabb v. Arun D.C.* [1976] Ch. 179, CA, *Pascoe v. Turner* [1979] 1 W.L.R. 431, CA, *Re Sharpe* [1980] 1 W.L.R. 219 and *Taylor Fashions Ltd v. Liverpool Victoria Trustees Co. Ltd* [1982] Q.B. 133.

[65] See *Pascoe v. Turner*, above.

[66] See *Clerk & Lindsell on Torts* (18th ed.), p. 933, para. 18–20 and *Wrexham Maelor Borough Council v. MacDougall* [1993] 2 E.G.L.R. 23, CA.

[67] See *e.g. Monsanto plc v. Tilly & ors, The Times,* November 30, 1999, CA and *Manchester Airport Plc. v. Dutton* [2000] 1 Q.B. 133, CA. The claimant in the latter case was granted a licence by the landowner to occupy a wood for the purpose of carrying out works of felling and lopping of trees in connection with the construction of an airport runway.

[68] Above.

[69] Chadwick L.J. dissenting, set out what might have been regarded as orthodoxy prior to the decision, namely that a licensee without exclusive possession with merely a personal, contractual right to enter could not use trespass to vindicate his rights. See *e.g.* p. 143 of the judgment.

[70] At p. 148.

[71] At p. 149.

specific nature of ejectment means only that it was not available to a licensee; it does not imply the further proposition that *no* remedy by way of possession can now be granted to a licensee not in occupation. Nowadays there is no distinct remedy of ejectment; a plaintiff sues for an order of possession, whether he is himself in occupation or not. The proposition that a plaintiff not in occupation may only obtain the remedy if he is an estate owner assumes that he must bring himself within the old law of ejectment. I think it is a false assumption.

I would hold that the court today has ample power to grant a remedy to a licensee which will protect but not exceed his legal rights granted by the licence. If, as here, that requires an order for possession, the spectre of history (which, in the true tradition of the common law, ought to be a friendly ghost) does not stand in the way. The law of ejectment has no voice in the question; it cannot speak beyond its own limits."

Kennedy L.J. agreed with Laws L.J. and stated[72]:

"The plaintiff does have a right to possession of the land granted to it by the licence. It is entitled "to enter *and occupy*" (my emphasis) the land in question. The fact that it has only been granted the right to enter and occupy for a limited purpose (specified in clause 2 of the licence) and that, as I would accept, the grant does not create an estate in land giving the plaintiff a right to exclusive possession does not seem to me to be critical. What matters, in my judgment, is that the plaintiff has a right to possession . . ."

Although it might be said that the *Dutton* case was concerned only with the requirements of the former R.S.C. Order 113, it is difficult to so restrict the judgments since they turned on the entitlement to possession.[73] However, the licence in that case expressly granted the right to occupy[74] and it is unlikely that the ratio can be extended to confer an entitlement to possession where the licence falls short of conferring some form of occupation or non-exclusive possession.

An invitee is in a position similar to that of a licensee in that a person invited onto land is normally granted a merely temporary permission to enter for certain purposes (*e.g.* to deliver goods, or carry out work or as a guest[75]) and not possession or occupation. Accordingly, subject to *Manchester Airport Plc v. Dutton*,[76] a mere invitee cannot bring an action in trespass if excluded or ejected by his invitor, or

---

[72] At p. 151.

[73] See also *Wiltshire County Council v. Frazer* (1983) 82 L.G.R. 313, CA, at p. 320 (Stephenson L.J.) considered by the Court in *Dutton*. Further support for a wider approach to the entitlement to sue in trespass can also be found in *Pemberton v. Southwark London Borough Council* [2000] 1 W.L.R. 1672, CA, below, where a "tolerated trespasser" was held able to sue in nuisance and trespass.

[74] See clause 1 of the licence ("licence to enter and occupy") quoted at [2000] 1 Q.B. 133 p. 137.

[75] *Smith v. Overseers of St Michael's, Cambridge* (1860) 3 E. & E. 383 (hotel guest).

[76] Above.

those deriving title under him, from land onto which he has been invited.

(5) "Tolerated trespassers"

1–014   Where a final order for possession has been obtained against a secure tenant under the Housing Act 1985, the local authority or housing association may assist the former tenant by allowing him to remain in occupation provided that certain conditions are complied with, usually including payment of rent and small sums towards any arrears. Under such circumstances, the former tenant becomes a "tolerated trespasser", no new secure tenancy is intended or created, and none of the usual covenants bind the former landlord and former tenant. If the former tenant breaches the conditions of the arrangement, he is liable to be evicted without the need for a further order for possession.[77]

Although they might appear to be a form of licensee or tenant, such "tolerated trespassers" are treated as neither tenants nor licencees. Their occupation depends upon compliance with the terms of their particular arrangement and the opportunities available under the Housing Act 1985 to apply for the order for possession to be varied or discharged. In *Burrows v. Brent London Borough Council* Lord Browne-Wilkinson held:[78]

> "The position in relation to secure tenancies is *sui generis* . . . In these circumstances I think it fair to characterise the former tenant as a trespasser whom the landlord has agreed not to evict — a 'tolerated trespasser' — pending either the revival of the old tenancy or the breach of the agreed conditions."

"Tolerated trespassers", whilst unable to sue for breaches of the usual implied covenants,[79] have been held to have standing to sue in trespass and nuisance. In *Pemberton v. Southwark London Borough Council*,[80] Roch L.J. gave the following reasons for permitting a tolerated trespasser to sue her former landlord for an admitted nuisance:[81]

> "The tolerated trespasser has, whilst remaining in the premises, the exclusive right to occupy the premises . . . the order for possession, although ending the contractual relationship does not end the tolerated trespasser's actual occupation of the property, nor does it end

---

[77] See *Thompson v. Elmbridge Borough Council* [1987] 1 W.L.R. 1425, CA, *Greenwich London Borough Council v. Regan* (1996) 28 H.L.R. 469, CA and *Burrows v. Brent London Borough Council* [1996] 1 W.L.R. 1448, HL.

[78] [1996] 1 W.L.R. 1448, HL, at 1455.

[79] See, further, Chapter 2 below. However, if the possession order is [varied or] discharged after a period during which the tolerated trespasser has paid the equivalent of full rent, the authority will become liable for any breach of a covenant to repair during the tolerated trespasser's occupation: *Rogers v. Lambeth London Borough Council* [2000] L.G.R. 198, CA.

[80] [2000] 1 W.L.R. 1672, CA.

[81] *ibid.*, at 1681.

the tolerated trespasser's obligation to pay for that occupation of the premises. The policy considerations which led to the evolving of the special status of the tolerated trespasser are hardly good reasons for depriving the tolerated trespasser of all remedies in trespass and nuisance. The local authority will not have an obligation to repair the premises, but there is no reason why the local authority should not have the obligations so to conduct itself in relation to the remainder of the premises as not to . . . interfere in a way which is tortious in the tolerated trespasser's occupation and use of the premises."

(6) Service occupiers

An employee who is required to occupy particular premises "for the better performance of his duties" is not granted a tenancy and his occupation is deemed to be that of his employer;[82] this is not the case if the occupation is merely a matter of convenience rather than requirement. The employment which is related to the occupation does not have to exist at, or before, the grant of the licence provided that it was contemplated by the parties that the occupier would take up the employment within a reasonable time.[83]

1–015

Accordingly, since possession of the premises is not granted to the employee, orthodox principle holds that such a person may not sue in trespass against his employer or those claiming under him.[84] Indeed, once the employment has been determined, the right to occupy determines immediately without the necessity for notice to quit.[85] However, whilst the Court of Appeal has adopted a broader approach to trespass in *Manchester Airport Plc v. Dutton*[86] based on a contractual entitlement to occupy, even on a non-exclusive basis, this should not affect the position of service occupiers since their occupation is deemed to be that of their employers.

Owners and occupiers under trusts of land

Prior to 1996, co-owners were not usually able to sue each other for trespass to the land since each co-owner was jointly entitled to possession of the whole of the land. However if one of them had dispossessed or ousted another, then the ousted co-owner may bring an action in trespass in order to vindicate his right to possession of the whole. However, this position

1–016

---

[82] *Smith v. Seghill Overseers* (1875) L.R. 10 Q.B. 422, *Street v. Mountford*, above, at 818, and *Norris v. Checksfield* [1991] 1 W.L.R. 1241, CA.

[83] See *Norris v. Checksfield*, above.

[84] *White v. Bayley* (1861) 10 C.B. (N.S.) 227 and *Hemmings v. Stokes Poges Golf Club* [1920] 1 K.B. 720, CA.

[85] See *Hemmings v. Stoke Poges*, above. Although the Protection from Eviction Act 1977, s. 5(1A), requires the giving of a notice to quit in the prescribed form in the case of licensees, this does not apply to service occupiers who occupy for the duration of their employment since the right to occupy terminates with the employment. Such a licence is not a "periodic licence to occupy" within s. 5(1A): *Norris v. Checksfield* [1991] 1 W.L.R. 1241, CA.

[86] [2000] 1 Q.B. 133, CA, above.

has changed following the Trusts of Land and Appointment of Trustees Act 1996. Under the 1996 Act, the trustees of a trust of land[87] have all the powers of an absolute owner[88] but a beneficiary entitled to possession under a trust for land is entitled to occupy trust land, which is available and suitable for the beneficiary, subject to reasonable conditions imposed by the trustees and, where there is more than one beneficiary so entitled, the trustees may determine who shall occupy.[89] Accordingly, more than one beneficiary may still occupy subject to the decision of the trustees and conditions imposed by them.

Since co-occupiers under the Trusts of Land and Appointment of Trustees Act 1996 will, by definition, both be entitled to occupy the land the effect of *Manchester Airport Plc v. Dutton*[90] appears to be that both are entitled in principle to sue in trespass.

Dispossession or ouster by another co-owner or beneficiary entitled to occupy is not restricted to blatant cases of exclusion or expulsion, but may occur where part of the property is destroyed or removed by another, *e.g.* by the excavation and removal of the soil or removal of a wall.[91] However, where the destruction or removal of part of the property is part of the normal use of that property[92] then this does not amount to an ouster — although there will be a duty to account for the profits of any operation.[93] Further, if part of the property is destroyed with the intention of renewing or rebuilding it,[94] then no ouster has occurred.

One joint tenant may sue for possession of premises which have been licensed jointly even where the licensee's right to occupy has been terminated by one co-owner without the knowledge or consent of the other.[95] Further, a notice served by one of a number of co-tenants is sufficient to terminate their joint interest without the knowledge or consent of the other tenant(s).[96] However, where rights under Article 8 of the European

---

[87] Defined by s. 1(1)(a).

[88] S. 6(1).

[89] S. 12 of the Trusts of Land and Appointment of Trustees Act 1996, which confers a right of occupation on a beneficiary who is entitled to an interest in possession in land subject to a trust of land, provided the land is available and suitable for occupation by him (s. 12(2)). This is subject to any reasonable conditions imposed by the trustees: s. 13(3). Where more than one beneficiary is so entitled, the trustees are given the power to determine who shall occupy: s. 13(1). Compensation to the excluded beneficiaries may be provided under s. 13(6). The new statutory right may imply that other beneficiaries, who are not so entitled, do not have a right to occupy.

[90] [2000] 1 Q.B. 133, CA, and see further above.

[91] *Stedman v. Smith* (1857) 8 E. & B. 1.

[92] *e.g.* where minerals are extracted from a mine or timber is cut.

[93] *Wilkinson v. Haygirth* (1849) 12 Q.B. 837.

[94] *Cubitt v. Porter* (1828) 8 B. & C. 257 and *Standard Bank of British South America v. Stokes* (1878) 9 Ch.D. 68.

[95] *Doe d. Aslin v. Summersett* (1830) 1 B. & Ad. 135, *Robson-Paul v. Farrugia* (1969) 20 P. & C.R. 820, CA and *Annen v. Rattee* [1985] 1 E.G.L.R. 136, CA. The position was different where one equitable tenant in common sought possession from another tenant in common: *Bull v. Bull* [1955] 1 Q.B. 234, CA, but this may require reassessment given the right conferred by s. 12 of the Trusts of Land and Appointment of Trustees Act 1996, above.

[96] *Hammersmith & Fulham L.B.C. v. Monk* [1992] 1 A.C. 478, HL, and *Notting Hill Housing Trust v. Brackley* [2001] EWCA Civ 601, CA. This applies in the absence of a term in the tenancy

Convention on Human Rights are engaged (see paragraphs 1–139 to 1–147 below), principally in the case of public authority landowners, consideration will have to be given to such rights.[96a]

The extent of protection of possession

Introduction

The tort of trespass provides remedies for those in possession of land. That **1–017** protection is not confined simply to the possession of the physical surface of the land itself, but extends to deal with intrusions both above and below the physical surface. Above the surface, trespass will be available in respect of buildings placed on the land[97] and plants and structures attached to the land. Certain types of rights on or over land may be protected where such rights confer possession on their holder although infringements of perhaps the commonest type of such rights, namely easements, are not actionable in trespass since easements do not confer an entitlement to possession.

Below the surface of the soil, trespass is not only available to remedy intrusions to the sub-soil, but also to minerals beneath the sub-soil. In addition, those in possession of structures and plants affixed to the soil will be able to protect their interest by action.

As well as the case of disturbance to property above and below the surface of the land itself, trespass will lie where there is interference with airspace

agreement to contrary effect: *Monk* at 483. See, however, *Hounslow L.B.C. v. Pilling* [1993] 1 W.L.R. 1242, CA. Further, this may now be affected in certain cases by the terms of any conditions imposed by trustees on the occupation of the beneficiary under the trust for land under s. 13(3) of the Trusts of Land and Appointment of Trustees Act 1996. See also *Qazi v. Harrow L.B.C.*, below, where the Human Rights Act 1998 applies.

[96a] In *Qazi v. Harrow L.B.C.* [2001] EWCA Civ 1834, CA, the Court of Appeal remitted the Council's possession claim to the county court to consider the application of Article 8(2) despite the fact that the Defendant's wife had properly given notice to terminate their joint secure tenancy. See per Arden L.J. at paras. 1.1.4 to 1.5.8 and Peter Gibson L.J. at paras. 1.1.62–1.1.66. The court held that a former tenant whose tenancy has come to an end by operation of law can, after that time, have a right to a home for the purposes of Article 8 of the Convention. The Court relied upon Strasbourg decisions to the effect that Article 8 rights were not excluded simply because the occupation of the home was unlawful (principally *Buckley v. UK* (1996) 23 E.H.R.R. 101 and *Chapman v. UK* (2001) 33 E.H.R.R. 339 — see, further, below at paras. 1–140 to 1–142). However, the extent to which the court might have to take consideration of article 8(2) was not explained by the court since the sole issue for the Court of Appeal was whether article 8 was engaged at all and the court did not consider the facts. This leaves open to question whether the courts are likely to require much persuading whether it is pursuant to a legitimate aim and proportionate to rely on the general common law rules as to the termination of tenancies. In the light of *Michalak v. Wandsworth L.B.C* [2002] EWCA Civ 271, CA, it must be strongly arguable that those common law rules do, in general, satisfy article 8(2) given that the common law rules define the nature and extent of the right to occupy. See per Brooke L.J. at paras. 43–47 and Mance L.J. at paras. 76–77. See also *Somerset C.C. v. Isaacs* [2002] EWHC 1014 (Admin).

[97] Although these may be legally categorised as land if they become affixed to the land: see, e.g. *Holland v. Hodgson* (1872) L.R. 7 C.P. 328 at 335, *Jordan v. May* [1947] K.B. 427, *Stokes v. Costain Property Developments Ltd* [1983] 1 W.L.R. 907 and Megarry & Wade (6th ed.), pp. 928–932. See further below, paras. 1–018 to 1–023.

above the land. Such an interference may be caused by structures intruding from adjacent property or, in certain circumstances, by objects passing overhead with no direct physical connection with the land, *e.g.* aircraft, balloons and projectiles. Although the Latin tag *usque ad coelum* is often used to indicate the vertical extent of the ownership of interests in land, in modern times the use of aircraft, satellites and spacecraft at very high altitudes would make a literal application of that expression an absurdity.

Land and fixtures

1–018 The physical surface of land includes not only the actual soil but those structures and other items which are affixed to it and which, as a matter of law, are regarded as part of the land itself. For example, a building which is constructed on land and which is permanently attached to the land will generally be regarded as part of the land itself — *quicquid planatur solo, solo cedit.*[98] More difficult questions arise where structures are less firmly attached or where there is a possibility that they might be removed.[99]

In such circumstances, whether or not the item placed on or attached to the land becomes part of it is said to depend on two matters:[1]

(i)   the degree to which the item has been annexed to the land, *i.e.* the extent and nature of the attachment; and

(ii) the object and purpose of the annexation.

(i) Degree of annexation

1–019 Whether or not a chattel has been annexed depends generally on whether it is actually attached to, or connected with, the land. A chattel (even if substantial) will prima facie not be a fixture if it is merely placed, or laid, on the surface of the land.[2] Similarly, the mere fact of a connection to a power supply which is annexed to the land is not sufficient itself to amount to annexation.[3] If a chattel which is placed on the land subse-

---

[98] Whatever is attached to soil becomes part of it: see *Minshall v. Lloyd* (1837) 2 M. & W. 450 at 459 and *Berkley v. Poulett* (1976) 241 E.G. 911, CA at 913.

[99] See Megarry & Wade, (6th ed.) pp. 928–938 and Cheshire & Burn (16th ed.) pp. 151–157.

[1] See *Leigh v. Taylor* [1902] A.C. 157, H.L., *Berkley v. Poulett* (1976) 241 E.G. 911, CA at 912 and *Megarry and Wade* (6th ed.) p. 929.

[2] See, *e.g. Mather v. Fraser* (1856) 2 K. & J. 536, *Elwes v. Maw* (1802) 3 East 38 (Dutch barn standing on brick columns let into the ground), *Hulme v. Brigham* [1943] K.B. 152 (heavy printing machine standing on the floor), *H.E. Dibble Ltd v. Moore* [1970] 2 Q.B. 181 (greenhouses resting on own weight), *Berkley v. Poulett* (1976) 241 E.G. 911 (statue of Greek athlete standing on a plinth), *Chelsea Yacht and Boat Co. Ltd v. Pope* [2000] 1 W.L.R. 1941 (D-Day landing craft, moored or resting on the river bottom)(but see *D'Eyncourt v. Gregory* (1966) L.R. 3 Eq. 382 and *Hamp v. Bygrave* (1982) 266 E.G. 720) and *Hynes v. Vaughan* (1985) 50 P. & C.R. 444 (growing frame and sprinkler system). The fact that the base upon which the chattel rests may itself be annexed is a separate issue. An unattached object requiring demolition for its effective removal from a resting place on land is likely to be treated as part of that land: *Elitestone Ltd v. Morris and another* [1997] 1 W.L.R. 687, HL, at pp. 692 and 696.

[3] *Vaudeville Electric Cinema v. Muriset* [1923] 2 Ch. 74 and see also *Hulme v. Brigham* [1943] K.B. 152 (batteries not fixtures).

quently sinks into the soil as a result of its weight or use, it appears that its character does not change as a result and it remains a chattel.[4]

On the other hand, keys[5] and certain other items[6] which are essential for the enjoyment of the land are regarded as part of the land even though there is not a physical attachment to the land.

Chattels which are attached by nails, screws or bolts are generally regarded as annexed to the land[7] although the ease with which they may be detached and removed may be strong evidence as to the purpose of the annexation (see below). This is particularly true in the case of matter affixed for trade or ornament.[8] Such cases are more likely to turn on questions of intention than the question of physical annexation.

Although the question of degree of annexation was originally the only relevant one it is now subject to consideration of the second issue, *i.e.* intention, although this means an objective assessment not the actual, subjective, intention of the person making the annexation.[9] The change in approach resulted from the fact that the earlier law proved harsh on those with only a limited form of ownership in the land[10] and who had affixed valuable property to the land.[11] However, the degree of annexation is still a relevant issue although in the light of the present importance of the second test of object and purpose, it should be remembered that physical attachment is not decisive and, in the present law, plays a role little more than that of an indicator of intention. As Scarman L.J. said in *Berkley v. Poulett & Others*:[12]

"Today so great are the technical skills of affixing and removing objects to land or buildings that the second test is more likely than the first to be decisive. Perhaps the enduring significance of the first test is a reminder that there must be some degree of physical annexation before a chattel can be treated as part of the realty."

(ii) Object and purpose of the annexation

In *Holland v. Hodgson*[13] Blackburn J. stated: 1–020

---

[4] *Beaufort v. Bates* (1831) 31 L.J. Ch. 481. In any event, the mere sinking, or settling, of the chattel would not of itself demonstrate a change in intention to treat the chattel as a chattel.
[5] *Liford's Case* (1614) 11 Co. Rep. 46b, 50a, 50b and *Moody v. Steggles* (1879) 12 Ch.D. 261.
[6] *Liford's Case*, above (millstone) and *Metropolitan Counties Society v. Brown* (1859) 26 Beav. 454 (handle of water pump).
[7] *Jordan v. May* [1947] K.B. 427 (engine and dynamo bolted to concrete).
[8] See below and *per* Lord Clyde in *Elitestone Ltd v. Morris and another* [1997] 1 W.L.R. 687, H.L, at pp. 695–696 following Lord Cairns L.C. in *Bain v. Brand* (1876) 1 App.Cas. 762, H.L., at p. 767 and *In re De Falbe; Ward v. Taylor* [1901] 1 Ch. 523 at p. 539.
[9] Which is to be assessed objectively: *Elitestone Ltd v. Morris and another* above, H.L, *per* Lord Clyde at p. 698, quoting Lord Cockburn in *Dixon v. Fisher* (1843) 5 D. 775 at , "no man can make his property real or personal by merely thinking it so."
[10] Principally tenants for life of settled land and tenants for years.
[11] See *per* Scarman L.J. in *Berkley v. Poulett & others* (1976) 241 E.G. 911, C.A. at 912 (second column) and *Leigh v. Taylor* [1902] A.C. 157 at 158–9.
[12] Above, at 913.
[13] (1872) L.R. 7 C.P. 328 at 335.

"Perhaps the true rule is, that articles not otherwise attached to the land than by their own weight are not to be considered as part of the land, unless the circumstances are such as to shew that they were intended to be part of the land, the onus of showing that they were so intended lying on those who assert that they have ceased to be chattels; and that, on the contrary, an article which is affixed to the land even slightly is to be considered as part of the land, unless the circumstances are such as to shew that it was intended all along to continue a chattel, the onus lying on those who contend that it is a chattel."

This demonstrates the importance which intention has come to play in the modern law.[14] Parke B. expressed the test in *Hellawell v. Easton*[15] as follows:

"Whether it was for the permanent and substantial improvement of the dwelling, in the language of the civil law, *perpetui usus causa*, or in that of the year book, *pour un profit del inheritance*, or merely for a temporary purpose and the more complete enjoyment of it as a chattel . . ."

Accordingly, a clear intention to benefit the land must be demonstrated in order to show annexation: if the intention is merely to enjoy the chattel better as a chattel, then there will be no annexation. Examples of the differences which may arise from superficially similar circumstances are set out below.

(a) Statutes and decorative items

1–021   In *D'Eyncourt v. Gregory*[16] a collection of statutes, tapestries, panelled pictures, figures and garden seats was held to have been annexed to the land since (however fixed) they were to be regarded as essentially part of the house or of the architectural design of the house and grounds. The clear inference was that the items had been intended to form part of the house, and hence the land, and such a conclusion did not arise merely as the result of the permanent fixing of the items.[17] Similar results were reached in *Re Whaley*[18] and *Lord Chesterfield's Settled Estates*[19] the latter of which cases concerned carvings by Grinling Gibbons which had been affixed to a suite of rooms for some 200 years. However, a different result was

---

[14] See *Berkley v. Poulett & Others*, above.
[15] (1851) 6 Exch. 295.
[16] (1866) L.R. 3 Eq. 382. And see *Hamp v. Bygrave* (1982) 266 E.G. 722. The status of *D'Eyncourt* must be doubtful given the judge's own lack of certainty and the statement in *Berkley v. Poulett* 241 E.G. 911 at 912 by Scarman L.J. that "there is now no need to enter into research in the case law prior to *Leigh v. Taylor* . . ." (see below and sub nom. *Re De Falbe*).
[17] See *D'Eyncourt v. Gregory* (1866) L.R. 3 Eq. 382, at 396–7.
[18] [1908] 1 Ch. 615.
[19] [1911] 1 Ch. 237.

reached in both *Leigh v. Taylor*[20] and *Berkley v. Poulett*.[21] In the former, tapestries tacked on frames and then nailed to walls were not annexed since the fixing of the tapestries to the wall was necessary for their enjoyment as chattels. In *Berkley v. Poulett* the court considered that a statue placed on a plinth[22] was not annexed. The "design" argument failed there since the court held that it was the position of the plinth rather than of the statue that was essential to the elevation of the house. Indeed, this was demonstrated by the fact that at least one other item had previously been placed on the plinth before the statue.

(b) Stones/building materials

As an example of the importance of intention, Blackburn J. in *Holland v.*   **1–022**
Hodgson[23] considered the legal position of stones placed on top of each other (without mortar or cement) to form a dry stone wall, which would be annexed to the land, and the same stones merely stacked on each other for convenience in a builder's yard, which would not. On that basis, materials, or components, merely stored on land would not be annexed to it but once used in the construction of a permanent structure would thereby become annexed to the land.[24]

(c) Mechanical equipment

Machines and equipment (even of substantial size and weight) will gener-   **1–023**
ally not be considered as being intended to be annexed if they are free standing,[25] although there is a greater degree of willingness to regard machinery as becoming annexed once it has been secured to the ground. *Hellawell v. Eastwood*,[26] where cotton spinning machines fixed to the floor to steady them were held to remain chattels, was disapproved by the court in *Crossley v. Lee*.[27] In the latter case, such machines were held to have become fixtures. The decision may be doubted to the extent that if the fixing of the machines was intended as a means of better enjoying them as chattels, and not improving the realty, they ought properly to be regarded as retaining their nature as chattels.[28] In any event, this must ultimately be a question of intention and the greater flexibility shown by the courts in more recent cases such as *Berkley v. Poulett* applies to all categories of fixtures, see above.

---

[20] [1902] A.C. 157, H.L. which affirmed the decision of the Court of Appeal *sub nom. Re De Falbe* [1901] 1 Ch. 523, C.A. Cited with approval by Lord Clyde in *Elitestone Ltd v. Morris and another* [1997] 1 W.L.R. 687, H.L, at pp. 695–696.
[21] See above.
[22] And a sundial placed on a pedestal.
[23] (1872) L.R. 7 C.P. 328.
[24] *Elitestone Ltd v. Morris*, above.
[25] See above, para. 1–019.
[26] (1851) 6 Ex. 295.
[27] [1908] 1 K.B. 86.
[28] See also *Trappes v. Harter* (1833) 2 C. & M. 153 and *Leigh v. Taylor* [1902] A.C. 157.

These cases and others illustrate the difficulties which may arise and the fine distinction between cases where the chattels are viewed as part of the land and those where they are merely fixed for their better enjoyment as chattels. The questions of degree of annexation and purpose cannot always be clearly separated since in many cases the degree of annexation has played an important part in the determination of the purpose[29] but even if the degree of physical connection is slight this does not preclude the finding that the chattels form part of the land if the purpose of annexation is to improve the land.[30]

Those entitled to grow and remove crops, although the crops do not become chattels until they are severed from the land, are also entitled to use trespass to prevent entry and damage to their interests. One of the results of the activities of environmental protestors in destroying genetically modified crops has been a reaffirmation of legal principles in this context. In *Back v. Daniels*[31], Scrutton L.J. had held that:

> "Now it is clear that at common law, for the same land, though hardly for the same portion of it, two persons may be in possession at the same time, and each can bring trespass. In the case of a grant by the owner of the soil of the right to herbage, *vestura terrae*, or growing crops, the owner can bring trespass for damage to his right to the soil; the person having a right to the herbage for damage to the herbage or crops; but neither could bring trespass for the damage to the other's right."

In *Monsanto plc v. Tilly*[32] it was confirmed that interference with crops will, in certain circumstances, amount to trespass both to land and goods. Stuart-Smith L.J. followed *Back v. Daniels* and stated:[33]

> "Ordinarily growing crops do not become goods until they are severed from the land. Once they are so severed the owner of the crop can maintain an action for wrongful interference with the goods. The defendant's actions in uprooting the crop amounted to severance, and therefore an action for trespass to goods will lie. For practical purposes it makes little difference in this case whether the tort is trespass to land or goods, though in my opinion it should properly be regarded as trespass to land which affords Monsanto somewhat wider protection, for example in relation to a poisoning of the crop without uprooting.
>   The arrangements between the farmer and Monsanto are governed by a standard form of agreement. It is unnecessary to set it out at

---

[29] e.g. in *Leigh v. Taylor*, above, at 160.
[30] See *D'Eyncourt v. Gregory* (1866) L.R. 3 Eq. 382, at 396–7.
[31] [1925] 1 K.B. 526, CA, at p. 542. See also *Wellaway v. Courtier* [1918] 1 K.B. 200 where the purchaser of a crop of turnips growing on a third party's land was entitled to maintain an action for trespass to land in respect of the damage to the turnips done by the defendant's sheep.
[32] *The Times*, November 30, 1999, CA. See also, below, at 1–086.
[33] At paras. 21–23.

length. The seed is the property of Monsanto; the drilling, spraying and co-ordination of the trial is done by Monsanto's contractor. More importantly it is provided that 'the crop resulting from the tests are all the property of Monsanto'. This is clearly sufficient to enable Monsanto to maintain the action for trespass both on sites which they do not own as well as those they do."

Sub-soil

The rights of a landowner are not limited to the physical surface of the   **1–024**
land nor any items affixed to it, but also extend to the sub-surface beneath and the airspace above. A commonly repeated maxim is that *cuius est solum, eius est usque ad coelum et usque ad inferos*[34] — implying that land ownership carries with it an ownership of infinite extent both above and below it. In *Corbett v. Hill*[35] Sir W.M. James V.-C. said:

"Now the ordinary rule of law is, that whoever has got the *solum* — whoever has got the site — is the owner of everything up to the sky and down to the centre of the earth. But that ordinary presumption of law, no doubt, is frequently rebutted, particularly with regard to property in towns, by the fact that other adjoining tenements, either from there having been once a joint ownership, or from other circumstances, protrude themselves over the site."

Practicality and modern thought have further relegated the old presumption to the realms of fancy especially with regard to airspace[36] — although a landowner's property rights certainly do extend both above and below the surface of the land. The question of trespass to airspace will be considered in the next section.

Unless the landowner has in some manner parted with his rights in the sub-soil and minerals beneath his land, his ownership extends to the sub-soil and those minerals. Unless a clear contrary intention is shown,[37] a disposition of land will normally carry with it the rights to the sub-soil and to exploit the minerals beneath the land.[38] Mineral rights are modified in certain special cases: for example, gold and silver in mines is vested in the Crown,[39] as is all petroleum in its natural state in strata.

Thus an action in trespass may be maintainable by a landowner in   **1–025**
respect of unauthorised interference beneath his land, *e.g.* the winning

---

[34] Co. Litt. 4a.
[35] (1870) L.R. 9 Eq. 671 at 673.
[36] See *e.g. Wandsworth Board of Works v. United Telephone Co. Ltd* (1884) 13 Q.B.D. 904 at 915 and *Bernstein (Baron) v. Skyviews & General Ltd* [1978] 1 Q.B. 485.
[37] See, *e.g. Earl of Lonsdale v. Attorney-General* [1982] 1 W.L.R. 887.
[38] *Grigsby v. Melville* [1974] 1 W.L.R. 80.
[39] See the Royal Mines Acts 1688 and 1693.

and working of minerals without authorisation.[40] However, whilst there is authority on the question of the extent to which a trespass may be committed by aircraft above the land, there is no corresponding authority on the issue whether a person may go beneath the land to such a depth that a trespass is not committed. There appear to be physical constraints on the depth to which a person might mine given the current state of technological progress which do not exist with travel in the air and space.

The better view must be that where the sub-soil is capable of access and working, then property rights extend to protect it. Thus sub-soil which may not be accessible at one time may become accessible in future and hence be the subject-matter of a trespass action.

Airspace

1–026   The unlawful invasion of airspace falls into two main categories: first, there may be overflying, *i.e.* invasion by an aircraft or other flying object which has no direct physical connection with any land. Secondly, intrusion may occur by overhanging, *i.e.* by projection over the land of another from adjacent land (*e.g.* by part of a building or other structure). The present state of the authorities requires a distinction to be drawn between the two for the purposes of ascertaining whether or not the height of the offending object or structure from the land is sufficient to prevent there being a trespass. A much stricter approach is taken in the first type of case than the second: in the second type of case, vertical distance from the land over which the projection lies is irrelevant. In the first type of case, the court must take such distance into account in determining whether or not it is necessary for the landowner's ordinary use and enjoyment of the land.

Overflying

1–027   An unauthorised[41] invasion of airspace may take the form of an intrusion by aircraft if that intrusion is low enough to interfere with the ordinary use and enjoyment of the land and buildings beneath it. This form of trespass may be committed though the offending object has no physical contact with either the land over which it is passing or adjacent land (as in the case of projections). Although a landowner is sometimes said to have rights above his land *usque ad coelum* this Latin tag is not to be interpreted literally.[42] Indeed, as had been noted already, such a literal interpretation would be absurd in the context of the present day intensive use of air and space (although different considerations apply in the case of projections).

---

[40] See, *e.g. Livingstone v. The Rawyards Coal Co.* (1880) 5 App.Cas. 25, H.L. (mistaken working of coal beyond boundary), and *Bulli Coal Mining Co. v. Osborne* [1899] A.C. 351, P.C. (furtive and wilful taking of coal).

[41] Subject to the provisions of the Civil Aviation Act 1982, below. 13 See *Corbett v. Hill* (1870) L.R. 9 Eq. 671.

[42] See *Corbett v. Hill* (1870) L.R. 9 Eq. 671.

In *Baron Bernstein of Leigh v. Skyways & General Limited*[43] the defendant's **1–028** business was to take aerial photographs of properties and to offer them for sale to the owners of the properties photographed. The plaintiff objected to this and brought an action for damages alleging, *inter alia*, that the defendant had committed a trespass by the intrusion of its aircraft into the airspace above his property. Griffiths J., having found that there had been an intrusion in fact, dismissed the plaintiff's claim. The learned judge accepted that a landowner has certain rights in the airspace above his land but rejected the view that a landowner has rights in the airspace literally *usque ad coelum*:

> "It may be a sound and practical rule to regard any incursion into the airspace at a height which may interfere with the ordinary user of the land as a trespass rather than a nuisance. Adjoining owners then know where they stand: they have no right to erect structures over-hanging or passing over their neighbours' land and there is no room for argument whether they are thereby causing damage or annoy-ance to the neighbours about which there may be much room for argument and uncertainty. But wholly different considerations arise when considering the passage of aircraft at a height which in no way affects the user of the land . . . I can find no support in authority for the view that a landowner's rights in the airspace above his property extend to an unlimited height. In *Wandsworth Board of Works v. United Telephone Co. Ltd* 13 Q.B.D. 904 Bowen L.J. described the maxim, *usque ad coelum*, as a fanciful phrase, to which I would add that if applied literally it is a fanciful notion leading to the absurdity of a trespass at common law being committed by a satellite every time it passes over a suburban garden."

The solution adopted by Griffiths J. was to balance the rights of property owners to enjoy their land against the right of the general public to take advantage of airspace:[44]

> "This balance is in my judgment best struck in our present society by restricting the rights of an owner in the airspace above his land to such height as is necessary for the ordinary use and enjoyment of his land and the structures upon it, and declaring that above that height he has no greater rights in the airspace than any other member of the public."

However, in *Anchor Brewhouse Developments Ltd v. Berkley House (Docklands Developments) Ltd*[45] Scott J., whilst not dissenting from the *Bernstein* decision, held that Griffiths J.'s reasoning did not apply to a crane overhanging land at a high level.

---

[43] [1978] 1 Q.B. 479.
[44] This solution can be compared with the principles underlying the tort of nuisance: see Chapter 2, *e.g.* paras. 2–012, 2–028 to 2–034.
[45] [1987] 2 E.G.L.R. 173.

Overhanging

1–029   A trespass of this nature may be caused by matters such as part of a build-ing, a sign or some other structure[46] which project without authorisation over the land of another. In *Gifford v. Dent*[47] Romer J. ordered the removal of a sign which projected some 4ft 8ins. over the plaintiff's forecourt on the basis that:

> " . . . the plaintiffs were tenants of the forecourt and were accordingly tenants of the space above the forecourt *usque ad coelum*, it seemed to him that the projection was clearly a trespass upon the property of the plaintiffs . . ."

Gifford was followed by McNair J. in *Kelsen v. Imperial Tobacco Co. (of Great Britain and Ireland)*,[48] where the court ordered the removal of a sign which projected a mere eight inches over the plaintiff's land.

The fact that a structure or other trespassing object only infringes the landowner's airspace at a high level does not prevent there being a trespass: see *Anchor Brewhouse Developments Ltd v. Berkley House (Dock-lands Developments) Ltd*.[49] In that case Scott J. did not consider it permissi-ble to apply the approach taken to aircraft in the *Bernstein* case to a high level crane which overhung the plaintiff's land and considered that the question of flying objects warranted a separate approach. He said:[50]

> "The difficulties posed by overflying aircraft or balloons, bullets or missiles seem to me to be wholly separate from the problem which arises where there is an invasion of air space by a structure placed or standing upon the land of a neighbour. One of the characteristics of the common law of trespass is, or ought to be, certainty. The extent of proprietary interests enjoyed by landowners ought to be clear. It may be that, where aircraft or overflying missiles are concerned, certainty cannot be achieved . . . but certainty is capable of being achieved where invasion of air space by tower cranes, advertising signs and other structures are concerned. In my judgment, if somebody erects on his own land a structure, part of which invades the air space above the land of another, the invasion is trespass."

1–030   It is clear from the *Anchor Brewhouse* decision that where an infringement of airspace is caused by an overhanging item or structure which is placed

---

[46] *Kelsen v. Imperial Tobacco* [1957] 2 Q.B. 334 (projecting sign). *Pickering v. Rudd* (1815) 4 Camp. 219 (board nailed to defendant's premises, projecting over plaintiff's land).
[47] [1926] W.N. 336.
[48] [1957] 2 Q.B. 334.
[49] [1987] 2 E.G.L.R. 173 and also *London & Manchester Assurance Co. Ltd v. O & H Construction Ltd* [1989] 2 E.G.L.R. 185 (crane swinging into neighbour's airspace) especially at 186 H-K.
[50] Above, at 175–6.

on adjacent premises, that infringement will amount to a trespass and no balance between the parties' respective rights will be struck. That is made plain by Scott J.'s summary of the problem in that case:[51]

"What is complained of in the present case is infringement of air space by a structure positioned upon a neighbour's land. The defendant has erected tower cranes on its land. Attached to each tower crane is a boom which swings over the plaintiff's land. The booms invade the air space over the plaintiff's land. Each boom is part of the structure on the defendant's land. The tort of trespass represents an interference with possession or with the right to possession. A landowner is entitled, as an attribute of his ownership of the land, to place structures on his land and thereby to reduce into actual possession the air space above his land. If an adjoining owner places a structure on his (the adjoining owner's) land that overhangs his neighbours land, he thereby takes into his possession air space to which his neighbour is entitled. That, in my judgment, is trespass. It does not depend upon any balancing of rights."

The learned judge noted that the difficulties posed by overflying aircraft or balloons, bullets or missiles seemed to be "wholly separate" from the case of an invasion of airspace by a structure placed on neighbouring land.

Since the question of the extent of damage is irrelevant to the commission of a trespass,[52] it is apparent from the authorities that a trespass by projection over another's land can be easily committed. Thus, whilst damages may be nominal or small, the primary remedy in such a case is by way of injunction.[53]

Should there be a single approach to trespass to air space?

As set out above, there appear to be two tests of what constitutes trespass to airspace depending on whether the trespass is by overflying or overhanging. The determination of which test applies depends solely on whether the trespassing object is attached to other land or has no physical contact with the ground. However, it might be thought that some modern cranes and high level structures stand at such a height so as not to interfere with the airspace which is necessary for the ordinary use and enjoyment of neighbouring property. The test of necessity for ordinary use and enjoyment (used in the case of overflying) would not of itself

1–031

---

[51] Above, at 175 M.

[52] *Woollerton & Wilson Ltd v. Richard Costain Ltd* [1970] 1 W.L.R. 411, *John Trenberth Ltd v. National Westminster Bank Ltd* (1979) 39 P. & C.R. 104, *Anchor Brewhouse*, [1987] 2 E.G.L.R. 173 and *Lemmon v. Webb* [1895] A.C. 1, HL.

[53] See below, Chapter 4, para. 4–084ff. In *London & Manchester Assurance Co. Ltd v. O & H Construction Ltd* [1989] 2 E.G.L.R. 185 the high-handed acts of the defendant, and the strength of the claim in trespass, led to the grant of a mandatory interlocutory injunction and an order restraining the swinging of the crane over the plaintiff's land.

appear to make actionable all[54] those objects or structures (however high) which are attached to adjacent land and which overhang. That conclusion would, on that test, only be justified by a proper consideration of the factual circumstances and the nature and use of the land affected.

Whilst a low flying aircraft, balloon or bullet is capable of being the subject matter of a trespass if it infringes that necessary airspace referred to by Griffiths J., the fact of attachment to the earth appears, in accordance with the principles in *Anchor Brewhouse*, to preclude the exclusion from trespass even of structures which are too high to interfere with necessary airspace.

Although logically it may be difficult to exclude the necessity test from the overhanging cases, the two approaches might be reconciled: in the case of an overhanging structure, the fact that it is attached to adjacent land suggests that the airspace into which it intrudes is also capable of beneficial use by the neighbouring owner — and thus, in that sense, fulfils Griffiths J.'s necessity criterion. Indeed, that capability of use is stressed by Scott J. in the passage set out above.[55]

The difficulty with the suggested reconciliation is that it assumes a particular "ordinary use and enjoyment" of a particular parcel of land by reference to the actual use of another parcel whereas the actual circumstances of the parcel under consideration might not support such an inference in fact, *e.g.* where there is a crane overhanging at a great height but the parcel whose air space is affected is too small to support a crane of such height.

Statute

1–032   If an aircraft complies with the conditions set out in section 76 of the Civil Aviation Act 1982, then the mere entry into the airspace above another's property will not amount to a trespass by reason only of the flight (or the ordinary incidents of such) providing that the conditions stipulated in section 76(1) are met[56] and that the flight is reasonable having regard to wind, weather and all the circumstances of the case. Similar rights to enter the property of another are granted by many statutes, in some cases to limited classes of person *e.g.* public authorities[57] and in others, to the public.[58]

Incorporeal rights

1–033   The law of trespass does not deal equally with all incorporeal rights which might be enjoyed over the land of another: it only protects those

---

[54] As in the *Anchor Brewhouse* decision, above.
[55] [1987] 2 E.G.L.R. 173 at 175 M.
[56] *i.e.* that the provisions of any Air Navigation Order have been complied with and there is no breach of s. 81 (dangerous flying).
[57] See, *e.g.*, s. 178(1) of the Town and Country Planning Act 1990.
[58] See, *e.g.*, Part I of the Countryside and Rights of Way Act 2000.

incorporeal rights which confer possession on the owner, or upon the owner jointly with persons other than the person infringing the right. Although an unwarranted interference with *profits à prendre* may be protected by the action of trespass, an action does not lie in respect of interference with easements since the latter do not confer possession, or an entitlement to possession, on the owner of the dominant tenement. In *Pain & Co. Ltd v. St. Neots Gas & Coke Co.*[59] Luxmoore L.J. drew the distinction between easements and profits as follows:[60]

> "... a *profit à prendre* is an interest capable of being assigned and dealt with according to the ordinary rules of property, being of a possessory nature and capable of existing in gross. Its owner can bring an action for trespass at common law for its infringement ... An easement differs from a *profit à prendre*, although both may be classed under the head of servitudes in that the owner of an easement cannot maintain trespass, the only remedies available to him for disturbance being by abatement or by an action for nuisance. In an action for nuisance the owner of the easement must plead that he is entitled, so that if his title to the easement alleged to be interfered with is put in issue (as in this case), he must establish that title, for he is asserting a right which of necessity excludes the possibility of possession of the servient tenement, or any part of it: see *Aldred's* case (1610) 9 Co. Rep 57b, *Higgins v. Betts* [1905] 2 Ch. 210."

Examples of those rights over the land of others which have been protected by trespass include the exclusive right to cut turf,[61] to cut timber,[62] to fish[63] and the right to a free warren.[64]

In *Fitzgerald v. Firbank*[65] Lindley L.J. stated, in the context of action by the owners of a several fishery against a person who had discharged polluted water into a nearby river which drove away the fish and injured their breeding, that such an owner:

1–034

> "has such possessory rights that he can bring an action for trespass at common law for the infringement of those rights ..."

The distinction between profits and easements might appear odd, given the similarity between the two types of third party rights. The rationale for it lies in the fact that whilst a *profit à prendre* generally confers upon its owner an exclusive right to a particular thing, *e.g.* to fell timber, which

---

[59] [1939] 3 All E.R. 812.
[60] *ibid.* at 823.
[61] *Wilson v. Mackreth* (1766) 3 Burr. 1824 and *Coverdale v. Charlton* (1878) 4 Q.B.D. 104.
[62] *Glenwood Lumber Co. Ltd v. Phillips* [1904] A.C. 405.
[63] *Holford v. Bailey* (1846) 8 Q.B. 1000, affirmed (1849) 13 Q.B.D. 426, *Fitzgerald v. Firbank* [1897] 2 Ch. 96 and *Nicholls v. Ely Beet Sugar Factory* [1931] 2 Ch. 84, CA.
[64] *Lord Dacre v. Tebb* (1777) 2 Wm. Bl. 1151.
[65] [1897] 2 Ch. 96 at 101–102.

amounts to a possessory right, an easement does not. Typically, a right of way granted to a person will permit passage over a certain parcel of land, with certain limitations, but will not entitle the easement owner to an exclusive right of way. Another person using that way will not wrongfully interfere with the easement simply by his use of the way, although if there is a substantial interference an action in nuisance may lie.

The distinction between the types of incorporeal rights may cause no substantial problem in practice since the disturbance of an easement is remediable by an action in nuisance or by abatement. The principle limitation arises from the fact that an action for the disturbance of an easement may only lie where there is substantial interference with that right,[66] whereas an interference with a *profit à prendre* is actionable *per se* and thus requires no element of substantial interference or disturbance.

The exclusion of easements from the category of interests which may form the subject-matter of a trespass action does not, however, prevent the existence of an easement providing a suitable defence to action of trespass against the user of the easement in appropriate cases,[67] if that easement authorises the activity which is alleged to constitute a trespass.

What amounts to a trespass

Direct injury

1–035   The action of trespass is said to lie only for cases of direct wrongdoing whereas cases of indirect wrongdoing form the subject-matter of actions on the case, *e.g.* for nuisance or actions that later became classed as negligence.[68] In *Scott v. Shepherd*,[69] Blackstone J. stated that he took:

> "the settled distinction to be that, where the injury is immediate, an action of trespass will lie; where it is only consequential, it must be an action on the case ... the lawfulness or unlawfulness of the original act is not the criterion ... if I throw a log of timber into the highway (which is an unlawful act), and another man tumbles over and is hurt, an action on the case only lies, it being consequential damage; but if in throwing it I hit another man, he may bring trespass, because it is an immediate wrong. Trespass may sometimes lie for the consequences of a lawful act. If in lopping my own trees a bough accidentally falls on my neighbour's ground and I go thereon to fetch it, trespass lies ... But then the entry is of itself an immediate wrong ... So that lawful or

[66] See below Chapter 2, paras. 2–007, 2–026 to 2–030.
[67] See below, paras. 1–074 to 1–082.
[68] See J.H. Baker, *An Introduction to Legal History* (4th ed., 2002) pp. 401–405, Milsom, *Historical Foundations of the Common Law* (2nd ed., 1981), pp. 305–313 and M.J. Pritchard, Scott and Shepherd (1773) and the *Emergence of the Tort of Negligence* (Selden Society Lecture 1976).
[69] (1773) W. Blackstone 892.

unlawful is quite out of the case; the solid distinction is between direct and immediate injuries on the one hand, and mediate or consequential on the other. And trespass never lay for the latter . . ."

Although, in general, the passage of time has tended to blur the distinction between the various forms of action[70] the distinction between direct and indirect wrongdoing is not merely of historical interest.[71] Further, as appears from the following section, a direct wrongdoing is not sufficient in itself to amount to a trespass. In practical terms it is often possible to frame actions in trespass and, in the alternative, in another form of tortious action, e.g. nuisance[72] or negligence. This results from the fact that all that need be pleaded is the factual circumstances giving rise to the cause(s) of action and then the allegation of the cause(s) of action itself. This should present no practical difficulty provided that facts sufficient to support each individual cause of action are pleaded. If, however, there is a proper distinction between trespass and other tortious actions arising from actions on the case, then it appears theoretically incorrect to sue in *both* trespass and that other tort save in the alternative. Whether this distinction would trouble a modern court, charged with giving effect to the overriding objective in Part 1 of the CPR, is open to doubt.

Intention

Although this question has been said to be "of little practical interest, for the majority of trespasses to land are, in the nature of things, self-evidently intentional,"[73] intention appears nonetheless to be required in order to establish a trespass.[74] A wholly involuntary interference with land does not constitute a trespass,[75] *i.e.* the trespass must be the act[76] of the defendant, but a wholly deliberate act is not required[77] since recklessness or negligence may be sufficient.[78] In *League Against Cruel Sports v. Scott*,[79] Park J.

1–036

---

[70] See *Letang v. Cooper* [1965] 1 Q.B. 232 CA, subject to *Stubbings v. Webb* [1993] A.C. 498, HL.

[71] See Baker and Milsom, *op. cit.* The direct/indirect distinction may only have resulted from an attempt at rationalisation of principle in the eighteenth century. Some of the consequences appear to have endured until fairly recently: see Winfield & Goodhart (1933) 49 L.Q.R. "Trespass and Negligence", *Fowler v. Lanning* [1959] 1 Q.B. 426 (trespass to the person) and Goodhart (1959) 75 L.Q.R. 161.

[72] See below, Chapter 2, paras. 2–011 to 2–013, 2–016.

[73] Winfield, Tort (11th ed.), p. 335. See also the works cited in n. 74 below.

[74] See Pollock (1891) 7 L.Q.R. pp. 10–11, Goodhart & Winfield, *op. cit.*, Fleming, *Law of Torts* (1998, 9th ed.) (Australia), pp. 21–27 and Cane (1982) 2 O.J.L.S. 30 at 35–39 "Justice and Justification for Tort Liability". Whether or not intention is a necessary element of the tort is considered briefly below, paras. 1–037 to 1–042.

[75] See, *e.g.* *Braithwaite v. South Durham Steel Co. Ltd* [1958] 1 W.L.R. 986 and the defence of inevitable accident.

[76] Or omission, such as the failure to remove trespassing buttresses in *Holmes v. Wilson* (1839) 10 A. & E. 503. See also *Konskier v. B. Goodman Ltd* [1928] 1 K.B. 421, CA.

[77] *Holmes v. Mather* (1875) L.R. 10 Ex. 261 at 268–269, *Conway v. George Wimpey & Co. Ltd* [1951] 2 K.B. 266, at 273–274, *Joliffe v. Willmett & Co.* [1971] 1 All E.R. 478 and *League Against Cruel Sports v. Scott* [1986] 1 Q.B. 240.

[78] Subject to *Letang v. Cooper* and the matters considered below, paras. 1–037 to 1–042.

[79] [1986] 1 Q.B. 240.

considered that, in the case of trespassing hounds supervised by hunt members, if it were impossible to prevent the entry onto the land of another the inference might well be drawn that indifference to the risk of trespass "amounted to an intention that hounds should trespass on the land".

In summary the effect of the authorities appears to be as follows:[80]

(1)   in order to amount to trespass, an act must be intended in the sense that the person committing it must intend to carry out the physical act constituting the interference;

(2)   the act does not need to be wholly deliberate, or wilful, and will amount to a trespass if the person committing it was negligent or reckless as to its occurrence or consequences;

(3)   a mere involuntary physical movement, or act, will not amount to a trespass; but

(4)   there is no requirement that the person committing the act must intend that the act should have the character of a trespass, or be unlawful. Hence, mistake is no defence to trespass.

Trespass and fault

1–037   Notwithstanding doubts expressed *obiter* by a majority of the Court of Appeal in the context of trespass to the person,[81] the present state of the law with regard to trespass to land appears in *Holmes v. Mather*[82] where Bramwell B. explained the distinction between trespass and other forms of wrongful interference as follows:

> "If the act that does the injury is an act of direct force, *vi et armis*, trespass is the proper remedy (if there is any remedy), where the act is wrongful either as being wilful or as being the result of negligence. Where the act is not wrongful for either of these reasons no action is maintainable, though trespass would be the proper form of action if it were wrongful."

The above approach appears to be founded on the distinction drawn by the common law in the past between actions of trespass, which concerned direct wrongdoings, and actions on the case, which concerned indirect

---

[80]   Contrary to the view expressed in Fleming, *The Law of Torts* (9th ed., 1998) (Australia) at pp. 47–49.

[81]   *Letang v. Cooper* [1965] 1 Q.B. 232, CA. Following the decision of the House of Lords in *Stubbings v. Webb* [1993] A.C. 498 this decision appears to be confined to the interpretation of the Law Reform (Limitation of Actions etc) Act 1954, s. 2(1): see *per* Lord Griffiths at 127.

[82]   See above, also *League against Cruel Sports v. Scott*, [1986] 1 Q.B. 240, and Commonwealth decisions such as (Australia) *Williams v. Milotin* (1957) 97 C.L.R. 465, *Venning v. Chin* (1975) 10 S.A.S.R. 299 at 306–8, (New Zealand) *Beals v. Hayward* [1960] N.Z.L.R. 131, (Canada) *Cook v. Lewis* [1952] 1 D.L.R. 1 and *Larin v. Goshen* (1974) 56 D.L.R. (3d) 719.

wrongdoing.[83] However, it is clear that even in the case of "direct force", some form of fault is required to establish trespass.[84] Accordingly, a wrongful act amounts to a trespass whether it is wholly deliberate, or results from negligence[85] or recklessness and, to that limited extent, the act alleged to be a trespass must be shown to be intentional. This approach appears to be consistent with the more recent decision of Park J. in the *League Against Cruel Sports v. Scott*[86] where the defendants' submission that the real question in deciding whether or not a trespass had been committed was simply whether the acts in question were voluntary or involuntary was rejected. The learned judge stated:[87]

> "I have, therefore, come to the conclusion that, before a master of hounds may be held liable for trespass on land by hounds, it has to be shown that he either intended that the hounds would enter the land, or by negligence he failed to prevent them from doing so . . . where a master of staghounds takes out a pack of hounds and deliberately sets them in pursuit of a stag or hind, knowing that there is a real risk that in the pursuit hounds may enter or cross prohibited land, the master will be liable in trespass if he intended to cause hounds to enter such land, or if by his failure to exercise proper control over them he caused them to enter such land . . .
>
> Further, if it is virtually impossible, whatever precautions are taken, to prevent hounds from entering, yet the master knowing that to be the case, nevertheless persists in hunting in its vicinity, with the result that hounds frequently trespass on the land, then the inference might well be drawn that his indifference to the risk of trespass amounted to an intention that hounds should trespass on the land."

However, the view of the majority of the Court of Appeal in *Letang v. Cooper*[88] appears to exclude from the ambit of trespass those wrongful acts

---

[83] See *Scott v. Shepherd* (1773) W. Blackstone 892 and the works cited above, nn. 68 and 71.

[84] Even though, in the context of the distinction between direct and indirect wrongdoing, the question of intention was not of primary significance whereas the nature of the wrongdoing was.

[85] Although such negligence would not have to be such as to amount to actionable negligence (*i.e.* the tort) since trespass does not require proof of actual damage: see Diplock L.J. in *Letang v. Cooper* [1965] 1 Q.B. 232, at 244–245. Note also the overlap in the discussion of negligence and trespass in, *e.g. Konskier v. B. Goodman Ltd* [1928] 1 K.B. 421, CA, 425–427.

[86] Where *Letang* was cited in argument but, interestingly, the learned judge did not find it necessary to consider the majority's views on trespass and negligence in his judgment.

[87] [1986] 1 Q.B. at 251–252.

[88] In that case, the claimant sued in both negligence and trespass for personal injuries caused by the defendant driving his car over her legs. It was argued that, although the limitation period had expired for the action brought in negligence, the limitation period for "actions for damages for negligence, nuisance or breach of duty" did not apply to actions in trespass. The ratio of the decision appears to lie in the interpretation of the Limitation Act 1939 since it was held, in any event, that the action (whether viewed in trespass or negligence) involved a "breach of duty" within the 1939 Act, s. 2, and failed for

which arise otherwise than from direct, intentional conduct,[89] thereby excluding those cases where a wrong has been caused negligently or inadvertently. Apart from the construction of section 2 of the Limitation Act 1939, the majority of the Court of Appeal (Lord Denning M.R. and Danckwerts L.J.) also considered that where the act complained of was not "intentional" the cause of action lay in negligence, not trespass.[90] Diplock L.J., whilst concurring in the result that the claimant's action was statute-barred, chose to do so on a different footing[91] and appeared to reach a conclusion different from the views of the majority on the question of intentional acts:[92]

> "It is not, I think, necessary to consider whether there is today any respect in which a cause of action for unintentional as distinct from intentional trespass to the person is not equally aptly described as a cause of action for negligence. The difference stressed by Elwes J. that actual damage caused by failure to exercise reasonable care forms an essential element in the cause of action for negligence, but does not in the cause of action for trespass to the person, is, I think, more apparent that real when the trespass is unintentional: for, since the duty of care, whether in negligence or in unintentional trespass to the person, is to take reasonable care to avoid causing actual damage to one's neighbour, there is no breach of the duty unless actual damage is caused. Actual damage is thus a necessary ingredient in unintentional as distinct from intentional trespass to the person."

1–038   If the views of the majority in *Letang* were to be applied to the distinction between trespass and negligence generally it would lead to the conclusion that the cause of action for a negligent, but not intentional, interference with land would lie in negligence but not in trespass. However, this approach does not represent the present state of the authorities on trespass to land[93] nor does there appear to be justification for such a distinction. Further, the House of Lords in *Stubbings v. Webb*[94] has held that, whilst *Letang* was correctly decided in so far as the interpretation of section 2(1) was concerned, it was of no wider effect and was not applicable to the parallel provisions in the Limitation Act 1980.[95] Lord

that reason. See now the Limitation Act 1980, s. 2, which is worded differently — the term now used is "actions founded on tort".

[89] [1965] 1 Q.B. 232 — at least insofar as the reasoning there (which concerned an action for trespass to the person) is applicable to trespasses to land. See Dworkin (1965) 28 M.L.R. 92 ("Trespass and Negligence — A Further Attempt to Bury the Forms of Action").

[90] [1965] 1 Q.B. 232 at 239–40 (the views of the majority are found in the judgment of Lord Denning M.R.).

[91] Namely that since the cause of action was fundamentally that of negligence (notwithstanding the fact that the claimant sued in trespass) the Limitation Act 1939, s. 2, applied.

[92] [1965] 1 Q.B. 232 at 244–245.

[93] See *League Against Cruel Sports v. Scott* [1986] 1 Q.B. 240.

[94] [1993] A.C. 498, HL.

[95] He relied on the distinction between "negligence" and "breach of duty" in the Limitation Act 1980, s. 11(1). This case is also an example of the practice established by the House of

Griffiths,[96] whilst quoting the passage from the judgment of Lord Denning MR in *Letang* dealing with the question of negligence and trespass, was careful not to endorse it and to limit the effect of the decision to the construction of the particular statutory provision.

To adopt the views of the majority in *Letang* with respect to land would introduce a difficult and unnecessary division[97] between (a) acts of interference which were wholly intentional[98] and (b) acts which were still intentional, but were not wholly deliberate, *e.g.* where they were, wholly or in part, the result of negligence or recklessness. Although a particular act may be "intended" in the sense that the activity is deliberately carried out, not all aspects of it may be deliberately planned nor may the fact of the unlawful interference itself be intended, although there may be recklessness as to the interference. An example of this is where a pedestrian deliberately leaves the footpath without considering where his detour will take him or whether he has any right to enter the land off the path.

In defence of the *Letang* view it might be said that the distinction would present few problems in practice since, in cases of doubt, it would usually be open to the injured party to sue both in trespass and negligence. However, the advantage of trespass over negligence lies in the fact that trespass is actionable *per se* and does not require proof of loss: the *Letang* distinction might lead to unnecessarily complex arguments at applications for interim injunctions, or at attempts to strike out ill-framed actions, although there is little evidence of its doing so.

Wholly involuntary acts

Since the physical act of interference must be intentional[99] in order to constitute a trespass[1] it follows that a wholly involuntary act will not be a trespass.[2] In *Braithwaite v. South Durham Steel Co. Ltd*[3] Edmund Davies J. rejected the submission that a crane driver's mate had trespassed where, as a result of the negligence of one of the defendants, he had taken a "startled and un-premeditated step" of a few inches outside the area over which he was permitted to pass. Since trespass may be caused by a reckless or negligent act, it must be a question of fact in every case where involuntariness is in issue whether the act complained of was truly

1–039

Lords in *Pepper v. Hart* [1993] A.C. 593 whereby Hansard may be used by the Courts: see also: Practice Direction (Hansard: Citation) [1995] 1 W.L.R. 192.

[96] The other Law Lords agreed with Lord Griffiths.

[97] The view of the High Court of Australia, in *Hackshaw v. Shaw* (1984) 155 C.L.R. 614 at 619, that a jury might be confused by alternative claims in trespass and negligence has little to commend it in this jurisdiction where jury trial for such actions is obsolete.

[98] *i.e.* as to both the act of the interference and the form of interference itself.

[99] In the sense set out above, *i.e.* intentional, but not necessarily in the sense that it was intended as an act of interference.

[1] *Braithwaite v. South Durham Steel Co. Ltd* [1958] 1 W.L.R. 986.

[2] *Smith v. Stone* (1647) Style 65.

[3] [1958] 1 W.L.R. 986.

involuntary or whether it was the result of recklessness or negligence, *i.e.* "intentional" in the sense described in the previous section.[4]

Mistake

1–040 Mistake is no defence to trespass if the act of trespass was intentional in the sense explained above. A mistaken, though deliberate, act is nonetheless a trespass and it would introduce undesirable complexities into the law if an inquiry had to be conducted into a trespasser's knowledge of property boundaries (which are often not obvious or apparent). Further, the absence of this defence casts the burden upon the user of land to ascertain the proper boundaries of property and to be sure that he has the requisite leave to enter on or use the land.

Should intention be a necessary requirement of trespass?

1–041 Although it has been seen that the authorities do regard intention as a necessary element of the tort, it does not appear to have a significant role to play except to preclude involuntary actions from giving rise to liability. The scope of intention is wide, including the reckless or negligent, and mistake cannot provide a defence. Theoretically, there may be a residual category of non-mistaken, voluntary yet "innocent" acts (*i.e.* ones which are neither wilful, negligent or reckless), but it is difficult to envisage the circumstances when such a situation would arise. If a voluntary act is committed, it would be unlikely that it would not qualify as a trespass at least on grounds of recklessness, and most pleas of "innocence" would probably amount to no more than attempts to mount a defence based on mistake. In other words, the "innocent" acts category may for all practical purposes be co-extensive with involuntary acts.

Further, since the action of trespass lies to protect the rights of those entitled to possession of land, it is preferable and simpler that liability should arise from the act of interference itself and not from a categorisation of the act as "wrongful" in some additional sense. The rights of the owner or occupier of the land trespassed upon are interfered with regardless of intention and leaving a residual category of "innocent" acts of interference simply allows an uncertain, subjective element to be set up against the injury to the landowner. The better approach would be to make the issue an objective one only, as in the reasonable foreseeability criterion of the tort of negligence or the question of substantial interference in nuisance.[5]

1–042 Indeed, it might be better to eliminate altogether consideration of intention from the definition of trespass save to exclude involuntary acts:

---

[4] See above, para. 1–036. The use of the term "unintentional trespass" by Diplock L.J. in *Letang*, above, appears to mean reckless or negligent trespass as opposed to trespass which was wholly involuntary.
[5] See below, Chapter 2, paras. 2–025 and 2–030.

if this were done trespass would not wholly become a type of strict liability, dependent merely upon the act of interference, but there would be eliminated from consideration an unnecessary element which serves little useful function.[6] The principle function which the requirement of intention now performs appears to be that of excluding involuntary acts from the scope of trespass liability. An involuntary act might be better explained as an act which is not the act of the person committing it, rather than one which is not wrongful because of an absence of intention. Accordingly, liability should depend, in general, simply upon establishing an unwarranted intrusion upon the land, or interference with rights in possession, of another.

This view does not represent the current state of the law — as exemplified by the decision in the *League Against Cruel Sports v. Scott,*[7] where Park J. rejected the defendants' submission that the real question in deciding whether or not a trespass had been committed was simply whether the acts in question were voluntary or involuntary.[8] However, the discussion by Park J. of the responsibility of a master of staghounds for his dogs[9] does illustrate the difficulty of establishing a voluntary, yet "innocent" intrusion upon another person's land and the fact that it is likely that most intrusions will at least be regarded as reckless and, hence, intentional.

Continuing trespasses

A trespass may be a continuing trespass if the trespasser remains in occupation of the land which he has unlawfully entered or unlawfully remains in occupation following the termination of his right.[10] In those circumstances, a new cause of action accrues each day so long as the trespass continues and the limitation period applies to each such separate cause of action. A new owner who enters into possession of premises on which there is a continuing trespass has, from the time of such entry, a cause of action in trespass in respect of the continuing wrong.[11] In *Konskier v. B. Goodman Ltd,*[12] the fact that ownership changed during the course of a series of continuing trespasses did not prevent the new owner from bringing an action in trespass once title has been acquired, although he could not maintain an action in respect of wrongs which occurred prior to his acquisition of title.

1–043

---

[6] The infrequency of any discussion of intention in the authorities provides some support for this proposition.

[7] [1986] 1 Q.B. 240.

[8] *ibid.* at 251–252.

[9] In the passage quoted above at para. 1–037 from [1986] 1 Q.B. at 251–252.

[10] *Holmes v. Wilson* (1839) 10 A. & E. 503 and *Hudson v. Nicholson* (1839) 5 M. & W. 437.

[11] *Hudson v. Nicholson* (1839) 5 M. & W. 437 and *Konskier v. B. Goodman Ltd* [1928] 1 K.B. 421, CA.

[12] [1928] 1 K.B. 421, CA.

Forms of trespass to land

1–044   This section sets out principal examples of trespass to land which may be encountered, although the categories set out below are by no means exclusive. The common element running through each is the lack of authorisation, either by the law or the owner of the land in question, to act in a certain manner or carry on a particular activity which involves a direct interference with the possession of real property — whether that absence of authorisation exists from the outset or at some later stage.

Unlawful entry

1–045   This is the simplest form of trespass, and probably that most commonly thought of as trespass, namely the entry of a person without authorisation onto the land in the possession or ownership of another. The entry will also be unlawful if it is not onto the land itself but, in certain cases, into the airspace above it or the sub-soil beneath.[13] In such a case the actual entry is trespass *ab initio* being unlawful from the outset. If the trespasser remains on the land, or returns to it, then each daily continuation of the unlawful entry, or each repetition of it, is a new trespass.

It does not matter that the extent of the entry on to the land of another is small or insignificant:

> "It is clear that, in determining the question of trespass or no trespass, the Court cannot measure the amount of the alleged trespass; if the defendant place a part of his foot on the plaintiff's land unlawfully, it is in law as much a trespass as if he had walked half a mile on it."[14]

Dispossession

1–046   The unauthorised ousting of another from possession of land is also unlawful and may well be accompanied by some other form of trespass, *e.g.* entry. In a more extreme form, dispossession could take the form of a physical removal of the person of the lawful owner (whether with or without his chattels),[15] or may simply involve the barring of entry to that owner,[16] *e.g.* by changing the locks on the doors or erecting a gate. In the case of a landlord who unlawfully locks out a tenant from the premises let to him, not only will the act amount to a trespass but there will be additional liability under the landlord's covenant for quiet enjoyment.[17]

---

[13]   See above, paras. 1–024 to 1–032.
[14]   *per* Lord Coleridge C.J. in *Ellis v. The Loftus Iron Co.* (1874) L.R. 10 C.P. 10 at 12.
[15]   Which would probably also amount to a trespass to the person.
[16]   *Lavender v. Betts* [1942] 2 All E.R. 72 (removal of doors and windows by landlord); *Drane v. Evangelou* [1978] 1 W.L.R. 455, CA (forcible entry by landlord in tenant's absence and bolting of door from inside to exclude the tenant).
[17]   See below, Chapter 3, 3–024 to 3–041.

Remaining once the right to stay is terminated

This is a variation on trespass by unlawful entry since a trespass may be **1–047** committed where, although consent had been given to the entry onto the land, that consent has been terminated whether expressly or by the trespasser exceeding the permission given. This latter possibility is considered at paragraphs 1–048 and 1–073 and 1–076, below.

If a person has been granted a right to occupy land then, if such a right is properly terminated, the occupier's right to remain ceases with that termination and he becomes a trespasser if he remains on, or in occupation of, the land. However, there are two points which require further consideration:

(1) whether or not the right has been duly terminated;

(2) whether any time should be allowed to the occupier to vacate once the right has been so terminated.

These points are both examined in greater detail under *The Recovery of Possession*, below, paragraphs 4–057 and 4–083.

Where a person does remain in occupation as a trespasser, such a trespass is *continuing* and a separate cause of action accrues for each day of unlawful occupation.[18]

Abuse of right

If a person enters land (or carries out some other act which would other- **1–048** wise be a trespass) under some legal authority (other than the consent of the owner of the land) and abuses his right to enter, or be, on that land, then he is deemed to have been a trespasser from the moment of entry (or other act), *i.e.* is regarded as a trespasser *ab initio*.[19] The apparently illogical distinction drawn between abuse of legal right and that of express consent is a result of the origins of the doctrine in preventing the abuse of levying distress and has been strongly criticised. In *Chic Fashions (West Wales) Ltd v. Jones*,[20] Lord Denning MR[21] remarked:

> "The lawfulness of his conduct must be judged at the time and not by what happens afterwards. I know that at one time a man could be made a trespasser *ab initio* by the doctrine of relation back. But that is

---

[18] *Konskier v. B. Goodman Ltd* [1928] 1 K.B. 421. The limitation period applies to each separate cause of action, *i.e.* an action in trespass (where there is continuing unlawful occupation) does not become wholly statute-barred merely because the commencement of the occupation began more than six years ago. The plaintiff may still sue for the daily trespasses within the six year limitation period. Compare Chapter Two on continuing nuisances, paras. 2–014 to 2–015 and 2–030.

[19] *The Six Carpenters' Case* (1610) 8 Co. Rep. 146a.

[20] [1968] 2 Q.B. 299 (which concerned trespass to goods).

[21] At p. 313 (*obiter*). See also Salmon L.J. at 320 and Diplock L.J. at 317.

no longer true. The *Six Carpenters'* Case was a by-product of the old forms of action. Now that they are buried, it can be interred with them."

However, since the contrary view was expressed some 12 years later by the same judge in *Cinnamond v. British Airports Authority*,[22] it is clearly not safe to consider the doctrine as obsolete.

In any event, it is necessary to be careful in considering the extent to which the authority has been abused since an entry will only be considered to be unlawful to that extent.[23] Accordingly in *Elias v. Pasmore*,[24] where police inspectors had entered premises and seized certain documents, a trespass had been committed only with regard to those documents which the police were not entitled to seize. It appears that the court did not consider that the police officers had committed a trespass to the land entered but only to the documents unlawfully seized: this suggests that a partial abuse of authority, or an abuse only in respect of certain acts carried out on the land, will not render an otherwise lawful entry unlawful *ab initio*.[25]

Placing items on land

1–049   Whilst the placing of items on (or in) the land of another may, incidentally, involve an unlawful entry, the placing of the items itself also may amount to a trespass if it is unauthorised.[26] Indeed, such a form of trespass may well be a continuing trespass if the items are left on that land or, for example, if a structure is unlawfully erected on another's land.

Tenant holding over

1–050   Where a tenancy determines and the former tenant remains in possession without the consent of the landlord,[27] then although that occupation is dignified by the title tenancy at sufferance[28] the occupier has, in reality, a highly precarious interest (and not an estate in land) which may be

---

[22] [1980] 1 W.L.R. 582 at 588.

[23] *Harvey v. Pocock* (1843) 11 M. & W. 740, *Canadian Pacific Wine Co. v. Tuley* [1921] 2 A.C. 417, PC, and *Elias v. Pasmore* [1934] 2 K.B. 164.

[24] [1934] 2 K.B. 164.

[25] See *Harvey v. Pocock* (1843) 11 M. & W. 740, and *Canadian Pacific Wine Co. v. Tuley* [1921] 2 A.C. 417, PC.

[26] See *Sussex Investments Ltd v. Jackson, The Times*, July 27, 1993, CA, where the trespass occurred by the placing of a gangplank from a houseboat onto the towpath.

[27] If the landlord consents then, in the absence of agreed terms, the tenant will usually become a tenant at will: *Cardiothoracic Institute v. Shrewdcrest Ltd* [1986] 1 W.L.R. 368 and *Javad v. Aqil* [1991] 1 All E.R. 243, CA. If the landlord then accepts rent upon a periodic basis, that may convert the tenancy into a tenancy from year to year, although this is subject to proof of the intention of the parties in paying and accepting sums of money: *Longrigg Burrough & Trounson v. Smith* (1979) 251 E.G. 857, CA, *Cardiothoracic v. Shrewdcrest* and *Javad v. Aqil*, above.

[28] See *Hill & Redman's Law of Landlord and Tenant*, paras A[150]–A[161] and *Foa's General Law of Landlord and Tenant* (8th ed.), pp. 2–3.

determined at any time without notice[29] and merely by the landlord entering into possession or demonstrating an intention to retake possession.[30] Whilst a tenancy at will arises from right, a tenancy at sufferance does not.[31] On such determination, the tenant at sufferance becomes a trespasser. Such a situation does not arise where, for example, the original contractual tenancy determines but the tenant is entitled to remain in possession by virtue of some statutory right, *e.g.* under the provisions of the Housing Act 1988 or Part II of the Landlord and Tenant Act 1954.

If, however, the former tenant holds over where the reversionary owner is the Crown, then no tenancy at sufferance arises and the tenant becomes a trespasser on the determination of the tenancy. This distinction is said to arise since the tenancy at sufferance results from the negligence or laches of the owner of the reversion and the Crown is not capable of committing laches.[32]

On the related question of 'tolerated trespassers,' see para. 1–014 above.

Animals

Common law

Although the Animals Act 1971 abolished the ancient action for cattle-trespass the general liability in trespass for animals remains, such as for the placing, or sending, of animals onto the land of another without consent or authority. In general terms animals, as chattels, are merely the instruments of the persons owning or controlling them and those persons are liable if the chattels trespass.[33] In *League Against Cruel Sports Ltd v. Scott*[34] Park J. held that hunt members would have been liable in trespass for hounds straying onto lands held by the claimant even had it been impossible to prevent physical entry onto that land.

Animals which are *ferae naturae* (*i.e.* wild) and which pass onto or over the land of another will not found an action in trespass even if they come from the land of their erstwhile possessor. Ownership in general terms does not exist in animals *ferae naturae*[35] and only a qualified property right[36]

1–051

---

[29] *Doe d. Rogers v. Pullen* (1836) 2 Bing. N.C. 749 and *Randall v. Stevens* (1853) 2 E. & B. 641.

[30] *Jones v. Chapman* (1849) 2 Exch. 803 and *Doe v. Beaufort* (1851) 6 Ex. 498. Any re-taking of possession must be peaceable: see the Criminal Law Act 1977. In the case of a residential letting, a former tenant must be evicted by possession proceedings: the Protection from Eviction Act 1977, s. 3 (except in the case of a statutorily protected tenancy or an excluded tenancy).

[31] The landlord may not distrain upon the goods of the tenant at sufferance: *Alford v. Vicery* (1842) Car. & Marsh. 280.

[32] Co. Litt. 57b.

[33] See, *e.g. Ellis v. The Loftus Iron Co.* (1874) L.R. 10 C.P. 10 (horse kicked through fence) and *Ponting v. Noakes* [1894] 2 Q.B. 281 (horse stretching neck across ditch boundary and eating leaves from tree).

[34] [1986] Q.B. 240 and see above, paras. 1–036 to 1–042.

[35] See *The Case of Swans* (1592) 7 Co. Rep. 15b at 17b.

[36] Either obtained *per industriam, ratione impotentiae et loci* or *ratione soli* or *ratione privilegii,*

can be enjoyed: this right is lost if the animals regain their freedom or leave the land. Hence, animals which have left the land of another cease to be within the limited ownership of the owner of that land. In general, animals which are *ferae naturae* will cease to become the property of the landowner whose land they have left[37] and they will then be capable of becoming the qualified property of the landowner whose land has been entered.

However, bees which have been hived[38] and which forage over and onto the land of another are not regarded as trespassing. This is a consequence of the fact that, in normal circumstances, the keepers cannot control where the bees will fly in their foraging.[39] In *Tutton v. A.D. Walter Ltd*,[40] the plaintiff bee-keeper successfully sued the defendant in negligence for spraying its crop with insecticide which killed his bees and the defendant failed in a defence which alleged (*inter alia*) that the bees were trespassing. It does not appear to have been disputed that the bees were, at the time, the qualified property of the plaintiff. The Deputy Judge (Denis Henry Q.C.)[41] said:

> "I find great difficulty . . . in accepting the concept that bees may be invitees, licensees or trespassers. In my opinion it is unreal to divide bees into those categories and attempt to force on to them the subtleties of the common law when dealing with human beings who either had or had not permission to enter on to the land on which they were injured. Further, in my opinion, the common law concepts of bailment do not hold in considering the legal position as to bees . . . trespassers in the eyes of the law are wrongdoers. It is unreal to look at bees in this light. Bees are useful insects; for their use to the neighbourhood in which they forage is universal and not peculiar to certain neighbourhoods. True, that utility is limited or latent in the case of a neighbouring landowner whose crop for that year is self-pollinating, but the bees' utility to the neighbourhood remains. I am invited to make a distinction, dividing bees' foraging grounds for each season into areas where, on the one hand, they are currently useful and beneficial, improving the farmer's yield (for example, orchards) where they should be treated as invitees and owed a duty of care; and those areas, on the other hand, where they are at best tolerated, where it is said that they are trespassers and their negligent

---

[37] *i.e.* by industry in taming or containing the animal, by the retention of the young until they are able to leave, or the right arising from ownership of the soil (or grant of a right) to hunt or take animals on the land.

[37] See *e.g.* bees swarming, rabbits or game.

[38] In other words, reduced into the qualified ownership of the keeper *per industriam*.

[39] Although bees are *ferae naturae* they can become the qualified property of a person by that person hiving them but if they swarm and leave the hive, they remain the property of the keeper only for so long as the bees can be seen and followed: see *Hannam v. Mockett* (1824) 2 B. & C. 934 and *Kearry v. Pattinson* [1939] 1 K.B. 471, CA. Note that the keeper of bees may not rely on the defence of necessity to justify following that swarm onto the land of another: *Kearry v. Pattinson*.

[40] [1986] Q.B. 61.

[41] *ibid.* at 75–77.

destruction must be accepted as being within the law, provided it is not reckless.

I find this unreal, particularly as it is both beyond the power of their keepers to control where they go to forage, and beyond the practical control of the landowner to exclude them. Whether the landowner thinks he needs or wants bees to come on to his property, or whether he would rather be without them, he is bound, in the real world, to recognise that they will be wherever pollen and nectar are to be found . . ."

However, if a landowner brings on to his land more animals *ferae naturae* **1–052** than occur there naturally, *e.g.* by establishing a large quantity of game, he may be liable if those animals escape in circumstances where the number retained could not properly and reasonably have been kept there.[42] In *Farrer v. Nelson*,[43] where the defendant had kept 300–400 pheasants which damaged the plaintiff's crops, Pollock B. said[44]:

"As I understand the law, each person in this country is entitled to bring on his land any quantity of game which can reasonably and properly be kept on it, and so nothing extraordinary and non-natural is done . . . but the moment he [the lessee of shooting rights] brings on game to an unreasonable amount or causes it to increase to an unreasonable extent, he is doing that which is unlawful, and an action may be maintained by his neighbour for the damage which he has sustained."

It is accordingly a question of fact and degree whether the bringing on to land and keeping of quantities of animals *ferae naturae* is excessive and unreasonable. The mere fact that breeding stock produces an unusually large amount of offspring due to exceptional weather conditions, and which then causes damage to adjoining land, is not sufficient to establish liability.[45]

The Animals Act 1971

In certain areas, summarised in paragraph 5–038, liability under the **1–053** Animals Act 1971 has replaced the old common law liability in trespass — such as the statutory remedy for straying livestock under section 4 of that Act.

---

[42] *Hilton v. Green and Others* (1862) 2 F. & F. 821, *Farrer v. Nelson* (1885) 15 Q.B.D. 258, and *Seligman v. Docker* [1949] 1 Ch. 53. An action of this nature would appear to be more in the nature of a nuisance (or perhaps negligence) action than a trespass action: the case of the plaintiff in *Seligman* appears to have been put on the basis of nuisance and in *Farrer* the learned judge accepted that the action was founded on the breach of the principle *sic utere tuo ut alienum non laedas*.

[43] (1885) 15 Q.B.D. 258.

[44] *ibid.* at 260, affirming the judgment of the county court awarding damages to the plaintiff.

[45] See *Seligman v. Docker*, [1949] 1 Ch. 53, at 63–4.

Unlawful distress

1–054   Distress is a remedy with ancient origins and provides one of the few
remaining examples in English law of a "self-help" remedy. Typically,
distress is the taking of the chattels of a person by whom a specific type
of debt is owed in satisfaction of that debt or as security for payment of
that debt, *e.g.* as a means of recovering arrears of rent.[46] The right of distress enables a landlord to enter onto the demised premises (in respect of
which the arrears have arisen) to seize goods belonging to the tenant and
to retain them until the arrears are paid or to sell them if they are not
replevied within five days of the distress.[47]

The use of distress is narrowly confined and is hedged with safeguards
to prevent abuse, *e.g.* the relationship of landlord and tenant must exist at
the date the arrears arose and at the date of the distress, and the rent[48]
must be in arrears when distress is levied.[49]

However, a distress may be unlawful to the extent that it is should not
have taken place at all,[50] or be irregular[51] or excessive.[52] Further, exercise
of the right to distrain must be exercised with caution following the coming into force of the Human Rights Act 1998 and the extent of the ancient
remedy may now be ripe for reassessment since Lightman J. remarked
(obiter) in *Fuller v. Happy Shopper Markets Ltd*:[53]

> ". . . a landlord is bound to take the greatest care before levying dis-
> tress that there are no claims on the part of the tenant which may be
> available by way of equitable set off to be offset against and satisfy
> the rent outstanding. In any ordinary case he would be well advised
> to give notice of his intention and invite the tenant to agree what is
> owing and to inform him whether there are any cross-claims and (if
> so) to identify them. The ancient (and perhaps an anachronistic) self
> help remedy of distress involves a serious interference with the
> right of the tenant under Article 8 of the European Convention on
> Human Rights to respect for his privacy and home and under Arti-
> cle 1 of the First Protocol to the peaceful enjoyment of his posses-

---

[46] The right to levy distress for arrears of rent exists at common law subject to the Distress
for Rent Act 1737.

[47] S. 1 of the Distress for Rent Act 1689, s. 5 of the Landlord and Tenant Act 1730 and s. 10
of the Distress for Rent Act 1737.

[48] Which must be certain, *i.e.* ascertainable at any given time: see *Re Knight ex parte Voisey*
(1882) 21 Ch.D. 442.

[49] For fuller details on the right to distrain see Hill & Redman's *Law of Landlord and Tenant*,
Division A, Chap. 9; Halsbury's Laws, Vol. 13, paras 601–803 and Foa's *General Law of
Landlord and Tenant* (8th ed.), pp. 569–585.

[50] *e.g.* because there were no arrears outstanding at the time of the distress, the goods taken
were privileged, or the right to distrain had been lost.

[51] *i.e.* although the distress was lawfully commenced a wrongful act is committed at some
point in the process following seizure of the goods.

[52] *i.e.* where the distrainor seizes more goods than are reasonably necessary to meet the
arrears of rent and the costs of the distress.

[53] [2001] 1 W.L.R. 1681 at p. 1692, para. 27. See also consideration of the impact of the Human
Rights Act 1998 on self-help remedies generally, below, Chapter 4, paras. 4–105 to 4–113.

46

sions. The human rights implications of levying distress must be in the forefront of the mind of the landlord before he takes this step and he must fully satisfy himself that taking this action is in accordance with the law."

In the case of an illegal distress, the distrainor is regarded as a trespasser **1–055** *ab initio* since none of his acts were lawful. However, in the case of an irregularity which appears in the course of an initially lawful distress, the distrainor is not regarded as trespassing *ab initio* and the tenant's only remedy is in damages if he has suffered special loss[54] In the case of an excessive distress, the tenant may seek damages from the landlord or, if he acts quickly enough, an injunction to restrain the distress — or at least so much of it as may be excessive. The question of whether an excess has been seized is a question of degree and is subject to the fact that the value must be judged by reference to a forced sale. An injunction is therefore unlikely to be granted unless the tenant can show that the amount taken is clearly excessive.

It is an offence (although almost obsolete) to commit either rescue or pound-breach.[55] Rescue is the prevention of impounding after distress has been levied[56] and pound-breach is the forcible release of goods or animals lawfully impounded or of damaging or destroying the pound with a view to releasing the animals, knowing such animals or goods to have been impounded or secured.[57]

Defences

The following categories comprise the principle defences which may be **1–056** available to a defendant against whom a trespass is alleged.

Justification

If the entry onto land is authorised in some manner, either by actual **1–057** licence or by legal authority, then such entry is not unlawful and is not a trespass. Such licence may take a number of forms, from a mere grant of permission to enter to a grant of a more enduring right or interest in the land itself. The defence of justification should be specifically pleaded and, in order to provide a complete defence, should cover all the acts of alleged trespass.[58]

---

[54] The Distress for Rent Act 1737, s. 19.
[55] Bl. Com. (14th ed.) 146 and see the alternative remedy under the Distress for Rent Act 1689, s. 3.
[56] Co. Litt. 160a and 160b and *Iredale v. Kendall* (1878) 40 L.T. 362.
[57] *Green v. Duckett* (1883) 11 Q.B.D. 275 and *R. v. Butterfield* (1893) 17 Cox, C.C. 598.
[58] *Taylor v. Cole* (1789) 3 Term. 292 and (1791) 1 Hy. and Bl. 555, *Curlewis v. Laurie* (1848) 12 Q.B. 640 and *Hope v. Osborne* [1913] 2 Ch. 349. C.P.R. Part 16.5 requires a defence to provide a comprehensive response to the particulars of claim, and, in particular, must give reasons for denying an allegation (*e.g.*, trespass): r. 16.5(2)(a).

Tenancy

1–058   If a person in occupation of land has been granted a tenancy, of whatever nature or duration, as tenant in occupation he is entitled to possession (unless he has himself granted some right in possession such as a sub-tenancy) and cannot lawfully be ousted from possession unless his interest is appropriately terminated. The question of termination and the right to sue for the possession of land is considered at paragraphs 4–057 to 4–083 below.[59] The sole exception to this is the so-called "tenancy at sufferance"[60] which is not a tenancy at all but is the precarious right which arises by operation of law where premises are occupied by a former tenant following the termination of his tenancy without any statutory right to do so and without either the assent or dissent of the landowner.[61] Such a right can be terminated by the landlord's entry of the premises at any time.

Grant of licence

1–059   If a person on the land of another has been granted permission to enter (whether expressly or by implication)[62] then entry following such permission will be lawful while that licence continues in force and providing that its terms are not exceeded.

FORMS OF GRANT

1–060   At the least, a licence is a bare permission to enter land, whether generally or for limited purposes.[63] However, there is a considerable range of interests greater than a bare licence which grant more substantial rights — whether of a contractual nature or conferring some right or interest in or over the property itself.[64] The distinction between the nature of the various types of interest is of significance to the issues of the extent of the licence granted and of revocability of the permission.

---

[59] See also *Hill & Redman's Law of Landlord and Tenant* Division A Chap. 14 ("Determination of the tenancy").

[60] For a more detailed account see Hill & Redman, paras A[7843]–A[7848]. See also para. 1–050, above.

[61] But not the Crown: a tenancy at sufferance does not arise where the Crown is the landowner. See Co. Litt. 57b.

[62] *e.g.* where an obligation or entitlement to repair is imposed on a person, the law generally implies the right to enter in order to carry out such repair. See *Gale on Easements* (16th ed.) pp. 109–121.

[63] See, *e.g. Wood v. Leadbitter* (1845) 13 M. & W. 838.

[64] *e.g.* where an obligation or entitlement to repair is imposed on a person the law generally implies the right to enter in order to carry out such repair. See *Gale on Easements* (15th ed.) pp. 94–105.

DURATION OF GRANT

(1) Bare licence

The grant of a bare licence is very precarious since it may be revoked at will by the licensor. If a bare licence is revoked, the licensee thereupon becomes a trespasser although, if it is revoked while he is in occupation of the property which formed the subject-matter of the licence, he must be allowed a reasonable time to leave that property.[65] Such reasonable time may include time to remove any goods which the licensee has placed there.[66] It is unlikely that, in the absence of exceptional circumstances, such time will be extensive given that a court also has a limited discretion to postpone the date on which an order for possession will take effect.[67]

1–061

(2) Contractual licence

The question of the revocability of a contractual licence is more complex and generally depends on whether the contractual licence is coupled with some interest. If the licence has not been granted together with some interest, then at common law the licence is generally revocable notwithstanding that revocation would be a breach of contract and the licensor would be liable in damages.[68] The common law position was stated by Vaughan C.J. in *Thomas v. Sorrell*:[69]

1–062

> "A dispensation or licence properly passeth no interest, nor alters or transfers property in any thing, but only makes an action lawful, which without it had been unlawful."

However, the apparently simple position of the contractual licence at common law[70] has been complicated by the possibility that a term may be implied into the contract preventing revocation either absolutely or

---

[65] If the licensor purports to terminate the license without giving reasonable notice that notice will be effective, but only after a reasonable time has elapsed: *Minister of Health v. Bellotti* [1944] Q.B. 298. See Kerbel (1996) C.L.J. 229 who asserts that a notice which fails to specify a period that is in fact reasonable ought to be invalid.

[66] *i.e.* "packing-up time". *Cornish v. Stubbs* (1870) L.R. 5 C.P. 334, *Canadian Pacific Railways v. The King* [1931] A.C. 414, *Ministry of Health v. Belotti* [1944] K.B. 289, CA, *Robson v. Hallett* [1967] 2 Q.B. 939, *G.L.C. v. Jenkins* [1975] 1 W.L.R. 155, CA at 158, *Re Hampstead Garden Suburb Institute* (1995) 93 L.G.R. 470 and, below, paras. 1–072 and 4–063.

[67] Generally 14 days or six weeks if exceptional hardship can be proved: see the Housing Act 1980, s. 89. This restriction apparently does not apply to the High Court (to the extent that the High Court will now hear possession actions, post-C.P.R.): *Bain & Co. v. Church Commissioners for England* [1989] 1 W.L.R. 24. See also below, para. 4–071.

[68] *Wood v. Leadbitter* (1845) 13 M. & W. 838, *Kerrison v. Smith* [1897] 2 Q.B. 445, *King v. David Allen & Sons (Billposting) Limited* [1916] 2 A.C. 54, HL and *Thompson v. Ward* [1944] K.B. 408.

[69] (1674) Vaug. 330 at 351. See also *Frank Warr & Co. Ltd v. London County Council* [1904] 1 K.B. 713 at 722, *King v. David Allen & Sons (Billposting) Ltd* [1916] 2 A.C. 54, H.L., and *Clore v. Theatrical Properties Ltd* [1936] 3 All E.R. 483, CA.

[70] *Hill v. Tupper* (1863) 2 H. & C. 121.

conditionally.[71] If a contract creating a licence is enforceable in equity, then equity will treat the licensee as having an equitable right to remain on the land and will protect that right, where appropriate, by decreeing specific performance or granting an injunction to restrain a threatened breach or the enforcement of a purported revocation.[72] In certain cases the form of an injunction to require a licensor to re-admit an expelled licensee is a form of indirect specific performance.

1–063   If there is an express contractual stipulation which limits or defines the rights of the licensor to revoke the licence, then it is likely that the courts will intervene to prevent revocation in a manner inconsistent with that stipulation. Indeed, although at one stage it was suggested that a licence might be revoked in breach of agreement,[73] the present position is that an injunction will issue to prevent a wrongful repudiation of the licence agreement.[74]

The forms of protection which have been offered to licensees by the courts over the years led to the argument that they had now matured into a species of legal interest which were capable of binding third parties to the licence.[75] The view of the Court of Appeal in *Errington v. Errington & Woods*[76] that a contractual licence could create an interest in land binding on third parties[77] was decisively rejected by both the House of Lords in *Street v. Mountford*[78] and the Court of Appeal in *Ashburn Anstalt v. Arnold.*[79]

Although the licensee may not have an interest in the land, his protection from eviction in such circumstances may be substantial as against the licensor. In the case of the effect of such contractual licences on third parties, the position is not so clear. As the following sections demonstrate, even where there are no statutory restrictions on revocation, the courts have used a number of different means to prevent the inequitable revoca-

---

[71] *Feltham v. Cartwright* (1829) 5 Bing. N.C. 569, *Tanner v. Tanner* [1975] 1 W.L.R. 1346, *Chandler v. Kerley* [1978] 1 W.L.R. 693, *Hardwick v. Johnson* [1978] 1 W.L.R. 683, and *Re Sharpe* [1980] 1 W.L.R. 219.

[72] *Verall v. Great Yarmouth B.C.* [1981] Q.B. 202, CA (purported revocation of a licence to hire a hail for a 2 day conference enforced by a decree of specific performance).

[73] *Wood v. Leadbitter* (1845) 13 M. & W. 838 and *Thompson v. Park* [1944] K.B. 408.

[74] *Winter Garden Theatre (London) Limited v. Millennium Productions Limited* [1948] A.C. 173, HL at 194 and 202–3. See below, para. 1–064. Indeed, there is no reason why a licensee with an express contractual agreement governing revocation should not be in at least as good a position as the licensee who requires the implication of a term to prevent revocation.

[75] See Megarry & Wade (6th ed.), pp. 1046–1047 and 1054–1057 and Cheshire & Burn (16th ed.), pp. 643–646. Now see also s. 116 of the Land Registration Act 2002 which provides that equities are interests capable of binding successors in title.

[76] [1952] 1 K.B. 290.

[77] See also *Binions v. Evans* [1972] Ch. 359, *per* Lord Denning M.R. and *D.H.N. Food Distributors Ltd v. Tower Hamlets Borough Council* [1976] 1 W.L.R. 852 at 859. Doubts as to the correctness of *Errington* were expressed as early as *National Provincial Bank Ltd v. Ainsworth* [1965] A.C. 1175, HL *per* Lord Wilberforce at 1250–1252 and Lord Upjohn at 1239–1240.

[78] [1985] A.C. 809 *per* Lord Templeman at 814.

[79] [1989] Ch. 1 especially at 22 and the criticisms of the Master of the Rolls' approach in *Binions v. Evans,* [1972] Ch. 359, at 25 *per* Fox L.J. *Ashburn Anstalt* was overruled, on other grounds relating to the uncertain duration of tenancies, by the House of Lords in *Prudential Assurance Co. Ltd v. London Residuary Body* [1992] 3 W.L.R. 279. The decision on the point here was not criticised by the House of Lords.

tion of licences. In *Ashburn Anstalt v. Arnold*,[80] the Court accepted both the distinction between contractual and proprietary rights and the availability of other means, principally the constructive trust, to limit the revocability of a licence.[81] Accordingly, if the circumstances are sufficient to give rise to an estoppel or constructive trust, then in practical terms the licence may at least affect the position of third parties[82] — although a contractual licence in itself cannot now be said to bind them. In the light of the means available to the court to prevent revocation and to confer some form of protection of the licensee, it would still be unwise to regard a contractual licence as inherently revocable notwithstanding the disapproval of *Errington v. Errington*.

(a) Implied term

Even in cases where equitable assistance is not available, the courts have modified the basic common law principle that a licence may be revoked. A term restricting revocation of the licence, or a term requiring reasonable notice,[83] may be implied if it can be demonstrated either that the parties intended that the licence would endure for a specific period or purpose, or that such a term is necessary for the efficacy of the agreement.[84] Particular problems arise in cases of informal arrangements for the sharing of occupation and, among the numerous solutions reached by the courts,[85] one approach has been to imply from the arrangement a licence which is only revocable in certain circumstances, *e.g.* so long as the children remain at school,[86] or until expenditure on the occupied property is repaid,[87] or on 12 months' notice.[88]

1–064

---

[80] See above and the over-ruling of the decision by the House of Lords in the *Prudential* case on other grounds.

[81] "... a beneficial adaptation of old rules to new situations ..." [1989] Ch. at 22 *per* Fox L.J.

[82] See, *e.g. Binions v. Evans* [1972] Ch. 359, CA and *Bannister v. Bannister* [1948] 2 All E.R. 133, CA. See also s. 116 of the Land Registration Act 2002.

[83] *Australian Blue Metal Ltd v. Hughes* [1963] A.C. 74, PC. For an example of an implied period of reasonable notice in a "long-term" contractual licence see *Mehta v. Royal Bank of Scotland and Others* [1999] E.G.L.R. 153.

[84] Based on the standard principles for the implication of terms: *e.g.* Lewison, *The Interpretation of Contracts* (2nd ed., Sweet & Maxwell), Chapter 5 and *Hurst v. Picture Theatres Ltd* [1915] 1 K.B. 1, *Winter Garden Theatre (London) Limited v. Millennium Productions Limited* [1948] A.C. 173, H.L., *Hounslow v. Twickenham Garden Developments Ltd* [1971] Ch. 233, *Shell U.K. v. Lostock Garage* [1976] 1 W.L.R. 1187, CA and *Verrall v. Great Yarmouth* [1981] Q.B. 202, CA. In accordance with standard principles, necessity and not reasonableness is the criterion for implication: *Liverpool City Council v. Irwin* [1977] A.C. 239, H.L. and *Duke of Westminster v. Guild* [1985] 1 Q.B. 688, CA.

[85] See S. Moriarty (1984) 100 L.Q.R. 376, *Cheshire & Burn* (16th ed.), Chap. 19, Megarry & Wade (6th ed.), pp. 1050–1063, *Snell's Equity* (30th ed.), pp. 637–643 and, *e.g. Dillwyn v. Llewellyn* (1862) 4 De G., F. & J. 517, *Williams v. Staite* [1979] Ch. 291, CA, *Pascoe v. Turner* [1979] 1 W.L.R. 431, CA, *Dodsworth v. Dodsworth* [1973] E.G.D. 233, CA. and *Re Sharpe* [1980] 1 W.L.R. 219.

[86] *Tanner v. Tanner* [1975] 1 W.L.R. 1346, CA.

[87] *Dodsworth v. Dodsworth* [1973] E.G.D. 233.

[88] *Chandler v. Kerley* [1978] 1 W.L.R. 693.

In *Winter Garden Theatre (London) Limited v. Millennium Productions Limited*[89] the House of Lords implied a term permitting revocation of a licence to use a theatre to produce and present plays and granted an injunction to restrain the purported revocation of the licence in breach of the implied term. Lord Uthwatt stated[90]:

> "The next question is whether the notice given must be a reasonable notice or whether it may be a notice operating at once to determine the licence, the licensees in that event having a reasonable time within which to vacate the theatre. In my opinion it is the former. I cannot think that any other notice would reflect the intention of reasonable men in the position of the licensors and licensees in the present case. No reasonable man would in that connexion deny the relevance of the general proposition that he who sows should be allowed to reap . . ."

At the same time, the House of Lords cast doubt on the principle in *Thompson v. Park*[91] that a contractual licence may be revoked notwithstanding the consequent breach of agreement. Lord Uthwatt added[92]:

> "The settled practice of the courts of equity is to do what they can by an injunction to preserve the sanctity of a bargain. To my mind, as at present advised, a licensee who has refused to accept the wrongful repudiation of a bargain which is involved in an unauthorized revocation of the licence is as much entitled to the protection of an injunction as a licensee who has not received any notice of revocation; and, if the remedy of injunction is properly available in the latter case against unauthorized interference by the licensor, it is also available in the former case."

This approach was adopted by the Court of Appeal in *Verall v. Great Yarmouth B.C.*[93] although it was not necessary to do so since the decision was to decree specific performance of the agreement.

In other circumstances, the courts have held that a contractual licence is subject to an implied term that the licence cannot be revoked or cannot be revoked save in certain circumstances. In general, the question of revocability is determined by construing the terms of the agreement and ascertaining the intention of the parties[94] — although plainly if the parties

---

[89] [1948] A.C. 173. See also *Australian Blue Metal Ltd v. Hughes*, [1963] A.C. 74, at 98–99.
[90] [1948] A.C. 173, at 199.
[91] *ibid.*
[92] *ibid.* at 202–203. See also Lord Porter at 194.
[93] [1981] Q.B. 202 at 216 and 219.
[94] *Re Spenborough U.D.C.'s Agreement* [1968] Ch. 139, *Winter Garden Theatre* case, [1948] A.C. 173, and Lewison, *The Construction of Contracts* pp. 147–149. As Lewison suggests, it is unlikely that a term would be implied where a licence is stipulated for a fixed period or

expressly limit the right to revoke then that agreement will be enforced. However, the fact that a licensor may have agreed not to revoke a licence does not mean that an assignee of the licensor will be bound by that agreement in the absence of privity of contract. For an assignee to be bound, something more is needed: see below.

(b) Constructive trust

The device of the constructive trust has been developed by the Courts as **1–065** a means by which they can prevent revocation of a right to occupy, and confer greater rights if appropriate, by imposing a trust on the owner of the land.[95] The circumstances where such a trust is imposed are typically where parties have informally agreed that they were to have an interest in particular property, but none is granted (or legal title does not vest in both), or where the circumstances are such that it would be equitable to impute an intention to grant a beneficial interest since the occupier has made some contribution to the acquisition of the property.[96] In strict common law terms the person in mere occupation would have little protection as a bare licensee but the intervention of equity mitigates the otherwise harsh consequences of the parties' lack of formality. Fox L.J. has described the impact of the constructive trust doctrine thus:[97]

"The constructive trust principle . . . has been long established and has proved to be highly flexible in practice. It covers a wide variety of cases from that of a trustee who makes a profit out of his trust or a stranger who knowingly deals with trust properties, to the many cases where the courts have held that a person who directly or indirectly contributes to the acquisition of a dwelling-house purchased in the name of and conveyed to another has some beneficial interest in the property. The test, for the present purposes, is whether the owner of the property has so conducted himself that it would be inequitable to allow him to deny the claimant an interest in the property . . ."

The basic requirement for equity to intervene and impose a trust which prevents the party bound from revoking a licence or reneging on an

express provision is made for termination: *Kirklees M.B.C. v. Yorkshire Woollen District Transport Co. Ltd* (1978) 77 L.G.R. 448.

[95] See A.J. Oakley, *Constructive Trusts* (3rd ed.), especially pp. 53–84, John Dewar, *Law and the Family* (2nd ed.) at pp. 182–204, *Snell's Equity* (30th ed.), pp. 213–219 and 227–228. S. 116 of the Land Registration Act 2002 confirms that estoppels and equities are interests capable of binding successors in title.
[96] Either by direct contribution to the purchase price or payment of mortgage instalments: see below, para. 1–066. If the purchase price were provided wholly by one party and title vested in the other then a resulting trust might arise: see *Snell's Equity*, pp. 206–213.
[97] *Ashburn Anstalt v. Arnold* [1989] Ch. 1, CA at 22. Although this case has been overruled by the House of Lords in *Prudential Assurance Co. Ltd v. London Residuary Body* [1992] 3 W.L.R. 279 (see at 286) on the question of uncertainty of duration of tenancies, there appears no reason at present to doubt the correctness of the passage quoted.

informal understanding or agreement is that the conscience of the estate owner should have been affected.[98] Further, the court will require convincing evidence of the circumstances said to affect the conscience of the party alleged to be bound by the trust and will not imply such a trust on "inferences from slender materials".[99] However, once the trust arises on that basis, it will not be defeated by the failure of the parties to comply with any formal requirements such as the lack of a written agreement or memorandum.[1]

1–066   Constructive trusts have been held to arise in a number of cases: for example, in circumstances where there has been a contribution to the purchase price of a home,[2] or where there has been an informal agreement to permit one party to remain in occupation rent-free[3] or where land has been sold subject to an existing contract where it is intended that such a stipulation should create new rights in the grantor.[4]

In the case of contributions to the purchase price of a property, the courts (after a period of apparently greater liberality) now take the approach that, in the absence of an express agreement or understanding, any contributions relied upon as giving rise to a trust must be referable to the cost of acquisition of the property.[5] The test is not merely one of fairness, or equitability, in a general sense:

> "A resulting, implied or constructive trust . . . is created by a transaction between the trustee and the *cestui que trust* in connection with the acquisition by the trustee of a legal estate in land, whenever the trustee has so conducted himself that it would be inequitable to deny

---

[98] "The Court will not impose a constructive trust unless it is satisfied that the conscience of the estate owner is affected": *per* Fox L.J. in *Ashburn Anstalt v. Arnold* [1989] Ch. 1, at 25. In that case, the Court held that there were no indications of unconscionability such as the payment of a reduced purchase price.

[99] See *Ashburn Anstalt v. Arnold*, above at 26 E and see further *Lloyds Bank Plc v. Rosset* [1991] 1 A.C. 107, HL where the Court scrutinised the facts very carefully in seeking to determine whether an intention to confer an interest could be inferred.

[1] As required by the Law of Property Act 1925, s. 40 or s. 53(1)(b). S. 40 has been replaced by the Law of Property (Miscellaneous Provisions) Act 1989, s. 2. See, *e.g. Bannister v. Bannister* [1948] 2 All E.R. 133, CA.

[2] See, *e.g. Neale v. Willis* (1968) 19 P. & C.R. 839, *Gissing v. Gissing* [1971] A.C. 886, H.L., *Heseltine v. Heseltine* [1971] 1 W.L.R. 342, *Cowcher v. Cowcher* [1972] 1 W.L.R. 425, *Cooke v. Head* [1972] 1 W.L.R. 518, CA, *Hazell v. Hazell* [1972] 1 W.L.R. 301, *Hussey v. Palmer* [1972] 1 W.L.R. 1286, *Eves v. Eves* [1975] 1 W.L.R. 1338, *Re Densham* [1975] 1 W.L.R. 1519, *Burns v. Burns* [1984] Ch. 317, *Grant v. Edwards* [1986] Ch. 638, CA, *Lloyds Bank Plc v. Rosset* [1991] 1 A.C. 107, H.L., *Lloyd's Bank v. Carrick* [1996] 4 All E.R. 630, CA and *Gillett v. Holt* [2000] 2 All E.R. 289, CA. Similar principles apply whether the persons contributing are married or unmarried: see *Cooke v. Head*, *Grant v. Edwards*, Dewar *op. cit.*, and others, above. This principle does not apply if the "contribution" is made by way of loan: see *Re Sharpe* [1980] 1 W.L.R. 219 as explained in *Ashburn Anstalt v. Arnold* [1989] Ch. 1, CA at 25.

[3] See *Bannister v. Bannister* [1948] 2 All E.R. 133, CA.

[4] *Lyus v. Prowsa Developments Ltd* [1982] 1 W.L.R. 1044 — although the mere insertion of the words "subject to" does not of itself have this effect.

[5] See, *e.g. Burns v. Burns* [1984] Ch. 317, and *Lloyds Bank Plc v. Rosset*, [1991] 1 A.C. 107, H.L., marking a return to the approach above in *Gissing v. Gissing* [1971] A.C. 886, H.L. Decisions such as *Nixon v. Nixon* [1969] 1 W.L.R. 1676 and *Wachtel v. Wachtel* [1973] Fam. 72 should now be treated with caution in the light of the return to the stricter *Gissing* principles.

to the *cestui que trust* a beneficial interest in the land acquired. And he will be held so to have conducted himself if by his words or conduct he has induced the *cestui que trust* to act to his own detriment in the reasonable belief that by so acting he was acquiring a beneficial interest in the land."[6]

There are clearly similarities between the analysis of this type of constructive trust and estoppel considered below. The concept of detrimental reliance is central to both since it provides the means by which equity is motivated to intervene and protect the disadvantaged party.

In *Lloyds Bank Plc v. Rosset*[7] the House of Lords distinguished two types of case:

(1) where an agreement, arrangement or understanding is reached by the parties at any time before acquisition (or "exceptionally" at a later date) that the property is to be shared beneficially "independently of any inference to be drawn from the conduct of the parties in the course of sharing the house as their home and managing their joint affairs;" and

(2) where there is no evidence to support the existence of an agreement or arrangement to share[8] and the court must rely entirely on the conduct of the parties from which to infer a common intention to share the property beneficially.

In the second case:

"... direct contributions to the purchase price by the partner who is not the legal owner will readily justify the inference necessary to the creation of a constructive trust. But, as I read the authorities, it is at least extremely doubtful whether anything less will do."[9]

The flexibility of the use of constructive trusts does not extend to cases where there is already an enforceable contract for the property. In *Lloyds Bank v. Carrick*[10] the Court of Appeal rejected the invitation to impose a constructive trust where an enforceable contract existed although it had not been registered and as such did not bind the claimant bank, a subsequent mortgagee of the property. The Court also rejected the imposition of a bare trust or estoppel. Morritt L.J. stated:[11]

---

[6] *per* Lord Diplock in *Gissing v. Gissing* [1971] A.C. 886 at 905.
[7] [1991] 1 A.C. 107, HL, at 132–133.
[8] "However reasonable it might have been for the parties to reach such an arrangement if they had applied their minds to the question:" *ibid. per* Lord Bridge at 132H.
[9] *ibid. per* Lord Bridge, at 133A.
[10] [1996] 4 All E.R. 630, CA.
[11] At p. 639.

"In this case there was a trust of the maisonette for the benefit of Mrs Carrick precisely because there had been an agreement between her and Mr Carrick which, for her part, she had substantially if not wholly performed... there is no room in those circumstances for the implication or imposition of any further trust of the maisonette for the benefit of Mrs Carrick. In *Lloyds Bank plc v. Rosset* there was no contract which conferred any interest in the house on the wife. As with all such statements of principle the speech of Lord Bridge of Harwich must be read by reference to the facts of the case. So read there is nothing in it to suggest that where there is a specifically enforceable contract the court is entitled to superimpose a further constructive trust on the vendor in favour of the purchaser over that which already exists in consequence of the contractual relationship.

It is true that on this footing the ultimate position of Mrs Carrick with the benefit of a specifically enforceable contract may be worse than it would have been if there had been no contract. But that is because she failed to do that which Parliament has ordained must be done if her interest is to prevail over that of the bank, namely to register the estate contract. Her failure in that respect cannot, in my view, justify the implication or imposition of a trust after the execution of the charge when the dealings between Mr Carrick and Mrs Carrick before such execution did not."

The mere conveyance of property "subject to" a particular contract or contractual right will not of itself give rise to a constructive trust since it may be consistent merely with an intention to protect the grantor against claims by the grantee.[12] However, where a licensor holds the land subject to a constructive trust in favour of the licensee, an assignee of the licensor will take subject to the trust always providing that there is compliance with the usual rules relating to the notice of existing interests.[13]

It follows from the rejection in *Ashburn Anstalt* of the *Errington* approach (that a contractual licence created an interest in land) that the mere grant of a licence cannot of itself give rise to a constructive trust.[14]

(c) Estoppel

1–067 Another approach which is adopted to the question of revocability is that in certain cases a licensor may be estopped from revoking the licence if

---

[12] See *Ashburn Anstalt v. Arnold* [1989] Ch. 1, CA at 26 and *Lyus v. Prowsa Developments Ltd* [1982] 1 W.L.R. 1044 (intention of the parties clearly to confer new rights on the claimants). The dicta to the contrary by the Master of the Rolls in *Binions v. Evans* [1972] Ch. 359 at 368 cannot now be regarded as good law.

[13] See *Megarry and Wade* (6th ed.), pp. 138–150.

[14] As a result, the authority of *D.H.N. Food Distributors Ltd v. Tower Hamlets L.B.C.* [1976] 1 W.L.R. 852, CA must be in doubt for the same reason.

the circumstances are such that it would be inequitable to do so.[15] As in the case of the imposition of a constructive trust,[16] the mere grant of the licence is not sufficient in itself to give rise to a proprietary estoppel. In general, an estoppel will arise if the landowner permits or encourages the licensee to act to his detriment in such a way that the licensee understands that he will acquire a permanent right to remain on the land or an interest in the land.[17] The courts have not always adopted a consistent approach to the question of estoppel[18] and the stricter approach requires that the estoppel should be founded on a mistake as to ownership of the land. However, more recent cases display a greater flexibility and an attention to giving effect to what is perceived as the "equity" of the situation.[19] Robert Walker L.J. in *Gillett v. Holt*[20] recognised the modern, flexible approach:

"... it is important to note at the outset that the doctrine of proprietary estoppel cannot be treated as subdivided into three or four watertight compartments. Both sides are agreed on that, and in the course of the oral argument in this court it repeatedly became apparent that the quality of the relevant assurances may influence the issue of reliance, that reliance and detriment are often intertwined, and that whether there is a distinct need for a 'mutual understanding' may depend on how the other elements are formulated and understood. Moreover the fundamental principle that equity is concerned to prevent unconscionable conduct permeates all the elements of the doctrine. In the end the court must look at the matter in the round."

In *Crabb v. Arun D.C.*,[21] Scarman L.J. had stated:

"I think it is now settled law that the court, having analysed and assessed the conduct and relationship of the parties, has to answer three questions. First, is there an equity established? Secondly, what is the extent of the equity, if one is established? And, thirdly, what is the relief appropriate to satisfy the equity?"

---

[15] See Wilken & Villiers, *Waiver Variation & Estoppel* (Wiley, 1998), especially Chapter 11.

[16] On the similarity of approaches in cases of constructive trusts and estoppel see Moriarty, *op. cit.*, and Dewar, *op. cit.*, at pp. 187–190, and Morritt L.J. in *Lloyd's Bank v. Carrick* [1996] 4 All E.R. 630, CA, at p. 639. For a comparison with equitable forbearance and contract see Wilken & Villiers, *op.cit.* pp. 319–331

[17] See, *e.g. Crabb v. Arun* [1976] Ch. 179, CA, *Plimmer v. Mayor of Wellington* (1884) 9 App.Cas. 699, *Inwards v. Baker* [1965] 2 Q.B. 29, *Gillett v Holt* [2000] 2 All E.R. 289, CA and other cases cited above.

[18] Although note that the five elements or "probanda" referred to by Fry J. in *Willmott v. Barber* (1880) 15 Ch. D 96 at 105–106 are no longer pre-requisites to an estoppel: see *Taylor Fashions Ltd v. Liverpool Victoria Trustees Co Ltd* [1982] Q.B. 133 and *Lloyd's Bank v. Carrick* [1996] 4 All E.R. 630, CA, at p. 640.

[19] See, *e.g. Crabb v. Arun* [1976] Ch. 179, CA, *Taylors Fashions v. Liverpool Victoria Trustees* [1982] Q.B. 133, Moriarty (1984) 100 L.Q.R. 376, *Greasely v. Cooke* [1980] 1 W.L.R. 1306, CA (an extreme case where the question of the existence of detriment was greatly subordinated to that of reliance).

[20] [2000] 2 All E.R. 289, CA, at p. 301.

[21] [1976] Ch. 179, CA.

Indeed, the satisfaction of such an equity may go much further than merely preventing revocation: in *Pascoe v. Turner*[22] the Court of Appeal ordered the landowner to transfer the fee simple to his mistress who had incurred expenditure in reliance on his promise that the house was hers. This appears an extreme means of preventing the revocation of the right to occupy, particularly since the value of the property was considerably greater than the expenditure of the mistress. Indeed, the prevention or limitation of the revocation of the licence appears to be only one means by which the law protects those who have entered into informal and often improvident arrangements.[23]

In *Lloyd's Bank v. Carrick*[24] the Court of Appeal rejected the applicability of estoppel to a case where a defendant has an enforceable contract but had failed to protect herself by registration against a subsequent disposition of the land (to the mortgagee bank). Proprietary estoppel could not be used, in such circumstances, to defeat the consequences required by the Land Registration Act, Morritt L.J. held:

> First, as in the case of the constructive trust, I do not see how there is any room for the application of the principles of proprietary estoppel when at the time of the relevant expenditure there was already a bare trust arising in consequence of an enforceable contract to the same effect as the interest sought pursuant to the proprietary estoppel. As the evidence showed Mrs Carrick knew of the need for a conveyance and was content that it should be deferred. Thus at the time that she paid the price and committed herself to the expenditure on the subsequent improvements she believed, rightly, that she was spending the money in respect of her own property, albeit under an uncompleted contract . . .
>
> Second, this is not a case in which the expectations of Mrs Carrick have been defeated by Mr Carrick seeking to resile from the position he had encouraged her to expect . . . Mrs Carrick's expectations have been defeated because the contract was not registered at any time before the charge was granted and Parliament has decreed that in those circumstances the contract is void against the bank.
>
> Third, it was common ground that the right arising from a proprietary estoppel cannot exceed that which the party sought to be estopped encouraged the other to believe that she had or would acquire . . . It cannot be unconscionable for the bank to rely on the non-registration of the contract. I do not see how it could be right to confer on Mrs Carrick indirectly, and by means of a proprietary estoppel binding on the bank, that which Parliament prevented her from obtaining directly by the contract it has declared to be void.

---

[22] [1979] 1 W.L.R. 431, CA. See also *Re Basham* [1986] 1 W.L.R. 1498.

[23] For a much more detailed account see *Megarry & Wade* (6th ed.), pp. 734–748, *Cheshire & Burn* (16th ed.), Chap. 19 and Moriarty, *op cit.*

[24] [1996] 4 All E.R. 630, CA, above. See pp. 641–642.

To avoid any future misunderstanding I would emphasise that there was and is a valid and enforceable contract as against the vendor. Accordingly this case is quite unlike those which may become more prevalent where there is no contract at all, not because there was no agreement but because the agreement was not in writing as now required by section 2 of the Law of Property (Miscellaneous Provisions) Act 1989.

An unsuccessful attempt was made to extend the principles of estoppel so that rights might be conferred on the public at large. In *CIN Properties v. Rawlins*,[25] a shopping centre, which had no public rights of way though it, was argued to be subject to irrevocable licences[26] to the public which forbade the mall owners from excluding a group of disruptive teenagers. The court rejected this contention and Balcombe L.J. held:[27]

"In my judgment, this principle has no application in the circumstances of the present case. There was no representation by either the council or CIN that the public would have irrevocable rights to use the pedestrian malls in the centre, nor was there any evidence that any member of the public had altered his or her position in reliance upon any such representation. Indeed, I have the gravest doubts whether this principle could ever apply so as to create rights in favour of the public at large, since it is difficult to see how the acts or omissions of those individuals who rely on a representation could create rights in favour of the public. Counsel was unable to refer us to any reported authority in which an equity of this type had been created in favour of the public."

(d) Statutory limits on revocation

Statute intervenes in two principal ways to limit revocation: the first is by expressly fettering the right to terminate itself, whereas the second is to confer security of tenure on the licensee as if he were a tenant. **1–068**

(i) The right to terminate — Even in the case of a periodic licence to occupy residential premises[28] it is necessary to give four weeks' prior written notice containing prescribed information before the licence may be terminated.[29] It is very likely that an injunction would be available[30] to restore a licensee to occupation of land from which he had been **1–069**

---

[25] [1995] 2 E.G.L.R. 130, CA.
[26] Reliance was placed on as *Crabb v. Arun District Council* [1976] Ch. 179, CA, and *Williams v. Staite* [1979] Ch. 291, CA.
[27] Above, p. 134.
[28] Unless it is an excluded licence within the Protection from Eviction Act 1977, ss. 3A and 5(1B)(b).
[29] S. 5 of the Protection from Eviction Act 1977.
[30] Including an interim injunction — provided, of course, that the aggrieved party has acted reasonably promptly and has not done anything to disentitle himself from equitable relief.

ejected without due termination in accordance with the Protection from Eviction Act 1977 since, without the appropriate notice, the licence would not have been validly determined. Similar protection is conferred upon those stationing caravans for residential purposes by the Caravan Sites Act 1968.

1–070   *(ii) Security of tenure* — Apart from those more general provisions, there are particular statutory schemes conferring security of tenure even where the occupation of premises is attributable to the grant of a licence and not a tenancy. In particular, public sector residential licensees within Part IV of the Housing Act 1985 are classified as "secure,"[31] licensees of caravan sites within the Mobile Homes Act 1983 receive a form of security via prescribed forms of agreement which may only be terminated by the caravan owner or with the Court's consent,[32] and certain licensees of agricultural holdings within the Agricultural Holdings Act 1986[33] receive statutory security of tenure.

(3) Licence coupled with an interest

1–071   A licence which confers a right to do something once entry has been effected is not immediately revocable since the licensee must be allowed to realise his interest or fulfil the purpose of the licence. The interest, or the grant, does not have to be in the nature of a real property interest[34] but may be simply personal property, *e.g.* the right to enter property in order to collect a purchase.[35] *Thomas v. Sorrell*[36] Vaughan C.J. illustrated the distinction between a mere licence and a licence coupled with an interest:

> "But a licence to hunt in a man's park and to carry away the deer killed to his own use; to cut down a tree in a man's ground and to carry it away the next day after to his own use, are licenses as to the acts of hunting and cutting down the tree; but as to the carrying away of the deer killed and the tree cut they are grants."

[31] See the Housing Act 1985, s. 79(3). Of course, the licensee has to fulfil the relevant conditions for the creation of a secure tenancy other than that of the grant of a tenancy. See, for example, ss. 80–82. A secure tenancy may only be terminated in accordance with the provisions of the Act and, where the "tenant" remains in occupation of the dwelling as his only or principal home, then possession can be obtained if the provisions of s. 83 (notices of proceedings for possession of termination) and 84 (grounds for possession) are observed.

[32] See s. 2 and paras. 3 and 4 of Sched. 1 to the Mobile Homes Act 1983.

[33] See, in particular, s. 2(2)(b) of the Agricultural Holdings Act 1986. The provisions do not apply to grazing licences for a specified period of a year (s. 2(3)(a)) or to licences approved by the Minister prior to the letting (s. 2(1)). There are certain other exclusions which apply to tenancies and licences: see Scammell & Densham's *Law of Agricultural Holdings*, (8th ed.), S. 1, Part III. Note that the Agricultural Tenancies Act 1995 created a new regime for agricultural tenancies from September 1, 1995 (with certain exceptions set out in s. 4) although there are still arrangements in force which were entered into under the 1986 Act.

[34] *e.g.* entry for the purpose of exercising a *profit à prendre*.

[35] *Wood v. Manley* (1839) 11 A. & E. 34.

[36] (1673) Vaughan 330 at 351.

Once that interest has been realised, or the purpose of the grant fulfilled, the licence will then become revocable.[37] The terms of the licence may even provide for the termination of the licence automatically upon the fulfilment of the purpose of the grant. With regard to the effect of such licences upon third parties, if the grant with which the licence is coupled is of an equitable interest then the contract will require registration under section 2(4) of the Land Charges Act 1925 as an estate contract otherwise it will be void against a purchaser of the legal estate for money or money's worth.[38] In the case of registered land, the interest may be an interest within section 32(1) of the Land Registration Act 2002 and may be protected by a notice.[39] In certain circumstances, the interest will amount to an overriding interest[40] and bind future purchasers, for example, if it is coupled with actual occupation.[41] If the grant is of a legal interest, then it will bind the successors in title of the grantor.

(4) Licence granted to a body discharging a public function

Where a body which is conducting or discharging a public function is granted a licence to occupy land, the licence may not be terminated without first giving reasonable notice to the licensee and, as a guide as to what was reasonable, the court will have regard to the functions which the licensee is required to discharge under statute.[41a] In *Re Hampstead Garden Suburb Institute*,[42] Carnwath J. held that the Institute could not revoke a licence granted to a school which had become a voluntary aided school under the Education Act 1944 without first giving reasonable notice. The learned judge held that "reasonable notice" was notice which gave sufficient time to enable practical arrangements to be put in hand to safeguard the public service. On that basis, the nine months' notice given by the Institute was ineffective to revoke the licence since it was "impossibly short".[43] On the facts, the learned judge considered that at least two years' notice was required applying, as a guide to what was reasonable, the terms of the statute under which the licensee was operating and the fact

1–072

---

[37] See *Wood v. Leadbitter*, (1845) 13 M. & W. 838, at 844–845, *Jones v. Tankerville* [1909] 2 Ch. 440 at 442, *Clore v. Theatrical Properties* [1936] 3 All E.R. 483, CA.

[38] See s. 4(6) of the 1972 Act and *Midland Bank Trust Co. Ltd v. Green* [1981] A.C. 513, H.L.

[39] See ss. 32 to 39 of the LRA 2002 replacing ss. 54 to 56 of the Land Registration Act 1925, rr. 215 to 228 of the Land Registration Rules 1925 (S.I. No. 1093). See Megarry and Wade (6th ed.), pp. 244–261.

[40] Formerly s. 3 (xvi) of the Land Registration Act 1925 and see now the more limited categories in Schedule 3 to the Land Registration Act 2002.

[41] S. 70(1)(g) of the Land Registration Act 1925 and para.2 of Schedule 3 to the Land Registration Act 2002.

[41a] In the reverse case of a public body terminating a licence see below, paras. 1–134 ff and also *Wandsworth v. A* [2000] 1 W.L.R. 1246, CA.

[42] (1995) 93 L.G.R. 470. See also *Canadian Pacific Railway Co. v. R* [1931] A.C. 414 which Carnwath J.

[43] And, on the facts, had not been intended to be implemented since it was accompanied by a "without prejudice" letter which made it clear that the school could continue in occupation of the land on condition that it paid a market rent to the Institute.

that school governors had to give at least two years' notice to the Secretary of State for Education in order to discontinue a school.

EXCEEDING THE TERMS OF THE LICENCE

1–073   Apart from the proper termination or revocation of the licence, the question arises as to the consequences of a licensee acting in excess of the permission which he has been granted. To the extent that the licensee does more than his authority permits, such acts in excess of his authority will amount to a trespass.[44] In *Hillen & Pettigrew v. ICI (Alkali) Ltd*,[45] Lord Atkin stated:

> ". . . in my opinion this duty to an invitee only extends so long as and so far as the invitee is making what can reasonably be contemplated as an ordinary and reasonable use of the premises by the invitee for the purposes for which he has been invited. He is not invited to use any part of the premises for purposes which he knows are wrongfully dangerous and constitute an improper user. As Scrutton L.J. has pointedly said: 'When you invite a person into your house to use the staircase you do not invite him to slide down the banisters.' [*The Calgarth* [1926] P. 93, 110]. So far as he sets foot on so much of the premises as lie outside the invitation or uses them for purposes which are alien to the invitation he is not an invitee but a trespasser, and his rights must be determined accordingly."

See also the consideration of abuse of right,[46] on the question of whether exceeding the licence renders an entry unlawful *ab initio*.

It is the acts of the licensee which are material to the question of whether the terms of the licence are exceeded and not the motive of the licensee when entering the premises.[47]

Conduct outside the subject-matter of the licence is unlikely to affect the right of the licensee to do that which he is permitted to do by the licence: this includes conduct following the acquisition of an equity. In *Williams v. Staite*[48] Goff L.J. confirmed that once an equity had been acquired, it could not subsequently be forfeited although Lord Denning M.R. suggested that in extreme cases, the licence might become revocable as a result of conduct subsequent to creation of the equity.[49] It is difficult

---

[44] *Ancaster v. Milling* (1823) 2 Dow. & Ry. K.B. 714, *Brunner v. Williams* (1975) 73 L.G.R. 266, and *Wilcox v. Kettel* [1937] 1 All E.R. 223.

[45] [1936] A.C. 65, HL, at 69.

[46] Para. 1–048.

[47] *Byrne v. Kinematograph Renters Society Ltd* [1958] 1 W.L.R. 762 at 776. Compare the rejection of mistake as a defence to trespass: see para. 1–092.

[48] [1979] Ch. 291, CA at 300.

[49] Above at 297–298. Misconduct might be a reason for preventing the equity from arising in the first place — on the basis that a party seeking equitable relief must not himself act in an unconscionable manner: see *Snell's Equity* (30th ed.) at pp. 31–33 (the need for "clean hands") and *per* Cumming-Bruce L.J. in *Williams v. Staite* [1979] Ch. 291, CA at p. 300.

to see how such conduct could have such an effect in the absence of anything else which might establish an alteration in the legal position of the parties.

Tolerated Trespassers

A "tolerated trespasser"[50] will have a defence to a claim that he is a trespasser for so long as he abides by the terms of the arrangement under which he is allowed to remain in occupation of his premises following the making of a possession order. If he breaches the terms of the arrangement, he may be evicted on the date specified in a warrant of possession, which may be issued by the authority at any time after the tolerated trespasser's default without the need for fresh possession proceedings.

Easements and profits[51]

It is a valid defence to a claim in trespass that the alleged trespasser is entitled to enter the land in issue for certain purposes or by particular means, or generally, pursuant to an easement or profit. Since these rights are interests in or over land they provide a justification for the entry onto land and the carrying out of acts on that land in accordance with their terms. It follows that the terms of the particular right must be carefully considered in order to determine whether it provides a lawful authority for the act in question. Easements may be created expressly, by implication or be acquired by prescription and in each case the efficacy of the defence to trespass will depend on the exact nature of the right granted and the form of trespass alleged.[52]

1–074

EXPRESS GRANT OR RESERVATION

In the case of an easement created expressly by deed[53] or statute,[54] the question of the nature and extent of the authorisation is principally a matter of construction[55] of the terms of the grant of reservation or of the statutory provision creating the right.

1–075

---

[50] See above, para. 1–014.
[51] For a detailed discussion of easements and incorporeal rights, see Gale on Easements, generally, and *Megarry & Wade* (6th ed.), Chap. 15, Part 4.
[52] For a recent example, see *Peacock v. Custins* (2001) 81 P. & C.R. 479, CA.
[53] This can take the form either of a grant of rights or by reservation from land or property rights granted to another. A conveyance (which includes leases and mortgages) may operate as a grant of easements and profits by virtue of s. 62 of the Law of Property Act 1925 unless a contrary intention is expressed in the conveyance.
[54] *e.g.* pursuant to the Inclosure Acts or rights in the nature of easements granted in respect of the provision of public utilities such as electricity cables or water pipes. See, *e.g.* the Water Resources Act 1991, ss. 159 and 160.
[55] *Peacock v. Custins* (2001) 81 P. & C.R. 479, CA, at p. 487 para. 24 (Schiemann L.J.). It is often said that grants should generally be construed against the grantor, although this may have much less force where the deed is drafted by commercial parties or where there are lawyers acting for the parties: see, *e.g. Neill v. Duke of Devonshire* (1882) 8 App.Cas. 135,

Further problems may arise where the property concerned (especially the dominant tenement) has changed in character in the years since the making of the grant. Although the use of the dominant tenement may change from that contemplated by the parties to the grant at the time of the grant, the use of the right of way may continue provided that the burden on the servient tenement is not materially increased.[56]

RIGHTS OF WAY

1–076   One of the most familiar forms of easement is the right of way, which is the most likely form of authority to be encountered in the context of access to land. Such a right may exist over a road or path or even across land where the way is not visible and can only be ascertained from a consideration of the deed itself. The term "right of way" encompasses a considerable range of rights: the extent of the right requires consideration in terms not only of the physical extent of the right[57] but also the manner[58] and the time[59] in which the right may be exercised. For example, an easement conferring a general right of way across land along a particular lane whether with or without a motor vehicle will be adequate to authorise the driving of a car along that lane. However, if the easement were only a right of way exercisable on foot, then it would not authorise the use of the car and the entry would be unlawful. Such an entry would also be unlawful if the grant permitted the use of the way only at certain times of the day or year and those restrictions were not observed.

Although distinctions may readily be drawn between rights of way conferred on those proceeding on foot and those with vehicles, greater difficulties arise where the manner of the exercise is not clearly expressed — unless it is expressly made a general rights. In such circumstances, if the answer cannot be found by a proper construction of the words of the grant, then assistance may be derived from the physical condition of the

---

149. Although reservations at common law were treated in a similar fashion (*i.e.* construed against the vendor making the reservation), this is now not the case with reservations following s. 65 of the Law of Property Act 1925 which, in a somewhat anomalous fashion, are construed against the purchaser: *St. Edmundsbury and Ipswich Diocesan Board of Finance v. Clark (No. 2)* [1975] 1 W.L.R. 468, CA.

[56] See *White v. Grand Hotel, Eastbourne Ltd* [1913] 1 Ch. 133 (affirmed 84 L.J. Ch. 938) and, further, *Allen v. Gomme* (1840) 11 A. & E. 759, *Robinson v. Bailey* [1948] 2 All E.R. 791, CA, *Keefe v. Amor* [1965] 1 Q.B. 334, CA, *T. R. H. Sampson Associates Ltd v. British Railways Board* [1983] 1 W.L.R. 170 and *Graham v. Philcox* [1984] 3 W.L.R. 150, CA. If the character of the dominant tenement changes drastically, a right of way granted for the original purpose will not serve the new form of the dominant land, *e.g.* where a former access to open land is sought to be used for a new dwelling constructed on the land: above, *Allen v. Gomme*.

[57] *Keefe v. Amor* [1965] 1 Q.B. 334, CA; *West v. Sharp* (2000) 79 P.C. & R. 327, CA; *Groves v. Minor, The Times*, November 20, 1997, CA.

[58] *Brunton v. Hall* (1841) 1 Q.B. 792, *Cousens v. Rose* (1871) L.R. 12 Eq. 366, *British Railways Board v. Glass* [1965] Ch. 538, CA, *Jobson v. Record* (1997) 74 P. & C.R. D16, CA. (and see *Britel Developments (Thatcham) Ltd. v. Nightfreight (G.B.) Ltd.* [1998] 4 All E.R. 432).

[59] *Collins v. Slade* (1874) 23 W.R. 199 and *Hollins v. Verney* (1884) 13 Q.B.D. 304.

way at the time of the grant:[60] a way which was unmetalled at the date of grant and plainly unsuitable for use by motorised vehicles will provide a strong indication that the parties did not intend the right to include use by such vehicles. If a track were too narrow to permit its use by larger vehicles such as lorries and pantechnicons, then the user of the way would be limited to smaller vehicles such as cars and vans.

PROFITS À PRENDRE

As with easements, the existence of a profit will provide a lawful author- **1–077**
ity for an act which would otherwise be a trespass provided that the extent of the right is not exceeded. *Profits à prendre* are, in general terms, rights to take something off the land of another.[61] For example, a profit of pasture[62] may exist in a number of forms: if it is appurtenant[63] the terms of the grant, or the prescriptive user, must be examined to determine the animals which may be pastured and extent of the right[64]; if it is appendant[65] then the profit is limited to cows, oxen, sheep and horses and only to those which the dominant land might support during the winter months.[66] The commoners using a common of pasture *pur cause de vicinage*[67] may only place on the adjacent common so many animals as their own common would support, and a profit in gross[68] depends on the precise terms of the right and is not limited to specific numbers of animals

---

[60] *Cannon v. Villars* (1878) 8 Ch.D. 415 at 420, *Kain v. Norfolk* [1949] Ch. 163 and *St. Edmundsbury & Ipswich Diocesan Board of Finance v. Clark (No. 2)* [1975] 1 W.L.R. 468, CA; *Millman v. Ellis* (1996) 71 P. & C.R. 158.

[61] per Lindley L.J. in *Duke of Sutherland v. Heathcote* [1892] 1 Ch. 475, CA, 484. This definition is considered by *Megarry & Wade* (6th ed.), p. 1097 and, whilst correct to the extent that profits are of that nature described, is too wide in that it might appear to encompass rights which are not capable of being profits. There is also the essential requirement that the subject matter of the profit should form part of the land (*e.g.* crops) or at least be capable of ownership (*e.g.* game once killed).

[62] For other profits, such as turbary, piscary and estovers, see *Halsbury's Laws*, Vol. 6, paras. 576–586.

[63] A profit which is annexed to a dominant tenement in the vicinity, which is limited to the needs of that land and runs with that land: the nature of the right is similar to that of an easement (see *Megarry & Wade*, p. 1098). See *Halsbury's Laws*, Vol. 6, para. 557.

[64] It is not confined as a matter of law to specific animals but the numbers of the animals must be fixed either by the terms of the grant or prescriptive user or the number of animals the land is capable of maintaining during the winter (*i.e.* levancy and couchancy — *Robertson v. Hartopp* (1889) 43 Ch.D. 484, 516). See *Halsbury's Laws*, Vol. 6, paras. 559, 565 and 596–599.

[65] A profit of pasture appendant is one which is annexed to land by operation of law. See *Halsbury's Laws*, Vol. 6, paras. 547–556 and *Baring v. Abingdon* [1892] 2 App. Ch. 374.

[66] *i.e.* levancy and couchancy. See *Robertson v. Hartopp*, (1884) 43 Ch.D. 484, at 516–7.

[67] *i.e.* where two adjacent commons are open to each other and where the cattle placed on one common have been allowed to stray on to the other. Lack of physical contiguity or the existence of fencing will prevent the right from arising. See *Newman v. Bennett* [1981] Q.B. 726.

[68] A profit in gross is one which may exist independently of the ownership of the land held by the owner of the profit, *i.e.* there is no dominant tenement. See *Halsbury's Laws*, Vol. 6, paras. 564–565. A familiar form of a profit in gross is the right to catch and take fish (a profit of piscary).

except that no more animals may pasture than may be supported by the servient land.[69]

IMPLIED EASEMENTS

1–078   Rights may also be implied both as a matter of actual or imputed intention and as a matter of necessity. In the former case, the parties to a grant or reservation may not have set out in the grant or reservation all the elements to give effect to their common intentions: in such a case, the law will imply terms to give effect to those intentions.[70]

Easements of necessity are implied if land is conveyed and no access is either granted in favour of the land conveyed or reserved in favour of land retained, such that the land conveyed or retained (as the case may be) is completely landlocked.[71] Rights of support may also be implied as a matter of necessity.[72] A way of necessity will be implied in the circumstances described above, even if this affects the lands of persons who were not parties to the grant giving rise to the necessity. The necessity must exist at the time of the grant and will cease if the necessity ceases due to the acquisition of another right of way by the landowner.[73] An easement of necessity will not arise merely because the way which exists is not convenient[74]: the existence of an access to the dominant tenement will generally defeat a claim of necessity unless it is precarious.[75]

PRESCRIPTIVE RIGHTS

1–079   Easements (and profits) which arise by one of the methods of prescription,[76] by which the law seeks to uphold a right enjoyed for a lengthy period of time (the origins of which may be uncertain or even unlawful), are less easy to apply since the circumstances of the acquisition will dictate the nature and extent of the rights exercisable.[77]

---

[69] *Halsbury's Laws*, Vol. 6, para. 565.

[70] e.g. *Jones v. Pritchard* [1908] 1 Ch. 630 (right to a common flue), *Pwllbach Colliery Co. Ltd v. Woodman* [1915] A.C. 634, H.L. (right of way implied in easement to draw water from a spring), *Cory v. Davies* [1923] 2 Ch. 95 (right to common use of drive), *Wong v. Beaumont Property Trust Ltd* [1965] 1 Q.B. 173 (right to install ventilation system for cellar restaurant) and *Liverpool City Council v. Irwin* [1977] A.C. 239, H.L. (right to use common facilities on letting of flat).

[71] This arises as a matter of the intention of the parties: *Nickerson v. Barraclough* [1981] Ch. 426, CA.

[72] *Richards v. Jenkins* (1868) 18 L.T. 437.

[73] *Holmes v. Goring* (1824) 2 Bing. 76.

[74] *Dodd v. Burchell* (1862) 1 H. & C. 113.

[75] *Barry v. Hasseldine* [1952] Ch. 835.

[76] Either (i) at common law (user from time immemorial, *i.e.* prior to 1189, although there was a presumption of immemorial user if 20 years' user could be proved — see *Bryant v. Foot* (1867) L.R. 2 Q.B. 161 at 180–181 and *R. P. C. Holdings Ltd v. Rogers* [1953] 1 All E.R. 1029), (ii) in accordance with the Prescription Act 1932, or (iii) by the doctrine of lost modern grant (*e.g. Bryant v. Foot*, above, at 181, *Dalton v. Angus & Co.* (1881) 6 App.Cas. 740, H.L., *Tehidy Minerals Ltd v. Norman* [1971] 2 Q.B. 528, CA. For a detailed account see *Megarry & Wade*, (6th ed.), pp. 1124–1141.

[77] *Williams v. James* (1867) L.R. 2 C.P. 577, *United Land Co. v. Great Eastern Railway* (1875) 10 Ch. App. 586, and *Ironside v. Cook* (1978) 41 P. & C.R. 326.

The nature and extent of an easement acquired by prescription depends on the long user from which the prescriptive right arises: whether or not the act in relation to the land is authorised by such an easement may often require detailed considerations of the user giving rise to the easement and its precise nature and extent. In order to determine whether the right alleged has been acquired by long user, the actual user must be scrutinised[78] carefully to ensure that it provides authorisation for the entry and activities on the land of another. This is more difficult in the case of an easement by prescription than in that of one granted by deed since, in the latter case, the principle question is one of construction of the grant whereas, in the former, factual evidence of user over time must be examined. Evidence of a contrary intention will rebut a prescriptive grant,[79] but the intention cannot be purely nominal.[80] The extent of the right acquired depends on the physical extent of the user, the time of the exercise of that user and the manner of enjoyment. For example, if the prescriptive right of way has been established through at least 20 years' user by pedestrians, then it will not authorise the use of that way for the purposes of vehicular traffic.

As with licences, if the authority of the easement or profit is exceeded then any acts in excess of that authority will be acts of trespass. In *Mills v. Silver*,[81] the servient owner of a prescriptive right of way was awarded damages where the dominant owner had improved a farm track over which a right of way existed by laying a road using some 600 to 700 tons of stone. Although the dominant owner was entitled to repair the track which was the subject of the right of way, he was not entitled to improve it and so increase the burden on the servient tenement.

Custom

Although customary rights appear anachronistic, certain classes of such rights, which by custom have been exercised from time immemorial, still remain vested in specific classes of people — generally the inhabitants of a locality. For example, there may be a customary right for local inhabitants to use certain land for recreational purposes,[82] to dry fishing nets[83] or to hold a fair.[84] If such a right can be established, then it will provide a valid defence to a claim in trespass.

1–080

The nature of customary rights is quite different from that of easements since there is no requirement of dominant or servient tenements nor of a

---

[78] See *Williams v. James* (1867) L.R. 2 C.P. 577 at 580, *United Land Co. v. Great Eastern Railway* (1875) 10 Ch. App. 586 at 590, *Bradburn v. Morris* (1876) 3 Ch.D. 812, *Ironside v. Cook* (1978) 41 P. & C.R. at 336 and *Mills v. Silver* [1991] Ch. 271, CA.

[79] *R v. Secretary of State for the Environment, ex parte Dorset County Council* [1999] N.P.C. 72.

[80] *Secretary of State for the Environment v. Beresford Trustees* [1996] N.P.C. 128.

[81] [1991] Ch. 271, CA.

[82] *New Windsor Corporation v. Mellor* [1975] Ch. 380, *Hall v. Nottingham* (1875) 1 Ex. D. 1.

[83] *Mercer v. Denne* [1905] 2 Ch. 538.

[84] *Wyld v. Silver* [1963] Ch. 243.

capable grantee: customary rights exist, instead, as a "special local law"[85] which are exercisable by all those within the locality but not the general public.[86] However, a valid custom cannot exist which purports to permit local inhabitants to exercise rights outside their locality.[87]

The main prerequisites of a valid customary right are that it should have existed since "time immemorial," *i.e.* prior to 1189,[88] that it is reasonable, continuous and certain both as to the locality affected[89] and the extent of the right.

There appears to be no reason to doubt that if the terms of the customary right are exceeded, any act in excess of the acts permitted by that right will be a trespass.

Public rights of way — highways

1–081   A highway, or public right of way as it is sometimes called,[90] may comprise not only metalled roads but footpaths and bridleways.[91] A lawful use of the public highway is a defence to an allegation of trespass in respect of the land over which the highway runs. In *Harrison v. Duke of Rutland*,[92] Lord Esher M.R. stated:

"Highways are, no doubt, dedicated *prima facie* for the purpose of passage; but things are done upon them by everybody which are recognised as being rightly done, and as constituting a reasonable and usual mode of using a highway as such. If a person on a highway does not transgress such reasonable and usual mode of using it, I do not think that he will be a trespasser. Again, I do not think that such a trespass could be made out, except where acts other than the reasonable and ordinary user of a highway as such have been done on that particular portion of the highway, the soil of which belongs to the owner alleging a trespass to his land. If a person is passing along a part of the highway which belongs to a particular owner, in order to do something beyond, on land which does not belong to that owner, then, so

---

[85] *Megarry & Wade* (6th ed.), p. 1097.
[86] See above.
[87] *Edwards v. Jenkins* [1896] 1 Ch. 308, *Sowerby v. Coleman* (1867) L.R. 2 Ex. 96.
[88] Although this may be presumed if the right is demonstrated to have been enjoyed for a considerable time and there exists no indication of an origin later than 1189: *Mercer v. Denne*, [1905] 2 Ch. 538, and *Simpson v. Wells* (1872) L.R. 7 Q.B. 214.
[89] The nature and extent of the locality may vary, *e.g.* it may be a village, parish, town or even as wide as a county. See *New Windsor Corporation*, above, *Mercer v. Denne*, above, but see *Beckett v. Lyons* [1967] Ch. 449. A customary right cannot exist generally for a whole county: *Earl of Coventry v. Willes* (1863) 9 L.T. (N.S.) 384 and *R. v. Doncaster M.B.C. ex part Braim* (1987) 85 L.G.R. 233.
[90] Note that although a highway is sometimes described as a "public right of way" the characteristics of a highway do not correspond closely to those of private rights of way since, in particular, there is no requirement of a servient or dominant tenement in the case of a highway. For a full discussion of the meaning of "public highway", see *Halsbury's Laws*, Vol. 21, paras. 1–9 and Sauvain, *Highway Law* (2nd ed. 1997), Chap. 1.
[91] See, generally, the Highways Act 1980 and the Wildlife and Countryside Act 1981.
[92] [1893] 1 Q.B. 142 at 146–7.

far as that owner is concerned, he is merely passing along that part of the highway, and, whatever it may be his intention to do further on, there would be no trespasses against such owner. Again, if a man is passing along a highway, only intending, so far as the highway is concerned, to pass along it, though he intends to go from it and go into other land of the same owner, and does something contrary to his rights, I do not think that there will be any trespass on the highway. But the Plaintiff in this case, it should be observed, . . . was using this part of the highway solely for the purpose of interfering with the rights which the owner of the land was exercising on another part of his land. He did not intend to go on the land of the Duke by the side of the highway, and thence interfere with the Duke's sport. He knew that would be a trespass, he stood on the highway, and walked up and down on it for the purpose of doing things which interfered with the Duke's enjoyment of his land near the highway. He was, therefore, not there for the purpose of using the highway as such in any of the ordinary and usual modes in which people use a highway. Under those circumstances, I think that he was a trespasser."

As appears from the above, the right of members of the general public to use a public highway is not unfettered or unlimited: it is restricted to the right to pass and repass and to such other uses as are reasonable and usual on the highway.[93] However, that reasonable use is not restricted only to reasonable incidental uses associated with passage although they must not obstruct passage.[94] Examples of reasonable and usual use of the highway include taking a short rest[95] or leaving a vehicle for a short time whilst delivering goods. In *Iveagh v. Martin*[96] Paull J. said:

"On a highway I may stand still for a reasonably short time, but I must not put my bed upon the highway and permanently occupy a portion of it. I may stoop to tie up my shoelace, but I may not occupy a pitch and invite people to come upon it and have their hair cut. I may let my van stand still long enough to deliver and load goods, but I must not turn my van into a permanent stall."

What is a reasonable and usual use of the highway may alter from time to time. In *Hickman v. Maisey*,[97] Collins L.J. described the use as follows:

"The right of the public to pass and repass on a highway subject to all those reasonable extensions which may from time to time be recognised as necessary to its exercise in accordance with the enlarged

---

[93] *Hickman v. Maisey* [1900] 1 Q.B. 752 at 755.
[94] *Director of Public Prosecutions v. Jones* [1999] 2 A.C. 240, H.L.
[95] *ibid.*, at 756. See also *Rogers v. Ministry of Transport* [1952] 1 All E.R. 634, CA (use of lay-by for temporary stop) — but see *The Calgarth* [1927] P. 93 at 107–108.
[96] [1961] 1 Q.B. 232 at 273.
[97] [1900] 1 Q.B. 752, CA at 757–758, and see *DPP v. Jones*, further, below.

notions of people in a country becoming more populous and highly civilised, but they must be such as are not consistent with the maintenance of the paramount idea that the right of the public is that of passage."

The intention and purpose of the person using the highway may be relevant to the issue of whether his user is normal and reasonable for a public highway since it may demonstrate that a user which is, on its face, a perfectly normal use of the highway is nothing of the sort. In *Hickman v. Maisey*,[98] A.L. Smith L.J. said:

"For instance, if a man, while using a highway for passage, sat down for a time to rest himself by the side of the road, to call that a trespass would be unreasonable. Similarly, to take a case suggested during the argument, if a man took a sketch from the highway, I should say that no reasonable person would treat that as an act of trespass. But I cannot agree with the contention of the defendant's Counsel that the acts which this defendant did, not really for the purpose of using the highway as such, but for the purpose of carrying on his business as a racing tout to the detriment of the plaintiff by watching the trials of race horses on the plaintiff's land, were within such an ordinary and reasonable user of the highway as I have mentioned . . . I do not agree with the argument . . . to the effect that the intention and object of the defendant in going upon the highway cannot be taken into account in determining whether he was using it in a lawful manner. I think that his intention and object were all-important in determining that question."

1–082   Where the use of the highway exceeds what is usually permitted on the highway then the user may be sued in trespass by the owner of the soil on which the highway is constructed.[99] Accordingly, in *Harrison v. Duke of Rutland*,[1] where the claimant went on to the highway, the soil of which was vested in the defendant, not for the purpose of using the highway but to interfere with the defendant's use of the land for grouse driving, the claimant was held to be a trespasser and the defendant was entitled to use force to prevent such interference. Similarly, it was not a lawful use of the highway in *Liddle v. Yorkshire (North Riding) County Council*,[2] where children had climbed up a heap of waste soil temporarily left during road construction works and sat on a retaining wall by the highway.

[98]   [1900] 1 Q.B. 752, 756–757. See also Collins L.J. at 757.
[99]   See *Harrison v. Duke of Rutland* [1893] 1 Q.B. 142, CA, *Hickman v. Maisey*, above, *Liddle v. Yorkshire (North Riding) County Council* [1934] 2 K.B. 101, *Farrugia v. Great Western Railway* [1947] 2 All E.R. 565, and *Hubbard v. Pitt* [1976] Q.B. 142, CA. Even if there is a trespass to the highway, this does not relieve persons lawfully using the highway of the ordinary duty of care owed to other users: *Farrugia*, above.
[1]   Above.
[2]   [1934] 2 K.B. 101 at 112 and 122–3.

It is not a lawful use of the highway to congregate for the purpose of picketing premises[3] except for the purposes of "peacefully obtaining or communicating information or peacefully persuading any person to work or abstain from working" in contemplation or furtherance of a trade dispute.[4] This exception only applies[5] generally where the person involved is at or near his own place of work and does not authorise the stopping of vehicles on the highway[6] or sealing up the highway.[7] Further, the Act does not authorise the entry by persons (even if in furtherance of a trade dispute) onto private land without the consent of the landowner.[8] In accordance with the decision of the majority House of Lords in *D.P.P. v. Jones*, it may now be a normal and reasonable user of a highway to assemble peacefully for a reasonable period,[9] so long as no obstruction or nuisance is caused to those exercising the right of passage along the highway. Whether such a user is reasonable will depend upon the facts of the case.[10] As Lord Hutton held:[11]

> ". . . the issue which arises in the present appeal is whether the right of the public to use the highway, as stated by Lopes L.J. in *Harrison v. Duke of Rutland*, should be extended and should include the right to hold a peaceful public assembly on a highway, such as the A344, which causes no obstruction to persons passing along the highway and which the Crown Court found to be a reasonable user of the highway.
>
> In my opinion your Lordships' House should so hold for three main reason which are as follows. First, the common law recognises

---

3 *Hubbard v. Pitt* [1976] Q.B. 142, CA which involved the picketing of estate agents' premises to protest against changes in the character of Islington due to the influx of higher income house buyers.

4 S. 15 of the Trade Union and Labour Relations Act 1974 and *Vacher & Sons Ltd v. London Society of Compositors* [1913] A.C. 107, H.L. at 123 (on the Trade Disputes Act 1906).

5 S. 15(1)(a) unless he is a trade union official or normally works at more than one place: s. 15(1)(b) and (2). In the case of those unemployed for reasons connected with the trade dispute, see s. 15(3).

6 *Broome v. D.P.P.* [1974] A.C. 587, H.L. and *Kavanagh v. Hiscock* [1974] 1 Q.B. 600. It is lawful only to invite, or attempt to persuade, a driver to stop but not to require him to do so.

7 *Tynan v. Balmer* [1967] 1 Q.B. 91.

8 *British Airports Authority v. Ashton* [1983] 3 All E.R. 6 (applying *Larkin v. Belfast Harbour Commissioners* [1908] 2 I.R. 214) — ". . . It would be astonishing if Parliament intended such a right to be implied" (*per* Mann J. at 13).

9 Contrast earlier authority such as *R. v. Graham* (1888) 16 Cox C.C. 420, at pp. 429–430 and *Ex parte Lewis* (1888) 21 Q.B.D. 191 at p. 197.

10 *Director of Public Prosecutions v. Jones* [1999] 2 A.C. 240, H.L., *per* Lord Clyde and Lord Hutton. The case concerned the offence of trespassory assembly, as to which see para. 5–058 below. Lord Irvine L.C. favoured an even wider approach, stating that the highway was a public place and that any user would be reasonable if it did not breach the peace or cause a nuisance or obstruction. However, that wide principle was not adopted by the other members of the House of Lords, and strong dissenting judgments from Lord Slynn and Lord Hope argued that the user in the present case was not sufficiently connected with the core concept of the right of passage as required by previous authority. See *e.g.* Lord Hope at p. 274 — "In my opinion the distinction between the use of a highway for passage and its use as a place of assembly as an end in itself is a fundamental one, although the question is ultimately one of fact."

11 *ibid.*, at p. 287, citing with approval Collins L.J. in *Hickman v. Maisey*, above, at p. 758

that there is a right for members of the public to assemble together to express views on matters of public concern and I consider that the common law should now recognise that this right, which is one of the fundamental rights of citizens in a democracy, is unduly restricted unless it can be exercised in some circumstances on the public highway. Secondly, the law as to trespass on the highway should be in conformity with the law relating to proceedings for wilful obstruction of the highway under section 137 of the Highways Act 1980 that a peaceful assembly on the highway may be a reasonable use of the highway. Thirdly, there is a recognition in the authorities that it may be appropriate that the public's right to use the highway should be extended . . ."

The mere fact that a person leaves the highway and trespasses on adjoining land does not necessarily render the use of the highway a trespass if the trespass is separate and is not so intimately bound up with the use of the highway as to make the entire user of the highway unlawful.[12] This may be a difficult distinction to draw in practice if the use of the highway (apart from the exit in order to trespass) was such as would be considered normal and reasonable but the whole reason for the use of the highway was to facilitate the subsequent unlawful act. Since the question of intention and purpose may be relevant to whether a use of the highway is reasonable,[13] if such unlawful intention and purpose can be proved, it will convert a *prima facie* lawful use of the highway into a trespass. The fine line between such cases can be seen from *Hickman v. Maisey*[14] itself, where the use of the highway for observing and taking notes of race horses in training on nearby land was held to be so closely bound up in the unlawful act that the use of the highway amounted to a trespass. On the other hand, in *Randall v. Tarrant*[15] the parking of a car on the highway where the owner subsequently trespassed on nearby land was not regarded as sufficiently closely bound up with the unlawful act as to make the use of the highway itself a trespass. It appears from those cases that if the highway is used for ordinary purposes merely in preparation for some unlawful act which takes place off the highway and in a manner distinct from the use of the highway itself, then the user will be lawful. On the other hand, if the highway is itself used for an act which is not a lawful use of the highway, the whole user will be unlawful even if it would have been lawful but for the ultimate act, for example the observation of the race horses in *Hickman*.

---

[12] See *Harrison v. Duke of Rutland* [1893] 1 Q.B. 142, CA at 147 and *Randall v. Tarrant* [1955] 1 W.L.R. 255 at 260.
[13] *Hickman v. Maisey* [1900] 1 Q.B. 752, CA.
[14] *ibid.*
[15] [1955] 1 W.L.R. 255.

The foreshore

Whilst members of the public have the right to pass and repass over the foreshore[16] in order to fish and navigate,[17] or to anchor temporarily,[18] there is no general right to use the foreshore for recreational purposes such as bathing[19] or to gather sea coal[20] or to put down permanent moorings.[21]

1–083

Recovery or removal of goods (recaption)

If a person wrongfully takes the goods of another and places them on his own land, the owner of the goods may enter that land for the purposes of recovering the goods taken.[22] Although there are some suggestions that this right of recaption may extend to justify an entry onto the land of an innocent third party where goods have been unlawfully taken and deposited there by another, there is no clear support for such a proposition.[23] If the true explanation of the right to enter is that it is a type of licence, or authority, implied by law against a wrongdoer to enable the aggrieved party to take steps to recover his goods, it would not justify the entry onto the land of an innocent third party who was not a party to the wrongdoing. The position might be different if the innocent landowner were to refuse to return the chattels to their owner or allow them to be recovered, or if he were to convert them to his own use.

1–084

---

[16] The foreshore is the land between the high water mark of a medium high tide and low water mark: *Blundell v. Catterall* (1821) 5 B. & Ald. 268; *Scratton v. Brown* (1825) 4 B. & C. 485; *A.-G. v. Chambers* (1854) 4 De G.M. & G. 206. There is a presumption of ownership of the foreshore in favour of the Crown: *A.-G. v. Richards* (1795) 2 Anst. 63. At common law, the waters below the low water mark where great ships can go constitute the "high seas": *The Mecca* [1895] P. 95, CA, at 107. The Crown may from time to time declare sovereignty over the high seas which are then termed "territorial waters": *R. v. Kent JJ ex p. Lye* [1967] 2 Q.B. 153 at 172 (construing "territorial waters" in the Wireless Telegraph Act 1949). The breadth of the territorial waters adjacent to the UK is currently 12 nautical miles: s. 1(1)(a) of the Territorial Seas Act 1987. By s. 1(1)(b) and s. 1(4) of that Act, the baselines from which territorial waters are to be measured are to be found in the Territorial Waters Order in Council 1964 and the Territorial Waters (Amendment) Order in Council 1979: they are generally the low water mark.

[17] *Fowley Marine (Emsworth) Ltd v. Gafford* [1968] 2 Q.B. 618. See also *Llandudno U.D.C. v. Woods* [1899] 2 Ch. 705 and *Fitzhardinge v. Purcell* [1908] 2 Ch. 139 at 166. This includes purposes ancillary to those permitted, which includes the digging of bait by those intent on exercising their right to fish: *Anderson v. Arun District Council* [1993] 1 W.L.R. 1156, CA.

[18] See *Fowley Marine*, above.

[19] *Blundell v. Catterall* (1821) 5 B. & A. 268.

[20] *Beckett v. Lyons* [1967] Ch. 449, CA.

[21] See *Fowley Marine*, above.

[22] *Anthony v. Haney* (1832) 8 Bing. 186, *Patrick v. Colerick* (1838) 3 M. & W. 483, *Wood v. Manley* (1839) 11 Ad. & El. 34, and *Burridge v. Nicholetts* (1861) 6 H. & N. 383. In the light of the concerns expressed by Lightman J. in *Fuller v. Happy Shopper Markets Ltd.* [2001] 1 W.L.R. 1681 at p. 1692, para. 27, as to reliance on distress in the context of the Human Rights Act 1998, it would be prudent to consider the implications of such rights in this context. Although Strasbourg jurisprudence establishes that the European Convention on Human Rights does not apply to wholly private contract disputes, if the action involves the intervention of the court and the discretion of the court (which is a "public body" for the purposes of s. 6 of the 1998 Act) then human rights may well be engaged. See, further, Chapter 4 para. 4–113, below.

[23] Bl. Comm., Vol. 3, pp. 4–5, *Anthony v. Haney*, (1832) 8 Bing. 186, *per* Tindal C.J.

If the owner of goods unlawfully places those goods on the land of another, the landowner (or person entitled to possession or occupation) may remove those goods and enter the land of the owner of the chattels in order to leave the goods there.[24]

However, where there is no wrongful dealing with goods, e.g. where a former tenant seeks to re-enter premises formerly demised to recover goods accidentally left there,[25] the person entering land cannot use the mere presence of his goods to justify an entry. In those circumstances a landlord would be able to bring an action in trespass in respect of such entry. However, the owner of such chattels (and the owner of the goods placed by another on the land of another) may have a remedy in conversion if the landowner subsequently acts in such a way to convert the goods to his own use.[26]

Entry to abate a nuisance

1–085 Similar to the right of recaption is the right of a landowner to enter upon adjoining land to abate a nuisance.[27]

Necessity

1–086 The defence of justification by necessity must be approached with considerable care since it is based on a narrow ground in that the only form of necessity sufficient to give rise to an authority to enter land is that of preserving life or property.[28] Further, the necessity must not have arisen as a result of the negligence of the person effecting the entry[29] and the trespasser must in any event act reasonably.[30] Whether the defence of necessity is established must be determined by reference to the state of affairs in existence at the time of the entry.[31]

Necessity sufficient to amount to a defence has arisen where land has been entered to prevent a heather fire from spreading,[32] to shoot a dog to

---

[24] *Rea v. Sheward* (1837) 2 M. & W. 424.

[25] *Wilde v. Waters* (1855) 24 L.J.C.P. 193.

[26] See *Anthony v. Haney*, (1832) 8 Bing. 186, at 192–3. Denial of title is not itself sufficient to amount to conversion: s. 11(3) of the Torts (Interference with Goods) Act 1977. However, if the denial is coupled with a dealing in the chattels which is inconsistent with the right of its owner, then an action may lie in conversion. See *Clayton v. La Roy* [1911] 2 K.B. 1031, *Caxton Publishing Co. v. Sutherland Publishing Co.* [1939] A.C. 178 (esp. at 202) *Capital Finance Co. Ltd v. Bray* [1964] 1 W.L.R. 323 and *Bryanston Leasings Ltd v. Principality Finance Ltd* [1977] R.T.R. 45.

[27] See below, Chapter 4, paras 4–114 to 4–122.

[28] *Esso Petroleum Co. Ltd v. Southport Corp.* [1956] A.C. 218, H.L.

[29] *Cope v. Sharpe* [1910] 1 K.B. 168 and *Rigby v. Chief Constable of Northamptonshire* [1985] 1 W.L.R. 1242 at 1253–4 (the criteria for negligence in this context are the same as for the tort of negligence).

[30] *Monsanto plc v. Tilly & ors*, *The Times*, November 30, 1999, CA, below.

[31] *Cope v. Sharpe (No. 2)* [1912] 1 K.B. 496.

[32] *Cope v. Sharpe (No. 2)*, above.

prevent it from worrying sheep,[33] to remove goods to preserve them,[34] and where oil has been discharged on the foreshore to preserve the life of the crew of a tanker which would have otherwise broken its back.[35]

However, the narrowness of the defence is shown by the fact that an entry cannot be justified merely to assist the fire brigade which is already present.[36] It is not sufficient for a person to justify his entry onto his neighbour's land by his need to repair his own property, unless such need arises from the need to preserve life or property:[37] nor is it a good defence to allege that the need arises from the trespasser's own homelessness.[38] The keeper of bees may not rely on necessity to justify following a swarm onto the land of another.[39] Acts done merely "in the public interest" are likely to fall well below the level required for a defence of necessity to succeed. In *Monsanto plc v. Tilly*[40] Mummery L.J. held that:

"even in cases of emergency, trespass by the individual, in the absence of very exceptional circumstances, could not be justified as necessary or reasonable if there existed a public authority responsible for the protection of the relevant interests of the public . . ."

However, if that approach were to be applied beyond the particular circumstances in which it arose, it would create a number of difficulties, not the least that it would deny the defence of necessity to a person who entered a burning building to save a life since the fire brigade exists and is a "public authority responsible for the protection of the relevant interests of the public." If Mummery L.J.'s view intended to state a general requirement, rather than consider simply matters specific to the case, then it would require an assessment to be made of the extent to which the public authority is genuinely available to deal with the emergency at hand. Such unnecessary complexity perhaps underlines the fact that the principle enunciated was applied in that case where there was no pressing emergency or necessity and as such was merely a specific application of justifying necessity on the facts.[41] Pill L.J. expressed the issue in a manner consistent with earlier authority and more easily applicable:

---

[33] *Cresswell v. Sirl* [1948] 1 K.B. 241.
[34] *Kirk v. Gregory* (1876) 1 Ex. D. 55.
[35] See *Esso Petroleum Co. Ltd v. Southport Corp.*, above.
[36] *Carter v. Thomas* [1893] 1 Q.B. 673. The position may be different if the fire brigade is not able to deal with the fire and assistance is required in order to preserve life or property.
[37] *Kirby v. Chessum* (1914) 30 T.L.R. 660.
[38] *Carter v. Thomas*, above, and *London Borough of Southwark v. Williams* [1971] Ch. 734, CA at 744 (*per* Lord Denning M.R.).
[39] *Kearry v. Pattinson* [1939] 1 K.B. 471, CA and see above para. 1–050.
[40] *The Times*, November 30, 1999, and transcript dated November 25, 1999, CA. The case involved the uprooting of genetically modified crops for what were argued to be environmental and public health reasons. Summary judgment was granted and the Court declined to allow the case to proceed to a full trial despite the wishes of the defendants to publicise their cause.
[41] Underlined by Mummery L.J.'s express agreement with Stuart-Smith L.J.

"1. When Lord Goff[42] stated that the principle is one of necessity not of emergency, he was not intending to restrict the need to establish an "imminent danger" in the first two groups of cases he contemplated in his analysis, that is public necessity and private necessity. The examples Lord Goff gives in those groups are both examples of fire, where the danger is imminent and obvious. Lord Goff used the broader expression when analysing the third group of cases "concerned with action taken of necessity to assist another person without his consent". He was concerned with "action taken to preserve the life, health or well being of another who is unable to consent to it". To justify trespass, in cases such as the present, where the owner has the ability to refuse consent, the danger must be immediate and readily perceivable.

2. As pleaded, the alleged dangers are not in that category. . . . the case cannot be put as one of imminent danger.

. . . I acknowledge the possibility that a danger may be great while remaining insidious . . . The existence of a system of licensing and control by a public body, potentially susceptible to judicial review, is also to be welcomed when novel operations are conducted. The law of trespass does not however acknowledge a defence of justification based on allegations such as those pleaded by the defendants in this case."

Similarly, Stuart-Smith L.J. held:[43]

"Those cases show that the danger must be immediate and obvious and that a reasonable person would conclude that there was no alternative to the act of trespass."

It is also not a trespass for a member of the public to enter land in order to prevent the commission of a serious crime,[44] although plainly such a person is taking a risk that he will not be able to justify his entry.

Justification by law

1-087   A landlord's entry of demised premises in order to distrain for rent, is lawful since it is in exercise of the common law right to levy distress — although the distress must itself be lawful.[45] Bailiffs have power to enter premises in the course of executing a judgment as part of the ordinary civil process and providing that they do not break into the premises.[46] Although a bailiff may enter the land of a person who is not the judgment debtor to execute against the judgment debtor this is generally undesirable, unless he is certain of the existence of the debtor's property,

---

[42] Re F (Mental Patient) [1990] 2 A.C. 1, H.L., at p. 73.
[43] Para. 33 of his judgment.
[44] Handcock v. Baker (1800) 2 Bos. & P. 260 (entry to prevent murder).
[45] See above, paras. 1–053 and 1–054.
[46] Semayne's Case (1604) 5 Co. Rep. 91a, Southam v. Smout [1964] 1 Q.B. 308 and Vaughan v. McKenzie [1969] 1 Q.B. 557.

since if the bailiff seizes property belonging to a third party (and not the
debtor) the bailiff becomes a trespasser.[47]

An aircraft which complies with the provisions of section 76 of the Civil
Aviation Act 1982 will not commit a trespass by entering the airspace of
another.[48]

(1) ACCESS TO THE COUNTRYSIDE

(a) National Parks and Access to the Countryside Act 1949

Under the National Parks and Access to the Countryside Act 1949, section   **1–088**
60 and of the Countryside Act 1968, sections 16–19 members of the public
are given rights of entry to the "open countryside"[49] for recreational purposes where an access agreement or order[50] is in force and a member of
the public

> ". . . shall not be treated as a trespasser on that land or incur any other
> liability by reason only of so entering or being on the land . . ."[51]

(b) Countryside and Rights of Way Act 2000

The provisions of Part I of this Act ("Access to the Countryside") give   **1–089**
effect to what is popularly referred to as the "right to roam", from a date
to be appointed.[52] An important general right of access to countryside is
created by Part I together with the means of enforcing that right and other
associated rights of entry. The essential structure of Part I of the Act is as
follows:

(1) a general right for any person to enter and remain on "access
land" for the purposes of "open-air recreation"[53] is created by section 2(1) provided that

    (a) such person exercises the rights without breaking or dam-
aging any wall, fence, hedge, stile or gate[54] and observes the

---

[47] See *Southam v. Smout*, above.
[48] See above, para. 1–032.
[49] Defined by s. 59(2) of the 1949 Act and s. 16 of the 1968 Act as comprising wholly or predominantly mountain, moor, heath, down, cliff or foreshore and including woodlands,
rivers, and canals where situated in the countryside.
[50] See s. 59 of the 1949 Act.
[51] S. 60(1).
[52] S. 103(3). At the date of publication, these provisions are not yet fully in force. Although
much of Part I came into force on January 30, 2001 the key provisions in s. 2 are not yet in
force. For guidance as to the application of the provisions, see DETR Circular 04/2001
(February 5, 2001).
[53] "Open-air recreation" is not defined. It is likely that the words will be given their ordinary
meaning, although applied in the context of the Act. On the approach to interpreting
ordinary words, see *R. v. Monopolies & Mergers Commission ex p. South Yorkshire Transport
Ltd.* [1993] 1 W.L.R. 23, HL, at pp. 29 A-D & 32 (Lord Mustill).
[54] S. 2(1)(a).

general restrictions imposed pursuant to Schedule 2 (which are many and rigorous)[55] and/or under Chapter II of Part of the Act[56]; and

(b)   entering or remaining on land is not in contravention of any prohibition contained in or having effect under any enactment, other than an enactment contained in a local or private Act.[57]

"Access land" is defined by section 1(1) in wide terms as meaning land which:

(a)   is shown as "open country" on a map in conclusive form issued by the appropriate countryside body[58] for the purposes of this Part. "Open country" means land which appears to the appropriate countryside body to consist wholly or predominantly of "mountain, moor, heath or down",[59] which is not registered common land;[60]

(b)   is shown on such a map as registered common land,[61]

(c)   is registered common land in any area outside Inner London for which no such map relating to registered common land has been issued,

(d)   is situated more than 600 metres above sea level in any area for which no such map relating to open country has been issued, or

(e)   is dedicated for the purposes of this Part under section 16

However, "access land" does not include "excepted land" under Part I of Schedule I[62] or land which is treated by section 15(1) as being accessible to the public apart from this Act);

(2)   procedures are established for —

---

[55] Para. 1 of Schedule 2 imposes general restrictions (a) to (t) on access under s. 2(1). A person is not entitled to access under s. 2(1), *e.g.*, with vehicles (other than invalid carriages)(a), where accompanied by an animal other than a dog (c), where he commits a criminal offence (d), where he lights or tends or does anything likely to cause fires (e), where he takes, kills, injures or disturbs any animal, bird or fish (f) or nests and eggs (g), engages in hunting related activities (j), feeds livestock (h), bathes in non-tidal waters (i), and various other activities which might harm the land, the interests of the land owner, the interests of the public and anyone pursuing a lawful activity on the land. Also unauthorised is engaging in any activity which is organised or undertaken "for any commercial purpose" (t). Further restrictions are imposed on access with dogs (especially in the vicinity of livestock) in paras 4–6. The general restrictions may be relaxed by direction of the relevant authority with the agreement with the land owner: para. 7.

[56] S. 2(1)(b). See ss. 21 and 22, further, below.

[57] S. 2(3).

[58] Defined by s. 1(2) as the Countryside Agency in England and the Countryside Council for Wales in Wales.

[59] Defined by s. 1(2) as not including "land which appears to the appropriate countryside body to consist of improved or semi-improved grassland."

[60] S. 1(2).

[61] See also ss. 1(3) and (4).

[62] S. 1(2). See also Part II of Schedule 1.

(a) the preparation, publication, confirmation and review of maps showing all common land and "open country"[63] by the Countryside Agency (in England) and the Countryside Council for Wales;

(b) the dedication of open land as access land[64];

(c) the issue and revision of a Code of Conduct for the guidance of persons exercising the right of access under section 2(1) and of those interests in access land[65] by the Countryside Agency and the Countryside Council for Wales;

(d) ancillary matters such as powers to make byelaws,[66] appoint wardens,[67] and to erect and maintain notices which indicate boundaries, or which inform the public of the general restrictions in Schedule 2 or of the exclusion or restriction of access to land or of any other appropriate matters relating to the access to land under section 2(1);[68]

(3) provisions are made so that the exercise of the right of access under section 2(1) does not increase the liability of the land owner (whether under an enactment or "any rule of law");[69]

(4) "entitled persons"[70] may restrict or exclude access to land under section 2(1) for a limited period not exceeding 28 days in any calendar year.[71] Restrictions are placed on some of the days on which limitations may be placed, *e.g.* access may not be restricted or excluded on Christmas Day, Good Friday or Bank Holidays;[72]

(5) it is made a summary offence to place or maintain "on or near" access land or a way leading to access land a notice containing "false and misleading information likely to deter the public" from exercising the right of access under section 2(1).[73] Such an offence not only attracts the possibility of a fine on Scale 1 but also an order to remove the notice in not less than four days.[74] Failure to comply with a removal order is a further summary offence for which the maximum penalty is a fine not exceeding Scale 3;[75]

---

[63] S. 4–11.
[64] S. 16. Such dedications are irrevocable.
[65] S. 20.
[66] S. 17.
[67] S. 18.
[68] S. 19.
[69] S. 12 and 13. S. 13 introduced specific amendments to the Occupiers' Liability Acts 1957 and 1984.
[70] S. 22(3): it means the owner and any other persons having an interest in the land and "falling within a prescribed description" under regulations.
[71] Ss. 21 and 22. Where there are 2 "entitled persons", their rights to restrict or exclude are to be determined in accordance with regulations but the totality of their restrictions or exclusions must not exceed 28 days in any calendar year.
[72] S. 22(6). See also s. 22(7) which places restrictions on the number of weekend days in any year on which limitations may be imposed.
[73] S. 14(1).
[74] S. 14(2).
[75] S. 14(3).

(6)   whilst the right of access under section 2(1) justifies entry on to land for the statutory purposes, section 2(4) specifically provides that a person "becomes a trespasser" on access land by failing to comply with either section 2(1)(a),[76] the general restrictions in Schedule 2 or any other restriction imposed in relation to the land under Chapter II.[77]

(2) ACCESS TO NEIGHBOURING LAND ACT 1992

1–090   The Access to Neighbouring Land Act 1992 enables the owner of land to seek a court order[78] to grant him a right of access to adjoining or adjacent land[79] to carry out works[80] to his own land[81] if and only if the court is satisfied that:

(1)   the works are reasonably necessary for the preservation of the whole or any part of the applicant's land;[82] and

(2)   they cannot be carried out, or would be substantially more difficult to carry out, without entry upon the adjoining or adjacent land.[83]

Certain works, termed "basic preservation works" are deemed to fulfil (a) and include works for the maintenance, repair or renewal of any part of a

[76] Where a wall, fence, hedge, stile or gate is broken or damaged by the person entering or remaining on access land.
[77] Where access is restricted in accordance with s. 21 and 22.
[78] S. 1(1) and (2). The terms and conditions of access orders are specified in accordance with s. 2 and include a specification of the works which may be carried out, the land affected by the order and the time limit for the exercise of the right of access.
[79] S. 1(a).
[80] This can include an inspection to determine whether works within the Act are necessary: s. 1(7) deems the making of such an inspection to be the carrying out of works within s. 1. It is not certain whether the court has power under ss. 1 and 2 to authorise an inspection and at the same time to authorise any works falling within s. 1 which are then found to be reasonably necessary. There is a strong argument against such a composite order, namely that the court will not know the results of the inspection at the time it makes its order and will not be able to determine clearly whether the criteria for an access order for works under s. 1(2)-(6) will be met. The power to impose conditions under s. 2(2) and (3) does not appear to give the court power to impose the right to carry out certain works if the statutory criteria for authorisation are discovered to be met. It may be possible to specify in detail the precise circumstances in which the works can be done following inspection, but this is likely to lead to very complex orders which might be difficult to draw up and to enforce.
[81] Termed "the dominant land": s. 1(a): the adjoining or adjacent land is termed "the servient land" . The use of terminology appropriate to easements appears deliberate given that the effect of the Act is to enable the Court to grant a limited right of access.
[82] S. 1(2)(a). It is unlikely that the access order could cover works which were mere improvements and were not reasonably necessary to preserve the dominant land, its buildings, *etc.* A limited exception is found in s. 1(5)(a) where the improvement is merely incidental to the aim of preservation.
[83] S. 1(2)(b). This is clearly very much a question of fact and degree and leaves a great deal of discretion to the court. The criterion is one of difficulty not expense and it remains to be seen whether the courts will construe "substantially more difficult" as including difficulties caused by excessive expense. The statute also contains a number of other key provisions which leave much to the discretion of the court, *e.g.* ss. 1(3), (4) and (5).

building or structure or drain, sewer pipe or cable, works to vegetation which is in danger of becoming damaged, diseased or dangerous and the filling in or clearance of a ditch.[84] Access to carry out works which incidentally involve demolition, alteration, adjustment or improvement can be authorised under the Act but only where the court considers it to be fair and reasonable.[85] The court may not make an access order where it is satisfied that the disturbance or interference, or the hardship, to the respondent or others caused by the entry would be to such a degree that it would be unreasonable to make the order.[86] Even where the hardship or disturbance is not insuperable, the court has power to require the payment of compensation as a term of the exercise of the order[87] or a sum for the privilege of entering the servient land.[88]

The effect of an access order under the 1992 Act is two-fold:[89]

(1)   the respondent must permit the applicant or any of his associates[90] to do anything they are authorised or required to do by virtue of the order or by section 3 of the Act;[91] and

(2)   during the period authorised by the order, the applicant and his associates are authorised to enter upon the servient land for the purpose of carrying out the works specified by the order, and to bring onto the servient land and leave there equipment and materials reasonably necessary to carry out the works and waste arising from the works.[92]

If the applicant or his associates exceed the terms of the access order or attempt to enter the servient land outside the period during which entry may be effected, they will be trespassers in a position akin to a person who exceeds the terms of a licence.[93] In addition to the usual remedies for trespass, the court has power to award damages for breach of an access order under section 6(2) of the 1992 Act: the Act does not specify how such damages should be assessed. In principle, it seems appropriate that damages for breach should be assessed on the same footing as trespass damages since exceeding the terms of an access order appears to be a clear case of trespass where some legal authority to enter is exceeded, *i.e.* a form of "abuse of right". See paragraph 1–048, above.

---

[84] This is not a complete list: see s. 1(4).
[85] S. 1(5).
[86] Notwithstanding the court's power under s. 2 to impose terms and conditions on the access order under: s. 1(3).
[87] S. 2(4).
[88] S. 2(5) and (6).
[89] S. 3.
[90] Defined by s. 3(7) as such number of persons whom the applicant may reasonably authorise to exercise the power of entry conferred by the access order as may be reasonably necessary for carrying out the specified works.
[91] S. 3(1).
[92] S. 3(2).
[93] See above, paras. 1–048 and 1–073, and *Hillen & Pettigrew v. ICI (Alkali) Ltd* [1936] A.C. 65, HL at 69.

(3) PARTY WALL ETC. ACT 1996

See Chapter 5, paragraph 5–037. Section 8(1) of the Act contains a right of entry, subject to compliance with the notice procedure prescribed by section 8(3) and (4), entitling building owners (and their workmen and agents) to —

> "during usual working hours enter and remain on any land or premises for the purpose of executing any work in pursuance of this Act and may remove any furniture or fittings or take any other action necessary for that purpose."

If the premises are closed, the building owner (or workmen and agents) may pursuant to section 8(2) —

> "if accompanied by a constable or other police officer, break open any fences or doors in order to enter the premises."

Rights of entry "during usual working hours" are also granted by section 8(5) to a surveyor appointed or selected under section 10 of the Act "for the purpose of carrying out the object for which he is appointed or selected". Entry by a section 10 surveyor is subject to the notice procedure set out in section 8(6).

(3) Generally

1–091   There are numerous statutory powers conferred on local authorities,[94] acting in their capacity as public authorities, to enter land for various purposes: for example, a local planning authority may enter land for the purposes of executing works required by an enforcement notice where development has taken place without planning[95] or for enforcement purposes generally,[96] or a housing authority may enter property for certain purposes under the Housing Act 1985 relating to repair[97] area improvement,[98] slum clearance,[99]

---

[94] See, generally, Cross on *Local Government Law and the Encyclopaedia of Local Government Law* on the powers and duties of local authorities.

[95] S. 178 of the Town and Country Planning Act 1990 as amended by s. 7 of the Planning and Compensation Act 1991. There is no power to obtain a warrant in the case of such entry (contrast ss. 196A-C, below) which would appear to exclude any right of forcible entry. See also s. 209 of the Town and Country Planning Act 1990 (power to enter and plant trees where trees required to be replaced following the making of a tree preservation order) and, under the Planning (Listed Buildings and Conservation Areas) Act 1990, ss. 42 (to execute works following listed building enforcement notice), 54 (urgent works to preserve unoccupied listed buildings) and 76 (urgent works to preserve unoccupied buildings in conservation areas).

[96] S. 11 of the Planning and Compensation Act 1991 introduced ss. 196A-196C (rights of entry with and without warrant) into the Town and Country Planning Act 1990.

[97] S. 197 (as amended by the Local Government and Housing Act 1989).

[98] S. 260.

[99] S. 319.

overcrowding,[1] houses in multiple occupation,[2] and common lodging houses.[3]

The police have numerous powers conferred on them by statute which permit them to enter and search premises. For example, section 17 of the Police and Criminal Evidence Act 1984 permits entry and search to arrest a person who has committed an arrestable offence. Section 18 of the same Act authorises entry for the arrest of a person who has committed an arrestable offence and to search for evidence of that offence or in connection with similar offences.

On the consequences of exceeding the authority conferred by law, see above.[4]

Mistake no defence

It is no defence to trespass to plead that the trespass occurred by mistake **1–092** if that trespass was intentional in the sense considered above (*i.e.* excluding only wholly involuntary acts),[5] and notwithstanding that the defendant may have genuinely believed that he was entitled to enter the land, or even that he owned an interest in the land.[6]

Inevitable accident

Although a wholly deliberate act of interference is not required in order **1–093** to commit a trespass to land[7] it appears to be a valid defence[8] to allege that the trespass arose as a result of an inevitable accident,[9] *i.e.* from an entirely involuntary act.

Ius tertii no defence

Whilst a claim by a defendant that he was entitled to possession of the **1–094** land over which he is alleged to have committed a trespass is generally a good defence[10] a defendant may not set up the entitlement of a third party to possession as a defence to an action in trespass. In *Nicholls v. Ely Sugar Beet Factory*[11] Farwell J. noted that

> "It is well settled that in an action of trespass a defendant may not set up a *ius tertii*. He may set up a title in himself, or show that he acted

---

[1] S. 340.
[2] S. 395.
[3] S. 411.
[4] See above, paras. 1–048, 1–073.
[5] See paras. 1–039 to 1–042, above.
[6] *Basely v. Clarkson* (1682) 3 Lev. 37, *Conway v. Wimpey (No. 2)* [1951] 2 K.B. 266 at 273 and *R. v. Collins* [1973] Q.B. 100.
[7] See above, paras. 1–036 to 1–042.
[8] Although criticised as of no significance by Winfield and Jolowicz (15th ed.), pp. 872–873 on the basis that the burden of proof lies on the claimant.
[9] *National Coal Board v. J.E. Evans (Cardiff) Ltd* [1951] 2 K.B. 861.
[10] *Delaney v. T.P. Smith Ltd* [1946] K.B. 393 at 397 and 399.
[11] [1931] 2 Ch. 84 at 86.

upon the authority of the real owner, but he cannot set up a mere *ius tertii*. That is well settled . . ."

This defence is not available even though the party bringing the trespass action can show no other title than actual possession and notwithstanding the fact that he may himself have wrongfully acquired possession from that third party — and hence would not be able to prevent ejectment by that person with the right to possession. Although there are indications that this view is not accepted by all[12] the current weight of authority lends it support.[13] The basis of the principle appears to lie in the presumption which is made that the original entry by the claimant was lawful, and that the claimant is seised in fee, and also in the overriding need to avoid breaches of the peace which might otherwise be encouraged if the law permitted a party with no title himself to dispossess another with precarious title. Although the logic of this might suggest that the presumption could be rebutted by proof that the original entry was not lawful, namely by adducing evidence of the title of a stranger to the action, this is not the case. Indeed, it is questionable whether the need to avoid breaches of the peace is not now more appropriately dealt with by legislation such as the Criminal Law Act 1977 and the Protection from Eviction Act 1977 which prescribe both criminal penalties and civil damages.[14]

The justification for the principle appears further weakened not only by the fact that the validity of documentary evidence can be attacked by reference to the title or interests of another, but also by the existence of the defence that the defendant was in occupation as agent for or as licensee of a third party. Whilst the justification of the exclusion of *ius tertii* may lie in the desire to reduce delaying tactics in litigation by parties with unmeritorious defences, or to discourage breaches of the peace, there is some attraction in the approach exemplified by the abolition of the *ius tertii* rule with regard to trespass to chattels[15] — especially where ample means now exist to deal with breaches of the peace and violent entries onto land.[16] Indeed, it would be preferable for the law of trespass to give greater weight to better title rather than to more recent "title" acquired by the taking of possession.

A defendant may however rely on a *ius tertii* where he can establish that he acted in accordance with the authority of the third party owner.[17] If

---

[12] *Doe d. Carter v. Barnard* (1849) 13 Q.B. 945.

[13] See, *e.g. Asher v. Whitlock* (1865) L.R. 1 Q.B. 1, and the comments of Lord Macnaghten in *Perry v. Clissold* [1907] A.C. 73, HL, at pp. 79–80. See also *J.A. Pye (Oxford) Ltd. v. Graham* [2002] 3 W.L.R. 221, HL, at para. 42.

[14] See below, Chapter 5.

[15] See 18th Report of the Law Reform Committee, Cmnd 4774, s. 8(1) of the Tort (Interference with Goods) Act 1977 and the former R.S.C., Ord. 15, r. 10A (now revoked). See Battersby, (1992) Conveyancer 100.

[16] *e.g.* the Criminal Law Act 1977 and Protection from Eviction Act 1977 as amended by the Housing Act 1988 which, for the first time, introduced a statutory right to damages for unlawful eviction. Compare the pre-Housing Act position in *McCall v. Albelesz* [1976] Q.B. 585, CA.

[17] *Fitzgerald v. Firbank* [1897] 2 Ch. 96, *Glenwood Lumber v. Phillips* [1904] A.C. 405, H.L. and *Nicholls v. Ely Beet Sugar Factory* [1936] 1 Ch. 343, CA.

such a defence is to be raised it must be pleaded and the defendant must prove it.[18] The existence of the authority of the person entitled to possession is sufficient to support a defence even if the defendant did not actually rely upon it at the time of the alleged trespass.[19]

Where the claimant seeks to prove his superior title by reliance upon documentary evidence, this is then open to attack by the defendant, *e.g.* by establishing the invalidity of a mortgage deed or will. The ability to rely upon a superior title deriving solely from prior possession may be useful in certain cases, *e.g.* where one seeking to acquire title by adverse possession[20] is dispossessed by a person other than the landowner with "paper" title.

A further consequence of the *ius tertii* principle is that a defendant may not plead *ius tertii* in mitigation or diminution of loss: for example, by maintaining that since the claimant has no title other than by actual possession, he should not be entitled to recover mesne profits since he is not himself entitled to the benefit of the land. Since bare possession provides *prima facie* evidence of title[21] and is sufficient to maintain an action for trespass, the defendant trespasser is *prima facie* liable in damages to a mere possessor.[22] However, such a claimant has himself only a precarious title and may be liable himself to the lawful owner. Such liability may, if damages are recovered against the trespasser, include the necessity to account to the third party owner for the damages recovered.[23]

1–095

A person in actual possession cannot generally be defeated in a trespass action by a defendant claiming that his own act of trespass (if sufficiently extensive) has displaced the claimant's own possession and hence his very title to sue. Nonetheless, in practice it may be difficult for a claimant to recover possession in an action for the recovery of land if the sole basis of his claim was his own actual possession which he has now lost.[24] In *Thompson v. Ward*[25] a statutory tenant under the Rent Acts abandoned his statutory tenancy (within the principles of the Rent Acts[26]) but subsequently sought to recover possession of the dwelling-house from his licensee who was in occupation. He failed in an action for recovery of the dwelling on the basis that he had abandoned the possession necessary to maintain an action for trespass.

Limitation and adverse possession

A person who has, or is entitled to, possession of land may lose that possession or entitlement in two ways: he may be dispossessed by another

1–096

---

[18] *Ewer v. Jones* (1846) 9 Q.B. 623.

[19] *Trent v. Hunt* (1853) 9 Exch. 14 and *Phillips v. Whitsed* (1860) 2 E. & E. 804.

[20] See paras. 1–096 to 1–133, the Land Registration Act 2002, Part 9 and Sched. 6, and the Limitation Act 1980, ss. 15–19.

[21] *Delaney v. T.P. Smith Ltd* [1946] 1 K.B. 393.

[22] *Eastern Construction Co. v. National Trust Co.* [1914] A.C. 197, H.L. and *Glenwood Lumber Co. v. Phillips* [1904] A.C. 405, H.L.

[23] *Eastern Construction Co. v. National Trust Co.*, above, at 210.

[24] *Doe d. Carter v. Barnard* (1849) 13 Q.B. 945 and *Thompson v. Ward* [1953] 2 Q.B. 153.

[25] *ibid.*

[26] *Brown v. Brash* [1948] 2 K.B. 247, CA.

person[27] or discontinue his own possession, allowing another person to enter and occupy the land. In *Buckinghamshire County Council v. Moran*[28] Nourse L.J. explained the distinction as follows:

"Adopting the distinction between dispossession and discontinuance which was suggested by Fry J. in *Rains v. Buxton*, 14 Ch.D. 537, 539, I take the first case to be one where the squatter comes in and drives out the true owner from possession and the second to be one where the true owner goes out of possession and is followed in by the squatter."

As with other actions, the right to bring proceedings in trespass, whether for dispossession or for entry following discontinuance of possession, is subject to restrictions imposed by statute. This takes the form of a limitation period in the case of a right to claim damages, which must generally be brought within six years of the accrual of the cause of action in trespass.[29] In terms of the ability of the landowner to take proceedings to recover possession, this is also affected by statute although the reforms of the Land Registration Act 2002 ("LRA 2002") have radically affected the position with regard to registered land. Previously, there was a uniform 12 year limitation period applicable to both registered and unregistered land and title could generally be lost by 12 years' adverse possession of the land. However, following the coming into force of Part 9 of the LRA 2002 there are different regimes for unregistered and registered land. In the case of unregistered land, the time limits remain those imposed by the Limitation Act 1980[30] and, in the case of registered land,[31] the new regime created by the LRA 2002 applies. The LRA 2002 regime places significant limits on the ability of squatters to obtain title to registered land, notwithstanding proof of adverse possession.

Since the concept of "adverse possession" is common to both regimes, it will be considered first, although its function in the cases of registered and unregistered land is quite different.

●

---

[27] See, *e.g. Rains v. Buxton* (1880) 14 Ch.D. 537.

[28] [1990] Ch. 623, CA at 644. See also *J A Pye (Oxford) Ltd v. Graham* [2001] 2 W.L.R. 1293, CA. The House of Lords has granted leave to appeal in *Pye* and it remains to see what clarification of principles may be provided.

[29] S. 2 (time limit for actions founded on tort) subject generally to s. 29 (acknowledgment) and s. 32 (fraud, concealment and mistake).

[30] For the distinction between limitation and prescription see Megarry & Wade (6th ed.) pp. 1303–1304 and *Buckinghamshire v. Moran* [1990] Ch. 623, CA at 644 (Nourse L.J.). The principal provisions are ss. 15 and 17 and Schedule 1.

[31] Meaning registered estates and registered rentcharges: see s. 96(1) of the LRA 2002.

Adverse possession

Contrary to suggestions in some earlier authorities, "adverse possession"   **1–097**
means no more than "possession"[32] and bears[32a]

> "the traditional sense of that degree of occupation or physical control, coupled with the requisite intention commonly referred to as animus possidendi, that would entitle a person to maintain an action of trespass in relation to the relevant land . . . "

The addition of "adverse" to "possession" does not mean that there is some added requirement that the possession must be inconsistent or contrary to the interests of the actual owner (although such possession is likely to be contrary to such interests in any event). The use of "adverse" therefore adds nothing of legal relevance and as Lord Browne-Wilkinson recently stated in *J. A. Pye (Oxford) Ltd. v. Graham*[32b]:

> "Many of the difficulties with these sections . . . are due to a conscious or subconscious feeling that in order for a squatter to gain title by lapse of time he has to act adversely to the paper title owner. It is said that he has to "oust" the true owner in order to dispossess him; that he has to intend to exclude the whole world including the true owner; that the squatter's use of the land has to be inconsistent with any present or future use by the true owner. In my judgment much confusion and complication would be avoided if reference to adverse possession were to be avoided so far as possible and effect given to the clear words of the Acts. The question is simply whether the defendant squatter has dispossessed the paper owner by going into ordinary possession of the land for the requisite period without the consent of the owner."

Since a claim to title by means of adverse possession arises from what has been described as "possession as of wrong,"[33] the courts are understandably careful in assessing this type of claim and require clear evidence

---

[32] *J. A. Pye (Oxford) Ltd. v. Graham* [2002] 3 W.L.R. 221, HL, reversing the decision of the Court of Appeal [2001] Ch. 804, and restoring the order of Neuberger J. [2000] Ch. 676. See Lord Browne-Wilkinson (with whom the other members of the House of Lords agreed) at paras., 32–36 applying the analysis of Slade J. in *Powell v. McFarlane* (1977) 38 P. & C.R. 452 at 469 (which was described as "remarkable" at para. 31). Lord Browne-Wilkinson, in a speech which usefully clears away much confusion from the law of adverse possession (drawing principally on *Powell v. McFarlane*), explains at paras. 32–35 the history of the provisions and the unnecessary confusion which was caused by the reintroduction of the concept of adverse possession by the Limitation Act 1939.

[32a] Slade J. in *Powell v. McFarlane*, above, at p. 469.

[32b] *Ibid.* at para. 36.

[33] *per* Nourse L.J. in *Buckinghamshire v. Moran*, [1990] Ch. 623, CA, at 644.

before depriving the actual owner of his title.[34] In order to establish legal possession to land there are two necessary elements,[35] namely:

(1) a sufficient degree of custody or physical control of the land ("factual possession");

(2) an intention to exercise such custody and control on one's own behalf and for one's own benefit ("intention to possess" — sometimes also referred to as the *animus possidendi*).

It is also necessary to establish the appropriate possession of the land for the requisite period of time under statute.[36]

The concept of adverse possession was developed in the context of the Limitation Act 1980 and its predecessors, although the inappropriate use of "adverse" has created unecessary confusion.[36a] The same concept is applied for the different purposes of the LRA 2002 by paragraph 11(1) of Schedule 6[37]:

"A person is in adverse possession of an estate in land for the purposes of this Schedule if, but for section 96, a period of limitation under section 15 of the Limitation Act 1980 (c. 58) would run in his favour in relation to the estate."

However, since Part 9 of the LRA 2002 is no longer concerned with the accrual of a cause of action, paragraph 11(3) of Schedule 6 disregards (for the purpose of that paragraph) —

(1) the commencement of any legal proceedings; and

(2) paragraph 6 of Schedule 1 to the 1980 Act

in determining whether a period of limitation would run under section 15 of the 1980 Act.[38]

Specific modifications to adverse possession in the context of the LRA 2002 are dealt with under "Registered Land" below, at paragraphs 1–101 to 1–107.

---

[34] *per* Nourse L.J. in *Buckinghamshire v. Moran*, [1990] Ch. 623, CA, at 640.

[35] *J. A. Pye (Oxford) Ltd. v. Graham*, above, at paras. 40 (Lord Browne-Wilkinson) and 70 (Lord Hope).

[36] 12 years under the Limitation Act 1980 and 10 years for the purposes of para. 1(1) of Sched. 6 to the LRA 2002 (subject to para. 6 of Sched. 6)

[36a] *J. A. Pye (Oxford) Ltd. v. Graham*, above, at paras. 32–35 and n. 32, above.

[37] See Law Com No. 271 para. 14.20, pp. 310–311.

[38] Para. 11(3)(a) and (b) of Sched. 6 to the LRA 2002. See Law Com No. 271 para. 14.23, pp. 312–313.

(a) Factual possession

The first requirement is that a trespasser must establish (whether in a case **1–098** of dispossession or discontinuance of possession) that he has a sufficient degree of custody or physical control of the land for the relevant period of time[39]:

> "(3) Factual possession signifies an appropriate degree of physical control. It must be a single and [exclusive] possession, though there can be a single possession exercised by or on behalf of several persons jointly. Thus an owner of land and a person intruding on that land without his consent cannot both be in possession of the land at the same time. The question what acts constitute a sufficient degree of exclusive physical control must depend on the circumstances, in particular the nature of the land and the manner in which land of that nature is commonly used or enjoyed. . . . Everything must depend on the particular circumstances, but broadly, I think what must be shown as constituting factual possession is that the alleged possessor has been dealing with the land in question as an occupying owner might have been expected to deal with it and that no-one else has done so."

(b) Intention to possess

In addtion to factual possession, the squatter must also have an intention **1–099** for the applicable limitation period to exercise the custody and control necessary for factual possession on his own behalf and for his own benefit,[40] *i.e.* he must have the relevant intention to possess (or *animus possidendi*). There is no requirement that a squatter should intention to *own* the land.[41] In *J. A. Pye (Oxford) Ltd. v. Graham*, Lord Browne-Wilkinson held[42]:

> "There are cases in which judges have apparently treated it as being necessary that the squatter should have an intention to own the land in order to be in possession. In *Littledale v Liverpool College* [1900] 1 Ch 19, 24 Lindley MR referred to the plaintiff relying on "acts of ownership": see also *George Wimpey & Co Ltd v Sohn* [1967] Ch 487 at 510. Even Slade J in *Powell*, at pp 476 and 478, referred to the necessary intention as being an "intention to own". In the *Moran* case . . . the trial judge (Hoffmann J) had pointed out that what is required is "not an intention to own or even an intention to acquire ownership but an

---

[39] Slade J. in *Powell v. MacFarlane*, above, at pp. 470–471 approved and applied by the House of Lords in *J. A. Pye (Oxford) Ltd. v. Graham*, above, at para. 41.

[40] *J. A. Pye (Oxford) Ltd. v. Graham*, above, at para. 40 and *Buckinghamshire County Council v. Moran* [1990] Ch. 623, C.A., at 636C (Slade L.J.) and 644–5 (Nourse L.J.).

[41] This being one of the few issues where the House of Lords disagreed with the judgment of Slade J. in *Powell v. MacFarlane*, above.

[42] Above, at para. 42. See also Lord Hope at para. 71.

intention to possess". The Court of Appeal in that case [1990] Ch 623, 643 adopted this proposition which in my judgment is manifestly correct. Once it is accepted that in the Limitation Acts, the word "possession" has its ordinary meaning (being the same as in the law of trespass or conversion) it is clear that, at any given moment, the only relevant question is whether the person in factual possession also has an intention to possess: if a stranger enters on to land occupied by a squatter, the entry is a trespass against the possession of the squatter whether or not the squatter has any long term intention to acquire a title."

Further, the true intention to possess does not require that the squatter should intend to exclude the true owner[43] and the requirement to "exclude the world at large", often found in previous authorities, is difficult to apply since, as Lord Browne-Wilkinson held in *Pye*, quoting Slade J. in *Powell v. MacFarlane* —

"In *Powell's* case . . . [at] 471 Slade J found difficulty in understanding what was meant by this dictum since a squatter will normally know that until the full time has run, the paper owner can recover the land from him. Slade J reformulated the requirement (to my mind correctly) as requiring an 'intention, in one's own name and on one's own behalf, to exclude the world at large, including the owner with the paper title if he be not himself the possessor, so far as is reasonably practicable and so far as the processes of the law will allow'."

In general, intention should be inferred from the actual acts of the trespasser,[44] and the circumstances taken as a whole, although caution needs to be exercised with regard to subjective evidence which may be self-serving.[45]

As a matter of evidence, proof of intention can be difficult especially when the proof comprises a variety of sources, both direct, factual evidence, oral evidence of the squatter's own intentions, and circumstantial evidence as occurred in *J.A. Pye (Oxford) Ltd v. Graham*.[46] Restoring the judgment of Neuberger J.,[47] the House of Lords held that the intention of the defendants who held over following the expiry of a licence without

---

[43] Described by Lord Browne-Wilkinson in *Pye*, above, at para. 43 as a "similar manifestation of the same heresy" as that of requiring an intention to own.

[44] For a recent example of intention inferred from a number of acts of the trespasser, see *Prudential Assurance Co Ltd v. Waterloo Real Estate Inc* [1999] 2 E.G.L.R. 85, CA.

[45] *Tecbild Ltd. v. Chamberlain* (1969) 20 P. & C.R. 633, CA, at p. 643 and *Pye*, above, at para. 60. *Pye* is an example of a case where the court did rely on the expression of intention by the trespasser as part of the picture presented by the evidence as a whole. The subjective expressions of intention were consistent with the objective factual evidence. The Court of Appeal, indeed, was criticised for being selective in its reliance on the evidence.

[46] [2002] UKHL 30.

[47] [2000] Ch. 676.

any significant change of user was sufficient to amount to the requisite intention[48]:

> "Despite Pye's notification to quit the land in December 1983, its peremptory refusal of a further grazing licence in 1984 and the totally ignored later requests for a grazing licence, after 31 December 1983 the Grahams stayed in occupation of the disputed land using it for what purposes they thought fit. Some of those purposes (i.e. the grazing) would have fallen within a hypothetical grazing agreement. But the rest are only consistent with an intention, verified by Mr Michael Graham, to use the land as they thought best. That approach was adopted from the outset. In my judgment, when the Grahams remained in factual possession of the fully enclosed land after the expiry of the mowing licence they manifestly intended to assert their possession against Pye."

Lord Browne-Wilkinson rejected the artificiality which would have resulted from not treating the defendants as in possession of the land, despite the fact they would have been willing to pay, given that they alone had farmed the land[49]:

> ". . . although the Grahams would have been willing to pay for the use of the disputed land if asked, such willingness is not inconsistent with them intending to possess the land in the meantime as demonstrated by them treating the land as part of Manor Farm and maintaining it on the same basis as the rest of the farm.
>
> If the view of the Court of Appeal were to be correct, the result would be anomalous. Although from 1984 to 1997 the Grahams were the only people who did anything on the disputed land and Pye had throughout that period been physically excluded from the land, nevertheless Pye was throughout to be treated as in possession. In my judgment, however favourably one approaches the claim of a paper owner to possession, such a conclusion would be so unrealistic as to be an impossible one. For all practical purposes the Grahams used the land as their own and in a way normal for an owner to use it throughout the period from August 1984 onwards. During that whole period Pye did nothing on the disputed land from which they were wholly excluded save on foot."

As the above passage demonstrates, the willingness of a squatter to pay for occupation is not necessarily inconsistent with the relevant intention to possess. Lord Browne-Wilkinson preferred the view of Lord Diplock in

---

[48] *Pye*, above, at para. 64 *per* Lord Browne-Wilkinson.
[49] At paras. 60–61.

Ocean Estates Ltd v. Pinder[50] on this issue and disagreed with the Court of Appeal[51]:

> "The decision in *Pinder* is to be preferred because it is consistent with principle. Once it is accepted that the necessary intent is an intent to possess not to own and an intention to exclude the paper owner only so far as is reasonably possible, there is no inconsistency between a squatter being willing to pay the paper owner if asked and his being in the meantime in possession. An admission of title by the squatter is not inconsistent with the squatter being in possession in the meantime."

For dispossession to occurr for the purposes of adverse possession, it is not necessary that should have been an intention by the squatter to possess the land wrongfully, since the intention to possess by the squatter and dispossess the true owner may have occurred in the mistaken belief that the land was his.[52] Indeed, this conclusion appears to flow in any event from the clarification of the meaning of possession by the House of Lords in *Pye v. Graham*.

Whilst it is not inconsistent with such an intention that the trespasser might go out of possession for a time,[53] if the trespasser's absence amounts to a cesser of adverse possession then a fresh right of action accrues if he then goes back into possession.[54] In such a case, the trespasser cannot aggregate later periods of adverse possession with the period prior to the cesser and a full period of adverse possession must run from the resumption of possession before the true owner's title is extinguished.

Although, as set out above, the intention of the trespasser is an important factor, the intention of the true owner of the land has given rise to greater problems. For many years, decision of the Court of Appeal in *Leigh v. Jack*[54a] caused "repeated trouble"[54b] since it suggested that the acts of the squatter must be inconsistent with the intentions of the owner. Following

---

[50] [1969] 2 A.C. 19, P.C., at p. 24 where Lord Diplock referred to the admission as one "which any candid squatter hoping in due course to acquire a possessory title would be almost bound to make."

[51] *Pye*, above, at para. 46. Lord Browne-Wilkinson also considered *R v. Secretary of State for the Environment, Ex p Davies* (1990) 61 P. & C.R. 487 to have been wrongly decided since it had not referred to *Pinder*.

[52] See *Lodge v. Wakefield Metropolitan City Council* [1995] 2 E.G.L.R. 124 CA and *Prudential Assurance Co Ltd v. Waterloo Real Estate Inc* [1999]2 E.G.L.R. 85, CA, at pp. 87–88 (dealing with the "unconscious trespasser").

[53] See *R v. Secretary of State for the Environment, Ex p Davies*, above, at p. 495 if this aspect of the decision survives the criticism of it by the House of Lords in *Pye v. Graham*, above. See n. 51.

[54] See below, para. 1–110, and para. 8(2) of Sched. I to the 1980 Act.

[54a] (1879) 5 Ex. D. 264.

[54b] *Pye v. Graham*, above, at para. 44.

Buckinghamshire v. Moran and *Pye v. Graham*, it is now clear that this is not the case.[55] As Lord Browne-Wilkson explained in *Pye*[56]:

> "The suggestion that the sufficiency of the possession can depend on the intention not of the squatter but of the true owner is heretical and wrong. It reflects an attempt to revive the pre-1833 concept of adverse possession requiring inconsistent user. Bramwell B's heresy led directly to the heresy in the *Wallis's Cayton Bay* line of cases . . . which heresy was abolished by statute. It has been suggested that the heresy of Bramwell B survived this statutory reversal but in the *Moran* case the Court of Appeal rightly held that however one formulated the proposition of Bramwell B as a proposition of law it was wrong. The highest it can be put is that, if the squatter is aware of a special purpose for which the paper owner uses or intends to use the land and the use made by the squatter does not conflict with that use, that may provide some support for a finding as a question of fact that the squatter had no intention to possess the land in the ordinary sense but only an intention to occupy it until needed by the paper owner. For myself I think there will be few occasions in which such inference could be properly drawn in cases where the true owner has been physically excluded from the land. But it remains a possible, if improbable, inference in some cases."

In the light of the above, it is suggested that for all practical purposes, the intention of the true owner should be regarded as irrelevant. In the type of case which Lord Browne-Wilkinson considered might improbably arise, the facts might be capable of being dealt with in any event as part of the question of the squatter's own factual possession and intention.[57]

(c) Aspects of proof of possession

The principles, following the wide-ranging review of the law by the **1–100** House of Lords in *Pye v. Graham* have already been set out above. Whether or not there is adverse possession in a particular case must, of course, be decided by a careful consideration of the facts including not only the acts of the squatter, but also the character of the property, how it is normally used, what acts demonstrating ownership might be expected from the actual owner in the circumstances and also the relationship (if any) between the owner and trespasser.[58]

---

[55] See *Buckinghamshire v. Moran*, [1990] Ch. 623, CA, per Nourse L.J. at pp. 644–5 and Slade L.J. at pp. 639–640 and *Pye v. Graham*, above, at paras. 44–45. See, further, Megarry & Wade, *Real Property* (6th ed.) pp. 1310–1311 (para. 21–019).

[56] Above, at para. 45.

[57] A case such as *Bligh v. Martin* [1968] 1 W.L.R. 804 at 812 B–C (use of arable land during winter for grazing of cattle not sufficient) may be explained on this basis.

[58] *e.g.* if the occupation of the dispossessor is attributable to some other legal relationship (see *Hyde v. Pearce* [1982] 1 W.L.R. 560), or some family connection exists between the

It is generally fatal to a claim to adverse possession that the party making the claim has some right to occupy the land in question[59]:

> "Possession is never 'adverse' within the meaning of the Act of 1980 if it is enjoyed under a lawful title. If, therefore, a person occupies or uses land by licence of the owner with the paper title and his licence has not been duly determined, he cannot be treated as having been in 'adverse possession' as against the owner with the paper title."

The importance of an examination of the nature and character of the land can be illustrated by the following cases.[60] In *Red House Farms (Thorndon) Ltd v. Catchpole*[61] the defendant's shooting "fairly regularly"[62] over marshy and overgrown land, separated from the rest of the paper owner's land, was sufficient in the circumstances to amount to adverse possession since the nature of the land meant that its only value was as a place for shooting. On the other hand, it was considered significant in *Boosey v. Davis*[63] that the land, although waste or scrub, could still be developed or used for other purposes since it had value to the owner in its waste state.

It is often said that enclosure of land is the best evidence of adverse possession[64] but, whilst it may be very strong evidence in some cases, it is by no means decisive.[65] If the enclosure is referable to an intention only to exclude persons other than the true owner, then clearly such enclosure will be insufficient to amount to adverse possession.[66] In *Tecbild Ltd v. Chamberlain*[67] pp. 642–3 Sachs L.J. stated:

> ". . . even all-round fencing is not unequivocal if other explanations exist as to why it may well have been placed round the land in question, as, for instance, to protect the ground from incursions of others."

parties (*Hughes v. Griffin* [1969] 1 W.L.R. 23), an assertion of adverse possession may be negatived.

[59] See *Buckinghamshire v. Moran* [1990] Ch. 623, CA, at p. 636 (Slade L.J.)
[60] Contrast also *Williams Brothers Direct Supply Ltd v. Raftery* [1958] 1 Q.B. 159 with *Powell v. McFarlane*, (1979) 38 P. & C.R. 452.
[61] (1977) 244 *e.g.* 295, CA.
[62] *ibid.* at 295, column 2 (Cairns L.J.).
[63] (1987) 55 P. & C.R. 83, CA — although there the alleged acts of possession were also regarded as too trivial, *i.e.* grazing of goats for 2 or 3 days 2 to 3 times a year, cutting scrub and erecting a wire mesh fence to reinforce an existing fence.
[64] See *Seddon v. Smith* (1877) 36 L.T. 168 at 169 and also *Marshall v. Taylor* [1895] 1 Ch. 641 at 645, *Williams v. Usherwood* (1981) 45 P. & C.R. 235 (acts of adverse possession more extensive than enclosure).
[65] *e.g. Littledale v. Liverpool College* [1900] 1 Ch. 19 (fencing and securing land consistent not with exclusion of owner but with exclusion of the general public); *George Wimpey & Co. Ltd v. Sohn* [1967] Ch. 487 (fencing of garden square for 30 years equivocal since it might have been done to protect the common rights to use the garden); *Basildon D.C. v. Manning* (1975) 237 *e.g.* 878 (enclosure by chicken-wire too trivial in the circumstances); *Boosey v. Davis* (1987) 55 P. & C.R. 83, CA at 87 (wire fence to reinforce existing fence which did not in any event enclose the land) and *Marsden v. Miller*, (1992) 64 P. & C.R. 119, CA (fence did not give trespasser effective control of land).
[66] *e.g. Littledale v. Liverpool College*, above, and *George Wimpey & Co. Ltd v. Sohn*, above.
[67] (1969) 20 P. & C.R. 633, CA.

Where acts other than enclosure are relied upon, then in each case it must be demonstrated that the acts are sufficiently substantial to amount to the exclusion of the owner and are inconsistent with the owner's rights of ownership. If the acts relied upon are equivocal,[68] then the squatter will have failed to provide the necessary clear evidence that his possession is adverse.

Adverse possession may not be relied upon by the owner of land acquired by compulsory purchase, at least while there remains a specifically enforceable contract between the acquiring authority (which was beneficial owner) and the owner of the land, despite the owner's remaining in occupation long after the authority had entered the land and statutory compensation had been determined.[69]

It is no longer a good defence to a claim based on adverse possession to rely on an implied licence from the owner arising simply by virtue of the owner's lack of present use for the land.[70] This does not, of course, affect the position where actual licence can be demonstrated to have been granted. This is made clear by paragraph 8(4) of Schedule 1 to the Limitation Act 1980 which provides:

"(4) For the purpose of determining whether a person occupying land is in adverse possession of the land it shall not be assumed by implication of law that his occupation is by permission of the person entitled to the land merely by virtue of the fact that his occupation is not inconsistent with the latter's present or future enjoyment of the land.

This provision shall not be taken as prejudicing a finding to the effect that a person's occupation of any land is by implied permission of the person entitled to the land in any case where such finding is justified on the actual facts of the case."

---

[68] For example, the occupation in *Hyde v. Pearce* [1982] 1 All E.R. 1029, CA, at 1040j-1041c, which followed the termination of a contractual licence granted pending completion of a contract for the sale of land, did not amount to adverse possession because the occupier had not demonstrated clearly that he was no longer bound by the contract.

[69] *Rhondda Cynon Taff County B.C. v. Watkins* (Chancery Division, December 11, 2001), New Law Digest February 19, 2002. The CPO was made in 1964, notices to enter and treat served in 1965 and compensation determined by the Lands Tribunal in 1977. The Council sought summary possession of the land in 2000 and the order obtained from the county court was upheld by Neuberger J. on appeal.

[70] See cases such as *Wallis's Cayton Bay Holiday Camp Ltd v. Shell Mex and B.P. Ltd* [1975] Q.B. 94, CA now reversed on this point by para. 8(4) of Sched. 1 to the Limitation Act 1980. See *Buckinghamshire v. Moran* [1990] Ch. 623, CA, at 164 and 171 and, generally, where the dissenting judgment of Stamp L.J. in *Wallis* was preferred, and now, *J.A. Pye (Oxford) Ltd. v. Graham* [2002] 3 W.L.R. 221, HL, at paras. 44–45.

Registered Land

(a) The need for reform

1–101 The LRA 2002 reform of the law relating to limitation in the case of registered land followed the recommendations of the Law Commission in its report "Land Registration for the Twenty-First Century — a Conveyancing Revolution" (July 9, 2001) Law Com No. 271.[71] The Law Commission adopted[72] the criticisms of the concept of the acquisition of title by adverse possession made by Neuberger J. in *J A Pye (Oxford) Ltd v. Graham*[73]:

> ". . . the right to acquire title to land by adverse possession is often explained by reference to the uncertainties which sometimes arise in relation to the ownership of land, but it appears to me that with one or two exceptions those uncertainties are very unlikely to arise in the context of a system of land ownership involving compulsory registration; the owner of the land is readily identifiable by inspecting the proprietorship register of the relevant title at the Land Registry. In the days when land was unregistered one can well understand that uncertainties could arise where the owner was seeking to rely upon an old conveyance; the person in possession might claim to have lost the documents which established his title, and the legislature may have concluded that arguments about what happened long ago should be avoided, and that this should be achieved by depriving the person with apparently good if somewhat ancient paper title of his ownership if the squatter could establish more than 12 years uninterrupted possession of the land . . .
>
> A frequent justification for limitation periods generally is that people should not be able to sit on their rights indefinitely, and that is a proposition to which at least in general nobody could take exception. However, if as in the present case the owner of land has no immediate use for it and is content to let another person trespass on the land for the time being, it is hard to see what principle of justice entitles the trespasser to acquire the land for nothing from the owner simply because he has been permitted to remain there for 12 years. To say that in such circumstances the owner who has sat on his rights should therefore be deprived of his land appears to me to be illogical and disproportionate. Illogical because the only reason that the owner can be said to have sat on his rights is because of the existence of the 12–year limitation period in the first place; if no limitation period existed he would be entitled to claim possession whenever he actually wanted the land . . .
> I believe that the result is disproportionate because, particularly in a climate of increasing awareness of human rights including the right to

---

[71] See, in particular, Part XIV pp. 299–346.
[72] Law Com No. 271 paras. 14.1–14.4, pp. 299–301.
[73] [2000] Ch. 676 at 709–710.

enjoy one's own property, it does seem draconian to the owner and a windfall for the squatter that, just because the owner has taken no steps to evict a squatter for 12 years, the owner should lose 25 hectares of land to the squatter with no compensation whatsoever."

Whilst, as Neuberger J. acknowledged, different considerations apply to the recovery of damages after a lengthy delay, the system of registration of title adds an additional concern to the deprivation of title by adverse possession as the Law Commission explained[74]:

"Indeed, the doctrine of adverse possession runs counter to the fundamental concept of indefeasibility of title that is a feature of registered title. It is only where the register is not conclusive — as is the case, for example, in relation to boundaries and short leases that are not registrable — that the conveyancing justification for adverse possession is the same as it is in relation to unregistered land."

(b) Introduction to the new regime

The LRA 2002 creates a regime, found in Part 9 and Schedule 6 of the Act, **1–102** which is significantly different from the former requirements: the new regime does not turn on the application of a limitation period but a new procedure by which a squatter can apply to be registered as proprietor after 10 years' adverse possession.[75] However, that 10 year period is not a limitation period since the registered proprietor can object to the squatter's application for registration and the grounds on which the objection may be dismissed are wholly new factors which do not turn on the question of proof of adverse possession.[76] Indeed, adverse possession itself does not extinguish title but is merely a precondition to a squatter's ability to apply to be registered as proprietor[77] or to make further application if the initial application is rejected after two years.[78] The new regime dispenses with consideration of when the cause of action in trespass accrued since it centres on the application procedure set out in Schedule 6.

Sections 15 to 17 of the Limitation Act 1980 are disapplied so far as they apply to an estate in land or Rentcharge the title to which is registered[79] and section 98(1) of the LRA 2002 provides that a person now has a defence to an action for possession of land (which must mean registered land) if:

---

[74] Para. 14.3, p. 301.
[75] Para. 1(1) of Sched. 6 to the LRA 2002.
[76] Para. 5 of Sched. 6 to LRA 2002.
[77] Para. 14.20, pp. 310–311.
[78] Para. 6 of Sched. 6 to the LRA 2002.
[79] S. 96 of the LRA 2002.

(1)　Either —

    (a)　on the day immediately preceding that on which the action was brought he was entitled to make an application under paragraph 1 of Schedule 6 to be registered as the proprietor of an estate in the land, and

    (b)　had he made such an application on that day, the condition in paragraph 5(4) of that Schedule would have been satisfied.

(2)　Or, if on the day immediately preceding that on which the action was brought the defendant was entitled to make an application under paragraph 6 of Schedule 6 to be registered as the proprietor of an estate in the land.

Provisions are made in section 98(2) and (4) for judgments for possession to cease to be enforceable: see further below.

Section 97 gives effect to the provision of Schedule 6 which makes provisions about the registration of an adverse possessor of land or Rentcharge.

(c) Application by squatter to be registered

(a) Squatter's application after 10 years' adverse possession

1–103　A squatter may apply under paragraph 1(1) of Schedule 6 to the LRA 2002 to be registered as the proprietor of registered land if he has been in adverse possession of the estate for a period of 10 years ending on the date of the application (whether or not the estate had been registered for the whole of the 10 year period[80]).

Such an application may be made under paragraph 1(2) of Schedule 6 if[81]:

(1)　he has in the period of six months ending on the date of the application ceased to be in adverse possession of the estate because of eviction by the registered proprietor, or a person claiming under the registered proprietor;

(2)　on the day before his eviction he was entitled to make an application under Schedule 6 paragraph 1(1), namely he had at that time been in adverse possession of the estate for at least 10 years; and

(3)　the eviction was not pursuant to a judgment for possession.

The applicant must give written notice of the application for registration to a number of parties, including the proprietor of the estate and of any registered charge on the estate.[82] The notice must also include notice that

---

[80]　Para. 1(4) of Sched. 6 to the LRA 2002.
[81]　Para. 1(2) of Sched. 6.
[82]　Para. 2(1)(a)–(d). The categories can be expanded by statutory instrument: para. 2(1)(e).

if the application is not required to be dealt with under paragraph 5 of Schedule 6 he will be entitled to be entered in the register as the new proprietor of the estate.[83] In effect, this warns the parties notified that unless they object to the application it is likely to succeed. A notice which does not give the warning is likely to be regarded as invalid, given the mandatory nature and importance of the warning.

(b) Restrictions on applications

However, an application to be registered as proprietor may not be made if the applicant:

(1)   is a defendant in proceedings which involve asserting a right to possession of the land; or

(2)   judgment for possession of the land has been given against him in the last two years.

There are also more general restrictions on applications under Schedule 6 which, if they apply, may be noted on the Register.[84] No one may apply to be registered as the proprietor of an estate in land:

(1)   during, or before the end of 12 months after the end of, any period in which the existing registered proprietor is for the purposes of the Limitation (Enemies and War Prisoners) Act 1945 either an enemy, or is detained in enemy territory[85]; or

(2)   during any period in which the existing registered proprietor is —

(a)   unable because of mental disability to make decisions about issues of the kind to which such an application would give rise; or

(b)   unable to communicate such decisions because of mental disability or physical impairment.[86]

"Mental disability" means a disability or disorder of the mind or brain, whether permanent or temporary, which results in an impairment or disturbance of mental functioning[87].

(c) Objections

The persons duly notified by the applicant of an application under paragraph 1 of Schedule 6 may give a counter notice to the Registrar within

---

[83]   Para. 2 and 4 of Sched. 6.
[84]   Para. 8(4) of Sched. 6.
[85]   Para. 8(1) of Sched. 6.
[86]   Para. 8(2) of Sched. 6.
[87]   Para. 8(3) of Sched. 6.

such period as the rules may prescribe that the application should be dealt with under paragraph 5 to Schedule 6. If they fail to do so, then paragraph 4 of Schedule 6 applies:

> "If an application under paragraph 1 is not required to be dealt with under paragraph 5, the applicant is entitled to be entered in the register as the new proprietor of the estate."

(d) Grounds on which a squatter may defeat the proprietor's objections

1–103a If a duly made counter notice is received by the Registrar, then the applicant squatter may only be registered as proprietor if one of the three conditions set out in paragraph 5 of Schedule 6 is established. The relative narrowness of the grounds marks the significant shift away from the position prior to the Act which depended solely on proof of adverse possession for the requisite period of time. As the Law Commission stated[88]:

> "The general rule is, therefore, that if the registered proprietor or registered chargee brings proceedings for the recovery of land in the possession of a squatter, those proceedings will succeed, regardless of how long the squatter has been in adverse possession. Under our scheme, as we have explained, the rights of the registered proprietor are not barred by lapse of time. To this general rule there are, necessarily, exceptions."

The exceptions are:

(1) *estoppel*,[89] namely —

    (a) it would be unconscionable because of an equity by estoppel for the registered proprietor to seek to dispossess the applicant, and

    (b) the circumstances are such that the applicant ought to be registered as the proprietor.

(2) *some other right to the land* — the applicant is for some other reason entitled to be registered as the proprietor of the estate[90]

(3) *reasonable mistake as to a boundary*,[91] namely —

    (a) the land to which the application relates is adjacent to land belonging to the applicant;

---

[88] Law Com No. 271 para. 14.83, p. 338.
[89] Paras. 14.39–13.42 and note examples given at para. 14.42.
[90] See Law Com No. 271 para. 14.43.
[91] Paras. 14.44–14.52 and note examples at para. 14.46.

(b) the exact line of the boundary between the two has not been determined under rules under section 60;

(c) for at least ten years of the period of adverse possession ending on the date of the application, the applicant (or any predecessor in title) reasonably believed[92] that the land to which the application relates belonged to him. The reference to the date of the application has effect for the purposes of an application under paragraph 1(2) as if that reference were to the day before the date of the applicant's eviction; and

(d) the estate to which the application relates was registered more than one year prior to the date of the application.

If there is a dispute as to whether the squatter is entitled to be registered then, unless the parties can reach agreement, the matter will be referred by the registrar to the Adjudicator for resolution: see sections 73 and 107 of the LRA 2002. The Law Commission anticipated that, in practice, most such cases would be referred to the Adjudicator.[93]

(e) Right to make further application for registration

Even if an application under paragraph 1 of Schedule 6 does not succeed, a squatter may reapply to be registered under paragraph 6 if he is in adverse possession of the estate from the date of the application under paragraph 1(1) until the last day of the period of two years beginning with the date of its rejection. The Law Commission thought that two years was a reasonable time in which the proprietor could either evict the squatter or regularise the occupation.[94]

However, an further application may not be made under paragraph 6 if[95]:

(1) the applicant is a defendant in proceedings which involve asserting a right to possession of the land,

(2) judgment for possession of the land has been given against the applicant in the last two years, or

(3) the applicant has been evicted from the land pursuant to a judgment for possession.

---

[92] The Law Commission did not consider that this "mental element' was likely to be very demanding, given the need to show an *animus possidendi* for adverse possession in any event: see para. 14.50 and 14.51.

[93] Para. 694, p. 578.

[94] Paras. 14.53 to 14.57.

[95] Para. 6(2)(a) to (c) of Sched. 6.

(d) Effect of a successful application

(a) Generally

1–104   If a squatter is successful in an application to register, paragraph 9 of Schedule 6 provides that:

(1)   the title by virtue of adverse possession which the applicant had at the time of the application is extinguished;

(2)   the registration of a person under the Schedule as the proprietor of an estate in land does not affect the priority of any interest affecting the estate (subject to (3));

(3)   where a person is registered under the Schedule as the proprietor of an estate, the estate is vested in him free of any registered charge affecting the estate immediately before his registration. This does not apply where registration as proprietor is in pursuance of an application determined by reference to whether any of the conditions in paragraph 5 applies.

(b) Apportionment and discharge of charges

Paragraph 10 of Schedule 6 makes provision for the apportionment or discharge of charges affecting the registered estate which is subject to the application under Schedule 6, in accordance with rules to be made as to procedure, valuation, the calculation of costs incurred by the chargee as a result of apportionment, and payment of costs to the chargor.[96]

Where a registered estate continues to be subject to a charge notwithstanding the registration of a person under Schedule 6 as the proprietor, and the charge affects property other than the estate, the proprietor of the estate may require the chargee to apportion the amount secured by the charge at that time between the estate and the other property on the basis of their respective values.[97]

The person requiring the apportionment is entitled to a discharge of his estate from the charge on payment of —

(1)   the amount apportioned to the estate, and

(2)   the costs incurred by the chargee as a result of the apportionment.[98]

Where a discharge is made under paragraph 10, the liability of the chargor to the chargee is reduced by the amount apportioned to the estate.[99]

---

[96] Para. 10(4) of Sched. 6.
[97] Para. 10(1) of Sched. 6.
[98] Para. 10(2) of Sched. 6.
[99] Para. 10(3) of Sched. 6.

(e) Meaning of "adverse possession" in the case of registered land

In general, "adverse possession" bears the same meaning as it does under the Limitation Act 1980 and is considered above at paragraphs 1–097 to 1–100. Paragraphs 11 and 12 of Schedule 6 to the LRA 2002 creates specific modifications to the law under the 1980 Act. **1–105**

(a) Cases treated as adverse possession

A person in the following cases is to be treated as having been in adverse possession[1]:

(1) where he is the successor in title to an estate in the land, during any period of adverse possession by a predecessor in title to that estate, or

(2) during any period of adverse possession by another person which comes between, and is continuous with, periods of adverse possession of his own.

(b) Trust interests

In the case of trusts a person is not to be regarded as being in adverse possession of an estate for the purposes of Schedule 6 at any time when the estate is subject to a trust, unless the interest of each of the beneficiaries in the estate is an interest in possession.[2] Thus, the provisions of the LRA 2002 adopt the same principle as under the 1980 Act,[3] namely that adverse possession cannot arise against successive equitable interests under a trust, which renders it very difficult indeed for a squatter to make an application under Schedule 6 of the LRA 2002 since the 10 year period of adverse possession cannot begin to run for the purposes of paragraph 1(1) while beneficial interests exist which have not fallen into possession. This was plainly the intention of the legislation in adopting the recommendations of the Law Commission.[4] **1–106**

(c) Rentcharges

Paragraph 14 of Schedule 6 to the LRA 2002 provides for rules to make provision to apply the provisions of the Schedule to registered rentcharges, subject to such modifications and exceptions as the rules may provide.

---

[1] Para. 11(2) of Sched. 6 to the LRA 2002.
[2] Para. 12 of Sched. 6.
[3] See para. 1–119, below.
[4] Law Com No. 27 paras. 14.91 to 14.96, pp. 341–343.

(d) The Crown

1–107   Where the adverse possession relied on for the purposes of an application under Schedule 6 is of Crown foreshore,[5] 60 years' adverse possession is required before an application can be made. "Foreshore" means the shore and bed of the sea and of any tidal water, below the line of the medium high tide between the spring and neap tides.[6] For the purposes of these provisions, land is to be treated as foreshore if it has been foreshore at any time in the previous ten years.[7]

(e) Transitional arrangements

1–107a   Under the LRA 2002[7a] where a registered estate in land is held in trust for a person by virtue of section 75(1) of the Land Registration Act 1925[7b] immediately before the coming into force of the new regime, he is entitled to be registered as the proprietor of the estate. Such a person has a defence to any action for the possession of land (in addition to any other defence he may have) if he is entitled for this reason to be registered as the proprietor of an estate in the land.[7c]

Where in an action for possession of land a court determines that a person is entitled to a defence for this reason, the court must order the registrar to register him as the proprietor of the estate in relation to which he is entitled under this paragraph to be registered.[7d]

Unregistered Land

1–108   In the case of unregistered land, possession proceedings must still be brought within 12 years of the accrual of the right of action.[8] Section 15(1) of the 1980 Act provides:

> "(1) No action shall be brought by any person to recover any land after the expiration of twelve years from the date on which the right of action accrued to him or, if it first accrued to some person through whom he claims, to that person."

Part I of Schedule 1 to the 1980 Act sets out detailed provisions as to the accrual of the right of action. Paragraph 1 defines the accrual of the right of action to recover possession upon discontinuance or dispossession:

---

[5] *i.e.* belongs to Her Majesty in right of the Crown or the Duchy of Lancaster or to the Duchy of Cornwall. See para. 13(1)(b) of Schedule 6.
[6] Para. 13(3) of Sched. 6.
[7] Para. 13(2) of Sched. 6.
[7a] See Sched. 12 para. 18(1).
[7b] See below para. 1–112.
[7c] Sched. 12 para. 18(2).
[7d] Sched. 12 para. 18(3).
[8] S. 15 (time limit for action to recover land).

"1. Where the person bringing an action to recover land, or some person through whom he claims, has been in possession of the land, and has while entitled to the land been dispossessed or discontinued his possession, the right of action shall be treated as having accrued on the date of the dispossession or discontinuance . . ."

A right of action to recover land includes rights to enter into possession of the land or to distrain for arrears of rent or tithe.[9]

It is clear from these provisions that the limitation period cannot run until possession of the land has been taken by someone other than the true owner. It is important to note that the passage of time does not of itself provide sufficient defence since the right of action does not accrue unless the land in question is taken into adverse possession. Paragraph 8 of Part I of Schedule 1 to the 1980 Act provides:

"8.—(1) No right of action to recover land shall be treated as accruing unless the land is in the possession of some person in whose favour the period of limitation can run (referred to below in this paragraph as "adverse possession"); and where under the preceding provisions of this Schedule any such right of action is treated as accruing on a certain date and no person is in adverse possession on that date, the right of action shall not be treated as accruing unless and until adverse possession is taken of the land."

In other words, in addition to the discontinuance or dispossession, there must be adverse possession by the trespasser before the limitation period can begin to run.

Adverse possession

See Paragraphs 1–097 to 1–100 above. **1–109**

Cesser of adverse possession before limitation period has run

Paragraph 8(2) of Part I to Schedule 1 of the 1980 Act provides as follows: **1–110**

"(2) Where a right of action to recover land has accrued and after its accrual, before the right is barred, the land ceases to be in adverse possession, the right of action shall no longer be treated as having accrued and no fresh right of action shall be treated as accruing unless and until the land is again taken into adverse possession."

Accordingly, where a squatter abandons possession of the land before the full period of twelve years' adverse possession has run, the period which has run is effectively lost and any subsequent squatter is unable to rely

---

[9] S. 38(7).

upon it.[10] Any fresh dispossession will then give rise to a new cause of action and the limitation period will begin to run again from the date that new cause of action accrues.

Successive squatters with continuous adverse possession

1–111   Unlike the situation considered above, where adverse possession is actually abandoned for a period of time, the dispossession of the squatter in adverse possession by another who continues in adverse possession will not cause the limitation period to start afresh and paragraph 8(2) of Schedule 1 to the 1980 Act will not apply since the land will not have ceased to be in adverse possession. The combined effect of paragraphs 1 and 8(1) of Schedule 1 is that a landowner's cause of action accrues as soon as he is dispossessed and adverse possession begins.

Accordingly, as against the owner, the "successor" squatter can rely upon his own period of adverse possession together with that of the previous squatters provided the land has continued to be in adverse possession.[11]

Further, a squatter may assign or devise the right which has accrued to him by means of adverse possession even before the full limitation period has run and, provided that there is no break in the adverse possession, the assignee or devisee can aggregate his own period of adverse possession with that of his predecessor.[12]

Landlord and tenant

1–112   Whilst a lease or tenancy is in existence, a tenant cannot be in adverse possession against his landlord since he is lawfully in possession with the consent of the landlord. Further, a tenant is estopped from denying his landlord's title[13] and cannot, for that reason, claim title by adverse possession. The limitation period will only begin to run against a landlord once the lease has determined and he becomes entitled to possession.[14] The right of action will not accrue if the term is extended by statute, *e.g.* pursuant to Part II of the Landlord and Tenant Act 1954.[15] Where a tenant under a long lease is dispossessed by a squatter, the landlord's right of action does not accrue until the lease has determined. Although the tenant's interest may have been extinguished by the squatter's adverse pos-

---

[10]   See *Trustees, Executors & Agency Co. Ltd v. Short* (1888) 13 App.Cas. 793: the effect of this case is made statutory by para. 8(2) of Sched. 1 to the 1980 Act.

[11]   *Willis v. Earl Howe* [1893] 2 Ch. 545.

[12]   *Asher v. Whitlock* (1865) L.R. 1 Q.B. 1.

[13]   *Industrial Properties (Barton Hill) Ltd v. Associated Electrial Industries Ltd* [1977] Q.B. 580.

[14]   Para. 4 of Sched. 1, *Walter v. Yalden* [1902] 2 K.b. 304 and *Chung Ping Kwan v. Lam Island Development Co. Ltd* [1977] A.C. 38, P.C., at 46.

[15]   But see below in connection with the Rent Acts and *Moses v. Lovegrove* [1952] 2 Q.B. 533 and *Jessamine Investment Co. v. Schwartz* [1978] Q.B. 264, CA.

session, the landlord cannot recover possession unless he would be otherwise entitled to forfeit the lease or determine it by other means.[16]

Whilst a squatter may obtain title on the expiry of 12 years' adverse possession against a tenant under a long lease, time does not begin to run against the reversioner until the expiry of the lease since the reversioner's own entitlement to possession does not arise until that time[17]:

". . . so long as the legal estate created by the lease remains in existence, the landlord has no right to obtain possession of the land from a squatter. The squatter dispossessed the lessee, not his landlord. If the lessee seeks to recover possession it will be sufficient for him to prove he was in possession and that the squatter dispossessed him. But if the landlord, not having been dispossessed by the squatter, comes along and seeks to eject the squatter he must set up and rely upon his title. He has to show a better title to possession than the squatter. Herein will be his difficulty. So long as the lease is extant, his title to present possession of the land is deficient. This is so even if the title of the lessee, as between himself and the squatter, has been extinguished."

Indeed, if the landowner were to grant the dispossessed tenant a new lease, that tenant would then (unless the new lease were granted pursuant to an option under the former lease[18]) be able to recover possession against the squatter on the basis that he had obtained a new title from the reversioner[19]:

"A lessee's ability to regain possession in reliance on a new lease is no more than a striking illustration of the principle that dispossession of a lessee sets time running against the lessee and those claiming through him as lessee, but not against the landlord and those claiming through him as reversioner. A trespasser on leased property is more vulnerable than a trespasser on property occupied by the freeholder. In the latter case the title which the squatter bars is the freehold title. In the former case the title which is barred is leasehold only, because that is the extent of the title of the person who has been dispossessed. Adverse possession defeats the rights, whatever they may be, of the person against whom the possession is adverse. It does not defeat the rights of others."

One exception to the barring of the tenant's title is the surrender of the lease by the tenant whose title has become barred, since on the current state of the law the owner of the reversion of unregistered land can then evict the

---

[16] See below, para. 1–130 (effect of the expiry of the limitation period).
[17] *Chung Ping Kwan v. Lam Island Development Co. Ltd*, above, at p. 46 (*per* Lord Nicholls, who delivered the judgment of the Privy Council).
[18] *ibid.*, pp. 48–9. In such a case the tenant's rights under that lease had already been barred.
[19] *ibid.*, at pp.46–47.

squatter,[20] although in the case of land registered under the Land Registration Act 1925 the operation of section 75(1) of that Act 1925 achieves the contrary result since the reversioner is bound by the squatter's overriding interest.[21]

Although a tenant cannot be in adverse possession of the demised premises during the continuation of a tenancy, different considerations apply where the adverse possession relates to land not included within the original demise to the tenant:

(1) where the tenant remains in adverse possession of land owned by the landlord but not included within the demise, there is a presumption that, once the limitation period has expired, the additional land becomes subject to the terms of the lease for the remainder of the term.[22] This presumption can be rebutted, *e.g.* if the tenant sells the land to a third party during the continuation of the term and the landlord has notice of the sale.[23] However, if the landlord is allowed to continue in the belief that the tenant only occupies the additional land as part of the demised premises, then the presumption will not be rebutted; and

(2) if the tenant goes into adverse possession of land in the ownership of a third party for the duration of the limitation period, the land so acquired may be held for the landlord's benefit unless a contrary intention is demonstrated by the conduct of both landlord and tenant.[24]

Forfeiture

1–113 Where a landlord is entitled to determine a lease for breach of condition or forfeiture, the right of action accrues upon the date of the breach of condition or the date on which the forfeiture was incurred.[25]

---

[20] *Fairweather v. St Marylebone Property Co. Ltd* [1963] A.C. 510, criticised by Wade (1962) 78 L.Q.R. 541, but not revisited in *Chung Ping Kwan v. Lam Island Development Co. Ltd* [1997] A.C. 38, PC, although described by Lord Nicholls as "controversial" at p. 47.

[21] *Central London Commercial Estates Ltd v. Kato Kagaku Ltd* [1984] 4 All E.R. 948.

[22] *Kingsmill v. Millard* (1855) 11 Exch. 313 and *Smirk v. Lyndale Developments Ltd* [1975] Ch. 317, CA. In *Smirk* the Court of Appeal approved the veiws of Pennycuick V.-C., reviewing the "tangle" of authorities, at 323–332: see 337G–H and 340E.

[23] See *Smirk v. Lyndale*, above, at 324, citing with approval Alderson B. and Parke B. in *Kingsmill v. Millard* (1855) 11 Exch. 313, at 316 and 318.

[24] *Whitmore v. Humpries* (1871) L.R. 7 C.P. 1 at pp. 4–5, *East Stonehouse U.D.C. v. Willoughby Bros Ltd* [1902] 2 K.B. 318, *King v. Smith* [1950] 1 All E.R. 553 and *Kensington Pension Developments Limited v. Royal Garden Hotel (Oddenino's) Limited* [1990] 2 E.G.L.R. 117. Presumably this can be rebutted as in the case of adverse possession of other land belonging to the landlord: *Kingsmill v. Millard*, above. There appears to be no reason in principle why a landlord should be in a better position with regard to land not formerly within his ownership and which comes to him, at best, as a "windfall".

[25] Para. 7 of Sched. 1.

If a landlord does not seek to enforce a forfeiture his right of action is barred after 12 years. Section 38(7) of the 1980 Act defines the right to recover possession of the land as including the right to enter into possession and further defines the reference of the bringing of such an action to recover possession as including the making of such an entry. Accordingly, the 12 year limitation period for the recovery of possession applies equally to the exercise of rights of re-entry.

The failure of the landlord to enforce a right of forfeiture within the limitation period does not have an effect on the landlord's title but merely bars the right to forfeit. Subsequent breaches of condition or events giving rise to rights of re-entry constitute fresh causes of action and in respect of each a fresh limitation period runs. Certain breaches of covenant, such as breaches of the covenant to repair or user covenant, are classified as "continuing" breaches.[26] Since these breaches continue, the limitation period accrues on a continuing basis also — thus making it difficult for a landlord effectively to be barred from enforcing such breaches by forfeiture.[27]

Periodic tenancies

If a periodic tenancy arises under a written agreement, then the normal rule applies, namely that the limitation period accrues only on the determination of the tenancy, *e.g.* on the expiry of a notice to quit. However, Schedule 1 contains special rules concerning yearly or other periodic tenancies where there is no lease in writing.[28] Paragraph 5 of Schedule 1 provides:

1–114

"(1) Subject to sub-paragraph (2) below, a tenancy from year to year or other period, without a lease in writing, shall for the purposes of this Act be treated as being determined at the expiration of the first year or other period; and accordingly the right of action of the person entitled to the land subject to the tenancy shall be treated as having accrued at the date on which in accordance with this sub-paragraph the tenancy is determined.

(2) Where any rent has subsequently been received in respect of the tenancy, the right of action shall be treated as having accrued on the date of the last receipt of rent."

The limitation period begins to run from the end of the first period of the oral tenancy[29] unless it is extended by the receipt of rent[30] or there is a

---

[26] See Hill and Redman's Law of Landlord and Tenant, Vol. 1, pp. A965–A967.
[27] Although a right of action for damages would become barred after the usual limitation period.
[28] *i.e.* oral periodic tenancies. See *Long v. Tower Hamlets Longdon Borough Council* [1996] 2 All E.R. 683.
[29] Which will depend on the periodicity of the tenancy under consideration. This rule was criticised by the Law Reform Committee in its Twenty-First Report (*Final Report on Limitation of Actions* July 1977), paras. 3.54–3.56. However, the recommendation (Conclusion 27, para. 6.1) was not implemented.
[30] Para. 5(2) of Sched. 1. See also *Price v. Hartley* [1995] E.G.C.S. 74.

written acknowledgement of the landlord's title.[31] Where rent is paid, the limitation period recommences with receipt of each payment.

In *Moses v. Lovegrove*[32] the tenant originally held under an oral weekly tenancy which was subsequently brought within the provisions of the Rent Restriction Acts. The tenant ceased payment of rent in 1938, some 14 years prior to the issuing of possession proceedings. The Court of Appeal held that the effect of the Rent Acts did not defeat the application of the provisions of the Limitation Act and that, since the claimant's right of action had accrued in 1938, the landlord was statute-barred from recovering possession. Sir Raymond Evershed M.R. stated[33]:

> ". . . possession, as I have said, for the purposes of this Limitation Act
> 1939, is nonetheless adverse, because Parliament has thought fit to put
> certain serious qualifications upon the right of a person whose land is
> in adverse possession to enter and recover the possession of that prop-
> erty. After all, in order that the tenant or the occupant may invoke the
> Rent Acts at all, he must assert the tenancy, either a contractual ten-
> ancy or a statutory tenancy; it obviously would not lie easily in the
> mouth of the tenant to assert an actual contractual tenancy, if for years
> and years he has paid no regard whatever to any of the terms of the
> contract he alleges. The same, I think, would apply to a statutory ten-
> ancy . . . I cannot see anything, in the impact of the Rent Acts or other-
> wise, which qualifies or alters the character of the possession which
> had begun as adverse possession, and I think continued as adverse
> possession until the proceedings in the present case were initiated."

1–115   It is not entirely clear what the effect *Moses v. Lovegrove* has upon a statutory tenancy which does not arise from a written tenancy and which runs for more than 12 years. One interpretation of the above decision is that the interposition of a personal right to occupy does not prevent the occupation of the statutory tenant amounting to adverse possession. However, this conclusion is insupportable since it cannot have been Parliament's intention to give a statutory tenant of more than 12 years' standing an interest in the property particularly since there is no ground for possession under Schedule 15 of the 1977 Act which allows possession to be obtained to prevent acquisition of title by adverse possession. The better view is that so long as a statutory tenancy is in existence any claim for adverse possession will not succeed:

> (1)   provided the tenant pays the rent and generally observes the
> terms of the tenancy, his possession ought not to be considered
> adverse since he is still observing the terms of the original con-

---

[31] Ss. 29 and 30.

[32] [1952] 2 Q.B. 533, CA. *Moses* was applied by the Court of Appeal in *Jessamine Investment Co. v. Schwartz* [1978] 1 Q.B. 264. See also *Hayward v. Challoner* [1968] 1 Q.B. 107, *Lodge v Wakefield M.D.C.* [1995] E.G.C.S. 51, CA and *Price v. Hartley* [1995] E.G.C.S. 80.

[33] [1952] 2 Q.B. 533, CA, at 541–543.

tractual bargain between landlord and tenant as carried forward into the statutory tenancy. *Moses* was a case where the tenant had not paid rent, or apparently observed the terms of the tenancy, and it is important to note the stress laid by the Master of the Rolls on asserting the tenancy (either contractual or statutory);

(2) the concept of estoppel between landlord and tenant does not appear to have defeated the adverse possession claim in *Moses* but it ought to apply (notwithstanding the fact that the statutory tenancy is a creation of statute) where the tenancy is asserted by the parties; and

(3) although the proviso in paragraph 5(2) of Schedule 1 does not apply where there is no written tenancy agreement, if rent is actually paid by the statutory tenant then this is capable of amounting to an acknowledgment of the landlord's title within section 29 of the 1980 Act.[34]

It is clearly much easier for an oral periodic (or statutory) tenant to acquire title by adverse possession where the tenant is in arrears of rent than in the case of a written lease or tenancy agreement where the limitation period applies only to the recovery of the rent itself. The barring of the right to recover rent in such a case does not affect the title of the landlord.[35]

Tenancy at will

Although the law was originally more complicated,[36] the position of tenants at will under the 1980 Act is now brought into line with that of other tenancies. The right of action does not accrue until the tenancy at will is actually determined.[37]   1–116

Tenancy at sufferance

In the case of the so-called tenancy at sufferance,[38] the limitation period accrues immediately on commencement of the "tenancy" since such a tenancy is not a true tenancy at all but is merely the occupation of land by a former tenant where the landlord has neither consented to the tenant holding over nor has taken steps to prevent it.[39] The tenant at sufferance is in possession without the agreement of the landlord[40] and, in consequence, the landlord is entitled to recover possession immediately, *i.e.* his   1–117

---

[34] See below, para. 1–128.
[35] See below, para. 1–132.
[36] See s. 9 of the Limitation Act 1939 and *Colchester B.C. v. Smith* [1991] Ch. 448 at 481 (affirmed by the Court of Appeal [1992] Ch. 421 but not commenting on this aspect).
[37] Para. 4 of Sched. 1 and the Law Reform Committee's Twenty-First Report, above, at paras. 3.55 and 3.56.
[38] See above, para. 1–050.
[39] *Remon v. City of London Real Property Co. Ltd* [1921] 1 K.B. 49 at 58.
[40] In other words, the tenant at sufferance is in adverse possession.

right to bring an action to recover possession accrues at the moment the tenant begins to hold over.

Vendor and purchaser

1–118 Where a person has entered into a contract for the purchase of land, the contract may provide for his occupation of the land as licensee prior to completion.[41] Whilst that licence continues, it is clear that the prospective purchaser cannot be in adverse possession since he has lawful title to occupy deriving from the owner. However, if that licence is terminated then time will begin to run against the owner subject to circumstances such as those which arose in *Hyde v. Pearce*[42] where it was unclear whether the purchaser still regarded himself as bound by the contract.

If there is a contractual entitlement for the vendor to terminate the licence by notice, even though the contract remains alive, it is likely that time will begin to run against the vendor from the termination of the licence. Where a vendor becomes entitled to terminate or rescind[43] the contract, his right of action does not accrue until he exercises that right.[44]

Trusts

1–119 Section 18(1) of the Limitation Act 1980[45] provides that the Act (and Schedule 1 in particular) is applicable to equitable interests in land as to legal estates.[46] However, the application of the Act is specially modified by section 18 in the cases of trust interests. Where land is held on trust, the trustee's right to bring an action to recover possession does not become barred until the rights of action of all those with beneficial interests (or interests in the proceeds in sale) either have accrued or been barred. Only when the rights of all those with beneficial interests have been barred is the trustee's title extinguished.[47]

The result of these provisions can be a very long limitation period, particularly if there is a life interest followed by an interest in remainder. In such a case, time cannot start to run against the remainderman until his right of action accrues, *i.e.* when his interest falls into possession[48] upon the termination of the life interest.

Provision is made, to enable the trustee to bring an action for the recovery of possession on behalf of the beneficiaries[49]:

---

[41] See *Walters v. Roberts* (1980) 41 P. & C.R. 210, CA and also *Vangean v. Benjamin* (1976) 239 *e.g.* 647.

[42] [1982] 1 W.L.R. 560.

[43] For the distinction between rescission and termination see *Johnson v. Agnew* [1980] A.C. 367, HL.

[44] *Lakshmijit v. Faiz Sherani* [1974] A.C. 605, PC.

[45] As modified by Trusts of Land and Appointment of Trustees Act 1996, s. 25(2) and Sched. 4.

[46] Subject to s. 21(1) and (2) — see below.

[47] S. 18(2)–(4).

[48] See para. 4 of Sched. 1.

[49] S. 18(4).

"... an action to recover the land may be brought by the ... trustees on behalf of any person entitled to a beneficial interest in possession in the land ... whose right of action had not been barred by this Act, notwithstanding that the right of action of the ... trustees would apart from this provision have been barred by this Act."

This usefully enables the trustee to oust a squatter, to the benefit of the trust, even where the trustee had otherwise failed to act to recover possession during the initial 12 years' adverse possession.

The possession of land by a beneficiary is not regarded as adverse to others interested in the settled land or land held on trust where the beneficiary is not solely entitled in equity.[50] As a result, the persons in whom the title to the land is vested, or other persons having beneficial interests in the land, cannot be barred from recovering possession from a beneficiary by reason of the Limitation Act.

A trustee[51] cannot normally obtain title by adverse possession against the beneficiaries because the six year limitation period for breach of trust[52] does not apply in a number of cases which would normally include most trustees in breach. No limitation period prescribed by the Act applies in these cases, namely where there has been fraud or a fraudulent breach of trust to which the trustee was privy, or where an action is brought to recover trust property, or the proceeds of the trust property, in the possession of the trustee or previously received by the trustee and converted to his own.[53]

Future interests

Section 15(2) provides for two alternative limitation periods in the case of future interests: the person interested in reversion or remainder must sue by the end of the longer of the two periods. The first is a 12 year period which runs from the date upon which the right of action accrued to the person with the preceding estate or interest if the cause of action accrued prior to the falling into possession of the future interest. The second period is one of six years which runs from the date when the future interest falls into possession.

1–120

Accordingly, even if there has been 12 (or more) years' adverse possession prior to the falling into possession of the future interest, the right of action will not accrue[54] until the remainderman or reversioner becomes entitled to possession and then the limitation period has six years to run. If the right of action does not accrue until after the future interest has fallen into possession, then the ordinary 12 year period applies.

The alternatives provided by section 15(2) do not apply to the falling into possession of an interest by reason of the determination of an entailed

---

[50] Para. 9 of Sched. 1.
[51] Defined by s. 38 of the Act.
[52] S. 21(3).
[53] S. 21(1). See also *Paragon Finance plc v. D B Thakerar & Co. (a firm)* [1999] 1 All E.R. 400, CA.
[54] See para. 4 of Sched. 1.

interest[55] which might have been barred by the person entitled to the entailed interest. In that case, the normal 12 year period under section 15(1) runs from the commencement of adverse possession.

Co-owners

1–121　Since the mechanism of co-ownership of land is that the interests of the owners subsist behind a trust of land,[56] the rules regarding limitation are subject to the provisions of section 18 which expressly include interests "subject to a trust of land".[57]

Mortgages

1–122　A mortgagee who wishes to recover possession of his security must do so within 12 years of when the mortgagor became liable to make repayment[58] unless there is written acknowledgment of the mortgagee's title or he makes a payment in respect of the mortgage debt.[59] In those cases, time runs afresh from the acknowledgment or payment.

Wrongful receipt of rent

1–123　There is a special provision in paragraph 6(1) of Schedule 1[60] for the case where rent is received by a person wrongfully claiming to be entitled to the reversion to the lease and no rent is subsequently received by the reversioner rightfully entitled to the rent. If the lease reserves not less than £10 a year rent, then the right of the reversioner to recover the land is treated as having accrued on the date when the rent was first received by the person wrongfully claiming to be so entitled and not at the date of the determination of the lease. The payment of an unapportioned rent to one reversioner following severance of the reversion is not wrongful for the purposes of paragraph 6.[61]

The Crown

1–124　The Crown is in the privileged position of having a limitation period of 30, not 12, years. Under Sched. 1 para. 10 of the Limitation Act 1980:

---

[55]　Note that no entailed interests may be created after 1996: S. 2(6) and para. 5 of Sched. 1 to the Trusts of Land and Appointment of Trustees Act 1996. The effect of attempting to do so is to create a declaration of a trust of land.

[56]　See the Trusts of Land and Appointment of Trustees Act 1996 replacing SS. 34–36 of the Law of Property Act 1925. "Trust of land" is defined by s. 1. See, further, Megarry & Wade (6th ed.) pp. 501–524.

[57]　Amended by the Trusts of Land and Appointment of Trustees Act 1996, Sched. 3 para. 18.

[58]　*Lloyds Bank Ltd v. Margolis* [1954] 1 W.L.R. 644 and *Cotterell v. Price* [1960] 1 W.L.R. 1097.

[59]　S. 31.

[60]　Which does not apply to the Crown.

[61]　*Mitchell v. Mosley* [1914] 1 Ch. 438, CA, *Grigsby v. Melville* [1974] 1 W.L.R. 80, CA, and Woodfall Vol. 1 para. 7.156.

"10. Subject to paragraph 11 below, section 15(1) of this Act shall apply to the bringing of an action to recover any land by the Crown or by any spiritual or eleemosynary corporation sole with the substitution for the reference to twelve years of a reference to thirty years."

However, where the Crown conveys property from which it has been dispossessed to another, para. 12 of Sched. 1 provides that the transferee's title is barred either on the expiration of 30 years' from the Crown's dispossession or 12 years from the date of the conveyance, whichever is the earlier:

"12. Notwithstanding section 15(1) of this Act, where in the case of any action brought by a person other than the Crown or a spiritual or eleemosynary corporation sole the right of action first accrued to the Crown or any such corporation sole through whom the person in question claims, the action may be brought at any time before the expiration of —
(a) the period during which the action could have been brought by the Crown or the corporation sole; or
(b) twelve years from the date on which the right of action accrued to some person other than the Crown or the corporation sole;
whichever period first expires.'

Effect of issuing proceedings

Whilst the issue of proceedings before the end of the limitation period will generally prevent the limitation period from expiring,[62] this operates because it leads to a determination of the entitlement to possession of the true owner in circumstances where the limitation period has not expired. A compulsory winding-up order will also suspend the running of a limitation period.[63] A mere demand for possession,[64] the making of an administration order,[65] or the issue of a claim form where an action is dismissed for want of prosecution will not prevent the true owner becoming time-barred nor will it start time running again[66]:

1-125

"The issue of a writ, for the purposes of the action which it begins, prevents the true owner from being time barred under s 15 providing 12 years' adverse possession have not already accrued. It serves no other purpose."

---

[62] *BP Properties Ltd v. Buckler* (1987) 55 P. & C.R. 337 CA at p. 344.
[62] *Re General Rolling Stock Co.* (1872) LR 7 Ch. App. 646.
[64] *Mount Carmel Investments Ltd v. Peter Thurlow Ltd* [1988] 1 W.L.R. 1078, CA, at p. 1085.
[65] *Re Maxwell Fleet and Facilities Management Ltd (in administration)* [2001] 1 All E.R. 464.
[66] *Markfield Investments Ltd v. Evans* [2001] 2 All E.R. 238, CA, *per* Simon Brown L.J. at p. 243, para. 21.

Note however, that if an action is successful and possession is ordered against the trespasser, the owner may not enforce the order without the court's permission if more than six years have expired since the order was made.[67]

Extensions to the limitation period

1–126 The limitation period prescribed for a particular action may be extended in a number of situations which are relevant to trespass actions: these are where there has been fraud, concealment or mistake, where the defendant has acknowledged the claimant's title and where the claimant is under a disability.

Although certain limitation periods are extended by the Latent Damage Act 1986, including cases of negligent damage to land,[68] the extensions appears to be available only in cases of the tort of negligence.[69] The Act specifically refers to "negligence"[70] in contradistinction to the wider "tort",[71] or "breach of duty",[72] and to actions "to recover land"[73] or "to recover rent".[74] In *Iron Trade Mutual Insurance Co Ltd v. J K Buckenham Ltd*[75] the Deputy Judge appears, in construing section 14A of the 1980 Act as applicable to tortious negligence only, to have considered that the provisions extending the limitation period in negligence cases might apply to an action for trespass damages "when negligence is a necessary ingredient of the cause of action"[76] — although he later made it clear that section 14A applied to "the tort of negligence." Moreover, the mischief at which the 1986 Act was aimed was set out in the Law Reform Committee's 24th Report,[77] *i.e.* latent damage arising in the context of the tort of negligence.[78] Indeed, para. 1.2 of the Report noted that:

---

[67] CPR Sched. 1, RSC Order 46 r. 2(1)(a), Sched. 2 CCR Order 26 r. 5(1)(a). See also *Lowsley v. Forbes* [1999] 1 A.C. 329, HL, where it was held that "an action . . . upon any judgment" in s. 24(1) of the Limitation Act 1980 meant a fresh action and did not include proceedings by way of execution of a judgment in the same action.

[68] S. 3 of the 1986 Act.

[69] And, further, tortious negligence as opposed to the breach of a contractual duty of care: *Iron Trade Mutual insurance Co. Ltd v. J K Buckenham Ltd* [1990] 1 All E.R. 808.

[70] As do ss. 14A and 14B introduced into the 1980 Act by the 1986 Act.

[71] S. 2 of the 1980 Act.

[72] S. 11 of the 1980 Act.

[73] S. 15 of the 1980 Act.

[74] S. 19 of the 1980 Act.

[75] See [1990] 1 All E.R. 808, cited with approval by the Court of Appeal in *Société Commerciale de Reassurance v. ERAS Ltd* [1992] 2 All E.R. 82.

[76] Although this remark is plainly *obiter*, and was made in the context of distinguishing *Letang v. Cooper* [1965] 1 Q.B. 232, CA — discussed above at paras. 1–036 and 1–037. The reference to negligence and trespass derives from the Australian case of *Kruber v. Grzesiak* [1963] V.L.R. 621 (quoted at [1990] 1 All E.R. 808 at 822–823).

[77] Cmnd. 9390.

[78] Following the House of Lord's decision in *Pirelli General Cable Works Ltd v. Oscar Faber & Partners* [1983] 2 A.C. 1.

"Our study is . . . confined to a very limited class of negligence case."[79]

Further, in *Société Commerciale de Reassurance v. ERAS Ltd*,[80] Mustill L.J. (giving the judgment of the Court of Appeal) stated[81]:

"Even when the section is read in isolation, the words 'any action for damages in negligence' denote to our minds an action asserting that the defendant has committed the tort of negligence . . . this reading is reinforced by the express overriding of the ordinary provision for tort claims in section 2. . ."

(a) Fraud, concealment or mistake

In this group of cases,[82] the limitation period is extended for reasons based on the conduct of the defendant, namely:

1–127

(1)   where the action is based on the defendant's[83] fraud;

(2)   where any fact relevant to the claimant's right of action has been deliberately concealed from him by the defendant[84]; and

(3)   where the action is for relief from the consequences of a mistake.[85]

In the above cases, the limitation period does not begin to run until the claimant has discovered the fraud, concealment or mistake or could have discovered it with reasonable diligence. In *Sheldon v. R.H.M. Outhwaite (Underwriting Agencies) Ltd*[86] a majority of the House of Lords held that, for the purpose of invoking section 32(1)(b), the concealment of relevant facts did not have to be contemporaneous with the accrual of the cause of action, but could occur subsequently. As to the nature of concealment, such an act must be deliberate but the specific legal consequences do not have to be understood or intended. It was held in *Brocklesby v. Armitage & Guest (A firm)*,[87] contrasting the case of fraud, that[88]

". . . it is not necessary for the purpose of extending the limitation period pursuant to s 32(1)(b) to the 1980 Act to demonstrate that the fact relevant to the claimant's right of action has been deliberately

---

[79] See also, *e.g.* Part V (Conclusions and Recommendations) at, *e.g.* paras. 5.3(a) "a cause of action in negligence" and (c) "negligence cases".
[80] [1992] 2 All E.R. 82.
[81] Also in the context of rejecting the application of s. 14A to "contractual negligence" cases.
[82] S. 32(1).
[83] "Defendant" in the context of these provisions includes the defendant's agent and any person through whom the defendant claims and his agent: s. 38(1).
[84] See above.
[85] See *Kleinwort Benson Ltd v. Lincoln City Council* [1999], 1 A.C. 153, HL.
[86] [1996] A.C. 102, HL.
[87] [2001] 1 All E.R. 172, CA, followed in *Liverpool Roman Catholic Archdiocese Trustees Incorporated v. Goldberg* [2001] 1 All E.R. 182.
[88] *ibid.*, at pp. 180–181 *per* Morritt L.J.

concealed in any sense greater than that the commission of the act was deliberate in the sense of being intentional and that that act or omission, as the case may be, did involve a breach of duty whether or not the actor appreciated that legal consequence."

The provisions governing fraud, concealment and mistake do not, however, enable the rights of innocent third parties to be prejudiced. Section 32(3) provides that nothing in section 32 shall enable any action to recover property (or its value) or enforce any charge against, or set aside any transaction affecting, property to be brought against an innocent third party who has purchased the property for valuable consideration since the fraud, concealment or mistake occurred. "Innocent third party" means:

(a) in the case of fraud or concealment, a person who was not a party to the fraud or concealment and did not at the time of the purchase know or have reason to believe that the fraud or concealment had taken place[89]; or

(b) in the case of mistake, a person who at the time of the purchase did not know or have reason to believe that the mistake had been made.[90]

(b) Acknowledgment or part payment

1–128   Section 29 provides that where any right of action to recover land[91] has accrued, if the person in possession of that land acknowledges the title of the person to whom the right of action has accrued then the right shall be treated as having accrued "on and not before" the date of that acknowledgment.[92] There are broadly equivalent provisions for mortgagee possession[93] and foreclosure[94] actions. Although acknowledgments can repeatedly extend the limitation period, they can only do so if they are made within the relevant limitation period[95] and cannot revive a cause of action in respect of which the limitation period has previously expired.[96]

For there to be a valid acknowledgment for the purposes of section 29, the acknowledgment must be in writing[97] and signed by the person mak-

---

[89] S. 32(4)(a).
[90] S. 32(4)(b).
[91] Including an advowson.
[92] S. 29(2)(a). S. 29(2)(b) contains a special rule actions accruing to those entitled to land on the determination of an entailed interest.
[93] S. 29(4).
[94] S. 29(3).
[95] Or within the limitation period as validly extended by another means, *e.g.* an earlier acknowledgment.
[96] S. 29(7).
[97] See s. 5, Sched. 1 of the Interpretation Act 1978 and *Browne v. Perry* [1991] 1 W.L.R. 1297, HL.

ing it[98] although it may be made by an agent[99] of the person by whom it is required to be made. The agent must, however, be a person authorised to make the acknowledgment.[1] The requirement of writing will be satisfied if the written acknowledgment has been lost but parol evidence can be produced to prove its existence.[2]

An acknowledgment does not have to be intended to be such and, for example, an offer to purchase the land in adverse possession by the occupier will suffice for section 29 purposes.[3] However, although the question of whether a particular document amounts to an acknowledgment is a matter of the construction of that document, it must amount in substance to an acceptance in some form of the title or right of the paper owner. If it does not accept such right, or in some way challenges it, then it cannot be an acknowledgment.[4] Although payment of part of the rent may amount to an acknowledgment, since the payment of rent clearly implies acceptance of the landlord's right to receive it, such payment will not extend the period in which the remainder of the rent due can be recovered.[5]

(c) Disability

Section 28(1) of the 1980 Act provides that where a cause of action accrues to a person who is under a disability, then the limitation period will be extended for a period of six years running from the date on which the disability ceases or death (whichever is the earlier). Persons under a "disability" are persons who are minors[6] or of unsound mind.[7] **1–129**

However, this suspension of the running of the limitation period does not apply to any case where the right of action accrues to some person not under a disability through whom[8] the person under a disability claims.[9] Nor does the disability suspend the running of the limitation period for actions to recover land or money charged on land beyond a period of 30 years from the date upon which the right of action first accrued to the claimant or the person through whom he claims.[10]

If the original person under a disability dies still under that disability, and his right of action passes to another person under a disability, there is

---

[98] S. 30(1).
[99] S. 30(2). The agency need not be express but may be implied: *Wright v. Pepin* [1954] 2 All E.R. 52.
[1] *Curwen v. Milburn* (1889) 42 Ch.D. 424, *Re Edwards' Will Trusts, Brewer v. Gething* [1937] Ch. 553 and *Wright v. Pepin* [1954] 1 W.L.R. 635.
[2] *Read v. Price* [1909] 2 K.B. 724 and *Jones v. Bellegrove Properties Ltd* [1949] 2 K.B. 700.
[3] *Edginton v. Clark* [1964] 1 Q.B. 367.
[4] *ibid.*
[5] S. 29(6).
[6] S. 38(2).
[7] S. 38(3) and (4).
[8] Defined by s. 38(5). This does not include any person becoming entitled to any estate or interest by virtue of the exercise of a special power of appointment: s. 38(6).
[9] S. 28(2).
[10] S. 28(4).

no further suspension of the limitation period by reason of the successor's disability.[11]

Effect of the expiry of the limitation period

1–130   If the limitation period has expired then the unregistered landowner is deprived of his ability to sue for damages for trespass in respect of any claim arising outside that period and is unable to bring an action to recover possession. Further, the expiry of the limitation period also extinguishes the paper owner's title[12] in favour of the title founded on adverse possession. The dispossessor obtains a new title, based on his own adverse possession.

Since a successful claimant to title by adverse possession will not have acquired his interest for value, he will obtain title subject to all prior existing third party interests capable of binding the land.[13] The title obtained by adverse possession may also be subject to rights exercised by the dispossessed owner during the period of his dispossession which appear to be analogous to easements.[14] The landlord of a dispossessed tenant has no right to recover possession against the successful dispossessor unless he is entitled to forfeit the lease (or otherwise terminate it) in accordance with its terms although, curiously, the dispossessor may be ejected if the dispossessed tenant surrenders his interest to the landlord[15] or otherwise acquires the freehold reversion himself.[16]

The dispossessor of a leasehold interest is not personally liable on the lessee's covenants and the dispossessed tenant can still be sued on those covenants by the landlord except where the landlord becomes entitled to forfeit or otherwise determine the lease.[17] In such circumstances the dispossessor is disadvantaged in that he is not entitled to seek relief from forfeiture[18] and can be ejected or, if the landlord so wishes, effectively compelled to perform the terms of the lease.

---

[11] S. 28(3).

[12] See s. 17 of the 1980 Act.

[13] *Re Nisbet & Potts' Contract* [1906] 1 Ch. 386.

[14] *Marshall v. Taylor* [1895] 1 Ch. 641, *Williams v. Usherwood* (1981) 45 P. & C.R. 235, CA at 253–255.

[15] See *St Marylebone Property Co. Ltd v. Fairweather* [1963] A.C. 510, HL. This decision was considered by the Law Reform Committee in its Twenty-First Report (1977), above, paras. 3.44–3.46. Although the Committee criticised the logic of the decision (*i.e.* that it is difficult to see how a lessee whose interest has been extinguished has anything left to surrender), it was unable to reach a concluded view since some members of the Committee considered that the law should not assist squatters.

[16] *Taylor v. Twinberrow* [1930] 2 K.B. 16.

[17] *e.g.* where the lease contains a "break clause" permitting early termination.

[18] *Tickner v. Buzzacott* [1972] Ch. 426.

Limitation provisions common to registered and unregistered land

Damages

Any claim for damages for trespass is subject to the usual six year limitation **1–131** period under section of the Limitation Act 1980.[19]

Non-payment of rent

Section 19 of the Act imposes a six year limitation period on any proceed- **1–132** ings to recover arrears of rent or damages in respect of arrears of rent. The period runs from the date on which the rent falls due. A separate limita- tion period runs in respect of each rent payment which falls due. The provisions also apply to sureties for the rent.[20]

In the case of unregistered land, as in the case of the right to forfeit, the barring of the right to recover rent arrears has no effect on the title to the landlord's reversion.[21]

Delay and equitable remedies

Save in the case of specific provisions,[22] there are no general limitation **1–133** periods prescribed by the Limitation Act 1980 for equitable remedies.[23] In the case of trespass, the principle concern lies with the availability of injunctions. Unless there is an effect on beneficial interests,[24] equity gen- erally follows the law and applies limitation periods which mirror the periods prescribed for common law remedies.

Public law remedies as a defence

In a number of cases, judicial review has been used as a means of defeat- **1–134** ing possession proceedings commenced by public authorities even though, in private law terms, there was no defence on the merits to a claim in trespass. Although a detailed consideration of the scope of judi- cial review is outside the terms of this book, it is well-established that if a public authority[25] in the discharge of its public functions[26] has acted

---

[19] S. 2 (time limit for actions founded on tort) subject generally to s. 29 (acknowledgment) and s. 32 (fraud, concealment and mistake), considered at 1–126 to 1–128, above.

[20] *Romain v. Scuba TV Ltd* [1996] 2 All E.R. 377, CA.

[21] Although see above, para. 1–114, as to the effect of non-payment of rent in the case of oral periodic tenancies in the case of unregistered land.

[22] See *e.g.* ss. 21 and 22.

[23] Indeed, s. 36(1) excludes from the scope of many of the principal limitation provisions of the 1980 Act claims for specific performance, injunction or other equitable relief.

[24] See *Williams v. Greatrex* [1957] 1 W.L.R. 31.

[25] See *R. v. Panel on Takeover and Mergers ex p. Datafin* [1987] Q.B. 815, CA.

[26] And not if it is merely exercising private law rights: *R. v. East Berkshire Health Authority ex p. Walsh* [1985] Q.B. 152 at p. 162.

unreasonably[27] in resolving to take proceedings, or in taking them, the decision can be challenged as ultra vires.[28] To these common law grounds, incompatibility with Convention rights in contravention of section 6 of the Human Rights Act 1998 may also be added.[29] A successful challenge will result in the decision being quashed and the dismissal of the proceedings.

In order to bring an application for judicial review, the permission of the High Court must first be obtained[30] and the application must be made "promptly" and, in any event, within three months[31] of the decision or act which is challenged unless there exist good reasons for extending the period. Further, there must not be undue delay in applying for relief, since it may be refused if it would be likely to cause substantial hardship to, or substantially prejudice the rights of, any person or would be detrimental to good administration.[32]

1–135   It is important to distinguish between three classes of case:

(1)   where the public law issue provides a genuine defence to the claim. For example, in *Wandsworth LBC v. Winder*[33] the Council's claim for possession based on arrears of rent failed since the

---

[27] See *Associated Provincial Picture Houses Ltd v. Wednesbury Corporation* [1948] 1 K.B. 223, CA— the origin of familiar terms such as "*Wednesbury* unreasonable" — and also *Council of Civil Service Unions v. Minister for the Civil Service* [1985] A.C. 374, HL at 410. The principle of "Wednesbury unreasonableness" which has been, for many years, one of the root concepts of public law is gradually being replaced by the broader concept of "abuse of power." See, *e.g. R. v. North Devon Health Authority ex p. Coughlan* [2001] Q.B. 213, CA, and *R. v. Secretary of State for Education ex p. Begbie* [2000] 1 W.L.R. 1115, CA. The influence of the Human Rights Act 1998 may accelerate further the development of judicial review, *e.g.* in terms of the concept of "proportionality." See *R. (Daly) v. Home Secretary* [2001] 2 W.L.R. 1622, HL, paras. 25–28, and *R. v. Shayler* [2002] UKHL 7, HL, at paras. 33–34 and 75–78. Two examples of decisions which show that public authorities are not unfettered in respect of the administration and control of their own property are *R. v. Coventry City Airport ex p. Phoenix Aviation* [1995] 3 All E.R. 37 and *R. v. Somerset C.C. ex p. Fewings* [1995] 1 W.L.R. 1037, CA. See, further, Wade & Forsyth, *Administrative Law* (8th ed.), and especially at Chap. 12 ("Abuse of Discretion").

[28] For the procedure see C.P.R. Part 54 and the Part 54 Practice Direction (which replaced the old R.S.C. Order 53) and Gordon, *Judicial Review and Crown Office Practice* (Sweet & Maxwell, 1999).

[29] See Wade & Forsyth, *op. cit.*, pp. 186–199 & 389–391, Clayton & Tomlinson, *The Law of Human Rights* (OUP, 2000) and Grosz, Beatson & Duffy, *Human Rights* (Sweet & Maxwell, 2000). "Public authorities" within s. 6 includes central and local government and extends more widely to other public bodies. See *e.g. ex parte Datafin*, above, Grosz, Beatson & Duffy, *op. cit.*, at pp. 60–75.

[30] C.P.R. Part 54.4. The High Court's jurisdiction is exercised by the Administrative Court (formerly the Crown Office List).

[31] See C.P.R. Part 54.5. These requirements are separate and an application may be refused, in a proper case, for lack of promptness even within the three month period: see *R. v. Stratford-upon-Avon District Council ex p. Jackson* [1985] 1 W.L.R. 1319, CA; *R. v. Swale Borough Council ex p. R.S.P.B.* [1991] 1 P.L.R. 6, *R. v. Dairy Produce Quota Tribunal ex p. Caswell* [1990] 2 A.C. 738, HL, *R. v. Criminal Injuries Compensation Board ex parte A* [1999] 2 W.L.R. 974, HL, (and see Simon Brown L.J. in the Court of Appeal at [1998] Q.B. 659 at 676 F–G), *R. v. Camden LBC ex parte Williams* [2000] 2 P.L.R. 93 and *R (Burkett) v. Hammersmith & Fulham L.B.C.* [2002] 1 W.L.R. 1593, HL, Doubt was cast, *obiter*, over the compatibility of the 'promptness' rule and the requirements of legal certainty: see Lord Hope at pp. 1612–1614.). See also s. 31(6) of the Supreme Court Act 1981.

[32] S. 31(6) of the Supreme Court Act 1981 and *R. v. Swale B.C. ex p. R.S.P.B.*, above.

[33] [1985] A.C. 461, HL.

Council's decision to raise the defendant's rent was void for unreasonableness. This collateral challenge to the legality of the Council's decision gave rise to a genuine defence since the effect of the challenge was that there were no arrears of rent. Such genuine defences can properly be raised in the course of ordinary civil proceedings and do not require resort to judicial review.[34] Where a public body seeks to terminate a licence, such as where school seeks to exclude parents who have a legitimate interest in the education of their children[35], the validity of the termination of the licence may be challenged in exclusion proceedings on public law grounds. The extent of the duty of public bodies to act lawfully in the public law sense will depend on the context, the nature of the duties and the demands of the public work[36];

(2) where the challenge on public law grounds does not raise a genuine defence on the merits, but goes to the exercise of the authority's power to bring proceedings, then the proper course of action is usually to seek an adjournment of the civil action and to seek judicial review.[37] An adjournment should not be granted as a matter of course, but only if there is a real possibility of the defendant being granted leave to apply for judicial review.[38] If the public law issue is raised late in the day, the defendant may find himself unable to pursue it if it is clear that he will not obtain leave for judicial review, *e.g.* if there has been lack of promptness and/or undue delay[39] or prejudice to good administration.[40] In determining the correct approach, the courts have

[34] *Wandsworth L.B.C. v. A* [2000] 1 W.L.R. 1246, CA. See the general observations of the Court of Appeal on public law defences in private law proceedings, and the undesirability of allowing them, at pp. 1253–1254 (Buxton L.J., giving the judgment of the Court). However, the Court of Appeal recognised that, however undesirable, such defences enjoyed the authority of the House of Lords in *Winder* and accepted that the parent in the particular case ought to be allowed to raise public law issues by way of defence in the county court.

[35] *Wandsworth v. A*, above, at pp. 1256–1258.

[36] See *Wandsworth v. Winder, ibid.* The House of Lords considered that the protection which what is now C.P.R. Part 54 and judicial review provides for public authorities should not take precedence over the preservation of "the ordinary rights of private citizens to defend themselves against unfounded claims" (per Lord Fraser). It is important to note the emphasis placed on the use of ordinary rights to defend: it appears that this statement refers to genuine defences to claims (as in that case) as opposed to challenges to the legality of the decision to institute proceedings (see below). See, further, *Steed v. Home Secretary* [2000] 1 W.L.R. 1169, HL, where the right to compensation (and its quantification and payment) under a scheme under statute requiring the surrender of certain firearms was held to be justiciable in the county court even though it involved the discharge of a public function. The claim was essentially one for late payment of money due and interest due on that sum which involved questions of fact and the assessment of valuation evidence which could more conveniently be dealt with by a judge in ordinary civil proceedings.

[37] *Avon County Council v. Buscott* [1988] 1 Q.B. 656, CA, especially at pp. 661 and 663–4 and *Trustees of Dennis Rye Pension Fund v. Sheffield City Council* [1994] 4 All E.R. 747, CA, at pp. 753–6 (Lord Woolf M.R.)

[38] *Avon v. Buscott, ibid.*, at p. 664 F–H (per Parker L.J.).

[39] See above.

[40] See s. 31(6) of the Supreme Court Act 1981 and para. 1–122, above.

shown an increasing disinclination to rely on distinctions between public and private law and to adopt a flexible, pragmatic approach. As Lord Woolf M.R. held in *Trustees of Dennis Rye Pension Fund v. Sheffield City Council.*[41]

"(1) If it is not clear whether judicial review or an ordinary action is the correct procedure it will be safer to make an application for judicial review than commence an ordinary action since there then should be no question of being treated as abusing the process of the court by avoiding the protection provided by judicial review. In the majority of cases it should not be necessary for purely procedural reasons to become involved in arid arguments as to whether the issues are correctly treated as involving public or private law or both. (For reasons of substantive law it may be necessary to consider this issue). If judicial review is used when it should not, the court can protect its resources either by directing that the application should continue as if begun by writ or by directing it should be heard by a judge who is not nominated to hear cases in the Crown Office List. It is difficult to see how a respondent can be prejudiced by the adoption of this course and little risk that anything more damaging could happen than a refusal of leave.

(2) If a case is brought by an ordinary action and there is an application to strike out the case, the court should, at least if it is unclear whether the case should have been brought by judicial review, ask itself whether, if the case had been brought by judicial review when the action was commenced, it is clear leave would have been granted. If it would, then that is at least an indication that there has been no harm to the interests judicial review is designed to protect. In addition the court should consider by which procedure the case could be appropriately tried. If the answer is that an ordinary action is equally or more appropriate than an application for judicial review that again should be an indication the action should not be struck out.

(3) Finally, in cases where it is unclear whether proceedings have been correctly brought by an ordinary action it should be remembered that after consulting the Crown Office a case can always be transferred to the Crown Office List as an alternative to being struck out."

The procedural reforms of the C.P.R. and the case management powers in the High Court should ease the transfer of applications from the general civil tracks to the Administrative Court[42]; and

---

[41] Above, at p. 755. Applied by the House of Lords in *Steed v. Home Secretary* [2000] 1 W.L.R. 1169.
[42] See C.P.R. Parts 30 and 54.20.

(3) Where the case involves action by the public authority which is incompatible with Convention rights under the European Convention on Human Rights ("ECHR") as applied by the Human Rights Act 1998. This might take the form of a defence to a possession claim or a public law challenge, although the approach of the Courts in recent years (typified by the Master of the Rolls' judgment in the *Dennis Rye* case, above) ought to mean that the precise manner of raising the issue in proceedings should not be controversial.

Strictly speaking, a public law challenge is not a defence to an action in trespass but rather a challenge to the legality of the decision to institute such proceedings.[43] However, the result may be the same if it leads to the dismissal of the proceedings. Nonetheless, quashing the decision may only provide a temporary respite since the authority may reconsider its decision in a lawful manner and issue fresh proceedings to which there is no valid defence either in private or public law terms unless to do so would be irrational in the circumstances to do so or would be "incompatible with a Convention right" within the meaning of section 6(1) of the Human Rights Act 1998. **1–136**

The above distinction between cases where a genuine defence is put forward by way of a collateral vires challenge and where the challenge is to the legality of the institution of proceedings forms part of the difficulties which have arisen in the courts in determining where the boundary lies between private law and public law actions and to what extent they should be regarded as exclusive.[44] The present position appears to be that, provided the litigant is seeking to enforce genuine private law rights, the raising of a defence which has public law aspects will not be regarded as an abuse of ordinary civil procedure and will be permitted to be made in the absence of challenge by way of judicial review.[45]

The challenge to the legality of the institution of proceedings has been utilised frequently in cases where public authorities have sought to evict gipsies[46] from council sites[47] although the remedy is not restricted to **1–137**

---

[43] *West Glamorgan County Council v. Rafferty* [1987] 1 W.L.R. 457, CA at pp. 468–9.

[44] *O'Reilly v. Mackman* [1983] 2 A.C. 237, HL; *Cocks v. Thanet D.C.* [1983] 2 A.C. 286, HL, *Wandsworth v. Winder* [1985] A.C. 461, HL; *Mohram Ali v. Tower Hamlets LBC* [1993] Q.B. 407, CA and *Roy v. Kensington & Chelsea Family Practitioner Committee* [1992] 1 A.C. 624, H.L, *Mercury Communications Ltd. v. Director General of Telecommunications* [1996] 1 W.L.R. 48, H.L., *Trustees of Dennis Rye Pension Fund v. Sheffield City Council* [1994] 4 All E.R. 747, CA, *Steed v. Home Secretary* [2000] 1 W.L.R. 1169, HL and *Clark v. University of Lincolnshire and Humberside* [2000] 3 All E.R. 752, CA. For discussion of these issues see, *e.g.* Wade and Forsyth, *Administrative Law* (8th ed.) pp. 649–666, Wade (1985) 101 L.Q.R. 250, Woolf [1986] Public Law 220 at 233, and Beatson (1987) 103 L.Q.R. 34.

[45] See *Roy v. Kensington* [1992] 1 A.C. 624, HL, *Dennis Rye*, above, *Steed v. Home Secretary*, above, and the endorsement of the views of Robert Goff L.J. in *Wandsworth v. Winder* [1985] A.C. 461 at 480.

[46] The duty of local authorities to make provision for gipsy caravan sites formerly contained in Part II of the Caravan Sites Act 1968 was repealed by s. 80 of the Criminal Justice and Public Order Act 1994 with effect from November 3, 1994: see Chap. Five, below and comments by Sedley J. in *R. v. Lincolnshire C.C. ex parte Atkinson* [1997] J.P.L. 65.

[47] See *West Glamorgan C.C. v. Rafferty*, below; *R. v. London Borough of Brent ex p. McDonagh* (1989) 21 H.L.R. 494; *R. v. Avon County Council ex p. Rexworthy* (1989) 21 H.L.R. 544 and *R.*

"gipsy" cases.[48] In *West Glamorgan County Council v. Rafferty*,[49] the council sought to evict gipsies from council owned land in circumstances where it was in breach of its duty "to provide adequate accommodation for gipsies residing in or resorting to their area".[50] The Court of Appeal set aside an order for possession under R.S.C., Order 113 since there was an arguable case that the council had acted unreasonably in taking proceedings. Ralph Gibson L.J. stated[51]:

> "The continuing breach of duty by the plaintiffs under section 6 of the Act of 1968 . . . does not in law preclude the right of the plaintiffs to recover possession of any land occupied by the trespassing gipsies, but that does not remove that continuing breach of duty from the balance or reduce its weight as a factor. The reasonable council in the view of the law is required to recognise its own breach of legal duty for what it is and to recognise the consequences of that breach of legal duty for what they are. The reasonable council, accordingly, was not in my judgment free to treat the interference with the intended reclamation and redevelopment of the site, for such period of time as would have resulted from the holding up of complete eviction from the entire site while temporary accommodation was provided elsewhere, as outweighing the effects of eviction on the gipsies then present and on those to whom the impact of trespassing by gipsies would necessarily be transferred. The decision is only explicable to me as one made by a council which was either not thinking of its powers and duties under the law or was by some error mistaken as to the nature and extent of those powers and duties."

1–138   A public authority instituting proceedings against persons such as gipsies who enjoy a degree of protection either under statute or as a result of the application of government policy, or through "considerations of common humanity",[52] must exercise a greater degree of caution than the ordinary landowner seeking possession and:

(1)   the authority must be satisfied that there is an entitlement to possession. This is the ordinary private law requirement;

---

[*] *v. Essex County Council ex p. Curtis* [1991] C.O.D. 9. See also cases on injunctions, *e.g. City of Bradford Metropolitan Council v. Brown* (1986) 19 H.L.R. 16, CA, *Runnymede Borough Council v. Ball* [1986] 1 W.L.R. 353, CA, *Waverley Borough Council v. Hilden* [1988] 1 W.L.R. 246, *Reigate & Banstead Borough Council v. Brown* (1992) 90 L.G.R. 557, CA and *South Bucks v. Porter* [2002] 1 All E.R. 425, CA.

[48] See *Bristol District Council v. Clark* [1975] 1 W.L.R. 1443, CA, *Cannock Chase District Council v. Kelly* [1978] 1 W.L.R. 1, CA and the *Lincolnshire C.C.* case, above, applying a similar approach to the Criminal Justice and Public Order Act 1994, ss. 77–79, although see *R. v. Barnet London Borough Council ex p. Grumbridge* (1992) 24 H.L.R. 433 where relief was refused.

[49] [1987] 1 W.L.R. 457, CA. See also *South Hams D.C. v. Shough* (1992) 91 L.G.R. 202, CA.

[50] S. 6 of the Caravan Sites Act 1968 (repealed by the Criminal Justice and Public Order Act 1994).

[51] At p. 447.

[52] *R. v. Lincolnshire C.C. ex p. Atkinson*, per Sedley J., [1997] J.P.L. 65.

(2)   the authority must take into account any relevant matters which arise under statute[53] or policy which might include the reason for taking the action and the consequences of eviction, particularly on those to be evicted; and

(3)   effect must be given to the human rights of any persons likely to be affected by the decision in accordance with the duty under section 6(1) of the Human Rights Act 1998. In many cases, this may add nothing to requirements (1) and (2), since many of the protections conferred by pre-Human Rights Act domestic law on administrative decision making already give effect to rights which are also protected by the ECHR.[54]

Point (1) is dealt with below at paragraphs 4–061 to 4–063. On issue (2), the considerations may include relevant statutory duties or policy relevant to the exercise of statutory discretions. For example, government policy which urges public authorities not to evict gipsies without good reason must be considered: the authority should assess its reasons for seeking possession and how seeking possession will impact upon those who might otherwise merit particular consideration. If there are other factors which may have an effect on the decision to evict, a public authority would be well advised to consider their relevance and significance to a decision to evict, *e.g.* if the authority is in breach of a relevant statutory duty or it was the breach of the authority's own duty which lead to the defendants becoming trespassers.[55] Plainly perverse or irrational decisions will be open to challenge. To these factors will also be added consideration arising in respect of rights under Articles 8 and 14 of the ECHR.

However, a rational decision which clearly has been reached after a careful consideration of the relevant issues will be unlikely to be struck down. An example of this is *Secretary of State for the Environment v. Widowfield*[56] where Brooke J. upheld the validity of a decision to evict travellers from a former depot which was required for the purposes of sale[57] since that decision had plainly been reached after a proper

---

[53] Powers under legislation (primary or secondary) must be construed so far as possible compatibly with Convention rights pursuant to s. 3 of the Human Rights Act 1998. See *Grosz, Beatson & Duffy, op. cit.,* at pp. 33–52 and *J. A. Pye (Oxford) Ltd. v. Graham* [2001] 2 W.L.R. 1293, CA, p. 1310 at para. 48 (Keene L.J.).

[54] See, *e.g.*, *R (Alconbury Developments Limited & others) v. Secretary of State for the Environment, Transport & the Regions* [2001] 2 W.L.R. 1389, HL at paras. 50–53 (Lord Slynn). See also *J. A. Pye (Oxford) Ltd. v. Graham*, above, pp. 1307–1310 at paras. 36–43 (Mummery L.J.) and 46–48 (Keene L.J.)

[55] As in *Rafferty*, above. In *Grumbridge*, above, Otton J. did not find the decision to evict perverse since there was no link between the duties of the authority as landlord and its duty under Part III of the Housing Act 1985. Unlike the "gipsy" cases, the applicant was not a trespasser as the result of a breach of duty by the authority.

[56] Unreported, dated September 9, 1993.

[57] Ironically, to the Avon County Council for use as a gipsy site. The applicant had submitted that, in view of the County Council's breach of its statutory duty to provide gipsy sites, in the absence of any attempts by the Secretary of State to seek alternative sites for him to move to if he were evicted from this land, it was irrational for the Secretary of State to evict him.

consideration of the relevant issues including the impact of the decision to evict on the occupiers and complaints from local residents as to nuisances caused by the travellers:

"In my judgment, it would be quite wrong for this Court to criticise this decision . . . It is quite clear to me that Mr Dalton [the decision-maker] carried out a proper and careful balancing exercise as to whether or not to take proceedings to obtain possession of the land. There were strong reasons which impelled him to seek vacant possession of the land. . . . Mr Dalton was well aware of the Secretary of State's policy in relation to gypsies, and of the human misery and the waste of time and financial resources that are involved when gypsies are moved from site to site because a County Council does not comply with its statutory duty to provide appropriate sites. He took all this into account, and balanced against that the countervailing reasons. He came to a decision to which, in my judgment, he was lawfully entitled to come."

It is advisable for a public authority, embarking upon the decision making process which might lead to eviction, to record by minutes or notes the issues which it considers and its decision-making process so that it can clearly be proved if the decision is challenged by way of judicial review. Such a practice was clearly useful in the *Widowfield* case, above, where Brooke J. noted the full and careful explanation of the decision-making process in that case. In *R. v. Horsham District Council ex p. Wenman*,[58] Brooke J. stated[59]:

". . . it would be wise for all local authorities to adopt the growing practice of setting out in clear terms the criteria they will use when deciding to move "gipsies" off land in their local authority area and to make it clear on the face of any resolution to take enforcement or possession action that they have had those criteria well in mind and the way in which they have applied them on the facts before them."

Human Rights

1–139 The prospect of raising the incompatibility of possession action with human rights under the ECHR is likely to be most concerned with substantive rights under Article 8 and Article 1 to the First Protocol, although other rights may be engaged more rarely.[60] In terms of the right to a fair trail, Article 6 is applicable but this is unlikely to prove an issue since (with the exceptions considered at 4–113 under "Self Help") prop-

---

[58] [1995] 1 W.L.R. 680. Judgment was given a month after that in *Widowfield*, above.
[59] At p. 704.
[60] *e.g.* under Article 14 (prohibition on discrimination).

erty rights are generally dealt with by the High Court and county courts which fulfil the requirements of Article 6.[61]

Article 8(1)[62] provides:

1–140

"Everyone has the right to respect for his private and family life, his home and his correspondence."

These rights are not absolute, but may give way to the considerations set out in Article 8(2) where it is "necessary in a democratic society", *i.e.* proportionate.[63] As with all human rights issues under the ECHR, it is of particular importance to consider the specific facts of the case, and to apply the provisions of the ECHR in order to give effect to their aim and object, as part of a "living instrument".[64]

The protection of the "home" under Article 8(1) is construed broadly, and applies to both domestic premises and in certain cases to business premises where there is a sufficiently close link between the private life of the occupier and the premises, to business premises.[65] Moreover, "home" does not only mean the actual home but premises which are intended to be the home although the victims have not been able to take up lawful occupation.[66] It is not essential that the occupation of the premises should have been lawful but recent Strasbourg case law is less generous in this respect than it has been in the past. In *Buckley v. United Kingdom*[67] the European Court of Human Rights suggested that a home could arise from unlawful occupation, but more recently in *Chapman v. United Kingdom*[68] at paragraphs 98–104 of its judgment, the Court rejected the argument that the refusal of a local authority to accept the unlawful occupation of gypsies amounted to a violation of Article 8 and emphasised the fact that "Article 8 does not in terms give a right to be provided with a home." At paragraph 101 of its judgment, the Court held:

". . . if the establishment of a home in a particular place was unlawful, the position of the individual objecting to an order to move is less

---

[61] Although see R (*McLellan*) v. *Bracknell Forest D.C. & Others* [2002] 1 All E.R. 899, CA, on the special issues arising in the context of introductory tenancies and the adequacy of judicial review as a means of ensuring compliance with Article 6.

[62] See, generally, Grosz, Beatson & Duffy, *Human Rights* pp. 265–291 and Clayton & Tomlinson, *The Law of Human Rights*, Chapter 12.

[63] See *per* Sedley L.J. in *London Borough of Lambeth v. Howard* (2001) 33 H.L.R. 58, CA, at para. 30.

[64] See *e.g. Golder v. United Kingdom* (1975) 1 E.H.R.R 524 and *Tyrer v. United Kingdom* (1978) 2 EHRR 1); also see Grosz, Beatson & Duffy, *op. cit.*, pp. 162–173 for a succinct account of fundamental Convention concepts.

[65] The European concept of "home" is more akin to that of "domicile". See *Niemietz v. Germany* (1992) 16 E.H.R.R. 97, where a lawyer's office fell within the meaning of "home" given the close connection between his private life and his office.

[66] *Gillow v. United Kingdom* (1989) 11 E.H.R.R. 335.

[67] (1997) 23 E.H.R.R. 101.

[68] (2001) B.H.R.C. 48

strong. The Court will be slow to grant protection to those who, in conscious defiance of the prohibitions of the law, establish a home on an environmentally protected site. For the Court to do otherwise would be to encourage illegal action to the detriment of the protection of the environmental rights of other people in the community."

1–141 However, the fact that "home" may encompass premises which were not lawfully occupied gives rise to difficulties where trespassers are allowed to remain in occupation for some time or are tolerated. It is likely that there will be cases where trespassers can demonstrate that their occupation of the building or land is genuinely occupation as their "home". Whilst *Chapman* provides a recent basis for arguing that Article 8 is not engaged, it may not take much acceptance by the person entitled to possession to change this. The *Chapman* case concerned the enforcement of planning control and it remains to be seen whether it extends to other areas, although it appears likely that it will do so given the Court's view that it should not support defiance of the law. Public authorities should therefore act with caution when even tolerating occupation, since it may confer legitimacy on the initially unlawful occupation sufficient to engage Article 8 rights. *Chapman* also makes it relevant to consider the existence and adequacy of alternative accommodation[69]:

"A further relevant consideration, to be taken into account in the first place by the national authorities, is that if no alternative accommodation is available, the interference is more serious than where such accommodation is available. The more suitable the alternative accommodation is, the less serious is the interference constituted by moving the applicant from his or her existing accommodation.

The evaluation of the suitability of alternative accommodation will involve a consideration of, on the one hand, the particular needs of the person concerned — his or her family requirements and financial resources — and, on the other hand, the rights of the local community to environmental protection. This is a task in respect of which it is appropriate to give a wide margin of appreciation to national authorities, who are evidently better placed to make the requisite assessment."

1–142 The greatest likely impact which the ECHR will have on an authority seeking to recover possession is in requiring them to consider its aim for seeking possession and whether that aim is proportionate[70] to the impact on the home, family and private life of the occupiers against whom action is contemplated. Sedley L.J. considered the general application of Article

---

[69] Above, at paras. 103–104.
[70] On proportionality and its growing influence see *R (Daly) v. Home Secretary* [2001] 2 W.L.R. 1622, HL.

8 to possession cases in *London Borough of Lambeth v. Howard*[71] where he held at paragraphs 30–32 of his judgment:

> "30. . . . It seems to me that any attempt to evict a person, whether directly or by process of law, from his or her home would on the face of it be a derogation from the respect, that is the integrity, to which the home is prima facie entitled.
>
> 31. The real question is the one the judge goes on to address: is the interference justified? This question arises by virtue of the Human Rights Act, section 6(1), where the lessor is itself a public authority. It also arises, and more generally, by virtue of section 3 of the Act as a matter of statutory construction, whoever the lessor may be; that is to say, the meaning given to the word "reasonable" in a statute such as the Housing Act 1985 must now, so far as possible, be Convention-compliant. As this court has said more than once, there is nothing in Article 8, or in the associated jurisprudence of the European Court of Human Rights, which should carry county courts to materially different outcomes from those that they have been arriving at for many years when deciding whether it is reasonable to make an outright or a suspended or no possession order. Nevertheless, as the judge in the present case has demonstrated in the final passage of his judgment, it can do no harm, and may often do a great deal of good, if the exercise is approached for what it is, an application of the principle of proportionality.
>
> 32. A legal threat to a secure home will, in the ordinary way, engage Article 8.1."

However, the impact of Article 8 must not be overestimated, especially where (but for the HRA) the Court would have no discretion to refuse to make the order as a result of statutory provisions. Where a statute regulating security of tenure (such as the Housing Act 1985) applies, the Court does not in each case have to review the application of mandatory provisions in the "micro" sense of requiring evidence to justify the order in the indvidual case, if the justification for the order lies at the "macro" scale of the enactment of the regime by Parliament.[72] As Brooke L.J. held in *Michalak v. Wandsworth L.B.C.*[73]

> "The objective justification for the possession order lies in the statutory arrangements devised by Parliament for identifying who may succeed to successor tenancies and who may not following the death of a secure tenant. There is ample Strasbourg authority for the

---

[71] (2001) 33 H.L.R. 58, CA.

[72] *R (McLellan) v. Bracknell Forest D.C.* [2002] 1 All E.R. 899, CA, *Sheffield C.C. v. Smart* [2002] EWCA Civ 4, CA, and *Michalak v. Wandsworth L.B.C.* [2002] EWCA Civ 271, CA followed in *Somerset C.C. v. Isaacs* [2002] E.W.H.C. 1014 (Admin).

[73] Above, at paras. 43–47 relying on *James v. UK* (1986) 8 E.H.R.R. 123. See also Mance L.J. at paras. 62–82.

proposition that appropriate justification may be derived from a statutory scheme, and that it need not always be demonstrated on a case by case basis."

Even in such cases, the Court should not wholly exclude "micro" level, case specific considerations:

"there might be the rare case where something wholly exceptional has happened since service of the notice to quit, which fundamentally alters the rights and wrongs of the proposed eviction, and the county court might be obliged to address it in deciding whether or not to make an order for possession."[74]

A more difficult question arises where there is no carefully devised statutory scheme, regulating security of tenure, and it is, therefore, difficult to conclude on a "macro" scale that Parliament has made the necessary proportionate arrangements and the Court need do little more than comply with the statutory provisions in order to give effect to Convention rights. This is particularly significant in the case of trespassers *ab initio* where the Court's discretion is otherwise circumscribed not by statute but by the common law.[75] In such a case, there appears to be a stronger case for considering the case on its own facts and to be careful to ensure that the requirements of Article 8(2), and of proportionality in particular, have been observed if Article 8 rights are engaged. Nonetheless, there are *obiter* suggestions in *Michalak* that the position would not be changed[76]:

"76. . . . the effect of this court's decision in *Sheffield C.C. v. Smart* was that the scheme of the homelessness legislation confined the county court's role in granting a possession order to considering (a) whether there was any arguable case for judicial review in the Administrative Court of the local authority's conduct, if judicial review was sought (in which case the court would adjourn the matter pending such review in the Administrative Court) and (b) whether anything wholly exceptional had happened since service of the notice to quit (in which case the county court judge would himself have to consider the implications of Article 8). Thus, although this court might, perhaps, have taken a different view after the Human Rights Act, it preferred to maintain an approach which in the result (a) mirrors that established prior to that Act and (b) places the onus, on a person challenging the consistency with Article 8 of the Convention of a local

---

[74] *per* Laws L.J. in *Sheffield C.C. v. Smart*, above, at para. 43. See also Mance L.J. in *Michalak*, above, at paras. 72–76.

[75] See 4–071 below, which includes a discussion of the potential impact of such issues on the discretion of the Court in making a possession order. See *Sheffield Corp v. Luxford* [1929] 2 K.B. 180, *Jones v. Savory* [1951] All E.R. 820 and *McPhail v. Persons Unknown* [1973] Ch. 447.

[76] Mance L.J. in *Michalak*, above, at paras. 76–77.

authority's attempts to obtain possession, to pursue that challenge by the conventional route of judicial review.

77. The judgment in *Sheffield C.C. v. Smart* does not refer to the line of cases establishing the court's duty at common law, prior to the Human Rights Act, to make a possession order against a trespasser with no defence: cf *Sheffield Corp v. Luxford, Jones v. Savory* and *McPhail v. Persons Unknown* . . . or to the statutory restrictions on the right to suspend a possession order once made. The effect of *Sheffield C.C. v. Smart* is, however, to preserve the relevance and operation of both."

It could be argued, against the above approach, that it does not take consideration of the fact that the common law approach is judge made and does not rest on any principles of proportionality derived from the enactment of a scheme by a democratically elected Parliament. It can also be pointed out that the decision of the Court of Appeal in *Smart* arose in the context of a statutory scheme and the question of "exceptional circumstances" arising following a notice to quit cannot arise in cases of trespass *ab initio* where notices to quit (or terminate) are unnecessary and inappropriate.

On the other hand, it can properly be maintained that the protection afforded under article 8 is qualified: there is to be no interference with the right to respect for the home except to the extent that the interference is "necessary in a democratic society . . . for the protection of the rights and freedoms of others". Since the person at common law who is entitled to possession against the trespasser *ex hypothesi* has a proprietary interest in the land in question, that person has rights which themselves are protected under article 1 of the First Protocol to the ECHR. On that basis, the common law approach is the correct one and is necessary both to protect the rights of the person with title to the land and to maintain the rule of law. The only way of giving effect to the rights of the person entitled to possession would be for the Court to make an order for possession. Any issues of infringement of the ECHR could be left to a judicial review of the decision of the authority to evict.[76a]

This issue is one which requires further judicial consideration, especially in the light of recent injunction cases where the principles on which the court operates are also judge made, and the Court of Appeal has accepted the need to consider Convention rights and proportionality when deciding whether to grant the discretionary remedy of an injunction.[77]

[76a] See *Somerset C.C. v. Isaacs* [2002] EWHC 1014 (Admin) *per* Stanley Burnton J. at paras. 25–27.

[77] See e.g. *South Bucks D.C. v. Porter* [2002] 1 W.L.R. 1359, CA, at para. 41, & Chapter Four, at para. 4–103 and generally. Consideration of whether to grant an injunction, and how Convention rights influence the exercise of the court's discretion, is plainly at the factual, "micro" level.

1–143   The first United Kingdom cases considering the effect of the ECHR[78] on property issues support a wide margin of the margin of appreciation conferred on Parliament for limiting rights as part of the social control of the occupation of land through statute[79] and a straightforward approach to the application of Article 8.[80] In *Poplar Housing & Regeneration Community Association Ltd v Donoghue*,[81] Lord Woolf C.J. (giving the judgment of the Court of Appeal) approved the manner in which the county court dealt with Article 6 and 8 arguments relating to the lack of protection afforded by assured shorthold tenancies[82]:

> "7.   The judge then turned his attention to the Human Rights Act 1998 argument. It was contended that to make an order for possession would contravene articles 6 and 8 of the Convention for the Protection of Human Rights and Fundamental Freedoms and would involve interpreting section 21(4) in a manner which is not compatible with the Human Rights Act 1998. The judge rejected these contentions as well. He said:
>
> 'If I were to read section 21(4) in the way in which I am being enjoined to do, this would, in effect, enable people who were intentionally homeless—and that is a finding that has been made already by the local authority, which has been reviewed and has not been challenged, the final decision having been made a year ago, in November 1999—to jump the housing queue, that would impede the human rights of others and that is the proviso to article 8(2) that I have got in mind, "the protection of the rights and freedoms of others." '
>
> 8.   He did, however, postpone the date on which the order came into force for 42 days. This was the maximum extension which he was entitled to give. This was because of the defendant's exceptional personal circumstances. In addition, as already stated, the judge gave permission to the defendant to appeal directly to the Court of Appeal.
>
> 9.   It is the defendant's contention that the judge should have adjourned the hearing so as to enable her to place before the court the substantial evidence, which is now before this court, in sup-

---

[78] *Poplar Housing & Regeneration Community Association Ltd v. Donoghue* [2001] 3 W.L.R. 183, CA, *London Borough of Lambeth v. Howard*, above, *R (McLellan) v. Bracknell Forest D.C. & Others* [2002] 1 All E.R. 899, CA, *Qazi v. Harrow L.B.C.* [2001] EWCA Civ 1834, CA, *Sheffield C.C. v. Smart* [2002] EWCA Civ 04, CA and *Michalak v. Wandsworth L.B.C.* [2002] EWCA Civ. 271, CA.

[79] *Poplar v. Donoghue*, above, at paras. 73–77 of the judgment. A similar approach was taken by the European Court of Human Rights in *Gillow v. United Kingdom* (1989) 11 E.H.R.R. 335 and *Mellacher v. Austria* (1989) 12 E.H.R.R. 391.

[80] See also, in the context of planning injunctions, *Tandridge B.C. v. Delaney* [2000] 1 P.L.R. 11. for an example of the consideration of Article 8 rights in the domestic context.

[81] Above.

[82] See also the views expressed on the procedural issues at paras. 25–31 of the judgment.

port of her appeal. The evidence is directed to the issues of whether the housing association is a public body or performing a public function and whether any breach of article 8 could be justified on the grounds set out in article 8(2).

10. In our judgment, where it is possible for a judge to give a decision summarily, as the judge did here, in a case where there will almost certainly be an appeal, there can be substantial advantages in adopting this approach. It can avoid expense and delay being incurred both at first instance and in the Court of Appeal."

In R (*McLellan*) v. *Bracknell Forest D.C. & Others*[83] the Court of Appeal con- **1–144** sidered the effect on Article 8 on introductory tenancies[84] under the Housing Act 1996. Waller L.J. (giving the judgment of the Court) held that Article 8 was engaged at both the "macro" and "micro" levels, *i.e.* first, in terms of the general compatibility of the applicable statutory provisions and, secondly, the application of the particular statute and the ECHR to the specific facts of the case. On the first question, the Court of Appeal approved the judgment of Longmore J. at first instance[85]:

"42. There remains the question of proportionality. Here it is important to note how the interference with the tenant's right is limited. The Council must give reasons for issuing a notice of possession proceedings. If the tenant requests, there must be a review; if the decision of the review confirms the decision to seek possession, reasons must be given for that second decision. The interference with the tenant's rights of respect for his home is thus little more than that the assessment of the grounds for possession is not made by the County Court. Moreover, the interference is only for twelve months. Once the year is up, the tenant becomes a secure tenant."

However, the Court added that it was necessary also to consider the application of Article 8, and the statutory provisions, to the specific circumstances of the case. Waller L.J. pointed out the differences between the instant case and *Poplar*:

"50. The distinction between *Poplar* and the cases under the introductory tenancy scheme which create the difficulty seems to me to be the fact that the circumstances of the particular tenant are brought directly into focus under the introductory tenancy scheme by virtue of the requirement under section 128(3) to provide reasons for seeking possession, and the machinery for the reviewing of those reasons.

---

[83] [2002] 1 All E.R. 899, CA.
[84] Where there is no requirement to prove grounds or satisfy the Court as to reasonableness before a possession order is made during the introductory period.
[85] Above, Waller L.J. at paras. 46–47.

51. In other words so far as individual tenants are concerned their positions have to be considered at the micro level, and the decision of a council to use section 127 may itself have to be tested. Do those reasons have to be tested by reference to Article 8(2), i.e. do the reasons on their face have to demonstrate that if they are right, it is necessary for the protection of the rights and freedom of others for the procedure under section 127 to be used? If so, is there machinery which allows the tenant to establish that the exceptions in Article 8(2) do not apply?"

Waller L.J. answered this question in the affirmative:

"58. It seems to me that a tenant under an introductory tenancy must have the right to raise the question whether it is reasonable in his or her particular case to insist on eviction *i.e.* the question whether Article 8(2) justifies the eviction. That much has in reality to be conceded because under the relevant section reasons must be given and there is then an entitlement to review *i.e.* an opportunity to argue, that it is not reasonable in the particular case."

Waller L.J., applying the decision of the House of Lords in *R. (Alconbury Developments Limited and others) v. Secretary of State*,[86] then went on to hold that judicial review provided an adequate means to ensure compliance with the ECHR (and to ensure compliance with Article 6).[87]

Approach to Article 8

1–145   In approaching a case with Article 8 implications, a public authority should follow a five-stage approach to the issues which can be seen in the Strasbourg Article 8 cases such as *Buckley v. United Kingdom*.[88] This approach requires consideration to be given to:

(a)   the identification of any Article 8 rights which may be engaged;

(b)   whether there has been an interference with those Article 8(1) rights;

(c)   whether such an interference was "in accordance with the law";

(d)   whether that interference had a legitimate aim or aims (*i.e.* one of those listed in Article 8(2)); and

(e)   whether that interference was "necessary in a democratic society", *i.e.* proportionate.

---

[86]   [2001] 2 W.L.R. 1389, HL. See Elvin & Maurici [2001] J.P.L. 883.
[87]   Above, at paras. 59–66 and 69–103 of the judgment.
[88]   (1996) 23 E.H.R.R. 101 and see the similar process in *Chapman v. United Kingdom*, above, at paras. 71–116 (identified as headings A to E) of the judgment.

The express articulation of Article 8 issues in the decision-making process appears not to be strictly necessary provided that it is complied with in substance: see *R. (on the application of Malster) v. Ipswich Borough Council and Ipswich Town Football Club*[89] and also the Strasbourg Article 8 decisions in *Buckley v. United Kingdom*[90] and *Chapman v. United Kingdom*[91] where no violations were found to have occurred, yet the decisions under challenge had not expressly referred to Article 8 considerations. Nonetheless, prudence suggests that it would be better for ECHR considerations to be expressly addressed in the decision-making process to avoid later dispute.

Applying the above approach to Article 8 the implications of the ECHR for the termination of occupation might be approached in the following manner:

1–146

(1) termination of a right to occupy is unlikely of itself to be a violation of Article 8 rights if it is carried out correctly and is simply the exercise of one of the incidents of the right to occupy, *e.g.* the service of a notice to quit or to determine a licence;

(2) proceedings for the recovery of possession under the CPR must be "in accordance with the law" and, therefore, any errors in the procedure which might render the recovery of possession unlawful as a matter of common law will prevent reliance by the authority on Article 8(2).[92] This would in any event lead to the dismissal of the proceedings as a matter of the general law;

(3) the recovery of possession must have a legitimate aim. There may be a variety of aims within Article 8(2) for seeking possession, including cases where the authority is protecting the rights of others, *e.g.* by terminating a tenancy due to disturbance caused to others, or even to protect its own rights, *e.g.* where the tenant is in arrears of rent or the property is needed for a more important purpose;

(4) seeking possession must be proportionate to such interference as may be caused on the facts with the home, family or private life of the occupier. This is capable of giving rise to difficulties in cases where the proceedings are brought for reasons which provide little justification for eviction, *e.g.* where an authority pursues possession for arrears of rent which are insignificant compared to the impact of eviction on the occupier's family, or where it has not considered other means to resolve the problem. These matters are

---

[89] [2001] EWHC Admin. 711 *per* Sullivan J. Permission to appeal was refused by the Court of Appeal [2001] EWCA Civ. 1715.
[90] (1997) 23 E.H.R.R. 101.
[91] (2001) B.H.R.C. 48
[92] Although minor procedural defects may be waived or sanctioned by order of the Court. In such an event, they would be in accordance with the law.

no doubt ones which would in any event be relevant factors where the court has a discretion to order possession.[93] Whilst a court may not be persuaded of the appropriateness of a possession order in any event, the existence of Article 8 rights is an additional factor which both the authority and the court[94] will have to consider in exercising their respective powers.

Approach to Article 1 of the First Protocol

1–147 Article 1 of the First Protocol[95] has been analysed by the European Court of Human Rights as comprising three distinct strands[96]:

(1) "Every natural person or legal person is entitled to the peaceful enjoyment of his possessions." This is a rule of a general character declaring "the principle of peaceful enjoyment of property";

(2) "No one shall be deprived of his possessions except in the public interest and subject to the conditions provided for by law and by the general principles of international law." The deprivation of possessions is made subject to a number of conditions; and

(3) Rules (1) and (2) should not in any way impair the right of a State to enforce such laws as it deems necessary to control the use of property in accordance with the general interest or to secure the payment of taxes or other contributions or penalties. This derives from the second paragraph of the Article.

Unsurprisingly, the deprivation of possessions is regarded as inherently more serious than the control of its use where ownership is retained. "Possessions" is given a very wide meaning under Strasbourg case law and encompasses rights which would not be regarded as such under the common law.[97]

As with Article 8, Article 1 Protocol 1 rights are not absolute but may be overridden if the public interest in depriving or restricting possession is proportionate to the private interest in retaining it, or retaining in a less regulated form. The approach to be taken to this Article is similar to that in relation to Article 8. The margin of appreciation accorded is especially wide in terms of this provision of the ECHR. In *Spörrong*[98] the Court held:

---

[93] *e.g.* under the secure tenancy provisions of the Housing Act 1985.

[94] Which is itself subject to the s. 6 duty.

[95] See, generally, Grosz, Beatson & Duffy, *op. cit.*, pp. 333–356 and Clayton & Tomlinson, *op. cit.*, Chapter 18.

[96] *Spörrong & Lonnroth v. Sweden* (1982) 5 E.H.R.R. 35 and *James v. United Kingdom* (1986) 8 E.H.R.R. 123.

[97] See *e.g. Tre Traktörer AB v. Sweden* (1989) 13 E.H.R.R. 309 at para. 53 (liquor licence) and *Fredin v. Sweden (No. 1)* (1991) 13 E.H.R.R. 784 at para. 53 (gravel extraction licence).

[98] Above.

"The Court must determine whether a fair balance has been struck between the demands of the general interests of the community and the requirements of the protection of the individual's fundamental rights . . ."

In most cases, rights under Article 1 Protocol 1 will add little to considerations under Article 8. It is noticeable that claims under this provision rarely succeed in Strasbourg. The termination of property rights in accordance with the law, or their own provisions, does not amount to a breach of Article 1 Protocol 1[99] and interferences resulting from matters of a purely private contractual nature do not fall within the provisions of the ECHR.[1]

---

[99] *JS v. The Netherlands* (1995) 20 E.H.R.R. CD 42 and *Gudmunsson v. Iceland* (1996) 21 E.H.R.R. CD 89.
[1] *Gustafsson v. Sweden* (1996) 22 E.H.R.R. 409 at para. 60.

Chapter Two

Nuisance

οὐδ᾽ ἂν βοῦς ἀπόλοιτ᾽ εἰ μὴ γείτων κακὸς εἴη
[Hesiod, Works and Days, line 348.]

Introduction

"Nuisance, nocumentum, or annoyance, signifies anything that **2–001** works hurt, inconvenience or damage. And nuisances are of two kinds: public or common nuisances, which affect the public, and are an annoyance to the King's subjects; . . . and private nuisances, which . . . may be defined, anything done to the hurt or annoyance of the lands, tenements or hereditaments of another."[1]

This part of the book is concerned with the second kind of nuisance.

The principle underlying the tort of private nuisance is the maxim *sic utere tuo ut alienum non laedas.*[2] Nuisance involves a hurt or damage. But this maxim and Blackstone's definition quoted above are too wide. It is not every "hurt or annoyance" to lands, tenements or hereditaments of another that will amount to a private nuisance. There must be some right in the person whose lands, tenements or hereditaments are damaged to immunity from the damage of which complaint is made.[3] A better description of private nuisance is:

". . . unlawful interference with a person's use or enjoyment of land, or some right over or in connection with it."[4]

---

[1] Bl. Comm. III, c. 13, p. 216.
[2] *Aldred's Case* (1610) 9 Co. Rep. 57b, 59a; *Tenant v. Goldwin* (1709) 2 Ld. Raym. 1089, 1092 and see para. 2–027.
[3] *Hammerton v. Dysart* [1916] A.C. 57.
[4] *Winfield and Jolowicz on Tort* (15th ed., 1998), p. 494; this statement from earlier editions was adopted in *Read v. J. Lyons & Co. Ltd* [1945] K.B. 216, 236; *Howard v. Walker* [1947] K.B. 860, 863; *Newcastle-under-Lyme Corporation v. Wolstanton Ltd* [1947] Ch. 97, 107 (dictum of Evershed J. unaffected on appeal, [1947] Ch. 427, 467–468); *Hargrave v. Goldman* (1963) A.L.J.R. 277, 283 affirmed [1967] 1 A.C. 645, P.C.; *Home Brewery Co. Ltd v. William Davis & Co. Ltd* [1987] 1 Q.B. 339. Also, see *Hunter v. Canary Wharf Ltd* [1997] A.C. 655, HL at 687C–688D *per* Lord Goff, 702F –704C *per* Lord Hoffmann; *Jan de Nul (U.K.) Ltd v. N.V. Royale Belge* [2000] 2 Lloyd's Rep 700, 711–712.

Of course, this description begs the question of when an interference is unlawful. In order to maintain an action in nuisance a claimant must establish:

(1)   that he has a right or interest in land with which there has been an interference, *i.e.* he is within the categories of person who can sue,

(2)   that the defendant is legally responsible for the interference, and

(3)   that the interference is the sort of interference which the law will consider to be a nuisance.

This chapter will consider each of these ingredients before considering defences which are generally available and providing a catalogue of the sorts of interference with land which have been held to be actionable as nuisances.[5]

Who can sue

Introduction: rights or interests in land

2–002   Private nuisance may be an unlawful interference either with a man's "natural" rights of property, namely those rights which are necessary for the enjoyment of the property, or in respect of his easements over the property of another.[6] Private nuisance may occur in respect of either corporeal or incorporeal hereditaments.[7] Unless, however, there is interference with some *right* in or appurtaining to the claimant's land with which there is interference, there can be no nuisance.[8] Thus a claimant was held to have no cause of action for interference with television signals as a result of development by the defendant because the plaintiff as landowner had no right to receive television transmissions.[9]

Nuisance may also occur where, although the claimant has no proprietary interest, he has an entitlement to possession against the defendant:

---

[5]   Who can sue: see para. 2–002 *et seq.*; who can be sued: see para. 2–010 *et seq.*; nature of interference: see para. 2–025 *et seq.*; defences para. 2–035 *et seq.*; catalogue of nuisances: see para. 2–049 *et seq.*

[6]   Pearce and Meston, *Law of Nuisances*, (1926), p. 13; J.H. Baker, *An Introduction to English Legal History* (3rd ed., 1990), pp. 484–486; *Tate & Lyle Industries Ltd v. Greater London Council* [1983] 2 A.C. 519, 536.

[7]   Bl. Comm. III, c. 13, pp. 216–218.

[8]   See, for instance, *Bland v. Mosely* (1857) 9 Co Rep 58a, *Aldred's Case* (1610) 9 Co Rep 57b *Dalton v. Angus* (1881) 6 App Cas 740, 794–795 *per* Lord Selborne L.C. and 823 *per* Lord Blackburn *Chastey v. Ackland* [1895] 2 Ch. 389, CA at 402 *per* Lindley L.J.

[9]   *Hunter v. Canary Wharf Ltd* [1997] A.C. 655, HL; see too *Anglian Water Services Ltd v. Crawshaw Robbins Ltd* February 6, 2001 QBD (interruption of gas supply by third party's works outside the claimants' land did not constitute a nuisance since there was no property right in the gas supply) and see para. 2–033 below ("Normal uses of the defendant's land and the defendant's motives").

thus a licensee with an entitlement to exclusive possession may maintain an action for nuisance.[10]

Where a claimant has a right to exclusive possession it is not necessary for him to prove his title in order to bring an action in nuisance where the defendant himself has no title to the land. It is not open to the defendant to raise *ius tertii* as a defence to nuisance; the claimant has a better title to the land by the fact of possession than the defendant has.[11] Thus in the case of *Foster v. Warblington UDC*[12] the plaintiff was entitled to maintain an action for nuisance in respect of the discharge of sewage into oyster beds of which he was the exclusive licensee notwithstanding that he could not prove title.[13] Likewise, in the case of *Charing Cross Electricity Supply Co v. Hydraulic Power Co*[14] a plaintiff which had a statutory right to lay and maintain gas mains had a sufficient right to maintain an action in nuisance for an interference with its pipes. Similarly, in the case of *Pemberton v. Southwark LBC*[15] a tolerated trespasser who retained possession after the termination of her secure tenancy had sufficient possession against her local authority landlord for her to be able to maintain a claim for nuisance against it.[16]

On the other hand, it is clear that to maintain an action for nuisance the claimant must have some right to the enjoyment of real property or some right in, over or in connection with land which gives the claimant better title than the defendant.[17] Thus it was held by the Court of Appeal in the case of *Malone v. Laskey*[18] that a bare licensee with no legal right to possession of the land which she occupied was not entitled to maintain an action based on private nuisance. This case was approved in *Hunter v. Canary Wharf Ltd*[19] in which it was held by the House of Lords that occupants of flats who were not householders had an insufficient interest in the land to maintain an action for nuisance.[20] So too companies which were subsidiaries of the

---

[10] *Foster v. Warblington UDC* [1906] 1 K.B. 648, CA; and see *Hunter v. Canary Wharf Ltd* [1997] A.C. 655, HL.

[11] See *Hunter v. Canary Wharf Ltd* [1997] A.C. 655, HL and paras. 2–006, 2–048 below.

[12] [1906] 1 K.B. 648, CA.

[13] The grant of exclusive possession for a term will create a tenancy rather than a licence: *Street v. Mountford* [1985] A.C. 809, HL. See 2–005 below in relation to the right of tenants to bring claims for nuisance.

[14] [1913] 3 K.B. 442, [1914] 3 K.B. 722, CA; see too *Newcastle-under-Lyme Corporation v. Wolstanton* [1947] Ch. 97 (on appeal [1947] Ch. 427, CA).

[15] [2001] 1 W.L.R. 1672, CA.

[16] For the law relating to the status of "tolerated trespassers" see *Burrows v. Brent LBC* [1996] 1 W.L.R. 1448, HL.

[17] See above and *Hunter v. Canary Wharf* [1997] A.C. 655, HL. See also *Cunard v. Antifyre Ltd* [1933] 1 K.B. 551, 557, DC; *Sedleigh-Denfield v. O'Callaghan* [1940] A.C. 880, 902–903, HL; *Read v. J. Lyons & Co. Ltd* [1947] A.C. 156, 183, HL; *Southport Corp v. Esso Petroleum Co. Ltd* [1954] 2 Q.B. 182, 193, CA.

[18] [1907] 2 K.B. 144.

[19] [1997] A.C. 655.

[20] See in particular pp 691–692, 698, 703–705. See also *Blackburn v. ARC Ltd t/a Greenways Landgill* [1997] P.L.S.C.S. 317 (Official Referee), H.H.J. Humphrey Lloyd Q.C. (unmarried partner of householder had no claim for nuisance caused by smell and litter); *Jan de Nul (U.K.) Ltd v. N.V. Royale Belge* [2000] 2 Lloyd's Rep 700, Moore-Bick J (licences to moor boats on river gave insufficient interest for claim).

owner of the land but themselves without any interest in or entitlement to possession of land affected by building works have been held not to have a sufficient interest in the land to maintain an action in nuisance.[21]

Malone v. Laskey was purportedly followed by Goddard LJ in *Metropolitan Properties v. Jones*.[22] In that case the defendant had been the tenant of one of the plaintiff's flats but had assigned the lease. The assignee disappeared and the tenant went back into possession. The original tenant remained liable for the rent for which the landlord sued. The defendant counterclaimed seeking damages for noise nuisance from the central heating system on the landlord's retained premises in which she lived. Goddard LJ dismissed the counterclaim because the defendant did not have title. In *Hunter v. Canary Wharf Ltd*, however, Lord Hoffman[23] considered this decision to be wrong since the defendant was in *de facto* exclusive possession and this was sufficient to enable him to bring an action (the fact that the assignee had a better title was no defence for the landlord).

2–003   The requirement that a claimant must have a right to enjoyment of property obviously limits the scope of the tort of nuisance. It had been held in *Khorasandjian v. Bush*[24] that a young girl who lived with her mother had sufficient standing to bring an action for nuisance against a man who pestered her with telephone calls notwithstanding that she was not entitled to possession of the premises in which she lived. This case was overruled by the House of Lords in *Hunter v. Canary Wharf Ltd*.[25] The House of Lords followed *Malone v. Laskey*[26] and re-asserted the traditional view on the limits of the law of nuisance as a tort against land and interests in land.[27]

The tort of harassment created by the Protection from Harassment Act 1997[28] has gone some way to providing protection for those who have no legal right to possession of their homes.[29] This Act is limited in its scope.[30] It is possible, however, that (apart from statute) the common law may develop to provide still further protection from nuisances for those who do not have the right to possession of their homes. In his dissenting judgment in *Hunter v. Canary Wharf Ltd*, Lord Cooke of Thorndon[31] referred to Article 8 of the European Convention on Human Rights (aimed at protecting the home). This provision has been construed so as to give protection against nuisances[32] and appears to go beyond the protection of

---

[21] *Butcher Robinson & Staples Ltd v. London Regional Transport* [1999] 3 E.G.L.R. 63, Q.B. (TCC), HHJ Bowsher Q.C.

[22] [1939] 2 All E.R. 202, 205.

[23] [1997] A.C. 655, HL at 704E.

[24] [1993] Q.B. 727, CA.

[25] [1997] A.C. 655, HL.

[26] [1907] 2 K.B. 141, CA.

[27] See in particular [1997] A.C. 655, HL at p. 691 G-692 B, 698 B-C, 707 G, 725 C-F.

[28] Which came into force on [*check*]

[29] See generally p. 448 *et seq.* below

[30] *ibid.*

[31] [1997] A.C. 655, HL at 714 A-D.

[32] *Arrondelle v. United Kingdom* Application No. 7889/77 (1982) 26 D & R 5 (aircraft noise); *Lopez Ostra v. Spain* (1994) 20 E.H.H.R. 277 (fumes and smells from waste treatment plant); *Guerra v. Italy* (1998) 26 E.H.R.R. 357.

possession and property rights.[33] Lord Cooke stated that[34] "this is a legitimate consideration in support of treating residence as an acceptable basis of standing at common law". If so, it may be open to the Court (as a public authority which is now bound to act in accordance with the Convention[35]) to develop the common law to give redress against nuisances to those whose homes are affected but who have no rights of exclusive possession to their homes. Indeed, the Convention was a material factor in the Court of Appeal's consideration that the law of nuisance extended to protect "tolerated trespassers" holding over after the determination of their secure tenancies from nuisances for which their local authority landlords were responsible.[36] The development in the law to include those who had no entitlement to possession as against the defendant would, however, be a radical departure and inconsistent with the traditional view of private nuisance as re-asserted by the majority of the House of Lords in *Hunter v. Canary Wharf Ltd.*

It follows from the above discussion that an occupier with a right of possession by virtue of a tenancy or his freehold ownership of the land in question clearly has a sufficent interest in the land to maintain an action in nuisance.[37] The following paragraphs consider in more detail the categories of people who have been held to have a sufficient interest to maintain a claim in nuisance.

Freeholders entitled to possession

It is clear that a freehold owner with an entitlement to possession is entitled to maintain an action in nuisance for interferences with his enjoyment of property.[38] Thus, for instance, a freeholder who is entitled to possession of property but who is not in actual occupation is entitled to damages if a nuisance affects the reasonable enjoyment of the property so that tenants cannot be found for it.[39]

2–004

Tenants entitled to possession

It follows from what has been said[40] that tenants with a right to immediate possession will be able to maintain an action for nuisance because it is in such a tenant that the rights to the use and enjoyment of the land vest.

2–005

---

[33] Harris, O'Boyle and Warbrick, *Law of the European Convention on Human Rights* (1995) p. 319.
[34] [1997] A.C. 655, HL at 714 A-D.
[35] Human Rights Act 1998, s. 6.
[36] *Pemberton v. Southwark LBC* [2001] 1 W.L.R. 1672; [2000] 21 E.G. 135, CA in particular *per* Clarke LJ.
[37] See *Wood v. Conway Corporation* [1914] 2 Ch. 47, CA at 58 *per* Buckley LJ.
[38] See generally *Hunter v. Canary Wharf Ltd* [1997] A.C. 655, HL. But in relation to freeholders who are not entitled to possession, see below, para. 2–008.
[39] See para. 2–008.
[40] See above, paras. 2–002 to 2–003.

Tenants under tenancies of even short duration can maintain an action: weekly tenants[41] and even tenants at will[42] can do so.[43]

Other Occupiers

2–006   As indicated above[44] it has long been held that mere licensees[45] cannot maintain an action in nuisance. However, licensees with a right of possession will be able to bring an action in nuisance even if they have no title to the land in question.[46] Further, an occupier with *de facto* possession will be able to found an action in nuisance since actual possession is protected against all but the rightful owner.[47] Similarly, it has been held that "tolerated trespassers" whose secure tenancies under the Housing Act 1985 have determined but who enjoy possession are entitled to maintain an action for nuisance even against their former landlord.[48]

Owner of incorporeal hereditaments

2–007   Owners of incorporeal hereditaments such as easements even though they do not carry with them the right to exclusive possession of land may maintain an action in nuisance for the disturbance of their rights.[49]

Reversioners

2–008   Although a reversioner to a lease does not have a right to immediate possession he does have a sufficient interest to maintain an action in nuisance, but to do so he must show some damage to his reversionary interest. It seems that for a reversioner to have such a cause of action he must show that the damage is of a permanent nature.[50]

In *Jones v. Llanrwst UDC*.[51] Parker J. stated that it was "reasonably certain" that a reversioner could not maintain an action "in the nature of trespass" (the context here indicates that nuisance is covered by this phrase):

> "... including, I think, actions for the infringement of natural rights arising out of the ownership of land, without alleging and proving injury to the reversion. If the thing complained of is of

---

[41] *Jones v. Chappell* (1875) L.R. Eq.539.

[42] *Burgess v. Woodstock* [1955] 4 D.L.R. 615.

[43] But see *Cunard v. Antifyre Ltd* [1933] 1 K.B. 551 at 557, DC.

[44] Para. 2–002.

[45] See *Malone v. Laskey* [1907] 2 K.B. 141, CA; *Hunter v. Canary Wharf Ltd* [1997] A.C. 655, HL.

[46] *Foster v. Warblington UDC* [1906] 1 K.B. 648, CA; *Charing Cross Electricity Supply Co. v. Hydraulic Power Co.* [1913] 3 K.B. 442, [1914] 3 K.B. 772, CA; *Newcastle-under-Lyme Corpn v. Wolstanton* [1947] 1 Ch. 92 *per* Evershed J at 104, 108; [1947] 1 Ch. 427, CA.

[47] See *Hunter v. Canary Wharf Ltd* [1997] A.C. 655, HL in particular at 704 *per* Lord Hoffman.

[48] *Pemberton v. Southwark LBC* [2000] 1 W.L.R. 1672, CA; see para. 1–014 above.

[49] See para. 2–093 below.

[50] *Jones v. Llanrwst UDC (No. 2)* [1911] 1 Ch. 393, 404.

[51] *ibid.*

such a permanent nature that the reversion may be injured, the question whether the reversion is or is not injured is a question for the jury."

However, Parker J. went on to define what was meant by "permanent"[52]:

"I take 'permanent', in this connection, to mean such as will continue indefinitely unless something is done to remove it. Thus a building which infringes ancient lights is permanent within the rule, for, though it can be removed before the reversion falls into possession, still it will continue until it be removed. On the other hand, a noisy trade, and the exercise of a right of way, are not in their nature permanent within the rule, for they cease of themselves unless there be some one to continue them."

Accordingly, it has been held that a reversioner can have no cause of action in respect of interference with the land by noise or smoke or other nuisance of a "temporary nature"[53] even if such a nuisance drives away the tenant or reduces the letting value of the property.[54] It has been stated, in the context of an action where a defendant admitted negligently damaging a landlord's property, that the "general rule . . . that a reversioner can only sue in respect of damage which will affect the property when the reversion falls in . . . is not of universal applicability"[55]; but in the context of the law of nuisance where inteference with enjoyment of land itself is the basis of the action[56] it seems to be settled that a reversioner has no cause of action save where a nuisance is "permanent". A reversioner does not enjoy any right to possession until the lease is determined, so it is hard to see how interferences which will not affect his enjoyment of possession when the lease determines can be actionable in the tort of private nuisance. On the other hand, a reversioner can sue for acts which tend either to destroy evidence of the existence on adjoining land of a servitude[57] in his favour or to establish against him that his own land is burdened with a servitude in favour of the adjoining land.[58] Thus, a reversioner can sue in respect of the erection of a hoarding which interferes with his ancient

---

[52] ibid. See also *Rust v. Victoria Graving Dock Company* (1887) 36 Ch.D. 113, CA.

[53] *Simpson v. Savage* (1859) 1 C.B. N.S. 347; *Mott v. Shoolbred* (1875) L.R. 20 Eq. 22; *Cooper v. Crabtree* (1882) 20 Ch.D. 589, CA; *House Property and Investment Co. v. HP Horse Nail Co.* (1885) 29 Ch.D. 190; *Mayfair Property Co v. Johnston* [1894] 1 Ch. 508.

[54] *Mumford v. Oxford, Worcester etc. Ry Co.* (1856) 1 H. & N. 34; *Simpson v. Savage* (1859) 1 C.B., N.S. 347.

[55] *Harris v. Hall*, The Independent, August 18, 1992, CA.

[56] See above, para. 2–002.

[57] *i.e.* a burden on land which affects the owner's right to use the land in a certain way or puts an obligation on the owner to allow another to use the land in a certain way or take something from that land. See 2–093 below for examples of nuisances affecting such rights.

[58] See 2–027 below; proof of damage is not required to maintain an action for such interferences.

lights,[59] the locking of a gate across a right of way,[60] and the discharge of sewage from a drain.[61] Physical injury such as is caused by vibration may also give the reversioner a cause of action.[62]

As stated above, a reversioner can only bring an action in nuisance in respect of interferences with the land which will inevitably affect his interest when it falls into possession.[63] A reversioner cannot bring an action for interferences which might cease before his interest falls into possession because his action would not be based upon what is done but upon a fear that it will continue.[64] Actionable nuisances are limited to injuries to those rights which are appurtenant to the right of possession and physical enjoyment of the land: an interference with the rental value of the land during the subsistence of a lease is not sufficient. Although this is conceptually intelligible, this is not an entirely satisfactory position since a "temporary" nuisance (which may cease before the end of the term of the lease) might affect the rent of the property upon a rent review during the term of the lease but have no effect on the landlord's rights to possession at the end of the term. A landlord would probably have no remedy in negligence since his loss in such a case would be purely economic.[65]

Persons who acquire their interest in the property subject to a nuisance

2–009 Where there is a continuing actionable nuisance, the person in possession of an interest in property can recover the loss incurred by him in remedying the damage caused by a continuing nuisance whether the damage occurred before or after he acquired the land.[66] The principle is that where there is a continuing nuisance of which the defendant knew or ought to have known, reasonable remedial expenditure may be recovered by the owner who has to incur it.[67]

---

[59] *Shadwell v. Hutchinson* (1831) M. & W. 350, *Metropolitan Association v. Petch* (1858) 5 C.B., N.S. 504.

[60] See *Kidgill v. Moor* (1850) 9 C.B. 364; see also *Bell v. Midland Ry* (1861) 10 C.B., N.S. 287.

[61] *Jones v. Llanrwst UDC (No. 2)* [1911] 1 Ch. 393, 404.

[62] *Meux's Brewery Co. v. City of London Electric Co.* [1895] 1 Ch. 287, 317; *Colwell v. St Pancras Borough Council* [1904] 1 Ch. 707.

[63] *Simpson v. Savage* (1859) 1 C.B., N.S. 347, 362.

[64] See *Jones v. Llanrwst UDC (No. 2)* [1911] 1 Ch. 393.

[65] *Cf. Spartan Steel & Alloys Ltd v. Martin & Co. (Contractors) Ltd* [1973] Q.B. 27; *Candlewood Navigation Corp. Ltd v. Mitsui O.S.K. Lines Ltd* [1986] A.C. 1; *Murphy v. Brentwood District Council* [1991] 1 A.C. 398. However, in the case of *Harris v. Hall, The Independent*, August 18, 1992, the Court of Appeal compensated a landlord for loss of rent under a lease where the landlord's premises were physically damaged as a result of the defendant negligently driving his car into the demised premises resulting in an abatement of the tenant's rent.

[66] *Thompson v. Gibson* 7 M. & W. 456; *Masters v. Brent LBC* [1978] 1 Q.B. 841.

[67] *Delaware Mansions Limited v. Westminster City Council* [2001] UKHL 55 especially at para. 38 *per* Lord Cooke.

Who can be sued

Generally

"Nuisance involves doing something on adjoining or nearby land which 2–010 constitutes an interference with the utility of the plaintiff's land. The primary defendant is the person who causes the nuisance by doing the acts in question".[68] In principle there seems to be no good reason why the primary defendant should have any legal interest in the land on which he causes the nuisance.

In the case of *Hussain v. Lancaster City Council*[69] the defendant council was held not to be liable for interference with the plaintiffs' enjoyment of their land by racial harassment taking place outside the council's land. It was held that the acts complained of "did not involve the tenants' use of the tenants' land and therefore fell outside the scope of the tort"[70] and it was held that the landlord was not responsible for the tenants' acts. This statement appears to be correct in the context of that case. The issue was whether the landlord could be held to be liable for the conduct of its tenants. There is no good reason why a landlord qua landlord should be liable in nuisance for the conduct of a tenant on land which has no connection with the relationship between landlord and tenant. On the other hand, we suggest that this statement should not be taken to indicate that in general a defendant must have some interest in land to be liable for a nuisance which he causes on that land. In general, there is:

"no reason why if the defendant as a licensee or trespasser misuses someone else's land, he should not be liable for a nuisance in the same way as an adjoining occupier would be".[71]

It is suggested that it remains correct to state that:

"the person liable for a nuisance is the actual wrongdoer, whether or not he is in occupation of the land".[72]

In addition to the person who has created the nuisance, others may be liable. Thus, the owner of land may be liable for nuisances caused by occupants where he authorises or continues the nuisance, landlords may

---

[68] *Southwark LBC v. Mills* [2001] 1 A.C. 1 at 15D; [1999] 4 All E.R. 449 at 459g *per* Lord Hoffman. See also *per* Lord Millett at 464 c.

[69] [1999] 4 All E.R. 125, CA. This case is dealt with more fully below.

[70] at 144 e-f *per* Hirst LJ.

[71] *Southport Corporation v. Esso Petroleum Co Ltd* [1956] A.C. 218 at 224–225 *per* Devlin J, *obiter*, see also Morris L.J. [1954] 2 Q.B. 182, 204 (but at p. 242 Lord Radcliffe agreed with Lord Denning who took a contrary view (see [1954] 2 Q.B. 182, 196–197).

[72] Clerk and Lindsell on *Torts*, 18th ed, para. 19–49; *Lippiatt v. South Gloucestershire Council* [1999] 4 All E.R. 149 at 152 g-h *per* Evans LJ (see also at 160 e-f *per* Sir Christopher Staughton). See also *Sedleigh-Denfield v. O'Callaghan* [1940] A.C. 880, 918; *Hall v. Beckenham Corporation* [1949] 1 K.B. 716; *Halsey v. Esso Petroleum Co Ltd* [1961] 1 W.L.R. 683, 699–700.

be liable for the condition of their tenanted premises, parties may be vicariously liable for their servants, agents and (in some circumstances) independent contractors, and occupiers of land may be liable for adopting or continuing existing nuisances which they did not themselves create. It is clear, however, that in order to be liable for nuisance, a defendant must either have caused the nuisance or have some *de facto* or *de jure* control over land on which the nuisance occurs. Accordingly, while a local highway authority in which trees on the highway are vested may be liable for damage caused by the trees to adjoining property,[73] a local planning authority is not liable at common law for nuisances caused by development on a developer's land merely because it has granted planning permission[74] (and, indeed, it has no statutory duty under the planning legislation to individuals in relation to interferences with the enjoyment of land caused by development resulting from the grant of planning permission).[75]

Defendants, fault and foreseeability

GENERALLY

2–011   Fault of some kind is almost always necessary for a defendant to be liable for a nuisance and fault generally involves foreseeability.[76] The touchstone of nuisance, however, is the unreasonableness of the interference and not its foreseeability. In practice a foreseeable interference may often be unreasonable and an unforeseeable interference one which a claimant should be expected to tolerate,[77] but this is not necessarily so in all circumstances. In some cases, the defendant's behaviour which results in an interference may be of such a nature that any interference resulting from that behaviour would be unreasonable even if unforeseeable.

The degree of fault (if any) and the extent to which this involves the foreseeability of the harm done in order for an actionable nuisance to be established depends upon the circumstances and the nature of the interference with the claimant's land. These circumstances may be examined in three categories: (1) where the defendant causes the nuisance; (2) where by neglect of some duty the defendant allows the nuisance to arise; (3) where, when the nuisance has arisen without the defendant's own act or

---

[73] See *Hurst v. Hampshire CC* [1997] 2 E.G.L.R. 164, CA and see 2–050 below ("trees").

[74] *Lam v. Brennan* [1997] 3 PLR 22, CA.

[75] *ibid*. See also *Buxton v. Minister for Housing and Local Government* [1961] 1 Q.B. 278, 283 *per* Salmon J; see also 2–031 below in relation to the effect of the grant of planning permission.

[76] *The Wagon Mound (No. 2)* [1967] 1 A.C. 617, 639 PC. See also *Cambridge Water Co. Ltd v. Eastern Counties Leather plc* [1994] 2 A.C. 264. See generally, Dias, "Trouble on oiled waters: Problems of Wagon Mound (No. 2)" [1967] C.L.J. 62.

[77] The rule is a rule of "give and take, of live and let live"; *Kennaway v. Thompson* [1981] Q.B. 88, CA; and see also *Cambridge Water Co. Ltd v. Eastern Counties Leather plc* [1994] 2 A.C. 264, HL 299–300 *per* Lord Goff; *Jan de Nul (U.K.) Ltd v. N.V. Royale Belge* [2000] 2 Lloyd's Rep 700, 713 *per* Moore-Bick J.

default, he omits to remedy it within a reasonable time after he became, or ought to have become, aware of it.[78]

DEFENDANT CAUSING NUISANCE

First, where a person has created a nuisance by actions for which he is responsible, the fact that he has taken all reasonable care will not exonerate him from liability; the relevant test is whether the user of land which gives rise to the nuisance is a reasonable one.[79] The touchstone of what constitutes an actionable nuisance is whether the interference is reasonable or unreasonable "according to the ordinary usages of mankind living in society, or more correctly in a particular society".[80] The foreseeability of harm must be a factor to be considered in assessing whether the activities of a particular defendant are reasonable; but foreseeability in itself is not a sufficient determinant of whether a defendant's activities amount to a nuisance.

2–012

Accordingly, some interferences, even though foreseeable and preventable, must be tolerated by the claimant:

> "The question is whether the neighbour is using his property reasonably, having regard to the fact that he has a neighbour. The neighbour who is complaining must remember, too, that the other man can use his property in a reasonable way and there must be a measure of 'give and take, live and let live.'"[81]

On the other hand, where foreseeability of harm makes the defendant's activities unreasonable, the foreseeability must be distinguished from the foreseeability which is present where a defendant has been negligent. For instance, in nuisance, "an occupier may incur liability for the emission of noxious fumes or noise although he has used the utmost care in the building of the premises."[82] Similarly, in the case of *Rapier v. London Tramways Co.*[83] it was held that the company could be liable for the nuisance caused by the smell of its horses notwithstanding that the company had taken all reasonable care to prevent it. The activity of the defendant was such that its unpleasant consequences were foreseeable and thus it was an unreasonable interference constituting a nuisance even though the activity was not carried out negligently.

---

[78] See *Noble v. Harrison* [1926] 2 K.B. 332, 338 DC; *Leakey v. National Trust* [1980] Q.B. 485, 516, CA.
[79] See *Cambridge Water Co. Ltd v. Eastern Counties Leather plc* [1994] 2 A.C. 264, HL 300 *per* Lord Goff. See also Friedman (1943) 59 L.Q.R. 63: strictness of liability in these circumstances.
[80] *Sedleigh-Denfield v. O'Callaghan* [1940] A.C. 880, 903 HL; see *Cambridge Water Co. Ltd v. Eastern Counties Leather plc* [1994] 2 A.C. 264, HL 300, 299 *per* Lord Goff.
[81] *Kennaway v. Thompson* [1980] 3 All E.R. 329, CA 333, *per* Lawton L.J.
[82] See *The Wagon Mound (No. 2)* [1967] 1 A.C. 617, PC.
[83] [1893] 2 Ch. 588, CA; and see *Rosewell v. Prior* (1701) 12 Mod. 635. But contrast *Ilford UDC v. Beal* [1925] 1 K.B. 671; criticised by Friedman (1943) 59 L.Q.R. 63.

However, although negligence is not a prerequisite of liability for a nuisance,[84] the negligent behaviour of the defendant or indeed his deliberate behaviour may be taken into account in determining whether the interference with the claimant's land is unreasonable and unlawful so as to constitute a nuisance.[85]

NEGLECT OR DEFAULT IN A DUTY GIVING RISE TO NUISANCE

2–013   Secondly, where the defendant does not create a nuisance, he may be responsible for it if it has arisen due to his breach of duty. The imposition of a duty in respect of nuisances will usually depend upon the foreseeability of some harm from the defendant's activities. On the other hand, breach of such a duty will not always depend upon the foreseeability of the particular harm constituting the breach.

Instances where the imposition of a duty upon a defendant depends upon the foreseeability of the nuisance include those cases where landlords have been held liable for an interference with adjoining occupiers' rights through letting premises in a condition which will lead to a nuisance. In such circumstances a landlord generally will only be held liable where he knew or ought to have known of the nuisance at the commencement of the tenancy.[86]

There are other situations in which a defendant's breach of duty will not depend upon the foreseeability of the particular nuisance in respect of which the action is brought. For instance, an employer is liable for nuisances arising from dangerous operations caused by his independent contractors notwithstanding that he has taken all reasonable steps to ensure that the independent contractor is competent.[87] The strict duty on the employer in these circumstances arises because the operations which result in the nuisance might foreseeably, or in the natural course of things, lead to the nuisance.[88] However, the breach of the duty does not depend upon the foreseeability of the particular interference in respect of which an action is brought since the employer will be responsible if there is a failure by the contractor to take the necessary precautions to prevent the nuisance from arising;[89] liability may arise even if the employer employs a reasonably competent contractor and takes reasonable (though not all necessary) precautions to avoid the nuisance arising.

---

[84] *The Wagon Mound (No. 2)* [1967] 1 A.C. 617, PC. *Cambridge Water Co Ltd v. Eastern Counties Leather plc* [1994] 2 A.C. 264, HL; *Jan de Nul (U.K.) Ltd v. N.V. Royale Belge* [2000] 2 Lloyd's Rep 700, 713 Moore-Bick J *cf. Sedleigh-Denfield v. O'Callaghan* [1940] A.C. 880, 897, 904 HL.

[85] See *Christie v. Davies* [1893] 1 Ch. 316, 326; *Hollywood Silver Fox Farms v. Emmett* [1936] 2 K.B. 469; *Christie v. Davies* [1893] 1 Ch. 316, 326. See 2–033 below.

[86] See below, para. 2–019.

[87] See below, para. 2–021.

[88] See *Bower v. Peate* (1876) 1 Q.B.D. 321, 326, D.C.

[89] *Matania v. National Provincial Bank* [1936] 2 All E.R. 633, 646, CA.

Similarly under the rule in *Rylands v. Fletcher*,[90] which is historically and conceptually part of the law of nuisance,[91] a duty arises where a person brings onto his own land and collects and keeps there anything that is likely to do mischief if it escapes, *i.e.* it is foreseeable that mischief would result; but the duty will be breached if the thing escapes and causes harm notwithstanding that the particular escape is not foreseeable.

It seems that in some rare circumstances foreseeability may play a part neither in the creation of the duty nor in the liability for its breach. In *Wringe v. Cohen*[92] the Court of Appeal laid down a principle that:

> "if, owing to want of repair, premises on a highway become danger-
> ous and, therefore, a nuisance and a passer-by or an adjoining owner
> suffers damage by their collapse, the occupier, or the owner if he has
> undertaken the duty of repair is answerable whether he knew or
> ought to have known of the danger or not."

This case of public nuisance is hard to reconcile with other instances where the nuisance is not directly caused by the defendant. It may well be that if the House of Lords were to review the authorities it would overrule *Wringe v. Cohen*. Certainly that case seems to be inconsistent with the case of *Caminer v. Northern & London Investment Trust Ltd*[93] in which an occupier of land was held not liable for public nuisance where the tree on his land adjoining a highway injured a passer-by, because the tree was apparently sound and inspection by an expert would not have revealed that it was dangerous. Although *Wringe v. Cohen* does not appear to have been cited to the House of Lords in the *Caminer* case, it is hard to justify an owner of land with a tree on it which causes damage being in a different position from an owner of land with a building on it which causes damage.[94]

CONTINUANCE OF A NUISANCE

Thirdly, when the nuisance has arisen without the defendant's own act or default, he will only be liable if he continues the nuisance. In *Sedleigh Denfield v. O'Callaghan*,[95] it was held that an occupier of land continues a nuisance "if with knowledge or presumed knowledge of its existence he fails to take any reasonable means to bring an end to it though he has had ample time to do so".[96] Applying this principle in that case, the House of

2–014

---

[90] (1866) L.R. 1 Ex. 265; (1868) L.R. 3, H.L. 330; see below, paras. 2–056 *et seq.*; and *Cambridge Water Co. Ltd v. Eastern Counties Leather plc* [1994] 2 A.C. 264, HL.
[91] See Newark (1949) 65 L.Q.R. 480, 488.
[92] [1940] 1 K.B. 229.
[93] [1951] A.C. 88; see also *Chapman v. Barking and Dagenham LBC* [1997] 2 E.G.L.R. 141.
[94] Particularly since the case of *Leakey v. National Trust* [1980] Q.B. 485, CA, which extended the scope of nuisances to include liability for natural occurrences. See following paragraphs.
[95] [1940] A.C. 880, HL; below, 2–023.
[96] [1940] A.C. 880, HL *per* Viscount Maugham p. 894.

Lords held that the defendants were liable for flooding caused by a culvert which had been placed on their land by a trespasser, which became blocked.

Likewise, applying this principle, it has been held by the Court of Appeal that a highway authority which had constructed a culvert to take a natural stream under the highway which was adequate at the time of construction but which subsequently became inadequate because of development by others in the area and which could no longer cope with the velocity of flow during heavy rain was under a duty to take reasonable steps to ensure that the culvert did not cause flooding.[97]

It is implicit within this principle that if the defendant is to be liable there must be some foreseeability of harm since (a) the defendant must know or be presumed to know of the nuisance and (b) he must fail to use "reasonable" steps to bring the nuisance to an end — what is reasonable in any given situation will usually involve some consideration of the foreseeable consequences of *not* taking those steps.

If, on the basis of *Sedleigh-Denfield v. O'Callaghan*, an occupier of land can be under duties in relation to the condition of his land caused by trespassers, there is some force in the view that it is illogical to hold that a landowner can be under no duty in relation to similar conditions which occur naturally.[98] Accordingly, although a departure from the traditional view of nuisance as being concerned with non-natural uses of land,[99] the principle in *Sedleigh-Denfield v. O'Callaghan* has been extended to hazards caused by nature. The Privy Council has applied the principle to the spreading of fire from a smouldering tree,[1] and the Court of Appeal has done so to the falling of soil from an embankment,[2] and the loss of support due to progressive slippage (albeit in the latter case the defendant was not liable).[3] In considering how far an occupier of land may be liable for naturally occurring hazards, the Courts have held that there are limits both on when the duty arises and on what is required of a defendant in order to comply with the duty. In setting both limits foreseeability plays a part.

First, in relation to when the duty arises, it was held in *Holbeck Hall Hotel Ltd v. Scarborough Borough Council*[4] that:

---

[97] *Bybrook Barn Centre Ltd v. Kent County Council*, [2001] B.L.R. 55, CA. Contrast *Radstock Co-operative & Industrial Society Ltd v. Norton-Radstock Urban District Council* [1968] Ch. 605, CA (Sachs LJ dissenting).

[98] See Prof. A. L. Goodhart (1930) 4 C.L.J.13, in particular at 26–27 ("Liability for Things Naturally on the Land").

[99] See in particular the reluctant conclusion of Shaw LJ in his judgment in *Leakey v. National Trust* [1980] 1 Q.B. 485, CA at 527–529.

[1] *Goldman v. Hargrave* [1967] 1 A.C. 645, P.C.

[2] *Leakey v. National Trust* [1980] 1 Q.B. 485. See also *Bradburn v. Lindsay* [1983] 2 All E.R. 408: defendant held liable for spread of dry rot to adjoining premises where he could reasonably have appreciated danger.

[3] *Holbeck Hall Hotel Ltd v. Scarborough Borough Council*, [2000] Q.B. 836, CA and see 2–112.

[4] [2000] Q.B. 836, CA, para. 42 *per* Stuart-Smith LJ.

"The duty arises when the defect is known and the hazard or danger to the Claimants' land is reasonably foreseeable, that is to say it is a danger which a reasonable man with knowledge of the defect should have foreseen as likely to eventuate in the near future. It is the existence of the defect coupled with the danger that constitutes the nuisance; it is knowledge or presumed knowledge of the nuisance that involves liability for continuing it when it could reasonably be abated".

The defect referred to is one which:

"must be patent; that is to say that it is a defect which can be observed; it is no answer for the landowner to say that he did not observe it, if a responsible servant did so; or if a reasonable landowner he, or the person to whom he entrusted the responsibility of looking after the land, should have seen it. But if the defect is latent, the landowner or occupier is not to be held liable simply because, if he had made further investigation, he would have discovered it[5]".

Secondly, the steps which must be taken to discharge the duty which arises to abate a nuisance which is not caused by the defendant are also qualified. The duty is to take reasonable means to bring the nuisance to an end. In *Leakey v. National Trust*,[6] Megaw LJ said: **2–015**

"The duty is a duty to do that which is reasonable in all the circumstances, and no more than what, if anything, is reasonable to prevent or minimise the known risk of damage or injury to one's neighbour or to his property."

What is reasonable in the circumstances must to some extent depend on what the foreseeable consequences of the nuisance might be. However, unlike the tort of negligence where liability is imposed upon those who fail to do that which objectively a reasonable or prudent man would do whether the actual extent of the damage caused is foreseeable or not provided that the harm caused is of a type which is foreseeable, the duty upon landowners in respect of nuisances naturally occurring on their land, is a "measured duty".[7] The duty in the case of a defendant who finds that his land contains a naturally occurring nuisance is less strict than the objective duty imposed under the law of negligence. In the case of liability for continuing a nuisance which occurs naturally, harm is caused by reason of the "non-feasance" of the defendant who has done nothing to create the

---

[5] *ibid*; see also *Rees v. Skerrett* [2001] EWCA Civ. 760 *per* Lloyd J.
[6] [1980] 1 Q.B. 485, CA, at 524; see also *Rees v. Skerrett* [2001] EWCA Civ. 760.
[7] *Holbeck Hall Hotel Limited v. Scarborough Borough Council*, [2000] Q.B. 836, CA paras 45–49; see also *Bybrook Barn Centre Ltd v. Kent County Council*, [2001] B.L.R. 55, CA; *British Gas plc v. Stockport MBC* [2001] EWCA Civ. 212 paras 49–53. *Marcic v. Thames Water Utilities Ltd* [2002] EWCA Civ. 65, para. 94; *Southwark L.B.C. v. Long* [2002] EWCA Civ. 403, para.66

danger which has arisen. In *Leakey v. National Trust*, Megaw L.J. described the duty in such circumstances as follows[8]:

> "The defendant's duty is to do that which it is reasonable for him to do. The criteria of reasonableness include, in respect of a duty of this nature, the factor of what the particular man — not the average man — can be expected to do, having regard, amongst other things, where a serious expenditure of money is required to eliminate or reduce the danger, to his means. Just as, where physical effort is required to avert an immediate danger, the defendant's age and physical condition may be relevant in deciding what is reasonable, so also logic and good sense require that, where the expenditure of money is required, the defendant's capacity to find the money is relevant. But this can only be in the way of a broad, and not a detailed, assessment; and in arriving at a judgment on reasonableness a broad assessment may be relevant in some cases as to the neighbour's capacity to protect himself from damage, whether by way of some form of barrier on his own land or by way of providing funds for expenditure on agreed works on the land of the defendant."

Although the duty is objective to the extent that the defendant must do what is reasonable, the objectivity is limited: to fulfil his duty the defendant is only required to do that which it is reasonable for him to do in the circumstances in which he finds himself. These circumstances will include his relationship with and the position of the claimant. Thus in the case of *Holbeck Hall Hotel Limited v. Scarborough Borough Council*[9] where natural land slippage on the defendant's land caused damage to the claimant's hotel, Stuart-Smith LJ[10] considered that it was not "just and reasonable . . . to impose liability for damage which is greater in extent than anything that was foreseen or foreseeable (without further geological investigation), especially where the defect and danger existed as much on the Claimants' land as the Defendant's" (and in the particular circumstances of the case, liability was not imposed). On the other hand in *Rees v. Skerrett*[11] the Court of Appeal held a landowner to be liable to his neighbour where it could have been foreseen that his neighbour's house would suffer harm unless weatherproofing was provided, and where in the circumstances (demolition having taken place) weatherproofing was not provided when it was reasonable to do so.

From the above, one can conclude that although foreseeability of harm to the claimant's land is not the determining factor in whether or not liability is to be imposed on a defendant on whose land there exists a hazard not of his own making, either because the hazard occurs by natural

---

[8] [1980] 1 Q.B. 485, CA at 526. See too *Marcic v. Thames Water Utilities Ltd* [2002] EWCA Civ. para. 94.

[9] *Holbeck Hall Hotel Limited v. Scarborough Borough Council*, [2000] Q.B. 836, CA.

[10] See para. 51.

[11] [2001] EWCA Civ. 760.

causes or by the acts of a person for whom the defendant is not responsible,[12] it is clearly an important matter to consider both in the imposition of a duty (to the extent that foreseeability may lead to presumed knowledge of the hazard) and in determining what steps are required to discharge the duty (to the extent that what steps are reasonable may depend to some degree on the foreseeable consequences of failing to take those steps).

Fault: nuisance, negligence and the evidential burden

Even where liability for nuisance is dependent upon the breach of a duty of care,[13] there is an important practical distinction between the torts of nuisance and negligence. Pleading a claim in nuisance as opposed to negligence:

2–016

> "greatly affects the burden of proof. It puts the legal burden . . . on the defendant, whereas in negligence it is on the plaintiff."[14]

In the tort of negligence the burden of proof is upon the claimant to show that there has been a lack of care on the defendant's part. In the tort of nuisance, once the interference with the land has been established the burden is on the defendant to show that there has been no lack of care or that the interference is a reasonable one.

Examples of potential defendants

CREATOR OF THE NUISANCE AND CONTROLLER OF LAND FROM WHICH NUISANCE EMANATES

As indicated in the preceding paragraphs, a person who by himself or his servants causes a nuisance will be liable for it and its continuance whether or not he is owner or occupier of the land on which the nuisance occurs. This may be so whether or not he is able to stop the nuisance. Accordingly, in *Thompson v. Gibson*[15] where the defendants superintended and directed the construction of a building on land belonging to a third party and that building interfered with the plaintiff's market, it was held that the defendants could be liable for the continuance of the nuisance notwithstanding their inability to remove it.[16] In

2–017

---

[12] Compare *Cambridge Water Co. Ltd v. Eastern Counties Leather plc* [1994] 2 A.C. 264, HL 300 at which Lord Goff refers to both sorts of cause together.

[13] See above, paras 2–013 to 2–015.

[14] *Martin v. Wheeler*, The Times, February 1, 1956, *per* Denning L.J. See also *Southport Corpn v. Esso Petroleum* [1954] 2 Q.B. 152, 197; *Home Brewery Co. Ltd v. William Davies & Co. (Leicester) Ltd* [1987] 1 Q.B. 339, 350, 351. *Marcic v. Thames Water Utilities Ltd* [2002] EWCA Civ. 65, paras 84–86; *Southwark L.B.C. v. Long* [2002] EWCA Civ. 403, para. 65.

[15] (1841) 7 M. & W. 456.

[16] See para. 2–012 above.

Dalton v. Angus[17] a contractor who pulled down a house could be liable (as well as the owner of the house) for an interference with an easement of lateral support to an adjoining house.

An owner of land from which a nuisance emanates will be liable for a nuisance if he retains sufficient control over the land such that he can be said to be responsible for the manner of use of the land even though others are in occupation of the land as licensees.[18] An owner of such land may also be liable for a nuisance even though the premises are empty if they are in such a state as to cause a nuisance.[19]

LANDOWNERS LIABLE FOR OTHER OCCUPIERS

2–018   A lessor or licensor of land will be liable for the nuisances caused by his lessees or licensees if he authorises them to cause or to continue a nuisance.[20] The landlord's authorisation may be express or implied. Further, where land is occupied by trespassers, in principle there seems to be nothing to prevent the landlord being liable for nuisances caused by their presence if it can be established that the landlord has tolerated their presence or has acted in such a way that he can be said to have adopted the nuisance.[21]

Where the landlord has granted a lease or licence, he will be liable for a nuisance which was likely to result from the purposes for which the lease or licence was granted.[22] Accordingly, in *Tetley v. Chitty*[23] a local authority landlord which had licensed, then let, land to a go-kart club for the express purpose of developing and using the site as a go-kart track was held liable in nuisance for the interference with the enjoyment of neighbouring property caused by the noise of go-karting. McNeill J. in his judgment indicated[24] that the law does not require that the nuisance be a necessary consequence of the use of land for a landlord to be liable: it is sufficient for a landlord to authorise his tenant to do an act which was likely to cause a nuisance. Similarly, where unreasonable use of a roof area demised with a residential flat caused a nuisance to the flat below and this was authorised by the landlord, the landlord was liable for a nuisance.[25]

---

[17] (1881) 6 App.Cas. 740, HL.

[18] *A-G v. Stone* (1895) 13 T.L.R. 76 (land occupied by gypsies: owner liable); see also *Lippiatt v. South Gloucestershire District Council* [1999] 4 All E.R. 149, CA and para 2–018 below *cf. Page v. Epsom & Ewell Borough Council* [1980] J.P.L. 396, CA.

[19] *Coventry City Council v. Doyle* [1981] 2 All E.R. 184 (Public Health Act 1936, s.92).

[20] *Smith v. Scott* [1973] Ch. 314 at 321 *per* Pennycuick V-C; *Southwark LBC v. Mills* [2001] 1 A.C. 1 at 15; [1999] 4 All E.R. 449, HL at 459 *per* Lord Hoffman. See also *Chartered Trust plc v. Davies* [1997] 2 E.G.L.R. 83, CA (landlord liable for continuation of nuisance where it failed to take steps to prevent nuisance caused by activities associated with a pawn brokers shop).

[21] See *Lippiatt v. South Gloucestershire District Council* [1994] 4 All 149; see below, 2–018a.

[22] *Harris v. James* (1876) 45 L.J.O.B. 545 (burning Lime); *Jenkins v. Jackson* (1888) 40 Ch. 1071 (dancing); *R. v. Shorrock* [1993] 3 All E.R. 917 (public nuisance: "acid house" party).

[23] [1986] 1 All E.R. 663.

[24] [1986] 1 All E.R. 663, 671.

[25] *Sampson v. Hodson-Pressinger* [1981] 3 All E.R. 710 CA as explained by Lord Hoffmann in *Southwark LBC v. Mills* [2001] 1 A.C. 1 at 16; [1999] 4 All E.R. 451, HL at 460.

A lessor may also be liable for a nuisance on or emanating from the premises which he has let when the nuisance was known or ought to have been known to have existed at the commencement of the tenancy or licence. In such circumstances, it may be inferred that the landlord has impliedly authorised the nuisance.[26]

In *Smith v. Scott*[27] on the other hand, a local authority landlord was not liable for the nuisance caused by a family of tenants who had previously been homeless because there was no express or implied authority for the homeless family to cause a nuisance: the local authority had let the house from which the nuisance emanated to the tenants on conditions of tenancy which expressly prohibited the committing of a nuisance.[28] Likewise in *Hussain v. Lancaster City Council*[29] a local authority landlord was not liable for nuisance caused by racial harassment of the plaintiffs which was unauthorised and not adopted by the landlord.

Further, for the landlord to be liable for the activities of his tenants, the activities of the tenants about which complaint is made must themselves constitute a nuisance. Accordingly, in *Southwark LBC v. Mills*[30] where the landlord let residential premises to tenants who used those premises in the usual way for everyday activities which disturbed the enjoyment of their neighbours by reason of inadequate soundproofing, the landlords were not liable to the neighbours in nuisance since the ordinary use of residential premises did not amount to a nuisance.

A landlord may also be strictly liable for fires caused by occupiers of his premises: this is considered further below.[31]

The liability of a landlord for nuisances on or emanating from his land will not exclude the liability of his tenant for a nuisance on premises occupied by him.[32] For instance, a tenant may be liable for a nuisance caused by the dilapidated state of his premises though the landlord has positively covenanted with the tenant to carry out repairs to the dilapidations which have caused the nuisance;[33] but in such a case the tenant will have a remedy on the covenant against the landlord.

---

[26] *Rosewell v. Prior* (1701) 2 Salk 460 (stopping of ancient lights); *Todd v. Flight* (1860) 9 C.B. N.S. 377; *Brew Bros Ltd v. Snax (Ross) Ltd* [1970] 1 Q.B. 612, 636 (dilapidated premises); see also *Ribee v. Norrie* [2001] L&TR 239, CA (landlord granting licence over common parts liable for fire caused by licensee). See para 2–019 in relation to the landlord's responsibility for dilapidations.

[27] [1973] 1 Ch. 314.

[28] See also *Habinteg Housing Association v. James* [1994] N.P.C. 132: landlords not liable for cockroach infestation from tenanted premises over which they had no control; *Mowan v. London Borough of Wandsworth* [2001] 1 E.G.C.S. 4, CA: landlords not liable for nuisances caused by tenants which they had not authorised.

[29] [1999] 4 All E.R. 125.

[30] [2001] 1 A.C. 1; [1999] 4 All E.R. 451, HL.

[31] See 2–043 (Act of Stranger) and 2–067 (*Rylands v. Fletcher*)

[32] *Wilchick v. Marks and Silverstone* [1934] 2 K.B. 56, 68.

[33] *St Anne's Well Brewery Co. Ltd v. Roberts* (1929) 140 L.T. 1, 8.

LANDOWNERS LIABLE FOR OFF-SITE ACTIVITIES OF OTHER OCCUPIERS

2–018a   A landowner may be liable for a nuisance caused by the occupiers of his land even where their activities take place outside that land.[34] However, if such liability is to be imposed on a person as owner of land the nuisance must in some way be connected with the occupation of the land.

Thus, in the case of *Lippiatt v. South Gloucestershire District Council*[35] the Court of Appeal held there was an arguable claim for nuisance against the defendant council which was alleged to have tolerated on its land the presence of travellers who habitually misbehaved, trespassed on the claimant's land, obstructed access to the claimant's land, and dumped rubbish and tethered animals on the claimant's land.

This case can be distinguished from *Hussain v. Lancaster City Council*[36] where the defendant council was held not to be liable where the claimants had been the victims of a campaign of racial harassment by tenants on the council's housing estate or people living with them. As indicated above, in *Hussain's* case the landlord had neither authorised nor adopted the nuisance.[37] Additionally, in *Hussain's* case the conduct causing the nuisance was not in any sense linked to nor did it emanate from the homes in which those causing the interference lived. In *Lippiatt's* case, by contrast, the allegation was that the travellers were allowed to congregate on the council's land and that they used it as a base for the unlawful activities of which complaint was made (albeit that some of these activities occurred outside the council's land).[38] The alleged nuisance in *Lippiatt's* case itself consisted of the council allowing the travellers to congregate on its land whereas in *Hussain's* case the activities of which complaint was made all occurred outside the council's land on which those perpetrating the unlawful activities lived.[39]

LANDLORDS: DILAPIDATIONS

2–019   A landlord will be liable for a nuisance due to a breach of a covenant by him to put the premises in repair.[40] Even if there is no covenant with a tenant to repair, a landlord will still be liable for a nuisance resulting from a failure to repair if he has expressly[41] or impliedly[42] reserved the right to do repairs.

---

[34] *Thompson-Schwab v. Costaki* [1956] 1 WLR 335, CA (brothel owner liable for nuisance; nuisance consisted of "perambulations of the prostitutes and their customers" outside the defendant's premises at 339 *per* Lord Evershed MR).

[35] [1999] 4 All E.R. 149, CA.

[36] [1999] 4 All E.R. 125, CA.

[37] See 2–018 above.

[38] *per* Evans LJ [1999] 4 All E.R. 149 at 157; see also *per* Mummery LJ at 159 and *per* Sir Christopher Staughton at 160.

[39] *Ibid.*

[40] *Payne v. Rogers* (1794) 2 Hy. Bl. 350.

[41] *Wilchick v. Marks and Silverstone* [1934] 2 K.B. 56; *Heap v. Ind Coope and Allsopp Ltd*; [1940] 2 K.B. 476.

[42] *Mint v. Good* [1951] 1 K.B. 517.

Further, if the landlord lets premises in a ruinous condition at the date of the letting the landlord will also be liable for nuisances resulting from the dilapidations, if he knew or ought to have known of the defective state of the premises. The landlord will not be able to escape liability in these circumstances simply by letting the premises and taking a covenant to repair by the tenant.[43] A landlord will also be liable if he re-lets premises after they have become a nuisance,[44] but the continuation of a tenancy from year to year[45] or from week to week[46] will not amount to a reletting of the premises for these purposes.

Those cases where landlords have been held liable for nuisances resulting from disrepair of premises may be explained by there being an implied authorisation of the nuisance by the landlord either from his actual or his constructive knowledge of its existence at the commencement of the tenancy, or from his covenant to repair (since a landlord who undertakes to repair may be regarded as having authorised the tenant to leave the premises in disrepair[47]), or from his reservation to himself of a right to enter the premises to repair (thereby retaining the power to remedy the nuisance).

It is hard to fit the case of *Wringe v. Cohen*[48] into this analysis. It was held in that case that liability for public nuisance, so far as dangerous premises on the highway are concerned, occurs "whether [the Defendant] knew or ought to have known of the danger or not".[49] However, if the nuisance is created "not by want of repair but, for example, by the act of a trespasser, or by a secret and unobservable operation of nature, such as subsidence under or near the foundations of the premises, neither the occupier nor an owner responsible for the repair is answerable, unless with knowledge or means of knowledge he allows the danger to continue."[50] It is appropriate to regard this case as turning on the particular context of public nuisances affecting highways rather than being of general application to the law of private nuisance.

LANDLORDS: LIABILITY TO TENANT

In *Sampson v. Hodgson-Pressinger*[51] the Court of Appeal assumed that a landlord could be liable to his tenant in nuisance. The point, however, was expressly decided subsequently in the case of *Guppys (Bridport) Ltd v. Brookling*[52]:

2–020

---

[43] *Todd v. Flight* (1860) 9 C.B. N.S. 377, 389; *Gwinnell v. Earner* (1875) L.R. 10 C.P. 658, 661; *St Anne's Well Brewery Co. v. Roberts* (1929) 140 L.T. 1; *Brew Brothers v. Snax (Ross) Ltd* [1970] 1 Q.B. 612, CA.

[44] *R v. Pedley* (1834) Ad & El 822.

[45] *Gandy v. Jubber* (1865) 9 B. & S. 15.

[46] *Bowen v. Anderson* [1894] 1 Q.B. 164

[47] Salmond & Heuston on the *Law of Torts* (21st ed.), p. 69.

[48] [1940] 1 K.B. 229.

[49] *ibid* at 233.

[50] *ibid* (Contrast *Noble v. Harrison* [1926] 2 K.B. 332; *Chapman v. Barking and Dagenham LBC* [1997] 2 E.G.L.R. 141).

[51] [1981] 3 All E.R. 710.

[52] (1983) 269 E.G. 846, 942, CA esp. at 946, 947.

> "If a landlord uses his own property — it may be lawfully — in a way which unduly interferes with the enjoyment of his tenant's property, . . . he falls fairly and squarely within the category of wrongdoers who commit the tort of nuisance."

Accordingly, in the case of *Chartered Trust plc v. Davies*[53] the landlord was held liable to its tenant for continuing a nuisance by failing to stop adjoining premises within its control being used in connection with a pawnbroking business which seriously interfered with the tenant's enjoyment of her premises.[54]

A landlord's liability in nuisance to a tenant will only arise where the interference with the tenant's land is caused by activities outside the demised premises which indirectly affect the tenant's enjoyment of the demised premises.[55] Direct interferences will be actionable as trespasses.

VICARIOUS LIABILITY

2–021   A defendant will be liable for a nuisance created by his servants in accordance with the general principles governing vicarious liability for torts.[56] A defendant will also be liable for nuisances created by his agents. Since an occupier of premises is generally liable for a nuisance emanating from those premises while he is in occupation of the land, occupation by the agency of another of land from which a nuisance emanates will suffice.[57]

On the other hand, in general an occupier is not liable for a nuisance caused by an independent contractor[58] unless the nuisance is caused in circumstances in which it could reasonably have been foreseen that the work which the defendant instructed the independent contractor to do would have injurious consequences for the claimant. In these circumstances the occupier is under a duty to see that the injurious consequences from such "extra-hazardous" activities are avoided.[59]

In *Bower v. Peate*,[60] the plaintiff and defendant were owners of two adjoining houses, the plaintiff being entitled to the support for his house of the defendant's soil. The defendant employed a contractor to pull down his house and rebuild it and the contractor undertook the work of supporting the plaintiff's house and making good any damage. During

---

[53] [1997] 2 E.G.L.R. 83.

[54] See paras. 2–014 above and 2–023 below in relation to continuing nuisances. See also Chapter 3 para 3–042 in relation to the landlord's obligations not to derogate from grant.

[55] See below, para. 2–026. See also *Habinteg Housing Association v. James* [1994] N.P.C. 132 and *Mowan v. London Borough of Wandsworth*, [2001] 1 E.G.C.S. 4, CA.

[56] See generally, Atiyah, *Vicarious Liability in the Law of Torts* (1967).

[57] *ibid*. pp. 143–144; *Bower v. Peate* (1876) L.R. 1 Q.B.D. 321, 327; *Job Edwards Ltd v. Birmingham Navigations* [1924] 1 K.B. 341, 355.

[58] See *Salsbury v. Woodland* [1970] Q.B. 324; *Quarman v. Burnett* (1840) 6 M. & W. 499.

[59] *Dalton v. Angus* (1881) 6 App.Cas. 740, 831; *Douglas Alexander Alcock v. Wraith* (1992) 59 B.L.R. 16, CA (withdrawal of support; liability for independent contractors).

[60] (1876) L.R. 1 Q.B.D. 321 at 326 D.C.

the course of the works the plaintiff's house was damaged due to insufficient support. It was held that the defendant was liable to the plaintiff for
the nuisance even though he had employed an independent contractor.
Delivering the judgment of the court, Cockburn C.J. stated[61]:

> "A man who orders a work to be executed, from which, in the natu-
> ral course of things, injurious consequences to his neighbour must be
> expected to arise, unless means are adopted by which such conse-
> quences may be prevented, is bound to see to the doing of that which
> is necessary to prevent the mischief and cannot relieve himself of
> responsibility by employing someone else — whether it be the con-
> tractor employed to do the work from which the danger arises or
> some independent person — to do what is necessary to prevent the
> act which he has ordered to be done from becoming wrongful."[62]

The principle that a defendant will be liable for an independent contractor only where he has authorised "dangerous operations" has been
affirmed in subsequent cases.[63]

In *Matania v. National Provincial Bank Ltd*[64] the defendant employed a
contractor to carry out extensive works of alteration to the first floor of the
building which it occupied. The plaintiff was a tenant of the second floor.
It was held that the defendant was liable to the plaintiff for the noise and
dust created by the alterations. The basis of the defendant's liability was
that the operation to be performed involved in its very nature the risk of
damage being done to the plaintiff:

> "If the act done is one which in its very nature involves a special dan-
> ger of nuisance being complained of, then it is one which falls within
> the exception for which the employer of the contractor will be
> responsible if there is a failure to take the necessary precautions that
> the nuisance shall not arise."[65]

On the other hand, in *Blake v. Woolf*,[66] the defendant instructed a competent plumber to repair a water cistern which had leaked on his premises.
As a consequence of the plumber's negligence the cistern overflowed
and damaged goods on the plaintiff's premises. Wright J. held that the
defendant was not liable for the nuisance caused by the plumber: the

---

[61] *ibid.* at 326.
[62] See also *Dalton v. Angus* (1881) 6 App.Cas. 740, HL; *Lemaitre v. Davis* (1881) 19 Ch.D. 281;
Joliffe v. Woodhouse (1894) 10 T.L.R. 553, CA *cf. Hughes v. Percival* (1883) 8 App.Cas. 443, HL.
[63] *Hardaker v. Idle District Council* [1896] 1 Q.B. 335, 346, CA. See also *Black v. Christchurch
Finance Co.* [1894] A.C. 48; *Brooke v. Bool* [1928] 2 K.B. 578, 587; *H. & N. Emanuel Ltd v.
Greater London Council* [1971] 2 All E.R. 835; *Douglas Alexander Alcock v. Wraith* (1992) 59
B.L.R. 16, CA.
[64] [1936] 2 All E.R. 633, CA.
[65] *ibid.* at 646.
[66] [1898] 2 Q.B. 426.

ordinary rule that a person is not responsible for the negligence of an independent contractor applied.[67]

The narrow circumstances in which an employer has been held vicariously liable for nuisances caused by independent contractors are hard to reconcile with the case of *Spicer v. Smee*[68]: where it was stated that the principle in *Bower v. Peate* was:

"where danger is likely to arise unless work is properly done, there is a duty to see that it is properly done."

Accordingly a defendant was liable for nuisance resulting from a fire caused by faulty electrical wiring which had been installed negligently by an independent contractor. It is suggested that this is too wide: the liability of an employer in nuisance for the acts of his independent contractors only arises where the activities for which the independent contractors have been engaged are in themselves dangerous (this follows from the *Matania* case, which was not cited in *Spicer v. Smee*). Further *Spicer v. Smee* is hard to reconcile with the case of *Blake v. Woolf*. That an employer is not generally liable for the negligence of an independent contractor working on his land, even where injury is caused to the user of an adjoining highway (a public nuisance), was affirmed in *Salsbury v. Woodland*.[69]

OCCUPIER BRINGING DANGEROUS THINGS ONTO LAND

2–022   A person who brings on his land and keeps there anything likely to do mischief if it escapes may be liable upon the principles in *Rylands v. Fletcher*. This is dealt with more fully at 2–056 below.

OCCUPIER CONTINUING NUISANCE

2–023   As indicated above in para 2–014, an occupier may be liable for "continuing" a nuisance or "adopting" it even though he did not create it.

An occupier will be liable for continuing a nuisance even though it commenced prior to his acquisition of the land on which the nuisance occurs, if he knew or ought to have known of the existence of the nuisance when he acquired the land.[70] Thus in the case of *Broder v. Saillard*[71] the defendant tenant was held liable for a continuing nuisance to an adjoining house, caused by the percolation of water, where the nuisance existed at the commencement of the tenancy. However, where an occupier

---

[67]   *ibid.* at 429.
[68]   [1946] 1 All E.R. 489, Atkinson J.
[69]   [1970] 1 Q.B. 324 (but in the case of works taking place on the highway an employer will be liable for the negligence of his independent contractor, at 338). See also *Elle Ltd v. Manches & Co.* (unreported) June 13, 1990 in which Morland J. held that a landowner was not liable for dust created by building works carried out by experienced architects and builders as independent contractors. See also *Rowe v. Herman* [1997] 1 WLR 324, Q.B.
[70]   *Roswell v. Prior* (1701) 12 Mod. 635; *Ryppon v. Bowles* (1615) Cro. Jac. 375.
[71]   (1876) 2 Ch.D. 692.

acquires premises in circumstances where he neither knows nor ought to know of the nuisance he will not be liable for it[72] unless he can be said to have adopted the nuisance: accordingly where land vests in the Crown as bona vacantia the Crown will not be liable for a nuisance on that land merely by failing to disclaim the land.[73]

An occupier of land may also be liable for continuing or adopting a nuisance created by others after his acquisition of the land. In *Sedleigh-Denfield v. O'Callaghan*,[74] Lord Maugham said:

> "The statement that an occupier of land is liable for the continuance of a nuisance created by others, *e.g.*, by trespassers, if he continues or adopts it . . . throws little light on the matter, unless the words 'continues and adopts' are defined . . . . [A]n occupier of land 'continues' a nuisance if with the knowledge or presumed knowledge of its existence he fails to take any reasonable means to bring it to an end though with ample time to do so. He 'adopts' it if he makes any use of the erection, building, bank or artificial contrivance which constitutes the nuisance."[75]

In that case the occupiers were held liable for continuing a nuisance where a pipe laid by a trespasser became blocked causing a nuisance to adjoining occupiers: the occupiers knew of the pipe's existence and failed to take reasonable steps to prevent the nuisance by placing a grid before the pipe.[76]

In the case of *Attorney-General v. Tod-Heatley*[77] occupiers were held liable for continuing a public nuisance where land became a receptacle for "dead dogs and cats, vegetable refuse, fish, offal, rubbish and all kinds of filth" deposited by others.[78]

An occupier may, it seems, be held liable for the continuation of nuisances created by natural causes or an act of God as well as those created by human agency. The cases in which defendants have been held to be so liable appear to go beyond the previous extent of the law of nuisance,[79]

---

[72] *British Road Services v. Slater* [1964] 1 W.L.R. 498: no liability in respect of tree overhanging road even though "nuisance" was not latent.

[73] *Toff v. McDowell* (1993) 25 H.L.R. 650.

[74] [1940] A.C. 880.

[75] *ibid.* at 894. See also: *Barker v. Herbert* [1911] 2 K.B. 633, 642, 645; *Saxby v. Manchester Sheffield and Lincolnshire Ry Co.* (1869) L.R. 4 C.P. 198; *Broder v. Saillard* (1876) 2 Ch.D. 692; *R.H. Buckley & Sons v. N. Buckley & Sons* [1898] 2 Q.B. 608; and the dissenting judgment of Scrutton L.J. in *Job Edwards Ltd v. Birmingham Navigations* [1924] 1 K.B. 341, which was preferred to the judgment of the majority by Lord Maugham in *Sedleigh-Denfield v. O'Callaghan* [1940] A.C. 880.

[76] See also *Smeaton v. Ilford Corpn* [1954] Ch. 450; *Pemberton v. Bright and Devon County Council* [1960] 1 W.L.R. 436; *King v. Liverpool City Council* [1986] 1 W.L.R. 890.

[77] [1897] 1 Ch. 560.

[78] See also *Leanse v. Lord Egerton* [1943] 1 K.B. 323 (a piece of glass damaged three days previously fallen onto highway held a nuisance).

[79] *Goldman v. Hargrave* [1967] 1 A.C. 645; *Leakey v. National Trust* [1980] Q.B. 485, 518; also *Slater v. Worthington's Cash Stores* [1941] 1 K.B. 488 (snow fallen from roof onto highway held a nuisance). See 2–015 above.

though in such cases the standard of care to be adopted is measured by the occupier's capacities and circumstances and not on a purely objective basis.[80]

PREVIOUS OCCUPIERS

2–024 Where land from which a nuisance emanates changes hands, the question is whether the person who has transferred the land should remain liable. Where liability is dependent upon occupation and the occupier has not himself created the nuisance, liability ought to be confined to those nuisances occurring during his occupation and the consequences of such nuisances. Similarly the liability of a landlord dependent upon his covenant to repair should last for the duration of his interest in the property (unless the landlord has caused the disrepair). If this were not so there would be liability for a nuisance over which the occupier or landlord has no control (and which he has not himself caused). However, where liability is not dependent upon occupation or a landlord's covenant to repair, it does not matter that occupation has ceased.[81]

The nature of the interference

Introductory

2–025 The interferences with a person's land or rights over land which can constitute a nuisance are very varied.[82] It is not every interference which is actionable. It is not possible comprehensively to categorise all the nuisances which may exist. There are a number of factors, however, to consider when determining whether an interference with land is of a sort which is actionable. In general, to be actionable as a nuisance the interference must:

(1) be "indirect"
(2) cause damage and
(3) be unreasonable.

The following paragraphs deal with each ingredient in turn.

(1) 'Indirectness of interference'

2–026 "The forms which activities constituting actionable nuisance may take are exceedingly varied and there is the highest authority for saying that they

---

[80] See para. 2–015 *et seq.* above.
[81] See *A-G v. Tod Heatley* [1897] 1 Ch. 560; *Roswell v. Prior* (1701) Mod. 635.
[82] See *e.g. Brand v. Hammersmith & City Railway Co* (1867) LR 2 Q.B. 223, 247 *per* Erle CJ; *Sedleigh-Denfield v. O'Callaghan* [1940] A.C. 880, HL, 903 *per* Lord Wright, *Thompson-Schwab v Costaki* [1956] 1 W.L.R. 335, CA, 338.

are not capable of precise or close definition."[83] Actionable nuisances may consist of such different activities as the setting up of a "sex shop",[84] or the blocking of a right of way.[85] One factor which links the various activities is the "indirectness of the wrong done"[86] which may be contrasted with the directness of acts which amount to trespass.[87] Trespass to land is the entering upon land in the possession of another, or placing, or throwing, or erecting some material object thereon without the legal right to do so.[88] Trespass involves a direct interference with the land of another. Where there is no direct entry, placing, throwing or erection there will be no trespass. There may, however, be a nuisance. This distinction between the directness of trespass and the indirectness of private nuisance is made also between forms of trespass other than trespass to land and other actions "on the case", *e.g.* public nuisance.

Accordingly:

"If a man throws a log into the highway, and in that act hits me, I may maintain trespass, because it is an immediate wrong; but if as it lies there I tumble over it, and receive an injury, I must bring an action upon the case, for which originally I could have no action at all."[89]

The encroachment of the boughs and roots of a tree over and within the land of an adjoining owner is not a trespass, it is a nuisance[90]; but to plant a tree on the land of another is trespass. It is not a trespass where the top of a fence originally built by a defendant flush with the boundary between a claimant's and a defendant's land subsequently encroaches a few inches over the claimant's land as a result of the action of the frost and snow, but it may be a nuisance.[91] It is a trespass for a defendant to discharge water directly onto the claimant's land, but if the water spills from the defendant's land over intermediate land onto the claimant's land this may be a nuisance.[92]

---

[83] *Thompson-Schwab v. Costaki* [1956] 1 W.L.R. 335, 338, CA *per* Lord Evershed M.R.

[84] *Laws v. Florinplace* [1981] 1 All E.R. 659.

[85] See below, para. 2–115. See *Sedleigh-Denfield v. O'Callaghan* [1940] A.C. 880, 888.

[86] Pearce and Meston, *Law of Nuisances*, (1926), p. 2; Clerk and Lindsell on *Torts* (18th ed.), para. 19–02.

[87] The distinction between trespass being an immediate wrong, and nuisance as an action "on the case" being an indirect wrong, has its origins in attempts in the eighteenth century to rationalise the forms of action. See J.H. Baker, *Introduction to Legal History*, (3rd ed., 1990), pp. 73–75. See above, para. 1–035.

[88] See para. 1–035.

[89] *per* Fortescue J. in *Reynolds v. Clarke* (1725) 1 Sta. 634, 635.

[90] See 2–050 below. *Lemmon v. Webb* [1894] 3 Ch. 1, 24 (affirmed [1895] A.C. 1, HL); *Smith v. Giddy* [1904] 2 K.B. 448; *Butler v. Standard Telephones and Cables Ltd* [1940] 1 K.B. 399; *Delaware Mansions Ltd v. Westminster City Council* [2001] UKHL 55.

[91] *Mann v. Saulnier* (1959) 19 D.L.R. (2d) 130; Hudson, *Trespass and Nuisance*, (1960) 23 M.L.R. 188. But to erect a structure so as to invade another's airspace will be a trespass: *Kelson v. Imperial Tobacco Co. (of Great Britain and Ireland)* [1957] 2 Q.B. 334; *Anchor Brewhouse Developments Limited v. Berkley House (Docklands) Developments Ltd* [1987] 2 E.G.L.R. 173; see above, para. 1–026.

[92] *Nobilo v. Waitemata* [1961] N.Z.L.R. 1064; compare *Home Brewery plc v. Davis & Co* [1987] Q.B. 339 and *Palmer v. Bowman* [2000] 1 W.L.R. 842.

The distinction between nuisance and trespass is sometimes difficult to perceive: as the above examples illustrate, the line between direct and indirect interferences can be a fine one. Since the abolition of the forms of action the distinction is of less importance because a sufficient statement of the facts in a pleading will support an action. However, the distinction does retain practical significance: trespass is actionable *per se*,[93] but in nuisance it is necessary not only for there to be an infringement of rights but also for there to be some damage as a result, which it may be necessary to plead.[94]

(2) Interference must generally cause damage

2–027   For there to be an actionable nuisance there must in principle be some damage resulting from the interference to the land in question.[95] As stated at the beginning of this chapter the maxim underlying the origin of this tort is *sic utere tuo ut alienum non laedas* ("use your [land] so that you do not harm another's"). But in practice the proof of damage is sometimes unnecessary.

First, the Court will readily presume damage. Where, for instance, a cornice projects over the claimant's garden, the Court will presume that there is a nuisance and an injury to the claimant's land in the absence of evidence to the contrary.[96]

Secondly, where there is interference with easements, profits à prendre or certain natural rights, damage is not necessary for the interference to be actionable: "damage is not the gist of the action".[97] There is an historical reason for this. Under the old forms of pleading an action for trespass did not lie for interference with an easement,[98] but an action "on the case" became the remedy as a matter of course. The fact that disturbances with such rights were interferences with rights absolutely protected was recognised to the extent of importing the rule that no proof of damage was required.[99]

There are good reasons why many nuisances ought to be actionable without proof of damage. If damage were not presumed and no action lay, the party interfering with a right might in time himself gain a prescriptive right to interfere with a claimant's enjoyment of his land. Once such a prescriptive right has been acquired it might become possible for interference which results in damage to be caused with impunity.

---

[93] See, paras. 1–002, 4–003.

[94] *Mann v. Saulnier* (1959) 19 D.L.R. (2d) 130, 133.

[95] Nuisance is both "tortious and hurtful", see Bracton, Bk. IV, c 43; *Anchor Brewhouse Developments Ltd v. Berkley House (Docklands) Ltd* [1987] 2 E.G.L.R. 173, 174.

[96] *Fay v. Prentice* (1845) 1 C.B. 825; *Baten's Case* (1610) 9 Co. Rep. 53b.

[97] *Nichols v. Ely Beet Sugar Factory Ltd* [1936] Ch. 343, 349, *per* Lord Wright. See also *Pennington v. Brinsop Hall Co.* (1877) L.R. Ch.D. 769, 772 (prescriptive and natural riparian rights); *A-G v. Conduit Colliery Co.* [1895] 1 Q.B. 301, 312 (a case of support). But see *Thorpe v. Brumfitt* (1873) 8 Ch.App. 650, 656.

[98] *Nichols v. Ely Beet Sugar Factory Ltd* [1936] Ch. 343. Trespass is not maintainable in the modern law for infringement of an easement: see Chapter One, para. 1–032.

[99] *ibid.* The same rule is true in respect of disturbance of rights to hold a market, see *Halsbury's Laws* (4th ed.), Vol. 29, para. 654.

Thirdly, it is not necessary to prove damage has occurred where a *quia timet* injunction is being sought.[1]

Since nuisance consists of an interference with the enjoyment of land, the sort of damage which will sustain a claim in nuisance is harm to the land itself or to its value. Private nuisance is not primarily concerned with harm to persons on the land. It is considered by some that personal injury claims should be excluded from the scope of the tort of nuisance.[2] On the other hand, there seems to be no reason in principle why a claimant should not recover damages for personal injury to himself or illness which is the reasonably foreseeable consequence of an actionable interference with his land amounting to a private nuisance.[3] If a landowner has a right recognised in the law of private nuisance, for instance, to enjoy his land without the inconvenience caused by an unreasonable interference as a result of an unpleasant noise, it would be strange if the law of private nuisance did not protect his right to enjoy his property free from interferences causing personal injury (for instance, a noise causing deafness) and did not enable him to recover damages resulting from such interferences. Damages for personal injury are recoverable in the context of public nuisance.[4] In the context of the rule in *Rylands v. Fletcher* it seems that such damages are also recoverable[5] though the House of Lords has reserved its opinion on the matter.[6]

(3) Interference must be unreasonable

GENERALLY

We have already noted that to give rise to an action in nuisance there must be an "indirect" interference with the claimant's land.[7] But not all indirect interferences with land will give rise to an action in nuisance even if they harm the defendant. For a nuisance to be actionable there must be an unreasonable interference with the claimant's land:

2–028

> "It is impossible to give any precise or universal formula, but it may broadly be said that a useful test is perhaps what is reasonable according to the ordinary usages of mankind living in society, or more correctly in a particular society."[8]

---

[1] See below, 4–084 *et seq.* (Remedies).
[2] See discussion in *Hunter v. Canary Wharf Ltd* [1997] A.C. 655 at 687–688, HL *per* Lord Goff.
[3] See 4–036 below (Remedies).
[4] *Mint v. Good* [1951] 1 K.B. 517, CA.
[5] *Miles v. Forest Rock Granite Co. (Leicestershire) Ltd* (1918) 34 T.L.R. 500; *Hale v. Jennings Bros* [1938] 1 All E.R. 579. Compare *Shiffman v. Grand Priory in British Realm of Venerable Order of St John of Jerusalem* [1936] 1 All E.R. 557.
[6] *Read v. J. Lyons & Co. Ltd* [1947] A.C. 156.
[7] See 2–026 above.
[8] *Sedleigh-Denfield v. O'Callaghan* [1940] A.C. 880, HL 903, *per* Lord Wright.

This lack of a universal formula was recognised as long ago as the case of *Brand v. Hammersmith & City Railway Co.*[9] in which Erle C.J. noted and explained the difficulty[10] in his undelivered judgment:

> "This cause of action is immersed in undefined uncertainty; there is no standard by which to measure degrees of annoyance, or to estimate the effect of circumstances; each neighbour is a source of some annoyance; proximity necessitates mutual forbearance; the degree of forbearance to be required is measured by the sensibility to feelings of delicacy of the tribunal which has to decide the case . . ."

In judging whether an interference is actionable much will depend on considering all the circumstances of each case and the "principle of reasonable user".[11] In *Southwark LBC v Mills*,[12] Lord Millett stated[13]:

> "The use of the word 'reasonable' in this context is apt to be misunderstood. It is no answer to an action for nuisance to say that the defendant is only making reasonable user of his land . . . What is reasonable from the point of view of one party may be completely unreasonable from the point of view of the other. It is not enough for a landowner to act reasonably in his own interest. He must be considerate of the interests of his neighbour. The governing principle is good neighbourliness, and this involves reciprocity. A landowner must show the same consideration for his neighbour as he would expect his neighbour to show for him."

The question is, therefore, one of balancing the competing interests of claimant and defendant. Each case will substantially depend on its own context. In some cases the degree of fault of the defendant will be material in assessing whether the interference is one which must be tolerated (this is dealt with above at para. 2–011 *et seq.*). It is possible, however, to identify some other factors which the Courts have been willing and unwilling to take into account in deciding whether an interference is unreasonable and actionable.

WHETHER NUISANCE CAUSES PHYSICAL DAMAGE OR ENCROACHMENT

2–029   Where complaint is made of physical damage to, or of substantial encroachment upon, the claimant's land, the interference with the land is

---

[9] (1867) L.R. 2 Q.B. 223.
[10] *ibid.* at 247.
[11] *Cambridge Water Co Ltd v. Eastern Counties Leather plc* [1994] 2 A.C. 264, HL at 299 *per* Lord Goff; see also *Andreae v. Selfridge & Co Ltd* [1938] 1 Ch. 1, CA at p. 7 *per* Greene MR; *Blackburn v. ARC Ltd t/a Greenways Landfill* [1997] PLSCS 317, HHJ Humphrey Lloyd QC; *Wildtree Hotels Ltd v. Harrow LBC,* [2001] 2 A.C. 1 at 12; [2000] 3 W.L.R. 165 at 175 *per* Lord Hoffmann; *Video London Sound Studios Ltd v. Asticus (GMS) Ltd,* March 6, 2001, TCC.
[12] [2001] 1 A.C. 1; [1999] 4 All E.R. 449, HL.
[13] [2001] 1 A.C. at 20; [1994] 4 All E.R. 449 at 464.

usually by its very nature unreasonable. In such cases it will not generally be necessary to consider the surrounding context such as character of the neighbourhood or for how long the interference continues in determining whether or not there is a nuisance.[14] For such an interference to be actionable, however, it will still be necessary to find a defendant who is legally responsible for it.[15] Where no physical harm or encroachment is caused to the claimant's property it will be highly material to consider questions of the duration of the interference and the character of the neighbourhood.

DURATION OF INTERFERENCE

It has been said that to constitute a nuisance there must be an injury "of **2–030** a substantial character, not fleeting or evanescent".[16] Further it has been said that "private nuisances, at least in the vast majority of cases, are interferences for a substantial length of time by owners or occupiers of property with the use or enjoyment of neighbouring property."[17]

Despite these dicta it is clear that single or intermittent occurrences can give rise to an action in nuisance. The isolated escape of water,[18] gas,[19] metal foil,[20] or fire[21] may constitute nuisances as may an intermittent interference such as noise.[22] However, although there need be no continuity in the actual interference for it to give rise to an action in nuisance, it does seem that the interference must usually result from some "state of affairs" constituting a potential hazard to the claimant's land.

In *S.C.M. (United Kingdom) Ltd v. W.J. Whittall & Sons Ltd*,[23] Thesiger J. said:

> "While there is no doubt that a single isolated escape may cause the damage that entitles a plaintiff to sue for nuisance, yet it must be proved that the nuisance arose from the condition of the defendant's land or premises or property or activities thereon that constituted a nuisance."

In *Spicer v. Smee* a fire which destroyed the plaintiff's bungalow was caused by faulty wiring at the defendant's premises. It was held by

---

[14] *St Helen's Smelting Co v. Tipping* (1865) 11 HLC 642, 650 *per* Lord Westbury LC; *Halsey v. Esso Petroleum* [1961] 1 WLR 683, 689–692; *Video London Sound Studios Ltd v. Asticus (GMS) Ltd*, March 6, 2001, TCC.

[15] See 2–010 *et seq.*

[16] *Benjamin v. Storr* (1874) L.R. 9 C.P. 400, 407, *per* Brett J.

[17] *Cunard v. Antifyre Ltd* [1933] 1 K.B. 551, 557; *Southport Corpn v. Esso Petroleum Co. Ltd* [1956] A.C. 218, 224.

[18] *Rylands v. Fletcher* [1866] L.R. 1 Ex. 265.

[19] *Midwood & Co. Ltd v. Manchester Corpn* [1905] 1 K.B. 597; *Northwestern Utilities Ltd v. London Guarantee and Accident Co. Ltd* [1936] A.C. 108.

[20] *British Celanese Ltd v. A.H. Hunt (Capacitors) Ltd* [1969] 1 W.L.R. 959.

[21] *Spicer v. Smee* [1946] 1 All E.R. 489.

[22] *Rapier v. London Tramways* [1893] 2 Ch. 558, 591; *Halsey v. Esso Petroleum Co. Ltd* [1961] 1 W.L.R. 683, 700.

[23] [1970] 1 W.L.R. 1017, 1031.

Atkinson J.[24] that the "state of the defendant's bungalow . . . did consti-tute a nuisance on the defendant's property and . . . in the end, caused the escape of a dangerous thing, to wit, fire." In the case of *Stone v. Bolton*[25] there was (*inter alia*) an issue as to the liability of a cricket club in public nuisance where a pedestrian on the highway was hit by a cricket ball struck by a visiting batsman. The Court of Appeal considered the gist of nuisance in these circumstances to be the causing or permitting of a state of affairs from which damage is likely to result: on the facts it was held that there was no such nuisance. In *Halsey v. Esso Petroleum Co. Ltd*[26] the interference with the plaintiff's enjoyment of his property as a result of passing lorries belonging to the defendant was held to give rise to an actionable nuisance because the noise was attributable to the "defendant's mode of operation".

It is clear that the state of affairs which gives rise to a nuisance can be only temporary. Thus where access to the highway is only temporarily interrupted this may constitute a nuisance if for instance it harms the claimant's business.[27] Likewise in the case of *Crown River Cruises Ltd v. Kimbolton Fireworks Ltd*[28] Potter J held that a firework display that lasted for only 15 or 20 minutes could give rise to a liability in nuisance for dam-age to the plaintiff's barge and rejected a submission that that was too short a period to amount to a nuisance.

Even though the "continuity" of the interference with land is not a pre-requisite of a nuisance, the duration and interference with the land is an important factor to be considered in deciding whether or not the interfer-ence is unreasonable (at least where the interference is not one resulting in physical damage to the land). For instance, noise and dust created by temporary building operations may not amount to an actionable nuisance (even though they seriously interfere with the claimant's enjoyment of his land) where the defendant has used all reasonable skill to minimise the annoyance, whereas if the same level of noise and dust were created by permanent operations (or wantonly) they would amount to an actionable nuisance[29];

> "For the law, in judging what constitutes a nuisance, does take into consideration both the object and duration of that which is said to constitute the nuisance."[30]

---

[24] [1946] 1 All E.R. 489, 493. Compare also *Sedleigh-Denfield v. O'Callaghan* [1940] A.C. 880, HL 895–896: Lord Atkin said that the defendant had "created a state of things . . . from which . . . flooding of the plaintiff's ground might be reasonably expected."

[25] [1949] 2 All E.R. 851, CA (See [1951] A.C. 850: the House of Lords considered only negli-gence). Compare *Castle v. St Augustine's Links* (1922) 38 T.L.R. 615, where golf balls repeat-edly sliced onto the highway there was a nuisance since there was a substantial interference with the use of the highway and a state of affairs in which danger was foreseeable.

[26] [1961] 1 W.L.R. 683, 700.

[27] See *Fritz v. Hobson* (1880) 14 Ch.D. 542; compare *Iveson v. Moore* 1 Ld. Raym. 486.

[28] [1996] 2 Lloyd's Rep. 533

[29] *Harrison v. Southwark & Vauxhall Water Co.* [1891] 2 Ch. 409, 414, Vaughan Williams J.; compare *Andreae v. Selfridge & Co. Ltd* [1938] Ch. 1.

[30] [1891] 2 Ch. 409, 414. See also below, paras. 2–033, 2–082.

LOCALITY: CHARACTER OF NEIGHBOURHOOD AND PLANNING PERMISSION

In considering whether or not an interference with land is unreasonable **2–031** and actionable the character of the neighbourhood may be taken into account in those cases where the interference affects the enjoyment of the land rather than causes physical damage. In *Sturges v. Bridgman*[31] where the plaintiff complained of noise nuisance caused by the defendant's confectionery business in Wigmore Street, Thesiger L.J. said:

> "Whether anything is a nuisance or not is a question to be determined, not merely by abstract consideration of the thing itself, but in reference to its circumstances: what would be a nuisance in Belgrave Square would not necessarily be a nuisance in Bermondsey; and where a locality is devoted to a particular trade or manufacture carried on by the traders or manufacturers in a particular or established manner not constituting a public nuisance, judges and juries would be justified in finding, and may be trusted to find that the trade or manufacture so carried on in that locality is not a private or actionable wrong."

Even if the defendant carries on a business or activity which is similar to others in the neighbourhood he may still be liable in nuisance if he intensifies or increases the interference caused by his business so as materially to interfere with the claimant's comfort as previously enjoyed.[32]

If an activity in a particular locality would constitute a nuisance because of the interference to a claimant's enjoyment of land, the mere grant of planning permission will not render lawful that activity: the grant of planning permission does not of itself extinguish private law rights.[33] However, it appears that in some circumstances the grant of planning permission for a comprehensive redevelopment may alter the character of a locality in such a way as to make lawful an activity which might (prior

---

[31] (1879) 11 Ch.D. 852. See also *Bamford v. Turnley* (1862) 3 B. & S. 66, 79; *Adams v. Ursell* [1913] 1 Ch. 269: fried fish shop near a dwelling-house held a nuisance; *Murdoch v. Glacier Metal Co Ltd, The Times*, January 21, 1998, CA: noise of factory not a nuisance, where character of neighbourhood already affected by the by-pass.

[32] *Crump v. Lambert* (1867) L.R. 3 Eq. 409; *Polsue & Alfieri Ltd v. Rushmer* [1907] A.C. 121. See also *Milner v. Spencer* (1976) 239 E.G. 573. Compare *Heath v. Brighton (Mayor of)* (1908) 98 L.T. 718.

[33] *Wheeler v. JJ Saunders* [1995] 2 All E.R. 671, CA. See too, *Allen v. Gulf Oil Refining* [1980] Q.B. 156, at p. 174, CA, where Cumming-Bruce L.J. stated that the requirement of planning permission was an "additional safeguard" and a "neutral" point since a planning authority has no jurisdiction to authorise a nuisance. The House of Lords was silent on this point [1981] A.C. 101. See *Hunter v. Canary Wharf Ltd* [1997] A.C. 655 at 710 *per* Lord Hoffmann and at 721–722 *per* Lord Cooke. See also *Delyn BC v. Solitaire (Liverpool) Ltd* [1995] N.P.C. 11; *Blackburn v. ARC Ltd t/a Greenways Landfill* [1997] P.L.S.C.S. 317 (H.H.J. Humphrey Lloyd Q.C.).

to the grant of planning permission) have constituted a nuisance[34] or may have a bearing on whether the Court will grant an injunction to restrain the permitted activity.[35] On the other hand, if a defendant develops his land in breach of planning control, this may be a material indication that an interference caused by the development is unreasonable (such an interference being unacceptable to the community).[36]

The locality, therefore, does affect whether or not an interference with the enjoyment or use of property is reasonable. But where an interference causes physical injury to the claimant's property the locality will not affect whether or not the interference is unreasonable. In the case of *St Helen's Smelting Co. v. Tipping*[37] the defendant's copper smelting works located in a manufacturing area produced vapours which harmed the trees on the plaintiff's estate. The defendant was unsuccessful in its argument that the character of the neighbourhood prevented the plaintiff from complaining of the nuisance. Lord Westbury L.C. said:

"It appears to me to be a very desirable thing to mark the difference between an action brought for a nuisance upon the ground that the alleged nuisance produces material injury to the property, and an action brought for a nuisance on the ground that the thing alleged to be a nuisance is productive of sensible personal discomfort. With regard to the latter, namely, the personal inconvenience and interference with one's enjoyment, one's quiet, one's personal freedom, anything that discomposes or injuriously affects the senses or the nerves, whether that may or may not be denominated a nuisance, must undoubtedly depend greatly upon the circumstances of the place where the thing complained of actually occurs ... But when an occupation is carried on by one person in the neighbourhood of another, and the result of that trade or occupation or business, is a material injury to property, then there unquestionably arises a very different consideration. I think ... that in a case of that description the submission which is required from persons living in society to that amount of discomfort which may be necessary for the legitimate and free exercise of the trade of their neighbours, would not apply to circumstances the immediate result of which is sensible injury to the value of property."

This distinction between nuisances creating personal discomfort and injury to the property itself is not without difficulty: a noxious smell may affect the value of property and cause losses to a business carried on there

---

[34] *Gillingham BC v. Medway (Chatham) Dock Ltd* [1992] 3 All E.R. 923 (*cf. Wheeler v. Saunders,* [1995] 2 All E.R. 671).

[35] *Wheeler v. Saunders,* per Gibson L.J. [1995] 2 All E.R. 671; *cf.* paras. 2–047, 4–084 *et seq.* Remedies below.

[36] *Hunter v. Canary Wharf Ltd* [1997] A.C. 655 at 721 *per* Lord Cooke.

[37] (1865) 11 H.L.C. 642.

yet leave the property physically unharmed.[38] The character of the neighbourhood may be considered in such a case whereas it could not in respect of vapours from the same source causing physical harm with (perhaps) less severe economic consequences.[39]

SENSITIVITY OF THE CLAIMANT

The Court will not take into account any abnormal sensitivity of the claimant or his property in assessing whether or not an interference is reasonable. "A man cannot increase the liability of his neighbour by applying his own property to special uses whether for business or pleasure."[40]

2–032

In *Robinson v. Kilvert*[41] the plaintiff was unable to succeed in nuisance where his abnormally sensitive property was affected. In that case the defendant manufactured paper boxes in the cellar of premises the upper part of which was occupied by the plaintiff. The plaintiff stored brown paper in his part of the premises. The defendant needed hot and dry air to manufacture his boxes. The hot air raised the temperature of the upper storeys and damaged the plaintiff's brown paper. It was held by the Court of Appeal that the defendant was not liable in nuisance. "A man who carries on an exceptionally delicate trade cannot complain because it is injured by his neighbour doing something lawful on his property, if it is something which would not injure anything but an exceptionally delicate trade."[42]

Similarly, in *Heath v. Brighton (Mayor of)*[43] the incumbent and trustees of a church sought to restrain a "low humming sound or note" arising from the defendant's electrical power station. The plaintiffs failed since most ordinary people could attend church without annoyance, even though in the course of his judgment[44] Joyce J. accepted that the sound caused "irritation or annoyance to certain persons who are more sensitive than others; especially such persons who cannot apply their minds, or give attention, to anything unless there be absolute silence."[45]

---

[38] See Ogus and Richardson, *Economics and the Environment: A Study of Private Nuisance* [1977] C.L.Y. 284, 299.

[39] *cf.* Conor Gearty, *The Place of Private Nuisance in a Modern Law of Torts*, (1989) 48 C.L.Y. 214 where he argues that indirect physical damage to land properly belongs to the law of negligence not nuisance.

[40] *Eastern and Southern African Telegraph Co. v. Cape Town Tramways* [1902] A.C. 381, 393.

[41] (1889) 41 Ch.D. 88.

[42] *ibid.* at 97, *per* Lopes L.J. See also *Phillipay v. Pacific Power & Light Co.* (1922) 207 P. 957 (interference with telegraph line not a nuisance) and *Bridlington Relay Ltd v. Yorkshire Electricity Board* [1965] 1 Ch. 436 (no nuisance for interference with sensitive relay system). See too *Amphitheaters Inc. v. Portland Meadows* (1922) 198 P. (2d.) 847 (floodlighting affecting an outdoor cinema not a nuisance); *Grandel v. Mason* [1953] 3 D.L.R. 65 and *Rattray v. Daniels* (1959) 17 D.L.R. (2d.) 134 (concerning mink farming).

[43] (1908) 98 L.T. 718.

[44] *ibid.* at 721.

[45] Compare *Gaunt v. Fynney* (1872) L.R. 8 Ch.App. 8, 12; *Vanderpant v. Mayfair Hotel Co.* [1930] 1 Ch. 135; *Bloodworth v. Cormack* [1949] N.Z.L.R. 1058, 1064; *Murray v. Laus* [1960] N.Z.L.R. 126; *Stretch v. Romford Football Club Ltd* (1971) 115 S.J. 741.

But once nuisance has been proved in that the right to ordinary enjoyment has been infringed, damages or an injunction may be sought in respect of harm to delicate operations. In *McKinnon Industries Ltd v. Walker*[46] the ordinary enjoyment of the plaintiff's property was impaired by fumes and gas from the defendant's works. It was argued by the defendant that if an injunction was granted, it should exclude protection for the plaintiff's orchid growing which is a "particularly difficult and delicate operation". The Privy Council rejected this: once the plaintiff's ordinary enjoyment of his land was harmed unreasonably there was "no reason to treat damage to orchids differently to damage to any other flower, plant or shrub".[47]

NORMAL USES OF DEFENDANT'S LAND AND DEFENDANT'S MOTIVE

2–033 The purposes for which a defendant is using his property are relevant when deciding whether an interference with a neighbour's land resulting from that use is reasonable. Where operations can be described as "the usual and normal use of land by people in this country" an interference resulting from such use will not be a nuisance.[48] Thus, if a defendant uses his property for "ordinary" purposes, for example, he plays the pianoforte in his house, or there is noise in his children's nursery, any interruption resulting from these uses must be "to a considerable extent put up with".[49] Accordingly, in *Southwark LBC v Mills*[50] a local authority was not liable even though noise from its tenants' ordinary everyday activities seriously interfered with the enjoyment of property of other tenants due to inadequate sound-proofing. In that case it was stated by Lord Millett[51] that there would be no actionable nuisance even for a substantial interference with the claimant's land provided that the acts complained of were (a) necessary for the common and ordinary use and occupation of the defendant's land and (b) were done with proper consideration for neighbouring occupiers.

On this basis, demolition and construction operations carried out in a reasonable way are usual and normal and will not, therefore, constitute a nuisance.[52] Thus noise and dust resulting from demolition operations reasonably carried out must be tolerated, whereas if the same noise and dust arises through "sheer wantonness" they might well constitute an actionable nuisance.[53]

---

[46] [1951] 3 D.L.R. 577.
[47] *ibid.* at 581, *per* Lord Simonds.
[48] *Andreae v. Selfridge & Co.* [1938] Ch. 1, 6 CA.
[49] *Ball v. Ray* (1872) L.R. 8 Ch.App. 467, 471, *per* Mellish L.J.; see also *Bamford v. Turnley* (1862) 3 B & S 62 at 83–84 *per* Bramwell B; *Sanders-Clark v. Grosvenor Mansions Co. Ltd* [1900] 2 Ch. 373; *Kennaway v. Thompson* [1981] Q.B. 88, 94.
[50] [2001] 1 A.C. 1, HL.
[51] *ibid.* at pp. 464–465.
[52] *Andreae v. Selfridge & Co.* [1938] Ch. 1, CA.
[53] *Harrison v. Southwark & Vauxhall Water Co.* [1891] 2 Ch. 409, 414, *per* Vaughan Williams J.

If the purpose of the defendant's activities and the resulting interference with the claimant's land or enjoyment of land is motivated by malice and his intention is to annoy the claimant, the defendant's acts may amount to a nuisance notwithstanding that they would not have given rise to a cause of action if reasonably motivated.

In *Christie v. Davey*[54] the defendants "deliberately and maliciously for the purpose of annoying the Plaintiffs" hammered and beat trays against a party wall. North J. held that this constituted a nuisance but stated[55] that:

> "if what had taken place had occurred between two sets of persons both perfectly innocent, I should have taken an entirely different view of the case. But I am persuaded that what was done by the Defendant was only done for the purpose of annoyance, and in my opinion it was not a legitimate use of the Defendant's house to use it for the purpose of vexing and annoying his neighbours."

Similarly, in *Hollywood Silver Fox Farm Ltd v. Emmett*[56] malice on the part of the defendant was a factor to be taken into account. In that case the plaintiff bred silver foxes on its land. The defendant, during the breeding season, maliciously ordered his son to discharge guns on his own land to interfere with the breeding. This was held by Macnaghten J. to be a nuisance even though the firing occurred on the defendant's own land.

These cases must be contrasted with that of *Bradford Corporation v. Pickles.*[57] In that case the defendant abstracted water which percolated in undefined channels beneath his land which would otherwise have reached the plaintiff's adjoining reservoir. It was held by the House of Lords that the defendant had a right to abstract the water and his right was the same whether his motive was bona fide to improve his land or maliciously to harm the plaintiff or to induce the plaintiff to buy him out. Lord MacNaghten stated[58]:

2–034

> "It is the act, not the motive for the act which must be regarded. If the act, apart from motive, gives rise merely to damage without legal injury, the motive, however reprehensible it may be, will not supply that element."

Bradford Corporation v. Pickles can be distinguished from *Christie v. Davey* and *Hollywood Silver Fox Farm Ltd v. Emmett*. It is a natural right incident to the ownership of property not to have the enjoyment of that property unreasonably interfered with by, for instance, noise; what is or is not unreasonable will be a question of fact determined in the circumstances of

---

[54] [1893] 1 Ch. 316.
[55] *ibid.* at 326–327.
[56] [1936] 2 K.B. 468; see also (1936) 52 L.Q.R. 460–461; (1937) 53 L.Q.R. 1–4.
[57] [1895] A.C. 587.
[58] *ibid.* at 601.

each case depending on a balancing of the interests of the claimant and of the defendant; there is nothing to prevent the motives of the defendant being taken into account in assessing what is or is not reasonable. On the other hand, it is established law that there is no natural right to water percolating in no defined channel[59]: if there is no such right to percolating water, there can be no unlawful interference with the percolating water whatever the defendant's motive since in these circumstances there can be no injury to legal rights.[60]

This is consistent with the approach of the majority of the House of Lords in the case of *Hunter v. Canary Wharf Limited*[61] in which it was held that the plaintiffs had no cause of action in respect of the interference with television transmissions caused by the erection of the defendant's tall building because the plaintiffs had no *right* to receive television transmissions.

Defences

Introduction

2–035 There are a number of ways in which a defendant may seek to defend a claim that he is liable for a nuisance.

An otherwise unlawful interference with a claimant's enjoyment of his land and interests in land, may be rendered lawful in a number of circumstances. The interference may be justified: it may be permitted by the licence or consent of the claimant,[62] made lawful by reason of an easement or right acquired by the defendant by prescription or otherwise,[63] or authorised by statute.[64] The claimant himself may be wholly[65] or partly responsible for the harm of which he complains. Where liability results from the negligence of the defendant, a plea of contributory negligence subject to the Law Reform (Contributory Negligence) Act 1945 may be made.[66] Where liability is not strictly imposed, defences based on inevitable accident,[67] ignorance of the defendant,[68] and a plea that the nuisance was caused by the act of a stranger[69] may be available. The defence of act of God may also be made.[70]

---

[59] Compare *Bamford v. Turnley* (1862) 3 B. & S. 62, 83; *Kennaway v. Thompson* [1981] Q.B. 88, 94.
[60] *Acton v. Blundell* (1843) 12 M. & W. 324; *Broadbent v. Ramsbotham* (1856) 11 Exch. 602; *Chasemore v. Richards* (1859) 7 H.L.C. 376; *Bradford v. Pickles* [1895] A.C. 587. See *Home Brewery Co. Ltd v. William Davis & Co. (Leicester) Ltd* [1987] 1 Q.B. 339 and see *Palmer v. Bowman* [2000] 1 W.L.R. 842, CA.
[61] [1997] A.C. 655, HL at 692 *per* Lord Goff, at 699 *per* Lord Lloyd, at 709 *per* Lord Hoffmann at 726 *per* Lord Hope but *cf.* the judgment of Lord Cooke at 711 *et seq.*
[62] See para. 2–037.
[63] See para. 2–038.
[64] See para. 2–039.
[65] See para. 2–040.
[66] See para. 2–040.
[67] See para. 2–041.
[68] See para. 2–044.
[69] See para. 2–043.
[70] See para. 2–042.

The nature of the tort of private nuisance being an unreasonable interference with the enjoyment of land has led some defendants to argue that other defences are available so as to render an interference reasonable or lawful. However, as set out below, it will not avail a defendant that a claimant has come to a nuisance[71] or that the nuisance has a public benefit.[72] These matters will not render an otherwise unreasonable and unlawful interference either reasonable or lawful.

Further, provided that the claimant has a better title to possession of his land than the defendant, the defendant will not be able to assert that a third party has better title to the land than the claimant (*i.e. ius tertii* is no defence).[73]

Justification

A defendant may justify his interference with the claimant's land as being lawful because: (a) the claimant has consented to the nuisance, (b) the defendant has an easement or the benefit of some right by which he is entitled to commit the nuisance or (c) the defendant has statutory authority to commit the nuisance.

2–036

CONSENT OF CLAIMANT

If a claimant has consented to the defendant creating a nuisance he cannot then complain of an interference with his land to the extent that the interference was permitted.[74] The principle of *volenti non fit injuria* applies in the tort of private nuisance as it does elsewhere (though the claimant's "coming to" a nuisance after its creation will provide no defence as set out below).[75] It applies equally in the context of the rule in *Rylands v. Fletcher*.[76]

Consent to a nuisance may be implicit. For instance, consent may be implied where the dangerous thing is brought onto the defendant's land for the common benefit of both the claimant and the defendant. Thus, where different floors in the same building are occupied by different persons, they can usually be taken to consent to the presence of water on the premises if the supply is of a character usually found in such premises; accordingly there will be no liability under the strict rule in *Rylands v.*

2–037

---

[71] See para. 2–046.
[72] See para. 2–047.
[73] See para. 2–048.
[74] *Gill v. Edouin* (1894) 71 L.T. 762; 72 L.T. 579; *Att.-Gen. v. Cory Bros Ltd* [1921] 1 A.C. 521, 538, 543, 550; *Ross v. Fedden* (1872) L.R. 7 Q.B. 661; *Bishop v. Consolidated London Properties* (1933) 102 L.J.K.B. 257; *Kiddle v. City Business Properties Ltd* [1942] 1 K.B. 269. *Gibson v. Kerrier RDC* [1976] 1 W.L.R. 904 at 912–913, 914. See also *Leakey v. National Trust* [1980] Q.B. 485, 515 A–B.
[75] For a general discussion of *Volenti*, etc., see Clerk and Lindsell *Torts* (18th ed.), para. 3–57 *et seq.*
[76] See below.

Fletcher for the escape of water.[77] In similar situations, consent may be implied in relation to the presence of fire extinguishing apparatus,[78] gas,[79] and electricity.[80] In such a situation, however, there will not be implied consent to an interference with the enjoyment of premises caused by a negligent escape.[81]

EASEMENTS AND OTHER RIGHTS

2–038 A defendant may have a right to do acts which would otherwise amount to a nuisance by reason of an easement or right (such as a profit) granted over the claimant's land entitling him to do those acts.

An easement is a right which attaches to one piece of land (the dominant tenement) which gives its owner a right to use or interfere with the enjoyment of the land of another (the servient tenement). A *profit à prendre* is (in general terms) a right to take something off the land of another.[82]

An easement may be acquired by an express or implied grant upon a conveyance.[83] In *Lyttleton Times Co. Ltd v. Warners Ltd*[84] a landlord let the upper part of a building to a tenant to use for hotel bedrooms. The lower part of the building retained by the landlord was to be used for printing works and this was known to the tenant (though it was not believed that this would cause a nuisance). It was held that the tenant could not complain of the nuisance caused by the noise of the printing works: there was no evidence that the work was carried out improperly or negligently. Lord Loreburn L.C. said:[85]

> "If it be true that neither has done or asks to do anything which was not contemplated by both, neither can have any right against the other."[86]

A right to cause an interference which would otherwise constitute a nuisance may also be acquired as an easement by prescription.[87] In brief, in

---

[77] See *Kiddle v. City Business Properties Ltd* [1942] 1 K.B. 269, 274; see too *Blake v. Woolf* [1898] 2 Q.B. 426 at 428 cf. *Humphries v. Cousins* (1877) 2 C.P.D. 239.

[78] *Peters v. Prince of Wales Theatre (Birmingham) Ltd* [1943] 1 K.B. 73

[79] *Miller v. Addie & Sons Collieries* 1934 S.C. 150

[80] *Collingwood v. Home and Colonial Stores Ltd* [1936] 3 All E.R. 200

[81] *Prosser v. Levy* [1955] 1 W.L.R. 1224, 1233. Compare *Akerib v. Booth Ltd* [1960] 1 W.L.R. 454 at 458 (reversed on other grounds [1961] 1 W.L.R. 367).

[82] See para. 1–033.

[83] See, generally, *Gale on Easements*, (16th ed.).

[84] [1907] A.C. 476.

[85] *ibid.* at 481; compare *Pwllbach Colliery Co. v. Woodman* [1915] A.C. 634, esp. at 646, *per* Lord Parker. See also *Sovmots Investments Ltd v. Secretary of State for the Environment* [1979] A.C. 144, 175, *per* Lord Edmund-Davies.

[86] cf. *Vanderpant v. Mayfair Hotel Co.* [1930] 1 Ch. 138 (grant of immunity for obstruction of right to light, etc., by a hotel did not imply a right to cause nuisance from hotel kitchen); *Horton v. Tidd* (1965) 196 E.G. 697 (grant of lease to cricket club did not imply a right to hit balls onto adjoining land).

[87] See generally *Gale on Easements* (16th ed.), p. 232, for the principles of prescription. Compare *Viner's Abridgment Nuisance*, G; *Elliotson v. Feetham* (1835) 2 Bing. N.C. 134; *Crump v.*

order to establish a defence of prescription to an action for nuisance the defendant must show, first that he or his predecessors in title have been doing the acts complained of *nec vi nec clam nec precario* (neither by force, nor secretly nor with the permission of the servient owner) and secondly that the nuisance (rather than simply the operations which now cause the nuisance)[88] has been continuously in existence since time immemorial,[89] in such circumstances that the loss of a modern grant may be inferred[90] or for the statutory periods of 20 or 40 years.[91] To acquire a right by prescription there must be certainty and uniformity "for the measurement and determination of the user by which the extent of the prescriptive right is to be ascertained".[92] Accordingly it may be extremely difficult (if not impossible) to acquire an easement to interfere with one's neighbours enjoyment by means of smoke, noise or vibration where the extent of the interference is constantly varying.[93] Similarly it is hard to see how a prescriptive right to commit a nuisance within *Rylands v. Fletcher* can ever arise in practice given the intermittent or solitary nature of an escape within that rule.

The difficulties in establishing a defence based upon a prescriptive right to commit a nuisance are illustrated by the case of *Sturges v. Bridgman*.[94] In that case the defendant had carried on the business of a confectioner for more than 20 years and his business entailed him using a noisy pestle and mortar. The plaintiff then constructed a consulting room for his practice as a physician in the garden adjoining the defendant's premises. The noise from the defendant's machinery interfered with the plaintiff's enjoyment of his new consulting room. It was held that the defendant could not rely on a defence of prescriptive right because there had been no actionable nuisance which the plaintiff or his predecessors could have prevented until the plaintiff had constructed his consulting room and thus the nuisance had not continued for the necessary period of 20 years.

Further, it seems that one will not acquire an easement by prescription for one's trees to grow so as to overhang one's neighbour's premises or for

---

Lambert (1867) L.R. 3 Eq. 409, 413; *Wright v. Williams* (1836) 1 M. & W. 77; *Brown v. Dunstable Corporation* [1899] 2 Ch. 378; *Royal Mail Steam Packet Co. v. George and Branday* [1900] A.C. 480.

[88] See *Halsey v. Esso Petroleum Co. Ltd* [1961] 1 W.L.R. 683, 702; and see also *Flight v. Thomas* (1839) 10 A. & E. 590; *Murgatroyd v. Robinson* (1857) 7 E. & B. 391; *Goldsmid v. Tunbridge Wells Improvement Commissioners* (1866) 1 Ch.App. 349; *Crossley & Sons v. Lightowler* (1867) 2 Ch.App. 478; *Liverpool Corporation v. Coghill* [1918] 1 Ch. 307.

[89] See *Gale, op.cit.,* para. 4–03.

[90] See *Gale, op.cit.,* para. 4–06.

[91] See *Gale, op.cit.,* para. 4–17 (Prescription Act 1832).

[92] *per* Eve J. in *Hulley v. Silversprings Bleaching Co.* [1922] 2 Ch. 268, 281; compare *Cargill v. Gotts* [1981] 1 W.L.R. 441, 448.

[93] Compare *Halsey v. Esso Petroleum Co. Ltd* [1961] 1 W.L.R. 683, 702.

[94] (1878) 11 Ch.D. 852. See also *Elliotson v. Feetham* (1835) 2 Bing N.C. 134 (noise); *Bliss v. Hall* (1838) 4 Bing N.C. 183 (smell); *Crump v. Lambert* (1867) L.R. Eq. 409 (smoke and noise).

the roots of trees to encroach: it seems that such a nuisance constantly varies in the quantity of inconvenience caused.[95]

Like an easement, a profit may be acquired by express or implied grant[96] or by prescription.[97] The exercise of a profit may not only provide a defence to a claim based upon trespass on the claimant's land for its exercise,[98] but also for any nuisance caused as a result of the exercise of the rights granted with the profit. For instance, if game reared pursuant to sporting rights causes an interference with the servient owner's land, then such interference will not be actionable if it is within the ambit of the sporting rights granted though there will be liability to the extent that those rights are exceeded.[99]

STATUTORY AUTHORITY

2–039 Statute may render lawful what would otherwise be an unreasonable and unlawful interference with land. With the increase in the provision of public utilities and the spread of the railways in the nineteenth century, Parliament gave powers to and imposed duties upon many bodies to carry out works and use land in ways which interfered with the private enjoyment of land. Whether or not a particular nuisance will be authorised by such statutes either expressly or by statutory implication is a matter of the construction of the statute in each case.[1]

Thus in the case of *Dunne v. North Western Gas Board*[2] it was held upon the construction of the Gas Act 1948 that the defendant was not liable for damage caused by the escape of gas. The statute authorised the defendant and put it under a duty to supply gas and expressly envisaged the escape of gas providing the defendant with duties in those circumstances. The defendant did what the statute imposed upon it without negligence, and was held not liable for the escape upon the basis of *Rylands v. Fletcher*. Sellars L.J. delivering the judgment of the Court said[3]:

> "Gas, water and also electricity services are well-nigh a necessity of modern life, or at least are generally demanded as a requirement for the common good, and one or more are being taken with considerable

---

[95] Compare *Lemmon v. Webb* [1894] 3 Ch. 1, [1895] A.C. 1; *Khyatt v. Morgan* [1961] N.Z.L.R. 1020, 1024; [1962] N.Z.L.R. 791; *Morgan v. Khyatt* [1964] 1 W.L.R. 475, P.C.

[96] See generally, Megarry & Wade, *Law of Real Property* (6th ed.), (1999), para 18–090 *et seq.*

[97] *ibid.*

[98] See Chapter 1, para. 1–077 above.

[99] See *e.g. Pole v Peake* [1998] E.G.C.S. 125, CA and see too 3–044.

[1] See for instance *R. v. Pease* (1832) 4 B. & D. 30 (interference with public highway); *Vaughan v. Taff Ry* (1860) 5 H. & N. 679 (fire damage caused by sparks from engines where no negligence); *Hammersmith Ry v. Brand* (1869) L.R. 4 H.L. 171 (vibrations caused by trains without negligence); *London, Brighton and South Coast Ry v. Truman* (1885) 11 App.Cas. 45 (noise from cattle in railway yard). See also K. Davies (1974) 90 L.Q.R. 361; Craig, (1980) 96 L.Q.R. 413.

[2] [1964] 2 Q.B. 806.

[3] *ibid.* at 832; contrast *Pearson v North Western Gas Board* [1968] 2 All E.R. 669, at 672 *per* Rees J.

despatch to every village and hamlet in the country with either statutory compulsion or sanction. It would seem odd that facilities so much sought after by the community and approved by their legislators should be actionable at common law because they have been brought to the places where they are required and have escaped without negligence by an unforeseen sequence of mishaps."

In the case of *Allen v. Gulf Oil Refining Ltd*[4] the Court had to construe the Gulf Oil Refining Act 1965. The Act authorised the use of certain land for the construction of an oil refinery and associated works. There was no provision for the payment of compensation for any damage caused. There was provision for the construction of subsidiary works such as railways which required the statutory undertaker, the defendant, to make reasonable compensation for any damage caused by the exercise of its powers under this provision. The defendant constructed its refinery and the plaintiff complained of noxious odours, vibrations and offensive noise. On a preliminary point of law as to whether or not the defendant could rely on the Act of 1965 as having authorised the nuisance resulting from the construction and operation of the oil refinery it was held by May J. and the House of Lords (reversing the decision of the Court of Appeal, Lord Keith of Kinkel dissenting) that the Act conferred upon the defendant statutory immunity from action for nuisance to the extent that it could show that it had used all due diligence and that the resulting harm was the inevitable consequence of the authorised operations of the refinery. The Act was construed as authorising the construction of the refinery and by necessary implication both as authorising its use and as conferring immunity against proceedings for any nuisance which was the inevitable result of such use: if such a nuisance could be actionable the plaintiff could prevent the operation of the refinery by an injunction and thwart the purpose of the Act. The onus of proof was on the plaintiff to prove the nuisance alleged but if the defendant was to rely upon statutory immunity in its defence the onus was upon it to show that it was impossible to construct or to operate the refinery without creating the nuisance alleged or at least a nuisance.[5]

The principles upon which the Courts have approached the construction of statutes in this context may be summarised as follows[6]:

"1. In the absence of negligence, a body is not liable for a nuisance which is attributable to the exercise by it of a duty imposed on it by statute . . .[7]

---

[4] [1981] A.C. 1001.
[5] *ibid.*, 1013; see also *Manchester Corporation v. Farnworth* [1930] A.C. 171, 183, *per* Lord Dunedin.
[6] *Department of Transport v. North West Water Authority* [1983] 1 All E.R. 892, 895, *per* Webster J.; [1983] 3 All E.R. 273, 275–276, HL. *Marcic v. Water Utilities* [2002] EWCA Civ 65 at para. 57–60; also *Bristol Waterways Board v. Severn Trent Water Ltd* [2001] EWCA Civ. 276.
[7] See *Hammond v. St Pancras Corporation* (1874) L.R. 9 C.P. 316.

"2. It is not liable in those circumstances even if by statute it is expressly made liable, or not exempted from liability, for nuisance . . .[8]

"3. In the absence of negligence, a body is not liable for a nuisance which is attributable to the exercise by it of a power conferred by statute if, it is not expressly made liable, or not exempted from liability, for nuisance . . .[9]

"4. A body is liable for a nuisance by it attributable to the exercise of a power conferred by statute, even without negligence, if by statute it is expressly either made liable, or not exempted from liability, for nuisance . . .[10]

"In these rules, references to the absence of negligence are references to:

'the qualification, or condition, that the statutory powers are exercised without "negligence", that word here being used in a special sense so as to require the undertaker, as a condition of obtaining immunity from action, to carry out the work and conduct the operation with all reasonable regard and care for the interests of other persons . . .'"[11]

It will also be appropriate in construing a statute to consider whether or not the statute provides for compensation for acquisition of, intrusion upon or interference with private rights: without such provisions it may be that Parliament did not intend that private rights should be interfered with (in the absence of express or necessarily implied indications to the contrary).[12]

These rules of construction apply both to liability for nuisance *simpliciter* and to liability under the rule in *Rylands v. Fletcher*.[13] For this

---

[8] See *Stretton's Derby Brewery Co. v. Derby Corporation* [1894] 1 Ch. 431 and *Smeaton v. Ilford Corporation* [1954] Ch. 450.

[9] *Midwood & Co. Ltd v. Manchester Corporation* [1905] 2 K.B. 597; *Longhurst v. Metropolitan Water Board* [1948] 2 All E.R. 834 and *Dunne v. North Western Gas Board* [1964] 2 Q.B. 806.

[10] See *Charing Cross Electricity Supply Co. v. Hydraulic Power Co.* [1914] 3 K.B. 772. See also *Rapier v. London Tramways* [1893] 2 Ch. 588; *Batcheller v. Tunbridge Wells Gas Co.* (1901) 84 L.T. 765; *Pride of Derby, etc. v. British Celanese Ltd* [1953] Ch. 149; *Smeaton v. Ilford Corporation* [1954] Ch. 450.

[11] See *Allen v. Gulf Oil Refining Ltd* [1981] A.C. 1001 at 1011, *per* Lord Wilberforce. See too *Tate & Lyle Industries Limited v. Greater London Council* [1983] 2 A.C. 509. For consideration of duties of statutory bodies in other contexts, compare *Home Office v. Dorset Yacht Co. Ltd* [1970] A.C. 1004; *Anns v. London Borough of Merton* [1977] 2 All E.R. 492, 501–503; *Fellowes v. Rother District Council* [1983] 1 All E.R. 513; *Rowling v. Takaro Properties Ltd* [1988] 1 All E.R. 163.

[12] *Allen v. Gulf Oil Refining Ltd* [1981] A.C. 1001, 1016, *per* Lord Edmund-Davies, compare [1979] 3 All E.R. 1008, 1016, *per* Lord Denning M.R.

[13] *Department of Transport v. North West Water Authority* [1983] 1 All E.R. 892, 895. See *Geddis v. Proprietors of Bann Reservoir* (1878) 3 App.Cas. 430; *Green v. Chelsea Waterworks Co.* (1894) 70 L.T. 547 (statutory duty to maintain water supply; held, defence available); *Charing Cross Electricity Co. v. Hydraulic Power Co.* [1914] 2 K.B. 772 (statute only permitted laying of water mains; held, defence not available). See too *Pride of Derby etc v. British Celanese* [1953] Ch. 149 at 189 *per* Denning LJ. But see section 7 of the Nuclear Installations Act 1965 and *Merlin v. British Nuclear Fuels plc* [1990] 3 All E.R. 711 at 714.

defence to be available in a claim based upon *Rylands v. Fletcher* the statute must authorise the use of the dangerous thing itself either expressly or by necessary implication.[14] For the statute simply to permit the use of the dangerous thing will not suffice.[15]

In each case, it will be necessary to consider the extent to which a statute authorises the interference. Thus, for example, under the London Building Act (Amendment) Act 1939 provided that the statutory procedure was followed, the owner of a building would not be liable to his neighbour for the carrying out of works specified in the Act.[16] On the other hand, if the procedures were not followed *e.g.* because the correct statutory notices were not served prior to the commencement of works, the nuisances would not be authorised.[17]

It should be noted that the mere grant of planning permission under the Town and County Planning Acts will not authorise a nuisance.[18] In the case of incorporeal hereditaments over land, there are also statutory provisions which allow for the overriding of such rights in certain circumstances upon the development of land[19] or in the context of the compulsory acquisition of land.[20]

Acts of the Claimant and Contributory Negligence

The claimant may himself be responsible for an escape from the defendant's land which harms him. If so, this will provide a defence. Accordingly, in the context of the rule in *Rylands v. Fletcher*, if the claimant himself causes the escape of the dangerous thing or the damage which results, it is proper that he should not be entitled to a remedy for its escape.[21] Thus, in the case of *Dunn v. Birmingham Canal Co.*[22] the defendant canal owner was not liable for the escape of water from its canal into the plaintiff's mine where the escape of water had been caused by the plaintiff working his mine under the canal knowing that the water would escape as a result. Further, if the damage caused by an escape or **2–040**

---

[14] *West v. Bristol Tramways* [1908] 2 K.B. 14.
[15] *Jones v. Festiniog Ry* (1868) L.R. 3 Q.B. 733.
[16] See *Standard Bank of British South America v. Stokes* (1878) 9 Ch. D 68; *Selby v. Whitbread & Co.* [1917] 1 K.B. 736; see now Party Walls Act 1996.
[17] *Louis v. Sadiq* [1997] 1 E.G.L.R. 136, CA.
[18] *Allen v. Gulf Oil Refining* [1980] Q.B. 156, 174, CA, *per* Cumming-Bruce L.J. (House of Lords is silent on the point at [1981] A.C. 101); *Wheeler v. JJ Saunders* [1996] Ch 19 [1995] 1 All E.R. 671; *Gillingham BC v. Medway (Chatham) Dock Co. Ltd* [1992] 3 All E.R. 923. See para. 2–031, above.
[19] See Town and Country Planning Act 1990, s.237; see *R v. City of London Corporation ex p the Master Governors and Commonality of the Mystery of the Barbers of London* (1997) 73 P & CR 59, Q.B., Dyson J; *Thames Water Utilities Ltd v. Oxford City Council* [1999] 1 E.G.L.R. 167, Ch D, H.H.J. Rich.
[20] Whether incorporeal hereditaments are to be acquired will depend upon the construction of the enabling Act (compare Compulsory Purchase Act 1965, s.1(3)).
[21] See *Rylands v. Fletcher* (1868) L.R. 3 H.L. 330, 340; *Lomax v. Scott* (1870) 39 L.J. Ch. 834; *Holgate v. Bleazard* [1917] 1 K.B. 443; *Postmaster-General v. Liverpool Corp.* [1923] A.C. 587.
[22] (1872) L.R. 7 Q.B. 224 at 246.

emission from the defendant's land would not have occurred but for some special or non-natural use of the claimant's own land, the defendant will not be liable because "a man cannot increase the liabilities of his neighbour by applying his own property to special uses, whether for business or pleasure".[23] This is the same principle which arises when dealing with the "sensitivity" of a claimant in the law of nuisance generally.[24] If, on the other hand, the claimant merely contributes to the harm by his own negligence, then his damages may be reduced under the provisions of the Law Reform (Contributory Negligence) Act 1945.

"Contributory negligence" is a phrase which refers to the claimant's own want of care which contributes to his damage.[25] This defence, subject to the provisions regarding apportionment in the Law Reform (Contributory Negligence) Act 1945, appears to be available in an action for nuisance, save where the consequences of the nuisance were intended by the defendant.[26] In practice, however, the defence rarely appears to arise in the case of private nuisance which usually involves some escape or emission from premises outside the control of the claimant which the claimant is unable to influence (except in the case of exacerbation of damage).

Inevitable Accident and the Defendant's Care and Skill

2–041   An inevitable accident is an accident "not avoidable by any such precaution as a reasonable man, doing such an act then and there could be expected to take."[27] Where liability for a nuisance depends upon the negligent behaviour of the defendant, this defence may be of significance: if the defendant has taken all reasonable precautions against the interference with the claimant's land the interference may not be unreasonable and thus not be actionable. However, where a nuisance is actionable notwithstanding the precautions taken, it will afford the defendant no defence to the action that he has carried out his trade or business or other activities with all due care and skill and has made every effort to prevent the nuisance.[28] Thus, if the making of noise unreasonably interferes with the claimant's enjoyment of his property, it is no answer that the "best-known means have been taken to reduce or prevent the noise, or that the cause of the nuisance is the exercise of a business in a reasonable and proper manner."[29] Where liability is imposed under the principle in

[23] *Eastern and South Africa Telegraph Co. v. Cape Tramways Co. Ltd* [1902] A.C. 381 at 393.
[24] See above, para. 2–032.
[25] *Craze v. Meyer-Dumore Bottlers' Equipment Ltd* [1936] 2 All E.R. 1150, 1151.
[26] *Trevett v. Lee* [1955] 1 W.L.R. 113, 122, *per* Evershed M.R. (a case of public nuisance). See also Winfield, [1930 — 2] C.L.J. 189, 200 (defence never available); Williams, *Joint Torts* (1951), pp. 203–5.
[27] Pollock, *Torts* (15th ed.), p. 97.
[28] See *Rapier v. London Tramways Co.* [1893] 2 Ch. 588; *Adams v. Ursell* [1913] 1 Ch. 269; *Farrell v. John Mowlem & Co. Ltd* [1954] 1 Lloyd's Rep. 437, 440; *Bone v. Seal* [1975] 1 W.L.R. 797.
[29] *Vanderpant v. Mayfair Hotel Co.* [1930] 1 Ch. 138, *per* Luxmoore J.

Rylands v. Fletcher[30] because the existence of a duty is established and an escape in breach of the duty proven, it seems that nothing less than an act of God will suffice to provide a defence.[31]

Act of God

An act of God is an occurrence outside human agency and which cannot **2–042** reasonably be anticipated.[32] The defence has arisen where liability would otherwise be strict, in particular in the context of the rule in *Rylands v. Fletcher*.[33] Where liability is not strict, the defendant will not need to go so far as to establish that harm was caused as the result of an act of God; all that will be necessary will be for him to establish that he has taken those precautions which are sufficient for him to have complied with his duties (see the preceding paragraphs).

The defence of "act of God" recognises that some occurrences are so unexpected and so much outside the control of the defendant that the connection between the defendant's acts or omissions and the harm which the claimant has suffered is simply too remote for legal liability to be imposed.

This exception to the rule in *Rylands v. Fletcher* was expressly recognised by Blackburn J in that case. An act of God is the operation of natural forces "which no human foresight can provide against, and of which human pretence is not bound to recognise the possibility".[34]

In *Nichols v. Marsland*[35] the defendant was in possession of artificial ornamental pools formed by the damming of a stream. An extraordinary rainfall "greater and more violent than any within the memory of witnesses" broke down the artificial embankments containing the water. The water escaped and damaged four bridges in respect of which the plaintiff brought the action. It seems that the defendant was found to be not liable as the result of an act of God. In *J.J. Makin Ltd v. L.N.E.R.*[36] it seems that Lord Greene M.R. accepted that liability under *Rylands v. Fletcher* can be avoided for an escape of water if it can be shown that the water escaped without the defendant's negligence.

Despite these cases, it appears to be difficult to establish this defence to a claim made on the basis of *Rylands v. Fletcher*. In *Greenock Corporation v. Caledonian Railway*[37] the Corporation constructed a concrete paddling

---

[30] See below, paras 2–056 *et seq.*
[31] See below, paras 2–064 *et seq.*
[32] See Clerk and Lindsell *Torts* (18th ed.), paras. 2–38, 19–69.
[33] See para. 2–064.
[34] *Tennent v. Earl of Glasgow* (1864) 2 M. (H.L.) 22 at 26–27, *per* Lord Westbury; see also *Greenock Corp. v. Caledonian Railway* [1917] A.C. 556; *A.M.F. International Ltd v. Magnet Bowling Ltd* [1968] 1 W.L.R. 1028 at 1039, *per* Mocatta J.
[35] (1876) 2 Ex. D. 1.
[36] [1943] 1 K.B. 467 at 470 (citing counsel).
[37] [1917] A.C. 556.

pool for children in the bed of a stream. The construction of the pool involved altering the course and obstructing the flow of a natural stream. There was a very heavy rainfall ("a heavy, it may be an extraordinary and it may be an unprecedented, spate") which resulted in an escape of water and damage to the plaintiff's land. The House of Lords held that the rainfall in this case was not an act of God and the Corporation were liable. It was the Corporation's duty "so to work as to make proprietors or occupiers on a lower level as secure against injury as they would have been had nature not been interfered with". Further, in the case of *Attorney-General v. Cory*,[38] Scrutton L.J. stated:

"the fact that an artificial danger escaped through natural causes was no excuse to the person who brought an artificial danger there."[39]

It seems that the Courts are reluctant to permit the defence of act of God in cases where the defendant is under a duty under *Rylands v. Fletcher*: the duty arises because he has brought onto his land something which would *foreseeably* cause damage if it escaped. In such circumstances, there is force in arguing that it is the defendant who should assume the risk of all losses resulting from an escape. In any event, if the test of what constitutes an act of God is whether the escape or harm resulted from an operation of natural forces "which no human foresight can provide against, and of which human pretence is not bound to recognise the possibility" it would seem that the test is hard to satisfy since human foresight can provide against most disasters; and where it cannot, human pretence is usually bound to "recognise the possibility" of a disaster (albeit that the possibility is remote). Extraordinary weather would certainly appear to be recognised as possible in Britain (though perhaps other natural phenomena such as a serious earthquake would not). For this reason the House of Lords in the *Greenock Corporation* case were correct in casting doubt on the findings in *Nichols v. Marsland*.

Act of Stranger

2–043   In *Sedleigh-Denfield v. O'Callaghan*[40] Lord Wright said:

"An occupier is not prima facie responsible for a nuisance created without his knowledge and consent. If he is to be liable a further condition is necessary, namely, that he had knowledge or had means of knowledge, that he knew or should have known of the nuisance in time to correct it and obviate its mischievous effects."

---

[38] (1919) 25 T.L.R. 570, CA reversed at [1921] 1 A.C. 521, HL (fall of debris probably caused by saturation of strata by extraordinary rainfall).
[39] *ibid.* at 574, dissenting; [1921] 1 A.C. 521 at 536 *per* Lord Haldane.
[40] [1940] A.C. 880, 904.

It follows that if a stranger causes a nuisance on the defendant's land and the defendant has no knowledge or presumed knowledge of it, he will not be liable. In these circumstances, there is no duty upon the defendant. However, if the defendant has or acquires knowledge of the nuisance, he may be liable for adopting or continuing the nuisance caused by the stranger if he fails to take appropriate steps to abate it.[41] Thus, in the case of *Page v. Epsom and Ewell Borough Council*[42] a local authority was liable to the plaintiff where gypsies parked on the local authority's land without permission causing a nuisance to the plaintiff but the local authority failed to take reasonable steps to abate the nuisance when they had knowledge of it. On the other hand, in *Smeaton v. Ilford Corporation*[43] the defendant was held not liable for a nuisance caused by an overflowing of sewage from its sewers because the overflow was caused by an overloading of the sewers by third parties which the defendant had no power to prevent. Likewise in *King v. Liverpool City Council* where trespassers broke the pipes in the defendant's premises causing a flood affecting the plaintiff's premises, the defendant was not liable.[44]

In the context of the rule in *Rylands v. Fletcher* where a duty is imposed on a defendant who brings a dangerous thing onto his land, it has been held that if a defendant has not been negligent, he will not be liable if the dangerous thing escapes as the result of the independent act of a third party. Although the defendant is under a duty in respect of the dangerous thing, his duty does not extend to these circumstances. If this were not so, the rule in *Rylands v. Fletcher* would:

> "make a householder liable for the consequences of an explosion caused by a burglar breaking into his house during the night and leaving the gas tap open."[45]

In the case of *Rickards v. Lothian*,[46] from which this latter dictum is taken, the occupier of a lavatory on an upper floor was held not responsible to the occupier of a lower floor for the damage caused by an escape of water where a malicious and unknown third party turned on the tap and blocked the waste pipe causing an overflow. Of course, if the defendant

---

[41] See above para. 2–014.
[42] (1982) 80 L.G.R. 337, CA (and see too *Lippiatt v. South Gloucestershire Council* [1999] 4 All E.R. 149, CA). See para 2–014 *et seq.* above. See also *Leanse v. Lord Egerton* [1943] 1 K.B. 323 (glass falling from house damaged by enemy action, defendant had presumed knowledge); *Pemberton v. Bright and Devon County Council* [1960] 1 W.L.R. 436 (culvert fixed without adequate protection, defendants had knowledge).
[43] [1954] 1 Ch. 450.
[44] [1986] 1 W.L.R. 890, CA. See also *Barker v. Herbert* [1911] 2 K.B. 633 (trespassers damaged railing adjoining highway through which child fell, defendant not liable); *Cushing v. Peter Walker & Sons Ltd* [1941] 2 All E.R. 693 (loose slate blown from roof damaged by enemy action was the act of a trespasser); *Smith v. Littlewoods Organisation Ltd* [1987] 1 A.C. 241, HL (no duty of care where trespassers started fire in defendant's vacant cinema which spread to plaintiff's property).
[45] *Rickards v. Lothian* [1913] A.C. 263 HL at 282 *per* Lord Moulton.
[46] *Rickards v. Lothian* [1913] A.C. 263 HL.

turns on the water knowing of the obstruction he will be liable for the escape of the water.[47]

In the case of *Perry v. Kendricks Transport Ltd*[48] the defendant was held not liable for injury to the plaintiff resulting from an explosion caused by a stranger throwing a match into the petrol tank of a motor coach. The defendant had not been negligent in the way he had kept the motor coach. The principle was that:

> "If the mischievous, deliberate and conscious act of a stranger causes the damage, the occupier can escape liability; he is absolved."[49]

As indicated in the preceding paragraphs, it is only where the defendant has not been negligent that he will not be liable under *Rylands v. Fletcher* for an escape caused by a stranger. In other words, the defendant will not be absolved from liability where the stranger's act which results in the escape of that which the defendant has brought onto his land is of the sort which he could have guarded against with reasonable care. In such circumstances the liability based on *Rylands v. Fletcher* will merge with a claim in negligence.[50]

From the case of *Perry v. Kendricks Transport Ltd*[51] it seems that in order to defend a claim based on *Rylands v. Fletcher* on the grounds that that the escape was caused by the act of a stranger, the onus of proof is on the defendant to show affirmatively that the escape was due to the deliberate or conscious act of a third party over whom he had no control. If he does so, he will avoid liability unless the *claimant* can go on to show that the act which caused the escape "was an act of the kind which the occupier could reasonably have anticipated and guarded against".

However, this approach to the burden of proof in respect of acts which the occupier could reasonably have anticipated seems to conflict with the case of *Hanson v. Wearmouth Coal Co. Ltd and Sunderland Gas Co.*[52] in which Goddard L.J. stated[53]:

> "A person who brings a dangerous thing on to his land and allows it to escape, thereby causing damage to another, is liable to that other *unless he can show* that the escape was due to the conscious act of a third party, *and without negligence on his own part*. Obviously the burden of showing that there was no negligence is on the defendants, and it is not for the plaintiff to prove negligence affirmatively [emphasis supplied]."

---

[47] *Harrison v. G.N.R.* (1864) 3 H. & C. 231.
[48] [1956] 1 W.L.R. 85 CA.
[49] *ibid.* at 87, *per* Singleton L.J.
[50] *ibid. per* Jenkins L.J.
[51] *ibid.*
[52] [1939] 3 All E.R. 47.
[53] *ibid.*, at 53.

In the case of *Northwestern Utilities Ltd v. London Guarantee and Accident Co. Ltd*[54] the appellant was a public utility company which carried gas at high pressure under the street. Gas had percolated from the appellant's gas main into the basement of a hotel owned by the respondent. The gas ignited and damaged the respondent's property. The gas had percolated from the main because of a fracture caused during the construction of a storm sewer by a third party. The Privy Council held the appellant liable because it knew of the works carried out to the storm sewer and was negligent in failing to inspect the main to see if it had been damaged. The Privy Council seem to have taken an approach to the burden of proof similar to that of Goddard L.J., above.[55] The onus, therefore, appears to be on the defendant seeking to escape liability under *Rylands v. Fletcher* to establish (a) that the escape of the dangerous thing was due to the conscious act of the stranger and (b) that he had taken all reasonable steps to safeguard against the escape. This approach is consistent with what appears to be the general rule in nuisance that once a nuisance has been established the onus is on the defendant to show that he has an excuse.[56]

A stranger is someone over whom the defendant has no control.[57] A stranger for the purposes of raising a defence to an action for nuisance will not include the defendant's servants or agents since the usual rules with regard to vicarious liability apply to the tort of nuisance.[58] Likewise where a landowner grants a licence over land to a licensee who causes a nuisance in such circumstances that he retains sufficient control to prevent the nuisances, the licensee will not be a stranger.[59] An independent contractor, however, will usually be a stranger for these purposes[60] except where the operations for which the contractor has been engaged are dangerous in themselves: thus a defendant may be liable for the spread of fire[61] or damage caused as a result of works on gas installations[62] by independent contractors notwithstanding that the defendant has no knowledge of the actual nuisance resulting.

---

[54] [1936] A.C. 108, PC.

[55] *ibid.* at 120; compare *A. Prosser & Son Ltd v. Levy* [1955] 3 All E.R. 577 at 587 *per* Singleton L.J.

[56] See above.

[57] *Perry v. Kendricks Transport Ltd*, [1956] 1 W.L.R. 85 CA at 90, *per* Jenkins L.J.; *Balfour v. Barty-King* [1957] 1 Q.B. 496 at 505 (control over independent contractor where defendants "chose him, . . . invited him to their premises, and he could have been ordered to leave at any moment"). *Hale v. Jennings Bros* [1938] 1 All E.R. 579; *H. & N. Emanuel Ltd v. G.L.C.* [1971] 2 All E.R. 835; *E. Hobbs (Farms) Ltd v. The Baxendon Chemical Co. Ltd* [1992] 1 Lloyd's Rep. 54 at 69.

[58] See above 2–021.

[59] *Ribee v. Norrie*, [2001] PIQRP 128; [2001] L&TR 239, CA.

[60] See above 2–021.

[61] *H. & N. Emanuel Ltd v. GLC* [1971] 2 All E.R. 835; see also *Black v. Christchurch Finance Co.* [1884] A.C. 48.

[62] *Hardaker v. Idle District Council* [1896] 1 Q.B. 335; *Brooke v. Bool* [1928] 2 K.B. 578, 587, *per* Talbot J.

Ignorance of the Defendant

2–044   Where liability is not strictly imposed regardless of the foreseeability of the nuisance, the ignorance of the defendant of the nuisance or state of affairs giving rise to the nuisance will be a defence unless the ignorance is due to his omission to use reasonable care or skill to discover the facts or he otherwise ought to have known of the facts. This "defence" is based on a wider principle which also underlies the narrower defence of "the act of a stranger" dealt with above.

Thus in the case of *Ilford UDC v. Beal*[63] an owner of land was not liable for damage to a sewer lying beneath her land which was caused by acts done or omitted to be done by her on her land, where she did not know and could not reasonably be expected to have known of the existence of the sewer. Branson J. in thus holding relied upon the case of *Barker v. Herbert*[64] in which a defendant was held not liable for a nuisance caused by the acts of trespassers where he did not know of those acts. On the other hand, where liability is imposed on an occupier of land who employs an independent contractor to carry out an operation which is in itself dangerous, the ignorance of the occupier of the precise activities of the independent contractor which cause a nuisance can provide no defence.[65] Liability in this context does not rest on a duty based on the simple foreseeability of the harm in the particular context, but depends upon the nature of the activities undertaken.[66]

In the context of strict liability in *Rylands v. Fletcher* where a duty to the claimant is established the ignorance of the defendant will only avail him in limited circumstances: for instance, where the escape is caused by a stranger and the defendant has taken all reasonable care to guard against the nuisance.[67]

Similarly, in other contexts where liability does not depend upon the reasonable foreseeability of the particular nuisance, the ignorance of the defendant will only be of limited assistance to a defendant. Thus in *Wringe v. Cohen*[68] it was held with regard to artificial structures projecting over the highway causing a public nuisance that:

"if premises become dangerous as the result of something done by an occupier and they cause damage, the occupier is liable although he did not know of the danger and was not negligent in not knowing . . . On the other hand, if premises become dangerous, not by the occupier's act or neglect of duty, but as a result of the act of a third party, or of a

---

[63] [1925] 1 K.B. 671. See also *St Anne's Well Brewery Co. v. Roberts* (1928) 140 L.T. 1; *Wilkins v. Leighton* [1932] 2 Ch. 106. See too *Holbeck Hall Hotel Limited v. Scaborough Borough Council* [2000] Q.B. 836, and see para. 2–014 above.

[64] [1911] 2 K.B. 633. See above, para. 2–043 (Act of Stranger).

[65] See para. 2–021, 2–043 above.

[66] See para. *ibid.*, above

[67] See para. 2–043 above.

[68] [1940] 1 K.B. 229, 248. See above, para. 2–013.

latent defect, the occupier is not liable without proof of knowledge or means of knowledge and failure to abate it."

However, the availability of a defence that the harm was caused by a "latent defect" in the structure indicates that even in this context the law recognises that the defendant's ignorance in some circumstances will provide him with a defence.[69]

Limitation

Under section 2 of the Limitation Act 1980 an action "founded on tort shall not be brought after the expiration of six years from the date upon which the cause of action accrued."[70] This defence is available to an action in nuisance. Where the nuisance is a continuing nuisance, a cause of action will accrue on a daily basis each time the nuisance is continued.[71] Accordingly a separate limitation period will run for each day the cause of action accrues. Where the nuisance is actionable upon proof of damage, time does not run until damage occurs.[72] To the extent that a nuisance may cause an actionable personal injury,[73] the limitation period applicable to the damages claimed for personal injury is three years: see section 11 of the Limitation Act 1980.

2–045

Ineffective Defences

CLAIMANT COMING TO NUISANCE

It is no defence to liability for a nuisance that the claimant has come to the nuisance after its creation even if he has done so without knowledge of the existence of the nuisance. Indeed, where there is a continuing nuisance of which the defendant knew or ought to have known, remedial expenditure may be recovered by the owner of the land affected even where that owner acquired the land after the creation of the nuisance and the harm done.[74] Thus in the case of *Bliss v. Hall*[75] the fact that a tallow-chandlery

2–046

---

[69] See cases in the context of trees overhanging highways: if harm is caused by the secret unobservable processes of nature, there will be no liability upon the owner of the tree if he has taken reasonable precautions; *Noble v. Harrison* [1926] 2 K.B. 332; *Cunliffe v. Bankes* [1945] 1 All E.R. 459; *Caminer v. North London Investment Co.* [1951] A.C. 88; *Quinn v. Scott* [1965] 1 W.L.R. 1004; *Chapman v. Barking and Dagenham LBC* [1997] 2 E.G.L.R. 141. See above, para. 2–027; and see para. 2–050 below in relation to Trees.

[70] See, generally, Clerk & Lindsell *Torts* (18th ed.), Chap. 33. On fraudulent concealment and extensions to the limitation period generally see above, paras. 1–116 *et seq.* (Trespass)

[71] See below, para. 4–037 *et seq.* (Remedies), and, *e.g. Shadwell v. Hutchinson* (1831) 4 C. & P. 333.

[72] See above, paras. 2–027, 4–038, and, *e.g. Backhouse v. Bonomi* (1861) 9 H.L.C. 503 and *Darley Main Colliery Co. v. Mitchell* (1886) 11 App.Cas. 127. On the question of when damage occurs see also *Forster v. Outred & Co.* [1982] 1 W.L.R. 86, *Pirelli General Cable Works Ltd v. Oscar Faber & Partners* [1983] A.C. 1, HL, *D.W. Moore & Co. Ltd v. Ferrier* [1988] 1 W.L.R. 267, *Murphy v. Brentwood DC* [1991] 1 A.C. 398, HL.

[73] See 2–027 above and 4–036 below (Remedies).

[74] See *Delaware Mansions Ltd v. Westminster City Council* [2001] UKHL 55; and see 2–009.

[75] (1838) 4 Bing. N.C. 183. See *Elliotson v. Feetham* (1835) 2 Bing. N.C. 134.

which emitted "divers noisome, noxious, and offensive vapours, fumes, smells and stenches" had existed for three years prior to the arrival of the plaintiff afforded the defendant no defence for the nuisance caused by the works. Similarly, in the case of *Miller v. Jackson*[76] the majority of the Court of Appeal[77] held that there was no defence available for a nuisance from cricket-balls to the occupiers of houses adjacent to a cricket pitch, notwithstanding that the pitch had been used without complaint for 70 years and the houses were recently built at a distance of only 102 feet from the centre of the pitch. Geoffrey Lane L.J.[78] noted that:

> "It does not seem just that a long established activity, in itself innocuous, should be brought to an end because someone else chooses to build a house nearby and so turn an innocent pastime into an actionable nuisance."

However, he regarded the matter as settled by the case of *Sturges v. Bridgman*[79] where it was assumed:

> "That it is no answer to a claim for nuisance for the defendant to show that the plaintiff brought the trouble on his own head by building or coming to live in a house so close to the defendant's premises that he would inevitably be affected by the defendant's activities where no one had been affected previously."

Although the absence of a defence that a claimant came to the nuisance may appear unfair in the circumstances of the case of *Miller v. Jackson*, it can be justified on the ground that it would be unfair to deny the purchaser of land a cause of action which would have been available to his predecessor in title simply on the ground that the nuisance affecting his land pre-dated his arrival. Further, the absence of this defence does not affect the defences of prescription[80] nor of consent to the nuisance.[81] Additionally, it will be remembered that where a nuisance consists of an interference with the enjoyment of property which does not result in physical damage, the locality of the claimant's property will be a factor to consider in deciding whether the nuisance is actionable[82]: thus a claimant who moves into an industrial area cannot expect the same standards of convenience as in a residential one.[83]

---

[76] [1977] Q.B. 966.
[77] Lord Denning M.R. dissenting.
[78] [1977] Q.B. 966, 986.
[79] (1879) 11 Ch.D. 852.
[80] See above, para. 2–038.
[81] See above, para. 2–037.
[82] See above, para. 2–031.
[83] *Sturges v. Bridgman* (1879) 11 Ch.D. 852. See para. 2–031.

Public Benefit

If a nuisance is otherwise actionable it will be no defence that the nuisance **2–047** has a public benefit.[84] Notwithstanding this principle it has been argued that in some circumstances even though a nuisance may be actionable an injunction should not be granted in the Court's discretion because of the harm to the public that would thereby follow. However, the Courts are extremely reluctant to refuse relief for a private wrong even though this may have public benefit. Thus in *Adams v. Ursell*[85] a fried fish shop was held to be a nuisance in a residential part of a street and an injunction was granted notwithstanding that it would not only cause hardship to the defendant but would also cause hardship to his customers.

In the case of *Miller v. Jackson*[86] the Court of Appeal appears to have taken a different approach, Lord Denning M.R.[87] considering that the public interest should be balanced against the private interest in deciding what should constitute a nuisance where an action was brought by neighbours of a cricket field from which balls regularly escaped, and Cumming-Bruce L.J.[88] concluding that the public interest justified refusing an injunction and confining the remedy to damages. This approach has, however, not been followed by the Court of Appeal in subsequent cases which have re-affirmed its previous decisions. In the case of *Kennaway v. Thompson*[89] a nuisance was caused by the noise from power boats and motor boats on a lake near the plaintiff's premises: the Court of Appeal rejected an argument that public benefit would justify the refusal of an injunction. Reliance was placed upon the case of *Shelfer v. City of London Electric Light Co.*[90] in which Lindley L.J. stated that:

> ". . . ever since Lord Cairns's Act was passed, the Court of Chancery has repudiated the position that the Legislature intended to turn that Court into a tribunal for legalising wrongful acts; or in other words, the Court has always protested against the notion that it ought to allow a wrong to continue simply because the wrongdoer is able and willing to pay for the injury he may inflict. Neither has the circumstances that the wrongdoer is in some sense a public benefactor (*e.g.* a gas or a water company or a sewer authority) ever been a sufficient reason for refusing to protect by injunction an individual whose rights are persistently infringed. . ."

---

[84] *St Helens Smelting Co v. Tipping* (1865) 11 H.L. Cas. 642; *Bamford v. Turnley* (1860) 3 B.& S. 62. Compare *Shelfer v. City of London Electricity Co.* [1895] 1 Ch.D. 287. See too 4–100 *et seq.*
[85] [1913] 1 Ch. 269.
[86] [1977] Q.B. 966.
[87] *ibid.* at 981–982.
[88] *ibid.* at 988.
[89] [1981] 1 Q.B. 88.
[90] [1895] 1 Ch.D. 287.

Similarly, in the case of *Elliott v. London Borough of Islington*[91] a plaintiff was entitled to an injunction ordering the defendant to remove a tree which was causing damage to his wall and encroaching on his land. The Court rejected the argument that it would be harsh upon the public to remove the tree because of its amenity value on the ground that:

> "It is not generally appropriate that specific private rights should be denied in order to give rise to indefinite advantages to the general public."[92]

IUS TERTII?

2–048   A defendant cannot claim in his defence to an action for nuisance that a third party has a better right to the claimant's land with which he has interfered than the claimant (the defence of *ius tertii*).[93]

In the case of *Fitzgerald v. Firbank*[94] the defendant wrongfully discharged sediment into a stream which damaged the fish in the stream and harmed their breeding. The plaintiffs had been granted a right to fish the stream which the defendant sought to challenge on the basis that it was insufficient to maintain an action in nuisance. Kekewich J. rejected this argument[95]:

> "I should have thought, without argument, . . . that this would fall within the principle that a possessory right was sufficient to constitute a title to maintain an action in the nature of trespass. I am not impressed with that objection to the plaintiffs' action."

This approach has subsequently been taken by the Court of Appeal in *Foster v. Warblington UDC*[96] in which it was held that since *ius tertii* was no defence to an action for nuisance, a person who has exclusive possession of land may sue even though he cannot prove title to it; the plaintiff was thus able to maintain a claim in nuisance against the defendant council in respect of the discharge of sewage into the plaintiff's oyster beds of which the plaintiff had possession.

Likewise on the basis of this case Farwell J. in the case of *Nicholls v. Ely Sugar Beet Factory*[97] held that the defence of *ius tertii* was not available where a defendant discharged effluent damaging several fisheries in the possession of the plaintiff. A similar approach was taken by Evershed J. in the case of *Newcastle-under-Lyme Corp. v. Wolstanton Ltd* though his deci-

---

[91] [1991] 10 E.G. 145.
[92] *ibid.* at 149.
[93] See above, para. 2–002.
[94] [1897] 2 Ch. 96.
[95] *ibid.* at 97.
[96] [1906] 1 K.B. 648, CA.
[97] [1931] 2 Ch. 84.

sion was overruled on other grounds in the Court of Appeal[98-99]: it seems that the plaintiff in that case had a statutory right to possession of the land interfered with (for the purposes of its gas mains) albeit that it had no title at common law.

Since *de facto* possession is all that is required to maintain an action in nuisance,[1] it follows that provided that the claimant establishes that he has such possession, it is not open to the defendant to assert that a stranger has a better title.[2] This is consistent with the law relating to trespass where a claimant in possession of land may maintain an action against a defendant who ejects him without showing better title.[3] It would be illogical if an occupier in possession of land was protected by the law of trespass from direct interferences by a defendant notwithstanding that a third party had better title but had no protection from indirect interferences in similar circumstances.

NUISANCE DUE TO MANY

Although it may provide a defence to an action that the nuisance was caused by a stranger without the knowledge or presumed knowledge of the defendant,[4] it is no defence to an action that the nuisance has been caused because of the contributory acts of others as well as the defendant even if none of the acts (including those of the defendant) would have been sufficient in themselves to result in an actionable nuisance.[5] If the defendant knows or ought to know that his actions cumulatively with those of another will unreasonably interfere with the enjoyment of his neighbour's land, it will be no defence that his action alone would not have amounted to a nuisance. Thus, in the case of *Lampton v. Mellish*[6] two merry-go-round operators each with an organ carried on their businesses near the plaintiff's house. In granting an injunction Chitty J. said: "If the acts of two persons, each being aware of what the other is doing, amount in the aggregate to what is an actionable wrong, each is amenable to the remedy against the aggregate cause of complaint." Further, even if the act of one defendant is in itself sufficient to constitute a nuisance, the others will not be relieved from liability for their contribution to the total wrong.[7]

2–048a

[98-99] [1947] Ch. 92, 109–110, Evershed J.; [1947] Ch. 427, 467–468, CA.

[1] See 2–002 above.

[2] See *Hunter v. Canary Wharf Ltd* [1997] A.C. 655 at 688 *per* Lord Goff and at 702–704 *per* Lord Hoffmann.

[3] See 1–003, 1–094 above (Trespass).

[4] See 2–043 above.

[5] *Thorpe v. Brumfit* (1873) L.R. 8 Ch. 650, 656, *per* James L.J.; *Blair and Sumner v. Deakin* (1887) 57 L.T. 522; *Polsue and Alfieri v. Rushmer* [1907] A.C. 121.

[6] [1894] 3 Ch. 163.

[7] See *Pride of Derby v. British Celanese* [1952] 1 All E.R. 1326, 1333, *per* Harman J. (affirmed on other grounds [1953] Ch. 149).

Types of nuisance

Introduction

2–049   Because of the many various forms which actionable nuisances may take it is sometimes hard to categorise them into satisfactory "types". Nuisances may, however, be examined in a variety of ways: by examining the different degrees of fault which are necessary for a nuisance to be actionable[8]; by distinguishing between the types of activity which give rise to a nuisance, for instance, the creation of noise or smells, or the withdrawal of support to land[9]; by distinguishing between the different sorts of harm done to the claimant, for instance, by differentiating between physical harm to or encroachment upon the claimant's land and interference with the enjoyment of land falling short of physical interference[10]; or by distinguishing between the types of right interfered with, such as interferences with "natural" rights which are necessary for the enjoyment of property, on the one hand, and interferences with easements on the other.[11]

In *Hunter v. Canary Wharf Ltd* Lord Lloyd[12] categorised nuisances as being of three kinds[13]:

(1)   nuisance by encroachment on a neighbour's land

(2)   nuisance by direct physical injury to the neighbour's land and

(3)   nuisance by interference with a neighbour's quiet enjoyment of his land.

To these categories it is necessary to add a fourth, namely interference with servitudes. Each will be considered in turn giving examples of the sorts of interferences which have been held to be nuisances. Caution, however, must be exercised. The categories should be treated as being for ease of exposition only and should not be treated as closed. The question in any case should still be whether or not the interference is an unreasonable one according to the principles which have been examined above.

---

[8] See above, para. 2–011.

[9] *e.g.* Artis, *Odour Nuisances and their Control* (1984), Penn, *Noise Nuisances* (1979), Clerk & Lindsell *Torts*, (18th ed.), para. 19–89, *Withdrawal of Support*.

[10] Compare Pearce and Meston, *Law of Nuisances* (1926), Chap. 2 and Chap. 3, Salmond & Heuston, *The Law of Torts* (21st ed., p. 57 *et seq.*) Clerk & Lindsell, *loc. cit.* para.19–09. But see Gearty, 48 Camb. L.J. 214 where it is argued that physical damage to property is better subsumed into the law of negligence and private nuisance should be restricted to the "protection of property from non-physical damage, *i.e.* noxious fumes and noise and the like."

[11] Salmond & Heuston, *loc. cit.* at p. 81 Pearce and Meston, *loc. cit.* at p. 13. For instance, the owner of land has a right of support of his land in its natural state from the adjoining and subjacent land of his neighbours: such a right is a natural incident of ownership; but there is no natural right of support for buildings, though such a right may be acquired as an easement by prescription: *Dalton v. Angus* (1881) 6 App.Cas. 740; compare para. 2–112 *et seq.* below.

[12] [1997] A.C. 655.

[13] *ibid.* at 441.

The rule in *Rylands v. Fletcher* will be considered under the second category, namely direct physical injury to the neighbour's land, since it is within this category that the rule in *Rylands v. Fletcher* originates.

Encroachments: trees and other things

As has already been noted,[13a] where there is a physical encroachment **2–050** upon the claimant's land by a defendant, damage will be presumed.[14] A nuisance may be caused by a projecting building,[15] or by overhanging spouts[16] or boards.[17] Perhaps most commonly nuisances of this sort are caused by trees whose branches overhang the claimant's land[18] or whose roots grow into it.[19] An encroachment by tree branches or roots will in itself constitute a nuisance without proof of any further damage.[20]

Although damage is presumed in circumstances of encroachment, it is clear that such nuisances may actually cause damage. The extent to which a defendant will be liable for damages by reason of an encroachment will generally depend upon the foreseeability of the harm done. Thus, a defendant will be liable for damage caused by the encroachment of tree roots where such damage is reasonably foreseeable and the defendant fails to take appropriate steps to prevent the encroachment.[21] Whether or not harm is foreseeable will depend upon the type of tree, the distance from the claimant's land at which it is planted and the technical data available.[22] In areas where local authorities publish guidance to householders and developers on safe planting distances, it will be difficult for those parties to assert that harm was not reasonably foreseeable if the guidance is not followed.

Damages for encroachment will usually be calculated by reference to the diminution in value of the claimant's land (which will usually be equivalent to the cost of reinstatement)[23] or (if reasonable) remedial expenditure.[24]

[13a] See above, para. 2–027.

[14] *Baten's Case* (1610) 9 Co. Rep. 53b.

[15] *ibid.*

[16] *Fay v. Prentice* (1845) 1 C.B. 828.

[17] *Pickering v. Rudd* (1815) 4 Camp. 219, 221.

[18] *Earl of Lonsdale v. Nelson* (1823) 2 B. & C. 302, 311; *Lemmon v. Webb* [1895] A.C. 1, HL, *Smith v. Giddy* [1904] 2 K.B. 448.

[19] *Butler v. Standard Telephones & Cables Ltd* [1940] 1 K.B. 399, *McCombe v. Read* [1955] 1 W.L.R. 635, *Davey v. Harrow Corporation* [1958] 1 Q.B. 60 *Solloway v. Hampshire CC* (1981) 79 LGR, 449, CA, *Russell v. Barnet LBC* (1984) 271 E.G. 699; *Elliott v. Islington LBC* [1991] 1 E.G.L.R. 167, CA, *Hurst v. Hampshire CC* [1997] 44 E.G. 206, CA, *Delaware Mansions Ltd v. Westminster City Council* [2001] UKHL 55. See also *Morgan v. Khyatt* [1964] 1 W.L.R. 475, P.C.

[20] *Lemmon v. Webb* (1894) 3 Ch. 1, at p. 11 *per* Lindley LJ and at p. 24 *per* Kay LJ; *Davey v. Harrow Corporation* [1958] 1 Q.B. 60; see 2–027 above.

[21] *Solloway v. Hampshire CC* (1981) 79 LGR 449, CA; *Russell v. Barnet LBC* [1984] 271 EG 699; *Paterson v. Humberside County Council* [1995] E.G.C.S. 39, *The Times*, April 19, 1995. See generally para. 2–011 *et seq.* above concerning foreseeability.

[22] Compare *Paterson v. Humberside County Council* [1995] E.G.C.S. 39, *The Times*, April 19, 1995 *cf Greenwood v. Portwood*, January 4, 1984, unreported, QBD (HHJ Fallon QC) in which it was held in the particular circumstances then prevailing that the risk of subsidence was not foreseeable.

[23] *Hunter v. Canary Wharf Ltd* [1997] A.C. 655 at 695. See para. 4–031 *et seq.* below (Remedies).

[24] *Delaware Mansions Ltd v. Westminster City Council* [2001] UKHL 55. See para. 4–031 *et seq.* below (Remedies).

However, there will be cases in which encroachments cause other harm to the claimant's property in respect of damages may be awarded. For instance, the owner of a yew tree which overhung a neighbour's land was held liable when the neighbour's horse died from eating it.[25] (If, however, the horse had reached the yew tree by itself encroaching upon the defendant's land there would have been no liability in nuisance: the harm would have been caused as the result of a trespass by the horse[26] and not an encroachment upon the claimant's land). The owners of a decaying wire fence were held liable where the wire from the fence encroached onto the plaintiff's land and poisoned a cow which was grazing.[27] If a non-poisonous tree causes injury, for instance, to crops an action for damages will also lie.[28]

Nuisances causing direct physical injury

2–051 There are numerous other cases where nuisances have occurred which have resulted in physical damage being caused to a claimant's property. The following are examples. As can be seen, some of the cases can be categorised under more than one heading. As has been noted above, where a nuisance causes a direct physical injury, questions of the nature of the locality will seldom, if ever, be relevant in considering whether the interference was an unreasonable one.[29]

ESCAPE OF THINGS ON THE DEFENDANT'S LAND

2–052 Where things are present or collected on the defendant's land and escape, these may amount to nuisances. Where a defendant collects dangerous things on his land, strict liability may also be imposed upon the principles in *Rylands v. Fletcher*. The rule in *Rylands v. Fletcher* is dealt with at paras 2–056 *et seq*. Naturally occurring hazards present on the defendant's land may also be the subject of a duty to prevent their escape.[29a] Escaping fires[30] and fumes,[31] explosions caused by

---

[25] *Crowhurst v. Amersham Burial Board* (1878) L.R. 4 Ex. 5, *Cheater v. Cater* [1918] 1 K.B. 247.
[26] *Ponting v. Noakes* [1894] 2 Q.B. 281; *cf.* Occupiers' Liability Act 1984 for duties owed to trespassers.
[27] *Firth v. Bowling* (1878) 47 L.J.C.P. 358.
[28] *Smith v. Giddy* [1904] 2 K.B. 448.
[29] See 2–029 above; *St Helens Smelting Co. v. Tipping* (1865) 11 H.L.C. 642, 645.
[29a] *Goldman v. Hargrave* [1967] A.C. 645, PC. See generally, para. 2–014, 2–023 above concerning the extent of liability for naturally occurring nuisances.
[30] *Goldman v. Hargrave* [1967] A.C. 645, PC; *cf Smith v. Littlewoods Ltd* [1987] 1 A.C. 241 HL (fire caused by trespasser, held no liability on defendant). See 2–056, 2–067 below (*Rylands v. Fletcher*).
[31] *St Helen's Smelting Co. v. Tipping* (1865) 11 H.L.C. 642; *Salvin v. North Brancepeth Coal Co* (1874) L.R. 9 Ch. 705; *Wood v. Conway Corporation* [1914] 2 Ch. 47. *Manchester Corp. v Farnworth* [1930] A.C. 171; *Halsey v. Esso Petroleum Co. Ltd* [1961] 1 W.L.R. 683. See also *Cavey v. Ledbitter* (1863) 13 C.B. (N.S.) 470; *West v. Bristol Tramways* [1908] 2 K.B. 14. See 2–072 below (*Rylands v. Fletcher*).

explosives,[32] dislodged building debris[33] water or effluent escaping from faulty drains, sewers and culverts,[34] water entering the claimant's land because a drive was constructed in such a way that it caused water to overflow,[35] and gas[36] have all been held to amount to nuisances. It should be noted that even without escape, the mere storage of dangerous things may in itself amount to an interference with the reasonable enjoyment of neighbouring premises where such storage unreasonably exposes a claimant to danger.[37]

HARM CAUSED BY ANIMALS PRESENT ON OR ATTRACTED BY THE DEFENDANT'S LAND

The common law relating to animals and in particular to cattle trespass included many special rules. The law is now, however, to be found primarily in the Animals Act 1971.[38] Where farm animals in the nature of "livestock" stray and cause damage, there may be a cause of action under section 4 of that Act. However, the presence of animals may still give rise to liability at common law in nuisance. A defendant may be liable for any damage caused to his neighbour's land by overstocking his own land with game beyond levels which are reasonable in the circumstances.[39] A defendant may also be liable for harm caused to a claimant's land by rats[40] or flies[41] which are attracted by the defendant having unreasonable heaps of bone or manure. The imposition of liability for nuisance of this sort depends on whether the user of the defendant's land is excessive or beyond what can be regarded as reasonable.

2–053

---

[32] *Arnold v. Furness Railway Co.* (1874) 22 W.R. 613; *Miles v. Forrest Rock Granite Co.* (1918) 34 T.L.R. 500; see *Crown River Cruises Ltd v. Kimbolton Fireworks Ltd* [1996] 2 Lloyd's Rep 533. See 2–069 below (*Rylands v. Fletcher*).

[33] *Video London Sound Studios Ltd v. Asticus (GMS) Ltd*, 6/3/01, TCC.

[34] *Jones v. Llanrwst UDC* [1911] 1 Ch. 393; and see also *Humphries v. Cousins* (1877) 2 C.P.D.239 and *Ilford UDC v. Beal* [1925] 1 K.B. 671. *Sedleigh-Denfield v. O'Callaghan* [1940] A.C. 880; *Pemberton v. Bright* [1960] 1 W.L.R. 436; *Ryeford Homes Ltd v. Sevenoaks D.C.* [1989] 2 E.G.L.R. 281. *Cf Radstock Co-operative & Industrial Society Ltd v. Norton-Radstock UDC* [1968] Ch. 605, CA and *Bybrook Barn Centre Ltd v. Kent County Council* [2001] B.L.R. 55; [2000] 20 E.G. 158. See too 2–066 below (*Rylands v. Fletcher*).

[35] *Bennetts v. Honroth* [1959] S.A.S.R. 171.

[36] See 2–070 below (*Rylands v. Fletcher*).

[37] See 2–070 below. See *R. v. Lister* (1857) 1 Dears & B.C.C. 209 (storage of wood naptha) *Crowder v. Tinckler* (1816) 19 Ves. 617 and *R. v. Taylor* (1742) 2 Str. 1167 (gun powder); *Hepburn v. Lordan* (1865) 34 L.J. Ch. 293 (wet jute); *Bannister v. Bigge* (1865) 34 Beav. 287 (dangerous use of rifle butts).

[38] See para. 5–038.

[39] *Farrer v. Nelson* (1885) 15 QBD. 258 (excessive number of pheasants damaged plaintiff's crops); but see *Seligman v. Docker* [1949] Ch. 53 (where a defendant was not liable for damage due to the number of his pheasants where the number had increased in a favourable season). See too *Pole v. Peake* [1998] E.G.C.S. 125.

[40] *Stearn v. Prentice Bros* [1919] 1 K.B. 394.

[41] *Bland v. Yates* (1914) 58 Sol. J. 612 (defendant's use excessive compared with reasonable use in market garden area).

HARM CAUSED BY OR AS A RESULT OF ACTIVITIES ON THE DEFENDANT'S LAND

2–054   It is not only things which are collected on the land which escape and which cause damage that can give rise to liability in nuisance. For instance, liability can be imposed for damage caused by activities on the defendant's land such as those which cause vibrations[42] or heat[43] which affect the claimant's premises.

Similarly, where the consequences of the defendant's activities harm the claimant's premises there may be liability for nuisance. For instance, the working of mines so as to damage the claimant's land by subsidence will amount to a nuisance[44] (withdrawal of support is dealt with more fully below[45]). Likewise the defendant may be liable in nuisance if by raising the level of or building on his land he makes rain-water drain off his land which causes damp to penetrate the claimant's premises[46] or if he constructs a concrete paved drive which causes water to flow onto the claimant's land.[47] However, a defendant may not be liable if the drainage system is a reasonable one in the circumstances or is of benefit to the claimant.[48] The question must be one of balance, but the Court will be reluctant to hold that it is reasonable that a defendant should cause any significant physical harm to the claimant's property.[49]

HARM CAUSED BY INACTIVITY ON THE DEFENDANT'S LAND

2–055   Not only may activities on the defendant's land cause nuisances, a failure to take adequate steps to keep land in good condition may give rise to a liability in nuisance. Accordingly, if premises are allowed to fall into disrepair so that they harm the claimant's land the owner of the land[50] (both occupier and, in some instances, the landlord,[51]) may be liable.

Further, it has now been held that if a hazard occurs naturally on the defendant's land he may be under a duty to take reasonable steps to prevent harm to the claimant's land when he knows or is presumed to know of the

---

[42] *Grosvenor Hotel Co. v. Hamilton* [1894] 2 Q.B. 836; *Hoare & Co. v. McAlpine* [1923] 1 Ch. 167; *Barette v. Franki Compressed Pile Co. of Canada* [1955] 2 D.L.R. 665.
[43] Compare *Lyttleton Times Co Ltd v. Warners Ltd* [1907] A.C. 476 (defence to nuisance because of bargain between landlord and tenant): see 2–038 above. See too *Sanders-Clark v. Grosvenor Mansions Co* [1900] 2 Ch. 373; *Reinhardt v. Mentasti* (1889) 42 Ch. D 685 (heat from stoves rendering wine cellar unfit).
[44] See 4–038 below.
[45] See 2–112.
[46] *Hurdman v. N.E. Ry Co.* (1878) L.R. 3 C.P.D. 168; *Broder v. Saillard* (1876) 2 Ch.D. 692; *Maberley v. Peabody & Co.* [1946] 2 All E.R. 192; *Bradburn v. Lindsay* [1983] 2 All E.R. 408 (dry rot).
[47] *Bennetts v. Honroth* [1959] S.A.S.R. 171.
[48] *Gill v. Edouin* (1894) 11 T.L.R. 93.
[49] See 2–029 and see 2–098 *et seq.*
[50] See *e.g. Todd v. Flight* (1860) 9 C.B. (N.S.) 377; *St Anne's Well Brewery Co. Ltd v. Roberts* (1929) 140 L.T. 1, 8.*Wilchick v. Marks and Silverstone* [1934] 2 K.B. 56, 68.
[51] See 2–019 above.

hazard: a failure to take such steps will render him liable.[52] Such liability has been imposed in relation to fires ,[53] landslips[54] and the escape of damp.[55]

RYLANDS V. FLETCHER

The Rule

In the case of *Rylands v. Fletcher*[56] Blackburn J. said: 2–056

> "We think that the true rule of law is, that the person who for his own purposes brings on his lands and collects and keeps there anything likely to do mischief if it escapes must keep it in at his peril, and, if he does not do so, is prima facie answerable for all the damage which is the natural consequence of its escape. He can excuse himself by showing that the escape was owing to the plaintiff's default; or perhaps, that the escape was the consequence of *vis major* or the act of God; but as nothing of the sort exists here, it is unnecessary to inquire what excuse would be sufficient[57]."

The House of Lords concurred with this judgment, but Lord Cairns L.C. introduced another element to this rule, namely that for it to apply the defendant must have made a "non-natural" use of his land.[58]

Origins

In *Rylands v. Fletcher* the defendants constructed a reservoir upon their   2–057
land for the supply of water to a mill. On the site of the reservoir there was a disused mine shaft which was apparently filled up but which connected with the plaintiff's mine on his own land. The defendants' contractors who were not the employees of the defendants negligently failed to discover the connection and failed to take steps to protect the plaintiff's mine from flooding. When the reservoir was filled water escaped through the disused mine shaft and flooded the plaintiff's mine. The defendants were held liable to the plaintiff because of the rule as formulated in the preceding paragraph.

It is clear that the authorities relied upon by the Court in formulating this rule were drawn from the law of nuisance and Blackburn J. seems to have regarded the doctrine which he was formulating as being part of that tort: he could see no distinction between a man "whose mine is flooded

---

[52] *Goldman v. Hargrave* [1967] A.C. 645, PC; *Leakey v. National Trust* [1980] Q.B. 485, CA; see para. 2–014 *et seq.* above.
[53] *Goldman v. Hargrave* [1967] A.C. 645, PC.
[54] *Leakey v. National Trust* [1980] Q.B. 485, CA; see too *Holbeck Hall Hotel Limited v. Scarborough Borough Council*, [2000] Q.B. 836, CA.
[55] *Bradburn v. Lindsay* [1983] 2 All E.R. 408 (dry rot).
[56] (1866) L.R. 1 Ex. 265.
[57] *ibid.* at 279.
[58] (1868) L.R. 3 H.L. 330, 338–340.

by the water from his neighbour's reservoir" and a man "whose cellar is invaded by the filth of his neighbour's privy, or habitation is made unhealthy by the fumes and noisome vapours of his neighbour's alkali works": each is "damnified without any fault of his own".[59] Indeed in the House of Lords, Lord Cairns held the case he was considering indistinguishable from the case of nuisance in *Baird v. Williamson*[60] and distinguished it from *Smith v. Kenrick*[61] (another case of nuisance) on the ground that the latter case involved an "ordinary use" . Much of the later case law supports the view that the rule in *Rylands v. Fletcher* is an example of liability for nuisance in certain circumstances[62] though there are dicta which indicate that it might be regarded as a form of trespass.[63]

The speech of Lord Goff in the House of Lords in *Cambridge Water Co. Ltd v. Eastern Counties Leatherwork plc*[64] supports the view that although introducing an extension of the law of nuisance to isolated escapes, the decision in *Rylands v. Fletcher* should not be regarded as a revolutionary one:

> "Seen in its context, there is no reason to suppose that Blackburn J intended to create a liability any more strict than that created by the law of nuisance; but even so he must have intended that, in the circumstances specified by him, there should be liability for damage resulting from an isolated escape."

Lord Goff foresaw difficulties in treating *Rylands v. Fletcher* as the basis for a general rule of strict liability for damage caused by extra-hazardous activities[65] and stated.[66]

> "I incline to the opinion that, as a general rule, it is more appropriate for strict liability in respect of operations of high risk to be imposed

---

[59] (1866) L.R. 1 Ex. 265, 280. See also *Cambridge Water Co. Ltd v. Eastern Counties Leatherwork plc* [1994] 2 A.C. 264, 298; [1994] 1 All E.R. 53 at 70.

[60] 15 C.B.(N.S.) 376 (pumping water caused nuisance).

[61] (1849) 7 C.B. 515.

[62] *Cambridge Water Co Ltd v. Eastern Counties Leatherwork plc* [1994] 2 A.C. 264, 298; [1994] 1 All E.R. 53, 70; *Read v. J. Lyons & Co. Ltd* [1947] A.C. 156 at 173; *Rickards v. Lothian* [1913] A.C. 263 at 275; *Eastern and South African Telegraph Co. v. Cape Town Tramways Co.* [1902] A.C. 381 at 394. Other jurisdictions appear to take a similar view: see *Shell-Mex & B.P. v. Belfast Corporation* [1952] N.J. 72 at 75; *J.P. Porter Co. Ltd v. Bell* [1955] 1 D.L.R.62 at 64 (nuisance and negligence contrasted); *Benning v. Wong* (1969) 43 A.L.J.R. 467 at 484.

[63] *Foster v. Warblington UDC* [1906] 1 K.B. 648 at 672 (Stirling L.J.); *Jones v. Llanwrst UDC* [1911] 1 Ch. 393 at 403 (Parker J.); *Hoare & Co. v. McAlpine* [1923] 1 Ch. 167, 175 (Astbury J.). But see *Rigby v. Chief Constable of Northamptonshire* [1985] 2 All E.R. 985, 996 (Taylor J.). In *Read v. J. Lyons & Co. Ltd* [1947] A.C. 156, at 173, Lord Macmillan saw both trespass and nuisance as the "congeners" of this form of liability.

[64] [1994] 2 A.C. 264 at 299.

[65] *ibid.*, at 304–306.

[66] *ibid.*, at 305. The High Court of Australia by a majority of five to two has held that *Rylands v. Fletcher* no longer provides an independent head of liability but should, instead be regarded as "absorbed by the principles of ordinary negligence": *Burnie Port Authority v. General Jones Pty Ltd* (1994) 120 ALR 42. In Australia the principle now is that a "person who takes advantage of his or her premises to introduce a dangerous substance, to carry on a dangerous activity, ot to allow another to do these things" owes a "non-delegable duty" in the tort of negligence to those who suffer damage as a result.

by Parliament, than by the courts. If such liability is to be imposed by statute, the relevant activities can be identified, and those concerned can know where they stand. Furthermore statute can where appropriate lay down precise criteria establishing the incidence and scope of liability".

Who can sue

There are dicta which indicate that a claimant can maintain an action on the basis of the rule in *Rylands v. Fletcher* notwithstanding that he has no interest in land nor is he an occupier of it.[67] However, the modern dicta to that effect are obiter[68] and are hard to square with the rule being an extension of the law of private nuisance. Indeed in the leading case of *Read v. J. Lyons & Co. Ltd*[69] the rule in *Rylands v. Fletcher* was said by Lord Macmillan and Lord Uthwatt to be "a principle applicable between occupiers in respect of their land,"[70] and Lord Simonds held that the position in *Rylands v. Fletcher* was analogous to that in the law of nuisance and that "its foundation is to be found in the injunction *sic utere tuo ut alienum non laedas.*"[71]

    Accordingly, it appears that a claimant must have some right or interest in land,[72] and "the better view"[73] is that "liability under *Rylands v. Fletcher* requires proof of interference with the use of the land of another".[74] In any event as in other instances of nuisances it is beyond doubt that the rule does at least apply to interferences harming land or the enjoyment of land.

2–058

Things brought onto the land

The thing which gives rise to the harm in respect of which an action based upon the rule in *Rylands v. Fletcher* can be maintained must have been brought onto the land from which it escapes.[75] The escape of things which

2–059

---

[67] See *Miles v. Forest Rock Granite Co.* (1918) 34 T.L.R. 500; *Shiffman v. Order of St John* [1936] 1 All E.R. 557; *Perry v. Kendricks Transport Ltd* [1956] 1 W.L.R. 85; *British Celanese Ltd v. Hunt* [1969] 2 All E.R. 1252 at 1257.

[68] *Perry v. Kendricks Transport Ltd* [1956] 1 W.L.R. 85, was decided on the basis that the harm was caused by the act of a third party; *British Celanese Ltd v. Hunt* [1969] 2 All E.R. 1252, was decided on the basis that the foil which escaped was a natural use of the land (the plaintiff was in fact the occupier of land affected).

[69] [1947] A.C. 156.

[70] *ibid.* at 173–74, *per* Lord Macmillan ("The duty is to refrain from injuring not alium [another] but alienum [another's property]"); see also 185–86 by Lord Uthwatt.

[71] *ibid.* at 173, *per* Lord Macmillan. See also *Cambridge Water Co. Ltd v. Eastern Counties Leatherwork plc* [1994] 2 A.C. 264 at 305.

[72] See also *Weller v. Foot and Mouth Disease Research Institute* [1966] 1 Q.B. 569, 588. See too, paras. 2–005 and 2–008, above.

[73] Salmond & Heuston *Law of Torts* (21st ed.) p. 310.

[74] *N.Z. Forest Products Ltd v. O'Sullivan* [1974] N.Z.L.R. 80 at 83.

[75] (1866) L.R. 1 Ex. 265, (1868) L.R. 3 H.L. 330. See also *Cambridge Water Co. Ltd v. Eastern Counties Leatherwork plc* [1994] 2 A.C. 264.

are naturally on the land will not give rise to liability under the rule[76]; indeed, until recently a thing which was naturally on the land was not thought to give rise to liability in nuisance at all. Thus in *Smith v. Kenrick*[77] there was no liability for the escape of rain-water which had accumulated naturally upon the defendant's land; and in *Giles v. Walker*[78] it was held that an occupier was not liable for the escape of thistle down to his neighbour's land. However, it is now possible for a defendant to be liable for a nuisance arising from natural causes upon the principles set out in *Leakey v. National Trust*.[79]

Who can be sued

2–059a   The defendant need not be the freehold or leasehold owner of the land onto which the thing was brought.[80] The rule has been applied to a local authority which is required by statute to receive sewage into its sewers[81]; and to defendants with franchises, *e.g.* for the laying of gas pipes or electricity cables.[82] Licensees who bring onto the land the thing which escapes may also be liable.[83] Further an owner of land not in occupation who has authorised the accumulation of the dangerous thing on his land may be liable[84] (this accords with the principles which apply to nuisance generally[85]). The person who collects the dangerous thing and controls it at the time of its escape will be liable notwithstanding he does not own the land from which the escape takes place.[86] It also seems that liability may arise where the escape takes place from the highway.[87]

Non-natural use of land

2–060   As is noted above, the rule in *Rylands v. Fletcher* as explained by Blackburn J. does not apply to escapes of things which are naturally on the defendant's land. However, in the House of Lords, Lord Cairns referred to the "non-natural use" of the defendant's land. This has been taken to add an additional element to the rule, although there is no very satisfactory

---

[76] (1866) L.R. 1 Ex. 265; see also *Giles v. Walker* 24 Q.B.D. 656; *Seligman v. Docker* [1948] Ch. 53; *Pontardawe RDC v. Moore-Gwyn* [1929] 1 Ch. 656.

[77] (1849) 7 C.B. 515.

[78] (1890) 24 Q.B.D. 656 (but see the Weeds Act 1959).

[79] [1980] Q.B. 485. See above, para. 2–014 *et seq.*

[80] See 2–010 *et seq.* (Who may be sued).

[81] *Smeaton v. Ilford Corp.* [1954] 1 Ch. 450 at 469, 472.

[82] *Northwestern Utilities Ltd v. London Guarantee Ltd* [1936] A.C. 108 (gas pipes); *Charing Cross Electricity Supply Co. v. Hydraulic Power Co.* [1914] 3 K.B. 772 (electricity cables).

[83] *Rainham Chemical Works v. Belvedere Fish Guano Co.* [1921] 2 A.C. 465.

[84] *ibid.*

[85] See above, paras. 2–014 *et seq.*, 2–018 *et seq. cf. St Anne's Well Brewery Co. Ltd v. Roberts* (1928) 140 L.T. 1 at 5.

[86] *Rainham Chemical Works v. Belvedere Fish Guano Co.* [1921] 2 A.C. 465.

[87] *Rigby v. Chief Constable of Northamptonshire* [1985] 2 All E.R. 985 (but this was not a case of "escape" but an intentional act). *Powell v. Fall* (1880) 5 Q.B.D. 597 and compare *Halsey v. Esso Petroleum Co. Ltd* [1961] 1 W.L.R. 683 (nuisance from lorries on highway).

explanation of what this element comprises.[88] Blackburn J. seemed to limit the rule to an escape of a thing which was artificially on the defendant's land, but Lord Cairns has been regarded as further limiting it to a thing which is not only artificial but the use of which is also excessive in its context. In the case of *Rickards v. Lothian*[89] Lord Moulton said:

> "It is not every use to which land is put that brings into play that principle [the rule in *Rylands v. Fletcher*]. It must be some special use bringing with it increased danger to others, and must not merely be the ordinary use of land or such a use as is proper for the general benefit of the community."

And in the case of *Read v. J. Lyons & Co. Ltd*[90] Lord Porter said that it:

> ". . . seems to be a question of fact subject to a ruling of the judge whether the particular object can be dangerous or the particular use can be non-natural, and in deciding this question I think that all the circumstances of the time and place and practice of mankind must be taken into consideration so that what might be regarded as dangerous or non-natural may vary according to those circumstances."

These formulations seems to be analogous to the usual test for assessing whether a nuisance has been committed, *i.e.* whether the interference alleged to be a nuisance is "reasonable according to the ordinary usages of mankind living in society, or more correctly in a particular society".[91] It seems that the "gravity of the harm threatened must be weighed against the utility of the defendant's conduct, etc."[92]

In *Cambridge Water Co Ltd v. Eastern Counties Leatherwork plc*[93] Lord Goff highlighted the difficulties caused by this element of liability under *Rylands v. Fletcher*. He stated[94]:

> "It is obvious that the expression 'ordinary use of the land' in Lord Moulton's statement of the law is one lacking in precision. There are some writers who welcome the flexibility which has thus been introduced into this branch of the law, on the ground that it enables judges to mould and adapt the principle of strict liability to the changing needs of society; whereas others regret the perceived absence of principle in so vague a concept, and fear that the whole idea of strict

---

[88] See *Cambridge Water Co. Ltd v. Eastern Counties Leatherwork plc* [1994] 1 All E.R. 53, at 78–79; [1994] 2 A.C. 264, 307–309.

[89] [1913] A.C. 263 at 280, approved by Lord Simon in *Read v. J. Lyons & Co. Ltd* [1947] A.C. 156 at 169.

[90] [1947] A.C. 156 at 176.

[91] *Sedleigh-Denfield v. O'Callaghan* [1940] A.C. 880 at 908, *per* Lord Wright.

[92] Dias & Markesinis, *Tort Law* (1994, 3rd ed.), p. 465. See also *Stallybrass.* (1929) 3 Camb. L.J. 376; Newark, (1961) 24 M.L.R. 557.

[93] [1994] 2 A.C. 264.

[94] *ibid.*, at 308.

liability may as a result be undermined. A particular doubt is introduced by Lord Moulton's alternative criterion—'or such a use as is proper for the general benefit of the community'. If these words are understood to refer to a local community, they can be given some content as intended to refer to such matters as, for example the provision of services; indeed the same can, without too much difficulty, be extended to, for example, the provision of services to industrial premises, as in a business park or an industrial estate. But if the words are extended to embrace the wider interests of the local community or the general benefit of the community at large, it is difficult to see how the exception can be kept within reasonable bounds."

However, the House of Lords did not need to resolve the difficulties in that case because the storage of a chemical in substantial quantities on industrial premises was "an almost classic case of non-natural use".[95] Similarly, where gas, water or electricity are used outside an ordinary domestic context or on an unusually large scale it is more likely that their use will be regarded as "non-natural".[96]

The following are examples of uses which have been regarded as "natural" uses of a defendant's land: domestic water installations,[97] domestic fires,[98] electric wiring and gas pipes serving a dwelling or a shop,[99] stubble burning in the ordinary course of farming,[1] the ordinary working of mines and minerals,[2] and the carrying out of construction works on a disused airfield.[3]

Dangerous things — foreseeability

2–061   The rule in *Rylands v. Fletcher* applies to "anything likely to do mischief if it escapes".[4] There is thus an element of foreseeability in the imposition of the duty under this rule and it has now been clearly settled that "foreseeability of damage of the relevant type should be regarded as a prerequisite of liability in damages under this rule". Accordingly where chemicals were brought onto a defendant's land which nobody at the time could reasonably have foreseen would cause contamination to the plaintiff's water supply if they escaped, no duty under *Rylands v. Fletcher* was

---

[95] *ibid.*, at 309.
[96] See examples below, 2–065 *et seq.*
[97] *Rickards v. Lothian* [1913] A.C. 263; *British Gas plc v. Stockport MBC* [2001] EWCA Civ. 212 (supply of water to flats in tower block through a pipe below the basement of the tower).
[98] *Sochacki v. SAS* [1947] 1 All E.R. 344.
[99] *Collingwood v. Home and Colonial Stores Ltd* [1936] 3 All E.R. 200 (electrical wiring); *Miller v. Addie & Sons (Collieries) Ltd* 1934 S.C. 150 (gas).
[1] *Perkins v. Glyn* [1976] R.T.R. ix (note), *cf. Tuberville v. Stamp* (1697) 1 Ld. Raym. 264.
[2] *Rouse v. Gravelworks Ltd* [1940] 1 K.B. 489.
[3] *Ellison v. Ministry of Defence* (1997) 81 BLR 101.
[4] (1866) L.R. 1 Ex. 265 at 280. See also *Crowhurst v. Amersham Burial Board* (1878) 4 Ex. D. 5 at 12; *West v. Bristol Tramways Co.* [1908] 2 K.B. 14 at 21; *Mullholland & Tedd Ltd v. Baker* [1939] 3 All E.R. 253 at 256; *Cambridge Water Co. Ltd v. Eastern Counties Leatherwork plc* [1994] 2 A.C. 264 and see *Hamilton v. Papakura District Council* [2002] UKPC 8 at paras. 46–49.

imposed and the defendant was not liable for the subsequent escape of the chemicals which contaminated the plaintiff's water supply.[5] But this does not mean liability for the breach of the duty by allowing the escape of the thing is not strict, since where a duty is imposed under this rule, the defendant is under a duty to keep the thing "at his peril". What is or is not "likely" to do mischief if it escapes is a question of fact.

Escapes

"It is a rule which makes a person liable for the extent of an escape rather than for his actions."[6]   **2–062**

For liability to be imposed under the rule in *Rylands v. Fletcher* the harm to the claimant must result from an escape. The thing which does the damage must escape from a place where the defendant has occupation or control over land to a place outside his occupation or control. Thus in *Read v. J. Lyons & Co. Ltd*[7] a worker in a munitions factory could not recover damages under this rule because she was injured upon the defendant's land. But the thing escaping need not always be the thing accumulated: in *Miles v. Forest Rock Granite Co.*[8] liability was imposed under this rule for the escape of rocks caused by the blasting of explosives.

Once the duty under this rule is established because the defendant has been shown to have brought onto his land something likely to do mischief if it escapes, a breach of that duty will occur if the thing escapes regardless of the negligence or otherwise of the defendant: the defendant keeps the thing "at his peril" and liability for its escape is strict. This strict liability is, however, subject to certain defences or exceptions which are dealt with below.

Because the "essence" of the rule is "escape" it has been suggested that it does not apply to an intentional or voluntary release of a dangerous thing.[9] This suggestion is correct where the release is aimed at the claimant's land. If the defendant deliberately releases or discharges a dangerous thing the appropriate cause of action would be trespass: since the rule originates in the tort of nuisance it applies to indirect or "consequential" interferences rather than to direct ones.[10] Where, however, the release takes place without any intention of the dangerous thing entering the claimant's land, the interference may still be categorised as "indirect" and within the scope of the rule.[11]

---

[5] *Cambridge Water Co. Ltd v. Eastern Counties Leatherwork plc* [1994] 2 A.C. 264.
[6] per Mann L.J. in *Cambridge Water Co. Ltd v. Eastern Counties Leatherwork plc* [1994] 2 A.C. 264 at 276.
[7] [1947] A.C. 156.
[8] (1918) 34 T.L.R. 500.
[9] *Rigby v. Chief Constable of Northamptonshire* [1985] 2 All E.R. 985.
[10] See above, para. 2–026.
[11] See *Crown River Cruises Ltd v. Kimbolton Fireworks Ltd* [1996] 2 Lloyd's Rep 533 in which Potter J considered there was no good reason to limit the rule to releases which were not intentional or voluntary, at least where the intentional release was not deliberately aimed at the claimant with the intention of causing him damage.

2–063 Damage

As with nuisances which arise in other contexts, damage must be proven to establish a claim under the rule in *Rylands v. Fletcher*. Two problems arise, however, in relation to this rule: first, the extent to which liability might arise for personal injury; secondly, the question of the remoteness at which damage might be recoverable.

In the case of *Read v. J. Lyons & Co. Ltd*[12] the plaintiff was unable to establish liability under the rule in *Rylands v. Fletcher* for personal injury suffered in an explosives factory. Although in that case it was held that the defendant was not liable for the personal injuries suffered by the plaintiff, this seems to have been because she had no interest in land which was harmed. In principle there seems to be nothing to prevent recovery of damages for personal injury where the personal injury is a consequence of an unlawful interference with the claimant's reasonable enjoyment of his land.[13] On the basis of the decision of the House of Lords in *Read v. J. Lyons & Co. Ltd* it seems that there will be no liability for personal injury unless the claimant has an interest in land sufficient to maintain a claim in nuisance.[14]

The question of remoteness of damage in the tort of nuisance is dealt with generally elsewhere[15]; there are particular difficulties however in relation to the extent that losses may be recoverable under the rule in *Rylands v. Fletcher*.

In his judgment in the case of *Rylands v. Fletcher* itself, Blackburn J. said that where a defendant is liable under the rule he is "prima facie answerable for all the damage which is the natural consequence of its escape". It is unclear what is meant by a "natural consequence", but Farwell L.J. in *West v. Bristol Tramways Co.*[16] suggested that this meant "the consequences which are natural according to the common experience of mankind". The Privy Council in the *Wagon Mound (No.1)*[17] left open the position with regard to remoteness of recoverable damage under the rule in *Rylands v. Fletcher*.

In *Cambridge Water Co Ltd v. Eastern Counties Leatherwork plc*[18] the House of Lords made clear that the foreseeability of harm of the relevant type was a prerequisite of liability under the rule in *Rylands v. Fletcher*.[19] Accordingly, although the foreseeability of the manner in which the dangerous thing may escape may not be material in determining liability

---

[12] [1947] A.C. 156.
[13] See *Hale v. Jennings Bros* [1938] 1 All E.R. 579; compare *Benning v. Wong* (1969) 43 A.L.J.R. 467. See also 2–027 above and 4–036 below (Remedies).
[14] See above, para. 2–058 above and also *Cambridge Water Co. Ltd v. Eastern Counties Leatherwork plc* [1994] 2 A.C. 264 at 305.
[15] See below, Remedies.
[16] [1908] 2 K.B. 14, at 24, CA.
[17] [1961] A.C. 388, 426–427; also *British Celanese Ltd v. A.H. Hunt (Capacitors) Ltd* [1969] 1 W.L.R. 959.
[18] [1994] 2 A.C. 264.
[19] *ibid.* 309.

(and in this respect liability is strict), in order for damages to be recoverable they must be of the sort which can be reasonably foreseeable in the event that an escape takes place.

Exceptions to the rule: defences

In his judgment in *Rylands v. Fletcher* Blackburn J. indicated that there were exceptions to the rule of strict liability as laid down in that case. A defendant, **2–064**

> "can excuse himself by showing that the escape was owing to the plaintiff's default; or, perhaps, that the escape was the consequence of *vis major* or the act of God; but as nothing of the sort exists here, it is unnecessary to inquire what excuse would be sufficient."

The case law indicates that the following defences may be open to a defendant against whom a case is pleaded on the basis of *Rylands v. Fletcher*: (a) default or act of the claimant; (b) consent of the claimant; (c) act of God; (d) the independent act of a third party; (e) statutory authority.[20] These defences are also available generally in the law of nuisance and are dealt with above.[21]

If the rule can apply to intentional or voluntary releases of a dangerous thing, it seems that the defence of "necessity" will be available on the same basis as it is in the tort of trespass[22]; but as indicated above, the better view is that the rule does not apply to such releases which should fall within the scope of the law of trespass.[23]

Examples

There are numerous examples of cases in which the rule in *Rylands v. Fletcher* has been applied. It is convenient to list some of them according to the nature of the dangerous thing which has escaped. **2–065**

(1) Water

The case of *Rylands v. Fletcher*[24] itself was a case where an artificial accumulation of water (which was a non-natural use of the land of the defendants) escaped causing damage to the plaintiff for which the defendants were liable.[25] Defendants have also been held liable where they have laid hydraulic mains which burst without any negligence[26] or have **2–066**

---

[20] *E. Hobbs (Farms) Ltd v. The Baxenden Chemical Co. Ltd* [1992] 1 Lloyd's Rep. 54 at 69.
[21] See above, para. 2–058 *et seq.*
[22] *Rigby v. Chief Constable of Northamptonshire* [1985] 2 All E.R. 985, 996.
[23] See above, para. 2–062.
[24] (1866) L.R. 1 Ex. 265; (1868) L.R. 3 H.L. 330.
[25] See above, para. 2–057.
[26] *Charing Cross Electricity Supply Co. v. Hydraulic Power Co.* [1914] 3 K.B. 772.

constructed a watercourse to bring water to a mill and water has escaped and caused damage when the mechanism regulating the flow fell into disrepair.[27] Liability has also been imposed where a defendant has altered the level of his land so that rain-water percolated through the plaintiff's wall[28] and where a defendant allowed water to collect in his cellar which escaped and damaged the plaintiff's property.[29] Where the defendant accumulated quantities of water for the processing of cinematograph films it was held liable for the damage caused by the escape to a lower floor of the building occupied by the defendant.[30] The principle in *Rylands v. Fletcher* applies to owners of sewers whether they constructed the sewer or not.[31] Where a defendant diverts or alters a natural stream in such a way that the new stream is unable to carry off the water to the extent that the old stream could, he will be liable for the damage caused by the deficiency of the new stream.[32] The defences of default or act of[33] or consent of the claimant,[34] act of God,[35] the independent act of a third party[36] and statutory authority[37] apply to escapes of water where a claimant seeks to rely upon *Rylands v. Fletcher* in this context.

(2) Fire

2–067 At common law the rules relating to liability for fires are ancient and a remedy was provided by an action on the case, the allegation in the action being that the defendant *tam negligenter custodivit ignem suum.*[38] The use of the word *"negligenter"* did not mean "negligent" in the modern sense.[39]

The position at common law appears to be that a defendant will be liable for damage done by his fire if it has been caused wilfully or negligently, or

---

[27] *R.H. Buckley & Sons Ltd v. N. Buckley & Sons* [1898] 2 Q.B. 608.

[28] *Hurdman v. North Eastern Railway* (1878) 3 C.P.D. 168; compare *Broder v. Saillard* (1876) 2 Ch.D. 692.

[29] *Snow v. Whitehead* (1884) 27 Ch.D. 588.

[30] *Western Engraving Co. v. Film Laboratories Ltd* [1936] 1 All E.R. 106.

[31] *Humphries v. Cousins* (1877) 2 C.P.D. 239; *Jones v. Llanrwst UDC* [1911] 1 Ch. 393, 405; *Pride of Derby and Derbyshire Angling Association v. British Celanese Ltd* [1953] Ch. 149. But see *Ilford UDC v. Beal* [1925] 1 K.B. 671. See also *Sedleigh-Denfield v. O'Callaghan* [1940] A.C. 880 at 888–889; *Pemberton v. Bright and Devon County Council* [1960] 1 W.L.R. 436.

[32] *Greenock Corp. v. Caledonian Ry* [1917] A.C. 556 at 572. Contrast *Bybrook Barn Centre Ltd v. Kent County Council,* [2001] B.L.R. 55, CA, where on the facts found there was no strict liability (reversing [2000] LGR 302 but not on this point). See also *Booth v. Thomas* [1926] Ch. 109 (affirmed on other grounds [1926] Ch. 397).

[33] *Dunn v. Birmingham Canal Co.* (1872) L.R. 7 Q.B. 244, 246; see above, para. 2–040.

[34] *Prosser & Sons v. Levy* [1955] 1 W.L.R. 1224; see above, para. 2–037.

[35] *Nichols v. Marsland* (1876) 2 Ex. D. 1; see above, para. 2–042.

[36] *Rickards v. Lothian* [1913] A.C. 263; see above, para. 2–043.

[37] See the principles summarised by Webster J. in *Department of Transport v. North West Water Authority* [1983] 1 All E.R. 892 at 895. Contrast *Green v. Chelsea Waterworks Co.* (1894) 70 L.T. 547 with *Charing Cross Electricity Co. v. Hydraulic Power Co.* [1914] 2 K.B. 772; see para. 2–039.

[38] See *Beaulieu v. Finglam* (1401) Y.B. Pasch. 2 Hen. 4, f. 18, p. 1.6. See generally Winfield, (1926) 42 L.Q.R. 46; Newark, (1945) 6 N.I.L.Q. 134; Ogus, [1969] C.L.J. 104.

[39] *Hargrave v. Goldman* (1964) 110 C.L.R. 24 at 56. See *Collingwood v. Home and Colonial Stores Ltd* [1936] 3 All E.R. 200 at 203; *Mullholland and Tedd Ltd v. Baker* [1939] 3 All E.R. 253 at 255; *cf. Tuberville v. Stamp* 2 Salk. 776.

by its escape without negligence if it has been brought into existence by some non-natural user of the land.[40] Until the Fires Prevention (Metropolis) Act 1774 it also seemed that there was liability for the mere escape of fire.

The rules of liability for fire brought into existence by a non-natural use of land are effectively the same as for liability under the rule in *Rylands v. Fletcher*, except that in the case of fire liability arises where:

(a)　the defendant brings onto his land something which is likely to catch fire and keeps it there in such conditions that if it did ignite the fire would be likely to spread to the claimant's land;

(b)　he did so in the course of a non-natural use; and

(c)　the thing ignited and the fire spread.[41]

The basis for this type of liability is the maxim *sic utere tuo ut alienum non laedas.*[42]

Fires are dangerous things but clearly some uses of fires such as a fire **2–068** in a domestic grate will be regarded as "natural" and outside the scope of the rule.[43] But if a hayrick is so constructed by a defendant that it is dangerous if it catches fire, he may be liable on the principle of *Rylands v. Fletcher* if the fire escapes and causes damage. Similarly, a motor car with petrol in its tank has been held to be a dangerous thing and a defendant liable where it caught fire and burned down a garage.[44] The owner of a steam locomotive may be liable for the damage caused by sparks escaping from the engine.[45]

The Fires Prevention (Metropolis) Act 1774 modified liability for the spreading of fire from the defendant's land. Section 86 of that Act provides:

". . . no action, suit or process whatever shall be had, maintained or prosecuted against any person in whose house, chamber, stable, barn or other building, or on whose estate any fire shall . . . accidentally begin, nor shall any recompense be made by such person for any damage suffered thereby, any law, usage or custom to the contrary

[40] *Musgrove v. Pandelis* [1919] 2 K.B. 43 at 46.
[41] *Mason v. Levy Auto Parts of England Ltd* [1967] 2 Q.B. 530 at 542. See also *Balfour v. Barty-King* [1957] 1 Q.B. 496.
[42] *Mason v. Levy Auto Parts of England Ltd* [1967] 2 Q.B. 530.
[43] *Sochacki v. SAS* [1947] 1 All E.R. 344.
[44] *Vaugham v. Menlove* (1837) 3 Bing. N.C. 468 (haystack catching fire); *Musgrove v. Pandelis* [1919] 2 K.B. 43 (petrol in motor car). See *Balfour v. Barty-King* [1957] 1 Q.B. 496 (blow lamp in proximity to lagging); *H & N Emmanuel Ltd v. G.L.C.* [1971] 2 All E.R. 835 (burning of rubbish); *N.Z. Forest Products Ltd v. O'Sullivan* [1974] 2 N.Z.L.R. 80; *Holderness v. Goslin* [1975] N.Z.L.R. 46; *E. Hobbs (Farms) Ltd v. The Baxenden Chemical Co. Ltd* [1992] 1 Lloyd's Rep. 54 at 69 (spark from machinery causing fire which spread).
[45] *Mansell v. Webb* [1919] 88 L.J.K.B. 323; see too *Jones v. Festiniog Railway Co.* (1868) L.R. 3 Q.B. 733; *Powell v. Fall* (1880) 5 Q.B.D. 597; *Slater v. McClellan* 1924 S.C. 854. Compare Railways Fires Acts 1905 and 1923 and see *Langlands (Swanley) v. British Transport Commission* [1956] 1 W.L.R. 890.

notwithstanding: . . . provided that no contract or agreement between landlord and tenant shall be hereby defeated or made void."

The word "accidentally" in this provision has been interpreted restrictively and embraces only "a fire produced by mere chance or incapable of being traced to any cause".[46] Fires caused by negligence or creating a nuisance as a result of negligence are outside the scope of the statute.[47] Fires created by a landlord or by those for whom the landlord is responsible are also excluded.[48] Further, it seems that the rule in *Rylands v. Fletcher* is not affected so far as it is applicable to fires.[49]

In *Musgrove v. Pandelis*[50] the plaintiff occupied rooms above premises which he let to the defendant as a garage. The defendant kept a car in the garage. The defendant's chauffeur started the engine of the car and the petrol in the carburettor caught fire. The fire started without the fault of the chauffeur but if he had acted with reasonable competence he could have prevented its spread. However, the fire did spread to the rest of the car and burnt the plaintiff's property. It was held by the Court of Appeal that the defendant was liable and could not rely on the Act of 1774. Although the original fire in the carburettor was accidental, this fire was distinguished from the fire which spread and caused the damage which the chauffeur could have prevented: the statute therefore did not apply.[51] It was further held that a motor-car with its tank full was a mischievous thing within *Rylands v. Fletcher*, and that the Act did not apply to liability under the rule in that case; accordingly the defendant was liable for the damage caused by the escape of the fire.

(3) Explosives

2–069 Explosives are clearly dangerous and harm resulting from an explosion will fall within the rule in *Rylands v. Fletcher*. It is not necessary that the explosive itself should "escape": it is sufficient that the explosive causes some thing to escape which causes harm. Thus in *Miles v. Forest Rock Granite Co.*[52] the defendants were liable independently of negligence where the plaintiff was injured by a piece of rock which escaped from the defendants'

---

[46] *Filliter v. Phippard* (1847) 11 Q.B. 347 at 357, *per* Lord Denman C.J. Compare *Collingwood v. Home and Colonial Stores Ltd* (1936) 155 L.T. 550 (defective wiring caused fire but defendant was not negligent: defendant not liable).

[47] *Musgrove v. Pandelis* [1919] 2 K.B. 43; *Spicer v. Smee* [1946] 1 All E.R. 344 (electrical wiring negligently installed by contractor: owner liable in nuisance and negligence).

[48] *Spicer v. Smee* [1946] 1 All E.R. 489; *Williams v. Owen* [1955] 1 W.L.R. 1293.

[49] *E. Hobbs (Farms) Ltd v. The Baxenden Chemical Co. Ltd* [1992] 1 Lloyd's Rep. 54 at 69.

[50] [1919] 2 K.B. 43. But see *Job Edwards Ltd v. Birmingham Navigations* [1924] 1 K.B. 341, 361, *per* Scrutton L.J. which indicates that the 1774 Act protects from liability under *Rylands v. Fletcher*.

[51] This is a somewhat strained construction of "begin" in the circumstances since it is difficult to distinguish between the fire which caused the damage and that which had begun accidentally. The analysis of Scrutton L.J. in *Job Edwards Ltd v. Birmingham Navigations* [1924] 1 K.B. 341 at 361, is more convincing.

[52] (1918) 34 T.L.R. 500. Also *Arnold v. Furness Railway Co.* (1874) 22 W.R. 613.

quarry while it was engaged in blasting: "the case was like that of the escape of a dangerous and mischievous animal". The principle in *Rylands v. Fletcher* also applies to the storing of explosives and the carrying on of the business of their manufacture[53] and to firework displays.[54]

(4) Gas

Gas is a thing which is likely to cause harm if it escapes and so falls within the scope of *Rylands v. Fletcher*.[55]

2–070

Gas is supplied by statutory undertakers and it is accordingly necessary to examine the detailed statutory provisions relating to the undertaker in order to establish whether the defence of "statutory authority" will apply in the given circumstances.[56] In general the statutory undertaker will not be liable for damage resulting from the escape of gas from installations within its control in the absence of negligence.[57] But where gas does escape the statutory undertaker may be liable either for negligence in the escape or for its remedy.[58] The escape of gas from pipes will itself be evidence of negligence.[59]

Where a gas installation is outside the control of the supplier, the supplier will not be liable for damage caused by gas which has escaped due to the fault of the owner or occupier of the premises in which the installations are placed.[60] If gas pipes form part of the ordinary domestic installation of gas, the owner or occupier of the premises in which they are situated is not liable for its escape causing damage to the occupiers of other parts of the premises in the absence of negligence because the other owners or occupiers are deemed to have consented to the presence of gas on the premises.[61]

---

[53] *Rainham Chemical Works v. Belvedere Fish Guano Co.* [1921] 2 A.C. 465. But see *Read v. J. Lyons & Co. Ltd* [1947] A.C. 156 at 169–170 and 173–174, where doubts where expressed as to whether it was a non-natural use of land to manufacture explosives during war-time or in an industrial community.

[54] See *Crown River Cruises v. Kimbolton Fireworks Ltd* [1996] 2 Lloyd's Rep 533.

[55] *Northwestern Utilities v. London Guarantee and Accident Co.* [1936] A.C. 108; also *Parry v. Smith* (1879) 4 C.P.D. 325; *Goodbody v. Poplar Borough Council* (1915) 84 L.J.K.B. 1230; *Dominion Natural Gas Co. v. Collins* [1909] A.C. 640.

[56] See the Gas Acts 1972 and 1986; para. 2–039 above.

[57] See *Price v. South Metropolitan Gas Co.* (1895) 65 L.J.Q.B. 126; *Dunne v. North Western Gas Board* [1964] 2 Q.B. 806.

[58] *Burrows v. March Gas & Coke Co.* (1870) L.R. 5 Ex. 67 (negligence in trying to locate a leak with a candle); *Paterson v. Blackburn Corp.* (1892) 9 T.L.R. 55 (negligence in failing to cut off supply to disconnected meter).

[59] *Hanson v. Wearmouth Coal Co.* [1939] 3 All E.R. 47 at 53; *Pearson v. North West Gas Board* [1968] 2 All E.R. 669.

[60] *Henderson v. Newcastle and Gateshead Gas Co.* (1893) 37 Sot. J. 403; *Holder v. Liverpool New Gas and Coke Co.* (1846) 3 C.B. 1. See also *Glennister v. Condon and Eastern Gas Board* [1951] 2 Lloyd's Rep. 115; *Lloyde v. West Midlands Gas Board* [1971] 1 W.L.R. 749.

[61] See above, para. 2–037.

(5) Electricity

2–071   Electricity is a dangerous thing within the rule in *Rylands v. Fletcher*: anyone may be liable who discharges it into the earth beyond his control or allows it to escape in any way.[62]

Where electricity is supplied or used under statutory authority it is usually necessary to show negligence on the part of the statutory undertaker.[63] The question is one of the construction of the statute empowering and imposing duties on the undertaker in question.[64] The ordinary domestic installation of electricity should, in principle, be treated in the same manner as that of gas and water.[65]

If a small escape of electricity interferes with an unusually sensitive mechanism such as a telegraph[66] there will be no liability.

(6) Fumes

2–072   In *West v. Bristol Tramways*,[67] the defendant paved its tramway with wood coated with creosote which gave off fumes so as to damage the plants grown by the plaintiff in his market garden. The defendant was held liable for the damage: "Creosote is like the wild animals in the old cases, the water in *Rylands v. Fletcher*, and the electric fluid in *National Telephone Co. v. Baker*".[68]

(7) Poisons

2–073   The escape of poisonous substances will fall within the scope of *Rylands v. Fletcher*.[69]

(8) Other things

2–074   The categories of things which are regarded as likely to cause harm so as to fall within the scope of *Rylands v. Fletcher* are not closed. It will be a question of fact in each case whether a thing is likely to cause harm if it escapes.[70]

---

[62]   *National Telephone v. Baker* [1893] 2 Ch. 186. See also *Eastern and South African Telephone Co. v. Cape Town Tramways* [1902] A.C. 381.

[63]   *National Telephone Co. v. Baker* [1893] 2 Ch. 186. Now see the Electricity Act 1989 and para. 2–039 (statutory authority).

[64]   See above, para. 2–039.

[65]   Compare *Collingwood v. Home and Colonial Stores* [1936] 3 All E.R. 200.

[66]   *Eastern and South Africa Telephone Co. v. Cape Town Tramways* [1902] A.C. 381. para. 2–032, above (sensitivity of claimant).

[67]   [1908] 2 K.B. 14.

[68]   [1893] 2 Ch. 186.

[69]   *Crowhurst v. Amersham Burial Board* (1878) 4 Ex. D. 5, *cf. Newberry v. Wilson* (1871) L.R. 7 Q.B. 31; *Firth v. Bowling Iron Co.* (1878) 3 C.P.D. 254; *Ponting v. Noakes* [1894] 2 Q.B. 281; *Cheater v. Cater* [1918] 1 K.B. 247; *Cambridge Water Co Ltd v. Eastern Counties Leatherwork plc* [1994] 2 A.C. 264.

[70]   See para. 2–061.

Enjoyment of Property

The ways in which a claimant's reasonable enjoyment of his property can   2–075
be interfered with are numerous and the categories of this sort of nuisance
are certainly not closed. The principles upon which it will be assessed
whether a particular interference amounts to an actionable nuisance have
been dealt with more fully in the preceding parts of this chapter. It will be
convenient to collect some of the situations in which the Court has held
nuisances to exist in the absence of physical damage.

NOISE

One of the most common (if not the most common) interferences with the   2–076
enjoyment of property is noise. Whether a nuisance is caused by a particular noise will be determined according to the general principles which
we have already examined.[71] The interference as a result of noise must be
such as to make it unreasonable in the circumstances. Noise resulting
from the ordinary use of residential premises will not be unreasonable.[72]
The following are examples of noises which in their particular contexts
have been held to constitute nuisances.

(1) Musicians

The noise caused by singing lessons or musical instruments will not usu-   2–077
ally amount to a nuisance[73] unless it is so loud or cacophonous that it
unduly interferes with a claimant's comfort or stops him transacting his
business.[74] The malicious hammering of trays against a party wall will
amount to a nuisance, notwithstanding the hammerer's assertion that
"he has a perfect right to amuse himself on any instrument he may
choose".[75]

(2) Bell-ringing

The constant daily ringing of a heavy peal of bells from a Roman Catholic   2–078
chapel has been held to be a nuisance.[76] The duration of the bell-ringing
and its frequency are clearly important factors to be weighed in the
balance of whether the interference caused is an unreasonable one.

---

[71] See above, para. 2–025 et seq.
[72] See Southwark LBC v. Mills [2001] 1 A.C. 1, HL and see 2–028, 2–033 above.
[73] Christie v. Davey [1893] 1 Ch. 316.
[74] See Motion v. Mills (1897) 13 T.L.R. 427; Hampstead & Suburban Properties Ltd v. Diomedous
[1968] 3 All E.R. 545.
[75] Christie v. Davey [1893] 1 Ch. 316.
[76] Soltau v. de Held (1851) 2 Sim. (N.S.) 133.

(3) Entertainments

2–079   Nuisances have been caused by (and injunctions granted restraining) fêtes,[77] a circus which was to continue performing for eight weeks,[78] regattas,[79] an open rifle range[80] and a rifle gallery,[81] merry-go-rounds,[82] steam-organs,[83] a bowling alley,[84] a noisy exhibition,[85] and horse races.[86] Dancing and music will be restrained where they interfere with a claimant's reasonable enjoyment or business use of his property.[87] The causing of crowds to collect may amount to a nuisance.[88] The noise of a playground may also amount to a nuisance.[89]

(4) Machinery

2–080   The noise caused by machinery may amount to a nuisance especially when the noise is of such a frequency as to cause vibration. Saws,[90] steam-hammers,[91] printing machines (especially at night),[92] power stations,[93] mills,[94] and the manufacture and testing of aeroplanes[95] have all given rise to nuisances.[96]

(5) Business

2–081   The noise of traffic generated by a business may amount to a nuisance especially at night: the noise of carts and shouting drivers between 2 a.m. and 6 a.m.,[97] the passing of heavy lorries to and from an oil distribution

---

[77] *Walter v. Brewster* (1867) L.R. 5 Eq. 25 (rockets and band causing regular disturbance to nearby dwelling).
[78] *Inchbald v. Robinson* (1869) L.R. 4 Ch.App. 388.
[79] *Bostock v. North Staffordshire Railway Co.* (1867) 5 De G. & S. 584.
[80] *Howley v. Steele* (1877) L.R. 6 Ch.D. 521.
[81] *Winter v. Baker* (1886) 3 T.L.R. 569.
[82] *Lampton v. Mellish* [1894] 3 Ch. 163; *Bedford v. Leeds Corporation* [1913] 77 J.P. 430.
[83] *Spruzzen v. Dossett* (1896) 12 T.L.R. 246.
[84] *Barham v. Hodges* [1876] W.N. 234.
[85] *Becker v. Earls Court* (1911) 56 Sol. J. 73.
[86] *Dewar v. City & Suburban Racehorse Co.* [1899] 1 Ir. Ch. 345.
[87] *Jenkins v. Jackson* (1888) L.R. 40 Ch.D. 71.
[88] *Walker v. Brewster* (1867) L.R. 5 Eq. 25; *Bellamy v. Wells* (1891) 39 W.R. 158; *Barber v. Penley* [1893] 2 Ch. 447; *Chase v. London County Council* (1898) 62 J.P. 184; *Lyons, Son & Co. v. Gulliver* [1914] 1 Ch. 631. See too, para. 2–101.
[89] *Dunton v. Dover District Council* (1977) L.G.R. 87.
[90] *Gort v. Clark* (1868) 18 L.T. 343; *Husey v. Bailey* (1895) 11 T.L.R. 221.
[91] *Goose v. Bedford* (1873) 21 W.N. 449; *Scott v. Firth* (1864) 10 L.T. 240.
[92] *Polsue and Alfieri v. Rushmer* [1907] A.C. 121.
[93] *Colwell v. St Pancras Borough Council* [1904] 1 Ch. 707, *cf. Heath v. Mayor of Brighton* (1908) 24 T.L.R. 414.
[94] *Fenwick v. East London Railway Co.* (1875) L.R. 20 Eq. 544.
[95] *Bosworth-Smith v. Gwynne's* (1920) 89 L.J. Ch. 368.
[96] See also *Metropolitan Properties v. Jones* [1939] 2 All E.R. 202 (electric motor); *Newman v. Real Estate Debenture Corp.* [1940] 1 All E.R. 131 (banging of doors to lift).
[97] *Bellamy v. Wells* (1890) 63 L.T. 635.

depot,[98] and the noisy crowds and whistling for cabs at a sports club[99] have all amounted to nuisances. The noise of a creche for babies may amount to a nuisance[1]; so too the banging of cans and general noise associated with a dairy[2] and the noise of an hotel kitchen.[3] The noise of pestle and mortar caused by a confectioner has also been held to be a nuisance.[4] The noise of stables may also create a nuisance.[5]

(6) Building works

Where building works are reasonably carried out there will be no actionable nuisance.[6] However, if a defendant fails to carry out the operations reasonably or fails to take all reasonable and proper steps to ensure that there is no undue inconvenience to his neighbours, then the noise caused by the building operations may amount to a nuisance.[7] In *Harrison v. Southwark & Vauxhall Water Co.* Vaughan Williams L.J. said[8]:

2–082

> "A man who pulls down a house for the purpose of building a new one no doubt causes considerable inconvenience to his next-door neighbours during the process of demolition; but he is not responsible as for a nuisance if he uses all reasonable skill and care to avoid annoyance to his neighbour by the works of demolition. Nor is he liable to an action even though the noise and dust and the consequent annoyance be such as would constitute a nuisance if the same, instead of being created for the purpose of demolition of the house, had been created in sheer wantonness, or in the execution of works for a purpose involving a permanent continuance of the dust and noise. For the law, in judging what constitutes a nuisance does take into consideration both the object and the duration of that which is said to constitute the nuisance."

---

[98] *Halsey v. Esso Petroleum Co. Ltd* [1961] 1 W.L.R. 683.

[99] *Germaine v. London Exhibitions* (1896) 75 L.T. 101.

[1] *Moy v. Stoop* (1909) 25 T.L.R. 262.

[2] *Tinkler v. Aylesbury Dairy Co.* (1888) 5 T.L.R. 52; *cf. Fanshaw v. London & Provincial Dairy Co.* (1887) 4 T.L.R. 694.

[3] *Vanderpant v. Mayfair Hotel Co. Ltd* [1930] 1 Ch. 138.

[4] *Sturges v. Bridgman* (1878) L.R. 11 Ch.D. 852.

[5] *Broder v. Saillard* (1876) 2 Ch.D. 692; *Rapier v. London Tramways Co.* [1893] 2 Ch. 588.

[6] See above, para. 2–033. Compare *Gosnell v. The Aerated Bread Co. Ltd* (1894) 10 T.L.R. 661 (no nuisance caused by internal structural alterations where work was of temporary duration); *Clark v. Lloyd's Bank Ltd* (1910) 79 L.J. 645 (no relief although works commenced at 6.30 a.m. and affected plaintiff's hotel).

[7] See *Andreae v. Selfridge & Co. Ltd* [1938] Ch. 1; *De Keyser's Royal Hotel v. Spicer Bros Ltd and Minter* (1914) 30 T.L.R. 661 (pile driving at night, a nuisance); *Webb v. Barker* [1881] W.N. 158 (building works limited to daytime); *Boynton v. Helena Rubenstein and Hall, Bedall & Co.* (1960)176 E.G. 443 (builders restrained from using hoist to between hours of 9 a.m. and 6 p.m. and from running engine save when hoist in operation).

[8] [1891] 2 Ch. 409 at 413. See also *Phelps v. City of London Corp.* [1916] 2 Ch. 255; *Harper v. G.N. Haden & Sons Ltd* [1933] Ch. 298.

(7) Animals

2–083　The noise caused by animals may amount to a nuisance. Particular problems have been caused by cockerels.[9]

(8) Noises intended to annoy

2–084　As indicated above, noises created with the intention of annoying another will constitute a nuisance.[10]

DUST

2–085　Dust is another common cause of nuisance. Dust caused by building works will be judged by the same considerations as noise in that context[11]: the builder will be expected to take all reasonable and proper steps to minimise the inconvenience to his neighbours. Dust created by other activities or in other situations may also give rise to an actionable nuisance.[12]

SMELLS

2–086　If fumes or smoke by their odour materially interfere with the ordinary physical comfort of human existence enjoyed by an occupier of land, an action in nuisance will lie.[13] The following acts, when done so as to pollute the air of neighbours and to interfere with the reasonable enjoyment of their property, have been held to be nuisances: the burning of bricks[14]; the burning of mineral refuse[15]; operating a chemical[16] or a cement[17] or dye[18] works; operating a gas works[19]; the carrying of manure[20] and the operating of manure works[21] the keeping of a pig-sty[22] or stables[23] the

---

[9]　*Leeman v. Montagu* [1936] 2 All E.R. 1677.

[10]　See above, paras. 2–033, 2–077. *Christie v. Davey* [1893] 1 Ch. 316; *Hollywood Silver Fox Farm Ltd v. Emmett* [1936] 2 K.B. 468.

[11]　See above, para. 2–082; and compare *Matania v. National Provincial Bank Ltd* [1936] 2 All E.R. 633.

[12]　*Pwllbach Colliery v. Woodman* [1915] A.C. 634 (coal dust).

[13]　Compare *Crump v. Lambert* (1867) L.R. 3 Eq. 409 at 412; also *St Helen Smelting Co. v. Tipping* (1865) 11 H.L.C. 642.

[14]　*Bamford v. Turnley* (1862) 31 L.J.Q.B. 286.

[15]　*Fleming v. Hislop* (1886) 11 App.Cas. 691.

[16]　*Brooke v. Wigg* (1878) 8 Ch. 510; *St Helens Chemical Co. v. St Helens Corporation* (1876) L.R. 1 Ex. 196; and compare *St Helens Smelting Co. v. Tipping* (1865) 11 H.L.C. 642 (smelting).

[17]　*Umfreville v. Johnson* (1875) 10 Ch.App. 580.

[18]　See *Jones v. Powell* (1629) Hutton 136.

[19]　*Wood v. Conway Corporation* [1914] 2 Ch. 47.

[20]　*Swain v. G.N.R.* (1864) 33 L.J. Ch. 399.

[21]　*Knight v. Gardner* (1869) 19 L.T. 673.

[22]　*Aldred's Case* (1611) 9 Co. Rep. 5Th; *Bone v. Seal* [1975] 1 W.L.R. 797; *Wheeler v. JJ Saunders Ltd* [1996] Ch. 19; [1995] 1 All E.R. 671.

[23]　*Rapier v. London Tramways Co.* [1893] 2 Ch. 588.

making of tar or varnish[24] operating an oil storage depot[25] running a smithy,[26] a tan pit[27] or a fried-fish shop[28]; melting fat,[29] boiling soap,[30] or running the business of a tallow chandler[31]; the deposit of household or street refuse[32] or of night soil and other waste[33]; operating a sewage works[34]; the boiling of horse-flesh[35] and bones.[36] Further the running of a slaughter-house[37] or a brewery[38] may amount to a nuisance.

HEAT AND LIGHT

Causing heat to interfere with the ordinary comfort of physical existence enjoyed by a claimant may amount to a nuisance[39] as may the abstraction of heat so as to reduce the premises to "arctic" conditions.[40] In New Zealand, it has been held that where a building deflected the sun's rays into the plaintiff's buildings in such a way that it was too bright for the human eye to bear and which dazzled the building's occupants, this was a nuisance.[41]

2–087

HOSPITALS

If a hospital actually causes the spread of an infection so as to harm the claimant's land this might be a nuisance of the sort dealt with in the preceding section because it would cause physical harm. However, the very presence of a hospital may amount to a nuisance if it causes its neighbours to live in fear of the risk of infection.[42] With the advance of medical science

2–088

---

[24] *R. v. Neil* (1826) 2 C.& P. 485; *Bigsby v. Dickinson* (1876) 4 Ch. 24.

[25] *Halsey v. Esso Petroleum Co. Ltd* [1961] 1 W.L.R. 683.

[26] *Gullick v. Tremlett* (1872) 20 W.R. 358.

[27] *R. v. Pappineau* (1726) Str. 686.

[28] *Adams v. Ursell* [1913] 1 Ch. 269.

[29] *Att.-Gen. v. Cole* [1901] 1 Ch. 205.

[30] *R. v. Pierce* (1683) 2 Show. 327.

[31] *Bliss v. Hall* (1838) 7 L.J.C.P. 122.

[32] *Att.-Gen. v. Keymer Brick and Tile Co.* (1903) 67 J.P. 434; *Blackburn v. ARC Ltd t/a Greenways Landfill* [1997] P.L.S.C.S. 317 (waste disposal site); compare too *Att.-Gen. v. Tod Heatley* [1897] 1 Ch. 560.

[33] *G.C. Railway Co. v. Doncaster RDC* (1917) 118 L.T. 19.

[34] *Bainbridge v. Chertsey UDC* (1914) 84 L.J. Ch. 626.

[35] *Grindley v. Booth* (1865) 4 H. & C. 669.

[36] *Verco v. Morris* (1881) 26 Sol. J. 126.

[37] *Jones v. Powell* (1629) Hutton 136.

[38] *ibid.; cf. Gorton v. Smart* (1822) L.J. Ch. 36; *Rapley v. Smart* [1894] W.N. 2.

[39] *Sanders-Clark v. Grosvenor Mansions Co.* [1900] 2 Ch. 373; *Reinhardt v. Mentasti* (1889) 42 Ch.D. 685.

[40] *Dublin (South) City Market Co. v. McCabes Ltd* [1953] I.R. 283 at 311

[41] *Bank of New Zealand v. Greenwood* [1984] 1 NZLR 525 (see *Hunter v. Canary Wharf Ltd* [1997] A.C. 655 at 432–433 *per* Lord Goff.)

[42] *Metropolitan Asylum District v. Hill* (1881) 6 App.Cas. 193 (small pox hospital); *cf. Att.-Gen. v. Rathmines Hospital Board* [1904] 1 Jr. R. 161 and *Att.-Gen. v. Manchester Corporation* [1893] 2 Ch. 87; *Att.-Gen. v. Nottingham Corporation* [1904] 1 Ch. 673 (theory of aerial dissemination of small pox not definitely accepted by medical science, therefore no nuisance proved). *cf. Frost v. King Edward VII Association* [1918] 2 Ch. 180 (hospital for surgical tuberculosis not a nuisance). *cf. National Schizophrenia Fellowship v. Ribble Estates SA* [1994] 03 E.G. 132 (accommodation of schizophrenics in quiescent state not a nuisance).

it is now doubtful whether the risk of infection from most hospitals and similar institutions is such as to interfere unreasonably with the enjoyment of their neighbours' land.

URINALS

2–089   A urinal may amount to a nuisance to an adjoining occupier[43]; but the mere erection of a urinal will not in itself be a nuisance in the absence of some evidence of interference with the claimant's enjoyment of his land.[44]

IMMORALITY

2–090   The use of a house for prostitution may amount to a nuisance[45] as may the use of premises for a "sex-shop" in a residential area.[46]

UNSAVOURY OCCUPIERS

2–091   An owner of land has been restrained from permitting gipsies to settle on his land so as to cause a risk to the health of the neighbourhood.[47] Likewise a landowner may be liable where it permits or tolerates its land to be used by occupiers who use the land as a base for repeated interferences with the claimant's enjoyment of his property.[48] However, as noted above[49] an owner of land will not usually be liable for the nuisances caused by others unless he has either authorised or adopted the nuisance.[50]

WATCHING AND BESETTING

2–092   To "watch and beset" (*i.e.* to picket) a man's house with a view to compelling him to do or not to do what is lawful not to do or to do will be an interference with his ordinary enjoyment of his house: it will be a nuisance at common law unless there is some lawful excuse.[51]

---

[43] *Vernon v. Vestry of St James* (1880) L.R. 16 Ch.D. 449.
[44] See *Mudge v. Penge Urban Council* (1917) 86 L.J. Ch. 126.
[45] *Thompson-Schwab v. Costaki* [1956] 1 W.L.R. 335.
[46] *Laws v. Florinplace* [1981] 1 All E.R. 659.
[47] *Att.-Gen. v. Stone* (1895) 12 T.L.R. 76.
[48] See *Page Motors v. Epsom and Ewell Borough Council* (1980) 78 L.G.R. 505, CA; *Lippiatt v. South Gloucestershire Council* [1999] 4 All E.R. 149, CA. Contrast *Hussain v. Lancaster City Council* [1999] 4 All E.R. 125, CA.
[49] See above, paras. 2–014, 2–018.
[50] *See Smith v. Scott* [1973] Ch. 314; *Tetley v. Chitty* [1985] 1 All E.R. 663
[51] *J. Lyons & Sons Ltd v. Wilkins* [1896] 1 Ch. 811; [1899] 1 Ch. 255; *Thomas v. National Union of Mineworkers* [1985] 2 All E.R. 1.

Easements and other servitudes

A servitude is a burden on land which affects the owner's right to use the land in a certain way or puts an obligation on the owner to allow another to use the land in a certain way or take something from that land. There are three sorts of servitude which fall to be considered here: easements, *profits à prendre*, and natural rights. Restrictive covenants may also be characterised as servitudes but the remedy for their infringement is not in the law of tort so they will be dealt with elsewhere.[52] The next section will deal with specific examples of interferences with particular servitudes. This section deals briefly with the principles to be considered when dealing with nuisances affecting servitudes. An interference with an easement may be actionable in tort as a nuisance. As has already been stated above,[53] the action for disturbance of the *profits à prendre* by the person in enjoyment of such a right is historically in trespass though there seems to be nothing in principle to prevent such an action being framed in nuisance in the alternative. An action in nuisance is available for unlawful interferences with easements and servitudes consisting of natural rights. In addition to remedies in tort, the grantee of a servitude may have remedies on covenants. These remedies are dealt with in the next chapter.

2–093

EASEMENTS

An easement is an incorporeal hereditament the ownership of which gives the owner of one piece of land (the "dominant" tenement) rights over another's land (the "servient" tenement) which accommodate the dominant tenement.[54] An easement can only confer on the owner of the dominant tenement a right to use the servient tenement in a particular way. This may be contrasted with a *profit à prendre* which is an incorporeal hereditament which confers a right to take something from the servient tenement.[55]

2–094

Easements must also be distinguished from rights *ex iure naturae* or "natural rights". A natural right is an incident of property but, unlike an easement, is not acquired or presumed to have been acquired by a grant whether express or implied[56] but accrues to the ownership of the land as such.

Because the dominant owner does not have a possessory right to the servient owner's land, historically the interference with an easement by the servient owner or a third party has been characterised not as a trespass

[52] See paras 3–001 *et seq*. The late development of restrictive covenants has meant that the Courts have approached their enforcement distinctly from the law of easements.
[53] See above, paras. 1–001, 1–033.
[54] See generally *Gale on Easements* (16th ed.).
[55] See *Alfred F. Beckett Ltd v. Lyons* [1967] Ch. 449 and *Duke of Sutherland v. Heathcote* [1892] 1 Ch. 475.
[56] See *Baily & Co. v. Clark, Son and Morland* [1902] 1 Ch. 649 at 663–664.

but as a nuisance.[57] It also seems that in order to bring an action for disturbance of an easement it is necessary to prove one's title to the easement even against a stranger notwithstanding that there is *de facto* enjoyment of the easement (the dominant owner of an easement not possessing the servient tenement, he does not enjoy the possessor's right of protection against third parties without proof of title).[58] This position may be contrasted with that in relation to *profits à prendre* which are sufficiently possessory in their nature that their disturbance gives rise to an action in trespass for the person entitled to its enjoyment and without the need to prove title against a stranger.[59]

2–095   It has been noted above that there is no need to prove damage where an action is brought in respect of an interference with an easement since damage is not the "gist of the action", but rather the action is brought to protect or vindicate a claimant's rights.[60] For this reason nuisances to easements have been treated to some extent as sui generis.[61] However, the action for nuisances to easements and that for nuisances to the enjoyment of property share both historical antecedents and remedies available to a claimant:

> "Both injuries are called nuisances, and the same principles as to the nature of the remedies for them apply indiscriminately to both."[62]

The remedies (abatement, injunction and damages) are dealt with in Chapter 4.[63]

The test of whether an actionable nuisance results from an interference with an easement is whether the interference is such as to interfere substantially with the easement so that there is some sensible diminution in its enjoyment by the dominant owner.[64] Once a substantial interference with the enjoyment of the easement has been shown questions of the locality or the reasonableness of the defendant's conduct will not usually be relevant in considering whether the interference is an actionable nuisance[65] and the whims or peculiar sensitivity of the claimant will not

---

[57] See above, paras. 1–033, 2–002. *Nicholls Fitzgerald v. Firbank* [1897] 2 Ch. 96; *Paine & Co. Ltd v. St Neots Gas and Coke Co. Ltd* [1938] 4 All E.R. 492, [1939] 3 All E.R. 812; *Saint v. Jenner* [1973] Ch. 275.

[58] *Paine v. St Neots Gas and Coke Co. Ltd* [1938] 4 All E.R. 492, [1939] 3 All E.R. 812; but see *Jeffries v. Williams* (1850) 5 Exch. 792; *Bibby v. Carter* (1859) 4 H. & N. 153; and *Richards v. Jenkins* (1868) 18 L.T. 437 at 443, 444. See also *Keegan v. Young* [1963] N.Z.L.R. 720.

[59] *Fitzgerald v. Firbank* [1897] 2 Ch. 96. See also paras. 1–033, 2–002, 2–048.

[60] See above, para. 2–002, 2–006, 2–046. *Nichols v. Ely Beet Sugar Factory Ltd* [1936] Ch. 343 at 349. See also *Embrey v. Owen* (1851) 6 Ex. 353 at 368, per Parke B.; *Williams v. Morland* (1824) 2 B. & C. 910 at 916, per Littledale J.

[61] *Colls v. Home and Colonial Stores Ltd* [1904] A.C. 179.

[62] *Gale on Easements*, 16th ed., para. 13–01; *Saint v. Jenner* [1973] Ch. 275, CA at 280.

[63] See below.

[64] See *Jackson v. Duke of Newcastle* (1864) 3 De G.J. & Sm. 275 at 285; *Warren v. Brown* [1900] 2 Q.B. 722; *Colls v. Home and Colonial Stores Ltd* [1904] A.C. 179, HL at 182; *Pettey v. Parsons* [1914] 2 Ch. 653; *Keefe v. Amor* [1965] 1 Q.B. 334 at 346; *Celsteel Ltd v. Alton House Holdings* [1985] 2 All E.R. 562 at 572.

[65] See 2–028 *et seq.* above.

be considered when assessing the substantiality of the interference. The next section (para.2–097 *et seq.*) examines what interferences have been held to be nuisances in relation to some common easements.

Natural rights

A servitude in the nature of a natural right, unlike an easement, is not held **2–096** by a title distinct from the land occupied by a landowner, but is an incident to that land itself and part of the fee simple, *sine quo res ipsa haberi non debet.*[66] Such a right will attend a parcel of land unless expressly excluded upon a conveyance.[67] This is in contrast to rights in the nature of easements which can only be acquired by a grant (whether express or implied) or by the presumption of a grant or prescription.[68]

Natural rights recognised by law which amount to servitudes include the right of an owner of riparian land to use water from a stream for riparian purposes[69] and the right to support of land in its natural unbuilt state from adjoining land.[70] Another right which accrues to land itself at common law is the right of an owner of land adjoining the highway to have access to the highway.[71]

An interference with a natural right will be protected in accordance with the maxim *sic utere tuo ut alienum non laedas.*[72] The next section deals with riparian rights, rights of support and access to the highway and in what circumstances interferences have been held to constitute actionable nuisances.

INTERFERENCES WITH PARTICULAR SERVITUDES AND ANALOGOUS INTERFERENCES

This section examines examples of interferences with particular types of **2–097** servitude.

Water Rights

Nuisances can occur as a result of an interference with water. As with **2–098** other nuisances, in order to establish that an interference is actionable one must consider both whether the claimant has a right which has been

---

[66] "Without which the property itself should not be held": *Dalton v. Angus* (1881) 6 App.Cas. 740 at 791, *per* Lord Selborne L.C.; a natural right of support is one which is "essential to the protection and enjoyment of property", see *Humphries v. Brogden* (1850) 12 Q.B. 739 at 744.

[67] *North-Eastern Railway Co. v. Elliott* 1 J. & H. 145; *Dalton v. Angus* (1881) 6 App.Cas. 740 at 791. See now the Law of Property Act 1925, s.62.

[68] Compare *Baily & Co. v. Clark, Son & Morland* [1902] 1 Ch. 649 at 663–664; *Bonomi v. Backhouse* 1 E.B. & E. 639 at 655.

[69] See below, paras. 2–099 *et seq.*

[70] See below, paras. 2–112 *et seq.*

[71] See below, para. 2–109. Such a right is, perhaps, not strictly a "natural right" but can be treated as analogous to such rights.

[72] *Dalton v. Angus* (1881) 6 App.Cas. 740 at 791.

interfered with and also whether the defendant is entitled to interfere with the claimant's rights.

(1) Right to the flow of water

2–099   *Defined channels: natural watercourses—*

> "A riparian proprietor is entitled to have the water of the stream, on the banks of which his property lies, flow down as it has been accustomed to flow down to his property, subject to the ordinary use of the flowing water by upper proprietors, and to such further use, if any, on their part in connection with their property as may be reasonable in the circumstances. Every riparian proprietor is thus entitled to the water of his stream, in its natural flow, without sensible diminution or increase and without sensible alteration in its character or quality. Any invasion of this right causing actual damage or calculated to found a claim which may ripen into an adverse right entitles the party injured to the intervention of the Court."[73]

Water flowing underground in a defined channel is also a natural right to which these principles apply.[74]

2–100   *Defined channels: artificial watercourses—*These principles do not apply to a man-made watercourses unless the circumstances under which it is presumed to have been created and the mode in which it has been used and enjoyed are such that has acquired the status of a natural watercourse.[75]

2–101   *Undefined channels—*Likewise, these principles do not apply where water on the surface does not flow in a defined channel but squanders itself over an undefined area[76] nor do they apply to water which percolates underground in an undefined channel.[77]

2–102   *Nature and extent of right to water in defined channels—*These rights of ownership do not depend upon ownership of the soil of the stream, they are rights *ex iure naturae* and belong to the owner of adjoining lands.[78] But it is not every piece of land in the same occupation which includes the river bank that is a riparian tenement to which these rights accrue. Thus in the case of *Attwood v. Llay Main Collieries Ltd*[79] the defendant's colliery

---

[73] *John Young v. Bankier Distillery Co.* [1893] A.C. 691 at 698, *per* Lord NacNaghten.

[74] *Chasemore v. Richards* (1859) 7 H.L.C. 349.

[75] *Baily & Co. v. Clark Son & Morland* [1902] 1 Ch. 649; compare *Nield v. L. & N. W. Ry* (1874) 10 L.R. 4.

[76] *Rawstrom v. Taylor* (1855) 11 Ex. 369. See also *Broadbent v. Ramsbotham* (1856) 11 Ex. 602; *Palmer v. Bowman* [2000] 1 W.L.R. 842.

[77] See below, para. 2–106.

[78] *Lyon v. Fishmongers Company* (1876) 1 App.Cas. 662; *Chasemore v. Richards* (1859) 7 H.L.C. 349.

[79] [1926] 1 Ch. 444.

was too far from the river to be a riparian tenement entitling the defendant to abstract water for its purposes. The test of whether a tenement is a riparian tenement is one of "reasonable proximity" to the river bank.[80]

(2) Limits on right to flow of water

The abstraction of water is subject to statutory restrictions and licensing 2–103 by water authorities, detailed consideration of which is outside the scope of this work.[81] At common law, however, a riparian owner is entitled to make "ordinary use" of the water of the stream which his land adjoins.[82] For instance, he is entitled to the reasonable use of the water for his domestic purposes (washing and drinking) and for his cattle and he is entitled to make such use of the water without regard to the effect this may have upon proprietors down the stream even if this results in a deficiency of water for the lower proprietors.[83]

At common law a riparian owner is also entitled to make "extraordinary use" of a stream provided that he does not interfere with the rights of other proprietors above or below him.[84] Uses of a stream for the purposes of a mill or for irrigation are extraordinary uses in this context.[85] The extent to which a riparian owner is entitled to use water for other "extraordinary purposes", such as manufacturing, will depend upon the reasonableness of that use; what is a reasonable use will itself depend upon the nature of the stream in question.[86] An extraordinary user must also reasonably relate to the riparian tenement if the riparian owner is to have a right to make such a use of a stream: thus a defendant cannot divert a stream to create a reservoir for the benefit of parties who have no connection with the stream.[87] A riparian owner only has a right to use the water from a stream for extraordinary purposes if he does not substantially affect the flow of water for other riparian owners so as to cause them sensible injury; if he significantly diminishes the quantity or quality of the water in the stream he may have committed a nuisance.[88] If, however, a

---

[80] *ibid.* at 459, *per* Lawrence J.
[81] See in particular the Water Act 1989 and the Water Resources Act 1991.
[82] *John Young v. Bankier Distillery Co.* [1893] A.C. 691 at 698.
[83] *Miner v. Gilmour* (1858) 12 Moo. P.C. 131 at 156.
[84] *ibid.*
[85] *ibid.*
[86] *Swindon Waterworks Co. Ltd v. Wilts & Berks Canal Navigation Co.* (1875) 7 H.L. 697 at 704. See also *Rugby Joint Water Board v. Walters* [1967] Ch. 397; *cf. Cargill v. Gotts* [1981] 1 W.L.R. 441.
[87] *Swindon Waterworks Co. Ltd v. Wilts & Berks Canal Navigation Co.* (1875) 7 HL. 697, at 705. See also *McCartney v. Londonderry & Lough Swilly Ry Co. Ltd* [1904] A.C. 301 (filling of boilers for locomotives); *Attwood v. Llay Main Collieries* [1926] 1 Ch. 441 (colliery not proximate). Also *Roberts v. Gwyrfai RDC* [1899] 2 Ch. 608; *Stollmeyer v. Trinidad Lake Petroleum Co.* [1918] A.C. 485; *Ormerod v. Todmorden Mill Co.* (1883) 11 Q.B.D. 155.
[88] *Swindon Waterworks Co. Ltd v. Wilts & Berks Canal Navigation Co.* (1875) 7 HL 697. See also *McCartney v. Londonderry & Lough Swilly Ry Co. Ltd* [1904] A.C. 301; *Baily & Co. v. Clark Son & Morland* [1902] 1 Ch. 649; *Embrey v. Owen* (1851) 6 Ex. 353.

defendant abstracts water and returns it unpolluted and undiminished in volume, the abstraction will not be actionable.[89]

(3) Interference with flow of water

2–104   If a riparian owner interferes with the flow of a stream so as to increase or decrease its quantity or quality or affect its direction he commits a nuisance to other riparian owners.[90] Unless the interference causes abstraction or injury it will not be actionable.[91] Actionable interferences have been caused by excavations to a river bed which lessened the flow of water to the plaintiffs' mill,[92] the building of a mound or other structure which would divert the flow of the river onto the land of the opposite proprietor[93] and the damming of the river so as to diminish its flow.[94] The placing of a weir impervious to fish so as to obstruct the passage of fish along the river is an actionable interference.[95] An owner of land containing a spring which is the source of a natural stream cannot interfere with the flow of the water by abstraction from or interference with the spring so as to diminish the flow of the stream.[96] It seems also that a riparian owner may in some circumstances owe a duty to other riparian owners to prevent the natural accumulation of weed, silt or stones from impeding the flow of a stream.[97]

Although a riparian owner has a right to raise the river banks from time to time to prevent flood water within the banks of a river from overflowing his land,[98] he can only do so to the extent that he does no injury to the opposite owner or those above or below him. In *Menzies v. Breadalbane*[99] a riparian owner was held to have no right to build a mound which if completed would have thrown water onto the opposite bank in times of ordinary flood.[1] However, a riparian owner may protect his land from an extraordinary flood even if it results in water flowing onto the land of other riparian owners: a flood embankment placed some distance from the bank of the river may not give rise to a nuisance even if during heavy floods water flows in front of the embankment onto a neighbour's land

[89] *Kensit v. Great Eastern Ry* (1884) 27 Ch.D. 122.
[90] Compare *Orr Ewing v. Colquhoun* (1877) App.Cas. 839 at 856.
[91] *Kensit v. Great Eastern Ry* (1884) 27 Ch.D. 122.
[92] *Fear v. Vickers* (1911) 27 T.L.R. 558.
[93] *Menzies v. Breadalbane* (1828) Bli. (N.S.) 414; *Bickett v. Morris* (1866) L.R. 1 Sc. & Div. 47; compare *Marriage v. East Norfolk Rivers Catchment Board* [1949] K.B. 456.
[94] See *Sampson v. Hoddinott* (1857) 1 C.B. (N.S.) 590; *Roberts v. Gwyrfai RDC* [1899] 2 Ch. 608; *White v. White* [1906] A.C. 72.
[95] *Weld v. Hornby* (1806) 7 East 195; compare *Leconfield v. Lonsdale* (1870) L.R. 5 C.P. 657.
[96] *Mostyn v. Atherton* [1899] 2 Ch. 360.
[97] Assuming that a riparian owner may assume responsibility for a naturally occurring nuisance in accordance with the case of *Leakey v. National Trust* [1980] Q.B. 485; but see *Neath RDC v. Williams* [1951] 1 K.B. 115.
[98] *Trafford v. The King* (1832) 8 Bing. 204; *Ridge v. Midland Ry* (1888) 53 J.P. 55.
[99] (1828) 3 Bli. (N.S.) 414.
[1] See also *Bickett v. Morris* (1866) L.R. 1 Sc. & Div. 47; *Provinder Millers (Winchester) Ltd v. Southampton County Council* [1940] 1 Ch. 131.

since it is the "common enemy" of the river in flood which causes the damage rather than the party who erected the embankment.[2]

(4) Interference with quality of stream

A nuisance to a riparian owner may be caused by an interference with the natural quality of the stream. An actionable interference with the quality of a stream may be caused by pollution of the stream,[3] by affecting its temperature,[4] or changing its quality from soft to hard water.[5] For such an interference to be actionable it is not necessary for actual damage to be proven.[6]

    2–105

It is not every interference with the quality of a stream that will amount to an actionable nuisance: a person who causes pollution may be entitled to do so pursuant to his legal rights. A person may be entitled to pollute a stream because he is entitled to an easement[7] or is authorised to do so pursuant to statute.[8] He may also be entitled to pollute a stream by reason of an immemorial custom: for example, it may be an immemorial custom to wash in a stream impurities in minerals mined nearby; however, such a right must be definite and reasonable (and will be confined to the necessary working of the mine).[9]

(5) Underground water and water in undefined channels

As indicated above, water flowing underground in a defined channel is a stream to which the principles described above apply.[10] However, water which percolates underground in no defined channel[11] or in a channel which can only be ascertained by excavation, the continuation of which is uncertain,[12] has been treated differently. It has been held that a landowner through whose land water percolates underground has no natural right in the water which enables him to bring an action if a person interferes with

    2–106

---

[2] *Gerrard v. Crowe* [1921] 1 A.C. 395; *R. v. Pagham, Sussex Sewers Commissioners* (1828) 8 B. & C. 355; *Nield v. L. & N.W.R.* (1874) L.R. 10 Ex. 4.

[3] *Wood v. Waud* (1849) 3 Exch. 748; *Sharp v. Wilson Rotheray & Co.* (1905) L.T. 155; *Jones v. Llanrwst UDC* [1911] 1 Ch. 393; *Pride of Derby v. British Celanese Ltd* [1952] 2 All E.R. 1326 (affirmed on other grounds [1953] Ch. 149). See also *Fitzgerald v. Firbank* [1897] 2 Ch. 96.

[4] *Mason v. Hill* (1832) 5 B. & A. 1; *Ormerod v. Todmorden Mill Co.* (1883) 11 Q.B.D. 155; *Tipping v. Eckersley* (1855) 2 K. & J. 264; *Pride of Derby v. British Celanese* [1952] 2 All E.R. 1326.

[5] *Young v. Bankier Distillery Co.* [1893] A.C. 691.

[6] *Crossley & Sons Ltd v. Lightowler* (1867) L.R. 2 Ch. 478; *Pennington v. Brinsop Hall Coal Co.* (1877) 5 Ch.D. 769; see para. 2–027 (actionable if interference may ripen into an adverse right).

[7] See paras 2–060.

[8] See para. 2–061. Compare *Lee Conservancy Board v. Hertford Corp.* (1884) 48 J.P. 628; *Somerset Drainage Commissioners v. Brightwater Corp.* (1899) 81 L.T. 729.

[9] *Carlyon v. Lovering* (1857) 1 H. & N. 784; *Wright v. Williams* (1836) 1 M. & W. 77.

[10] See *Chasemore v. Richards* (1859) 7 H.L.C. 349.

[11] *ibid.*

[12] *Bradford Corporation v. Ferrand* [1902] 2 Ch. 655; *Bleachers' Association v. Chapel-en-le-Frith UDC* [1933] Ch. 356.

its supply.[13] Thus a landowner who had for more than 60 years enjoyed the use of a stream which was chiefly supplied by water percolating underground, had no cause of action where an adjoining landowner had dug a well on his own land which affected the supply of water.[14] Conversely, there was no actionable nuisance where a defendant who in carrying out mining operations on his own land drained away water percolating through the claimant's land leaving his well dry.[15] Similarly, it has been held that where water has percolated into the claimant's land and is collected in a well, no cause of action will lie if the water is abstracted due to workings on the defendant's adjacent property.[15a] Further, it has been held that there is no right for a landowner to have his land or water supported by water percolating through his land.[16]

Since a landowner has no right in water percolating in an undefined channel through his land, the motives with which a neighbour abstracts that water are irrelevant[17] and it has been held that there is no duty of care in abstracting percolating water to prevent causing subsidence.[18]

Although a lower occupier has no cause of action against an upper occupier for permitting the flow of water percolating in undefined channels to reach his land, the lower occupier is under no duty to receive the water and can take steps to prevent the influx of water, even if this causes damage to the upper owner.[18a] However, if the steps taken by the lower owner involve an unreasonable interference with the upper owner's enjoyment of his land (having regard to whether the lower owner is using his land reasonably), the lower owner may be liable to the upper owner for any damage caused as a result of the steps taken to prevent the influx of water to the lower land.[19]

The above case law may require revision in the light of the decisions of *Leakey v. National Trust*[20] and *Holbeck Hall Hotel Ltd v. Scarborough Borough Council*.[21] If a measured duty of care to a neighbour can be imposed on a landowner to prevent damage caused by natural slippage where the neighbour has no natural right appurtenant to his property to be protected from such slippage, it seems to us that similar duties may exist upon landowners where the abstraction of water may reasonably be foreseen to harm their neighbour's land by creating subsidence.

---

[13] See *Ballard v. Tomlinson* (1885) Ch.D. 115; *Cambridge Water Co. Ltd v. Eastern Counties Leatherwork plc* [1994] 2 A.C. 264 at 296; [1994] 1 All E.R. 53 at 68, HL.

[14] *Chasemore v. Richards* (1859) 7 H.L.C. 349, HL.

[15] *Acton v. Blundell* (1843)12 M. & W. 324.

[15a] *New River Co. v. Johnson* (1860) 2 E. & E. 435.

[16] *Popplewell v. Hodkinson* (1869) L.R. 4 Ex. 248; compare *Jordeson v. Sutton, Southcoates and Drypool Gas Co.* [1899] 2 Ch. 217; *English v. Metropolitan Water Board* [1907] 1 K.B. 588.

[17] *Bradford v. Pickles* [1895] A.C. 587, HL. See above, para. 2–034.

[18] *Stephens v. Anglian Water Authority* [1987] 1 W.L.R. 1381, CA; 18a *Palmer v. Bowman* [2000] 1 W.L.R. 842.

[19] *Home Brewery plc v. William Davies & Co. (Loughborough) Ltd* [1987] Q.B. 339.

[20] [1980] 1 QB.485 CA which was not cited in *Stephens v. Anglian Water Authority* [1987] 1 W.L.R. 1381. See 2–014 *et seq.* above.

[21] [2000] Q.B. 36, CA.

(6) Artificial watercourses, pipes and drains

Landowners may have rights in relation to artificial water courses which **2–107** adjoin or pass through their land. Such rights may be based upon express agreement or from agreement presumed from the user of the watercourse. One must take account of the nature of the watercourse, the circumstances of its creation and how it is used in determining what (if any) rights subsist in the absence of express agreement.[22] Pipes and drains are artificial watercourses over which easements may be acquired.[23] Interference with such rights, if substantial, will be actionable.[24]

Rights to lay pipes, drains and conduits for other services may also be granted, the extent of such rights being a matter of construction in each case.[25] Where rights are granted over pipes which may be laid in the future, such rights are subject to the rules regarding perpetuities.[26]

(7) Abstraction of water: statutory defence

Statute provides that no person shall abstract water or cause or permit **2–108** any other person to abstract any water except in pursuance of a licence granted by the water authority for the area in question.[27] A licence is not required for any abstraction of water not exceeding five cubic metres, if it does not form part of a continuous operation or series of operations, whereby in the aggregate more than 20 cubic metres of water are abstracted.[28] A licence is not required for abstraction from an inland water for one or both of the following purposes, namely, the domestic purposes of the occupier's household and agricultural purposes other than spray irrigation.[29] The detailed provisions relating to the grant of licences, "protected rights"[30] and the duties of water authorities are beyond the scope of this work; however, it will be noted that the requirement of a licence to abstract water does not extinguish the natural rights and easements of riparian owners, it simply prevents a riparian owner from exercising his rights unless he has obtained a licence.[31] It will also be noted that the statutory provisions do not prevent riparian owners from bringing an

---

[22] *Sutcliffe v. Booth* (1863) 32 L.J.Q.B. 136; *Baily & Co. v. Clark Son & Moreland* [1902] 1 Ch. 649; compare *Nield v. L. & N. W. Ry* (1874) 10 L.R. 4. See also *Manug Bya v. Manug Kyi Lyo* (1925) L.R. 52 Ind. App. 385, P.C.; *Epstein v. Reymes* (1972) 29 D.L.R.(3d) (Supreme Court of Canada).

[23] *Schwann v. Cotton* [1916] 2 Ch. 460; *Beauchamp v. Frome Rural District Council*, [1938] 1 All E.R. 595.

[24] *Rance v. Elvin* (1985) 50 P & CR 9, CA.

[25] See *e.g. Simmons v. Midford* [1969] 2 Ch. 415; *Trailfinders v. Razuki* [1988] 2 E.G.L.R. 46; *Coopind (UK) Ltd v. Walton Commercial Group Ltd* [1989] 1 E.G.L.R. 241. See too *Melluish v. BMI (No. 3) Ltd* [1995] 3 W.L.R. 630, 637 H–638 A.

[26] See Perpetuities and Accumulations Act 1964 and see too *Dunn v. Blackdown Properties Ltd* [1961] Ch. 433.

[27] See the Water Resources Act 1991, s. 24.

[28] See the Water Resources Act 1991, s. 27.

[29] *ibid.*

[30] See generally Part II of the Water Resources Act 1991.

[31] *Cargill v. Gotts* [1981] 1 W.L.R. 441.

action for an interference with their rights notwithstanding that those rights are only exercisable with a licence.[32]

However, it should be noted that section 48(2) of the Water Resources Act 1991 provides holders of licences under that Act with a defence to an action for nuisance brought as a result of the abstraction of water pursuant to and in compliance with the licence. That subsection provides:

> "In any action brought against a person in respect of the abstraction of water from a source of supply, it shall be a defence . . . for him to prove (a) that the water was abstracted in pursuance of a licence under this Act, and (b) that the provisions of the licence were complied with."

Access

(1) Highways

2–109 The public has rights to pass along the highway, interference with which may amount to a public nuisance. In addition to those rights shared in common with other members of the public, owners of land which adjoins the highway have common law private rights of access to the highway which benefit the land which they own interference with which may amount to an actionable private nuisance.[33] In the case of *Marshall v. Blackpool Corporation*[34] Lord Atkin said:

> "The owner of land adjoining a highway has a right of access to the highway from any part of his premises. This is so whether he or his predecessors originally dedicated the highway or not. The rights of the public to pass along the highway are subject to this right of access: just as the right of access is subject to the rights of the public, and must be exercised subject to the general obligations as to nuisance and the like imposed upon a person using the highway."

This private right is one of access only: when the highway is reached any interference, if it is to be actionable, must amount to a public nuisance. Thus in the case of *W.H. Chaplin and Co. Ltd v. Westminster Corpn*[35] it was held that the right to transfer goods from vans in the public roadway across the public pavement to premises adjoining the pavement was a right enjoyed by the owner of the premises as one of the members of the public entitled to use the highway: the owner of the premises was thus not entitled to an injunction restraining the local

---

[32] *ibid.*
[33] See *Lyon v. Fishmongers' Co.* (1876) 1 App.Cas. 662; *Chaplin v. Westminster Corp.* [1901] 2 Ch. 329; *St Mary's, Newington v. Jacobs* (1871) L.R. 7 Q.B. 47; *Tottenham UDC v. Rowley* [1912] 2 Ch. 633.
[34] [1935] A.C. 16 at 22.
[35] [1901] 2 Ch. 329.

authority from exercising its statutory powers to erect a lamp-post which interfered with his crossing of the pavement. Private rights of access to the highway are also to a large extent now qualified by the provisions of the Highways Act 1980.[36]

The common law right of access to the highway is not limited to access to the door of the house but includes a right of access to the walls of the house.[37]

An interference with the common law right of access is actionable per se[38]; though to be actionable the interference must be unreasonable. Damages for consequential losses can be recovered such as loss of business where customers are prevented from obtaining access to business premises.[39]

(2) Navigable Rivers

The public has rights to use navigable rivers which are analogous to its right to use highways.[40] Similarly, it is clear law that in general a riparian owner on a navigable river has a right of access to the river, subject to the public's right of navigation[41] and mooring.[42] Interference with this right of access may amount to a private nuisance. **2–110**

Rights of way

A private right of way is a type of easement.[43] In general a private right of way only confers a right to a reasonable use of the right of way in common with others.[44] Accordingly, the dominant owner may not substantially alter the nature of the road nor otherwise prejudice the servient tenement[45] and if he does so may himself be liable for a tortious interference with the rights of the servient owner or the rights of others who are entitled to use the way.[46] **2–111**

Further, an obstruction to a private right of way will only be actionable if it is substantial.[47] The test of whether an obstruction of a right of way is

---

[36] See also *Ching Garage Ltd v. Chingford Corp.* [1961] 1 W.L.R. 470; *L.C.C. v. Cutts* [1961] 1 W.L.R. 292.

[37] *Cobb v. Saxby* [1914] 3 K.B. 822 (obstruction to wall used for advertising).

[38] *Walsh v. Ervin* [1952] V.L.R. 361.

[39] *Fritz v. Hobson* (1880) 14 Ch.D. 542 at 554–556.

[40] *Orr Ewing v. Colquhourn* (1877) 2 App.Cas. 839; *Att.-Gen. v. Simpson* [1901] 2 Ch. 673, [1904] A.C. 476.

[41] *Lyon v. Fishmongers' Co.* (1876) 1 App.Cas. 662; compare *Tate & Lyle Food and Distribution Ltd v. G.L.C.* [1983] 2 A.C. 509. Also *Att.-Gen. v. Conservators of the Thames* (1862) 1 H. & M. 1.

[42] Compare *Att.-Gen. v. Wright* [1897] 2 Q.B. 318; *Denaby v. Anson* [1911] 1 K.B. 171.

[43] See above, para. 2–094.

[44] *Clifford v. Hoare* (1874) L.R. 9 C.P. 362 at 371.

[45] See *Alvis v. Harrison* (1990) 62 P & CR 10 at 15 *per* Lord Jauncey.

[46] See 1–033 above (trespass).

[47] *Thorpe v. Brumfitt* (1873) 8 Ch.App. 650 at 656. Compare *Pettey v. Parsons* [1914] 2 Ch. 662; *Celsteel Ltd v. Alton House Holdings Ltd* [1985] 1 W.L.R. 204 (reversed on other points [1986] 1 W.L.R. 374).

actionable was laid down in *Hutton v. Hamboro*[48] as being whether practically and substantially the right of way could be exercised as conveniently as before. Thus the dominant owner of a right of way can only object to such activities of the servient owner (including the erection and retention of obstructions) as substantially interfere with the dominant owner's use of the land in such exercise of his defined right as for the time being is reasonably required.[49] In considering whether or not an interference is actionable one must consider what use the dominant owner is entitled to make[50] and all the circumstances including the rights of others to use the way.[51]

The cause of action which a dominant owner may have in respect of interference with his right of way extends only to such loss as is occasioned by the interference. He does not have a cause of action for any physical damage to the servient land itself apart from its effect in obstructing his right of way.[52]

Actionable interferences have been caused by building on a way,[53] or over a way,[54] ploughing up a way,[55] and constructing ramps which disturbed a way when its surface subsequently deteriorated.[56] Placing a gate or door across the way may amount to an actionable interference with the way if the interference is substantial[57] but this may not always be so.[58] Whether or not there is an actionable interference will be a question of fact. By way of example, supplying the dominant owner with a key to a gate or door may render the interference by the gate or door such that it cannot be described as substantial if the way can be used as conveniently as before.[59] If, on the other hand, the dominant owner's rights include use by invitees and licensees to whom keys cannot conveniently be supplied, the supply of a key is unlikely to render insubstantial an interference caused by a gate or door.[60] Where a servient owner is entitled to place a gate across a right of way, the dominant owner may be under an obligation to shut the gate where it has been left open for his convenience.[61]

---

[48] (1860) 2 F. & F. 218.
[49] *Keefe v. Amor* [1965] 1 Q.B. 334 at 347.
[50] See above, n. 44.
[51] *Shoesmith v. Byerley* (1873) 28 L.T. 553.
[52] *Weston v. Lawrence Weaver* [1961] 1 Q.B. 402.
[53] *Lane v. Capsey* [1891] 3 Ch. 411; compare *Celsteel Ltd v. Alton House Holdings Ltd* [1985] 1 W.L.R. 204: *B&Q plc v. Liverpool and Lancashire Properties Ltd* 26/07/00 Ch. D Blackburne J.
[54] *V.T. Engineering Ltd v. Richard Barland Co. Ltd* (1968) 19 P. & C.R. 890.
[55] 2 Rolle, Ab., Nusans, G.1. Compare *Nicol v. Beaumont* (1883) 50 L.T. 112. See also *Charles v. Beach* [1993] N.P.C. 102 (flower bed interfering with way).
[56] *Saint v. Jenner* [1973] Ch. 275.
[57] *Pettey v. Parsons* [1914] 2 Ch. 662 at 666.
[58] *Deacon v. S.E. Ry* (1889) 61 L.T. 377; *Flynn v. Harte* [1913] 2 I.R. 327.
[59] *Dawes v. Adela Estates Ltd* (1970) 216 Estates Gazette 1405, Pennycuick V-C.
[60] See *Guest Estates Ltd v. Milner's Safes Ltd* (1911) 28 T.L.R. 59; *Dawes v. Adela Estates Ltd* (1970) 216 E.G. 1405; *Rafique v. Trustees of Walton Estates* (1992) 65 P & CR 356. See also *Johnstone v. Holdway* [1963] 1 Q.B. 601.
[61] *Geoghegan v. Henry* [1922] 2 IR 1; *Gohl v. Hendon* [1930] SASR 158; *cf Lister v. Rickard* (1969) 113 S J 981 (no obligation on *servient* owner to close gate).

In the absence of an express or implied grant or reservation to the servient owner, the servient owner has no right to divert the route of a right of way.[62] It has been left open whether a diversion in the absence of such a grant or reservation will always amount to a substantial, actionable interference with the dominant owner's rights even where the diverted way is as convenient as the original way.[63] Where a right is granted over specified land, the better view is that a diversion of the route available to the dominant owner onto other land will be actionable: the effect of such a diversion is to prevent the exercise of the right which was granted.[64] There may remain, however, the question of whether an injunction should be granted in the circumstances.[65]

Rights of support

Rights of support are of two kinds. First, there are natural rights of support: every owner of land has a right to the support of his land in its natural state from adjacent and subjacent land[66]; such a right is necessary for the enjoyment of any land.[67] Secondly, there are easements of support for buildings and land which is not in its natural state: these rights may be acquired by grant (express or implied) or by prescription like any other easement.[68] There was no natural right of support from adjacent or subjacent land for buildings.[69] However, since the development of the law of nuisance to embrace duties in relation to naturally occurring nuisances, an owner of land adjoining a building owes a duty to his neighbour:

2–112

> "to do that which is reasonable in all the circumstances, and no more than what, if anything, is reasonable to prevent or minimise the known risk of damage or injury to one's neighbour or to his property."[70]

Thus in the case of *Holbeck Hall Hotel Limited v. Scarborough Borough Council*.[70a] where natural land slippage on the defendant's land caused damage to the claimant's hotel, it was held that the defendant was under a duty to the claimant though in the circumstances of the case Stuart-Smith LJ[71] considered that it was not "just and reasonable . . . to impose liability for damage which is greater in extent than anything that was

---

[62] *Greenwich Healthcare NHS Trust v. London Quadrant Housing Trust* [1998] 1 WLR 204, 216–217.
[63] *ibid.*
[64] See *e.g. Nichols v. Ely Beet Sugar Factory Ltd* [1936], 343, 348 and 2–027 above.
[65] See 4–084ff (Remedies).
[66] *Humphries v. Brogden* (1850) 12 Q.B. 739; *Dalton v. Angus* (1881) 6 App.Cas. 740; *Backhouse v. Bonomi* (1861) 9 H.L.C. 503.
[67] *Sine quo res ipsa haberi non debet, Dalton v. Angus* (1881) 6 App.Cas. 740 at 791.
[68] *Dalton v. Angus* (1881) App.Cas. 740.
[69] *Wyatt v. Harrison* (1832) 3 B. & Ad. 871; *Dalton v. Angus* (1881) 6 App.Cas. 740 at 792.
[70] *Leakey v. National Trust* [1980] 1 Q.B. 485 *per* Megaw LJ; see 2–014ff above.
[70a] [2000] Q.B. 36, CA.
[71] *ibid.*, at para. 51

foreseen or foreseeable (without further geological investigation), especially where the defect and danger existed as much on the Claimants' land as the Defendants" (and in the particular circumstances of the case, liability was not imposed). In *Rees v Skerrett*[72] it was held that a landowner owes a duty of care when he pulls down a house, appreciating that it protects his neighbour's wall, to take reasonable steps to provide weatherproofing.

Interference with rights of support where they exist may be actionable as a nuisance

(1) Extent of natural rights of support

2–113   It has long been established that: "a man who has land closely adjoining my land cannot dig his land so near mine that mine would fall into his pit; and an action brought for such an act would lie."[73]

Similarly, where land is severed so that one plot is subjacent to another, the prima facie rule is that there are natural rights of support in favour of the upper plot.[74] Of course, this rule may be displaced by the intention of the parties to the instrument affecting the severance of the plots.[75] However, there is no natural right of support from any underground water percolating through the soil of an adjacent or subjacent owner in which no proprietary right can subsist[76]; but there may be a natural right of support from silt or liquid pitch or brine.[77] It was the law that a servient owner was only under an obligation to refrain from actively withdrawing support and he was not obliged either to take active steps to maintain the land that gave support[78] or to take steps to prevent subsidence where this was caused by the effect of nature after use of the servient land in a normal way.[79] How-

---

[72] [2001] E.W.C.A. Civ 760.
[73] Rolle's Abr. 565: *Trespass, Justification*, (I), pl. 1 (see *Gale on Easements op. cit.* at p. 313). *Davis v. Treharne* (1881) 6 App.Cas. 460; *Dalton v. Angus* (1881) 6 App.Cas. 740 at 808, 809. See also *Birmingham Corp. v. Allen* (1877) 6 Ch.D. 284.
[74] *Humphries v. Brogden* (1850) 12 Q.B. 739; *Backhouse v. Bonomi* (1861) 9 H.L.C. 503.
[75] *Butterknowle Colliery Co. v. Bishop Auckland Co-operative Society* [1906] A.C. 305; *Hext v. Gill* (1872) 7 Ch.App. 699; *Warwickshire Coal Co. v. Coventry Corp.* [1934] 1 Ch. 488. See also *Butterley Co. v. New Hucknall Colliery* [1910] A.C. 381; *Beard v. Moira Colliery* [1915] 1 Ch. 257; *Weldon v. Butterley Co.* [1920] 1 Ch. 130; *Jones v. Consolidated Anthracite Collieries* [1916] 1 K.B. 123. *cf. New Sharlston Collieries v. Westmorland* [1904] 2 Ch. 443; *Wath-upon-Dearne UDC v. Brown & Co.* [1936] 1 Ch. 172.
[76] *Popplewell v. Hodkinson* (1869) L.R. 4 Ex. 248; *English v. Metropolitan Water Board* [1907] 1 K.B. 588; *Langbrook Properties Ltd v. Surrey County Council* [1970] 1 W.L.R. 161.
[77] *Jordeson v. Sutton, etc., Gas Co.* [1899] 2 Ch. 217 (support by silt removed); *Trinidad Asphalt Co. v. Ambard* [1899] A.C. 594 (support by pitch removed); *Lotus v. British Soda Co.* [1972] Ch. 123 (liquefaction of mineral support). See also Brine Pumping (Compensation for Subsidence) Act 1891. *cf. Salt Union v. Brummer Mond & Co.* [1906] 2 K.B. 822. *Brace v. South East Regional Housing Association Ltd* (1984) 270 E.G. 1286 (shrinkage of subjacent clay).
[78] *Sack v. Jones* [1925] Ch. 235; *Bond v. Nottingham Corp.* [1940] Ch. 429 at 438; *Macpherson v. London Passenger Transport Board* (1946)175 L.T. 279.
[79] *Rouse v. Gravelworks Ltd* [1940] 1 K.B. 489.

ever, the law must now be considered in the light of *Leakey v. National Trust*[80] and *Holbeck Hall Hotel Limited v Scarborough Borough Council.*[81]

(2) Interference with natural right of support

Where there is a natural right of support, a withdrawal of that support **2–114** may be actionable where it causes subsidence to the claimant's land in its natural state.[82] But withdrawal of support is not in itself actionable: the right of support is simply a right not to have one's land appreciably affected by anything done, however carefully,[83] in the adjoining soil adjacent or subjacent.[84] Accordingly if the natural support of adjoining or subjacent land is removed but subsidence is avoided by artificial means, there is no cause of action.[85] It follows also that for the purposes of the Limitation Acts a cause of action does not arise until subsidence occurs[86]; and each subsidence (should more than one occur) gives rise to a separate cause of action.[87] It seems that liability for damage caused by withdrawal of support falls on the person who withdrew the support and not his successor in title even though subsidence does not occur until the excavated land is in the possession of the successor[88]; though a successor in title will be liable if he can be said to have "adopted" the nuisance.

It is not necessary for the claimant to prove pecuniary loss for a withdrawal of support to be actionable: it is sufficient for a claimant to prove that the condition of his land has been changed to a substantial extent.[89]

Injunctive relief is available to prevent a withdrawal of support.[90] It may also be available to compel a restoration of support after it has wrongfully been withdrawn; but such relief is discretionary.[91]

Damages for the loss of market value of the claimant's property due to the subsidence and any consequential losses will be recoverable; however, damages will not be recoverable to take account of the risk of future subsidence (unless damages are awarded in lieu of an injunction), since a new

---

[80] [1980] Q.B. 485. See above, para. 2–014; and 2–115 below (extent of rights of support for buildings).

[81] [2000] Q.B. 836, CA.

[82] See cases cited above, n. 73.

[83] *Humphries v. Brogden* (1850) 12 Q.B. 739 at 757; *Hunt v. Peak* (1860) John. 705 at 710.

[84] *Backhouse v. Bonomi* (1858) E.B. & E. 622 at 657; *Dalton v. Angus* (1881) 6 App.Cas. 740 at 808. See *Gale on Easements* (15th ed.), at p. 316.

[85] *Rowbotham v. Wilson* (1857) 8 E. & B. 123 at 157; *Bower v. Peate* (1876) 1 QBD 321 at 327.

[86] Limitation Act 1980, s. 2: "An action founded on tort shall not be brought after the expiration of six years from the date on which the cause of action accrued." See *Backhouse v. Bonomi* (1861) 9 H.L.C. 501; *West Leigh Colliery Co. v. Tunnicliffe & Hampson Ltd* [1908] A.C. 27. See 4–037 *et seq.*

[87] *Darley Main Colliery Co. v. Mitchell* (1886) 11 App.Cas. 127; *Crumbie v. Wallsend Local Board* [1911] 1 Q.B. 503; *Hall v. Duke of Norfolk* [1900] 2 Ch. 493 at 503; *Redland Bricks Ltd v. Morris* [1970] A.C. 652 at 664.

[88] *Greenwell v. Low Beechburn Coal Co.* [1897] 2 Q.B. 165; *Hall v. Duke of Norfolk* [1900] 2 Ch. 493; *cf. Manley v. Burn* [1916] 2 K.B. 121. See also Coal Industry Nationalisation Act 1946, s. 48(1) for an exception to this principle and now Coal Industry Act 1994.

[89] *Att.-Gen. v. Conduit Colliery* [1895] 1 Q.B. 301.

[90] See *Redland Bricks Ltd v. Morris* [1970] A.C. 652 at 665 B.

[91] *ibid.* at 665–667. See 4–084 *et seq.*

cause of action will arise in respect of such subsidence.[92] In addition to damages payable in respect of a breach of a natural right of support, compensation may be payable under the terms of conveyances[93] or under statute.[94] Statute may authorise a withdrawal of support.[95]

(3) Extent of rights of support for buildings

2–115   As indicated above,[96] it has been held that there is no natural right of support for buildings and a landowner may, in the absence of any rights in others restricting him, excavate his land[97] or pull down his own house even if it results in damage to or the collapse of his neighbour's building. The effect of this proposition is mitigated (1) by the existence of easements of support and (2) the imposition of a measured duty to take care to prevent foreseeable harm to one's neighbours.

First, a neighbour may acquire an easement of support with the result that withdrawal of support will be a nuisance. A right of support may be acquired by an express grant[98] or a grant implied[99] by an instrument. Such a right may also be acquired by prescription. In the case of *Dalton v. Angus*[1] the House of Lords held that the enjoyment of support for 20 years will be sufficient for the acquisition of a right of support by prescription (assuming that the other requirements for the acquisition of a right by prescription are fulfilled).[2] A landowner may acquire not only a right to have a building on his land supported by adjacent or subjacent land,[3] but also a right to have a building supported by an adjoining building.[4] Analogous rights may also be created by statute.[5]

---

[92] *West Leigh Colliery Co. v. Tunnicliffe* [1908] A.C. 27; *Midland Bank plc v. Bardgrove Property Services Ltd* (1992) 65 P & CR 153. See *Hooper v. Rogers* [1975] 1 Ch. 43 (which was not cited in *Midland Bank plc v. Bardgrove Property Services Ltd*). It seems that the cost of remedial works can be awarded as damages in lieu of an injunction.

[93] *Dyson v. Forster* [1909] A.C. 98; *Westhoughton UC v. Wigan Coal and Iron Co.* [1919] 1 Ch. 159; *Aynsley v. Bedlington Coal Co.* (1918) 87 L.J.K.B. 1031. See also *Snowdon v. Ecclesiastical Commissioners* [1935] 1 Ch. 181.

[94] See, *e.g.* Coal Industry Act 1975, s.2 and Sched. 1 and now Coal Industry Act 1994, s.38 and ss.44 *et seq.*

[95] *ibid.*

[96] See para. 2–114.

[97] *Wyatt v. Harrison* (1832) 3 B. & Ad. 871; *Dalton v. Angus* (1881) App.Cas. 740 at 792. See also *Ray v. Fairway Motors (Barnstable) Ltd* (1968) 20 P. & C.R. 261. *cf. Brown v. Robins* (1859) 4 H. & N. 186.

[98] Compare, *Gale on Easements* (16th ed), Pt. II.

[99] *ibid.*

[1] (1881) 6 App.Cas. 321.

[2] See generally *Gale on Easements* (16th ed.), p. 169 *et seq.* and p. 362 *et seq.*

[3] *Dalton v. Angus* (1881) 6 App.Cas. 321.

[4] *ibid.*; *Lemaitre v. Davis* (1881) 19 Ch.D. 281; *Waddington v. Naylor* (1889) 60 L.T. 480; *Selby v. Whitbread & Co.* [1917] 1 K.B. 736 at 751. See also *Tone v. Preston* (1883) 24 Ch.D. 739; *Lloyds Bank Ltd v. Dalton* [1942] Ch. 466. Compare *Colebeck v. Girdlers' Co.* (1876) 1 QBD 234 at 243.

[5] See London Building Acts (Amendment) Act 1939. *Gale on Easements* (16th ed.), Chap. 11 and now Party Walls Act 1996.

Where a right of support is acquired it will clearly relate to the dominant building as it then stands. However, the right of support will not be affected if over time the dominant building leans on the servient building to a greater extent due to settlement or decay[6]

In the case of *Bond v. Nottingham Corporation*[7] Sir Wilfred Greene M.R. said that:

> "The owner of the servient tenement is under no obligation to repair that part of his building which provides support for his neighbour. He can let it fall into decay. If it does so, and support is removed, the owner of the dominant has no cause for complaint . . . .. But what the owner of the servient tenement is not entitled to do is, by an act of his own, to remove the support without providing an equivalent."

It should be noted that an easement of support does not in itself result in the imposition of a duty of positive repair; the duty is simply a duty not actively to withdraw support.[8] A right of support does not in itself give the dominant owner a right to freedom from vibration.[9] On the other hand, although it was previously considered that a right of support did not provide a right to shelter,[10] the right appears to extend to protection of damage from wind suction.[10a]

Secondly, a measured duty of care not to withdraw support (or to take steps to mitigate such withdrawal) may be imposed in some circumstances. In the case of *Bradburn v. Lindsay*[11] it was held that a defendant was liable for damage caused by the penetration of rot from the defendant's property to the plaintiff's. The case of *Leakey v. National Trust*[12] was applied in these circumstances and the defendant was held liable because she should have appreciated the danger to the adjoining property and could reasonably have taken steps to prevent the damage. Similarly in the case of *Bar Gur v. Burton*[13] the Court of Appeal proceeded on the basis that *Leakey v. National Trust* was applicable to and might impose positive duties upon parties whose buildings adjoined one another and this approach was applied in *Rees v. Skerrett*.[14] A withdrawal of support from the dominant tenement resulting from an unreasonable neglect of the servient property would in the same way appear to amount to an actionable nuisance.

---

[6] *Byard v. Co-operative Permanent Building Society Ltd* (1970) 21 P. & C.R. 808.
[7] [1940] 429 at 438–439.
[8] *Sack v. Jones* [1925] Ch. 235; *Bond v. Nottingham Corp.* [1940] Ch. 429 at 438; *Macpherson v. London Passenger Transport Board* (1946) 175 L.T. 279.
[9] *Byard v. Co-operative Permanent Building Society Ltd* (1970) 21 P. & C.R. 808.
[10] *Phipps v. Pears* [1965] 1 Q.B. 76.
[10a] *Rees v. Skerrett* [2001] E.W.C.A. Civ. 760.
[11] [1983] 2 All E.R. 408.
[12] [1980] Q.B. 485. See above, para. 2–020. Also *Marchant v. Capital & Counties PLC* (1984) 267 E.G. 843 (a case concerning an award under the London Building Acts (Amendment) Act 1939).
[13] Transcript, July 28, 1993; considered in *Holbeck Hall Hotel Ltd v. Scarborough Borough Council* [2000] Q.B. 836, CA.
[14] [2001] E.W.C.A. Civ. 760.

(4) Interference with rights of support for buildings

2–116   If support is withdrawn, the dominant owner is entitled to take steps to ensure that support continues by effecting repairs to the servient land or building[15] or is entitled to bring an action for damages and an injunction.[16]

Rights to light

(1) Extent of rights to light

2–117   There are no natural rights to light. Rights to light must be acquired as easements. Acquisition may take place either by grant or by prescription.[17] A prescriptive right to light can only be acquired in respect of a building: a right to light cannot be acquired in respect of a vacant plot of land.[18] Further, if a right to light is acquired by prescription in respect of a building, it can only be acquired in respect of an aperture primarily intended to admit light: thus a right to light cannot be acquired in respect of a doorway.[19]

Once acquired by prescription, a right to light entitles the dominant owner to sufficient light for the ordinary purposes of the building. The amount of light to which there is a right depends upon the purposes to which the building is put. Thus in *Allen v. Greenwood*[20] Buckley L.J. stated:

> "the amount of light to which the dominant owner is entitled under a prescriptive claim is sufficient light, according to ordinary notions, for the comfortable or beneficial use of the building in question, again according to ordinary notions, for such purposes as would constitute normal uses of a building of its particular character. If the building be a dwelling-house, the measure must be related to reasonable standards of comfort as a dwelling-house. If it be a warehouse, a shop or a factory, the measure must be related to reasonable standards of comfort or beneficial use (for comfort may not be the most appropriate test in the case of such a building) as a warehouse, a shop or a factory as the case may be. These may very probably differ from the standards which would apply to a dwelling-house. If the building be a greenhouse, the measure must, in my opinion, be related to its reasonably satisfactory use as a greenhouse."

---

[15] *Bond v. Nottingham Corp.* [1940] Ch. 429 at 438–439.
[16] See generally *Redland Bricks Ltd v. Morris* [1970] A.C. 652.
[17] *Colls v. Home and Colonial Stores Ltd* [1904] A.C. 229. See generally, *Gale on Easements* (16th ed), for the law relating to prescription and easements of light generally.
[18] *Roberts v. Macord* (1832) 1 Mood. & R. 230; see also *Harris v. de Pinna* (1886) 33 Ch.D. 238; Prescription Act 1832, s. 3 ("dwelling-house, workshop, or other building").
[19] *Levet v. Gas Light & Coke Co.* [1919] 1 Ch. 24.
[20] [1980] Ch. 119 at 134–135. See also the leading case of *Colls v. Home and Colonial Stores Ltd* [1904] A.C. 179. Also *Higgins v. Betts* [1905] 2 Ch. 210; *Kine v. Jolly* [1905] 1 Ch. 480; [1907] A.C. 1; *Frogmore Developments Ltd v. Shirayama Shokusan Co Ltd* [2000] 1 E.G.L.R. 121.

In considering the extent of the right to light acquired, the Court will consider not only the present uses of the dominant tenement but any purpose to which it may be reasonably expected that in the future it will be applicable.[21] Thus if a right to light to a room in a residential building is interrupted so that the light received is no longer sufficient for the purposes of an ordinary room, there will be an actionable interference even if the room is currently used only as a scullery.[22]

It also seems that the fact that the dominant building is particularly badly lit and that the dominant owner was able to increase the size of his windows will not affect the extent of an easement acquired by prescription: the dominant owner will be entitled to sufficient light for the ordinary purposes of his building.[23]

Further, a right may be acquired which entitles the dominant owner to unusually good light.[24] However, if a right to such unusually good light is to be acquired by prescription, the dominant owner may have to show that he has enjoyed the unusually good light for the whole of the prescription period.[25] He will also have to show that his enjoyment of the unusually good amount of light was known to the servient owner.[26]

A right to light is not lost by the rebuilding or structural alteration of the dominant building: however, an alteration in the dominant building cannot increase the burden upon the servient land and the right of the dominant owner to light will be determined by reference to his entitlement as if the dominant building had been left unaltered[27] (unless, of course, a prescriptive right is claimed in respect of the dominant building in its altered state). Where a right to light is acquired by prescription, the dominant owner acquires the right for the building as a whole, not for particular portions of it, so his right to sufficient light is not affected by internal rearrangement of the dominant building nor does he have to prove the structural identity of the old windows has been preserved.[28]

(a) Interference with rights of light

An interference with light reaching a building may constitute a nuisance to the extent that it interferes with the dominant owner's rights. Once it is established that the dominant owner has a right to light the question is

2–118

---

[21] *Moore v. Hall* (1878) 3 QBD 178 at 183, *per* Cockburn C.J.; *Colls v. Home and Colonial Stores Ltd* [1904] A.C. 179 at 202–203, *per* Lord Davey, 211, *per* Lord Lindley; *Price v. Hilditch* [1930] 1 Ch. 500; *Carr-Saunders v. Dick McNeil Associates Ltd* [1986] 1 W.L.R. 922.

[22] *Price v. Hilditch* [1930] 1 Ch. 500.

[23] *Dent v. Auction Mart. Co.* (1866) L.R. 2 Eq. 238 at 251; see also *O'Connor v. Walsh* (1908) 42 J.L.R.T. 20; *McGrath v. Munster and Leinster Bank* [1959] I.R. 284. But see *Litchfield-Speer v. Queen's Gate Syndicate Ltd (No. 2)* [1919] 1 Ch. 407.

[24] *Allen v. Greenwood* [1980] Ch. 119.

[25] *Lanfranchi v. Mackenzie* (1867) L.R. 4 Eq. 421 at 430; see *Allen v. Greenwood* [1980] Ch. 119 at 132, 137–138.

[26] *ibid.*

[27] *Ankerson v. Connelly* [1907] 1 Ch. 678; *News of the World Ltd v. Allen Fairhead & Sons Ltd* [1931] 2 Ch. 402; *Smith v. Evangelization Society (Incorporated) Trust* [1933] 1 Ch. 515.

[28] *Carr-Saunders v. Dick McNeil Associates Ltd* [1986] 1 W.L.R. 922.

whether an interference with that right is so substantial as to amount to a nuisance.[29]

In determining whether or not the interference is a nuisance it is immaterial to consider how the dominant owner chooses to use the dominant tenement or how he chooses to arrange the internal structure of that tenement: the actual user will neither increase nor diminish the right.[30] In determining whether an interference is actionable, the right of light is not measured by the particular use to which the dominant tenement has been put in the past; the dominant owner is entitled to such access to light as will leave the property adequately lit for all ordinary purposes for which it may reasonably be expected to be used.[31]

Even though the Court is entitled to have regard to the locality in determining whether an interference is actionable,[32] it appears that no variation in the nature of the locality of the dominant tenement will justify a reduction in the level of light below a minimum standard:

"The human eye requires as much light for comfortable reading or sewing in Darlington Street, Wolverhampton, as in Mayfair,"[33]

2–119   Indeed, generally it appears that the nature of the locality will in practice be unlikely to affect whether or not the interference is actionable.[34] On the other hand, the Court may consider that higher standards of lighting are expected in modern times.[35]

Whether or not there has been an actionable interference will be a question of fact to be determined having regard to the extent to which the light to the dominant tenement is diminished. An interference will not be actionable if, notwithstanding that there is a change in the structure of the servient tenement the net light received by the dominant tenement is unaltered.[36] However, it is not sufficient for the servient owner who obstructs the light to the dominant tenement to offer glazed tiles to

---

[29] *Colls v. Home and Colonial Stores Ltd* [1904] A.C. 179, 204, HL.

[30] *ibid.*; *Carr-Saunders v. Dick McNeil Associates Ltd* [1986] 1 W.L.R. 922, 928; see too *Frogmore Developments Ltd v. Shirayama Shokusan Co Ltd* [2000] 1 E.G.L.R. 121.

[31] *Moore v. Hall* (1878) 3 QBD 178, 183; *Colls v. Home and Colonial Stores Ltd* [1904] A.C. 179, 204, HL; *Price v. Hilditch* [1930] 1 Ch. 500; *Carr-Saunders v. Dick McNeil Associates Ltd* [1986] 1 W.L.R. 922, 928.

[32] *Ough v. King* [1967] 1 W.L.R. 1547. Note also that by the custom of London a man might rebuild his house, or other edifice, upon the ancient foundation to what height he pleased, though thereby the ancient windows or lights of the adjoining house were stopped if there were no agreement to the contrary: Com. Dig. London, N. (5); *Wynstanley v. Lee* (1818) 2 Swan. 333 at 339; *Perry v. Eames* [1891] 1 Ch. 658, 667 *per* Chitty J; *Bowring Services Ltd v. Scottish Widows Fund & Life Assurance Society* [1995] 1 E.G.L.R. 158; *Gale on Easements* (16th ed), p. 311. This custom still applies where prescription at common law is relied upon but has no application where a case is made under Prescription Act 1832, s. 3 ("any local custom or usage notwithstanding").

[33] *Horton's Estate Ltd v. James Beattie Ltd* [1927] 1 Ch. 75 at 78, *per* Russell J.

[34] See *Colls v. Home and Colonial Stores Ltd* [1904] A.C. 179, 183–185 *per* Lord Halsbury, 210 *per* Lord Lindley; *Kine v. Jolly* [1905] 1 Ch. 480, 497 per Romer LJ; *Fishenden v. Higgs & Hill Ltd* (1935) 153 LT 128, 140 *per* Romer LJ and 142–143 *per* Maugham LJ.

[35] *Ough v. King* [1967] 1 W.L.R. 1547.

[36] *Davis v. Marrable* [1913] 2 Ch. 421.

mitigate the injury: there could be no positive covenant binding upon the servient owner's successors to maintain or clean such tiles.[37]

In determining whether or not light to a window has been diminished to such an extent that it is actionable, there is no rule, contrary to what appears from some early cases,[38] that if a person has 45 degrees of unobstructed light through a particular window left to him he cannot maintain an action for nuisance.[39] Conversely, a person may have no action in nuisance even if he is left with much less than forty-five degrees of light.[40]

> "But experience shows that it is, generally speaking, a fair working rule to consider that no substantial injury is done to him where an angle of forty-five degrees is left to him, especially if there is good light from other directions as well."[41]

The court will pay regard to light coming from sources other than that which has been obstructed in assessing whether an interference is substantial enough so as to leave the dominant tenement inadequately lit for ordinary purposes and to be actionable[42]: but such other sources of light will only be taken into account to the extent that the dominant owner has a right to them by grant or by prescription.[43]

Expert evidence is usually adduced to determine the extent to which light has been or will be diminished. It is common for experts in determining the extent to which a new building will interfere with light to assess the amount of direct sky which will reach a hypothetical table two feet nine inches high in a particular room and to regard the room adequately lit if 50 per cent or more of its area receives not less than one lumen of light at table level.[44] However, whether or not in any given case the interference will amount to a nuisance is a question for the Court. The question in each case is:

> "whether, as a matter of common sense, there is such a deprivation of light as to render the occupation of the house uncomfortable in accordance with the ordinary ideas of mankind".[45]

---

[37] *Dent v. Auction Mart. Co.* (1866) L.R. 2 Eq. 238 at 251–252. See also *Black v. Scottish Temperance Assurance* [1908] I.R. 541.

[38] See *Hackett v. Baiss* (1875) L.R. 20 Eq. 494.

[39] *Colls v. Home and Colonial Stores Ltd* [1904] A.C. 179 at 210.

[40] *Charles Semon & Co. v. Bradford Corp.* [1922] 2 Ch. 737.

[41] *Colls v. Home and Colonial Stores Ltd* [1904] A.C. 179 at 210, *per* Lord Lindley. Compare also *City of London Brewery Co. v. Tennant* (1873) 9 Ch.App. 220.

[42] *Smith v. Evangelization Society (Incorporated) Trust* [1933] Ch. 515.

[43] See *Colls v. Home and Colonial Stores Ltd* [1904] A.C. 179 at 211; also *Kine v. Jolly* [1905] 1 Ch. 480 at 493, 497; [1907] A.C. 7.

[44] Compare *Carr-Saunders v. Dick McNeil Associates Ltd* [1986] 1 W.L.R. 922, 927 B and *Deakins v. Hookings* [1994] 1 E.G.L.R. 190 (where the "50–50" rule was discussed).

[45] *Sheffield Masonic Hall Co. v. Sheffield Corporation* [1932] 2 Ch. 24; see too *Colls v. Home and Colonial Stores Ltd* [1904] A.C. 179; *Ough v. King* [1967] 1 W.L.R. 1547; esp. at 1552; *Gamble v. Doyle* (1971) 219 *Estates Gazette* 310; *Voyce v. Voyce* (1991) 62 P & CR 290.

An interference with a right of light may entitle the dominant owner to damages and to injunctive relief. Once a substantial interference is proven the dominant owner will usually be entitled to an injunction.[46] However, the grant of an injunction is a discretionary remedy: it will not be granted if the dominant owner by his conduct indicates that damages are acceptable to him and thus encourages the servient owner to continue with his interference or delays in seeking relief.[47] Further, injunctive relief is unlikely to be granted if the injury to the dominant owner's legal rights is small, capable of being estimated in money terms and being adequately so compensated, and in the circumstances it would be oppressive to grant the dominant owner an injunction restraining the interference with his light.[48] Damages will usually be the diminution in value of the dominant tenement caused by the interference with the owner's rights (and these may even include damages for the whole tenement of which the dominant tenement forms part).[49] Damages may in some circumstances be awarded for a threatened injury.[50]

[46] *Parker v. First Avenue Hotel Co.* (1883) 24 Ch.D. 282; *Litchfield-S peer v. Queen Anne's Gate Syndicate* [1919] 1 Ch. 407.
[47] *Blue Town Investments Ltd v. Higgs & Hill plc* [1990] 2 All E.R. 897.
[48] *Shelfer v. City of London Electric Lighting Co.* [1895] 1 Ch. 287; *Price v. Hilditch* [1930] 1 Ch. 500; *Fishenden v. Higgs & Hill Ltd* (1935) 153 L.T. 128; *Sampson v. Hodgson-Pressinger* [1981] 3 All E.R. 710.
[49] *Griffiths v. Richard Clay & Sons* [1912] 2 Ch. 291; *Wills v. May* [1923] 1 Ch. 317.
[50] See above, para. 4–100 (damages in lieu of an injunction). *Leeds Industrial Co-operative Society v. Slack* [1924] A.C. 851.

Chapter Three

Interference with land in breach of covenant or contract

We gabble o'er the oaths we mean to break
["Fears in Solitude", S.T. Coleridge]

Introduction

An interference with land may be wrongful in private law because the **3–001** person interfering with the land is prohibited from doing so by reason of his relationship with another party which has its origins in the law of contract and which restricts his ability to interfere with the land. For instance, if A grants to B a tenancy of land it will be an implied term of the tenancy that A will not interfere with the land so as to interrupt B's quiet enjoyment or to derogate from the grant; conversely there will be an implied obligation upon B to yield up possession at the end of the term granted (thus protecting A's right to enjoy the land at the determination of the term of the tenancy). Similarly if A grants to B a licence to use land the terms of the bargain between A and B may preclude interferences with their respective rights of enjoyment of the land, breach of which may result in an action for damages or injunctive relief. Further, A and B may otherwise agree that A will not interfere with B's enjoyment or use of his land, breach of which agreement may give B remedies by way of damages and injunction. This chapter will deal with these situations.

The enforceability of covenants[1]

Introduction

Generally

3–002   Parties may agree that land specified by them will be free from interference. Such agreements may be express or, in some circumstances, implied into contracts between the parties (or their predecessors in title).

> (i)   A may agree with B as a matter of contract that A will not interfere with B's use of B's land. B will have a remedy for breach of contract upon usual principles since there is privity of contract between A and B.

> (ii)   A may agree that he will not use his own land in such a way that he will interfere with B's enjoyment of B's land: privity of contract will exist between A and B, so if A uses his land in such a way that it interferes with B's enjoyment of his land then B will have a remedy against A for a breach of the contract since privity of contract exists between A and B. For instance, A may agree with B that A will not use his land so as to cause a nuisance and annoyance to B in his occupation of his land.

> (iii) In a contract such as that described in (i) and (ii), B may want to ensure that A's successors in title will also be bound not to interfere with his (B's) enjoyment of his own land. B may also want to ensure that his own successors in title enjoy the benefit of such an obligation imposed upon A and A's successors. The enforceability of such covenants will depend on the rules examined below.

There are, of course, many agreements which can be made between parties which affect the use and enjoyment of land which do not restrict the interferences which A may make with B's land (most restrictive covenants affect the way in which the covenantor may use his own land rather than deal with interferences the covenantor may cause to the covenantee's land). A detailed excursus of the law relating to the enforceability of such covenants is outside the scope of this book. However, before considering the sorts of covenant and contract which restrict interferences with land, it is appropriate to summarise the law relating to their enforceability.

---

[1]   For fuller treatments of the principles referred to in this chapter the reader is referred to *Megarry and Wade, Law of Real Property* (6th ed.) Chaps 14 to 18; *Preston and Newsom, Restrictive Covenants Affecting Freehold Land* (9th ed.); *Woodfall's Landlord and Tenant*; *Hill and Redman's Law of Landlord and Tenant*. Covenants may also be enforceable by the intervention of statute: see, *e.g.* Town and Country Planning Act 1990, s. 106; Local Government (Miscellaneous Provisions) Act 1982, s. 33.

The enforceability of covenants

Original parties: privity of contract

Where the parties are in a direct contractual relationship, *i.e.* there is priv- **3–003**
ity of contract, their mutual obligations are enforceable under the general
law of contract. Contractual liability may be enforceable at law by an
action for damages[2] or in equity by an action for specific performance or
an injunction[3]; such liability may also be enforceable by and against the
estate of a party who has died.

At common law, the obligations of the original parties to an agreement
will continue notwithstanding that the subject-matter of the agreement
has been assigned. So, at common law a lessee remains liable upon the
express covenants contained in a lease notwithstanding that there has
been an assignment of the lease by the tenant.[4] Likewise, the liability of the
original lessor on his covenants to the lessee continues notwithstanding
that the reversion to the lease has been assigned.[5]

Now, in the case of leases made (or entered into pursuant to agreements
made) prior to the coming into force of the Landlord and Tenant
(Covenants) Act 1995[5a] (and subject to statutory exceptions such as those
in the cases of perpetually renewable leases[6] and where leases are transferred upon divorce[7]), original lessees remain contractually liable on their
covenants even after assignment of the lease in the absence of a contractual provision to the contrary or the termination of the lease.[8] Although
they are entitled to be indemnified by subsequent assignees (and sureties
where existing) they retain a primary contractual liability which is not
that of surety.[9] However, notwithstanding earlier cases which indicated to
the contrary,[10] the Court of Appeal has held that the obligations of the
original lessee cannot be varied or increased by a subsequent agreement
made by the lessor with an assignee of the lease.[11]

---

[2] See below, para. 4–041.
[3] See below, paras. 4–084.
[4] See below, para. 3–004.
[5] *Stuart v. Joy and Nantes* [1904] 1 K.B. 362; *City & Metropolitan Properties v. Greycroft* [1987]
1 W.L.R. 1087.
[5a] See para. 3–005 below. The Act came into force on January 1, 1996.
[6] The Law of Property Act 1922, s. 145 and Sched. 15 para. 1.
[7] See Matrimonial Causes Act 1973.
[8] See, *e.g. Baynton v. Morgan* (1888) 22 QBD 74, CA, *Allied London Investments Ltd v. Hambro
Life Assurance* [1984] 1 E.G.L.R. 16 approved [1985] 1 E.G.L.R. 45, CA, *Johnsey Estates Ltd
v. Manley Ltd* [1987] 2 E.G.L.R. 69, CA, *City of Land Corporation v. Fell* [1994] 1 A.C. 458, HL,
and *Friends Provident Life Office v. BRB* [1996] 1 All E.R. 336, CA.
[9] *Baynton v. Morgan,* above. On the entitlement to an indemnity see *Johnsey Estates Ltd v.
Manley Ltd* and *Selous Street Fabrics v. Oronel* [1984] 1 E.G.L.R. 50; *Moule v. Garrett* (1872)
L.R. 7 Exch. 101 and *Becton Dickinson v. Zwebner* [1989] Q.B. 208.
[10] *Centrovincial Estates plc v. Bulk Storage Ltd* (1983) 46 P. & C.R. 393 and *Selous Street Fabrics
v. Oronel* [1984] 1 E.G.L.R. 50.
[11] *Friends Provident Life Office v. BRB* [1996] 1 All E.R. 336, CA.

In the case of leases to which the Landlord and Tenant (Covenants) Act 1995 applies, then the liability of original lessees is circumscribed. These provisions are summarised below.

Privity of estate

3–004   In the case of leases made (or entered into pursuant to agreements made) prior to the coming into force of the Landlord and Tenant (Covenants) Act 1995 a covenant may be enforceable by reason of privity of estate. Privity of estate between two parties means that there is a relationship of landlord and tenant between them.[12] Privity of estate may exist between persons who were not original parties to a lease and between whom there is no privity of contract. So if a landlord grants to a tenant a lease and the tenant assigns the lease to an assignee, there is no privity of contract between the landlord and the assignee but there is privity of estate because the assignee has acquired an estate in land upon which the landlord is entitled to the immediate reversion. Conversely if the landlord assigns the reversion to the lease, there will be privity of estate between the assignee of the reversion and the person entitled to the term of the lease. There will not, however, be privity of estate between a head landlord and a sub-tenant.

The burden of covenants or terms[13] contained in tenancies may bind parties between whom privity of estate exists but will only do so to the extent that the covenants and terms "touch and concern" the land.[14] A covenant which "touches and concerns" the land is one which "has reference to the subject-matter of the lease".[15]

In order to touch and concern the land a covenant must affect the landlord *qua* landlord and the tenant *qua* tenant.[16] The landlord's covenant for quiet enjoyment, express or implied[17] is clearly a covenant which touches and concerns the land. A tenant's covenant not to use the demised premises so as to cause nuisance and annoyance to adjoining occupiers is also such a covenant.[18] However, a covenant which is collateral to the relationship of landlord and tenant will not touch and concern the land[19]: thus, a covenant by the landlord or the tenant not to use premises other than the demised premises for purposes which do not benefit the demised

---

[12] See *Manchester Brewery Co. v. Coombs* [1901] 2 Ch. 608; *Purchase v. Lichfield Brewery Co.* [1915] 1 K.B. 184; *Milmo v. Carreras* [1946] K.B. 306.

[13] *i.e.* the obligation to comply with the covenant or terms.

[14] *Spencer's Case* (1583) 5 Co. Rep. 16a.

[15] See Law of Property Act 1925, ss 141 and 142. Also generally, *Hua Chiao Commercial Bank v. Chiaphua Industries Ltd* [1987] A.C. 99, PC; *P.A. Swift Developments v. Combined English Stores Group Ltd* [1989] A.C. 643; *System Floors Ltd v. Ruralpride Ltd* [1994] N.P.C. 127 and *Caerns Motor Services Ltd v. Texaco Ltd* [1995] 1 All E.R. 247.

[16] See *Spencer's Case* (1583) 5 Co. Rep. 16a.

[17] See below, para. 3–024 *et seq.*

[18] Compare *Tod-Heatly v. Benham* (1888) 40 Ch.D. 80. Also see *Hampstead and Surburban Properties Ltd v. Diomedous* [1968] 3 All E.R. 545.

[19] See *Spencer's Case* (1583) 5 Co. Rep. 16a.

premises but merely the other party to the lease because of his own particular personality will not touch and concern the land.

Thus, in *Thomas v. Hayward*[20] a covenant by a landlord not to open another beer or spirit house within half a mile of the hotel demised was a personal covenant and did not run with the land because the benefit which it secured benefitted the tenant rather than the premises which he occupied. On the other hand, a covenant by a landlord which restricts the landlord's building on premises adjoining the demised premises may touch and concern the land demised if the covenant benefits the demised premises.[21] A full analysis of those covenants which do and those which do not touch and concern the land is outside the scope of this book[22]: generally, covenants which restrict the landlord's interference with the demised premises will touch and concern the land, and covenants by the tenant not to use the demised premises themselves in such a way as to interfere with other premises will also touch and concern the land since such covenants clearly have reference to the subject matter of the lease.

Landlord and Tenant (Covenants) Act 1995

The above discussion deals with tenancies to which the provisions of the Landlord and Tenant (Covenants) Act 1995 do not apply. Under that Act,[23] where a tenancy is granted on or after the date on which the Act comes into force (otherwise than in pursuance of an agreement entered into before that date or an order of a court made before that date) new rules apply in relation to the transmission of the benefit and burden of covenants. The following is a summary of the main provisions of that Act.　　3–005

Assignments under the Landlord and Tenant (Covenants) Act 1995

An "assignment" for the purposes of the Landlord and Tenant (Covenants) Act 1995 includes (unless the context otherwise requires) an equitable assignment, an assignment in breach of covenant, and an assignment by operation of law.[24]　　3–006

Landlord and tenant covenants under the Landlord and Tenant (Covenants) Act 1995

A "tenant covenant" in relation to a tenancy means a covenant "falling to be complied with by the tenant of premises demised by the tenancy".[25] A　　3–007

---

[20] (1869) L.R. 4 Exch. 311.
[21] Compare *Ricketts v. Enfield Churchwardens* [1909] 1 Ch. 544.
[22] See generally *P.A. Swift Developments v. Combined English Stores Group Ltd* [1989] A.C. 643; *Systems Floors Ltd v. Ruralpride Ltd* [1994] N.P.C. 127.
[23] The 1995 Act came into force on January 1, 1996.
[24] Section 28(1).
[25] Section 28(1).

"landlord covenant" in relation to a tenancy means a covenant "falling to be complied with by the landlord of premises demised by the tenancy".[26]

The benefit and burden of all landlord and tenant covenants of a tenancy

> "(a) shall be annexed and incident to the whole, and to each and every part, of the premises demised by the tenancy and of the reversion in them, and
> (b) shall . . . pass on an assignment of the whole or any part of those premises or the reversion in them."[27]

Covenants expressed to be personal to the assignor are to be disregarded in determining whether any covenant bound the assignor immediately before the assignment.[28]

Assignment of the term under the Landlord and Tenant (Covenants) Act 1995

3–008   Where an assignment is made by the tenant under a tenancy, then as from the assignment the assignee

(a)   becomes bound by the tenant covenants of the tenancy except to the extent that

    (i)   immediately before the assignment they did not bind the assignor,[29] or

    (ii)   they fall to be complied with in relation to any demised premises not comprised in the assignment; and

(b)   becomes entitled to the benefit of the landlord covenants of the tenancy except to the extent that they fall to be complied with in relation to any such premises.[30]

An assignee of the term does not have any liability under any covenant relating to a time before the assignment and has no rights under a landlord covenant in relation to such time (though such rights may be assigned).[31]

If the tenant assigns the whole of the demised premises then he

(a)   is released from the tenant covenants of the tenancy; and

(b)   ceases to be entitled to the benefit of the landlord covenants of the tenancy, as from the assignment.[32]

---

[26] Section 28(1).
[27] Section 3(1).
[28] Section 3(4).
[29] Section 3(4).
[30] Section 3(2).
[31] Section 23(1).
[32] Section 5(2).

Where the assignment is of part only of the demised premises, then the tenant is released to the extent that the tenant covenants fall to be complied with in relation to the part assigned[33] and cannot enforce the landlord covenants to a similar extent.[34]

Although the rules applying to the privity of contract are abolished as indicated above, the original tenant may be liable after assignment if he has entered into an "authorised guarantee agreement".[35] The precise circumstances in which these can be required is outside the scope of this work.[36]

Guarantors of a tenant's liabilities will be released from their guarantee upon assignment.[37] Further, guarantors under authorised guarantee agreements will be released on any subsequent assignment.[38]

Assignment of reversion under there Landlord and Tenant (Covenants) Act 1995

Where the reversion of a tenancy is assigned, then as from the assignment, the assignee

3–009

(a) becomes bound by the landlord covenants except to the extent that

(i) immediately before the assignment they did not bind the assignor,[39] or

(ii) they fall to be complied with in relation to any demised premises not comprised in the assignment; and

(b) becomes entitled to the benefit of the tenant covenants of the tenancy except to the extent that they fall to be complied with in relation to any such premises.[40]

An assignee of the reversion does not have any liability under any covenant relating to a time before the assignment and has no rights under a landlord covenant in relation to such time (though such rights may be expressly assigned).[41]

A landlord is not automatically released upon assignment of the reversion. The landlord or former landlord will only be released if he complies with the procedural provisions of section 8 of the Act.[42] The landlord or former landlord must serve notice in a prescribed form (either before or within the period of four weeks beginning with the date of the

[33] Section 5(3).
[34] ibid.
[35] Section 16.
[36] See generally *Hill & Redman, op cit* and *Woodfall, op cit.*
[37] Section 24(2).
[38] Section 16(4).
[39] See section 3(4).
[40] Section 3(3).
[41] Section 23 (but see section 23(3) in relation to rights of re-entry).
[42] See section 6.

assignment) upon the tenant informing him of the assignment and requesting a release.[43] The landlord will be released from his covenants (to the extent mentioned in the notice) if

(a) within the period of four weeks beginning with the day on which the notice is served, the tenant does not serve on the landlord or former landlord a notice in writing objecting to the release; or

(b) the tenant does so serve such a notice but the county court,[44] on the application of the landlord or former landlord, makes a declaration that it is reasonable for the covenant to be so released; or

(c) the tenant serves on the landlord or former landlord, a notice in writing consenting to the release and, if he has previously served a notice objecting to it, stating that that notice is withdrawn

the Court has power to declare that it is reasonable to release the landlord from a covenant if reasonable so to do.[45] Upon release, the landlord ceases to be entitled to the benefit of the covenants contained in the tenancy (see section 6).

Enforcement of covenants in leases by and against persons other than landlord and tenant under the Landlord and Tenant (Covenants) Act 1995

3–010   Where any tenant covenant of a tenancy, or any right of re-entry contained in a tenancy, is enforceable by the reversioner in respect of any premises demised by the tenancy, it shall also be enforceable by:

(a) any person (other than the reversioner) who, as the holder of the immediate reversion in those premises, is for the time being entitled to the rents and profits under the tenancy in respect of those premises; or

(b) any mortgagee in possession of the reversion in those premises who is so entitled.[46]

Conversely, where any landlord covenant of a tenancy enforceable against the reversioner in respect of any premises demised by the tenancy, it is also enforceable against any such person.[47]

Where any landlord covenant of a tenancy is enforceable by the tenant in respect of any premises by the tenancy, it shall also be so enforceable by

---

[43] See generally section 8.
[44] Section 8(4)(c).
[45] Section 8(2).
[46] Section 15(1).
[47] Section 15(2). See generally *BHP Petroleum Great Britain Ltd v. Chesterfield Properties Ltd* [2001] EWCA Civ. 1797.

any mortgagee in possession of those premises under a mortgage granted by the tenant. Conversely, where any tenant covenant of a tenancy, or any right of re-entry contained in a tenancy, is enforceable, it shall also be so enforceable against any such mortgagee.[48]

Further, any landlord or tenant covenant which is restrictive of user of land shall, as well as being capable of enforcement against an assignee, be capable of being enforced against any other person who is the owner or occupier of any demised premises to which the covenant relates, even though there is no express provision in the tenancy to that effect.[49]

No privity of contract and no landlord and tenant relationship

In the absence of privity of contract and in the absence of the relationship of landlord and tenant or other relationship (to which either the principles of privity of estate or the Landlord and Tenant (Covenants) Act 1995 apply) in general, the benefit of a covenant or contract may be assigned but the burden may not.   **3–011**

There are some circumstances where a covenant restricting the use of land may still bind the owner of that land and may be enforceable not only by the covenantee but also by his successors. In order to see whether a particular covenant is enforceable in the absence of privity of contract or privity of estate one must consider in whom the benefit and in whom the burden of the covenant vests. Historically, the rules relating to the passing of the benefit and the burden of covenants are different depending on whether one is considering the position in law or in equity.

(1) The benefit of a covenant at law

The original covenantee may always enforce an express covenant against the original covenantor unless he himself has assigned the benefit of that covenant to another.[50] The party originally with the benefit of a covenant will be a party to a deed creating the covenant unless the covenant is a deed poll purporting to be for the benefit of the covenantee.[51]   **3–012**

Apart from the particular case of assignees of the original covenantee (which is dealt with below[52]) there are two particular circumstances in which persons who are not parties to a covenant may enforce a covenant.

First, a party may be able to take the benefit of the covenant by reason of the provisions of section 56 of the Law of Property Act 1925. Under section 56 of the Law of Property Act 1925 a person may take an interest in

---

[48] Section 15(3), (4).
[49] Section 3(5).
[50] See *Arlesford Trading Co. Ltd v. Servansingh* [1971] 1 W.L.R. 1080 (benefit of tenant's covenant only enforceable by assignee of reversion after assignment); see *Megarry and Wade, op. cit.* para. 16–04. See in relation to tenancies the Landlord and Tenant (Covenants) Act 1995.
[51] Compare *Chelsea & Waltham Green Building Society v. Armstrong* [1951] Ch. 853.
[52] See p. 250 and compare para. 3–019.

"land or other property" or the benefit of any condition, covenant or agreement respecting land or other property, "although he may not be named as a party to the conveyance or other instrument".[53]

Secondly, under the Contracts (Rights of Third Parties) Act 1999,[54] it is provided that a person not a party to a contract ('the third party') may enforce a term in the contract if (a) the contract expressly so provides, or (b) the term purports to confer a benefit on him[55] (unless on the proper construction of the contract it appears that the parties did not intend the term to be enforceable by the third party[56]). The benefit of the term may be conferred upon the third party expressly or by the third party being referred to as a member of a class or as answering a particular description (but need not be in existence when the contract is entered into).[57] The right of the third party to enforce the term is subject to and must be in accordance with the terms of the contract.[58] For the purpose of exercising his right to enforce a term of the contract, there shall be available to the third party any remedy that would have been available to him in an action for breach of contract if he had been a party to the contract (and the rules relating to damages, injunctions, specific performance and other relief apply accordingly).[59]

At common law, assignees of the original parties to a covenant may have the benefit of the covenant. The benefit of the covenant can run with the land at common law for the benefit of assignees of the original covenantor if two conditions are satisfied. First, if a covenant is to benefit an assignee of the land of the original covenantee, then the covenant must have been intended to be for the benefit of the land owned by the covenantee and not simply be for his personal convenience[60]: the covenant must touch and concern the land. Secondly, the person seeking to enforce the covenant must have a legal estate in the land benefitted (though by reason of the provisions of section 78 of the Law of Property Act 1925 the person seeking to enforce the covenant need not have the same legal estate as the covenantee but may enforce the covenant if he is a tenant or other successor in title of the covenantee.[61])

---

[53] See *Beswick v. Beswick* [1968] A.C. 58. Also *Re Foster* [1938] 3 All E.R. 357; *White v. Bijou Mansions Ltd* [1937] Ch. 610; *Lyus v. Prowsa Developments Ltd* [1982] 1 W.L.R. 1044.

[54] Royal assent was received on November 11, 1999 and the Act came into force on that date but does not apply, unless the contract expressly provides, to a contract entered into before the expiration of six months: section 10(2).

[55] Section 1(1).

[56] Section 1(2).

[57] Section 1(3).

[58] Section 1(4).

[59] Section 1(5).

[60] Co. Litt. 385a; *Rogers v. Hosegood* [1900] 2 Ch. 388; *Formby v. Barker* [1903] 2 Ch. 539 at 554; *Dyson v. Foster* [1909] A.C. 98; *Smith v. River Douglas Catchment Board* [1949] 2 K.B. 500 at 506.

[61] *Smith v. River Douglas Catchment Board* [1949] 2 K.B. 500. *cf.* (1956) Conv. (N.S.) 43 at 53 (D.W. Elliott). L.P.A. 1925, s. 78 provides that "a covenant relating to any land of the covenantee shall be deemed to be made with the covenantee and his successors in title and the persons deriving title under him or them, and shall have effect as if such successors and other persons were expressed." See below para. 3–019: the rules for the passing of the benefit of covenants in law and in equity are for most practical purposes co-extensive (but see *Megarry and Wade, Law of Real Property* (6th ed.) para. 16–014 *et seq.*).

(2) The burden of a covenant at law

At law the burden of a covenant will not pass upon an assignment of freehold land.[62] In practice, however, there are circumstances where in effect the burden of a covenant may pass even without the intervention of the equitable principles relating to the passing of the burden of restrictive covenants.[63] For instance, a chain of covenants may be created: thus, if V sells Blackacre to P and P covenants not to interfere with V's retained land Whiteacre, then P assigns Blackacre to A, P may take a covenant from A upon the assignment that A will indemnify P against any breaches of the covenant not to interfere with Whiteacre. P will remain liable to V in the event of an interference with Whiteacre by A because of privity of contract between V and P; P, however, may be able to enforce the indemnity covenant against A. An action by V against P may indirectly have the effect of enforcing the covenant not to interfere against A by reason of the chain of indemnity. Again, if upon a conveyance of Blackacre by P to A, A takes the benefit of covenants given by V to P, those covenants given by P to V may be enforceable against A under the doctrine that "a man cannot take the benefit under a deed without subscribing to the obligations thereunder"[64] or that a man to whom an estate is granted subject to conditions can take the estate only if bound by the conditions even if he was not party to the grant. However, a covenant or condition will only be enforceable in this way against a successor to the original covenantor when such a covenant or condition is "relevant" to the exercise of the beneficial rights enjoyed by such a successor: thus, the burden of a covenant to contribute to the repair of roads and sewers may be enforced against the successor to the original covenantor where that successor enjoys the benefit of the right to use such roads or sewers.[65]

3–013

(3) The burden of a covenant in equity

The position at law that the burden of a covenant cannot run with the land of the covenantor has been mitigated by the principles relating to restrictive covenants in equity.[66] Upon these principles, the burden of a covenant will run with the land where four conditions are fulfilled.

3–014

---

[62] *Rhone v. Stephens* [1994] 2 A.C. 310; [1994] 2 All E.R. 65, HL.

[63] See *Megarry & Wade, Law of Real Property* (6th ed.), para. 16–017 *et seq.*

[64] See *Halsall v. Brizell* [1957] Ch. 169 at 182, *per* Upjohn J.; *Tito v. Waddell (No. 2)* [1977] Ch. 106 at 290, *per* Megarry V-C. See also *E.R. Ives Investments Ltd v. High* [1967] 2 Q.B. 379; *Hopgood v. Brown* [1955] 1 W.L.R. 213.

[65] See *Rhone v. Stephens* [1994] 2 A.C. 310, 322; [1994] 2 All E.R. 65, 73 HL.

[66] See *Tulk v. Moxhay* (1848) 2 Ph. 774. Compare *L. & S.W. Ry v. Gomm* (1882) 20 Ch.D. 562 at 583, *per* Jessel M.R.: "This is an equitable doctrine establishing an exception to the rules of common law which did not treat such a covenant as running with the land, and it does not matter whether it proceeds on analogy to a covenant running with the land or on analogy to an easement"; and see *Whitgift Homes Ltd v. Stocks* [2001] EWCA Civ 1732 at para. 12.

First, the covenant must be restrictive or negative in its nature;[67] the Courts will look at the substance of the covenant in deciding whether it is in its nature negative.[68]

Secondly, the covenant must relate to two plots of land so that not only is one plot of land burdened but another plot of land is benefitted.[69] The equitable doctrine of the enforceability of restrictive covenants relates to covenants which are taken to preserve the value of the benefitted land.[70]

Thirdly, the burden of the covenant must have been intended to run with the covenantor's land.[71] If the covenant is worded in such a way that it is clear that it was intended only to be enforceable against the covenantor alone, it will not bind his successors in title.

Fourthly, a purchaser of the land must have notice of the covenant if it is to be enforceable against him. Restrictive covenants are not enforceable against bona fide purchasers of the legal estate which is the subject of the covenants who have no notice of the covenants (or persons claiming through such purchasers).[72] Thus, a restrictive covenant is enforceable against a squatter in possession of the land bound by the covenant because he is not a purchaser.[73] Notice will now be deemed to be given if registration has been made under the Land Charges Act 1972.[74] However, the provisions of this Act do not affect covenants made before 1926 nor do they affect the enforceability of covenants between landlord and tenant where there is privity of estate. In the case of registered land, restrictive covenants are protected by entering notice on the register (however old they may be).[75]

---

[67] *Tulk v. Moxhay* (1848) 2 Ph. 774. It seems that this condition exists because of the wariness of the courts of Equity to impose orders requiring positive acts demanding constant supervision, whilst restrictive covenants can be given effect, "by means of the land itself": compare *Re Nisbet and Potts' Contract* [1905] 1 Ch. 391 at 397, *per* Farwell J. See too *Rhone v. Stephens* [1994] 2 A.C. 310, HL.

[68] Compare *Shepherd Homes Ltd v. Sandham (No. 2)* [1971] 1 W.L.R. 1062.

[69] See *Formby v. Barker* [1903] 2 Ch. 539; *Millbourn v. Lyons* [1914] 2 Ch. 231; *L.C.C. v. Allen* [1914] 3 K.B. 642. The land benefitted may be part of a "scheme of development": see *Preston and Newsom, Restrictive Covenants*, (9th ed.) p. 43 *et seq.* It will be noted that a number of statutes make provision that public bodies may enforce covenants as if the body owned land adjacent to the burdened land in order to overcome this particular hurdle to enforceability: see, *e.g. Governors of Peabody Donation Fund v. London Residuary Body* (1987) 55 P. & C.R. 355.

[70] *Tulk v. Moxhay* (1848) 2 Ph. 744 at 777, *per* Lord Cottenham. Compare *Wrotham Park Estate Co. Ltd v. Parkside Homes Ltd* [1974] 1 W.L.R. 798.

[71] *Re Fawcett and Holmes' Contract* (1889) 42 Ch.D. 150; *Re Royal Victoria Pavilion, Ramsgate* [1961] Ch. 581. See the Law of Property Act 1925, s.79: unless expressed otherwise a covenant will be made by a covenantor for himself, his successors in title and those deriving title under him or them.

[72] See generally *Preston and Newsom, op. cit.*, pp 75 *et seq.*

[73] *Re Nisbet and Potts' Contract* [1906] 1 Ch. 386.

[74] A restrictive covenant entered into after 1925 is a Class D (ii) land charge Land Charges Act 1972, s. 4(6).

[75] A restrictive covenant is registrable under Land Registration Act 1925, s. 5. See Land Registration Act 2002, ss 32, 34.

(4) The benefit of the covenant in equity

If a claimant is to enforce a restrictive covenant in reliance upon his equitable interest, he must show that he is entitled to the benefit of the covenant in equity.[75a]   **3–015**

First, the original covenantee can sue the original covenantor's successors in title if he retains land for which the benefit of the covenant was taken. He cannot, however, enforce the restrictive covenant against the covenantor's successors in title if he has parted with the land for which the benefit of the covenant was taken.[76]

Secondly, the successors in title to the original covenantee can enforce the covenant where they are entitled to the benefit of the covenant at law, *e.g.* where the person seeking to enforce the covenant is entitled to the legal estate in the land which the covenant benefits.[77] In equity a successor in title to the original covenantee may enforce the covenant if he has some lesser estate such as a leasehold interest[78] or is only an owner in equity.[79] A successor in title to the covenantee may also be entitled to the benefit of the covenant by reason of the provisions of section 78 of the Law of Property Act 1925.[80] As at law, the benefit of the covenant must touch and concern the land of the covenantee if his successors in title are to be able to enforce the covenant[81]: the object of the rules allowing restrictive covenants to be enforceable is the preservation of the value of the land retained by the covenantee.

In addition to the covenant touching and concerning the covenantee's land, if a successor in title to the covenantee is to enforce a covenant the benefit must have passed to the person seeking to enforce it. The benefit of the covenant may pass to the original covenantee's successor in three ways[82]: by annexation, by assignment or under a scheme of development.

(a) Express Annexation

The benefit of a restrictive covenant may be annexed to the land by express agreement between the original parties[83]: where the benefit of the   **3–016**

[75a] *Whitgift Homes Ltd v. Stock* [2001] EWCA Civ. 1732 at para. 12.

[76] *Chambers v. Randall* [1923] 1 Ch. 149.

[77] See above, para. 3011, 3–012.

[78] *Taite v. Gosling* (1879) 11 Ch.D. 273. *Mander v. Falcke* [1891] 2 Ch. 554. Note, however, that a sub-lessee, whilst he may take the benefit of a lessor's covenant in the head lease cannot enforce the covenant against the assignee of the reversion under the Law of Property Act 1925, s. 142. This is because section 142 may be taken advantage of only by "the person in whom the term is vested." However, see the Landlord and Tenant (Covenants) Act 1995, s. 3(5).

[79] *Lord Northbourne v. Johnston* [1922] 2 Ch. 309; *Newton Abbot Co-operative Society Ltd v. Williamson & Treadgold Ltd* [1952] Ch. 286; *Earl of Leicester v. Wells-next-the-Sea UDC* [1973] Ch. 110; *Marten v. Flight Refuelling Ltd* [1962] Ch. 115. See also *Re Union of London and Smith's Bank Ltd's Conveyance* [1933] Ch. 611.

[80] See para. 3–012.

[81] See above para. 3–012. *Rogers v. Hosegood* [1900] 2 Ch. 388; *Re Union of London and Smith's Bank Ltd's Conveyance* [1933] Ch. 611; *Re Ballard's Conveyance* [1937] Ch. 473.

[82] See *Jamaica Mutual Life Assurance Society v. Hillsborough* [1989] 1 W.L.R. 1101.

[83] See generally *Preston and Newsom, Restrictive Covenants* (9th ed.) p. 15 *et seq.*

covenant has been so annexed a successor in title of the covenantee may enforce the covenant. In order for the benefit of a covenant to be expressly annexed to land there must be found in the conveyance creating the covenant sufficient intention of the parties that the benefit of the covenant[84] should pass and further the conveyance must sufficiently define the land to be protected.[85] In the absence of an express indication that a covenant is intended to benefit any part of the covenantee's land, it may be held that the covenant was intended to benefit only the whole and thus, can be enforced only by a successor of the whole of the covenantee's land[86]; however, even without clear words the Court may hold that the covenant was intended to benefit each part of the covenantee's land[87] and it now seems that if the benefit of a covenant is annexed to the land it will, prima facie, be annexed to any part of it in the absence of an intention to the contrary.[88]

(b) Implied Annexation

3–017   Although the Courts have traditionally been reluctant to find that the parties to a conveyance intended that the benefit of a covenant was to be annexed by implication,[89] in appropriate circumstances it seems that annexation may take place where that is the necessary implication of the covenant in question.[90]

(c) Statutory Annexation

3–018   As a result of section 78 of the Law of Property Act 1925, a covenant relating to any land of the covenantee is deemed to be made with him, and his successors in title and those deriving title under them and has effect as if they were expressed: in the case of restrictive covenants "successors in title" includes owners and occupiers for the time being of the land of the covenantee intended to be benefitted. The Court of Appeal in the case of *Federated Homes Ltd v. Mill Lodge Properties Ltd*[91] has interpreted this provision as providing a statutory method of annexation in the case of

---

[84]   *e.g. Rogers v. Hosegood* [1900] 2 Ch. 388: a covenant made "with intent that the covenant may enure to the benefit of the vendors their successors and assigns and others claiming under them to all or any of their lands adjoining."

[85]   See, *e.g. Wrotham Park Estate Company v. Parkside Homes Ltd* [1974] 1 W.L.R. 798.

[86]   See *Re Union of London & Smith's Bank Ltd's Conveyance* [1933] Ch. 611 at 628; *Russell v. Archdale* [1964] Ch. 38 (on appeal [1963] E.G.D. 366); *Re Jeff's Transfer (No. 2)* [1966] 1 W.L.R. 841; *Griffiths v. Band* (1974) 29 P. & C.R. 243.

[87]   See *Drake v. Gray* [1936] Ch. 451.

[88]   *Federated Homes Ltd v. Mill Lodge Properties Ltd* [1980] 1 W.L.R. 594 at 606G, *per* Brightman L.J.

[89]   See *Reid v. Bickerstaff* [1909] 2 Ch. 305 at 320; *Re Union of London and Smith's Bank Ltd's Conveyance* [1933] Ch. 611 at 628; *Marquess of Zetland v. Driver* [1939] Ch. 1 at 8; *Newton Abbott Co-operative Society v. Williamson & Treadgold Ltd* [1952] Ch. 286 at 289.

[90]   *Shropshire County Council v. Edwards* (1982) 46 P. & C.R. 271. *J. Sainsbury plc v. Enfield LBC* [1989] 1 W.L.R. 590, 597 cf. *Jamaica Mutual Life Assurance Society v. Hillsborough Ltd* [1989] 1 W.L.R. 1101 at 1105. See discussion at *Megarry & Wade, Law of Property* (6th ed.), pp. 1027 *et seq.*

[91]   [1980] 1 W.L.R. 594. The Court of Appeal also left open the possibility that the benefit of a covenant might pass by reason of Law of Property Act 1925, s. 62.

covenants entered into after December 31, 1925,[92] where the covenant touches and concerns the covenantee's land and where there is no contrary intention.[93] Such annexation will be to any part of the covenantee's land and not simply to the whole.[94]

(d) Assignment

A successor in title to the original covenantee may enforce a restrictive covenant if he has had the benefit of the covenant assigned to him. Such an assignment must be expressly made, at least to the extent that there must be an agreement between the parties that the benefit of the covenant should pass to the assignee rather than the conveyance simply taking place without reference to the covenant.[95] In the case of covenants entered into before 1926 where the provisions of section 78 do not provide for statutory annexation this method of ensuring the passing of the benefit of a restrictive covenant is still important in the absence of express annexation.

3–019

For an assignee to enforce a covenant against the original covenantor, it is sufficient that the assignee prove that the benefit of the covenant has been properly assigned to him as a chose in action.[96] However, if the assignee seeks to enforce the covenant against the successor in title to the original covenantor he must not only prove that the benefit of the covenant has been assigned to him but that it was assigned to him together with the land benefitted by the covenant as part of the same transaction[97] since the rules by which restrictive covenants are held to be enforceable owe their existence to equity's willingness to protect the value of the land to which the covenant relates.[98] If an assignee is to enforce a covenant against the covenantor's successors in title, the covenant must have benefitted ascertainable land at the date of the covenant[99] and the assignee seeking to enforce the covenant must have vested in him land which the covenant was intended to benefit: if the assignee is an assignee of only part of the covenantee's land he must show that the covenant benefitted that part of the land which vests in him.[1] Upon any further

---

[92] See *J. Sainsbury Plc and Haringey LBC v. Enfield LBC* [1989] 1 W.L.R. 590, in which it was held that the statutory predecessor to s. 78 (Conveyancing Act 1881, s. 58) did not effect annexation. See *Renals v. Cowlishaw* (1878) 9 Ch.D. 125.
[93] *Roake v. Chadha* [1984] 1 W.L.R. 40.
[94] See *Federated Homes Ltd v. Mill Lodge Properties Ltd* [1980] 1 W.L.R. 594.
[95] *Renals v. Cowlishaw* (1878) 9 Ch.D. 125 at 129–131; affirmed (1879) 11 Ch.D. 866. See also *Re Union of London & Smith's Bank Ltd's Conveyance* [1933] Ch. 611 at 628; *Drake v. Gray* [1936] Ch. 451 at 455.
[96] Compare the Law of Property Act 1925, s. 136 for formalities.
[97] *Re Union of London & Smith's Bank's Conveyance* [1933] Ch. 611 at 632, per Romer L.J. Compare also *Chambers v. Randall* [1923] 1 Ch. 149; *Re Rutherford's Conveyance* [1938] Ch. 396.
[98] See *Tulk v. Moxhay* (1848) 2 Ph. 774.
[99] *Formby v. Barker* [1903] 2 Ch. 539; *L.C.C. v. Allen* [1914] 3 K.B. 642; *Marten v. Flight Refuelling Ltd* [1962] Ch. 115 at 131. See also *Newton Abbot Co-operative Society Ltd v. Williamson & Treadgold Ltd* [1952] Ch. 286.
[1] *Re Union of London & Smith's Bank Ltd's Conveyance* [1933] Ch. 611 at 630; *Russell v. Archdale* [1964] Ch. 38 (on appeal [1963] E.G.D. 366). See also *Stillwell v. Blackman* [1968] Ch. 508.

assignments of the land, the further assignees will have to show a complete chain of assignments if they are to enforce the covenant.[2] However, it should be noted that in some circumstances it is not necessary for the covenantee or his express assigns to execute an assignment for it to be valid: it is sufficient if it be made by anyone in whom both the land and the benefits of the covenant are vested; for instance, if upon the death of the covenantee, the land is devised to a person (without an express assignment of the benefit of the covenant) and that person is also beneficially entitled to the enforcement of the covenant (such a covenant being a separate asset of the deceased) that person may assign the benefit of the covenant.[3]

(e) Schemes of development

3–020 Under schemes of development the benefit of a covenant may pass to successors in title to the original covenantee. The principles by which the benefit is held to run do not historically derive from the same principles as those by which the benefit of restrictive covenants strictly so called are held to run, but upon a wider principle that the benefit runs in equity according to the common intention and interest of the original parties.[4] In the case of a scheme of development, the restrictions are enforceable by and against all owners of the plots within the area of the scheme irrespective of the order in which the owners acquired their plots from a common vendor (the owner of Whiteacre could not seek to enforce a restrictive covenant against the owner of Blackacre, relying upon annexation or assignment as giving him the benefit of the covenant, if the common vendor of both Whiteacre and Blackacre had already parted with Whiteacre before taking the covenant from the owner of Blackacre: when the covenant in respect of Blackacre was taken, Whiteacre was not in the ownership of the vendor and could thus not benefit from the covenant.[5])

The prerequisites for establishing that a scheme of development exists were summarised by Buckley L.J. in *Reid v. Bickerstaff*[6]:

---

2   *Re Pinewood Estate Farnborough* [1958] Ch. 280; *Federated Homes Ltd v. Mill Lodge Properties Ltd* [1980] 1 W.L.R. 594 at 603 (first instance). But note that the older authorities suggest that the express assignment of the benefit of a covenant may have the effect of annexing the benefit of the covenant to the land so that it will thereafter pass without the need for express assignment: see *Renals v. Cowlishaw* (1878) 9 Ch.D. 125 at 130, 131; *Rogers v. Hosegood* [1900] 2 Ch. 388 at 408; *Reid v. Bickerstaff* [1909] 2 Ch. 305 at 320, 326, 328.

3   *Newton Abbot Co-operative Society Ltd v. Williamson & Treadgold Ltd* [1952] Ch. 286. See also *Lord Northbourne v. Johnston & Son* [1922] 2 Ch. 309; *Leicester v. Wells* [1952] Ch. 286.

4   See *Re Dolphin's Conveyance* [1970] Ch. 654. Also *Whatman v. Gibson* (1838) 9 Sim. 196; *Spicer v. Martin* (1888) 14 App.Cas. 12; *Reid v. Bickerstaff* [1909] 2 Ch. 305, esp. at 319; *Brunner v. Greenslade* [1971] Ch. 993, esp. at 1004.

5   However, it does not seem to have been considered that special rules relating to schemes of development may not now strictly be necessary because of the provisions of the Law of Property Act 1925, s. 56 (replacing the Real Property Act 1845, s. 5) by which covenants may be expressed to be made with the owners of lots previously sold.

6   [1909] 2 Ch. 305 at 323; see also 319, *per* Cozens-Hardy M.R. These passages were approved by the Privy Council in *Jamaica Mutual Life Assurance Society v. Hillsborough* [1989] 1 W.L.R. 1101.

"There can be no building scheme unless two conditions are satisfied, namely, first, that defined lands constituting the estate to which the scheme relates shall be identified, and secondly, that the nature and particulars of the scheme shall be sufficiently disclosed for the purchaser to have been informed that his restrictive covenants are imposed upon him for the benefit of other purchasers of plots within the defined estate with the reciprocal advantage that he shall as against such other purchasers be entitled to the benefit of such restrictive covenants as are in turn to be imposed upon them. Compliance with the first condition identifies the class of persons as between whom reciprocity of an obligation is to exist. Compliance with the second discloses the nature of the obligations which are to be mutually enforceable. There must be as between the several purchasers community of interest and reciprocity of obligation."

Four practical guidelines for establishing whether or not a scheme of development exists were set out by Parker J. *Elliston v. Reacher*[7]: **3–021**

"In my judgment, in order to bring the principles of *Renals v. Cowlishaw*[8] and *Spicer v. Martin*[9] into operation it must be proved (1) that both the plaintiffs and the defendants derive title under a common vendor; (2) that previously to selling the lands to which the plaintiffs and defendants are respectively entitled the vendor laid out his estate, or a defined portion thereof (including the lands purchased by the plaintiffs and defendants respectively), for sale in lots subject to restrictions intended to be imposed on all the lots, and which, though varying in details as to particular lots, are consistent and consistent only with some general scheme of development; (3) that these restrictions were intended by the common vendor to be and were for the benefit of all the lots intended to be sold, whether or not they were also intended to be and were for the benefit of other land retained by the vendor; and (4) that both the plaintiffs and the defendants, or their predecessors in title, purchased their lots from the common vendor upon the footing that the restrictions subject to which the purchases were made were to enure for the benefit of the other lots included in the general scheme whether or not they were also to enure for the benefit of the other lands retained by the vendors. If these four points be established, I think that the plaintiffs would in equity be entitled to enforce the restrictive covenants entered into by the defendants or their predecessors with the common vendors, irrespective of the date of the respective purchases . . . Further, if the first three points be established, the fourth point may readily be inferred, provided the purchasers have notice of the facts involved in the first three points;

---

[7] [1908] 2 Ch. 374 at 384.
[8] (1878) 9 Ch.D. 125.
[9] (1888) 14 App.Cas. 12.

but if the purchaser purchases in ignorance of any material part of those facts, it would be difficult, if not impossible, to establish the fourth point."[10]

If a plot within a scheme of development is later sub-divided, the covenants will be enforceable between the sub-purchasers as well as between them and the occupiers of the remainder of the scheme of development.[11]

Particular covenants

Introduction

3–022   Subject to covenants being enforceable in accordance with the principles summarised above, landowners are able to protect their land by taking covenants from others in a variety of form. This section considers a number of particular sorts of such covenant which are most commonly found and prayed in aid when there is interference with the enjoyment of land. In particular, we consider:

(1)   the covenant for quiet enjoyment which is found in leases[12];

(2)   the obligation not to derogate from grant under which it is implicit that where an interest in land is granted, the grantor may not derogate from his grant[13]; this obligation is found not only as between landlord and tenant but in other contexts where rights over land (such as easements and *profits à prendre*) have been granted;

(3)   the obligation on a tenant to deliver up possession at the end of the term of a lease and thus, to restore possession to the landlord[14];

(4)   obligations as between licensor and licensee which may protect the use of land under the terms of a licence[15]; and

(5)   particular forms of covenant found both in leases and as restrictive covenants over freehold land which restrict uses affecting the enjoyment of other land.[16]

Before considering each of these types of obligation, it is appropriate to consider the particular relationship of landlord and tenant in which the

---

[10] See also generally *White v. Bijou Mansions Ltd* [1938] Ch. 351; *Baxter v. Four Oaks Properties Ltd* [1965] Ch. 816; *Re Dolphin's Conveyance* [1970] Ch. 654; *Texaco Antilles v. Kernochan* [1973] A.C. 609; *Emile Elias and Company Ltd v. Pine Groves Ltd* (1993) 66 P. & C.R. 1. *Whitgift Homes Ltd v. Stocks* [2001] EWCA Civ 1732.
[11] See *Brunner v. Greenslade* [1971] Ch. 993.
[12] See para. 3–024.
[13] See para. 3–042.
[14] See para. 3–046.
[15] See para. 3–050.
[16] See para. 3–053.

first three of these obligations are invariably implied if they are not expressly found.

The relationship of landlord and tenant

A relationship of landlord and tenant usually has its origin in a contract, express or implied.[17] However, the contract by which the relationship of landlord and tenant is created brings into existence not only a contractual relationship between landlord and tenant, it confers on the tenant an estate in land.[18] It is in the nature of a tenancy that it entitles the tenant to exclusive possession[19] of land[20] for a term of years, either for a fixed period or for a period which can be ascertained.[21] Not only does the existence of a tenancy and the tenant's right to exclusive possession entitle the tenant to maintain an action for trespass against the landlord if he enters on the demised land without the tenant's consent or an entitlement to do so under the lease,[22] but there are also terms which, if not express, will be implied into the bargain between landlord and tenant that the landlord will not interfere with the tenant's quiet enjoyment of the demised premises[23] nor derogate from his grant.[24] Conversely, because the tenant's interest in the land demised is necessarily limited in duration, it is implicit in the agreement between landlord and tenant (if it is not expressly agreed) that at the end of the tenancy the tenant will yield up to the landlord possession of the land demised[25] (additionally, if the tenant fails to deliver up possession the landlord may have an action for trespass[26]). Although in any given tenancy agreement there will usually be other terms expressly agreed between the parties restricting the landlord's and tenant's rights, this section will concentrate on these three terms commonly found in or implied into tenancy agreements which protect the enjoyment of the land which is the subject-matter of the tenancy. The quality of occupation of the demised premises by a tenant and the value of those premises to the landlord will also commonly be determined by how the parties apportion the obligations (if any) to repair the demised premises

3–023

---

[17] Indeed, historically leaseholds were regarded merely as giving the tenant a contractual right to occupy land and no estate in land: see *Holdsworth, History of English Law*, iii, 213–217, iv 486.

[18] See the Law of Property Act 1925, s. 1(1)(b). See *Total Oil Great Britain Ltd v. Thompson Garages Biggin Hill Ltd* [1972] 1 Q.B. 318 at 324 where Lord Denning M.R. said that a lease conveyed an interest in land and did not come to an end like an ordinary contract on repudiation and acceptance. cf. *Hussein v. Mehlman* [1992] 2 E.G.L.R. 87 (Asst. Recorder S. Sedley Q.C.). See too *Chartered Trust plc v. Davies* [1997] 2 E.G.L.R. 87 cf; *Nynehead Developments Ltd v. R.H. Fireboard Containers* [1999] 1 E.G.L.R. 7.

[19] See *Taylor v. Caldwell* (1863) 3 B. & S. 826 at 832; *Street v. Mountford* [1985] A.C. 809; *A G Securities v. Vaughan* [1990] 1 A.C. 417.

[20] Compare Law of Property Act 1925, s. 205(1) (ix).

[21] See *Lace v. Chantler* [1944] K.B. 368; *Re Midland Railway Company's Agreement* [1971] Ch. 725; *Centaploy Ltd v. Matlodge Ltd* [1974] Ch. 1; *Prudential Assurance Co. Ltd v. London Residuary Body* [1992] 2 A.C. 386.

[22] See above, para. 1–011.

[23] See below, para. 3–024.

[24] See below, para. 3–042.

[25] See below, para. 3–046.

[26] See above, Chap. 1, para. 1–050.

and the extent to which alteration of the premises may be prohibited: these topics have much in common with the law relating to interferences with possession and occupation as such and the reader is referred to the standard works on the subject of the law of landlord and tenant. A discussion of the covenants which may protect the retained land of a landlord are found below ("Covenants restricting nuisance and annoyance etc").

Before dealing with each of the three terms mentioned above, it should be noted that because the contract which creates a tenancy also creates an estate in land, these implied terms will not only be enforceable by the original parties to the agreement (subject, where applicable, to the provisions of the Landlord and Tenant (Covenants) Act 1995) but will be enforceable by the assigns of the tenant in whom the term vests for the time being against the person in whom the reversion to the tenancy vests for the time being in the case of the landlord's implied covenants and vice versa in the case of the tenant's implied covenant.[27]

Landlord's covenant for quiet enjoyment

Introductory

3–024   Every tenancy contains a covenant by the landlord for quiet enjoyment. If the covenant is not express it will be implied: the word "demise" implies a covenant for quiet enjoyment[28] but the covenant will be implied in a letting whatever form the agreement takes[29]; "the basis of it is that the landlord, by letting the premises, confers on the tenant the right of possession during the term and impliedly promises not to interfere with the tenant's exercise and use of the right to possession during the term".[30] The tenant's right to quiet enjoyment will arise whether or not the tenant has actually entered the demised premises pursuant to the letting.[31] The covenant will also be implied into an agreement for a lease where it is equivalent to the grant of a lease.[32]

The meaning of "quiet enjoyment"

3–025   In the context of a covenant for quiet enjoyment, the word "enjoyment" has a technical meaning. It relates to the possession of the premises con-

---

[27] See above, para. 3–003 et seq.

[28] See Burnett v. Lynch (1826) 5 B. & C. 589 at 609; Iggulden v. May (1804) 9 Ves. 325 at 330; Mostyn v. West Mostyn Coal and Iron Co. (1876) 1 C.P.D. 145.

[29] See Markham v. Paget [1908] 1 Ch. 697. cf. Baynes & Co. v. Lloyd & Sons [1895] 2 Q.B. 610.

[30] Kenny v. Preen [1963] 1 Q.B. 499 at 511, per Pearson L.J. See also Budd-Scott v. Daniel [1902] 2 K.B. 351.

[31] Prior to 1926 a lessee did not acquire an estate until he had taken possession in accordance with the lease; until he had taken possession he had only an interesse termini: see Co. Litt. 270 a. A person with a mere interesse termini could not maintain an action for quiet enjoyment: Wallis v. Hands [1893] 2 Ch. 75. This doctrine was abolished by the Law of Property Act 1925, s. 149; see Miller v. Emcer Products Ltd [1956] Ch. 304.

[32] Compare Drury v. Macnamara (1855) 5 E. & B. 612; Walsh v. Lonsdale (1882) 21 Ch.D. 9.

cerned rather than to any pleasure of its occupants. Thus, in *Kenny v. Preen*[33] Pearson L.J. said:

> "I think the word 'enjoy' used in this connection is a translation of the Latin word 'fruor' and refers to the exercise and use of the right and having the full benefit of it, rather than to deriving pleasure from it."

Likewise "quiet" in this context does not mean free from noise. It means without interruption of the possession which is enjoyed.[34]

What may constitute an interference with possession sufficient to amount to a breach of covenant is considered more fully below.[35]

Extent of implied covenant

A covenant for quiet enjoyment will be implied in the absence of an express covenant.[36] Such a covenant gives the tenant (a) a right to be put into possession of the whole of the premises demised at the beginning of the tenancy[37] and (b) a right to enjoy the land free from interference by the landlord and persons claiming under the landlord.[38]

3–026

The implied obligation to put the tenant into possession at the start of the term is not a covenant that the landlord is entitled to grant the term which he purports to grant, but only that he is entitled to grant some term and that the lessee shall have the quiet enjoyment to which he is entitled under the covenant that the tenant may enjoy the land free from interference by the landlord (and others to whom the covenant extends).[39] The implied obligation determines with the landlord's interest[40] and does not extend to an implied general warranty of the land nor to an undertaking that the landlord has good title to the freehold and will deliver an abstract of title.[41] Accordingly the implied covenant does not give the tenant a remedy if he is ejected by title paramount.[42] It does, however, extend to those "claiming under the landlord".[43]

---

[33] [1963] 1 Q.B. 499, 511.

[34] See generally *Southwark LBC v. Mills* [1999] 4 All E.R. 449 HL, at 454 *per* Lord Hoffmann; see too *Hudson v. Cripps* [1896] Ch. 265 at 268; see too *Jenkins v. Jackson* (1888) 40 Ch. D 71.

[35] See para. 3–032.

[36] *Budd v. Scott-Daniel* [1902] 2 K.B. 351; *Kenny v. Preen* [1963] 1 Q.B. 499, CA.

[37] *Miller v. Emcer Products Ltd* [1956] Ch. 304. For the grant of leases after July 1, 1995 see Law of Property (Miscellaneous Provisions) Act 1994 which provides for implied covenants for title.

[38] See *Kenny v. Preen* [1963] 1 Q.B. 499, CA.

[39] *Miller v. Emcer Products Ltd* [1956] Ch. 304. But see now Law of Property (Miscellaneous Provisions) Act 1994 for dispositions after July 1, 1995.

[40] *Baynes & Co. v. Lloyd & Sons* [1895] 2 Q.B. 610 at 617, *cf. Fraser v. Skey* (1773) 2 Chit. 646.

[41] *Gwillim v. Stone* (1811) 3 Taunt. 433; *Temple v. Brown* (1815) 6 Taunt. 60.

[42] *Jones v. Lavington* [1903] 1 K.B. 253. However, if the tenant is evicted from the demised premises by a person with title paramount to that of the landlord the tenant will be entitled to an abatement of rent, and if he is evicted from part of the demised premises by such a person he will be obliged only to pay a rateable proportion of the rent in respect of the remainder of the demised premises: see *Smith v. Malings* (1607) Cro. Jac. 160; *McLoughlin v. Craig* (1856) 7 Ir. L.R. 117. See also *National Westminster Bank v. Hart* [1983] Q.B. 433. See also Law of Property (Miscellaneous Provisions) Act 1994 for dispositions after July 1, 1995.

[43] *Kenny v. Preen* [1963] 1 Q.B. 499, 511 CA.

Further, it seems that the obligation to put the tenant into possession of the whole of the premises at the start of the term only extends to the premises of which the tenant is to have exclusive possession, and will not extend to premises over which the tenant only has an easement.[44]

Express covenant

3–027 An express covenant for quiet enjoyment will exclude the implied covenant for quiet enjoyment including the implied covenant for title.[45] Unlike an implied covenant for quiet enjoyment, an express covenant for quiet enjoyment will usually endure for the whole term granted and not cease with the estate of the landlord.[46]

The obligations of a landlord which would otherwise be implicit in a lease by reason of the implied covenant for quiet enjoyment may be varied by the express agreement of landlord and tenant where there is an express covenant for quiet enjoyment. For instance, the landlord may expressly covenant that there will be no interference with the tenant's possession by a party with title paramount to the landlord (but such a covenant is unusual and express covenants for quiet enjoyment are usually in a qualified form).[47]

On the other hand, as well as being extended by agreement, the landlord's obligations may be circumscribed so long as the tenant remains entitled to legal possession of the premises demised: for instance, it is common for a tenant to covenant to allow the landlord access to the demised premises to carry out repairs where the tenant has failed to do so[48]; without such a covenant the landlord's entry onto the premises to carry out repairs might amount to a breach of the covenant for quiet enjoyment or a trespass; however, it is clear that there is no breach of the covenant for quiet enjoyment if the landlord enters the demised premises pursuant to the tenant's covenant to permit access: such an entry would not be such as to interfere with the tenant's right to legal possession since the tenant by his covenant has authorised the landlord's entry and the demise is subject to the landlord's rights in this respect.[49] But it is hard to see how a landlord could wholly exclude his own duty not to interfere with the tenant's quiet enjoyment of the demised premises because it is in the nature of the relationship of landlord and tenant that the landlord grants to the tenant exclusive possession of the premises demised.[50]

---

[44] *Miller v. Emcer Products Ltd* [1956] Ch. 304 at 318, *per* Romer L.J.

[45] See *Line v. Stephenson* (1838) 4 Bing. N.C. 678; 5 Bing. N.C. 183; *Miller v. Emcer Products Ltd* [1956] Ch. 304.

[46] *Evans v. Vaughan* (1825) 4 B. & C. 261.

[47] Compare *William v. Burrell* (1845) 1 C.B. 402.

[48] For example, see *Jervis v. Harris* [1996] Ch. 195, CA. See also the obligation implied into a statutory tenancy under Rent Act 1977, s. 3(2) and into a protected tenancy by Rent Act 1977, s. 148: compare *Empson v. Forde* [1990] 1 E.G.L.R. 131.

[49] See *Kent (Earl's) Case* (1588) Gouldsb. 76; *Greg v. Planque* [1936] 1 K.B. 669; *Plough Investments v. Manchester City Council* [1989] 1 E.G.L.R. 244.

[50] See *A.G. Securities v. Vaughan* [1990] 1 A.C. 417, 468H–469A, *per* Lord Oliver.

Usual form of express covenant and its extent

The extent of an express covenant for quiet enjoyment will depend upon   **3–028**
the precise words used by the parties. The usual form of express covenant
extends to "lawful interruption by the lessor his heirs and assigns or by
any other person or persons claiming by from or under him them or any
of them."

"Lawful interruptions"

Although the usual form of covenant is expressed to extend only to "law-   **3–029**
ful" interruptions by the lessor, where the interferences complained of are
by the landlord himself or those acting with the authority of the landlord[51]
the Court will not consider the word "lawful" in determining whether the
interference is within the scope of the covenant or not and will not force
the tenant to rely upon his remedies in tort.[52]

On the other hand where the interferences are by persons claiming
under the landlord, the words "lawful interruption" in the covenant are
given their full effect and the usual covenant is broken only to the extent
that the interferences by such persons are lawful: for the unlawful acts of
persons claiming under the landlord the tenant has his remedy against
them in tort.[53] It appears that even where the words "rightfully" or "lawfully" do not appear in the express covenant, interferences by persons
claiming from the landlord will only amount to breaches of the covenant
where they are "lawful" interferences.[54]

The case of *Sanderson v. Berwick-upon-Tweed Corpn*[55] illustrates the extent
of the landlord's liability upon his covenant for quiet enjoyment for interferences by those claiming under him and who "lawfully" claim under
the landlord. The tenant's farm adjoined two neighbouring farms each
held under different tenancies under a common landlord: the tenant's
farm was flooded from the neighbouring farms and the tenant suffered
damage. However, the flooding from one of the neighbouring farms was
caused by defective drains properly used, while the flooding from the
other neighbouring farm was caused by sound drains excessively used.
The landlord was held liable for the damage caused by the flooding from
the former neighbouring farm where the drains had not been used excessively: the interruption had resulted from the neighbouring tenant's

---

[51] See *Harrison, Ainslie & Co. v. Muncaster* [1891] 2 Q.B. 680 at 684.
[52] *Crosse v. Young* (1685) 2 Show 425 at 427; *Andrews v. Paradise* (1724) 8 Mod. Rep. 318; *Corus v. Anon* (1597) Cro. Eliz. 544. But the disturbance must be under a claim of right by the lessor: *Lloyd v. Tomkins* (1787) 1 Term. Rep. 671. However, an interruption by the landlord pursuant to a court order for possession will not be a breach even though the order is subsequently reversed: *Hillgate House Ltd v. Expert Clothes & Sales Ltd* [1987] 1 E.G.L.R. 65.
[53] See *Tisdale v. Essex* (1616) Hob. 34; *Hayes v. Bickerstaff* (1675) Vaugh. 118; *Dudley v. Folliott* (1790) 3 Term. Rep. 584; *Anon* (1774) Lofft 460; *Malzy v. Eicholz* [1936] 2 K.B. 308; *Matania v. National Provincial Bank Ltd* [1936] 2 All E.R. 633; *Toff v. McDowell* (1993) 25 H.L.R. 650.
[54] *Williams v. Gabriel* [1906] 1 K.B. 155.
[55] (1884) 13 Q.B.D. 547.

lawful acts; but the landlord was held not to be liable for the interruptions caused by the drains which were excessively used because such an interruption was caused by the unlawful acts of the neighbouring tenant which had not been authorised by the landlord.[56]

On the other hand, where the landlord lets property adjoining demised premises of which he is also the landlord, an interference with the demised premises by the adjoining tenant will not be "lawful" and thus, within the scope of the usual covenant for quiet enjoyment, simply because the landlord knows of the interruption: the landlord must have let the adjoining premises in such circumstances that their use would necessarily lead to the interruption[57] or the landlord must have consented to or participated in the interruption.[58] Where the tenant is interrupted by the activities of another tenant of adjacent premises holding from a common landlord, it is not necessary for the activities of that tenant to amount to a common law nuisance before they amount to a breach of covenant for quiet enjoyment by the landlord[59]; however, the ordinary use of residential premises by the adjoining tenant will not without more amount to a breach of covenant by the landlord.[60]

For these purposes it has been held that where land vests in the Crown as bona vacantia, its failure to disclaim the land will not in itself authorise or render "lawful" a nuisance occurring on that land so that it will amount to a breach of covenant for quiet enjoyment.[61]

"Claiming under" the landlord: to whose acts the covenant extends

3–030   The word "claiming" means claiming a lawful right to interrupt the tenant's occupation of the demised premises, and the words "claiming under the landlord" indicate a claim deriving from some act or disposition of the landlord.[62]

In the absence of an express limitation or extension of those within the scope of the landlord's usual covenant for quiet enjoyment, those "claiming under" the landlord will include his authorised servants,[63] a person claiming under a settlement made by the landlord under a power,[64] remainderman under a settlement made by the landlord before the lease,[65] the landlord's widow claiming under a settlement executed by the landlord before the lease,[66] a person claiming under a prior appointment

---

[56]   See too *Southwark LBC v. Mills* [2001] 1 A.C. 1 at 13–14 *per* Lord Hoffmann.
[57]   *Malzy v. Eicholz* [1916] 2 K.B. 308; *Matania v. National Provincial Bank Ltd* [1936] 2 All E.R. 633.
[58]   Compare *Celsteel Ltd v. Alton House Holdings Ltd (No 2)* [1987] 1 W.L.R. 291.
[59]   *Southwark LBC v. Mills* [2001] 1 A.C. 1 at 14–15 *per* Lord Hoffmann.
[60]   *ibid* (disapproving *Sampson v. Hodson-Pressinger* [1981] 3 All E.R. 712, CA).
[61]   *Toff v. McDowell* (1993) 25 H.L.R. 650.
[62]   *Celsteel Ltd v. Alton House Holdings Ltd (No 2)* [1987] 1 W.L.R. 291.
[63]   *Seaman v. Brownrigg* (1591) 1 Leon. 157.
[64]   *Carpenter v. Parker* (1857) 3 C.B. (N.S.) 206.
[65]   *Hurd v. Fletcher* (1778) 1 Doug. K.B. 43; *Evans v. Vaughan* (1825) 4 B. & C. 261.
[66]   *Butler v. Swinnerton* (1623) Cro. Jac. 656.

by the landlord and another,[67] and a person claiming under a prior lease where the landlord has been a party to the prior lease as trustee.[68]

On the other hand a tenant under a prior lease to which the landlord under the lease in question was not a party is not a person "claiming under" the landlord of the lease in question.[69] It has been held that where landlord A grants a tenancy to tenants and assigns the reversion to landlord B, those tenants do not "claim under" landlord B for the purposes of a lease of adjoining premises granted by landlord B and that landlord B is not liable to the tenants of the adjoining premises for interferences caused by the tenants under the tenancies originally granted by landlord A since landlord B had not granted those tenants any rights.[70] Similarly the remainderman under a settlement is not a person "claiming under" the landlord where the landlord is the life tenant.[71]

It is consistent with this construction that the acts of an assignee of the reversion will not be within the scope of the usual form of the covenant in cases where that assignee interrupts the tenant's quiet enjoyment in reliance on a title acquired independently of the reversion: for instance, where an assignee purchased from a stranger property adjoining the demised premises and built upon that property in such a way as to cause the tenant's chimney to smoke there was no breach of the covenant for quiet enjoyment.[72]

The landlord's usual covenant for quiet enjoyment will not extend to interferences by strangers since strangers are not persons "claiming by from or under" the landlord[73] even though the stranger pretends to be claiming under the landlord; but the landlord may expressly covenant that the tenant's enjoyment will not be interrupted by persons claiming or "pretending to claim" under the landlord.[74] Further, the landlord may expressly covenant that the tenant's enjoyment will not be interrupted by a named person or by persons identified by reference to a particular description or interest in property; in which case liability will be imposed upon the landlord for interruptions by the specified persons.[75] Where such an express covenant extends to interruptions by specified persons it extends both to lawful and unlawful interruptions.[76]

---

[67] *Calvert v. Seabright* (1852) 15 Beav. 156.

[68] *Markham v. Paget* [1908] 1 Ch. 697.

[69] *Re Griffiths* (1917) 61 Sol. Jo. 268. See also *David v. Sabin* [1893] 1 Ch. 523.

[70] *Celsteel Ltd v. Alton House Holdings Ltd (No 2)* [1987] 1 W.L.R. 291.

[71] *Pease v. Courtney* [1904] 2 Ch. 503.

[72] *Davis v. Town Properties Investment Corp. Ltd* [1903] 1 Ch. 797, CA. Compare *Tebb v. Cave* [1900] 1 Ch. 642. But the landlord's obligation not to derogate from his grant may prevent him from building on property acquired after the date of the lease if this frustrates the purpose of the lease: compare *Johnston & Sons v. Holland* [1988] 1 E.G.L.R. 264. See para. 3–042 *et seq.*

[73] Compare *Matania v. National Provincial Bank* [1936] 2 All E.R. 633; *King v. Liverpool City Council* [1986] 1 W.L.R. 890.

[74] *Chaplain v. Southgate* (1717) 10 Mod. Rep. 383; *Perry v. Edwards* (1721) 1 Stra. 400.

[75] *Foster v. Mapes* (1590) Cro. Eliz. 212, 213; *Nash v. Palmer* (1816) 5 M. & 5. 374 at 380; *Fowle v. Welsh* (1822) 1 B. & C. 29; *Queensway Marketing Ltd v. Associated Restaurants Ltd* (1984) 271 E.G. 1106; [1988] 2 E.G.L.R. 49, CA.

[76] *ibid.*

It is clear that an interruption by a person claiming by title paramount to that of the landlord will not be a person "claiming by from or under the landlord" within the meaning of the usual form of covenant.[77] This may leave a sub-tenant without remedy where he is evicted by the head landlord upon forfeiture of the headlease[78] (other than his right of abating the rent payable under the sub-lease[79]). A sub-tenant is thus best advised to seek from the mesne landlord either a wider form of covenant for quiet enjoyment[80] or an express covenant from the mesne landlord that he will pay the rent under and comply with the terms of the headlease. However, the usual form of covenant will provide a sub-tenant with a remedy against a mesne landlord who submits to judgment for possession against a claimant having no title to sue which has the effect of the sub-tenant being evicted.[81]

Similarly, there will be no breach of the covenant where an interruption takes place as a result of an interference by a statutory authority without the express or implied authorisation of the landlord.[82]

Provision that tenant to have quiet enjoyment while "paying the rent hereby reserved etc"

3–031 The usual form of express covenant for quiet enjoyment provides that the tenant is to have quiet enjoyment "paying the rent hereby reserved and performing the covenants". These words do not make it a condition precedent of the landlord's obligation that the tenant shall pay the rent and comply with his obligations: the landlord's obligation upon the usual form of covenant for quiet enjoyment will continue until the lease determines notwithstanding breaches of covenant or a failure to pay the rent by the tenant.[83]

Interference with possession: a question of fact

3–032 As stated above, the usual covenant for quiet enjoyment is a covenant which protects the tenant's possession of the demised premises and his enjoyment of the premises for the usual purposes of the demise. Enjoyment

---

[77] *Woodhouse v. Jenkins* (1832) 9 Bing. 431.

[78] *Kelly v. Rogers* [1892] 1 Q.B. 910.

[79] para. 4–053 *et seq.*

[80] Compare *Stevenson v. Powell* (1612) 1 Bulst. 182, but *cf. Spencer v. Marriott* (1823) 1 B. & C. 457.

[81] *Cohen v. Tannar* [1900] 2 Q.B. 609. The sub-tenant also has a right to seek relief from forfeiture against the head-landlord under Law of Property Act 1925, s.146(4); see also *Escalus Properties Ltd v. Robinson*, [1996] Q.B. 231, CA (relief under s. 146(2) of the CPA 1925).

[82] *Williams v. Gabriel* [1906] 1 K.B. 155. *Popular Catering Association Ltd v. Romagnoli* [1937] 1 All E.R. 167 (demolition of premises by local authority: no breach); *Crown Lands Commissioners v. Page* [1960] 2 Q.B. 274 (requisition under statutory powers: no breach). Compare *Trotter v. Louth* (1931) 47 T.L.R. 335

[83] *Hayes v. Bickerstaff* (1669) Vaugh. 118; *Dawson v. Dyer* (1833) 5 B. & Ad. 584; *Edge v. Boileau* (1885) 16 Q.B.D. 117; *Taylor v. Webb* [1937] 2 K.B. 283 (reversed on other grounds [1937] 2 K.B. 290). See also *Yorkbrook Investments Ltd v. Batten* [1985] 2 E.G.L.R. 100 and *Slater v. Hoskins* [1982] 2 N.Z.L.R. 541. *cf. Hussein v. Mehlman* [1992] 2 E.G.L.R. 87 indicating a failure to pay rent may be a repudiatory breach by the tenant, entitling the landlord to treat himself as discharged from his obligations.

in this context "refers to the exercise and use of the right and having the full benefit of it, rather than to deriving pleasure from it".[84] "Quiet" in this context means free from interference or disturbance by the exercise of adverse rights over the demised premises or neighbouring premises occupied by the landlord or a person claiming by from or under him.[85] Thus for an interference to amount to a breach of covenant, it must interfere with the tenant's title or possession of the demised premises and not be simply temporary disturbance.[86]

Acts or sometimes omissions by the landlord or those within the scope of the covenant which substantially interfere with the tenant's possession or ordinary quiet enjoyment of the demised premises will amount to breaches of covenant. Whether a particular interference amounts to a breach of covenant depends upon the nature of the interference in question. Thus, in the case of *Sanderson v. Berwick-upon-Tweed Corpn*[87] Fry L.J., giving the judgment of the Court of Appeal, stated:

> "It appears to us to be in every case a question of fact whether the quiet enjoyment of the land has or has not been interrupted; and where the ordinary and lawful enjoyment of the demised land is substantially interfered with by acts of the lessor or those lawfully claiming under him, the covenant appears to us to be broken, although neither the title to the land nor the possession of the land may be otherwise affected."

Interference with possession of *the premises*: the contemplation of the parties and the prospective nature of the covenant

If an interference is to amount to a breach it must interfere with the enjoyment of the premises: **3–033**

> "What are the premises? The things previously demised and granted. The covenant does not enlarge what is previously granted, but an additional remedy is given, namely an action for damages if the lessee cannot get, or is deprived of that which has previously been professed to be granted."[88]

Thus, the covenant does not of itself entitle the tenant to a right of light which he would not otherwise have.[89]

---

[84] *Kenny v. Preen* [1963] 1 Q.B. 499 at 511. See also *Branchett v. Beaney* [1992] 3 All E.R. 910.

[85] See *Hudson v. Cripps* [1896] 1 Ch. 265 at 268.

[86] *Manchester, Sheffield and Lincolnshire Ry Co. v. Anderson* [1898] 2 Ch. 394 at 401; *Phelps v. City of London Corp.* [1916] 2 Ch. 255.

[87] (1884) 13 Q.B.D. 547 at 551. See also *Robinson v. Kilvert* (1889) 41 Ch.D. 88 at 97.

[88] *Leech v. Schweder* (1874) 9 Ch. App. 463 at 474, per Mellish L.J. See also *Potts v. Smith* L.R. 6 Eq. 311 at 317; *Davis v. Town Properties Investment Corp. Ltd* [1903] 1 Ch. 797, CA.

[89] *Potts v. Smith* (1868) L.R. 6 Eq. 311; *Booth v. Alcock* (1873) 8 Ch. App. 663.

It follows also that the circumstances at the date of the lease must be considered in assessing whether there has been a breach of covenant since these may determine the scope of what has been granted: if it was contemplated that the landlord would be able to use his adjoining premises for a particular purpose, the existence of the covenant for quiet enjoyment cannot be used to prevent the landlord from using his adjoining premises for that purpose provided that he does so in a reasonable manner.[90]

So, where the demised premises formed part of a building estate at the date of the lease and this was known to both parties, the landlord was not deprived of his right to build by the existence of the covenant.[91] Similarly, the lease of sporting rights over a farm does not prevent the ordinary cultivation of the farm albeit that the cultivation disturbs the game.[92]

Conversely, if it was contemplated that the tenant should use the demised premises for a particular purpose, an interference with the premises so as to prevent the tenant from enjoying the premises for that purpose may amount to a breach of the covenant for quiet enjoyment.[93] However, if the tenant's use of the land was not contemplated by the lease then the landlord's use of his adjoining premises may not amount to a breach of covenant for quiet enjoyment even if it interferes with the tenant's business.[94]

In this context it is important to note that the covenant for quiet enjoyment is "prospective" in its nature[95]:

> "It is a covenant that the tenant's lawful possession *will* not be interfered with by the landlord or anyone claiming under him. The covenant does not apply to things done before the grant of the tenancy, even though they may have continuing consequences for the tenant."

Thus, in *Anderson v. Oppenheimer*[96] a pipe in an office building burst and water from a cistern installed by the landlord in the roof flooded the premises of the tenant of the ground floor. The Court of Appeal held that although the escape of water was a consequence of the maintenance of the cistern and water supply by the landlord, it was not a breach of the covenant for quiet enjoyment. It did not constitute an act or omission by

---

[90] *Lyttleton Times Ltd v. Warners* [1907] A.C. 476.

[91] *Potts v. Smith*, (1868) L.R. 6 Eq. 311; *Robson v. Palace Chambers Westminster Co.* (1897) 14 T.L.R. 56.

[92] *Jeffryes v. Evans* (1865) 19 C.B. (N.S.) 246; *Dick v. Norton* (1916) 85 L.J. Ch. 623. cf. *Peech v. Best* [1931] 1 K.B. 1 (where racing stables are built over land subject to a lease of sporting rights, this is a breach of covenant where the stables are not contemplated by the lease).

[93] *Andrews v. Paradise* (1724) 8 Mod. 318 (erection of gate to prevent use of close); *Shaw v. Stenton* (1858) 2 H. & N. 858, *Re Griffiths, Griffiths v. Riggs* (1917) 61 Sol. Jo. 268 (working of minerals so as to interfere with tenant's lease of lower stratum); *Grosvenor Hotel Co. Ltd v. Hamilton* [1894] 2 Q.B. 836 (vibrations interfering with business at premises contemplated by lease).

[94] *Robinson v. Kilvert* (1889) 41 Ch.D. 88.

[95] *Norton on Deeds* (2nd ed., 1928) pp 612–613; *Southwark LBC v. Mills* [2001] 1 A.C. 1 at 11 *per* Lord Hoffmann.

[96] (1880) 5 QBD 602.

the landlord or anyone lawfully claiming through him after the lease had been granted. The water system was there when the tenant took his lease and he had to take the building as he found it.

Similarly in *Spoor v. Green*[97] the plaintiff bought land and built houses upon it. The houses were damaged by subsidence caused by underground mining which had taken place before the sale. The Court of Exchequer held that there was no breach of the covenant for quiet enjoyment which had been given by the vendor. Cleasby B. said[98]

> "... it ... seems to me impossible to say that there is a breach of covenant for quiet enjoyment by reason of the subsidence of the house in consequence of the previous removal of the coal. This subsidence of the house is a necessary consequence of the condition of the property bought by the plaintiff ...."

In *Lyttleton Times Co Ltd v. Warners Ltd*[99] the plaintiffs owned a hotel next to the premises in which the defendants operated a printing press. They made an agreement under which the defendants would rebuild their premises and grant a lease of the upper floors to the plaintiffs for use as additional hotel bedrooms. The noise and vibrations of the press beneath caused substantial inconvenience to the occupants of the bedrooms. The plaintiffs claimed an injunction to restrain the defendants from working their press. They said that the defendants knew that they intended to use the premises as bedrooms and were under an implied obligation not to interfere with their convenient use. However, the plaintiffs also knew that the defendants intended to use their premises for printing and Lord Loreburn L.C. stated

> "When it is a question of what shall be implied from the contract, it is proper to ascertain what in fact was the purpose, or what were the purposes, to which both intended the land to be put, and, having found that, both should be held to all that was implied in this common intention ... if it be true that neither has done or asks to do anything which was not contemplated by both, neither can have any right against the other."[1]

In the case of *Southwark London Borough Council v. Mills*, Lord Hoffmann summarised the position as follows[2]

> "In the grant of a tenancy it is fundamental to the common understanding of the parties, objectively determined, that the landlord gives no implied warranty as to the condition or fitness of the premises.

---

[97] (1874) LR 9 Exch 99.
[98] *ibid* at 108.
[99] [1907] A.C. 476.
[1] *ibid* at 481.
[2] *Southwark LBC v. Mills* [2001] 1 A.C. 1 at 12 *per* Lord Hoffmann.

Caveat lessee. It would be entirely inconsistent with this common understanding if the covenant for quiet enjoyment were interpreted to create liability for disturbance or inconvenience or any other damage attributable to the condition of the premises"

Types of interference

3–034 The following categorises the sorts of activity (or inactivity) which may or may not amount to a breach of covenant for quiet enjoyment. These categories must not, however, be taken to be closed.

(1) Dispossession

3–035 Physical interferences with the demised premises which have the effect of dispossessing the tenant or substantially interfering with his possession of the premises will clearly amount to a breach of the covenant for quiet enjoyment. So if the tenant is evicted, and his belongings removed from the premises, this is a breach of convenant.[3] Similarly, it may amount to a breach if the landlord takes possession of the premises to carry out work (even having pressurised the tenant into consenting to the works).[4] The removal of the doors and windows of the demised premises in order to force the tenant to leave has also been held to be a breach of covenant.[5]

(2) Acts off the demised premises

3–036 There may be a breach of the covenant for quiet enjoyment without the landlord or those claiming under him entering onto the demised premises and directly dispossessing the tenant provided that what occurs substantially interferes with the tenant's title or possession of the demises premises[6]: for instance, where a lower stratum of minerals has been demised and the landlord works the upper stratum in such a way as to cause the roof of the lower stratum to fall in and the mine to be flooded this will be a breach of the covenant.[7]

Acts taking place off the demised premises may amount to breaches of covenant even though they do not lead to the actual dispossession of the tenant where such acts substantially interfere with the tenant's enjoyment of the premises or his ability to exercise his rights as a tenant.[8] However,

---

[3] *e.g. Millington v. Duffy* (1984) 17 H.L.R. 232.

[4] *Budd-Scott v. Daniel* [1902] 2 K.B. 351.

[5] *Cohen v. Tannar* [1900] 2 Q.B. 609; *Lavender v. Betts* [1942] 2 All E.R. 72.

[6] *Southwark LBC v. Mills* [2001] 1 A.C. 1, HL; *Southwark L.B.C. v. Long* [2002] EWCA Civ 403, para. 64.

[7] *Shaw v. Stenton* (1858) 2 H. & N. 858; *Re Griffiths, Griffiths v. Riggs* (1917) 61 Sol. Jo. 268 (discussed in *Celsteel Ltd v. Alton House Holdings Ltd (No. 2)* [1987] 1 W.L.R. 291).

[8] *Sanderson v. Berwick-upon-Tweed Corp.* (1884) 13 Q.B.D. 547 at 551; *McCall v. Abelesz* [1976] 1 All E.R. 727 at 730, *per* Lord Denning M.R. *cf. Browne v. Flower* [1911] 1 Ch. 219 at 228, *per* Parker J. and *Harmer v. Jumbil (Nigeria) Tin Areas Ltd* [1921] 1 Ch. 200 at 213 (reversed on other grounds [1921] 1 Ch. 215) which indicate that there must be some physical interference with the demised premises.

it seems that where a disturbance is due to an act done off the premises there will be no breach unless the disturbance to possession was intended or ought reasonably to have been foreseen.[9]

In *Owen v. Gadd*[10] where the landlord arranged for scaffolding to be erected for the purpose of repairing the landlord's premises situated above the demised premises and the scaffolding obstructed access to the tenant's shop window and door, there was a breach of covenant. Further, where a landlord without entering the demised premises deliberately intimidates the tenant and threatens physically to evict him this may interfere with the tenant's enjoyment of the demised premises so as to amount to a breach of covenant.[11] Similarly, there may be a breach of covenant where the landlord cuts off the electricity and gas to residential premises forcing the tenant to give up possession.[12] However, unless the acts complained of are such as to interfere with the rights by which the tenant enjoys possession of the premises they will not amount to a breach of covenant. Thus, if a landlord merely asserts that he is entitled to possession and threatens legal proceedings against the tenant there will be no breach.[13] Likewise, the erection of a staircase outside the demised premises which interferes with the tenant's privacy will not of itself amount to a breach of covenant.[14]

Although some cases may be read as indicating the contrary,[15] it should now be taken as settled that noise and disturbance created outside the premises may amount to a breach of this covenant if they are such as to interfere with possession.[16] So, where the landlord carries out building works which cause so much noise, dust and dirt that the tenant's occupation of the demised premises becomes intolerable, this will amount to a breach of covenant.[17]

(3) Omissions

A mere failure by a landlord to prevent an interference with the tenant's enjoyment of his occupation of the demised premises will not amount to a breach of covenant. Thus, in *Duke of Westminster v. Guild*[18] there was no   3–037

---

[9] *Manchester, Sheffield and Lincolnshire Ry Co. v. Muncaster* [1891] 2 Q.B. 680 at 689, CA.

[10] [1956] 2 Q.B. 99. See also *Queensway Marketing Ltd v. Associated Restaurants Ltd* (1984) 271 E.G. 1106, affirmed [1988] 2 E.G.L.R. 49.

[11] *Kenny v. Preen* [1963] 1 Q.B. 499; *Sampson v. Floyd* [1989] 2 E.G.L.R. 49.

[12] *Perera v. Vandiyar* [1953] 1 W.L.R. 672.

[13] *Browne v. Flower* [1911] 1 Ch. 219.

[14] Compare *Kenny v. Preen* [1963] 1 Q.B. 499.

[15] *Jenkins v. Jackson* (1888) 40 Ch.D. 71; *Jaeger v. Mansions Consolidated Ltd* (1902) 87 L.T. 690 at 694; CA. *Phelps v. City of London Corp.* [1916] 2 Ch. 255; also *Newman v. Real Estate Debenture Corp. Ltd and Flower Decorations Ltd* [1940] 1 All E.R. 131.

[16] See *Southwark L.B.C. v. Mills* [2001] 1 A.C. 1, HL; see too *Kenny v. Preen* [1963] 1 Q.B. 499.

[17] *Guppy's (Bridport) Ltd v. Brookling* (1983) 269 E.G. 846 at 942.

[18] [1985] Q.B. 688. See also *Anderson v. Oppenheimer* (1880) 5 QBD 601 (no breach of covenant where water pipes burst); *Blake v. Woolf* [1898] 2 Q.B. 426 (no breach of covenant where overflow of water where landlord had employed competent contractors to carry out works to water supply); *Hafton Properties Ltd v. Camp* [1995] 1 EGLR 67. But *cf. Hilton v. James Smith & Sons (Norwood)* [1979] 2 E.G.L.R. 44 (where a landlord had granted a right

breach of the covenant for quiet enjoyment where a landlord failed to keep a drain retained by him free from obstruction with the result that the tenant's premises were flooded. Further, the covenant does not amount to a covenant that the premises are fit for any particular purpose and does not oblige the landlord to put the premises into a better condition than they were at the date of the demise.[19] Accordingly, the covenant for quiet enjoyment does not oblige the landlord to rebuild or repair the premises if they are destroyed by fire, tempest or otherwise.[20]

On the other hand, where the landlord owes to the tenant a duty and a failure by the landlord to comply with that duty results in an interference with the tenant's enjoyment of the demised premises this may amount to a breach of the covenant for quiet enjoyment. Thus, in the case of *Gordon v. Selico Co Ltd,*[21] where the landlord was under an obligation to keep the exterior of a block of flats in repair but in breach of that covenant failed to keep the building watertight with the result that dry rot broke out in the demised premises, this was held to amount to a breach of the covenant for quiet enjoyment. Likewise in the case of *Hafton Properties Ltd v. Camp*[22] it was held that a landlord was in breach of his covenant for quiet enjoyment where it was under an obligation to keep the exterior of a block of flats in repair but failed to do so with the result that dry rot occurred in the tenant's flat.

(4) Claims and legal action

3–038   It seems that an action which results in the eviction of the tenant without determining his term as against the landlord or an action which disturbs the tenant's possession of the premises may amount to a breach of covenant for quiet enjoyment where the action is brought by a person within the scope of the covenant.

The wrongful levying of distress by a person claiming under the landlord may amount to a breach[23] as may a demand for rent from a sub-tenant where the rent is actually paid.[24] If proceedings are brought by a third party against the landlord for possession there will be no breach of covenant if the order is made with the result that the tenant is evicted, even though the landlord had a good defence but did not defend the proceedings.[25] However, if the landlord consents to judgment for possession this will amount to a breach of the covenant.[26]

---

of way to his tenant he was in breach of his covenant for quiet enjoyment when he failed to prevent other tenants from obstructing the right of way).

[19] *Southwark LBC v. Mills* [2001] 1 A.C. 1, HL.
[20] *Brown v. Quilter* (1764) Ambl. 384.
[21] [1985] 2 E.G.L.R. 79. See also *Booth v. Thomas* [1926] Ch. 397.
[22] [1995] 1 E.G.L.R. 67.
[23] *Dawson v. Dyer* (1835) 5 B. & Ad. 584.
[24] *Edge v. Boileau* (1885) 16 Q.B.D. 117; compare *Wichcot and Linsey v. Nine* (1612) 1 B. & G. 81.
[25] *Cohen v. Tannar* [1900] 2 Q.B. 609. Possession proceedings should be served upon sub-tenants where a claimant forfeiting a lease seeks possession: even if they are not parties. Compare CPR Pt 16 PD para. 6; Sched. 2, CCR Ord. 6 r.3 and CPR 55 PD para. 2.4.
[26] *ibid.*

(5) Interference with easements

An interference with an easement such as a right of way may amount to **3–039** a breach of covenant for quiet enjoyment, at least where the interference amounts to an assertion of title rather than simply a tortious interference.[27] However, the covenant does not alter the established principles of the law of easements and extend the scope of that which has been granted: thus, the existence of a covenant for quiet enjoyment will not oblige a landlord to repair the subject matter of an easement which he has not agreed to repair.[28]

Statutory powers and authorisation

Where a statute authorises an act, the act will generally not be in breach **3–040** of a covenant for quiet enjoyment. Thus, where a local authority exercises its powers to demolish the demised premises there will be no breach of covenant by the landlord.[29] However, if a landlord is to rely upon statutory powers to enter[30] and carry out works, he must comply with the requirements of the statute before being able to rely upon statutory authorisation for his defence.[31] Where a landlord is compelled by statute to enter upon premises it will not usually be a breach of covenant for quiet enjoyment if he does so.[32] However, if the landlord's liability under statute has arisen prior to the grant of the lease and the landlord could have reserved an express right under the terms of the lease to allow him to comply with his statutory obligations, then an entry by the landlord onto the premises in order to fulfil his pre-existing statutory obligations will be a breach of covenant.[33]

Where a public authority both is a landlord and seeks to exercise its statutory powers, the exercise by the public authority of its powers will not usually amount to a breach of covenant by the public authority: thus, in *Commissioner of Crown Lands v. Page*[34] there was no breach of covenant where the Crown requisitioned pursuant to its wartime powers premises which it had previously demised.

---

[27] See *Morris v. Edgington* (1810) 3 Taunt. 24; *Pomfret v. Ricroft* (1669) 1 Wms. Saund. 321; *Seddon v. Senate* (1810) 13 East 63, 72; *Hilton v. James Smith & Sons (Norwood) Ltd* (1979) 251 E.G. 1063; compare *B&Q plc v. Liverpool and Lancashire Properties Ltd* [2001] 1 E.G.L.R. 92, Ch. D, Blackburne J.

[28] *Duke of Westminster v. Guild* [1985] Q.B. 688, [1984] 3 All E.R. 144.

[29] *Popular Catering Association Ltd v. Romagnoli* [1937] 1 All E.R. 167.

[30] *e.g.* under the Party Walls Act 1996 or the Access to the Neighbouring Land Act 1992.

[31] *Trotter v. Louth* (1931) 47 T.L.R. 335.

[32] *Newby v. Sharpe* (1878) 8 Ch.D. 39.

[33] *Budd-Scott v. Daniel* [1902] 2 K.B. 354.

[34] [1960] 2 Q.B. 274. See too *Manchester, Sheffield and Lincolnshire Ry v. Anderson* [1898] 2 Ch. 394. Compare *Spurling v. Bantoft* [1891] 2 Q.B. 384; *Molton Builders Ltd v. City of Westminster* (1975) 30 P. & C.R. 182; *Dowty Bolton Paul v. Wolverhampton Corporation (No. 2)* [1973] 2 All E.R. 491, CA.

Remedies

3–041   The remedies available for a breach of the covenant for quiet enjoyment are

    (1)   damages;

    (2)   injunctions; and

    (3)   (where a tenant has been evicted) abatement of rent.

These remedies are dealt with in the section on remedies.[35] It should be noted that because the cause of action arises under the law of contract the measure of damages is contractual and exemplary and aggravated damages are not available.[36] However, in many instances, an interference in breach of covenant for quiet enjoyment may also amount to a tortious interference.

Obligation not to derogate from grant

The obligation

3–042   It is a general principle that a grantor may not derogate from his grant.[37] In other words if someone agrees that another is to have a particular benefit, he must not do anything by his voluntary act which prejudices those rights which he has created.[38]

In *Browne v. Flower*[39] Parker J. explained the nature of the obligation in these words:

> "The implications usually explained by the maxim that no one can derogate from his grant do not stop short with easements. Under certain circumstances there will be implied on the part of the grantor or lessor obligations which can restrict the user of the land retained by him further than can be explained by the implication of any easement known to law. Thus if the grant or demise be made for a particular purpose the grantor or lessor comes under an obligation not to use the land retained by him in such a way as to render the land granted or demised unfit for the purpose for which the grant or demise was made".

---

[35] See Chap. 4.
[36] See 4–044.
[37] *Palmer v. Fletcher* (1663) 1 Lev. 122; *Compton v. Richards* (1814) 1 Price 27; *Caledonian Ry v. Sprot* (1856) 2 Mac. 449; *North Easter Ry Co. v. Elliott* (1860) 1 John & H. 145; *London & North Western Ry Co. v. Evans* [1893] 1 Ch. 16; *Glamorganshire Canal Navigation Co. v. Nixon's Navigation Co. Ltd* (1901) 85 L.T. 53; *Harmer v. Jumbil (Nigeria) Tin Areas Ltd* [1921] 1 Ch. 200. See also (1964) 80 L.Q.R. 244 (D.W. Elliott).
[38] See *Birmingham, Dudley and District Banking Co. v. Ross* (1888) 38 Ch.D. 295.
[39] [1911] 1 Ch. 219 at 225.

Thus, the obligation may be implied wherever one man grants rights to another over land. The obligation is not only to be implied where there is a grant of rights by a landlord to a tenant, it may also be implied for instance where a tenant is in the position of grantor to his landlord as where a lease contains a reservation in favour of the landlord[40] or to the grant of a *profit à prendre*.[41] Although commonly found in the context of the grant of rights over real property, it should be noted that the principle by which the obligation is implied is not confined to the grant of such rights but is one of general application in the law of contract.[42]

In the context of the law of landlord and tenant the obligation has two particularly important aspects: first, if a landlord lets premises to a tenant for a particular purpose, he will not be able to act so as substantially to interfere with the use of the premises for that purpose[43]; secondly, the obligation not to derogate from grant is wider than the covenant for quiet enjoyment since the former may be broken without any interference with possession of the demised premises as such. These aspects are illustrated by the following two examples. In the case of *Aldin v. Latimer Clark, Muirhead & Co*,[44] where premises were let for the purpose of storing timber, it was held that the landlord was in breach of his obligation not to derogate from his grant by obstructing the flow of air necessary for drying the timber by building on adjoining land. In the case of *Harmer v. Jumbil (Nigeria) Tin Areas Ltd.*[45] where land was leased for the express purpose of storing explosives, the lessor and those claiming under him were prevented from using land adjoining the demised premises so as to put at risk the statutory licence necessary for the storage of explosives.

Limits on the obligation not to derogate from grant

A grantor may, of course, reserve to himself the right to do something which might otherwise amount to a derogation from grant. However, the courts will not construe the terms of a lease as giving the landlord power actually to derogate from his grant if the words are capable of another construction.[46]   3–043

In the absence of express reservations, the extent of the obligation will be ascertained by reference to the precise scope of the grant and by inferring the common intention of the parties as it existed at the date of the grant. Thus, where the purpose of the grant is the carrying on of a business, the obligation will only protect the grantee to the extent that he is

---

[40] *Johnston & Sons v. Holland* [1988] 1 E.G.L.R. 264.
[41] *Peech v. Best* [1931] 1 K.B. 1.
[42] *British Leyland Motor Corp v. Armstrong Patents Co.* [1986] A.C. 577 (copyright).
[43] See *Rigby v. Bennett* (1882) 21 Ch.D. 559; *Mundy v. Duke of Rutland* (1883) 23 Ch.D. 81, 96; *Myers v. Catterson* (1889) 43 Ch.D. 470; *Mitchell v. Cantrill* (1887) 57 L.J. Ch. 72 at 75; *Newman v. Real Estate Debenture Corp. Ltd and Flower Decorations Ltd* [1940] 1 All E.R. 131.
[44] [1894] 2 Ch. 437.
[45] [1921] 1 Ch. 200.
[46] Compare *White v. Harrow* (1902) 86 L.T. 4; see too *Saeed v. Plustrade Ltd* [2001] R.T.R. 30; [2001] PLSCS 283.

carrying on his business in an ordinary manner and will not extend to unusually sensitive uses of land by the grantee outside the scope of that originally contemplated by the parties.[47] The obligation will not preclude a lessor from the reasonable use of premises retained by him even if that use injures the tenant's business if the likelihood of injury was not common knowledge at the date of the grant.[48] It has been thus held not to amount to a derogation from grant for a landlord to use premises retained by him for a hotel even though this affected the amenities of the tenant to whom he had granted a residential lease.[49] Likewise it has been held not to be a derogation from grant for a landlord to let an adjoining shop to a competitor of the tenant.[50]

Further, the general principle is that the obligation will only be implied where the grantor is in a position to make an express grant: thus, in general, the obligation will not restrict the grantor's rights to use property which he acquires after the date of the grant.[51-52] In some circumstances, however, the obligation may extend to acts of the grantor on land acquired after the grant. Thus, in the case of *Johnson & Sons v. Holland*[53] it was held that where a lease reserved to the lessor/grantee the right to erect an advertising hoarding and subsequently the tenant/grantor acquired an interest in land which the hoarding faced and which the tenant used (out of spite) to erect structures obscuring the landlord's hoarding, this was held to be a derogation from grant. In so holding Nicholls L.J. stated[54]

"Can he in such a case . . . be at liberty to frustrate the whole purpose of the letting by erecting his own advertising hoarding hard up against the flank wall of the building? In my view common honesty permits of only one answer to that question. Of course in considering what is necessarily implicit in a transaction in a case where the grantor owns no other land, very great weight indeed must be given to that factor. It will be a very exceptional case for it to be necessarily implicit in a lease that the activities of a lessor who owns no adjoining land, and has no plans to buy any adjoining land, are to be restricted on the adjoining land should he ever become tenant or owner of that land. Whether it is so implicit or not will depend on all the circumstances, including the purpose of the grant and the nature of the activities sought to be restrained. But if the facts in a given case point clearly to such a

---

[47] *Robinson v. Kilvert* (1889) 41 Ch.D. 88; *Aldin v. Latimer Clark, Muirhead & Co.* [1894] 2 Ch. 437, 444 per Stirling J.

[48] *Robinson v. Kilvert* (1889) 41 Ch.D. 88; see too *Port v. Griffith* [1938] 1 All E.R. 295; *Johnston & Sons Ltd v. Holland* [1988] 1 E.G.L.R. 264; but see *Oceanic Village Ltd v. Shirayama Shokusan Co. Ltd* [2001] E.G.C.S. 20.

[49] *Kelly v. Buttershell* [1949] 2 All E.R. 830.

[50] *Romulus Trading Co. Ltd v. Comet Properties Ltd* [1996] 2 E.G.L.R. 70.

[51-52] *Myers v. Catterson* (1889) 43 Ch.D. 470; *Quicke v. Chapman* [1903] 1 Ch. 659; *Financial Times Ltd v. Bell* (1903) 19 T.L.R. 433.

[53] [1988] 1 E.G.L.R. 264.

[54] *ibid.*

restriction being implicit, I can see no reason in principle why the law should treat that case differently from one where the lessor already owns the adjoining land at the time of the lease".

Therefore, the extension of the obligation to include acts on land not held at the date of the grant will be exceptional.

Acts amounting to derogation from grant

In accordance with these principles, a direct physical interference with the exercise of a right can amount to a derogation from grant.[55] But landlords have also been held to be in derogation from their grants where they have used their adjoining land in such a way that vibrations have interfered with the stability of the demised premises[56] or in such a way that the support for buildings to be built on the demised premises has been substantially interfered with.[57] Likewise, it has been held that a landlord derogates from his grant if he uses a wall demised to the tenant as a party wall[58] and if he erects a building above the demised premises without an express reservation of the right to do so.[59]   **3–044**

Further, it is possible that a landlord may be in breach of his duty not to derogate from his grant without any physical interference, for instance by causing noise,[60] or intimidating[61] the tenant to such a degree that it can be said that he is taking away what he has granted, or by substantial interference with the light to the tenant's windows.[62] Similarly, if the grantor's act renders illegal use of the premises by the tenant for the purposes for which they were granted to the tenant, this may amount to a derogation from grant.[63] However, where a statutory authority exercises its statutory functions to prevent a use for which it has granted a lease, this will not be a derogation from grant.[64]

In general, where a landlord lets a retail unit in a shopping centre, the obligation not to derogate from grant does not extend to a general obligation not to do anything in the exercise of his reserved powers which might harm the tenant.[65] On the other hand, where a landlord lets premises within a shopping mall, he may be in derogation from his grant if he lets

---

[55] *e.g. Saeed v. Plustrade Ltd* [2001] R.T.R. 30; [2001] PLSCS 283, CA.

[56] *Grosvenor Hotel Co. v. Hamilton* [1894] 2 Q.B. 836.

[57] *Rigby v. Bennett* (1882) 21 Ch.D. 559; *Siddons v. Short* (1877) 2 C.P.D. 572. See also *Markham v. Paget* [1908] 1 Ch. 697 and *Jones v. Consolidated Anthracite Collieries Ltd* [1916] 1 K.B. 123.

[58] *Betts v. Pickfords* [1906] 2 Ch. 87.

[59] *Lawson v. Hartley-Brown* (1995) 71 P. & C.R. 242, CA.

[60] *Newman v. Real Estate Debenture Corp. Ltd* [1940] 1 All E.R. 131 (noise from altering a flat in same building as demised premises).

[61] Compare *Kenny v. Preen* [1963] 1 Q.B. 499 at 512, 513. *cf. Kelly v. Battershell* [1949] 2 All E.R. 830.

[62] *Coutts v. Gorham* (1829) Moo. & M. 396; *Cable v. Bryant* [1908] 1 Ch. 259.

[63] *Harmer v. Jumbil (Nigeria) Tin Areas Ltd* [1921] 1 Ch. 200.

[64] *Molton Builders Ltd v. Westminster City Council* (1975) 30 P. & C.R. 182.

[65] *Petra Investments v. Jeffrey Rogers* [2000] E.G.L.R. 120; compare *Oceanic Village Ltd v. Shirayama Shokusan Co. Ltd* [2001] E.G.C.S. 20. also *Romulus Trading Co. Ltd v. Comet Properties Ltd* [1996] 2 E.G. L.R. 70.

his retained premises for a purpose which results in a nuisance to the tenant and which he fails to take steps to prevent.[66] Similarly, if a landlord imposes restrictions on the access of the tenant's potential customers which was plainly contemplated at the date of the grant, this may amount to a derogation from grant.[67]

The obligation not to derogate from one's grant extends beyond the original grantor to those who claim under him whether by conveyance or lease.[68] Conversely, those claiming under the grantee may enforce the obligation.[69]

In the context of *profits à prendre*, there will be a breach if the grantor manages his property in a way not contemplated by the grant such as substantially to prejudice the rights granted.[70] However, the grantee of a profit cannot complain if the grantor manages his land in the ordinary way as contemplated at the time of the grant.[71]

Remedies

3–045   A derogation from grant may entitle a tenant to an injunction to restrain the landlord's breach of his obligation. It may also result in an action for damages. The principles relating to the grant of injunctions are set out elsewhere.[72] If the derogation from grant results in a tenant being evicted from the premises, then an abatement of rent may be appropriate.[73]

So far as an action for damages is concerned, since an action based upon a derogation from grant is an action for the breach of a contract, the principles upon which damages will be assessed will be similar to those for the assessment of damages for a breach of covenant for quiet enjoyment.[74] These principles are considered further in Chapter 4.

Tenant's obligation to deliver up

The obligation

3–046   It is in the nature of a tenancy that it is of limited duration; accordingly it is implicit in a lease that there is an obligation on the part of the tenant that he will deliver up the premises upon the expiration of the term.[75] It is usual to find such an obligation expressly formulated (often with an

---

[66] *Chartered Trust plc v. Davies* [1997] 2 E.G.L.R. 83, CA.
[67] *Platt v. London Underground Ltd* [2001] 20 E.G. 227, CS, Neuberger J. (exit from underground station closed affecting number of customers passing premises)
[68] *Aldin v. Latimer Clark, Muirhead & Co.* [1894] 2 Ch. 437. See now Landlord and Tenant (Covenants) Act 1995.
[69] See *Molton Builders Ltd v. City of Westminster LBC* (1975) 30 P. & C.R. 182.
[70] *Peech v. Best* [1931] 1 K.B. 1.
[71] *ibid.*; compare *Pole v. Carew* [1998] E.G.C.S. 125 and see 1–052.
[72] See para. 4–084.
[73] See 4–053.
[74] See para. 4–041.
[75] *Henderson v. Squire* (1869) L.R. 4 Q.B. 170 at 172; compare *Harding v. Crethorn* (1793) 1 Esp. 57.

obligation as to the state of repair at the time of delivery of possession). However, where the landlord is prevented from obtaining possession of the premises by reason of security of tenure conferred upon the tenant by statute, there is no obligation upon the tenant to deliver up the premises at the end of the contractual term.[76] It is also possible that landlord and tenant may agree that the obligation to deliver up will be limited or excluded[77] — but such agreement is very unusual.

Extent of the obligation: premises to which it extends

The obligation to deliver up the premises extends to those premises which form the subject-matter of the lease. These will usually be determined by construction of the lease itself.

3–047

The obligation upon a tenant to deliver up possession also obliges the tenant to yield up to the landlord any encroachments made by the tenant for the benefit of the tenancy.[78] Where a tenant encroaches on premises adjoining those demised during the term the encroachments are presumed to be made for the benefit of the tenancy: the encroachments may be enjoyed by the tenant during the term but after its expiry are for the benefit of the landlord.[79] This presumption is rebuttable. For instance, there may be evidence that when the encroachments were made the tenant intended to make them for his own exclusive benefit.[80] On the other hand, the mere fact that the landlord has consented to the encroachment during the term will not give the tenant the benefit of it after the determination of the lease.[81] It should be noted that these presumptions apply only between landlord and tenant.[82]

Where a tenant encroaches upon the landlord's adjoining land during the tenancy and occupies it for 12 years, the land upon which the encroachment has occurred cannot be recovered by reason of limitation.[83] However, at the end of the term, such land will presumed (in accordance with the principles set out in the preceding paragraph) to have been made for the benefit of the tenancy and will be recoverable by the landlord at the end of the term as with other encroachments.[84] Encroachments made by the tenant upon adjoining land before the tenancy commenced are not subject to this presumption and are not recoverable by the landlord.[85]

---

[76] See e.g. Landlord and Tenant Act 1954, ss. 3, 24; Rent Act 1977, ss. 2, 98; Housing Act 1988, ss. 5–7, 20–21.

[77] Hyatt v. Griffiths (1851) 17 Q.B. 505; Newsom v. Smythies (1858) 1 F. & F. 477.

[78] Smirk v. Lyndale Developments Ltd [1975] Ch. 317, CA; Kensington Pension Developments Ltd v. Royal Garden Hotel (Oddenino's) Ltd [1990] 2 E.G.L.R. 117.

[79] ibid.

[80] ibid.

[81] Whitmore v. Humphries (1871) LR 7 CP 1.

[82] Doe d. Baddeley v. Massey (1851) 17 Q.B. 373; Doe d. Buck v. Moyes (1849)13 LT OS 325.

[83] Limitation Act 1980, s. 15; see 1–096 et seq.

[84] Kingsmill v. Millard (1855) 11 Exch 313; Smirk v. Lyndale Developments Ltd [1975] Ch. 317, CA.

[85] Dixon v. Baty (1866) LR 1 Ex 259.

Extent of obligation: failure to deliver up

3–048　If the tenant fails to deliver possession of the premises to the landlord at the end of the term he will be in breach of his obligation. A breach will take place not only where the tenant remains in physical possession himself, but also where the tenant fails to give vacant possession because of his leaving rubbish or goods accumulated at the premises.[86] Similarly, if the tenant leaves an undertenant in possession of the premises.[87] or any part of the premises[88] at the end of the term this too will amount to a breach of covenant as will leaving a caretaker in occupation.[89] However, if the tenant has done all in his power to give vacant possession, he will not be liable for a failure to deliver up possession if an undertenant remains in occupation of the premises as a result of statutory protection.

A failure to deliver up possession at the end of the term may also amount to a trespass by the tenant.[91] However, the covenant to deliver up has important advantages over the landlord's rights to possession in the law of trespass: a covenant by a surety of the tenant that the tenant will observe and perform all the covenants in the lease extends to guaranteeing the performance of the covenant to deliver up the premises at the end of the term.[92]

Remedies

3–049　Remedies are dealt with more fully in Chapter 4. The landlord has available remedies against the former tenant as a trespasser as well as the contractual remedies upon the covenant. The remedies of double rent and double value may also be available.[93] In principle, it seems that injunctive relief may be available to enforce the covenant as will an action for contractual damages.[94]

Where the tenant is in breach of his covenant to deliver up possession of the premises, the landlord is entitled to damages which will not necessarily be limited to the value of the land: the landlord will be entitled to all damages which he has sustained as a result of the breach (subject to their remoteness).[95] Accordingly, a landlord may recover the reasonable

---

[86] See *Cumberland Consolidated Holdings Ltd v. Ireland* [1946] K.B. 264. The obligation will survive even a surrender of the tenancy: see *D'Arcy v. Lord Castlemaine* [1909] 2 I.R. 474.

[87] *Harding v. Crethorn* (1793)1 Esp 56; cf. *Roe v. Wiggs* (1806) 2 Bos & PNR 330. *Ibbs v. Richardson* (1839) 9 Ad & EL 849; *Thames Manufacturing Co. Ltd v. Perrott's (Nichol & Peyton) Ltd* (1984) 50 P. & C.R. 1.

[88] *Henderson v. Squire* (1869) LR 4 Q.B. 170.

[89] *Henderson v. Van Cooten* [1922] W.N. 340.

[90] *Reynolds v. Bannerman* [1922] 1 K.B. 719; *Watson v. Saunders-Roe* [1947] K.B. 437; *Regional Properties Ltd v. Frankenschwerth* [1951] 1 All E.R. 178 (not reported on this point at [1951] 1 KB 631).

[91] See above, para. 1–050.

[92] *Associated Dairies Ltd v. Pierce* (1982) 265 E.G. 127, CA.

[93] See 5–003, 5–004 below.

[94] See 4–050 below.

[95] *Watson v. Lane* (1856) 11 Exch. 769 at 774.

damages and costs incurred by him in respect of the failure to deliver possession: for example, where the landlord has contracted to re-let the premises but cannot so re-let the premises because the previous tenant has failed to deliver possession of the premises, leaving the landlord exposed to a claim for breach of contract by his new tenant.[96] Similarly the landlord will be able to recover from the tenant the costs of evicting an undertenant left in possession of the premises in breach of the covenant[97] as well as the value of the premises out of which he has been kept.[98]

Where one of two joint tenants holds over, both will be liable if the other assents to the holding over, but otherwise only the one who holds over.[99]

Obligations under a contract between licensor and licensee

Where one party to a contract licenses another to use land pursuant to that contract he may be prohibited by his contract from interfering with the rights which he has granted. Although a contract by which a person licenses another to use land does not create any legal or equitable interest in the property to which it relates but merely confers a right making that lawful which would otherwise be unlawful,[1] a licensee may have remedies against the licensor if his use of the land is interfered with contrary to the agreement between them.

3–050

The extent to which remedies may be available to the licensee for an interference with his enjoyment of the land will be determined by the construction of the contract between them and the extent to which it is agreed that the licensee is permitted to enjoy the land free from interruption. If the licensor interrupts or allows the interruption of the licensee's enjoyment of the land contrary to the terms agreed between them the licensee will have an action for damages for breach of contract. However, it is clear that because it is in the nature of a licence that the licensee is not granted exclusive legal possession of the land which he is licensed to occupy, the usual covenant for quiet enjoyment which is found in a tenancy has no place in a licence[2] either expressly or by implication. But there is no reason why it should not be implied into a contract creating a licence that the licensor will not interfere with the actual occupation of the land by the licensee if this is necessary to give efficacy to the contract.[3] So, in the case of *Smith v. Nottinghamshire County Council*[4] where students were granted licences of rooms in a hall of residence it was an implied term of the licences that the licensor would not without just cause disturb the students from getting on with their studies in their rooms in reasonable quietude.

---

[96] Compare *Bramley v. Chesterton* (1857) 2 C.B. (N.S.) 592.
[97] *Henderson v. Squire* (1869) L.R. 4 Q.B. 170; *Henderson v. Van Cooten* [1922] W.N. 340.
[98] *Harding v. Crethorn* (1793) 1 Esp. 57; *Ibbs v. Richardson* (1839) 9 Ad. & El. 849.
[99] *Tancred v. Christy* (1843) 12 M. & W. 316; *Draper v. Crofts* (1846) 15 M. & W. 166.
[1] *Thomas v. Sorrell* (1673) Vaugh. 350 at 351 and see above, Chap. 1, paras 1–062 *et seq.*
[2] *Addiscombe Garden Estate Ltd v. Crabbe* [1958] 1 Q.B. 513 at 529, *per* Parker L.J.
[3] See generally *Liverpool City Council v. Irwin* [1977] A.C. 239, upon the implication of terms.
[4] *The Times*, November 13, 1981, CA.

Similarly whether or not a licensee will have a remedy and the nature of that remedy if the licensor excludes him or evicts him from the land which is subject to the licence will be a question of the nature and construction of the licence and, in particular, whether or not the licensor is entitled to revoke the licence.[5] A bare licence without any contractual obligation between the parties may be revoked at any time.[6] Where the licence to use land is coupled with a grant, for instance a licence to enter land in exercise of a *profit à prendre*, the licence may not be revoked except to the extent that the interest which is the subject of the grant may be revoked: if the licence is purportedly revoked without a valid determination of the interest granted the determination will amount to a derogation from grant[7] and the licensee will be entitled to seek an injunction and damages as for other derogations from grant.

3–051　　Where a licence is granted pursuant to a contract and is not coupled with a grant, the licensee will have no remedy at common law[8] against the licensor for determining the licence if the licence has been determined in accordance with the contract[9] though before evicting the licensee the licensor may have to allow the licensee a reasonable time to leave the land.[10]

Where a licensor purports to revoke the contract and the revocation is in breach of contract the position is not entirely straightforward. It was previously believed that a licensor had power to revoke a licence and render the licensee a trespasser albeit in breach of contract; the licensee's remedy would be to seek damages for breach of the contract. Thus, in the case of *Wood v. Leadbitter*[11] the purchaser of a ticket who was forcibly ejected from a racecourse before the end of the racing was unable to sue for assault because he was a trespasser. However, if he had sued for damages for breach of contract he would have had a cause of action.[12]

However, where upon the true construction of the contract the licensor is not entitled to revoke the licence, the licensee may be able to enforce the

---

[5] *Winter Garden Theatre (London) Ltd v. Millenium Products Ltd* [1948] A.C. 173.

[6] *Aldin v. Latimer Clark, Muirhead & Co.* [1894] 2 Ch. 437 see para. 1–061. However, it seems that the courts have power to grant an injunction to prevent the revocation of a bare licence where the revocation would cause particular hardship at least where the licensor has acted to estop himself from revoking the licence: *Plimmer v. Wellington Corp.* (1894) 9 App.Cas. 699; *Dillwyn v. Llewellyn* (1862) 4 De G. F. & G. 517; *Att.-Gen. of Southern Nigeria v. John Holt & Co. (Liverpool) Ltd* [1915] A.C. 599; *Inwards v. Baker* [1965] 2 Q.B. 29.

[7] *Doe d Hanley v. Wood* (1819) 2 B. & Ald. 724 at 738; *Wood v. Leadbitter* (1845) 13 M. & W. 838 at 845; *James Jones & Sons Ltd v. Earl of Tankerville* [1909] 2 Ch. 440 at 442.

[8] But now see Protection From Eviction Act 1977 as amended by the Housing Act 1988: see below, para. 5–006 *et seq.*

[9] *Winter Garden Theatre (London) Ltd v. Millenium Productions Ltd* [1948] A.C. 173; *Allam & Co. v. Europe Poster Services Ltd* [1968] 1 W.L.R. 638. See also *Australian Blue Metal Ltd v. Hughes* [1963] A.C. 74; *Hopgood v. Brown* [1955] 1 W.L.R. 213.

[10] *Minster of Health v. Bellotti* [1944] K.B. 298; see above, Chap. 1, para. 1–061.

[11] (1845) 13 M. & W. 838. cf. *Hurst v. Picture Theatres Ltd* [1915] 1 K.B. 1.

[12] *Smart v. Jones* (1864) 15 C.B. N.S. 717; *Kerrison v. Smith* [1897] 2 Q.B. 445; cf. *Wilson v. Tavener* [1901] 1 Ch. 578.

terms of the contract by injunction or by specific performance and in those circumstances the licensee will be entitled to remain upon the land without becoming a trespasser notwithstanding the purported revocation of the licence, since the licensee has an enforceable right to remain upon the land.[13] This is, perhaps, the explanation of the decision in *Hurst v. Picture Theatres Ltd*[14] where the plaintiff had bought a ticket for the cinema and was forcibly ejected in the middle of the performance in the mistaken belief that he had not paid for his ticket: in that case it was held that as a matter of the construction of the contract it was not revocable during the performance.[15] In any event, it is clear that a licensee can in appropriate circumstances in accordance with the usual equitable principles enforce his contractual rights to a licence by injunction or specific performance and these remedies may be available to him in appropriate circumstances to prevent the licensor interfering with the licensee's contractual rights to use or occupy land.[16]

It is the better view that where a licence is created by contract, if the contract is not determined in accordance with its terms the licensee will not become a trespasser regardless of the question of the enforceability of the contract in equity. It seems that a "contractual licence is not an entity distinct from the contract which brings it into being, but merely one of the provisions of that contract"[17]; and if so, it is hard to see why the licence should not endure for so long as the contractual obligations of the licensor continue. This approach is at odds with the decision in *Thompson v. Park*.[18] In that case the owners of two schools agreed to share premises owned by one of them, and after revocation of the licence by the licensor, the licensee re-entered the licensor's premises by force. The Court of Appeal held that the licensee was a trespasser upon re-entering the premises even though the licence was revoked in breach of contract. Goddard L.J. stated that equity would not assist the licensee because "the court cannot specifically enforce an agreement for two people to live peaceably under the same roof".[19] As in *Wood v. Leadbitter*[20] a distinction can be drawn between the power of a licensor to revoke a licence and his contractual rights to do so. However, *Wood v. Leadbitter* has been doubted:

3–052

---

[13] *Verrall v. Great Yarmouth BC* [1981] Q.B. 202. See also *Winter Garden Theatre (London) Ltd v. Millenium Productions Ltd* [1946] 1 All E.R. 678 at 684, [1948] A.C. 173 at 202–203, *per* Lord Uthwatt.

[14] [1915] 1 K.B. 1.

[15] It is perhaps difficult to see how this particular contract could be specifically enforceable.

[16] *Verrall v. Great Yarmouth BC* [1981] Q.B. 202; *Luganda v. Service Hotels Ltd* [1969] 2 Ch. 209. See also *Foster v. Robinson* [1951] 1 K.B. 149; *Hounslow LBC v. Twickenham Garden Developments Ltd* [1971] Ch. 233.

[17] *Hounslow L.B.C. v. Twickenham Garden Developments Ltd* [1971] Ch. 233 at 254, *per* Megarry J. See *Winter Garden Theatre (London) Ltd v. Millenium Productions Ltd* [1946] 1 All E.R. 678 at 680, *per* Lord Greene M.R. (reversed on other grounds [1948] A.C. 173).

[18] [1944] K.B. 408.

[19] *ibid.* at 409.

[20] See above, para. 3–051.

in *Winter Garden Theatre (London) Ltd v. Millenium Productions Ltd*[21] where Lord Simon stated that *Wood v. Leadbitter* "should no longer be regarded as an authority".[22] But this repudiation of this doctrine in the House of Lords may be regarded as *obiter* since in the *Winter Gardens* case the House of Lords held that upon its true construction the licence in question in fact permitted revocation; and indeed, Lord Porter and Lord Uthwatt spoke only of cases where equity would have assisted the licensee. Although the better and more logical view appears to be that it is the construction of the contract between the parties that will determine whether or not a licence may be revoked so as to render the licensee a trespasser,[23] the matter would appear to be at large until *Thompson v. Park* is directly overruled.

Further restrictions upon the revocation of a licence are imposed by the doctrines of estoppel and constructive trusts. These remedies are not strictly contractual nor do they rely upon the doctrine of privity of estate and are, accordingly, not dealt within this part of this book.[24] It seems that apart from those cases where these doctrines apply the burden of a contractual licence which is not coupled with a grant will not fall upon successors in title to the original licensor since a contractual licence is not in itself an interest in land[25]: the licensee's remedy if the licensor's successor in title interferes with the licensee's occupation of the land is to bring an action against the licensor himself for breach of contract.[26] The benefit of a licence may be assigned in accordance with the usual principles for the transmission of the benefit of contracts.[27]

Covenant restricting nuisance and annoyance, etc

Introduction

3–053   What parties to a contract agree (whether in a conveyance, a lease or a licence), is a matter of the bargain between them. A covenantor may agree to restrict his activities in many ways which may be of benefit to others in their enjoyment of their own property. However, a common covenant found in such documents with the clear intent of prohibiting interferences with the land of others is a covenant restricting a party from causing nuisance and annoyance either to the covenantee or to others. Likewise, covenants restricting immoral, illegal or dangerous activities with the same intent may be found. Such covenants may be enforced so as to prevent or to provide a remedy for interferences with land in accordance

---

[21] [1948] A.C. 173.

[22] *ibid*. at 191.

[23] See also *Verrall v. Great Yarmouth BC* [1981] Q.B. 202, a case decided upon equitable principles but disapproving *Thompson v. Park*.

[24] These doctrines are briefly dealt with in Chap. 1, para. 1–065 *et seq.*

[25] *Ashburn Anstalt v. Arnold* [1989] Ch. 1.

[26] *Clore v. Theatrical Properties Ltd and Westby & Co. Ltd* [1936] 3 All E.R. 483.

[27] *Clore v. Theatrical Properties Ltd and Westby & Co. Ltd* [1936] 3 All E.R. 483 at 490, *per* Lord Wright M.R. See *Dawson & Pearce, Licences relating to the occupation and use of land*, (1979), pp 134, *et seq.*

with the principles relating to the enforceability of covenants summarised above. There are a number of forms of covenant restricting nuisances and annoyances. But the words which are commonly found in such a covenant have been discussed by the courts in a number of cases.

"Nuisance"

A covenant against causing a "nuisance" is a narrow covenant. In the case of *Harrison v. Good*[28] Bacon V.C. held that the establishment of an elementary school was not a breach of a covenant against "nuisance" and that this word meant an actionable nuisance at common law and no more.[29] However, this approach has been doubted in the case of *Tod-Heatly v. Benham*[30] in which the Court of Appeal considered this word in the context of a covenant against "nuisance and annoyance". Lindley L.J. said[31]:

3–054

> "When Bacon V.C. held . . . that the word 'nuisance' in the covenant meant only that which would be an actionable nuisance without the covenant I doubt whether he gave sufficient weight to the consideration that the whole object of having a covenant against nuisance is to give the covenantee some protection in addition to what he would have had without the covenant; but for a nuisance in the strict sense there would be an action, covenant or no covenant."

This criticism of *Harrison v. Good* certainly has force in the situation where the covenantee retains land interference with which would amount to an actionable nuisance entitling the covenantee to bring an action in tort. However, in the context of a covenant against a nuisance contained in a lease, it is sometimes the case that the landlord retains no neighbouring land which will be affected if the tenant causes a nuisance at common law: in such circumstances a covenant not to cause an actionable nuisance may have benefit to the landlord even though he suffers no nuisance himself since it may allow him to prevent nuisances to adjoining occupiers and prevent those adjoining occupiers arguing that the landlord has authorised a nuisance by letting the premises to the tenant.[32] Alternatively, the landlord may retain neighbouring land subject to leases which may be affected by the nuisance but not with sufficient "permanence" to entitle him to maintain an action in nuisance as a reversioner: again in such circumstances a restriction upon the committing of tortious nuisance by his tenants may benefit him (or prevent loss, *e.g.* upon the rent review of the neighbouring leases).[33] Accordingly, the precise extent of a covenant against nuisance may depend upon the context in which it is found,

---

[28] (1871) L.R. 11 Eq. 338.
[29] See above, paras 2–001 *et seq.*, for the common law meaning of "nuisance".
[30] (1888) 40 Ch.D. 80.
[31] *ibid.* at 95.
[32] See above, para. 2–018.
[33] See above, para. 2–008.

though the courts are likely to construe this word "according to robust common sense standards".[34]

"Annoyance"

3–055   The word "annoyance" on the other hand, when found in conjunction with the word "nuisance" in a covenant restricting "nuisance and annoyance" will clearly extend to interferences which do not fall within the scope of the law of tortious nuisance: it is settled "that effect must be given to the words 'annoyance or damage' where they occur in addition to the word 'nuisance'"[35] Annoyance means something more than "nuisance". Guidance as to what "annoyance" means was given in *Tod-Heatley v. Benham* by Bowen L.J. who said[36]:

> "if you find a thing which reasonably troubles the mind and pleasure, not of a fanciful person or of a skilled person who knows the truth, but of an ordinary sensible English inhabitant of a house, that seems to me to be an annoyance, although it may not appear to amount to a physical detriment to comfort."

In that case the Court of Appeal (in the context of what it perceived to be the reasonable apprehensions of ordinary sensible people in the late nineteenth century[37]) upheld the decision of Kekewich J. granting an injunction to prevent the establishment of a hospital for the treatment of outdoor patients suffering from "diseases of the throat, nose, ear, skin and eye, fistula and other diseases of the rectum and various deformities of the human frame" intended for poor persons and supported by voluntary contributions in breach of a covenant prohibiting "doing any act which shall or may be or grow to the annoyance, nuisance, grievance or damage of the lessor, his heirs or assigns. . ."

Other matters which have been held to constitute annoyances in breach of covenant have been the running of a school,[38] the business of a

---

[34]   *Hampstead Properties Ltd v. Diomedous* [1969] 1 Ch. 248 at 258, *per* Megarry J.

[35]   *Re Davis and Cavey's Contract* (1888) 40 Ch.D. 601 at 606, *per* Stirling J.

[36]   (1888) 40 Ch.D. 80 at 97. See too *Chorley Borough Council v. Ribble Motor Services* (1996) 74 P. & C.R. 182, CA.

[37]   See also *Bramwell v. Lacey* (1879) 10 Ch.D. 691; and *Watson v. Leamington College* (1880) 25 S.J. 30; *cf. Frost v. The King Edward VII Welsh National Municipal Association, etc.* [1918] 2 Ch. 180 (hospital not "hazardous or noisome or injurious or offensive" in breach of covenant where no risk of infection to neighbours). *cf. National Schizophrenia Fellowship v. Ribble Estates SA* [1994] 03 E.G. 132 (accommodation of schizophrenics in quiescent state not a nuisance or annoyance); see too *C. & G. Homes v. Secretary of State for Health* [1991] Ch. 365, CA. By Leasehold Reform, Housing and Urban Development Act 1993, s.89, any agreement made after the coming into force of that section and which relates to a lease of any property which comprises or includes a dwelling shall be void in so far as it would otherwise have the effect of prohibiting or imposing any restriction on the occupation of the dwelling, or any part of the dwelling, by persons with mental disorders (within the meaning of the Mental Health Act 1983) or the provision of the accommodation for such persons.

[38]   *Kemp v. Sober* (1851) 1 Sim. (N.S.) 517; *Wauton v. Coppard* [1899] 1 Ch. 92 (covenant against "any offensive or disagreeable noise or nuisance"); *cf. Johnstone v. Hall* (1856) 2 K. & J. 414 at 425.

char-a-banc and taxi-cab proprietor,[39] the holding of boxing exhibitions,[40] and the business of a fried-fish shop.[41]

What constitutes an annoyance will depend very much on the context of the acts complained of as well as the demised premises themselves. Thus, in *Heard v. Stuart*[42] the use of premises abutting a church and opposite a church door for the advertisement of, *inter alia*, alcoholic drinks, was an annoyance. In *Wood v. Cooper*[43] a large wooden screen placed just inside the boundary between two houses constituted an annoyance albeit that the defendant argued that its purpose was to prevent his neighbour overlooking his house. On the other hand, in *Our Boys Clothing Co. Ltd v. Holborn Viaduct Land Co. Ltd*[44] where a lessee of a shop put up a large advertisement along the front of its premises advertising a summer sale this was not an annoyance in breach of covenant; and in the case of *Gresham Life Assurance Society Ltd v. Ranger*[45] a blind, permanently lowered outside a shop, which obscured from the public the window displays of a neighbouring shop was held not to be an annoyance to the neighbourhood.

It has also been held to be a breach of a covenant not to do anything which might in the judgment of the landlord be or grow to be to his injury or annoyance or that of his tenants or occupiers to sub-let parts of the demised premises[46] or to convert the demised premises into flats.[47] The use of premises as a brothel will constitute an annoyance.[48]

"Detriment"

A covenant may be imposed to restrict use of land which causes "detriment". It has been held that "detriment" does not consist of purely financial detriment such as the impaired marketability of other property retained by the covenantee.[49]

3–056

"Dangerous and offensive trades"

Covenants are commonly imposed with a view to preventing interference with the enjoyment of land by restricting dangerous and offensive trades on the covenantor's land. Each such covenant will be construed in the context of the land to which it attaches and the transaction by which it

3–057

---

[39] *Ives v. Brown* [1919] 2 Ch. 314 at 321.
[40] *Seaward v. Paterson* (1896) 12 T.L.R. 525.
[41] *Errington v. Birt* (1911) 105 L.T. 373.
[42] (1907) 24 T.L.R. 104.
[43] [1894] 3 Ch. 671.
[44] (1896) 12 T.L.R. 344.
[45] (1899) 15 T.L.R. 454.
[46] *Barton v. Keeble* [1928] Ch. 517.
[47] *Day v. Waldron* (1919) 88 L.J.K.B. 937.
[48] *Mander v. Falcke* [1891] 2 Ch. 554; *Frederick Platts Co. Ltd v. Grigor* [1950] 1 All E.R. 941n, CA. Private sexual immorality may in some circumstances also amount to an annoyance: see *Benton v. Chapman* [1953] C.L.Y. 3099; *Whitbread v. Ward* (1952) 159 E.G. 494.
[49] *C & G Homes v. Secretary of State for Health* [1991] Ch. 365; *National Schizophrenia Fellowship v. Ribble Estates SA* [1994] 03 E.G. 132.

was imposed. Thus, if a particular trade was carried on at the premises when the covenant was imposed, this is a strong indication that the parties did not intend to prohibit that trade by the covenant.[50]

Such a covenant is not necessarily confined to restricting trades which are by their very nature dangerous or offensive. They may extend to trades which in themselves are inoffensive but which are carried out in a dangerous or offensive manner or are (in the particular context) dangerous or offensive.[51] On the other hand, activities which are not offensive in one context may be offensive in others.[52]

"Immoral or illegal" uses

3–058   Covenants are often imposed to prevent immoral or illegal uses with a view to preventing interference with the enjoyment of land.

What is "immoral" will be judged by reference to the kind of conduct which the majority of people in the country would condemn as immoral.[53] Accordingly, use of land for prostitution will be an immoral use[54] but for unmarried people to live together will not be.[55]

Where "illegal" use of land is restricted, it is not necessary for there to be a successful prosecution for there to be a breach of this covenant.[56]

Permitting or suffering a nuisance or annoyance, etc

3–059   If a covenantor simply covenants not to cause a nuisance or annoyance he will only be liable for nuisances or annoyances which he commits himself or by his servants or agents.[57] However, if a covenantor covenants not to "permit" nor to "suffer" a nuisance or annoyance, then he may be liable if a nuisance or annoyance is caused by someone other than himself or his agents (as well as being liable if he carries out the prohibited activity himself.)[58]

In *Tophams Ltd v. Sefton* (a case concerning a covenant not to "permit" the Aintree Racecourse to be used otherwise than for horse-racing and agriculture) the House of Lords considered the meaning of the word "permit". Lord Upjohn said[59]:

[50]   *Gutteridge v. Munyard* (1834) 7 C. & P. 129.
[51]   See *Duke of Devonshire v. Brookshaw* (1899) 81 L.T. 83.
[52]   *Moses v. Taylor* (1862) 11 W.R. 81 (mock auctions: breach); *Duke of Devonshire v. Brookshaw* (1899) 81 L.T. 83 (fried fish shop: breach); *Earl of Pembroke v. Warren* [1896] 1 IR 76 (private hospital: breach) *Knight v. Simmons* [1896] 1 Ch. 653] (public laundry: no breach) *Frost v. King Edward VII Welsh National Municipal Association* [1918] 2 Ch. 180 (well run tuberculosis hospital: no breach).
[53]   *London Scottish Properties v. Mehmet* (1970) 214 Estates Gazette 837.
[54]   *British Petroleum Pension Trust v. Behrent* [1985] 2 E.G.L.R. 97.
[55]   *Heglibiston Establishment v. Heyman* (1977) 36 P. & C.R. 351.
[56]   *Dunraven Securities v. Holloway* [1982] 2 E.G.L.R. 47; see too *Van Haarlem v. Kasner* (1992) 64 P. & C.R. 214, breach of covenant where tenant used property for acts preparatory to spying contrary to Official Secrets Act 1911; *cf. J Davy v. Guy Salmon (Services) Ltd* [1992] E.G.C.S. 89.
[57]   Compare *Tophams Ltd v. Sefton* [1967] 1 A.C. 50, 68; *Berton v. Alliance Economic Investment Co.* [1922] 1 K.B. 742 at 759.
[58]   *Oceanic Village v. United Attractions* [2000] Ch 234.
[59]   [1967] 1 A.C. 50 at 72.

"Apart from authority I would think that outside the sphere of purely polite social language, the word 'permit', used even between laymen bent on serious business, or other affairs intended to have legal consequences, would be used as a word connoting on the part of the one whose permission is asked the right effectively to refuse and on the part of the applicant the necessity to ask for and obtain permission, so as lawfully to undertake the proposed course of action. This, in my view, is its legal meaning."

Similarly Lord Guest said[60]:

"The ordinary meaning of 'to permit' is to give leave for an act to be done which the person permitting has power to prevent."

The majority of the House of Lords in this case relied on dicta of Atkins L.J. in the case of *Berton v. Alliance Economic Investment Co.*[61] that ". . . the word 'permit' means one of two things, either to give leave for an act which without leave could not be legally done, or to abstain from taking reasonable steps to prevent the act, where it is in a man's power to prevent it. Acts which fall short of that, though they be acts of sympathy or assistance, do not amount to permission at any rate in the covenants with which we are dealing."

It seems that the word "suffer" usually means little or no more than to "permit".[62] However, in some contexts, particularly where the word "suffer" together with the word "permit", the former word appears to have a slightly wider meaning.[63] However, the extent to which the two words have a different meaning is not clear.

Where a covenantor does all that can reasonably be done to prevent the acts prohibited by the covenant, it is clear that he will not "permit" or "suffer" that act. Thus, where a tenant covenanted not to do or permit to be done on the premises anything which might become a nuisance, she was not liable for the nuisance caused to the other tenants of the building in which she lived by the persistent telephoning, waiting, shouting and visiting of an admirer: she had installed an answerphone to prevent the persistent ringing of the telephone, she had disconnected the entryphone, and had begun proceedings against the admirer for an injunction.[64]

On the other hand, it is clear that where the covenantor encourages the prohibited act he will also be regarded as having permitted it. Thus, where the covenantor lets premises expressly for the purpose of the prohibited act he will have permitted it.[65]

---

[60] *ibid.* at 68.
[61] [1922] 1 K.B. 742 at 759.
[62] *Berton v. Alliance Economic Investment Co.* [1922] 1 K.B. 742 at 759, *per* Atkin L.J.
[63] *Barton v. Keeble* [1928] Ch. 517; *Barton v. Reed* [1932] 1 Ch. 362 at 375, *per* Luxmoore J. Compare *St Marylebone Property Co. Ltd v. Tesco Stores Ltd* [1988] 2 E.G.L.R. 40.
[64] *Commercial General Administration Ltd v. Thomsett* (1979) 250 E.G. 547.
[65] See *Ives v. Brown* [1919] 2 Ch. 314; *Teape v. Douse* (1905) 92 L.T. 319; *Evans v. Davis* (1878) 10 Ch.D. 747.

Between the two extremes of the covenantor doing all that is reasonably possible to prevent the prohibited act and the coventantee expressly encouraging it, a covenantor may be liable for having permitted the prohibited things either by consenting to those things or failing to take reasonable steps to prevent them. For instance, if the covenantor lets premises without taking a covenant restraining his tenant from the prohibited act, then he will be regarded as having permitted the act if it occurs.[66] Further, a covenantor may be liable for having permitted the prohibited act if he fails to take proceedings where they are reasonably open to him[67]: where however, the proceedings are doubtful, the covenantor will not be liable for having permitted the prohibited act merely by refraining from taking such proceedings.[68] Clearly if a covenantor is able to prevent the prohibited act but deliberately closes his eyes to what is going on, in such circumstances he will be liable for having permitted the prohibited act.[69]

Victims of the nuisance and annoyance

3–060 Some covenants against nuisance and annoyance prohibit nuisance and annoyance to particular persons or classes of persons. Commonly in the context of leases, nuisance and annoyance "to the landlord" or "the landlord's other tenants" is prohibited: there is no problem in such a case in identifying to whom the nuisance or annoyance must be caused before such a covenant is broken. Sometimes, however, the nuisance and annoyance prohibited is expressed to be to "the neighbourhood" or to "adjoining" or "neighbouring" property. In such cases, of course, only the covenantee or his successors in title are entitled to enforce such a covenant. In the case of restrictive covenants relating to freehold land, the covenant can only be enforced against the convenantor's successors where land for the benefit of which the covenant is taken is retained as indicated above at paragraphs 3–011 et seq.: thus such specification of the person to whom the nuisance or annoyance must be caused is usually superfluous.[70] However, in the case of such covenants by tenants in leases, the landlord may enforce the covenant whether or not he retains land near the demised premises: it is wise for a landlord to take such a covenant in order to prevent any argument that he has authorised a nuisance or annoyance caused by his tenant.

What constitutes "the neighbourhood", or "adjoining" or "neighbouring" property, will depend upon the precise circumstances of each

---

[66] See *Tophams Ltd v. Sefton* [1967] 1 A.C. 50; compare *St Marylebone Property Co. Ltd v. Tesco Stores Ltd* [1988] 2 E.G.L.R. 40 and *Prothero v. Bell* (1906) 22 T.L.R. 370. *cf. Toleman v. Portbury* (1870) L.R. 5 Q.B. 288, Ex. Ch., (1872) L.R. 7 Ex. Ch. 344.

[67] *Berton v. Alliance Economic Investment Co. Ltd* [1922] 1 K.B. 742; *Atkin v. Rose* [1923] 1 Ch. 522. See also *Hall v. Ewin* (1887) 37 Ch.D. 74; *Norton v. Charles Deane Productions Ltd* [1970] E.G.D. 268.

[68] *ibid.*

[69] *Borthwick-Norton v. Romney Warwick Estates Ltd* [1950] 1 All E.R. 362, [1950] 1 All E.R. 798, CA.

[70] See *Zetland v. Driver* [1939] Ch. 1, CA.

covenant. The word "adjoining" may be construed not only as meaning physically adjacent, but may be widely construed so as to embrace all those near enough to be affected by the covenantor's conduct.[71]

The judge of what constitutes a nuisance or annoyance

Covenants sometimes contain a prohibition not simply of an "annoyance" **3–061** but of "an annoyance in the opinion of" a specified person. For instance, in *Berton v. Alliance Economic Investment Co. Ltd*[72] there was a covenant against doing "anything which in the judgment of the lessors might be or grow to the injury or annoyance of the lessors". There seems to be no requirement that the person whose opinion is specified must act in a judicial manner, but if the covenant is to be broken the person specified must have formed his opinion,[73] and it is probably implicit that the person forming the opinion must do so in a reasonable manner.[74]

Remedies

Remedies in general are more fully dealt with below. Where covenants **3–062** exist in leases, a landlord may have a right of re-entry or forfeiture for a breach of such a covenant by the tenant.[75] A detailed account of the law of forfeiture is outside the scope of this work. The following points, however, should be noted.

Damages: limits on availability

Whether or not the remedy of damages for breach of covenant is available **3–063** depends upon the nature of the covenant of which enforcement is sought.

Where the covenant is one between landlord and tenant and is enforceable by virtue of privity of contract or privity of estate the usual principles of common law for the assessment of damages for breach of a contract will apply: the covenantee will be entitled to such damages as may reasonably be considered as arising from the breach of covenant itself.[76] There is no reason why this principle should also not apply as between any parties between whom there is privity of contract.

However, where the covenant is one which is enforceable against an owner of freehold land because the burden of the covenant binds him as a successor in title to the covenantor only because of the principles of

---

[71] See *Cobstone Investments Ltd v. Maxim* [1985] Q.B. 140.
[72] [1922] 1 K.B. 742. See also *Barton v. Reed* [1932] 1 Ch. 362 (opinion of the Governors of Dulwich College and their successors); *Zetland v. Driver* [1937] Ch. 652, [1939] Ch. 1 (opinion of vendor and successors in title).
[73] Compare *Zetland v. Driver* [1937] Ch. 652.
[74] Compare *Finchbourne v. Rodrigues* [1976] 3 All E.R. 581 (a case relating to service charge provisions in a lease).
[75] See 1–047, 4–061 (trespass).
[76] See above, para. 4–041.

equity,[77] it will not be possible to obtain common law damages from that successor in title: the successor in title is bound only in equity and thus he will be entitled only to relief afforded by equity[78] which is primarily an injunction, though now damages may be awarded in lieu of an injunction.[79]

Injunctions

3–064　Where a restrictive, negative covenant is enforceable against a covenantor or his successor in title the party entitled to the benefit of the covenant will usually be entitled to restrain breaches of the covenant by injunction[80] and this entitlement will follow regardless of whether the claimant has suffered any substantial damage.[81] It seems that where a covenant is enforceable against a successor in title to the original covenantor an injunction will usually be granted for a breach regardless of whether or not the successor had actual knowledge of the covenant.[82] However, an injunction is a discretionary remedy and the Court may take into account the fact that the defendant was ignorant of the existence of the covenant in determining how to exercise its discretion.[83]

Although injunctions to restrain breaches of covenant will usually follow as a matter of course, the Courts are more reluctant to grant mandatory injunctions requiring positive steps to compel the defendant to comply with his obligations. A discussion of the principles to be applied is found in Chapter 4 below.[84]

Defences and modification of restrictive covenants

3–065　There are a number of points that a defendant may take in his defence to an action alleging a breach of a restrictive covenant in addition to disputing whether the covenant is enforceable, whether or not the alleged acts happened or, if they happened, disputing whether as a matter of construction they are prohibited by the covenant.

First, where a claimant's interest is in reversion, an injunction will probably be refused unless the breach is such as to affect his interest.[85] Secondly, where an injunction is sought the conduct of the claimant may be taken into account.[86]

---

[77] See above, para. 3–014 *et seq.*
[78] See *Kelly v. Barrett* [1924] 2 Ch. 379.
[79] See below, para. 4–084.
[80] *Doherty v. Allman* (1878) 3 App.Cas. 709 at 719, *per* Lord Cairns; *Osborne v. Bradley* [1903] 2 Ch. 446 at 450, 451, *per* Farwell J.; *Elliston v. Reacher* [1908] 2 Ch. 374 at 395, *per* Parker J.
[81] *Doherty v. Allman* (1878) 3 App.Cas. 709, *per* Lord Blackburn; *Richards v. Revitt* (1877) 7 Ch.D. 224; see also *Elliston v. Reacher* [1908] 2 Ch. 274 at 395, *per* Parker J.
[82] *Wilson v. Hart* (1866) L.R. 1 Ch. 463; *Patman v. Harland* (1881) 17 Ch.D. 353 at 360; compare *Kelly v. Barrett* [1924] 2 Ch. 379.
[83] See *Marten v. Flight Refuelling Ltd* [1962] Ch. 115 at 150, *per* Wilberforce J.
[84] See 4–084.
[85] See *Johnstone v. Hall* (1856) 2 K. & J. 414; *Sharp v. Harrison* [1922] 1 Ch. 502.
[86] See para. 4–088 *et seq.* See *Shaw v. Applegate* [1977] 1 W.L.R. 970 in relation to the Court's discretion.

Thirdly, because of the discretionary nature of the Court's power to grant injunctions it may look at whether there have been any changes in the character of the neighbourhood since the covenant of which enforcement is sought was entered.[87] However, the Courts lend particular weight to this factor if the claimant has contributed to the change of the character by its acquiescence.[88]

Fourthly, statute may authorise an interference with the enjoyment of land in breach of covenant.[89]

Fifthly, by section 84(9) of the Law of Property Act 1925:

"(a) where any proceedings by action or otherwise are taken to enforce a restrictive covenant, any person against whom the proceedings are taken may apply to the court for an order giving leave to apply to the Land Tribunal under this section, and staying the proceedings in the meantime."[90]

The Lands Tribunal has a discretion under section 84 of the Law of Property Act 1925 to discharge, vary or modify covenants affecting freehold land[91] and leasehold land where the demise is for a term of more than 40 years and 25 years of the term have expired.[92] The reader is referred to these statutory provisions.[93] It would be surprising if these powers were exercised to discharge, vary or modify a covenant which prohibited the interference with the land of the covenantee and his successors of the sort that has been dealt with in the preceding Chapter. Where restrictive covenants are imposed as planning obligations on land pursuant to section 106 of the Town and Country Planning Act 1990, a statutory mechanism under that Act is provided for the discharge and modification of such covenants upon application to the local planning authority and (on appeal) to the Secretary of State[94]; similarly these provisions are unlikely to be of relevance in connection with the sorts of covenant dealt with above.

---

[87] See *Duke of Bedford's case* (1822) 2 My. & K. 552 at 576.

[88] See *Knight v. Simmonds* [1896] 1 Ch. 653; [1896] 2 Ch. 294; *German v. Chapman* [1877] 7 Ch.D. 271; *Sobey v. Sainsbury* [1913] 2 Ch. 513; *Chatsworth Estates Ltd v. Fewell* [1931] 1 Ch. 224.

[89] *Re Elm Avenue, NewMilton ex p. New Forest District Council* [1984] 1 W.L.R. 1398; *Cadogan v. Royal Brompton Hospital National Health Trust* [1996] 2 E.G.L.R. 115. See in particular Town and Country Planning Act 1990 s.237 in the context of development on land acquired or appropriated for planning purposes.

[90] For cases concerning the exercise of this discretion see *Feilden v. Byrne* [1926] Ch. 620; *Chatsworth Estates Co. v. Fewell* [1931] 1 Ch. 142; *Richardson v. Jackson* [1954] 1 W.L.R.447; *Hanning v. Gable-Jeffreys Properties Ltd* [1965] 1 W.L.R. 1390; *Shepherd Homes v. Sandham* [1971] Ch. 340; *Re Reynold's Application* (1987) 54 P. & C.R. 121; *Re Quartley's Application* (1989) 58 P. & C.R. 518.

[91] Law of Property Act 1925, s. 84(1).

[92] Law of Property Act 1925, s. 84(12).

[93] See generally *Preston and Newsom, Restrictive Covenants* (9th ed.).

[94] See sections 106–106C.

Chapter Four

Common Law remedies for interference with land

"Things without remedy should be without regard"
[Shakespeare, Macbeth]

Introduction

This Chapter deals with the remedies available at common law where **4–001**
there has been a tortious interference with land or an interference in
breach of covenant or contract. Statutory remedies are dealt with in
Chapter 5.

Where an interference is tortious, a claimant may seek damages for any
losses sustained by him[1] and, in the case of trespass where the tortfeasor
enjoys use and occupation of the claimant's land, these may be assessed
as mesne profits on a sui generis basis which resembles a restitutionary
claim[2]. The claimant may also be entitled in equity to injunctive relief or
damages in lieu of an injunction.[3] Where a tortious interference consists of
excluding the claimant from the lawful possession of his land he may seek
an order for possession.[4] In cases both of trespass and nuisance self-help
remedies are also available,[5] albeit with reservations.

Where there is an interference with land in breach a covenant enforceable by reason of privity of contract[6] or by reason of the relationship of
landlord and tenant,[7] both common law damages[8] and injunctive relief (or
damages in lieu of an injunction)[9] may be available. Where, however, an
interference occurs in breach of a covenant enforceable only in equity, an
injunction is the primary remedy, damages being awarded only in lieu of
an injunction.[10]

[1] See paras. 4–002 to 4–056 below.
[2] See paras. 4–017 to 4–019 below.
[3] See paras. 4–084 to 4–104 below.
[4] See paras. 4–057 to 4–083 below.
[5] See paras. 4–105 to 4–122 below.
[6] See paras. 3–003, 3–022 *et seq.*
[7] See paras. 3–023, *et seq.* above.
[8] See paras. 4–041 to 4–056 below.
[9] See paras. 4–100 to 4–103 below.
[10] See paras. 3–008 to 3–015 above and 4–100 to 4–103 below.

Damages

4–002   Damages are available where a tort has been committed. The general principle is *restitutio in integrum*,[11] namely that the Court will award

> "that sum of money which will put the party who has been injured, or who has suffered, in the same position as he would have been in if he had not sustained the wrong for which he is now getting his compensation or reparation"[12]

In addition to compensatory damages, exemplary and aggravated damages may be awarded for tortious interferences with land.[13] Mesne profits may also be awarded for a trespass which results in the tortfeasor enjoying the use and occupation of the claimant's land.[14]

Where there has been a breach of contract and damages are available at common law the general principle is that the claimant is entitled to an award of damages which will place him as far as possible in the same position as if the contract had been performed.[15]

In this section these broad principles are considered as they apply to:

(1)   trespass;

(2)   nuisance; and

(3)   interferences in breach of contract.

The award of damages in lieu of an injunction are considered in the section on injunctions.[16]

(1) Damages for Trespass

General principles

4–003   Proof of actual damage is not required to found an action in trespass: similarly, a claimant suing in trespass may recover nominal damages even though no actual loss has been suffered or proven.[17] Substantial damages are, available of course, where actual loss can be demonstrated and are based on the familiar general principle of providing compensation for that loss suffered (subject to the limitations set out below).[18] The compensatory

---

[11]   See *McGregor on Damages* (16th ed.) Chap. 1, para. 9–18.
[12]   *Livingstone v.. Rawyards Coal Co.* (1880) 5 App Cas 25, 39 *per* Lord Blackburn.
[13]   See paras. 4–023 to 4–030.
[14]   See paras. 4–017 to 4–019.
[15]   See, generally, *McGregor, op. cit.*, and *Chitty on Contracts* (28th ed.) para. 27–001.
[16]   See paras. 4–100 to 4–103.
[17]   *Kelsen v. Imperial Tobacco Co.* [1957] 2 Q.B. 334. On nominal damages, see further below, para. 4–013.
[18]   See *McGregor on Damages* (16th ed.), Chaps 2 and 32 and *Henderson v. Squire* (1869) L.R. 4 Q.B. 170.

approach may, exceptionally, be departed from in the case of exemplary damages.

(1) General principles: measure of damage

The measure of damages in trespass can be classified as follows: 4–004

(a)   mesne profits;

(b)   damage to real property;

(c)   severance of items from the land;

(d)   consequential losses.

(a) Mesne profits

Where the trespass does not cause actual harm but involves a user of land,   4–005
then damages in the form of *mesne profits* are recoverable. These are considered separately below.[19] There does not appear to be any reason in principle why mesne profits cannot be recovered in addition to damages for actual harm caused to property if there have been elements of both wrongful occupation and physical damage.

It should be noted that there are some similarities between an action for mesne profits and an action for use and occupation of the land. Although the two are sometimes used interchangeably, since both are broadly concerned with the recovery of sums for the use and occupation of land, the action for use and occupation is not appropriate to cases of trespass and wrongful use of land since it only arises where a person occupies land with the consent of the owner.[20] Mesne profits, on the other hand, are strictly damages for the *wrongful* use or occupation of land[21] or, where the actual loss cannot be demonstrated, a claim for restitution based on the value of the benefit obtained by the trespasser.[22]

(b) Damage to real property

Where the trespass involves actual physical harm to the land itself, the   4–006
question is more complicated. Although the basic principle is that, so far as possible, the claimant should be put in the same position as he would have been had the tort not occurred, *i.e. restitutio in integrum,*[23]

---

[19] See paras. 4–017 to 4–019.
[20] See *Foa's General Law of Landlord and Tenant* (8th ed.), pp. 403–414 and *Woodfall's Landlord and Tenant*, Vol. 1, Chap. 10.
[21] *Foa*, pp 723–724 and *Woodfall*, Vol. 1, paras. 19.012–19.013.
[22] *Ministry of Defence v. Ashman* (1993) 25 H.L.R. 513, CA and *Ministry of Defence v. Thompson* (1993) 25 H.L.R. 552, CA. These points are discussed in more detail below, paras. 4–017 to 4–019.
[23] *C.R. Taylor (Wholesale) Ltd v. Hepworths Ltd* [1977] 1 W.L.R. 659 at 667, *Stoke-on-Trent City Council v. Wass* [1988] 1 W.L.R. 1406 at 1410, CA, *Dominion Mosaics and Tile Co. Ltd v.*

the measure of damages was restricted for many years to the diminution in value of the claimant's land. Indeed, some still regard the diminution measure as the general basis for assessing damages.[24] However, it may no longer be correct to regard the diminution measure as the starting point[25] since such a measure will not always provide an accurate measure of the loss suffered by the claimant. Indeed, the diminution measure may be seen as reflecting only one aspect of possible losses resulting from trespassers.

Where the diminution measure is applied, it does not include the costs of repairing or replacing those parts of the land damaged except insofar as they may be comprised in the diminution calculation.[26]

Recent decisions concerning the approach to the award of damages for torts to land demonstrate that it is possible to recover damages based on reinstatement costs rather than diminution where reinstatement is a reasonable course of action in the circumstances[27] or, indeed, to recover damages assessed on another basis if this will more properly achieve the principal aim of *restitutio in integrum*.[28]

The justification for the general limitation to the diminution loss was that it prevented a trespasser being held liable in damages for an amount which might well exceed the actual loss in the value of the land.[29] This approach focussed on only one aspect of the claimant's loss, namely the value of the property interest in itself, to the exclusion of other matters incidental to that interest which were not themselves reflected (or fully reflected) in the value of the property. In particular circumstances, the application of the diminution measure can lead to the recovery of damages equal or close to the full repair costs,[30] but this would only occur when these could be proved to be the extent of the diminution and not otherwise.

As a result of applying the diminution measure, a claimant could not receive adequate compensation for such loss of enjoyment and use of the property if it was not reflected in the diminution in value. Accordingly, a claimant might be placed in the disadvantageous position of not being properly compensated, for example, to enable him to repair his property to the standard enjoyed immediately prior to the commission of the trespass. Whilst that approach may be defensible where the claimant intends

---

Trafalgar Trucking Co. Ltd [1990] 2 All E.R. 246, CA, *Farmer Giles Ltd v. Wessex Water Authority* [1990] 1 E.G.L.R. 177, CA at 180F-H and *Swingcastle Ltd v. Alastair Gibson (a firm)* [1991] 2 W.L.R. 1091, HL.

[24] *Salmond & Heuston's Law of Torts* (21st ed.) pp 50–51 and *Clerk & Lindsell* (18th ed.) para. 18–67.

[25] Although a number of recent cases still regard it as the general rule (whilst departing from it): see, *e.g. Ward v. Cannock Chase D.C.* [1982] 2 W.L.R. 660.

[26] *Salmond & Heuston op. cit.* pp 50–51, *Lodge Holes Colliery v. Wednesbury Corporation* [1908] A.C. 323, HL and *Nalder v. Ilford Corporation* [1955] K.B. 822

[27] See below.

[28] *Farmer Giles v. Wessex* [1990] 1 E.G.L.R. 177, CA.

[29] See *Nalder*, above, and *Jones v. Gooday* (1841) 8 M. & W. 146.

[30] *e.g.* where the market value of a house was reduced by the level of repair costs which a prospective purchaser would have to pay and, in the prevailing market would be able to demand as a reduction in the price equivalent to the repair costs.

to sell the land or to redevelop,[31] it is clearly not so where he wishes to remain in possession and continued enjoyment has been impaired by the trespass for which full repair value is not awarded. Indeed, to restrict the award of damages to a diminution measure may mean that a claimant is no longer able to use and enjoy the property damaged or to sell that property and obtain an adequate alternative.[32]

In consequence of this, more recent decisions have moved away from such a rigid approach to assessment of damages for torts to land. It appears now to be widely accepted that an award based on the cost of reinstating the land can be made where expenditure on repairs or rebuilding is reasonable in all the circumstances.[33] The guiding principle is whether the claimant has suffered loss and, if so, what measure would best achieve complete restitution (so far as monetary compensation is capable). For example, in *C.R. Taylor (Wholesale) Ltd v. Hepworths Ltd*[34] damages were not recovered[35] for a fire which destroyed the claimants' billiard hall since not only was it held solely for its redevelopment potential but the claimants had been saved the costs of demolition.[36] A similar result was reached in *Hole & Son (Sayers Common) v. Harrisons of Thurnscoe*[37] where a lorry had demolished cottages which merely "provided the claimant company with the opportunity to do that which they had previously had the intention of doing at their own expense, namely to build themselves new premises and to demolish the existing cottages" and consequently were awarded damages, not for the costs of rebuilding, but only in respect of temporary repairs and loss of rent. Although the learned judge considered the question of diminution measure as opposed to reinstatement costs, he did not have to apply either since he was satisfied that the claimant had suffered no significant loss in any event.

---

[31] *Taylor (Wholesale) v. Hepworths* [1977] 1 W.L.R. 659.

[32] Which would have occurred in *Ward v. Cannock Chase D.C.* [1982] 2 W.L.R. 660 had the court not awarded damages based on the costs of reinstatement. See below, para. 4–007.

[33] *McGregor, op. cit.,* paras 1474–1481; *Clerk & Lindsell, op. cit.,* para. 18–67; *Winfield & Jolowicz's Law of Tort* (15th ed.), pp 786–792; *Hollebone v. Midhurst and Fernhurst Builders* [1968] 1 Lloyd's Rep. 38; *Hole & Son (Sayers Common) v. Harrisons of Thurnscoe* [1973] 1 Lloyd's Rep. 345; *Dodd Properties (Kent) Ltd v. Canterbury City Council* [1980] 1 W.L.R. 433, CA at 456–457; *Ward v. Cannock Chase D.C.* [1982] 2 W.L.R. 660; *Dominion Mosaics and Tile Co. Ltd v. Trafalgar Trucking Co. Ltd* [1990] 2 All E.R. 246, CA and *Farmer Giles Ltd v. Wessex Water Authority* [1990] 1 E.G.L.R. 177, CA at 180F-H which goes further in pursuing a flexible approach to assessment. Although statements of principle in most of the cases cited above are made in the context of negligence actions, they can properly be taken to apply to trespass to land since they are expressed in general terms of torts causing damage to real property (see, *e.g. Dodd Properties* at 456 G-H and *Dominion Mosaics* at 249E). In any event, *Farmer Giles* was a case of trespass to land.

[34] [1977] 1 W.L.R. 659.

[35] Save of a consequential nature, *i.e.* clearing the debris, immediate remedial works and other minor sums.

[36] That approach is also consistent with the diminution measure since the value of the property lay in the development land and not in the billiard hall and the fire had not only failed to cause any damage to the development value but had provided a positive advantage to the claimants by destroying the hall.

[37] [1973] 1 Lloyd's Rep. 345.

4–007   In considering whether to award damages on a reinstatement cost basis, the court must be satisfied[38]:

(i)   the claimant genuinely intends to reinstate the land (and is legally able to do so); and

(ii)   it is reasonable for the claimant to seek reinstatement.

Question (i) is a matter of fact[39] and includes consideration of whether the claimant is legally able to rebuild. If a claimant is unable to build, then it is unlikely that a court will award damages on the reinstatement basis. In *Nalder v. Ilford Corporation*,[40] Sellers J. refused to award damages equivalent to the cost of putting up demolished buildings since the condition in which the former buildings had existed infringed by-laws and "it would be wrong to assess the damages as the cost of putting up once again a structure which would rightly be the subject-matter of complaint." In *Ward v. Cannock Chase D.C.*,[41] a question arose as to whether planning permission was required to carry out the rebuilding necessary and, if so, whether it would be granted. Scott J. made the award of damages on a reinstatement basis dependent upon whether planning permission was obtained (or determined not to be required) by the time of the assessment of the damages.[42]

Question (ii) requires the court to consider matters such as the financial and other implications of reinstatement as compared with the diminution measure, the nature and use of the property, the wrongful act causing the damage and the conduct of the parties. It also appears to be necessary to read these requirements in the context of the award of reinstatement costs being "exceptional" and a departure from the general diminution measure.[43] In *Ward v. Cannock Chase*,[44] Scott J. considered it reasonable to require the defendant council to repair two cottages which were of particular importance to the claimant since he required accommodation for a large family and to keep livestock. The council had been ordered by the court to repair the cottages but had not done so and had intentionally allowed them to fall into a state of severe dilapidation, and the claimant was unable to sell or repair them.

4–008   Other decisions indicate that the award of reinstatement costs may simply be an expression of the general rule, *i.e.* that damages are intended to

---

[38] See, *e.g. Ward v. Cannock Chase*, above, at 682–687 and, further, *Perry v. Sidney Phillips & Son* [1982] 3 All E.R. 705, CA where the reinstatement basis was abandoned since the claimant had sold the house prior to the hearing of the appeal.

[39] See *Hole & Son (Sayers Common) v. Harrisons of Thurnscoe*, above, n. 36, where the learned judge was not only not satisfied of this intention but also found that the claimant intended the opposite, *i.e.* to demolish.

[40] [1951] K.B. 822, at 830.

[41] [1982] 2 W.L.R. 660, at 686.

[42] By an Official Referee: [1986] 2 W.L.R. 660 at 686.

[43] See *Munnelly v. Calcon Ltd* [1978] I.R. 387 at 399–401 as approved and adopted by Scott J. in *Ward v. Cannock Chase*, above, at 684–6.

[44] [1982] 2 W.L.R. 660.

put the claimant in the position as if the tort had not occurred.[45] Indeed, with an increasing attention given to providing an award which properly meets the requirements of *restitutio in integrum*, the time has now come for a clear recognition[46] that there is no general rule based on diminution and that reinstatement costs are not "exceptional". The only proper question is to consider what damages will properly achieve full compensation for the wrong suffered by the claimant in the particular case. On that footing, diminution and reinstatement damages may not be the only alternatives. In *Farmer Giles Ltd v. Wessex Water Authority*,[47] where the trespass of the defendant in excavating a river bed caused the collapse of part of the claimant's premises into the river, it was argued that the court had only two alternatives: to award damages based on diminution measure or on the costs of reinstatement. The Court of Appeal rejected this contention and Purchas L.J. held:

> "I cannot accept that the law relating to damages in tort for trespass to property can be so simply stated. The trial judge rightly, in my view, approached the problem from the long recognised maxim *restitutio in integrum* . . . Obviously there may be cases in which the damages required to put the victim back into the position in which he would have been will be the same as the market value of the property concerned. On the other hand, there may be cases in which the victim cannot be put back into the position which he enjoyed unless there is complete physical reinstatement achieved or the cost of so doing. These two propositions do not mean, however, that the judge, in calculating the damages in accordance with the maxim, must look at one or other alternative . . . In my view, Peter Pain J. was correct when he said that he was not obliged to choose between the two alternative approaches."

The Court accordingly upheld the trial judge's award of the capitalised loss of rental from which was deducted the costs of refurbishment and the value of a cleared site and to which were added various relatively minor and consequential losses.

In *Dominion Mosaics and Tile Co. Ltd v. Trafalgar Trucking Co. Ltd*[48] the claimant's premises were damaged by fire caused by the defendant's contractors. The Court of Appeal, applying the principle of *restitutio in integrum*, rejected the application of the diminution measure in the circumstances and upheld an award of damages to the claimant based on the costs expended by it in acquiring new premises since the claimant had reasonably required premises to carry on business and the early provision

---

[45] See May J. in *Taylor v. Hepworths* [1977] 1 W.L.R. 659 at 667 and *Munnelly v. Calcon* [1978] I.R. 387 at 399–400 as adopted by Scott J. in *Ward v. Cannock Chase D.C.*, above, at 685–6B.

[46] See Purchas L.J. in the *Farmer Giles* case, below.

[47] [1990] 1 E.G.L.R. 177, CA. See in particular 178M–179J (Russell L.J.) and the passage from Purchas L.J.'s judgment cited below.

[48] [1990] 2 All E.R. 246, CA.

of a new building had mitigated its loss of profits. The court did not consider it necessary to reduce the damages as a result of the claimant's having acquired slightly better premises since there was no deliberate attempt to obtain better premises but merely to obtain existing premises which most nearly matched the claimant's requirements. Moreover, against the betterment there could be set the mitigation of loss of profits achieved by the quicker finding of alternative premises and the cost of adapting them for the claimant's purposes.

(c) Severance of items from the land

4–009   A particular problem in the assessment of damages for trespass arises where part of the land (*e.g.* a mineral) is severed by the trespasser from the land itself. In such circumstances, since the item severed has ceased to be part of the land it becomes (or reverts to being) a chattel, which may be worth more or less than it was when it formed part of the land from which it was severed. A question then arises as to whether damages should be assessed by reference to the value of the chattel as severed or by reference to the damage caused to the value of the land by reason of the severance.

In fact, there appears to be a choice of causes of action in that a claimant may sue for the conversion of the items once they have been severed from the land and taken away, or in trespass for the diminution in the value of the land itself. However, this would not allow a claimant to recover twice over for the same loss simply by suing in both trespass and conversion.[49]

In the case of the severance of minerals, a particular distinction is drawn in awarding damages between the case where the minerals have been severed *wilfully* and the case where the severance arises involuntarily, or by a mistake. In the latter case, a much less strict line is taken with regard to damages whereas, in the case of wilful severance, an approach akin to awarding exemplary damages is taken.[50]

In the case of *wilful severance* of minerals, the claimant is entitled to elect between the value of the chattels and the diminution to the land from which they were severed. As a result, the claimant may choose whichever measure will give him the larger damages. Further, notwithstanding the fact that the trespasser will have expended time and effort in removing the minerals and in taking them to the surface of the land, and that the claimant, had he mined the minerals himself would have incurred similar costs, the damages do not take into account the costs of winning and working, *i.e.* there is a punitive element to the damages in that the claimant recovers the full market value of the mineral without any discount for the costs of obtaining it. This appears to be an aspect both of a

---

[49] See *Unlawful Mining*, para. 4–011, below.
[50] See paras. 4–023 to 4–030, below. Indeed, Lord Diplock in *Broome v. Cassell & Co. Limited* [1972] A.C. 1027, HL at 1129B–D cited the severance cases as an example of punitive damages.

punitive approach and the notion of not permitting a wrongdoer to rely on his own wrongdoing.

As Lord Blackburn said in *Livingstone v. The Rawyards Coal Co.*[51]:

> "When something that was part of the realty (we are talking of coal in this particular case) is severed from the realty and converted into a chattel, then instantly on its becoming a chattel, it becomes the property of the person who had been the owner of the fee in the land whilst it remained a portion of the land; and then, in estimating the damages against a person who had carried away that chattel, it was considered and decided that the owners of the fee were to be paid the value of the chattel at the time when it was converted, and it would in fact have been improper, as qualifying his own wrong, to allow the wrongdoer anything for that mischief which he had done, or for that expense which he had incurred in converting the piece of rock into a chattel, which he had no business to do."

Where the trespass was not wilful, then a less punitive rule is applied and the claimant is only entitled to recover the diminution in the value of his land brought about by the removal of the mineral. The reason for this milder rule was stated by Lord Hatherley in *Jegon v. Vivian*[52]:

> "I think that the mild rule of law is certainly that which ought to guide this Court, subject to any case made of a special character which would induce the Court to swerve from it; otherwise, on the one hand, a trespass might be committed with impunity if the rule *in poenam* were not insisted upon; so, on the other hand, persons might stand by and see their coal worked, being spared the expense of winning and getting it."

This measure is based upon the value of the unworked mineral, *i.e.* as it lay *in situ* and such value would be measured by reference to considerations such as the value of the coal when worked, together with the costs of winning and working the mineral and bringing it to the surface.[53] It does not appear that the distinction between wilful and mistaken or accidental severance is confined to cases of trespass to coal[54] and should apply

---

[51] (1880) 5 App.Cas. 25, HL at 40 and see *Bulli Coal Mining Co. v. Osborne* [1899] A.C. 351, PC.

[52] (1871) L.R. 6 Ch. 742 at 762.

[53] See, *e.g. Livingstone v. The Rawyards Coal Company* (1880) 5 App.Cas. 25, HL, *Peruvian Guano Co. Limited v. Dreyfus Brothers & Co.* [1892] A.C. 166, HL at 173–177 (Lord Macnaghten) and *Trotter v. Maclean* (1879) 13 Ch.D. 574.

[54] See *Peruvian Guano Co. Limited v. Dreyfus Brothers & Co.*, above, at 176 *per* Lord Macnaghten "Those observations [Lord Cairns in *Livingstone v. The Rawyards Coal Company* (1880) 5 App.Cas. 25, H.L. at 32] . . . seem to me to be of the greatest importance, because I do not understand that they are necessarily confined to the case of coal trespass." Indeed, in the *Peruvian Guano* case, the principles were applied to the detention of cargoes of guano.

to the severance of any items from land, *e.g.* the cutting and severing of timber or other crops.[55]

The stricter rule appears to apply only in cases of "wilful and clandestine" mining and not to cases where the mining has occurred by reason of the trespasser's mistake[56] or where the trespasser was under the bona fide belief that he was about to obtain a contract authorising the mining.[57] It is possible to satisfy the milder rule even if there is no belief as to a current right to work the mineral: *Townend v. Askern Coal and Iron Company*[58] involved a trespass by the working of coal under adjoining property before the relevant statutory authorisation had been obtained. However, since the defendants were making an application for the relevant authorisation which was shortly afterwards obtained, Farwell J. awarded damages on the "non-wilful" basis.

(d) Consequential losses

4–010 Although there is scant authority on the recovery of consequential losses in trespass, there appears to be no reason in principle why they should not be recoverable in accordance with general principles.[59] In *Henderson v. Squire*[60] the landlord recovered from a tenant who had held over following the expiry of the term without consent not only mesne profits for the full value of the premises but also the costs of ejecting a sub-tenant to whom part of the premises had been let by the tenant.

In *Whitwham v. Westminster Brymbo Coal and Coke Co.*[61] the defendant had trespassed on part of the claimant's land by the tipping of soil and had thereby rendered the remainder of the land of limited use. The claimant not only recovered damages representing the diminution in the value of that part of the land upon which the soil had been tipped but also damages representing the diminution in value of the remainder of the land the use of which had been impaired.

It is also possible to recover damages arising out of anxiety, inconvenience and distress caused by the commission of the tort.[62] In the absence of medical evidence and special damage these damages are likely to be modest. However, since there is a considerable overlap with claims for exemplary or aggravated damages,[63] the sums may be much higher if the conduct of the tortfeasor is dealt with in the context of those damages.

---

[55] See, *e.g. Wasson v. California Standard Co.* (1964) 47 D.L.R. (2d) 71.

[56] *e.g. Livingstone v. The Rawyards Coal Company*, above.

[57] *Trotter v. Maclean* (1879) 13 Ch.D. 574.

[58] [1934] 1 Ch. 463.

[59] See *e.g. Rust v. Victoria Graving Dock Co.* (1887) 36 Ch.D. 113, and *Ward v. Cannock Chase D.C.* [1982] 2 W.L.R. 660, at 687–689, where the claimant also recovered damages for the cost of obtaining alternative accommodation and removal costs prior to the completion of the repair works. See also cases concerning loss of rent where premises are damaged, *e.g. Birch v. Clifford* (1891) 8 T.L.R. 103 and *Harris v. Hall*, The Independent, August 18, 1992.

[60] (1869) L.R. 4 Q.B. 170.

[61] [1896] 2 Ch. 538.

[62] *Millington v. Duffy* (1984) 17 H.L.R. 232, CA.

[63] See below, paras. 4–023 to 4–030.

(2) General Principles: unlawful mining

Where minerals have been taken from land or from below the surface of **4–011** the land of another without authorisation the main claim will usually be one for conversion of the minerals, but there may also be incidental claims in nuisance and trespass. Of course, the entry onto or beneath the land of another without due authority is a trespass and insofar as any damage is inflicted to the land itself there may be a claim for trespass damages.[64] However, damages for trespass will not always be awarded if to do so would effectively permit the claimant to recover twice over for his losses:

> "As it would necessarily follow, when you took away the coals that were below the land, that the surface of the land would come down, you must not take the sum which would be given as compensation for the injury to the surface twice over. You must not take that sum as being a matter which you are to be paid for, and also take the coals as if they had been got out without damage."[65]

The issue of damages in trespass for severance of the mineral is considered above.[66] Exemplary damages may be awarded in exceptional cases of such trespass, as is considered below.[67]

(3) General principles: negligence and nuisance

The overlap between remedies in damages in both trespass and conver- **4–012** sion has already been noted in connection with the mining cases, above. However, it is also quite possible for there to be a remedy in trespass where there has been the commission of a nuisance or an act of negligence in relation to land. The difficult question of intention and trespass,[68] and the fact that negligence is sufficient to establish trespass,[69] makes the possibility of overlap between the two torts a real one, although negligence as a tort can only be established upon proof of actual damage whereas trespass requires no such proof.

(4) General principles: nominal damages

Since trespass is actionable *per se* and loss is presumed, if the claimant fails **4–013** to establish that he has suffered actual damage[70], he may be awarded

---

[64] *Jegon v. Vivian* (1871) L.R. 6 Ch. App. 742 and *Livingstone v. Rawyards Coal Co.* (1880) 5 App.Cas. 25.
[65] per Lord Blackburn in *Livingstone v. Rawyards Coal Co.*, above.
[66] At para. 4–009.
[67] See paras. 4–023 to 4–030.
[68] See paras. 1–036 to 1–038.
[69] *League Against Cruel Sports v. Scott* [1986] 1 Q.B. 240.
[70] In *Nalder v. Ilford Corporation* [1951] K.B. 822, at 830–831, Sellers J. awarded nominal general damages since the claimant had failed to prove loss based on the correct diminution measure.

only a nominal sum, even though he has in all respects succeeded in his action and has established his right against the defendant.[71] Although the general rule is that the costs of an action follow the event,[72] costs are usually a matter for the court's discretion: where there is an award of nominal damages there is a risk that the court may not award the claimant his costs.[73] However, in such a case, the court will generally not order the claimant to pay the costs of the other parties unless the claimant has been guilty of some form of misconduct.[74] If the claimant seeks substantial relief other than, or in addition to, damages[75] then the risk of the claimant not being awarded costs is significantly reduced — provided that the other claims are well-founded.

(5) General principles: time at which damages should be assessed

4–014   Although the time at which damages should be assessed was, tradition- ally, the date of the commission of the wrong a more flexible approach is now taken and the courts now assess damages in such a way as will achieve full compensation to the claimant for the loss suffered.[76] As has already been noted above, the overriding principle is that the injured party should be put in the same position as if the wrong had not occurred and, such a principle should be applicable not only to the quantum of loss but also to the time of assessment. In *County Personnel (Employment Agency) Ltd v. Alan R Pulver & Co.,*[77] Bingham L.J. stated:

> "While the general rule undoubtedly is that damages for tort or breach of contract are assessed at the date of the breach (see, for example, *Milliangos v. George Frank (Textiles) Ltd* [1976] A.C. 443 at p. 468 *per* Lord Wilberforce), this rule should not be mechanistically

---

[71] In contexts other than trespass, see *Ashby v. White* (1703) 2 Ld. Raym. 938 and *Constantine v. Imperial London Hotels* [1944] K.B. 693.

[72] See s. 51 of the Supreme Court Act 1981, C.P.R. Part 44 and, for example, *Donald Campbell & Co. Ltd v. Pollack* [1927] A.C. 732, HL, *Scherer v. Counting Instruments Ltd* [1986] 1 W.L.R. 615n, CA and *Aiden Shipping Ltd v. Interbulk Ltd* [1986] A.C. 965, HL.

[73] *Anglo-Cyprian Trade Agencies Ltd v. Paphos Wine Industries Ltd* [1951] 1 All E.R. 873 (a contract case) and *Texaco Ltd v. Arco Technology inc., The Times,* October 13, 1989.

[74] *Kierson v. Thompson & Sons Ltd* [1913] 1 K.B. 587 and, in the context of contract, see *Anglo-Cyprian Trade Agencies Ltd v. Paphos Wine Industries Ltd* [1951] 1 All E.R. 873. How- ever, a defendant in a case of likely nominal damages may seek to pre-empt the decision of the court by making a payment into court of a nominal sum: if the claimant does not take the payment and nominal damages are then awarded, the defendant will receive his costs as from the date of payment in. See C.P.R. Part 36, which sets out the procedure to be used when making settlement offers, *Cutts v. Head* [1984] 1 All E.R. 597 at 610 and *Corby District Council v. Hoist & Co. Ltd* [1985] 1 W.L.R. 427, CA. It is open to question whether this approach should be reassessed in the light of the C.P.R. regime, although the operation of the overriding objective in C.P.R. Part I may lead to a different result if the facts of the case warrant it.

[75] *e.g.* an injunction or claim for possession.

[76] As with the traditional diminution measure of damages, above. See, *e.g. Dodd Properties Ltd v. Canterbury City Council* [1980] 1 W.L.R. 433, CA and *County Personnel (Employment Agency) Ltd v. Alan R. Pulver & Co.* [1986] 2 E.G.L.R. 246, CA at 249H-M.

[77] [1986] 2 E.G.L.R. 246, CA, at 249L-M.

applied in circumstances where assessment at another date may more accurately reflect the overriding compensatory rule . . ."

Indeed, if that general principle were not applied to permit flexibility with regard to the time for assessment then, as with the inflexible application of the diminution measure,[78] a claimant might find that he were not fully compensated for the loss actually suffered, e.g. where the costs of repairing the effects of a trespass escalate from the time of the commission of the wrong and the date of assessment. If the former were awarded, then the claimant would be unable to repair the effects of the wrong and would not have been adequately compensated.[79] On the other hand, if the costs reduced between the date of the trespass and assessment, there is no good reason why the claimant should receive a windfall through over-compensation.

(6) General principles: prospective losses and continuing wrongs

See Chapter 1, paragraph 1–043 and Chapter 4, paragraphs 4–037 and 4–038.

4–015

(7) General principles: remoteness

This issue is not frequently encountered in the context of trespass to land, perhaps due to the association of trespass with direct wrongdoing. A consideration of the general principles can be found under *Nuisance*,[80] below.

4–016

Wrongful occupation or use

An action for *mesne profits*, traditionally considered to be a particular species of damages for trespass[81] but recently considered to resemble a restitutionary remedy,[82] will arise where a party is wrongfully deprived of his use of land by the occupation of another: typically, such an action is brought together with an action for the recovery of land from the trespasser, although it may be brought independently. The action for mesne profits is an action which relates back to the commencement of the unlawful occupation.[83] Thus, a landlord may sue a tenant for mesne profits from the date of forfeiture of the lease until the time when possession is given. A claimant seeking to recover mesne profits, however, must elect whether to seek damages for a loss actually suffered or to seek the benefit which the unlawful occupier has obtained through the trespass.[84]

4–017

---

[78] See above, paras 4–006 to 4–008.
[79] See *Dodd Properties Ltd v. Canterbury City Council* [1980] 1 W.L.R. 433, CA.
[80] See below, para. 4–039.
[81] See, *e.g. Halsbury's Laws*, Vol. 12(1), para. 870.
[82] *Ministry of Defence v. Ashman* (1993) 25 H.L.R. 513, CA and *Ministry of Defence v. Thompson* (1993) 25 H.L.R. 552, CA and the discussion below.
[83] Trespass by relation is discussed above, para. 1–004.
[84] *Ministry of Defence v. Ashman* (1993) 25 H.L.R. 513, CA, at 518 and 519–20 (Lloyd L.J. dissenting on this point), and *Ministry of Defence v. Thompson* (1993) 25 H.L.R. 552, CA, at 554.

(1) Wrongful use and occupation: general measure

4–018   Regardless of whether the claimant would actually have used the land in question, he is entitled to recover a sum representing the fair value of the use of that land for the period for which it is used by the trespasser.[85] The basic principles governing the assessment of mesne profits were considered in *Clifton Securities Ltd v. Huntley*,[86] where Denning J. stated:

> "At what rate are the mesne profits to be assessed? When the rent represents the fair value of the premises, mesne profits are to be assessed at the amount of the rent, but, if the value is higher than the rent, then the mesne profits must be assessed at the higher value. In this case, the real value of the premises at the material time was £300 a year and the mesne profits are to be taken at that rate."

Further, the recovery of mesne profits does not depend on proof by the landowner that he would, or could, have let the premises. In *Swordheath Properties Ltd v. Tabet*[87] the trial judge declined to award damages since the claimant had failed to adduce evidence that it could or would have been able to let the premises during the period of the wrongful occupation. The Court of Appeal allowed an appeal from that decision and, in giving the judgment of the court, Megaw L.J. stated:

> "It appears to me to be clear, both as a matter of principle and of authority, that in a case of this sort the plaintiff, when he has established that the defendant has remained on as a trespasser in residential property, is entitled, without bringing evidence that he could or would have let the property to someone else in the absence of the trespassing defendant, to have as damages for the trespass the value of the property as it would fairly be calculated; and, in the absence of anything special in the particular case it would be the ordinary letting value of the property that would determine the amount of the damages."[88]

An even more striking example of this principle (sometimes referred to as "the user principle") is to be found in the Court of Appeal's decision in *Penarth Dock Engineering Co. Ltd v. Pounds*[89] which was considered in *Swordheath*. In the *Penarth* case, the owner of a dock recovered damages from a trespasser who failed to remove a pontoon although the owner

---

[85] *Stoke-on-Trent City Council v. W & J Wass Ltd* [1988] 1 W.L.R. 1406 at 1410–1411, CA, where the Court referred to this method of assessing damages as "the user principle": see 1416D-E (Nicholls L.J.).

[86] [1948] 2 All E.R. 283, at 284.

[87] [1979] 1 W.L.R. 285, CA. See also *Dean and Chapter of Canterbury Cathedral v. Whitbread plc* [1995] 1 E.G.L.R. 82.

[88] *ibid*, at 288D-E.

[89] [1963] 1 Lloyd's Rep. 359.

had suffered no actual loss since it would not have made use of the dock in any event. Although Megaw L.J. in *Swordheath* appeared to restrict his remarks to trespassers of residential premises, the *Penarth* decision makes it clear that this approach applies equally to business properties. There appears to be no reason in principle why a similar approach should not be followed regardless of the nature or character of the land occupied.

Further, although the basis of this approach appeared to depart from the principle that damages are generally awarded to compensate for actual loss, the Court of Appeal in the two *Ministry of Defence* cases[90] put mesne profits partly on the footing of a restitutionary remedy for the recovery of a benefit which the trespasser has obtained where an appropriate election is made by the landowne,[91] — although this analysis did not receive the complete endorsement of the House of Lords in *Attorney-General v. Blake*.[92] The approach was expressed by Hoffmann L.J. in the *Thompson* case[93] as follows:

"The principles in *Ashman* may, in my judgment, be summarised as follows: first, an owner of land which is occupied without his consent may elect whether to claim damages for the loss which he has been caused or restitution of the value of the benefit which the defendant has received.

Secondly, the fact that the owner if he had obtained possession would have let the premises at a concessionary rent, or even would not have let them at all, is irrelevant to the calculation of the benefit for the purposes of a restitutionary claim. What matters is the benefit the defendant has received.

Thirdly, a benefit may be worth less to an involuntary recipient than to one who has a free choice as to whether to remain in occupation or move elsewhere.

Fourthly, the value of the right of occupation to a former licensee who has occupied at a concessionary rent and who has remained in possession only because she could not be rehoused by the local authority until a possession order has been made, would ordinarily be whichever is the higher of the former concessionary rent and what she would have paid for local authority housing suitable for her needs if she had been rehoused by the time when the notice expired."

---

[90] *Ministry of Defence v. Ashman* (1993) 25 H.L.R. 513, CA and *Ministry of Defence v. Thompson* (1993) 25 H.L.R. 552, CA. In *Ashman*, Lloyd L.J. had dissented on this point but the subsequent decision of the Court in *Thompson* was unanimous. Hoffmann L.J., who had been in the majority in *Ashman*, gave the judgment of the Court in *Thompson*.
[91] See Goff & Jones, *The Law of Restitution* (5th ed.), pp. 775–786 and *Phillips v. Homfray* (1883) 24 Ch.D. 439, CA, criticised in Goff & Jones, but relied upon by Lloyd L.J. in his dissent in *Ashman* (1993) 25 H.L.R. 513, CA, at 521.
[92] [2001] 1 A.C. 268, see further below.
[93] (1993) 25 H.L.R. 552, CA, at 554.

However, the "user principle"[94] cannot be precisely categorised and is neither exclusively restitutionary nor exclusively compensatory. In *Inverugie Investments v. Richard Hackett*[95] Lord Lloyd, giving the opinion of the Privy Council, stated:

"In *Stoke-on-Trent City Council v. W & J Wass Limited* . . . Nicholls L.J., as he then was, called the underlying principle in these cases the 'user principle'. The Plaintiff may not have suffered any actual loss by being deprived of the use of his property. But under the user principle he is entitled to recover a reasonable rent for the wrongful use of his property by the trespassers. Similarly, the trespasser may not have derived any actual benefit from the use of the property. But under the user principle he is obliged to pay a reasonable rent for the use which he has and enjoyed. The principle need not be characterised as exclusively compensatory, or exclusively restitutionary; it combines elements of both. If this is the correct principle, how does it apply . . .

. . . The point is not altogether easy. But their Lordships have concluded that Mr Mowbray's argument is to be preferred. If a man hires a concrete mixer, he must pay the daily hire, even though he may not in the event have been able to use the mixer because of rain. So also must a trespasser who takes the mixer without the owner's consent. He must pay the going rate, even though in the event he has derived no benefit from the use of the mixer. It makes no difference whether the trespasser is a professional builder or, a do-it-yourself enthusiast. The same applies to residential property . . ."

In *Attorney-General v. Blake*,[96] the House of Lords considered (in the context of breach of confidence) the status of recovery under "the user principle" in the general context of remedies. After drawing an analogy with the recovery of reasonable royalties in intellectual property law, Lord Nicholls stated:

"This principle is established and not controversial. More difficult is the alignment of this measure of damages within the basic compensatory measure. Recently there has been a move towards applying the label of restitution to awards of this character: see, for instance, *Ministry of Defence v. Ashman* [1993] 2 E.G.L.R. 102, 105 and *Ministry of Defence v. Thompson* [1993] 2 E.G.L.R. 107. However that may be, these awards cannot be regarded as conforming to the strictly compensatory measure of damage for the injured person's loss unless loss is given a strained and artificial meaning. The reality is that the injured person's rights were invaded but, in financial

---

[94] See *Stoke-on-Trent City Council v. W & J Wass Ltd* [1988] 1 W.L.R. 1406, CA.
[95] [1995] 1 W.L.R. 713, PC. Lord Lloyd gave the dissenting judgment in *Ashman*.
[96] [2001] 1 A.C. 268.

terms, he suffered no loss. Nevertheless, the common law has found a means to award him a sensibly calculated amount of money. Such awards are probably best regarded as an exception to the general rule."

Since the context of the *Blake* case was that of breach of confidence, the consideration given to the nature of mesne profits was only as an example of a non-compensatory award of damages. It leaves a degree of uncertainty with regard to the Court of Appeal's restitutionary analysis, although Lord Nicholls did not criticise that analysis in terms.

(2) Wrongful use and occupation: quantum

The assessment of the quantum of the mesne profits claim will depend on whether the claimant elects to pursue a true damages claim or the alternative restitutionary remedy.[97] The need to elect requires a careful assessment to be made by the claimant prior to such election as to: **4–019**

(a)   whether actual loss can be proved and, if so, how much;

(b)   what is and/or was the likely benefit of the wrongful occupation to the occupier; and

(c)   whether (b) is likely to exceed (a).

In cases where there is little chance that the property would have been re-let, or occupied for a consideration, the landowner may have little difficulty in electing to pursue the restitutionary claim. In other cases, however, the decision may be more complicated. Although the language of election has been used by the Court of Appeal,[98] it does not appear that such election between the types of mesne profits claim has to be made prior to the hearing although, a choice should generally be made by the conclusion of the hearing. It is not clear whether the claimant will be allowed to plead both bases of claim in the alternative and elect during the course of the action or at the hearing. Since the question of value to the trespasser may depend on subjective factors unknown to the claimant prior to the action, it would be fairer not to insist on an irrevocable election until the claimant has at least had an opportunity to consider the trespasser's evidence. If this basis of claim is to be regarded as truly that of the recovery of a benefit following the "waiving of the tort"[99] then it

---

[97]   Assuming, following *Blake*, that this approach can be followed. The debate over the categorisation of mesne profits does not appear to affect the approach in the *Ministry of Defence* cases.

[98]   See the two *Ministry of Defence* cases, (1993) 25 H.L.R. 513, and (1993) 25 H.L.R. 552.

[99]   Goff & Jones, *op. cit.*, pp. 773–775.

appears that an election to seek restitution is not final until judgment is satisfied.[1]

(a) Quantum of damages for actual loss

4–020   In accordance with usual principle, if the property had been let prior to the wrongful occupation (or where the occupier is the former tenant of the property), the rent[2] will provide a useful guide to the damages to be awarded. However, as the *Clifton* decision makes clear, the former rent is a guide only and may be displaced by proof of greater loss — "the real value" — which is particularly important in a period of rising property prices.[3] The more "historic" the former rent, the less useful it is likely to be as a guide to damages.

The meaning of "real value" referred to above differs from the open market rent in the case of a property to which the Rent Act 1977 applied and in respect of which a fair rent had been registered. In such a case, the "real value" was the fair rental value and not the open market value[4] since the letting value was restricted by statute. In such a case the landlord would only have been able to recover a fair rent for the occupation of his land and he could not recover in damages more than he would have received in rent had the premises been let. Since the Rent Act ceased to apply to most new private residential lettings entered into after January 15, 1989[5] the application of this restriction is now very limited.

A particular problem which arises out of fluctuating property values is that of the trespasser who remains in occupation over a sufficiently long period of time that the market value of the land has risen or fallen within the period of his occupation. Since the assessment of mesne profits depends on the actual value[6] (usually the market letting value[7]) it follows that where a period of wrongful occupation coincides with changes in that value, the landlord should receive damages which compensate him in accordance with such changes. Indeed, since the wrongful occupation of land is a continuing trespass which accrues from day to day,[8] it should

---

[1]   Goff & Jones, *op. cit.*, at pp. 793–797, *United Australia Ltd v. Barclays Bank* [1941] A.C. 1, H.L. and *Tang Min Sit v. Capacious Investments Ltd.* [1996] A.C. 514, HL.

[2]   See *Clifton v. Huntley* [1948] 2 All E.R. 283, and cases on the Rent Acts.

[3]   And, of course, the general principle governing the measure of damages in trespass is *restitutio in integrum* — see above, para. 4–006.

[4]   See *Newman v. Dorrington Investments* [1975] 1 W.L.R. 1642.

[5]   Other than pursuant to a contract entered into prior that date (s. 1 and para. 1 of Pt I to Sched. 1 of the Housing Act 1988) and in the case of the exceptions found in section 34 of the Housing Act 1988. See also s. 96 of the Housing Act 1996 and s. 19A of the Housing Act 1988 which presumes any assured tenancy entered into after February 28, 1997 to be an assured shorthold tenancy is given that it is to be fully assured, and subject to other exceptions.

[6]   See *Clifton v. Huntley* [1948] 2 All E.R. 283, *Henderson v. Squires* (1869) L.R. 4 Q.B. 170 and *Viscount Chelsea v. Hutchinson* [1994] 2 E.G.L.R. 61, CA.

[7]   Except where the Rent Act 1977 might apply: and a "fair rent" only is recoverable.

[8]   See para. 1–043.

in theory be possible to obtain an assessment of damages which takes into account daily changes in value although this would probably be cumbersome and impracticable[9] and a more manageable period is likely to be selected. *Woodfall*[10] suggests that the valuation should be carried out on the basis of a short term letting at a rack rent as did the Court of Appeal in *Viscount Chelsea v. Hutchinson*,[11] but, if the compensatory principle is to be properly applied, this must depend on the actual loss which the landlord is able to establish and can, therefore, be no more than a rule of thumb.

Where the property is one which, but for the occupation of the trespasser, would have been let in the open market on a long lease at a fixed rent (although subject to rent reviews) it may be possible to limit the award of damages to the rent which would be achieved by such a letting. This approach, although without supporting authority, is consistent with the function of mesne profits which is to compensate the landowner for the actual loss of use and occupation. It would be consistent with that function to limit the award to the level of a rent which would have been achieved had the property been let on a long (or other) lease. This approach is also consistent with the judgment of Megaw L.J. in *Swordheath*,[12] and to the references there made to the value of the property as it would "fairly be calculated," to the absence of "anything special" and the "ordinary letting value".[13]

Where the user is not that of a trespasser in occupation, but involves the unauthorised user of a right of way, the damages are assessed by reference to a sum which would be reasonable to pay for the grant of a right for the purpose in question.[14]

Consequential losses and exemplary and aggravated damages are dealt with elsewhere.[15] Indeed, in *Henderson v. Squire*[16] consequential losses were awarded in addition to mesne profits.

---

[9] And unnecessary if property prices are not especially volatile.

[10] Vol. 1, para. 19.013 and see *Dean and Chapter of Canterbury Cathedral v. Whitbread plc* [1995] 1 E.G.L.R. 82.

[11] [1994] 2 E.G.L.R. 61, CA.

[12] [1979] 1 W.L.R. 285, CA.

[13] See *Henderson v. Squire* (1869) L.R. 4 Q.B. 170 at 174 where Blackburn J., in considering an award of mesne profits, stated that "he [the Plaintiff] is entitled to what the rent would have amounted to for the time he was kept out of possession . . ." See also *Viscount Chelsea v. Hutchinson* [1994] 2 E.G.L.R. 61, CA.

[14] *Jegon v. Vivian* (1871) L.R. 6 Ch. 743 and *Phillips v. Homfray* (1871) L.R. 6 Ch. 770 at 780–781 (damages to be assessed in both cases at the cost of a wayleave to carry coal unlawfully mined). See also *Wrotham Park Estate Co. Ltd v. Parkside Homes Ltd* [1974] 1 W.L.R. 798, *Bracewell v. Appleby* [1975] Ch. 409 at 419–420 (both concerned damages awarded in lieu of injunction for unlawful use of right of way) and *Stoke-on-Trent City Council v. W. & J. Wass Ltd* [1988] 1 W.L.R. 1406, CA.

[15] See below, paras. 4–023 to 4–030.

[16] (1869) L.R. 4 Q.B. 170.

(b) Quantum of damages for "restitutionary" claim

4–021   As explained by Hoffmann L.J. in *Thompson*,[17] because this claim involves the recovery of a benefit obtained by the trespasser through the wrongful occupation of land, the amount recovered will not depend on the letting value but on a careful assessment of the value to the trespasser. In *Ashman*[18] the defendant had no option but to remain in occupation of R.A.F. married quarters after she had separated from her husband and the mesne profits were assessed not by reference to the market rent but by reference to what the defendant would have had to pay for suitable local authority accommodation. The defendant would not have paid market rent had she had any choice and could not establish priority need for public sector housing until a possession order had been made against her. A further relevant factor was the fact that the premises were let at a concessionary rate and were not normally let on the open market. Accordingly, "subjective devaluation"[19] in the amount recoverable would not cause injustice to the landlord, particularly since it was always open to the landlord to elect to recover on the damages measure if a greater actual loss could be demonstrated.

    In assessing the value to the trespasser, it would be unfortunate if squatters were able to argue that the principle of "subjective devaluation" led to the conclusion that no sum was recoverable since the occupiers would not have taken rented premises in any event. This is unlikely if the court is satisfied that they have obtained a benefit from their unlawful occupation: as in *Thompson*, if no evidence is provided by the occupier of the value of the benefit, the court may be forced back to the market letting value as a guide to the benefit obtained by the occupier.[20]

(3) Wrongful use and occupation: period for which damages payable

4–022   The entitlement to mesne profits arises upon the commencement of the unlawful occupation and terminates when the trespasser delivers up possession to the landowner. Mesne profits are recoverable from a former tenant upon the forfeiture of his lease for breach of covenant or condition, but only from the date of the actual forfeiture — which is normally the time of service of the proceedings[21] or, less frequently, upon peaceable re-entry.[22] Mesne profits do not run from the time of the breach relied upon to found the forfeiture since it is only from the date of the actual termination of the lease that the occupation of the former tenant ceases to be lawful.[23]

---

17   (1993) 25 H.L.R. 552, CA, at 554.
18   (1993) 25 H.L.R. 513, CA.
19   *Ashman* (1993) 25 H.L.R. 513, CA, *per* Hoffmann L.J. at 520, quoting from Professor Birks' *Introduction to the Law of Restitution*.
20   See the discussion in Goff & Jones, pp 27–41.
21   *Canas Property Co. Ltd v. K.L. Television Services Ltd* [1970] 2 Q.B. 433, CA.
22   See *Woodfall's Landlord and Tenant*, Vol. 1, para. 17.089.
23   See *Elliot v. Boynton* [1924] 1 Ch. 236.

Mesne profits are not generally recoverable following the forfeiture, or termination, of an assured tenancy under the Housing Act 1988 or of a protected tenancy within section 1 of the Rent Act 1977. The regime under the 1988 Act applies to most private sector residential tenancies created on or after January 15, 1989. An assured tenancy cannot be terminated except by an order of the court[24]: a periodic assured tenancy will simply continue until so terminated[25] while, on the expiry of a fixed term assured tenancy, a statutory assured tenancy will arise.[26] Under the assured tenancy regime, companies are excluded altogether from the protection of the Act.[27] However, since the amendments introduced by the Housing Act 1996 the presumption is that new tenancies will be assured shorthold tenancies rather than assured tenancies with full security of tenure.[27a]

The position with remaining regulated tenancies under the Rent Act 1977 is similar since generally the termination of the protected tenancy will be followed by a statutory tenancy arising by virtue of section 2 of the 1977 Act.[28]

Exemplary and aggravated damages

Although the general measure of damages is based upon the principle of compensation for loss caused by the wrongdoing, in exceptional cases exemplary or aggravated damages[29] may be awarded in addition to the general measure where the wrongdoing has been particularly bad. Although aggravated damages are based on an extension of the compensatory principle, exemplary (or punitive) damages are not concerned with compensation but with marking the disapproval of outrageous acts of wrongdoing.   **4–023**

(1) Exemplary damages

(a) Rationale

Exemplary damages are punitive and intended to mark the law's disapproval of acts perpetrated in blatant or cynical disregard of the claimant's   **4–024**

---

[24] S. 5(1).
[25] S. 5(1) — notices to quit have no effect in the case of periodic assured tenancies.
[26] S. 5(2)-(7).
[27] S. 1(1)(a) — unlike under the Rent Act 1977, it is a prerequisite that an assured tenant be an "individual".
[27a] See s. 96 of the 1996 Act and s. 19A of the Housing act 1988.
[28] One exception to this situation is company lettings since, although a company may be a protected tenant it cannot become a statutory tenant since it cannot "occupy" within s. 2 of the 1977 Act. Accordingly, provided the company letting is genuine, a claim for mesne profits can be made against a company when its protected tenancy has terminated: see *Firstcross Ltd v. East-West (Import/Export) Ltd* (1980) 41 P. & C.R. 145, CA and *Hilton v. Plustitle* [1989] 1 W.L.R. 149, CA.
[29] For a discussion of the terminology see, *e.g. Cassell & Co. v. Broome* [1972] A.C. 1027, HL at 1073–1074 (Lord Hailsham) and 1124–1125 (Lord Diplock).

rights.[30] Unlike the award of aggravated damages, which is based on the compensatory principle, the purpose of exemplary damages is to punish and has been criticised as confusing the purposes of civil and criminal law.[31] Nonetheless, this head of damages is well-established (albeit restricted in scope to three categories of case) and, although it allows the claimant to recover what may be considered a "windfall" or "accidental benefit",[32] it only does so exceptionally,[33] in circumstances where the claimant has been subjected to flagrant wrongdoing. Indeed, it appears most satisfactory to regard this head of damages as based on a rule of policy which prevents a tortfeasor from profiting from his own deliberate wrong:

> "It . . . may be a blunt instrument to prevent unjust enrichment by unlawful acts. But to restrict the damages recoverable to the gain made by the defendant if it exceeded the loss caused to the plaintiff, would leave a defendant contemplating an unlawful act with the certainty that he had nothing to lose to balance against the chance that the plaintiff might never sue him, or if he did, might fail in the hazards of litigation. It is only if there is a prospect that the damages may exceed the defendant's gain that the social purpose of this category is achieved to teach a wrongdoer that tort does not pay."[34]

(b) Categories of exemplary damages

4–025   In *Rookes v. Barnard*[35] the House of Lords reconsidered the basis for awarding exemplary damages. Lord Devlin, in an authoritative restatement of the law, held that circumstances qualifying for an award of exemplary damages should be strictly confined, since it is not usually the function of the civil law to punish, and limited their award to three specific categories of case[36] The first category concerns oppressive, arbitrary

---

[30] *AB v. South West Water Services* [1993] 1 All E.R. 609, CA and *Ramdath v. Oswald Daley* (1993) 25 H.L.R. 273, CA.

[31] A clear example can be found in *Drane v. Evangelou* [1978] 1 W.L.R. 455, CA at 459, where the co-existence of criminal and civil penalties was expressly recognised by the Master of the Rolls. See, further, Lord Devlin in *Rookes v. Barnard* [1964] A.C. 1129 at 1221; Lord Wilberforce in *Cassell & Co. Ltd v. Broome* [1972] A.C. 1027 at 1114, McGregor, *op. cit.*, paras. 430–435 and *Winfield & Jolowicz, op. cit.*, pp 744–754.

[32] *per* Diplock L.J. in *McCarey v. Associated Newspapers Ltd (No. 2)* [1965] 2 Q.B. 86, CA at 107.

[33] See, *e.g. Rookes v. Barnard* [1964] A.C. 1129, and *Cassell v. Broome* [1972] A.C. 1027, and *Bradford City Metropolitan Council v. Arora* [1991] 2 Q.B. 507, CA, at 519A-B and E-F. Contrast the position in Commonwealth jurisdictions which take a generally less restrictive approach to the award of exemplary damages. See, *e.g.*, Fleming, *The Law of Torts* (9th ed., 1992) (Australia) pp 271–274.

[34] *per* Lord Diplock in *Cassell v. Broome*, above, at 1127 and 1130. See also Diplock L.J. in *McCarey v. Associated Newspapers Ltd (No. 2)*, above, at 107.

[35] [1964] A.C. 1129, HL approved by the later decision of the House of Lords in *Cassell & Co. Ltd v. Broome*, above.

[36] It is matter of some debate whether the award of exemplary damages should be further confined even within Lord Devlin's categories to only those torts for which exemplary damages would have been awarded prior to *Rookes v. Barnard*. There is a divergence of judicial opinion on the point: see *Cassell v. Broome* [1972] A.C. 1027, *per* Lord Diplock and

or unconstitutional acts of government servants and is not further considered here. However, with regard to the second category, Lord Devlin stated:

"Cases in the second category are those in which the defendant's conduct has been calculated by him to make a profit for himself which may well exceed the compensation payable to the plaintiff . . . Where a defendant with a cynical disregard for a plaintiff's rights has calculated that the money to be made out of his wrongdoing will probably exceed the damages at risk, it is necessary for the law to show that it cannot be broken with impunity. This category is not confined to money making in the strict sense. It extends to cases in which the defendant is seeking to gain at the expense of the plaintiff some object perhaps some property which he coverts which either he could not obtain at all or not obtain except at a price greater then he wants to put down. Exemplary damages can properly be awarded whenever it is necessary to teach a wrongdoer that tort does not pay."

Exemplary damages may also be awarded within a third category where they are authorised by specific statutory provisions.[37] There is now specific statutory provision for damages for unlawful eviction under sections 27 and 28 of the Housing Act 1988[38] and, although the section 28 measure appears intended to compensate the occupier "for his loss of the right to occupy the premises in question",[39] this appears to be at least partly punitive in character in that it is based on the value of the advantage gained by the landlord rather than the actual loss to the occupier. This value is consistent with the special measure now recognised in the assessment of mesne profits[40] as is the Commonwealth approach of using punitive damages to prevent the unjust enrichment of wrongdoers.[41] The award of damages under sections 27 and 28 does not exclude the award of damages at common law, especially where the occupier does not lose his rights of occupation[42] since section 27(3) expressly refers to the loss of the right to occupy. In *Tagro v. Cafane*[43] it appears to have been conceded that section

---

Lord Hailsham (1076 and 1130–1131); *Mafo v. Adams* [1970] 1 Q.B. 548; *Archer v. Brown* [1984] 2 All E.R.. 267 at 281; *Catnic Components v. Hill & Smith Ltd* [1983] F.S.R. 512. Note that exemplary damages are available only in the case of tortious misconduct and are not available for breaches of contract: *Perera v. Vandiyar* [1953] 1 W.L.R. 672, *Paris Oldham & Gustra v. Staffordshire B.G.* [1988] 2 E.G.L.R. 39 and *Reed v. Madon* [1984] 1 W.L.R. Ch. 408. See, in the context of quiet enjoyment, above, Chapter 3 at para. 3–024 *eq seq.*

[37] See the reference by Lord Devlin in *Rookes v. Barnard* to section 13(2) of the Reserve and Auxiliary Forces Act 1951.
[38] See below, Chap. 5, paras. 5–020 to 5–022.
[39] S. 27(3) of the 1988 Act.
[40] See paras. 4–017 to 4–022.
[41] Fleming, *The Law of Torts* (9th ed.) (Australia), p. 271.
[42] Other than purely temporary dispossession.
[43] [1991] 1 W.L.R. 378, CA.

27 damages excluded common law damages[44] whereas in *Mason v. Nwokorie*[45] general and aggravated damages were only set-off against section 27(3) damages by the Court of Appeal because in that case they represented damages for the loss of the right to occupy.[46] The latter decision appears to support the proposition that exemplary damages are not excluded in principle in that such damages are penal and not compensatory. Further, it does not appear that Parliament intended to exclude common law damages since this is not done expressly nor is it necessary that such an intention be implied (for the reasons given above). The award of both common law and statutory damages was confirmed by the Court of Appeal in *Kaur v. Gill*.[47]

(c) Lord Devlin's second category of exemplary damages

4–026   It is a pre-requisite to the recovery of exemplary damages in Lord Devlin's second category[48] that the wrong should have been committed with some degree of deliberation, *i.e.* with the aim of securing an advantage to the tortfeasor.[49] Whilst it is not necessary that the element of advantage be precisely calculated,[50] the tortfeasor should have at least had in mind the advantage to be gained and reached the conclusion that it was worth the exposure to the risk of being required to pay compensation.[51] Indeed, there may be cases where the advantage is not wholly a monetary one, such as where a landlord forces a tenant out of occupation so that he may utilise the premises for his own purposes.[52] In *Cassell v. Broome*[53] Lord Hailsham stated the requirements as follows:

> "(i) knowledge that what is proposed to be done is against the law or a reckless disregard whether what is proposed to be done is illegal or legal and (ii) a decision to carry on doing it because the prospects of material advantage outweigh the prospects of material loss . . ."

---

[44] Above at 379H-380A. The point was not argued since it does not appear that the Respondents were called upon by the Court of Appeal to make submissions: above at 384H.

[45] *The Times*, October 18, 1993, CA.

[46] And hence to be discounted in accordance with s. 27(5).

[47] *The Times*, June 15, 1995, CA.

[48] Above.

[49] See also *Cassell v. Broome* [1972] A.C. 1027, HL. In *Ramdath v. Oswald Dairy* (1993) 25 H.L.R. 273, the Court of Appeal overturned an award of exemplary damages against a landlord's agent (in fact, his son) on the basis that there was insufficient evidence to show that he had a sufficient interest of his own. His conduct on behalf of the landlord (including verbal abuse of the tenant) was taken into account as part of the actions of the landlord. The award of exemplary damages against the landlord was £1,000.

[50] See *Cassell v. Broome*, [1972] A.C. 1027, at 1078–1079, 1101 and the passage from Lord Diplock's speech cited below.

[51] Indeed "the defendant may calculate that the plaintiff will not sue at all . . ." *per* Lord Hailsham, *ibid*. at 1079.

[52] Where there may well be an element of financial gain, *e.g.* the saving of the cost of obtaining other premises, but the complete extent of the gain cannot be accurately calculated.

[53] See *Cassell v. Broome* [1972] A.C. 1027, at 1079.

Lord Diplock[54] put the matter in this way:

> ". . . it must be proved that the defendant, at the time that he committed the tortious act, knew that it was unlawful or suspecting it to be unlawful deliberately refrained from obvious steps which, if taken, would have turned suspicion into certainty. While, of course, it is not necessary to prove that the defendant made an arithmetical calculation of the pecuniary profit he would make from the tortious act and of the compensatory damages and costs to which he would render himself liable, with appropriate discount for the chances that he might get away with it without being sued or might settle the action for some lower figure, it must be a reasonable inference from the evidence that he did direct his mind to the material advantages to be gained by committing the tort and came to the conclusion that they were worth taking the risk of having to compensate the plaintiff if he should bring an action."

As well as emphasising the necessity of ascertaining whether the case in question can be brought within one of the established categories, Lord Devlin[55] stated that three matters should always be taken into account when considering an award of exemplary damages:

(1)   the claimant cannot recover exemplary damages unless he is the victim of punishable behaviour,[56]

(2)   the power to award exemplary damages could be used oppressively and the appellate courts should see that it is exercised with restraint[57]; and

(3)   the means of the parties are material in the assessment of exemplary damages since everything which aggravates or mitigates the defendant's conduct is relevant.[58]

It is clear that this category of exemplary damages encompasses an important series of circumstances where a landlord trespasses onto a tenant's demised property in order to dispossess him or perpetrate some other

---

[54] *ibid*. at 1130.

[55] *ibid*. at 1227–8.

[56] As Lord Diplock said *ibid*. at 1126, this means that a claimant "can only profit from a windfall if the wind was blowing his way".

[57] Even where the damages are assessed by a jury in the case of other torts. In *Cassell v. Broome* Lord Hailsham felt unable to support Lord Devlin's approach so far as interfering with awards by juries were concerned: above at 1066 — however, the jury's award in that case was upheld by only a bare majority. Clearly the appellate courts will be less reluctant to interfere with an award which has been fixed by a judge alone (see Lord Diplock, *ibid*. at 1122).

[58] See further, under *Assessment*, below at para. 4–028.

wrong.[59] In *Drane v. Evangelou*,[60] the landlord had sought to oust the tenant from possession by forcibly entering the premises when the defendant was away, putting the defendant's possessions in the back yard and locking them against the defendant, so that when the defendant returned he found the door bolted against him and a number of people on the premises without his consent. The landlord moved his parents-in-law into the premises and they all refused to obey injunctions ordering them to re-admit the tenant until the defendant applied to commit them for contempt. As a result, the defendant was not able to return to his home for over two months.

The court awarded exemplary damages of £1,000 to mark its disapproval of what was described as "monstrous behaviour". Lord Denning M.R. held that the case fell within Lord Devlin's second category and stated:[61]

"To my mind this category includes cases of unlawful eviction of a tenant. The landlord seeks to gain possession at the expense of the tenant — so as to keep or get a rent higher than that awarded by the Rent Tribunal — or to get possession from a tenant who is protected by the Rent Acts. So he resorts to harassing tactics. Such conduct can be punished now by the criminal law. But it can also be punished by the civil law by an award of exemplary damages."

Lawton L.J.[62] expressed himself in strong terms:

"To deprive a man of a roof over his head in my judgment is one of the worst torts which can be committed. It causes stress, worry and anxiety. It brings the law into disrepute if people like the defendant can act with impunity in the way he did . . . Parliament has said that this kind of conduct is sufficiently serious to be made a criminal offence. It follows, in my view, that the Court is entitled to approach cases of this kind on the basis that a very grave wrong indeed has been done to the tenant who is evicted in the sort of way that this plaintiff was evicted."

Other cases of landlords trespassing onto premises demised by them in order unlawfully to oust the tenants from possession have also attracted awards of exemplary damages. In *Ashgar v. Ahmed*[63] a claimant was awarded £1,000 exemplary damages where the landlord unlawfully evicted the claimant and his family from their home, had refused to

---

[59] See Lord Hailsham's comments on "Rachmanism" in *Cassell v. Broome*, [1972] A.C. 1027, at 1079.
[60] [1978] 1 W.L.R. 455, CA. A statutory remedy in damages is now available for tenants unlawfully evicted: see ss. 27 and 28 of the Housing Act 1988.
[61] *ibid.* at 459.
[62] *ibid.* at 459.
[63] (1984) 17 H.L.R. 25, CA.

re-admit them when ordered to do so by the court and had thrown their belongings out of the house.[64] Similar behaviour occurred in *McMillan v. Singh*[65] and *Millington v. Duffy*[66] and, although in the latter case the claim for exemplary damages was abandoned, the Court of Appeal was plainly of the view that it would have awarded such damages considerably in excess of £500 had the claim been maintained.[67]

In *McMillan v. Singh*,[68] Sir John Arnold P. held that the proper approach in such cases was to assess first ordinary damages for injury to property or person, then to consider whether the claimant had received such injury to his feelings that aggravated damages should be awarded and then, finally, when the quantification of other damage has been exhausted, whether the court should also assess exemplary damages.[69]

In the case of "wilful, clandestine trespass to minerals"[70] a punitive element arises in that the court may award to the injured party the value of the minerals without deducting the costs of extraction incurred by the trespasser, *i.e.* awarding to the claimant more than compensation for the loss.

(d) Pleading

A claim for exemplary damages should be expressly pleaded both in High Court and in county court proceedings.[71]   **4–027**

(e) Assessment

In *Rookes v. Bernard*,[72] Lord Devlin stressed that awards of exemplary damages should be "moderate" but what is appropriate is entirely a matter for the court to determine since the measure is not compensatory and the purpose of the award is to punish and, possibly, to act as a deterrent to others. Awards of exemplary damages for harassment of tenants are considered in more detail in connection with statutory remedies, but vary   **4–028**

---

[64] Special damages were awarded for damage to the claimant's property and an additional award of £500 aggravated damages was also made.

[65] (1984)17 H.L.R. 120, CA.

[66] Above. See also *Ramdath v. Oswald Daley* (1993) 25 H.L.R. 273, CA. In *Guppys (Bridport) Ltd v. Brookling & James* [1984] E.G.D. 294, CA *per* Stevenson L.J. at 319 the tortious conduct which attracted exemplary damages was not trespass but a nuisance. However, see the doubts expressed by the Court of Appeal in *AB v. South West Water Services Ltd* [1993] 1 All E.R. 609 at 620–21 and 627 (public nuisance). Both torts can comprise interference with the quiet enjoyment of a tenant: see below.

[67] Above, at 236 (Sir John Arnold P.).

[68] *ibid.* at 124.

[69] See below as to whether exemplary damages should be awarded in addition to compensatory damages.

[70] Lord Diplock in *Cassell v. Broome* [1972] A.C. 1027, at 1129C-D. See also *Livingstone v. The Rawyards Coal Co.* (1880) 5 App.Cas. 25, HL and *Bulli Coal Mining Co. v. Osborne* [1899] A.C. 351, PC. See above, paras. 4–009 and 4–011.

[71] C.P.R. Part 16.4(1)(c) and *Alexander v. Home Office* [1988] 2 All E.R. 118 at 123.

[72] [1964] A.C. 1129, HL, at 1227–8.

from the relatively low hundreds[73] to a few thousand pounds[74]: in general, serious acts of interference with lawful occupiers will merit an award of at least £500 to £1,000.[75] Awards for torts other than trespass have been higher than those for unlawful eviction.[76] It may be that certain torts (*e.g.* unlawful arrest and defamation) attract greater disapproval than others, though it is difficult to understand why a deliberate defamation should be regarded as more iniquitous than a deliberate trespass by a landlord with a view to ousting his tenant (considered to be "one of the worst torts"[77]) The discrepancy in the awards may also be a consequence of assessment of some tortious damages, such as in defamation actions, by juries.[78] In the final analysis, the quantum is in the discretion of the court and should reflect the court's assessment of the circumstances of the particular case, having regard to the three matters mentioned by Lord Devlin including the claimant's own conduct and any factors mitigating the defendant's action.

The principle of taking into account the claimant's conduct is akin to that of contributory negligence since a claimant who has aggravated circumstances himself should not receive the benefit of the same "windfall", and the defendant not be punished to the same extent, as in circumstances where the claimant is entirely blameless. It appears open to the court to decline to award any exemplary damages in circumstances where the unlawful conduct of the defendant was provoked by the claimant or where the claimant bears the greatest part of the blame for the act.[79] It is plainly undesirable for a claimant who has misconducted himself to receive the windfall of exemplary damages and to punish a defendant who has been provoked.

---

[73] *e.g. Hume v. Pratt* [1980] C.L.Y. 1647 (county court) and *Taylor v. Clayton* [1990] 9 C.L. 194 (county court).

[74] Contrast the potentially much higher levels of damages that can be awarded under ss. 27 and 28 of the Housing Act 1988: see *Tagro v. Cafane* [1991] 1 W.L.R. 378, CA (£31,000) and *Mason v. Nwokorie, The Times,* October 12, 1993 (£4,500). The award in *Tagro* was in part a result of the defendant's failure to adduce expert evidence on the question of loss before the trial judge: see pp. 385–6.

[75] *e.g. Drane v. Evangelou,* [1978] 1 W.L.R. 455, CA, (£1,000), *Taibi v. Foster & Foster* [1981] C.L.Y. 1596 (county court — £1,000), *Collier v. Burke* [1987] C.L.Y. 1143 (county court — £3,000) and *Ramdath v. Oswald Dairy* (1993) 25 H.L.R. 273, above, (£1,000). In *Ramdath* the award of exemplary damages against the landlord's agent was overturned by the Court of Appeal: it had been assessed by the County Court at £2,500. In *Kaur v. Gill, The Times,* June 15, 1995, CA, £500 was awarded.

[76] Contrast the awards referred to above with those in *Cassell & Co. Ltd v. Broome* [1972] A.C. 1027 (£25,000); *White v. Metropolitan Police Commissioner, The Times,* April 24, 1982 (£20,000) and *Riches v. News Group Newspapers* [1985] 2 All E.R. 845 (£25,000).

[77] *Drane v. Evangelou,* [1978] 1 W.L.R. 455, CA, *per* Lawton L.J. See para. 4–026.

[78] Although this does not affect trespass cases or cases of unlawful eviction. If this is the reason for higher awards of exemplary damages, then it provides considerable support for the view that exemplary damages should be assessed by the judge only since it involves the fixing of a penalty. See, *e.g.* Lord Kilbrandon in *Cassell & Co. Ltd v. Broome* [1972] A.C. 1027 at 1135.

[79] *O'Connor v. Hewitson* [1979] Crim.L.R. 46 (trespass to the person by a policeman provoked by claimant).

(f) Compensatory and punitive damages

The House of Lords in both *Rookes v. Barnard*[80] and *Cassell v. Broome*[81]   **4–029**
made it clear that there is a further principle limiting the award of exemplary damages, namely that they should not be awarded if the award of
ordinary compensatory damages is sufficient to act as a penalty for the
defendant's conduct.[82] In *Cassell v. Broome*,[83] Lord Diplock stated:

> "... even if the jury found that the case came within Lord Devlin's
> second category and that the defendants' conduct merited punish-
> ment, it did not necessarily follow that they must award as damages
> to the plaintiff a greater sum than was sufficient to compensate him
> for all the harm and humiliation that he had suffered as a conse-
> quence of the defendants' tortious acts. They should take into
> account as part of the punishment inflicted on the defendants any
> sum ... which they were minded to award to the plaintiff as com-
> pensatory damages; and only if they thought that sum to be inade-
> quate in itself to constitute sufficient punishment were they to award
> such additional sum as would, when added to the compensatory
> damages, amount to an appropriate penalty for the defendants'
> improper conduct."

It follows from the above that if the award of compensatory damages does
not provide an adequate penalty, then exemplary damages can be
awarded in addition to compensatory damages[84] in such sums as, when
added to the compensatory measure, will provide a suitable penalty.
   A more difficult question arises, where damages are awarded under
section 27(3) of the Housing Act 1988, whether exemplary damages can
also be awarded.[85] If the nature of a section 27(3) award[86] is that of a
penalty, then no additional punitive award should be made[87] since sufficient penalty will be exacted by that award.[88] If, on the other hand, the
character of a section 27(3) award is (at least in part) compensatory then
the court will have to consider the general question of whether the award
of such compensatory damages is sufficient penalty. The exclusion of

---

[80] [1964] A.C. 1129, HL, at 1228.
[81] [1972] A.C. 1027, at 1076–1077, 1089, 1096, 1104, 1118, 1134 and the passage from Lord
   Diplock's speech cited below.
[82] See also *Bradford City Council v. Arora* [1991] 2 Q.B. 507, CA at 519–520.
[83] [1972] A.C. 1027, 1121–1122.
[84] Examples of cases where both have been awarded include *Hume v. Pratt* [1980] C.L.Y. 1647
   (county court), *Ashgar v. Ahmed* (1984) 17 H.L.R. 25, CA, *Millington v. Duffy* (1984) 17
   H.L.R. 232, CA, *Reid & Reid v. Andreou* [1987] C.L.Y. 2250 (county court) and *McCormack v.
   Namjou* [1990] 9 C.L. 201 (county court).
[85] See above, and also below at paras. 5–020 to 5–022.
[86] Below, para. 5–022.
[87] This appears to have been conceded in *Tagro v. Cafane* [1991] 1 W.L.R. 378, CA.
[88] Which, if *Tagro v. Cafane* is a reliable guide, may be far greater than the usual levels of
   awards of exemplary damages in the case of a tortious act calculated to cause, or leading
   to, unlawful eviction (as to which, see above).

other liabilities "on account of the same loss"[89] strongly suggests that the statutory remedy was regarded by Parliament as principally a compensatory measure.

The first reported award[90] was considerably in excess of the usual range of awards of exemplary damages in similar cases and, on the *Rookes* and *Cassell* principle, it is doubtful that an additional, exemplary award will be justified unless the quantum of the section 27(3) award is relatively small. In *Mason v. Nwokorie*,[91] aggravated damages were set-off against statutory damages on the basis that they were an award for the loss of the right to occupy and hence excluded by section 27(5). This will not be the case with exemplary damages which are not compensatory in nature.[92] *Mason* was distinguished in *Kaur v. Gill*[93] on the basis that general damages had been awarded for breach of covenant for quiet enjoyment and the Court of Appeal held that exemplary damages were recoverable in addition to statutory damages under section 27.

(g) The future of exemplary damages

4–029a   In 1997 the Law Commission published its report *Aggravated, Exemplary and Restitutionary Damages*[94] proposing changes in the approach to be taken in awarding exemplary damages in all areas of law. The report recommended, in particular, making "punitive" damages available in all cases where the defendant's conduct is considered so outrageous by the court as to warrant punishment. With this as the guiding principle, Lord Devlin's three categories of case appropriate to an award of exemplary damages would be abolished, the first category being extended to acts by non-public servants and bodies, and the second being replaced by the development of the law of restitution.

Following the report, however, the Government declined to enact the proposals on exemplary damages, stating[95]:

> "The contending arguments for a complete legislative overhaul of exemplary damages, as recommended by the Law Commission, or abolition as preferred by many commentators, are finely balanced. In the absence of a clear consensus on the issue the Government have decided not to take forward the Law Commission's proposals for legislation on exemplary damages. It may be that some further judicial development of the law in this area might help clarify the issues."

---

[89] S. 27(5).
[90] *Tagro v. Cafane* [1991] 1 W.L.R. 378 (£31,000).
[91] *The Times*, October 18, 1993, CA.
[92] The trial judge in *Mason* had not distinguished between exemplary and aggravated damages in making an award of £1,000 and the Court of Appeal characterised the award as aggravated damages before discounting them under s. 27(5).
[93] *The Times*, June 15, 1995, CA.
[94] Law Com No. 247.
[95] House of Commons Debates, November 9, 1999, Col. 502.

Such 'judicial development' in this area has already begun. In *Kuddus v. Chief Constable of Leicestershire*,[96] the House of Lords reversed the Court of Appeal's decision in *AB & Others v. South West Water Authority*,[97] which had set out a "cause of action test" which restricted the availability of exemplary damages to torts which could be shown to have been subject to awards of exemplary damages before 1964, when *Rookes v. Barnard*[98] was decided. The tort of trespass, under which awards of exemplary damages have long been available, was unaffected by the *AB* case, but *obiter dicta* in *Kuddus* give some indication of how exemplary damages for this and other torts may be affected in the future.

While the House of Lords in *Kuddus* were unanimous in reversing the "rationally indefensible" cause of action test, opinions on the correct approach to awards of exemplary damages were sharply divided. Lord Nicholls, advocating reform along the lines suggested by the Law Commission, stated:

> "66. In *Rookes v. Barnard* [1964] A.C. 1129, 1226 , Lord Devlin drew a distinction between oppressive acts by government officials and similar acts by companies or individuals. He considered that exemplary damages should not be available in the case of non-governmental oppression or bullying. Whatever may have been the position 40 years ago, I am respectfully inclined to doubt the soundness of this distinction today. National and international companies can exercise enormous power. So do some individuals. I am not sure it would be right to draw a hard-and-fast line which would always exclude such companies and persons from the reach of exemplary damages. Indeed, the validity of the dividing line drawn by Lord Devlin when formulating his first category is somewhat undermined by his second category, where the defendants are not confined to, and normally would not be, government officials or the like.
> 67. Nor, I may add, am I wholly persuaded by Lord Devlin's formulation of his second category (wrongful conduct expected to yield a benefit in excess of any compensatory award likely to be made). The law of unjust enrichment has developed apace in recent years. In so far as there may be a need to go further, the key here would seem to be the same as that already discussed: outrageous conduct on the part of the defendant. There is no obvious reason why, if exemplary damages are to be available, the profit motive should suffice but a malicious motive should not."

In contrast, Lord Scott would have preferred to abolish exemplary damages in civil law altogether, stating:

---

[96] [2001] 2 W.L.R. 1789.
[97] [1993] Q.B. 507.
[98] Above.

"109.   Lord Devlin's second category, cases in which the defendant's wrongful conduct has made a profit for himself which exceeds the compensation payable to the victim of the conduct, has been largely overtaken by developments in the common law. Restitutionary damages are available now in many tort actions as well as those for breach of contract. The profit made by a wrongdoer can be extracted from him without the need to rely on the anomaly of exemplary damages: see the discussion of the topic in *Attorney General v. Blake* [2001] 1 A.C. 268, 278–280 by Lord Nicholls of Birkenhead.

110.   Whatever may have been the position in 1964, when *Rookes v. Barnard* [1964] A.C. 1129 was decided, or in 1972, when *Broome v. Cassell & Co Ltd* [1972] A.C. 1027 was decided, there is, in my opinion, no longer any need for punitive damages in the civil law, or, at least, no need sufficient to offset the disadvantages to which Lord Morris of Borth-y-Gest in *Broome v. Cassell & Co Ltd* cogently referred. These disadvantages are the more prominent now that, via the Human Rights Act 1998, article 6 of the Convention for the Protection of Human Rights and Fundamental Freedoms (1953) (Cmnd 8969) has become part of our domestic law.

111.   Thus far I have been considering some of the general issues that are prompted by the present appeal. For the reasons I have outlined, I would be receptive to a submission that exemplary damages awards should no longer be available in civil proceedings. However, Mr Mansfield, counsel for the defendant, has not made that submission and, having had the advantage of reading the texts of my noble and learned friends' speeches on this appeal, it is apparent that mine is a minority view."

As the law stands, the approach to exemplary damages awarded in trespass cases is unchanged, albeit ripe for development. The implications of *Kuddus* for nuisance cases and claims under *Rylands v. Fletcher* are discussed below at paragraph 4–040.

(2) Aggravated damages

4–030   Unlike exemplary damages, aggravated damages are based on the familiar principle of compensation and arise where the manner or motive of the defendant in committing a tort has been such as to heighten the injury. The additional compensation for the outrageous conduct of the wrongdoer is not to punish him but to provide compensation to the claimant for the aggravation of the injury.

Lord Hailsham in *Cassell v. Broome*[99] said:

---

[99] [1972] A.C. 1027, HL at 1073. See also, *e.g. Ramdath v. Oswald Daley* (1993) 25 H.L.R. 273, CA at 279.

"In awarding 'aggravated' damages the natural indignation of the court at the injury inflicted on the plaintiff is a perfectly legitimate motive in making a generous rather than a more moderate award to provide an adequate solatium. But that is because the injury to the plaintiff is actually greater and, as the result of the conduct exciting the indignation, demands a more generous solatium."

There can be a considerable overlap between circumstances giving rise to awards of aggravated damages and circumstances giving rise to awards of exemplary damages, e.g. where a landlord has trespassed onto tenanted property and attempted to evict the tenant by unlawful means. The conduct of the landlord can be sufficiently flagrant and serious that it attracts an award of both aggravated and exemplary damages.[1] The aggravated damages compensate the tenant for the outrageous and oppressive nature of the trespass and the exemplary damages (if the award of damages is not already sufficiently punitive[2]) punish the landlord for a wrong calculated to gain an advantage for himself.[3] Since aggravated damages are compensatory, if a claim is made under section 27(3) of the Housing Act 1988 they will fall to be discounted under section 27(5) if they amount to damages awarded in respect of the loss of the right to occupy.[4]

The Law Commission's report *Aggravated, Exemplary and Restitutionary Damages* recommended that aggravated damages should be awarded as "damages for mental distress" which "must not be intended to punish the defendant for his conduct".

(2) Damages for Nuisance

General principles

In general an interference with land must cause some damage before it is actionable as a private nuisance.[5] The measure of damages for an interference with land that is actionable as a private nuisance will, as with

4–031

---

[1] e.g. *Hume v. Pratt* [1980] C.L.Y. 1647 (county court) (£100 general damages, £100 aggravated damages and £100 exemplary damages where the claimant returned late at night to find the locks changed and his possessions in plastic bags left outside the door); *Reid & Reid v. Andreou* [1987] C.L.Y. 2250 (county court) (£3,000 general, exemplary and aggravated damages where locks were changed, the claimant's possessions put out whilst he was away and later the claimant was assaulted by two men at the landlord's behest); *Abouri & Abouri v. Ierodianconou* [1990] 9 C.L. 193 (county court) (£3,500 general, aggravated and exemplary damages where a landlord seized his tenants' possessions whilst the tenants were at work, dumped them on the pavement outside and changed the locks. The landlord then defied a High Court order to re-admit the tenants); *Patel v. Southwark LBC* (1993) C.L.Y. 1400 (£1,500 exemplary and aggravated damages; council failed to readmit tenant for three days once illegal eviction brought to housing officer's attention. Housing officer initially sceptical and abusive. General damages also awarded).

[2] See paras. 4–028 and 4–029.

[3] See para. 4–026.

[4] *Mason v. Nwokorie, The Times,* October 18, 1993, CA.

[5] See above para. 2–027.

damages for trespass, be such money as will compensate the claimant for the loss that he has suffered.[6] The general principle for the award of damages for a nuisance is the same as in the case of other torts, namely the Court will award:

"that sum of money which will put the party who has been injured, or who has suffered, in the same position as he would have been in if he had not sustained the wrong for which he is now getting his compensation or reparation."[7]

(1) Physical damage

4–032   Some nuisances cause physical damage.[8] Where physical damage is caused the measure of damage, as in the case of trespass, is often the diminution in the value of the land as a result of the tortious interference.[9]

However, if the claimant can establish that he reasonably intends to reinstate the land he may be entitled to the cost of reinstatement.[10] Thus, in *Bunclark v. Hertfordshire County Council*[11] it was held that where damage had been caused to a block of flats by encroaching tree roots and this damage was continuing, damages were recovered both for the diminution in value caused to the flats as a result of the bad reputation that the nuisance had given the flats and for the cost of repair and reinstatement. Also in *Dodd Properties (Kent) Ltd v. Canterbury City Council*[12] the cost of repair of the claimant's building, which had been damaged by the defendants' building operations, was the measure of damage.

In this context questions have arisen as to the date by reference to which the damages should be assessed. In *Bunclark*, the claimants were entitled to recover the cost of repair on the basis of building costs in 1976 and 1977 when the action was decided rather than the cost of repair in 1969 when the nuisance commenced because the defendants did not prove that the claimants had unreasonably failed to take steps to mitigate their losses in doing the works at an earlier date. Works of repair at the earlier date might have been more costly or pointless because the trees which had caused the damage were still standing. Further the claimants did not have sufficient resources. Similarly, in *Dodd Properties* the Court of Appeal accepted the claimants' argument that damages should be assessed as the cost of repair at the time of the hearing rather than when the damage occurred because it would not have made commercial sense to spend the money on repairing the building which could not produce a corresponding return in income

---

[6] See above para. 4–003.
[7] *Livinstone v. Rawyards Coal Co.* (1880) 5 App. Cas, 25, 29 *per* Lord Blackburn.
[8] See above 2–051 to 2–074.
[9] See para. 2–051 and, below, at paras. 4–006 to 4–037 *et seq.* in relation to prospective losses and continuing wrongs
[10] *Ward v. Cannock Chase District Council* [1986] 2 W.L.R. 660.
[11] (1977) 243 E.G. 381 and 455. Compare also *Masters v. Brent LBC* [1978] 1 Q.B. 841.
[12] [1980] 1 W.L.R. 433.

before the claimants could be sure of recovering the cost of repair from the defendants. This case was distinguished from that of *The Liesbosch*[13] in which it was held that the claimants could not recover damages to the extent that they were increased by their own impecuniosity because such losses were too remote: the *Dodd Properties* case was one where it was not financially prudent for the claimants to undertake the repairs earlier rather than a case where they were financially incapable of carrying out the repairs[14]; the delay in carrying out the repairs was thus reasonable and the increase in costs resulting from the delay was recoverable.

(2) Harm to amenity

Some nuisances consist in an interference with the enjoyment of property **4–033** falling short of physical interference and without causing physical damage, for instance the nuisance may consist of noise or smell.[15] Even where there is a physical encroachment[16] or there is interference with an easement,[17] there may also be a loss of amenity for which damages may be awarded. Where such an actionable interference is caused, damages are recoverable though the amount of the damages recoverable for such nuisances may be hard to quantify.[18]

In *Bone v. Seale*[19] the Court of Appeal considered the assessment of damages for the inconvenience caused over a long period by a nuisance consisting of the smell from the defendant's pig farm. In that case Stephenson L.J. said that damages should be fixed by analogy with damages for loss of amenity in an action for personal injury.[20] This approach, however, has been disapproved of by Lord Hoffmann in *Hunter v. Canary Wharf Ltd*.[21] The basis for the cause of action in nuisance is:

> "not causing discomfort to the person but . . . for causing injury to the land. True it is that the land has not suffered 'sensible' injury, but its utility has been diminished by the existence of the nuisance. It is for an unlawful threat to the utility of his land that the possessor or occupier is entitled to an injunction and it is for the diminution in such utility that he is entitled to compensation.

---

[13] [1933] A.C. 449.

[14] [1980] 1 W.L.R. 422, 453 *per* Megaw L.J., 459 *per* Donaldson L.J. See also *Radford v. De Froberville* [1977] 1 W.L.R. 1262, 1272 and 4–086 *et seq.* above (trespass).

[15] See para. 2–075 *et seq.* above.

[16] *Bunclark v. Hertfordshire County Council* (1977) 243 E.G. 381 and 455 (encroachment of tree roots).

[17] *Moore v. Buchanan* (1966) 197 E.G. 565 (obstruction of right of way).

[18] See *e.g. Halsey v. Esso Petroleum Co* [1961] 1 W.L.R. 683, especially at 702–703 *per* Veale J.

[19] [1975] 1 W.L.R. 797, CA.

[20] *ibid.* at 803–804.

[21] *Hunter v. Canary Wharf Ltd* [1997] A.C. 655 at 706; [1997] 2 All E.R. 426, at 451–452 *per* Lord Hoffmann; see also *Butcher Robinson & Staples Ltd & others v. London Regional Transport & Another* [1999] 3 E.G.L.R. 63, TCC, HHJ Bowsher Q.C.

"I cannot therefore agree with Stephenson L.J. in *Bone v. Seale* when he said that damages in an action for nuisance caused by smells from a pig farm should be fixed by analogy with damages for loss of amenity in an action for personal injury. In that case it was said that 'efforts to prove diminution in the value of the property as a result of this persistent smell over the years failed.' I take this to mean that it had not been shown that the property would sell for less. But diminution in capital value is not the only measure of loss. It seems to me that the value of the right to occupy a house which smells of pigs must be less than the value of the occupation of an equivalent house which does not. In the case of a transitory nuisance, the capital value of the property will seldom be reduced.[22] But the owner or occupier is entitled to compensation for the diminution in the amenity value of the property during the period for which the nuisance persisted. To some extent this involves placing a value upon intangibles. But estate agents do this all the time. The law of damages is sufficiently flexible to be able to do justice in such a case: compare *Ruxley Electronics & Construction Ltd v Forsyth*.[23]

"There may of course be cases in which, in addition to damages for injury to his land, the owner or occupier is able to recover damages for consequential loss. He will, for example, be entitled to loss of profits which are the result of inability to use the land for the purposes of his business. Or if the land is flooded, he may also be able to recover damages for chattels or livestock lost as a result. But inconvenience, annoyance or even illness suffered by persons on land as a result of smells or dust are not damage consequential upon the injury to the land. It is rather the other way about: the injury to the amenity of the land consists in the fact that the persons upon it are liable to suffer inconvenience, annoyance or illness".

It seems, therefore, that although damages for harm to amenity is recoverable, the starting point in assessing any such damages must be the effect upon the land itself.

(3) Nuisances causing economic loss

4–034   There is no doubt that losses of profits and expenses incurred as a result of interference with the claimant's property amounting to a nuisance will be recoverable (subject to their remoteness[24]). For instance, in *Rust v. Victoria Graving Dock Co.*,[25] the defendant was liable to the plaintiff for the flooding of the plaintiff's building estate; the plaintiff was entitled to recover damages in respect of the cost of repair of the houses which were

---

[22] See para. 4–037 below in relation to prospective losses and continuing wrongs.
[23] [1996] A.C. 344.
[24] See para. 4–039 below concerning remoteness.
[25] (1887) 36 Ch. D. 113.

in his possession and the economic loss of rental during the period of repairs. However, the claimant was not able to recover for the loss of rental arising from the prejudice to the neighbourhood caused by the flooding since such damage was not the "natural result of nor directly caused by the flood"[26]; nor was the claimant able to recover damages to the value of his reversionary interest in the properties of which he was not in possession since the nuisance was not of such a permanent nature as to affect the reversion when it came into possession.[27] In *Dodd Properties (Kent) Ltd v. Canterbury City Council*[28] the second claimants who were tenants of premises damaged by the defendants' building operations were entitled to recover as damages the dislocation of their business during the period which the first claimant, the freehold owner, would carry out repairs to the premises made necessary by the defendants' interference.

Economic losses may be recoverable even where the nuisance falls short of causing physical damage to the claimant's premises: thus in *Andreae v. Selfridge & Co.*[29] a hotel owner was entitled to recover damages for the loss of custom caused by noise and dust from the defendant's building operations in excess of what was reasonably tolerable.

Where incorporeal hereditaments are interfered with the claimant may be entitled to damages for economic losses resulting from the interference subject to their not being too remote. Thus in *Rose v. Groves*,[30] where the defendant obstructed a canal from which the plaintiff had a right of access, the claimant was entitled to recover for the resulting loss of custom.

(4) *Damage to chattels*

In addition to recovering damages for physical damage to his land, inconvenience to himself and economic losses resulting from the unlawful interference with his land, a claimant is entitled to recover damages for harm to chattels on the land caused by and consequential upon the nuisance.[31] Thus in *Halsey v. Esso Petroleum Co. Ltd*[32] the claimant was entitled to recover damages for harm to washing hanging on his property and his motor car as a result of acid smuts produced by the defendant.

4–035

---

[26] *ibid.*, at 113.
[27] *ibid.*, at 132; see above at para. 2–008. However, where physical damage to demised premises caused by negligence results in the landlord's entitlement to rent being abated the landlord appears to be entitled to recover the loss which he has suffered: *Harris v. Hall, The Independent*, August 19, 1992, CA.
[28] [1980] 1 W.L.R. 433. Compare *Dunton v. Dover District Council* (1977) 76 L.G.R. 87, 93.
[29] [1938] Ch. 1.
[30] (1843) 5 M & G 613. See also *Campbell v. Paddington Corporation* [1911] 1 K.B. 869 (loss of profits recoverable where stand constituting a public nuisance obstructed view of procession from plaintiff's premises). See also *Rose v. Limes* (1815) 5 M & S 101; *Tate & Lyle Food Distribution Ltd v. Greater London Council* [1982] 1 W.L.R. 149.
[31] *Hunter v. Canary Wharf Ltd* [1997] 2 All E.R. 426, at 451–452 *per* Lord Hoffmann.
[32] [1961] 1 W.L.R. 683, 702; [1997] A.C. 655 at 706.

(5) Personal injuries

4–036   Since an action in nuisance is an action for interference with *land*, damages for harm to a person as such will not be recoverable in a claim framed in nuisance.[33] However, as with harm to amenity generally, it seems that there is nothing in principle to prevent the court taking into account personal injury to an owner or occupier of land with a sufficient interest to bring a claim in nuisance in assessing the extent to which the claimant's right to enjoyment of his land has been affected.[34] Further, although it is clear that persons merely on the land will not be entitled to recover losses for personal injury consequent upon an interference with the land,[35] if (as appears to be the case) damages for harm to the chattels of an owner or occupier of land where such harm is consequential upon a nuisance, there seems to be no reason in principle, why analogous damages for personal injury to the land owner may not be recovered as harm consequential upon an unlawful interference with his land. Indeed, in the context of the rule in *Rylands v. Fletcher* it seems that such damages may be recoverable[36] though the House of Lords has reserved its opinion on the matter.[37]

(6) Prospective losses and continuing wrongs

4–037   The general rule in the law of torts is that damages for prospective losses are recoverable.[38] Where a nuisance consists of a single act which does not continue and which causes harm on a single occasion, there seems to be no reason in principle why this general principle should not apply and that damages for diminution in value to the claimant's land should not be recoverable.[39] However, this general proposition does not apply in the case of "continuing" wrongs. In *National Coal Board v. Galley*[40] it was accepted by the Court of Appeal that:

> "the general proposition that persistence in tortious conduct of particular kinds such as trespass or nuisance constitutes a continuing cause of action must be regarded as established."

It follows that a new cause of action arises each moment the nuisance continues and the claimant may bring a separate action in respect of it: a

---

[33] [1961] 1 W.L.R. 683, 702.

[34] See above para. 4–033 but see *Hunter v. Canary Wharf Ltd* [1997] 2 All E.R. 426, at 451–452 *per* Lord Hoffmann.

[35] *Hunter v. Canary Wharf Ltd* [1997] A.C. 655 at 706; [1997] 2 All E.R. 426, at 452 *per* Lord Hoffmann.

[36] *Miles v. Forest Rock Granite Co (Leicestershire) Ltd* (1918) 34 T.L.R. 500; *Hale v. Jennings Bros* [1938] 1 All E.R. 579. Compare *Shiffman v. Grand Priory in British Realm of Venerable Order of St John of Jerusalem* [1936] 1 All E.R. 557.

[37] *Read v. J. Lyons & Co Ltd* [1947] A.C. 156.

[38] *McGregor on Damages*, (16th ed.) p. 979 *et seq.*

[39] See above para. 4–032 (physical damage).

[40] [1958] 1 W.L.R. 16.

person committing a nuisance is under an obligation to abate it so long as the nuisance continues and each moment he fails to abate it he commits a tort and a new cause of action occurs. For example, where a defendant interferes with a right of light a new cause of action occurs each day the interference continued.[41] In the case of continuing wrongs, damages cannot be given at common law for nuisance continuing beyond the time of the commencement of the action, a new action being open to the claimant for each occasion after the commencement of the action that the nuisance continues. Thus, in *Battishill v. Reed*[42] a continuing nuisance had been committed by the construction of a building with eaves and gutters overhanging the claimant's wall. It was held that it was proper to exclude evidence of the diminution in value of the claimant's premises since only the loss until the date of the commencement of the action was recoverable.

The Court does however have powers to award damages for prospective losses in the case of continuing nuisances where it exercises its jurisdiction to award damages in lieu of or in addition to an injunction. These are dealt with below.[43]

There are some cases where a single act causes damage on two separate occasions and where a new cause of action occurs on each occasion damage occurs. In *Darley Main Colliery Co. v. Mitchell*[44] an excavation on the defendant's land caused subsidence to the claimant's land for which an action was brought and damages recovered. Subsequently the same excavation caused further subsidence. The new damage and the original wrongful excavation gave rise to a new cause of action in respect of which damages were recoverable in a second action. It is hard to analyse this case as a case in which the nuisance continued between the excavation and the second subsidence since an excavation does not create an actionable nuisance until subsidence occurs.[45] Further, where a defendant acquires title to the property which has been excavated only after the excavation has occurred no cause of action will lie against him in respect of subsidence caused by the excavation[46]: this would be strange if the nuisance were really continuing in its nature. However, in the *Darley Main Colliery* case, Lord Halsbury and Lord Fitzgerald appear to have proceeded in part at least on the basis that the nature of the tort in question was one arising from a continuing state of affairs created by the defendant which gave rise to a

4–038

---

[41] *Shadwell v. Hutchinson* (1831) 4 C & P 333. See also *Rosewell v. Prior* (1702) 2 Salk. 460.

[42] (1856) 18 C.B. 696. The common law position was affected by the Rules of Court: by R.S.C., Ord. 37, r. 6, damages for a continuing cause of action are allowed "to be assessed down to the time of the assessment". Thus in *Hole v. Chard* [1894] 1 Ch. 294, CA an action was commenced by the claimant in respect of a nuisance caused by the pollution of his stream with sewage. The claimant obtained an injunction to prevent future pollution and an inquiry as to damages was ordered. Three years later the damages were assessed and were assessed as at the date of the assessment, the defendant having wrongfully continued to pollute the stream in the meantime.

[43] See para. 4–100.

[44] (1886) 11 App. Cas. 127.

[45] *Backhouse v. Bonomi* (1861) 9 H.L.C. 503. See discussion in *McGregor on Damages* (16th ed.) pp. 266–267.

[46] *Greenwell v. Low Beechburn Co.* [1897] 2 Q.B. 165; *Hall v. Norfolk* [1900] 2 Ch. 493.

new cause of action when each event causing damage occurred. It may be that such cases should be regarded as being cases of "continuing" causes of action since they arise out of a continuing state of affairs caused by the defendant's act or omission which may be characterised as a nuisance albeit that no cause of action arises until damage occurs.

(7) Remoteness[47]

4–039   Damages for an actionable nuisance will not be recoverable if they are too "remote". In order for damages in the law of private nuisance to be awarded in respect of the nuisance it must be shown that the nuisance has actually caused the harm in question. Further, the nature of the harm caused may in itself be such that, even though it is (empirically speaking) caused by the nuisance, it is characterised as being too "remote" for liability to be imposed. The general principle for ascertaining whether damages are recoverable or whether a defendant is not liable because of their "remoteness" is found in *The Wagon Mound (No. 1)*.[48] This was a case of public nuisance. The defendant had chartered a ship which was berthed at a wharf in Sydney. While the ship was taking on oil, some was carelessly allowed to spill into the harbour. The oil floated to the claimant's wharf some 200 yards away where the claimant was refitting a ship. The refitting of the ship involved welding. The claimant noticed the oil but was reassured by the defendant that there was no danger. Two days later some molten metal fell from the claimant's wharf and ignited some cotton waste which was floating on the oil beneath the wharf; the cotton waste in its turn ignited the oil with the result that the claimant's wharf was badly damaged. The judge found on the facts of the case that the defendant could not reasonably have been expected to know that the oil could be ignited when floating on the water. However he also found that it was reasonably foreseeable that some damage would be caused to the claimant's wharf by the oil congealing on the slipways (as actually did happen). The judge at first instance applied the test laid down in *The Polemis*[49] namely that a defendant was responsible for all direct consequences of his negligent act whether or not they were reasonably foreseeable. Applying this test the defendant was held liable. The Privy Council, however, held the test was the wrong one. The recoverability of damages depended upon "whether the damage is of such a kind as the reasonable man should have foreseen".[50]

---

[47] See *Clerk and Lindsell on Torts* (18th ed.) para. 2–60 *et seq.* for an analysis of this concept.
[48] *Overseas Tankship (UK) Ltd v. Morts Dock & engineering Co Ltd* [1961] 1 A.C. 388, PC. (In *Hughes v. Lord Advocate* [1963] A.C. 837 HL (Scot) it was accepted that the *Wagon Mound (No.1)* case stated the law for England). See also *Overseas Tankship (UK) Ltd v. Miller SS Co Pty (the Wagon Mound)* [1967] 1 A.C. 617.
[49] [1921] 3 K.B. 560.
[50] [1961] A.C. 388, 426. It is sufficient that the general type of accident be foreseeable rather than the particular accident in question — see generally *Hughes v. Lord Advocate* [1963] A.C. 837. Also *Doughty v. Turner Manufacturing Co. Ltd* [1964] 1 Q.B. 518, 532; *Vacwell Engineering Co. Ltd v. B.D.H. Chemicals Ltd* [1971] 1 Q.B. 88, 100 (on appeal at 111n).

The principle found in the *Wagon Mound* case can be applied to nuisances where liability depends wholly or mainly upon the negligent behaviour of the defendant in causing or continuing a nuisance.[51] It is also possible to apply the "foreseeabiity" test to limit the damages recoverable for a breach of a duty imposed on the basis of *Rylands v. Fletcher*[52]: the strict test as to whether there is a breach of duty independent of issues of foreseeability does not mean that there must be a "strict" test governing the extent of the damages recoverable for a breach of duty. Indeed foreseeability plays a part not only in the imposition of a duty under *Rylands v. Fletcher*[53] (it is a pre-condition of liability that the defendant brings onto his land something "which is likely to do mischief if it escapes") but it also plays a part in determining the extent to which a defendant is liable for damages: the harm for which the defendant is liable must be the "natural and anticipated consequences" of the escape[54] (even though the escape itself was unforeseeable and the defendant took all reasonable steps to prevent it).[55]

The *Wagon Mound* formulation of the limit on the responsibility for damages by reason of their remoteness was made in the context of a defendant who is responsible for a nuisance as a result of his carelessness. It is hard to see why the same test should necessarily apply where the defendant has deliberately caused a nuisance. First, if the consequence is actually intended questions of foreseeability and remoteness should not arise.[56] Secondly, if the nuisance itself is intended or the defendant is reckless, it may be that the appropriate test is that of the "directness" of the consequence rather then whether it is reasonably foreseeable: it seems that in the tort of deceit where a defendant is liable for an intended or reckless misrepresentation the "directness" test remains even after the *Wagon Mound*.[57]

Exemplary and aggravated damages

The principles upon which the Court will award exemplary and aggra- **4–040**
vated damages have been examined generally above.[58] In *AB & Others v. South West Water Authority*,[59] the Court of Appeal indicated that exemplary damages should be restricted to torts which were recognised at the

---

[51] See [1967] 1 A.C. 617, esp. at 639 E-F. See above, paras. 2–011 *et seq.*
[52] (1868) L.R. 3 H.L. 330. See above, para. 2–061.
[53] See above para. 2–061.
[54] (1868) L.R. 3 H.L. 330 and see (1866) L.R. 1 Ex. 265, 279–80, *per* Blackburn J.; *Cambridge Water Co. Ltd v. Eastern Counties Leather plc* [1994] 1 All E.R. 53, 73.
[55] (1868) L.R. 3 H.L. 330; but see *The Wagon Mound*, where it was made clear that the remarks of the Privy Council did not apply in cases of strict liability. See [1961] A.C. 388, 426–7; compare [1967] A.C. 617, 639 G.
[56] Compare *Quinn v. Leatham* [1901] A.C. 495, 537.
[57] Compare *Doyle v. Olby (Ironmongers) Ltd* [1969] 1 Q.B. 158, 167, 168; *Smith New Court Securities Ltd v. Scimgeour Vickers (Asset Management) Ltd* [1996] 4 All E.R. 769, HL at 778–798 *per* Lord Browne-Wilkinson. Compare *Wilkinson v. Downton* [1897] 2 Q.B. 57.
[58] See para. 4–023 *et seq.*
[59] [1993] Q.B. 507.

time of *Rookes v. Barnard* as grounding a claim for exemplary damages. In this respect this decision has been reversed by the House of Lords in *Kuddus v. Constable of Leicestershire*.[60] In any event, it does appear that exemplary damages were available in the context of the law of private nuisance prior to *Rookes v. Barnard*. Indeed, in *Bell v. Midland Rly Co*.[61] exemplary damages were awarded where the defendant wrongfully interfered with the plaintiff's right of way and had been awarded in *Guppy's (Bridport) Ltd v. Brookling*.[62] It seems, therefore, that exemplary damages for private nuisance in accordance with the principles described above[63] may be awarded at least where:

> "there is deliberate and wilful interference with the plaintiff's rights of enjoyment of land where the defendant has calculated that the profit or benefit to him will exceed the damages he may have to pay."[64]

In other words, the damages fall within Lord Devlin's second category in *Rookes v. Barnard*.[65]

Damages in lieu of an injunction

These are considered in the section on injunctions.[66]

(3) Damages for breach of covenant

(1) General approach: basis of assessment

4–041 The wrong which damages for breach of contract seek to compensate is the *breaking* of the contract. Accordingly, such damages seek to put the claimant in the position he would have been in if the contract had never been broken, *i.e.* if the contract had been performed.[67] Accordingly, where the breach of contract in question amounts to an interference with land, the damages will be assessed by reference to the situation that would have prevailed if the contract had been performed, in other words as if there had been no interference. In practice, therefore, there will usually be no significant difference between the measure of damages for a breach of

---

[60] [2001] UKHL 29; [2001] 2 W.L.R. 1789.
[61] (1861) 10 C.B.N.S. 287.
[62] [1984] E.G.D. 294, CA (though the availability of exemplary damages does not appear to have been the subject of argument); see also para. 2–020 concerning this case.
[63] See para. 4–023 *et seq.*
[64] In *AB & Others v. South West Water Authority per* Stuart-Smith L.J.
[65] See para. 4–026 *et seq.* above.
[66] See paras. 4–100 to 4–103.
[67] See *Livingstone v. Rawyards Coal Co* (1880) 5 App. Cas. 25, 39 *per* Lord Blackburn; see generally *McGregor on Damages*, 16th ed., para. 810 *et seq.*

contract consisting of an interference with land and a tortious interference with land.[68]

(a) Remoteness

Damages for breach of contract for interference with land will be subject to the usual rules relating to remoteness applicable to damages for breach of contract.[69] In short, as stated by Alderson B in *Hadley v. Baxendale*[70]:   **4–042**

> "where two parties have made a contract which one of them has broken, the damages which the other party ought to receive in respect of such breach of contract should be such as may fairly and reasonably be considered either arising naturally, *i.e.* according to the usual course of things, from such breach of contract itself, or such as may reasonably be supposed to have been in the contemplation of both parties, at the time they made the contract, as the probable result of the breach of it. Now, if the special circumstances under which the contract was actually made were communicated by the plaintiffs to the defendants and were thus known to both parties, the damages resulting from the breach of such a contract, which they would reasonably contemplate, would be the amount of injury which would ordinarily follow from the breach of contract under these special circumstances so known and communicated. But, on the other hand, if these special circumstances were wholly unknown to the party breaking the contract, he, at the most, would only be supposed to have had in his contemplation the amount of injury which would arise generally, and in the great multitude of cases not affected by any special circumstances, from such a breach of contract."

(b) Mitigation

As in the case of other claims for contractual damages, the tenant will be under a duty to mitigate his losses.[71] In short, a claimant is under a duty to take reasonable steps to mitigate his loss consequent on the breach and he is unable to claim damages which are due to his failure to take such steps.[72]   **4–043**

(c) Exemplary damages

Exemplary damages are not recoverable in respect of a claim for damages for breach of contract.[73]   **4–044**

---

[68] See para. 4–002 *et seq.*
[69] See *McGregor on Damages*, 16th ed., para. 232 *et seq.*
[70] (1854) 9 Ex 341 at 355; see too *Victoria Laundry v. Newman* [1949] 2 K.B. 528, CA; *Czarnikow v. Koufos* [1969] 1 A.C. 350, HL.
[71] *McGregor on Damages*, 16th ed., para. 282 *et seq.*
[72] *British Westinghouse Co v. Underground Railway* [1912] A.C. 673, 689 *per* Viscount Haldane L.C.
[73] See para. 4–023 *et seq.*

(2) *Interference with land in breach of landlord's contract*

(a) Generally

4–045 Where there is an interference by a landlord with his tenant's possession of land this may amount to a breach of the covenant for quiet enjoyment[74] or the landlord's obligation not to derogate from his grant.[75] The damages which will be awarded will, as indicated above, be assessed by reference to the loss of bargain which the tenant suffers.[76] In this respect, it should be noted that the usual covenants between landlord and tenant do not extend to protection from mental distress but rather protect the use and benefit of the property which the tenant is entitled to enjoy.[77]

(b) Total eviction

4–046 Where a landlord evicts his tenant from the whole of the property or prevents the tenant from taking possession at all,[78] the tenant will be entitled to the value of the unexpired term.[79] In assessing this value it is clear that the rent which the tenant would have had to pay must be taken into account in the valuation.

In principle, it seems that the date for assessing such damages will be the date of the breach, namely the moment of eviction. Accordingly, any improvements made by the tenant prior to the eviction and any increases (or decreases) in value since the date of the lease will be taken into account.[80] It follows also that improvements to the property made by the landlord or increases (or decreases) in value since the eviction will not be taken into account.

In addition to the value of the land, damages for consequential losses (if not too remote and subject to the duty to mitigate) will also be recoverable. Thus in *Grosvenor Hotel Co v. Hamilton*[81] where the tenant was obliged to leave his premises and re-establish his business elsewhere as a result of the vibration of his landlord's machines on adjoining property, the tenant was entitled to recover the expenses of setting up business elsewhere. In principle, a tenant may also be able to recover loss of profit and goodwill which results from an eviction in breach of covenant.[82]

---

[74] See Chapter 3, para. 3–024 *et seq.*
[75] See Chapter 3, paras. 3–042 to 3–045.
[76] See 4–041 and 4–044.
[77] *Branchett v. Beaney* [1992] 3 All E.R. 910; see Chapter 3 para. 3–025.
[78] See Chapter 3 para. 3–035.
[79] See *Williams v. Burrell* (1845) 1 CB 402, 433 *per* Tindal CJ; *Lock v. Furze* (1866) L.R. 1 C.P. 441.
[80] *Rolph v. Crouch* (1867) L.R. 3 Ex. 44 (partial eviction — see below para. 4–047); see too *Bunny v. Hopkinson* (1859) 27 Beav. 565 (total eviction of purchaser). But *cf. Lewis v. Campbell* (1819) 8 Taunt 715.
[81] [1894] 2 Q.B. 836, CA.
[82] *Lawson v. Hartley Brown* (1995) 71 P. & C.R. 242, CA; *Connaught Restaurants v. Indoor Leisure* (1995) 71 P. & C.R. 242, CA; see too *Mira v. Aylmer Square Investments* [1990] 1 E.G.L.R. 45, CA (loss of profits from lost sub-lettings) and *Meadows v. Home Properties* [1993] E.G.C.S. 50 (loss of tenant architect's chance to win a competition).

(c) Partial Eviction

Where a landlord evicts his tenant from part of the property the tenant will be entitled to damages assessed by reference to the value of the property which has been lost (taking account of the rental payable for that property) as well as consequential losses. Thus, in the case of *Rolph v. Crouch*[83] the tenant was evicted from a part of the demised premises on which the tenant had built a conservatory which was used for the tenant's business as a florist. It was held that the tenant was entitled to damages for the loss of the value of the strip of land, the cost of the conservatory and loss of profit (or what the land might reasonably have expected to be worth to the claimant).

4–047

(d) Temporary eviction

Where a tenant has been evicted temporarily, damages may be assessed by reference to the value of the property only for the period of the eviction. The tenant may also recover damages for loss of business and for any temporary accommodation.[84]

4–048

(e) Disturbance without loss of possession

If the disturbance consists of an interference which does not result in the tenant losing possession, the matter is not as straightforward. If, for instance, the interference consists of the exercise by a person exercising an incumbrance over the tenant's land, unless it can be shown that the incumbrance will endure and be exercised for the term of the lease, then it will not be possible to recover damages for the loss in value of the premises for the entire term unexpired at the date of the breach.[85] One can only recover damages actually sustained at the commencement of the action.[86] On the other hand, there seems nothing in principle to prevent a tenant claiming damages for loss in value and any consequential losses in relation to the period before the commencement of the action.

4–049

Where an interference which consists of threats of eviction or disturbance by a third party, the cost of dealing with such a threat or claim may be recoverable.[87]

---

[83] (1867) L.R. 3 Ex. 44.
[84] See *Olidawura v. Fulmyk* [1975] C.L.Y. 1929 (county court); *Malloy v. Alexander* [1982] C.L.Y. 1747 (county court).
[85] See *Child v. Stenning* (1879) 11 Ch. D. 82; compare *Sutton v. Baillie* (1892) 65 L.T. 528 (covenant for title on sale of land).
[86] *ibid*; see too *Kenny v. Preen* [1963] 1 Q.B. 499, CA.
[87] *Lock v. Furze* (1866) L.R. 1 C.P. 441; compare too *Jones v. Hawkins* (1886) 3 T.L.R. 59.

(3) Tenant's Failure to deliver up possession in breach of covenant

4–050 Where a tenant fails to deliver up possession in accordance with his covenant to yield up possession,[88] the usual measure of damage is the value of the use of the property until such time as the landlord regains possession.[89] In addition, (subject to remoteness) consequential losses may be recovered. Thus, where the tenant's breach consists of leaving a third party in possession, the landlord is entitled to the reasonable cost of an action to eject the third party.[90] Similarly, where the tenant's breach puts the landlord himself in breach of an obligation to a third party (for instance, an incoming tenant), then the landlord may recover the damages and costs for which he is liable.[91] The extent to which such liability may arise will depend on whether the parties could have contemplated that the landlord would re-let,[92] but in modern circumstances, re-letting on usual market terms is something which parties to a lease might reasonably anticipate.

It will be noted that the lessor can claim damages only to the extent of his entitlement to possession. Thus in *Watson v. Lane*[93] where the landlord was also a mortgagor, the landlord could only recover damages for the tenant's breach of covenant for the three days which passed between the end of the lease and the day when the mortgagee took possession.

(4) Nuisances, annoyances, etc

4–051 Where an action for damages for breach of a restrictive covenant lies,[94] then any losses recoverable will be compensated in accordance with the principles set out above. Damages, however, will not be recoverable in relation to the loss of future value in the property unless it can be shown that the breach of covenant results in permanent damage.[95]

Additional remedies where there is a contractual relationship: set-off and suspension of rent

(1) Set-off

4–052 Historically there were limits on the extent to which a tenant was entitled to set-off claims for damages against a rent due to his landlord under a lease. It now, however, appears to be clear that the general equitable rule

---

[88] Chapter 3 para. 3–046.
[89] *Henderson v. Squire* (1869) L.R. 4 Q.B. 170; *Ibbs v. Richardson* (1839) 9 A. & E. 849.
[90] *Henderson v. Squire* (1869) L.R. 4 Q.B. 170; see too *Henderson v. Van Cooten* (1923) 67 Sol. Jo. 228.
[91] *Bramley v. Chesterton* (1857) 2 C.B.N.S. 592.
[92] *ibid.* at p 605 *per* Cockburn C.J. a "not unimportant fact".
[93] (1856) 11 Ex. 769.
[94] See para. 3–063.
[95] Compare paras. 4–049 (above) and 4–037 (damages for nuisance).

that where a cross-claim is so directly connected with a claim that it would be manifestly unjust to allow a claimant to recover, the defendant may set-off the cross-claim against the claim applies to claims for rent.[96] In principle, where a landlord (or licensor) wrongfully interferes with a tenant's (or licensee's) enjoyment of his property, a tenant may set-off damages for such breach against the rent (or contractual sums) due. A right of set-off may, however, be excluded by express agreement.[97]

(2) Suspension of Rent

(a) Generally

In the context of the law of landlord and tenant, where a tenant is deprived of his enjoyment of the demised premises, he may defend himself from an action by his landlord for rent. This remedy appears distinguishable from the right to set off damages for breach of covenant against the rent due to the landlord[98] the right to abate rent arising in some circumstances where the landlord is not in breach of covenant (for example, where a person with title paramount to the landlord evicts the tenant).[99]

4–053

(b) Eviction by landlord and persons claiming through the landlord

In the context of the law of landlord and tenant, it should be noted that where the tenant is wrongfully evicted by his or anyone claiming through his landlord, then his obligation to pay rent will be suspended.[1] Eviction for these purposes is:

4–054

> "something of a grave and permanent character done by the landlord with the intention of depriving the tenant of the enjoyment of the demised premises".[2]

It is something more than a temporary trespass.[3] On the other hand it is not necessary that the eviction consist of physical expulsion: it is sufficient for there to be activities which result in the tenant being deprived of possession.[4] Eviction has been held to occur where the landlord enters and

---

[96] See *British Anzani (Felixstowe) Ltd v. International Marine Management Ltd* [1980] Q.B. 137; *Eller v. Grovecrest Investments Ltd* [1995] Q.B. 272; [1994] 4 All E.R. 845, CA.

[97] See *Electricity Supply Nominees Ltd v. IAF Group Ltd* [1993] 2 E.G.L.R. 95; *Star Rider Ltd v. Intrepreneur Pub Co* [1998] 1 E.G.L.R. 53; contrast *Connaught Restaurants Ltd v. Indoor Leisure Ltd* [1994] 1 W.L.R. 501.

[98] See para. 4–052.

[99] See para. 4–055.

[1] *Morrison v. Chadwick* (1849) 7 C.B. 266; *London & County (A & D) Ltd v. Wilfred Sportsman Ltd* [1969] 1 W.L.R. 1215 and [1971] Ch. 764, CA. See too *Boodle v. Campbell* (1844) 7 Man. & G. 386.

[2] *Upton v. Townend* (1855) 17 C.B. 30 *per* Jervis C.J.

[3] *Henderson v. Mears* (1859) 1 F. & F. 636.

[4] See *Commissioners of Crown Land v. Page* [1960] 2 Q.B. 274; see too *Burn v. Phelps* (1815) 1 Stark 94; *Kirkman v. Jervis* (1839) 7 Dowl. 678; *Cowe v. Goodwin* (1840) 9 C. & P. 378.

uses the demised premises,[5] where he let it to a new tenant,[6] where he rebuilds the premises in a different form[7] and where he has demolished a party wall.[8]

The entry must not only be permanent but must be *wrongful*.[9] Thus rent will not be suspended if the landlord has reserved to himself the right to enter the premises: in such circumstances, there will be no trespass and the landlord is entitled to enter the premises.[10]

(c) Eviction by third parties: title paramount and trespassers

4–055   Even though a tenant may not have a claim for damages where he is evicted by someone with title paramount to that of his landlord,[11] then he will have a defence to a claim for rent by his own landlord.[12] There is no eviction by title paramount where the eviction is authorised by statute.[13]

On the other hand, eviction by a trespasser does not excuse the tenant from paying the rent.[14]

(d) Eviction from part

4–056   It appears that where the tenant is evicted from part of the land, the rent is apportionable if the eviction is by a person claiming by title paramount to the landlord.[15] On the other hand, if the eviction is by the landlord the whole rent is suspended[16] unless the eviction results from re-entry of part pursuant to a clause entitling the landlord to forfeit part of the premises.[17]

Although rent is suspended by eviction from part of the land, the tenant must still perform his other covenants under the lease.[18]

---

5   *Griffiths v. Hodges* (1824) 1 C. & P. 419.
6   *Pellatt v. Boosey* (1862) 31 L.J.C.P. 281.
7   *Upton v. Townend* (1855) 17 C.B. 30.
8   *Upton v. Greenless* (1855) 17 C.B. 30.
9   *Commissioners of Crown Land v. Page* [1960] 2 Q.B. 274; see Chapter 3 para. 3–040.
10 *Hunt v. Cape* (1775) Cowp 242; *Newton v. Allin* (1841) 1 Q.B. 518.
11 See Chapter 3 para. 3–030.
12 *Cuthbertson v. Irving* (1859–60) 4 H. & N. 742.
13 *Commissioners for Crown Land* [1960] 2 Q.B. 274; *Popular Catering Association Ltd v. Romagnoli* [1937] 1 All E.R. 167; *Swift v. Macbean* [1942] 1 K.B. 375; see Chapter 3 para. 3–040.
14 *Paradine v. Jane* (1647) Aleyn 26; *Cooper v. Young* (1733) Fortes Rep 36; see *Tasker v. Bullman* (1849) 3 Ex. 351.
15 Gilb. Rents 147; *Smith v. Malings* (1607) Cro Jac 160; *McLoughlin v. Craig* (1856) 7 Ir. C.L.R. 117; *Boodle v. Campbell* (1844) 7 Man. & Gr. 386.
16 *Furnival v. Grove* (1860) 8 C.B.N.S. 496; *London & County(A & D) Ltd v. Wilfred Sportsman Ltd* [1969] 1 W.L.R. 1215 ([1971] Ch. 764, CA).
17 *Walker's Case* (1587) Co. Rep. 22a; *Knight's Case* (1585) Moor 199.
18 *Newton v. Allin* (1841) 1 Q.B. 518; *Morrison v. Chadwick* (1849) 7 C.B. 266.

The recovery of possession

Introduction

Probably the most important of the remedies available to the dispossessed **4–057**
landowner is the remedy which restores possession, *i.e.* the action for the
recovery of land (*ejectment*). In procedural terms, the possession of land
must now be recovered in accordance with CPR Part 55,[19] which assumes
that most possession claims can be dealt with summarily. Sections 75 and
76 of the Criminal Justice and Public Order 1994 introduced a form of
accelerated summary procedure for "interim possession orders" which
still operate under Part II of CCR Ord. 24, preserved by Schedule 2 to the
CPR. This was intended to provide a more effective remedy for both residential and business occupiers who find their properties squatted.[20] The
"interim possession orders" introduced by the Criminal Justice and Public Order Act 1994 are supported by stringent criminal penalties: it is a
criminal offence not to leave premises subject to such an order within 24
hours of service of the order or to return within one year of service.[21] The
penalties include a maximum of six months' imprisonment.[22]

Action for the recovery of land

The action for ejectment developed initially as a special remedy for lease- **4–058**
holders[23] but was gradually adapted (through the use of fictions) for use
by freeholders as a speedier, and more reliable, alternative to the earlier
forms of action.[24] It is now the only remedy available in respect of trespass
to land which restores possession since the summary actions (including
applications for interim possession orders[25]) do not create new remedies
but merely provide new procedural means for obtaining the same remedy
as is available in ordinary actions in the High Court and the County Court
for the recovery of possession. The most significant difference between
ordinary actions and applications for interim orders is that breach of an
interim possession order is a criminal offence[26] and is enforceable by the
police.

---

[19] Introduced with effect from October 15, 2001 by the Civil Procedure (Amendment) Rules
2001 S.I. No. 256. These Rules revoked most of the old R.S.C. Order 113 (except for rule
7)) and C.C.R. Order 24 Part I (except for r. 6), which had survived the first 2½ years from
the introduction of the C.P.R. in April 1999. Only the enforcement provisions survive for
the time being.

[20] See the statement of the Home Secretary introducing the Bill: Hansard (Commons) 11.1.94
columns 29–30. See, further, paras. 4–076 to 4–003 and Chap. 5, para. 5–058.

[21] S. 76(2)-(4) of the 1994 Act.

[22] S. 76(5) of the 1994 Act.

[23] See Milsom, *Historical Foundations of the Common Law* (2nd ed.), Chapter 7, pp 152–157,
and in Selden Society, Vol. 80 (1963) (*Novae Narrationes*) pp clxxxviii-cxc, Baker, *An Introduction to English Legal History* (3rd ed.) pp 337–341.

[24] *Baker, op. cit.*, pp 341–343 and Sutherland, *The Assize of Novel Disseisin*, Chap. 5.

[25] Under ss. 75 and 76 of the Criminal Justice and Public Order Act 1994. See para. 4–057.

[26] S. 76(5) of the Criminal Justice and Public Order Act 1994. See Chap. 4, para. 4–053.

(1) Entitlement to possession

4–059   There are two essential elements to a claim for possession:

(a)   the claimant must prove that he has superior title to the defendant; and

(b)   the claimant must demonstrate that he was entitled to immediate possession of the land as at the date of the commencement of the proceedings.

(a) Proof of superior title

4–060   First, it is necessary for the claimant to prove the superiority of his own title to that of the defendant. He must be able to adduce evidence of his own good title, *e.g.* by production of the land certificate or office copy entries,[27] conveyance, mortgage or other title deeds. The claimant may also rely on evidence demonstrating an estoppel as between landlord and tenant[28] which would prevent the tenant/defendant disputing a claim to possession by the claimant brought by the claimant as landlord. A claimant may not rely principally on the fact that the defendant cannot prove his own title and must first set up his own. Once the claimant has proved his own title, then it is for the defendant to adduce evidence as to his own entitlement to remain in possession.[29]

As has already been stated,[30] a claimant need prove only that he was in possession prior to the defendant in order to demonstrate sufficient title to bring trespass against the defendant and the fact that a third party has better title provides no defence to the trespassing defendant. Nonetheless, it is clearly preferable for a claimant to be able to demonstrate better title than mere *de facto* possession since mere possession may prove precarious.

Where the claimant is a licensee, the terms of the licence will be of the greatest importance, as has been learned by developers seeking to evict protestors from sensitive construction projects. A licence giving the claimant a right of access and occupation will amount to better title than that of the trespasser[31] although; a mere right of access will not be sufficient.[32]

---

[27]   Which are admissible to the same extent as the land certificate — s. 113 of the Land Registration Act 1925.

[28]   See *Hill and Redman's Law of Landlord & Tenant* paras A[86]–A[149] ("Tenancies by Estoppel").

[29]   *Danford v. McAnulty* (1883) 8 App. Cas. 456 at 462.

[30]   See above, para. 1–003.

[31]   *Manchester Airport plc v. Dutton* [2000] 1Q.B. 133, CA *per* Laws L.J. "A licensee not in occupation can claim possession against a trespasser if that is a necessary remedy to vindicate and give effect to such rights of occupation as by contract with his licensor he enjoys".

[32]   *Countryside Residential (North Thames) Ltd v. Tugwell and others* [2000] 34 E.G. 87, CA.

(b) Immediate entitlement to possession

Secondly, the claimant must establish that as at the date of the commencement of the proceedings he was entitled to immediate possession of the land — whether by demonstrating that the defendant entered into occupation without licence or consent (*i.e.* as a trespasser *ab initio*) or that the defendant has remained in occupation following the termination of some limited right to occupy the land.

4–061

Where some right to occupy has been granted to the defendant, the claimant must prove that:

(i) the right of the defendant to occupy the premises was terminable by the claimant; and

(ii) such right was, in fact, duly terminated by the time proceedings were commenced.

Requirement (i) is largely a question of the nature and construction of the agreement between the parties and the nature of the right granted to the defendant. For example, it may be terminable only in certain specified circumstances such as upon a certain period of written notice or if certain facts arise.[33]

If the right to terminate exists, the claimant must ensure that he has properly determined the defendant's right to occupy. The entitlement to possession must have arisen by the date proceedings are commenced, otherwise they will fail. In the case of leasehold land, the reversioner must prove that the tenancy has been duly terminated — whether by surrender, forfeiture (or notice to determine) or notice to quit.[34] The right of the landlord to recover possession may then depend on the following:

(i) in the case of forfeiture, the right of the tenant to seek relief from forfeiture; and

(ii) any statutory restrictions on the termination of tenancies.

(i). A detailed consideration of forfeiture is to be found in the standard texts on the law of landlord and tenant.[35] In general, the courts lean against forfeiture and, on the footing that the purpose of forfeiture is to secure the tenant's compliance with his covenants, will grant relief in most cases if the tenant is able to restore the status quo[36] and to compensate the landlord in costs[37] for having had to bring the action. The effect of

---

[33] *e.g.* where a landlord chooses to exercise his rights under a redevelopment break clause.

[34] See *Hill and Redman*, para. A[7849] *et seq.*

[35] See, for example, *Hill and Redman*, para. A[8530] *et seq.*, *Woodfall*, Chapter 17, Part 5, and Pawlowski, *The Forfeiture of Leases*.

[36] *e.g.* by paying off arrears of rent or otherwise complying with the provisions of covenants which have been breached.

[37] See, *e.g. Gill v. Lewis* [1956] 2 Q.B. 1, CA, *Central Estates (Belgravia) v. Woolgar* [1971] 2 Q.B. 48, CA and *Scala House and District Property Co. Ltd v. Forbes* [1974] Q.B. 575, CA.

relief, except where an order is made under section 146(4) of the Law of Property Act 1925 (mortgages and sub-tenants),[38] is to restore the forfeited interest.[39]

(ii). There are a number of statutory codes conferring security of tenure on various classes of tenant and the particular rules of the statutory codes must be observed in order for the landowner to become entitled to possession of his land. See the principal codes conferring various forms of security of tenure: Part II of the Landlord and Tenant Act 1954 (business tenancies); the Rent (Agriculture) Act 1976, the Rent Act 1977, the Housing Act 1988 (all concerned with various forms of private sector residential tenancies); the Housing Act 1985 (public sector tenancies); the Agricultural Holdings Act 1986 and the Agricultural Tenancies Act 1995 (tenancies of agricultural land) and the Caravan Sites Act 1968 and the Mobile Homes Act 1983 (both concerned with protecting residents of mobile homes). For example, in the absence of the parties' agreement, or loss of security of tenure,[40] Rent Act statutory tenancies and Housing Act 1988 assured tenancies can only be terminated by court order.

In the case of most residential periodic tenants, section 5 of the Protection from Eviction Act 1977 (as amended) stipulates a minimum period of four weeks' notice and requires that the notice be in writing in such form as may be prescribed.[41] If the notice does not comply with both section 5 and the common law rules as to termination it will be ineffective to terminate the interest, and any action to recover possession based upon it will fail.[42] However, section 5 stipulates only a minimum period of notice and certain categories of periodic tenancies (*e.g.* monthly, quarterly and annual) require, in the absence of agreement to the contrary, a longer period at common law (respectively, in the case of the previous examples, a month, a quarter and six months expiring on the anniversary of the commencement of the tenancy).

4–062 If a licence was granted, and is terminable by the claimant, then at common law:

(a) reasonable notice must be given; and

(b) a reasonable time must be allowed to the defendant to remove himself and his possessions from the premises ("packing-up time").[43]

---

[38] Where a new interest is vested in the applicant: see *Cadogan v. Dimovic* [1984] 1 W.L.R. 609 and *Escalus Properties Ltd v. Robinson*, [1996] Q.B. 231.

[39] See *Hill and Redman*, para. A[8530] *et seq.*

[40] *e.g.*, in the case of a Rent Act statutory tenancy, by the tenant's ceasing to occupy the premises as his residence.

[41] See the Notices to Quit (Prescribed Information) Regulations 1988 (S.I. 1988 No. 2201) and *Hill and Redman*, para. C[3251]–C[3254].

[42] See *Hill and Redman*, para. A[8127].

[43] *Minister of Health v. Bellotti* [1944] K.B. 298, CA.

Any contractual provision regulating termination must, in any event, be complied with by the claimant.

Even if time period (b) is insufficient, the notice to revoke the licence is still effective. In the event of failure to give sufficient packing-up time, the proceedings will fail but a new notice need not be served. Inadequate packing-up time does not invalidate an otherwise valid revocation of a licence. In *Minister of Health v. Bellotti*,[44] the Court of Appeal clearly considered that the adequacy of time to move out went to the entitlement to possession and, hence, the right to commence proceedings. Accordingly, if proceedings are commenced after the revocation of the licence but before sufficient time to move has elapsed they must fail and cannot be cured by the lapse of what would be a sufficient time to move out between the issue of proceedings and the hearing (or the date fixed for possession).[45] The requirement of "packing-up time" appears to be applied generally in the case of licences although it has been said that the question of whether reasonable notice to terminate a licence is required is "to be answered in the light of the circumstances existing when the contract is made".[46] Similarly, the length of the notice required "is the time that is deemed to be reasonable in the light of the circumstances in which the notice is given".[47]

Further, in the case of many licences, the position has been modified by the amendments made to the Protection from Eviction Act 1977 by the Housing Act 1988. Section 5 of the 1977 Act, as amended, provides that a periodic licence of residential premises (providing it is not an excluded licence[48]) can only be validly determined by a notice in the prescribed form which gives the licensee at least four weeks' notice to vacate. Accordingly, the licensee must be served with a written notice which is very similar to the notice to quit which must be used to determine a periodic tenancy of residential premises.[49] Indeed, there is only one set of prescribed information[50] for both tenants and non-excluded licensees and most law stationers have devised forms of notice which can be used for either periodic tenants or licensees within the Act. In these circumstances, the common law requirement of reasonable notice has been replaced with a statutory minimum period although it may still be argued (as with notice to quit) that, since the period prescribed is a minimum period only, reasonable notice in certain cases may be longer than four weeks. If the parties to the licence have agreed a longer period for notice of revocation than is stipulated by the 1977 Act, that period of notice must be given. As with the relationship between the common law rules governing notices to

---

[44] *ibid.*

[45] See the judgment of Lord Greene M.R. in *Bellotti*, above, at 243–5.

[46] Lord Devlin in *Australian Blue Metal Ltd v. Hughes* [1963] A.C. 74, PC, at 99.

[47] *ibid.* at 99.

[48] See ss. 3A and 31 of the Housing Act 1988.

[49] S. 5 of the Protection from Eviction Act 1977 does not apply to agricultural holdings, whether or not they include a dwelling house used as a residence: *National Trust for Places of Historic Interest or Natural Beauty v. Knipe and Anr.* [1998] 1 W.L.R. 230, CA.

[50] S.I. 1988 No. 2201.

quit and the 1977 Act, the Act only prescribes a minimum period of notice. It is therefore open to the parties to agree a longer period.

The Housing Act 1988 amendments to the 1977 Act are silent as to the question of "packing-up time" and it appears possible, given the introduction of a statutory code for the determination of residential licenses (apart from those excluded), that no further time need be given to the licensee to move out following the expiry of the licence. Since the court has a discretion in such cases to postpone possession for a period,[51] there appears to be no useful purpose served by the requirement of additional time for packing-up. It must, however, be conceded that the same argument can be applied to the position at common law hence there is some scope for doubt whether packing-up time can be disregarded in the case of licences within the Protection from Eviction Act.

(c) Public authorities

4–063   The position of public authority landlords differs from that of ordinary private landlords in that the decision of such an authority to seek to evict a trespasser may be affected by the consideration of other statutory duties and considerations (such as government policy). If those matters are not properly considered as part of the decision to evict, then the decision may be open to challenge by way of judicial review. The issue of public law "defences" is considered earlier in paragraphs 1–122 to 1–135. Since the public law *vires* of a decision is closely bound up with the process of reaching the decision, that section also sets out certain broad principles which should be followed by public authorities when considering whether to evict trespassers from their own land.

Further, see the special considerations discussed above with regard to the time to be allowed for the termination of licences held by public authorities at paragraph 1–072, above.

The duty imposed on public authorities by section 6 of the Human Rights Act 1998 to act in a manner compatible with Convention Rights, and the interpretative requirements of section 3 of that Act, are capable of affecting decisions made by those authorities with regard to decision to take proceedings and with the enforcement of any orders obtained.[52] This is considered in more detail in Chapter 1.[53] Since the Court is itself a "public authority" any orders which the Court is asked to make will have to take account of the ECHR and ensure Convention Rights under the Act

---

[51] See *Bain & Co. v. Church Commissioners for England* [1989] 1 W.L.R. 24, subject to s. 89 of the Housing Act 1980 where the Court has no "reasonableness" discretion: though see the remarks of the Court of Appeal in *R. (McLellan) v. Bracknell Forest D.C. & Others* [2002] 1 All E.R. 899 and the Human Rights dimension, below. Since the Court is a "public authority" for the purposes of the Human Rights Act 1998 it must exercise its own discretion compatibly with Convention Rights.

[52] See e.g. *Poplar Housing and Regeneration Community Association v. Donaghue* [2001] 3 W.L.R. 183 (CA) where the claims for breach of Convention Rights and incompatibility failed.

[53] See 1–127 to 1–135 above. See also paras. 4–104 and 4–113.

are complied with. In *London Borough of Lambeth v. Howard*,[54] Sedley L.J. accepted the application of the Convention to possession proceedings and considered the implication of Article 8 in particular on the exercise of the Court's powers where the subject property was the defendant's home.[55]

(2) Procedure

From October 15, 2001 the procedural rules for possession of land were almost wholly replaced by the introduction of CPR Part 55, which provides a special procedure for all possession claims except those for interim possession orders, as introduced by the Criminal Justice and Public Order Act 1994. The procedures in force prior to October 15, 2001 under the Rules of the Supreme Court and the County Court Rules are not considered here,[56] other than Part II of CCR Ord. 24, which remains in force governing interim possession orders.

4–064

Possession proceedings against trespassers under CPR Part 55

(1) Introduction

In CPR Part 55,[57] account is taken of the differences which exist between various types of possession claims (even where combined with other disputes) now governed by the unified procedure. That unification is marred only by the omission of interim possession orders which remained governed by what remains of CCR Order 24. The thinking behind Part 55 includes the creation (or, more accurately, re-creation) of a fast and efficient procedure, capable of dealing with a high volume of claims for a single remedy, into the mechanics of a more general system. The solution has been to draft a special procedure with its own set of forms which brings together all "possession claims" made against trespassers, tenants and mortgagors (other than those using the interim possession order procedure set out below). Part 55 recognises that the value of the subject-matter of a possession claim is not an appropriate measure by which to classify it: there is now a presumption that most claims should be handled by the county court. Special allowances are also made for situations involving disputed facts and costs will be allowed even where the case is heard under small claims procedure.

4–065

The discussion in this book will be limited to the specific rules which apply to trespassers, except to the extent that the procedure against trespassers and other occupiers overlaps.[58]

---

[54] (2001) 33 H.L.R. 58, CA.
[55] Considered at paras. 1–128 to 1–134 above.
[56] See the first edition of this work, Chapter 1, paras. 1–154 to 1–182.
[57] See also the Part 55 *Practice Direction — Possession Claims* which accompanies it.
[58] See *Woodfall*, Volume 1, Chapter 19, Section 4.

(2) Availability of the Part 55 procedure

4–066   Unlike RSC Ord. 113 or CCR Ord. 24, Part 55 contains the procedure for all "possession claims", a term which means claims for the recovery of possession of land, including buildings or parts of buildings. One important change in emphasis between the old and new procedural rules is the requirement to use Part 55 in certain circumstances whereas, under Order 113 and Order 24, a defendant was more likely to attempt to exclude the summary jurisdiction of the court. The use of Part 55 is mandatory where a claim includes:

(1)   a possession claim brought by a landlord, mortgagee or licensee,[59]

(2)   a possession claim brought against trespassers,[60]

(3)   a claim by a tenant seeking relief from forfeiture.[61]

For the purposes of this work, the special rules for cases falling within Part 55.2(1)(b) above will be referred to as "the trespass procedure". The trespass procedure is not materially different to the procedure in Order 113 and Order 24, although claims using it require some elements beyond those necessary for other claims made under Part 55.

For a claim to be "a possession claim brought against trespassers", four requirements must be satisfied[62]:

(1)   the claimant must be entitled to possession of the land which is the subject of the proceedings;

(2)   the land must be in the sole occupation of the trespasser(s);

(3)   that occupation must be without the licence or consent of the person entitled to possession; and

(4)   that occupation must not be by a person or persons who are tenants or former tenants holding over.

(a) Entitlement to possession

4–067   This topic has already been discussed above.[63] As has already been mentioned, Part 55 does not create a new remedy but merely introduces a new unified procedure.

---

[59] CPR Part 55.2(1)(a).
[60] CPR Part 55.2(1)(b).
[61] CPR Part 55.2(1)(c).
[62] CPR Part 55.1(b).
[63] See paras. 4–061 and 4–063.

(b) Sole occupation

There are two points to note here. First, it is only necessary to prove occu- **4–068** pation — this is usually straightforward and generally involves a demonstration of the defendant's physical presence on the premises. Secondly, the requirement of sole occupation by the trespasser(s) prevents the use of the trespass procedure where premises are occupied by both trespassers and authorised persons. This protects the lawful occupier from the effects of a possession order which lies against all occupiers of the land named in Part 55 claim form.[64] Further, that limitation reflects the general rule that only the person with a claim to immediate possession of the land may bring an action to recover land, *i.e.* where the premises are lawfully occupied, it is for those lawful occupiers, who have an immediate entitlement to possession of the premises to bring an action for possession.[65]

(c) Without consent

It is clear from the wording of Part 55.1(b) that it is applicable both to cases **4–069** of trespass *ab initio* ("entered . . . the land") and where the right to occupy, though originally lawful, has been subsequently determined ("or remained on the land"). One difference between Part 55 and Order 113 and Order 24, is that it is inappropriate to treat former licensees as trespassers under the new rules. Former licensees now fall within the general application of Part 55[66]. It is nonetheless proper to use the trespass procedure for claims against service occupiers, parties to a conveyancing transaction which has fallen through or former occupiers pursuant to a old restricted contract within the Rent Act 1977.[67]

In the case of trespass *ab initio* it is only necessary to prove by affidavit that no or consent has been given: it is then for the defendant to adduce evidence to show licence or consent.

However, where the entry into occupation was lawful and the claimant relies on the "remained on the land" limb of Part 55.1(b), the claimant must prove that:

(i) the right of the defendant to occupy the premises was terminable by the claimant; and

(ii) the right was, in fact, duly terminated.

---

[64] *R. v. Wandsworth County Court ex parte London Borough of Wandsworth* [1975] 1 W.L.R. 1314.
[65] See above, paras. 4–061 and 4–063.
[66] Note the distinction between Part 55.2(1)(a)(iii) and 55.2.(1)(b) and between Part 55.5(2) and (3).
[67] Which has no effect on most agreements entered in or after January 15, 1989: see the Housing Act 1988, although note the terms of s. 34 of that Act which creates some exceptions.

(d) Nature of occupation

4–070   The trespass procedure should be used to obtain possession against all persons occupying without consent except:[68]

(i)   a tenant or sub-tenant; or

(ii)   a former tenant or sub-tenant.

For example, the trespass procedure may be used to recover possession against former service occupiers,[69] a prospective purchaser allowed into occupation under a contract for the sale of land where the transaction falls through.[70]

(3) Orders the court may make

4–071   In the case of a trespasser *ab initio,* and in the absence of the claimant's agreement, the court has no discretion at all and must make an order for possession forthwith without any suspension or delay. This point was considered at length by the Court of Appeal in *McPhail v. Persons Unknown*[71] where it was held that:

"... squatters were never able to enlist the aid of the Court of Chancery to resist a writ of possession and they cannot now" (*per* Lawton L.J.).[72]

Where persons remain in occupation as trespassers, following the termination of some right to remain,[73] it is likely that the court does have a discretion — particularly given that the analysis of the Court of Appeal in *McPhail* was based on the attitude of the court of equity to trespassers *ab initio, i.e.* where there had been wrongful conduct throughout. Where the occupation does not have a wrongful origin, the case for the complete exclusion of the court's discretion is not compelling.

---

[68]   CPR Part 55.1(b).

[69]   Who are generally not tenants: see *Street v. Mountford* [1985] 1 A.C. 809, HL, 818–9.

[70]   Occupation in such circumstances generally does not give rise to the relationship of landlord and tenant if it is referable to the relationship of vendor and purchaser: see *Street v. Mountford,* above, at 821B-C, *Walters v. Roberts* (1980) 41 P. & C.R. 210, *Bretherton v. Paton* [1986] 1 E.G.L.R. 172, *Essex Plan Ltd v. Broadminster Ltd* [1988] 2 E.G.L.R. 73 and *Bain and Co. v. Church Commissioners for England* [1989] 1 W.L.R. 24.

[71]   [1973] Ch. 447. See also *Swordheath Properties Ltd v. Floydd* [1978] 1 W.L.R. 550, where the Court of Appeal confirmed the application of *McPhail* to proceedings in the county court.

[72]   [1973] Ch. 447, CA at 462. In *Camden L.B.C. v. Persons Unknown* CA unreported, May 14, 1986, the Court of Appeal held that the entitlement to an immediate order for possession does not allow the order to be suspended or stayed.

[73]   Lawton L.J. in *McPhail,* [1973] Ch. 447, at 462, noted that the position there might be different.

If rights under the European Convention of Human Rights are in play, because section 6 of the Human Rights Act 1998 applies,[74] there may be circumstances where the Court should allow time even for trespassers *ab initio* since Article 8 rights[75] may make it disproportionate to evict the defendants from their home, even if it has arisen through unlawful occupation. For example, there may be no pressing public need to recover possession forthwith such as might justify the eviction of a family with young children without allowing them at least a short time in which to make alternative arrangements.

In a series of cases concerning the rights of gipsies to remain on land unlawfully used as their home, the European Court of Human Rights has recognised the existence of Article 8 rights notwithstanding the unlawful means by which they arose. In *Buckley v. United Kingdom*[76] the European Court of Human Rights considered Article 8 to be engaged even though the "home" was in part on land occupied in breach of planning control.[77] However, there are signs that such a generous approach may not always be taken, or at least that unlawfulness may affect the proportionality of the decision to evict, since in the recent decision in *Chapman v. United Kingdom*[78] the Court held at para. 101:

> ". . . if the establishment of a home in a particular place was unlawful, the position of the individual objecting to an order to move is less strong. The Court will be slow to grant protection to those who, in conscious defiance of the prohibitions of the law, establish a home on an environmentally protected site. For the Court to do otherwise would be to encourage illegal action to the detriment of the protection of the environmental rights of other people in the community."

In *Poplar Housing Association v. Donoghue*,[79] the Court of Appeal considered the significance of Article 8 rights where the landlord concerned was a "public authority" within the 1998 Act. Its decision, in effect, involved the determination whether the creation of non-secure, assured shorthold tenancies and the decision to evict were proportionate having regard to the application of Article 8.[80] Indeed, as Sedley L.J. elsewhere held[81]:

---

[74] *e.g.* because the claimant is a public authority within the 1998 Act or, more generally, if as seems to be the case that the Court will exercise its own discretion compatibly with the Convention as a "public authority" within s. 6(3)(a) of that Act. In the light of the Court of Appeal's decision in *London Borough of Lambeth v. Howard* (2001) 33 H.L.R. 58, especially paras. 30–32, it seems that the Court's exercise of its powers will at least take account of applicable Article 8 issues. See Clayton & Tomlinson, *The Law of Human Rights* (OUP, 2000) at paras. 5.80–5.99, 5.114 & 5.115 and Grosz, Beatson & Duffy, *Human Rights* (Sweet & Maxwell, 2000) paras. 4–01, 4–15 to 4–17 on the "horizontal effect" of the Convention.

[75] See, generally, on Article 8, Clayton & Tomlinson, *op. cit.*, Chapter 12 and pp. 265–291 and Grosz, Beatson & Duffy, *op. cit.*, pp. 265–291.

[76] (1996) 23 E.H.R.R. 101.

[77] See the Judgment, paras. 12 and 52–54.

[78] (2001) B.H.R.C. 48.

[79] [2001] 3 W.L.R. 183.

[80] See pp. 202–203 (paras. 67–72 of the judgment).

[81] *London Borough of Lambeth v. Howard* (2001) 33 H.R. 58 at para. 30. See also *St. Brice v Southwark L.B.C.* [2001] EWCA Civ. 1138, CA at paras. 9–18 and 24–26.

"It seems to me that any attempt to evict a person, whether directly or by process of law, from his or her home would on the face of it be a derogation from the respect, that is the integrity, to which the home is prima facie entitled."

Further, in *R (McLellan) v. Bracknell Forest D.C. & Others*,[82] the Court of Appeal held that the application of section 89 of the Housing Act 1980 (which limits the discretion of the Court in making possession orders[83]) was not incompatible with Article 8. Waller L.J. held[84]:

"The court has the power to adjourn if it is arguable that a tenant's right is being infringed. If it does that, section 89 is simply not in play. Section 89 only comes into play if either the court thinks its use with its limitations will prevent an infringement of human rights, or if there is no arguable infringement of those rights."

The implication of this is that where the Court may be faced with a limited power to suspend or postpone possession, it should consider whether or not the limitations on that power will infringe such Convention rights as may be engaged. Where, as in *McLellan*, the landlord is a public authority, there exists the option of adjourning the possession proceedings while a judicial review of the decision to evict is pursued.[85]

However, if the landlord is not a public body, judicial review is not available and more difficult questions arise especially if the Court considers that on the facts of the case the limitations on its powers are inconsistent with the applicable Convention rights. If the power is not of necessity incompatible with Convention rights,[86] then the Court appears to be under a duty under sections 6(1) and 8(1) of the 1998 Act to take such steps and grant such remedies as are open to it in order to give effect to those rights. While, at one level, a prolonged adjournment may not be a satisfactory means to resolve such rights,[87] it may of necessity be a solution in cases where other powers are not available. It may, for example, allow time for further efforts to be made to re-house the defendant in order to ensure a proportionate decision in due course. See also the discussion in Chapter 1, paragraphs 1–139 to 1–144, above.

---

[82] [2002] 1 All E.R. 899, CA. The context was the compatibility of introductory tenancies under Part v. of the Housing Act 1985.

[83] See *Bain & Co. v. Church Commissioners for England* [1989] 1 W.L.R. 24.

[84] At para. 68.

[85] See paras. 1–134 to 1–138.

[86] At what has been termed the "macro level": see *McLellan* para. 44.

[87] It appears on its face to undermine the limitations in section 89 since it is in effect a postponement of the order. However, such arguments may have to give way to the "reading down" duty in s. 3 of the 1998 Act.

(4) Court Procedure

(a) Jurisdiction

With certain exceptions, all claims made under Part 55 must be started in the county court for the district in which the land is situated.[88] This is a marked change to the rules under Order 113 and Order 24, under which the value of the claim would be assessed and the court chosen appropriately. This rule recognises that a possession claim brought in respect of a particularly valuable property does not necessarily deserve a greater share of the court's resources than one of lower value.

4–072

Where the claimant wishes to start a claim in the High Court, the claim form must be accompanied by a certificate, verified by a statement of truth, setting out the reasons for bringing the claim in that court.[89] The claim may be issued in either the Queen's Bench or Chancery Division. Practice Direction 55 sets out the 'exceptional' circumstances which may justify bringing a claim in the High Court[90]:

(1)   The claim involves a complicated dispute of facts;

(2)   The claim involves points of law of general importance;

(3)   The claim is against trespassers, and there is a substantial risk of public disturbance or of serious harm to persons or property which properly require immediate determination.[91]

Other factors which are relevant, but will not alone normally justify starting the claim in the High Court are[92]:

(a)   The value of the property; and

(b)   The amount of any financial claim.

The only circumstance in which possession claims may be issued in the High Court as of right, is where specific provision has been made in a particular enactment.[93]

Where a claim has been started in the High Court, and the court considers that it should have been started in the county court, the court will normally, of its own motion[94]:

---

[88] CPR Part 55.3(1) and Part 55 *Practice Direction — Possession Claims* ("PD 55").
[89] CPR Part 55.3(2).
[90] CPR Part 55.3(3) and PD 55, para. 1.
[91] Thus, cases such as the mass eviction of road protestors, might be justifiably brought in the High Court rather than the County Court.
[92] PD 55, para. 1.5.
[93] CPR Part 55.3(1).
[94] PD 55 para. 1.2.

(1)   Strike the claim out; or

(2)   Transfer proceedings to the county court.

The court will also punish the claimant for any unnecessary delay and administration by disallowing his costs of issuing in the High Court and of any transfer.[95]

(b) Form of proceedings

4–073   Proceedings under Part 55 are begun by way of the special claim form annexed to PD 55.[96] Where the claim is being brought against defendants whose identify is not known, as with the previous procedures these defendants must be referred to as "persons unknown".[97] Defendants whose identities are known should be named, with the advantage that costs can be recovered from them if the claim succeeds.

(i) *Particulars of claim* — In a claim against trespassers the particulars of claim must be filed and served with the claim form.[98] Much of the information which used to be contained in an affidavit in proceedings under Order 113 and Order 24 is now contained in the particulars of claim,[99] the contents of which must be verified by a statement of truth.[1] The particulars of claim must:

(a)   identify the 'land' (which includes a building or part of a building) to which the claim relates[2];

(b)   state whether the claim relates to residential property[3];

(c)   state that the defendant has never been a tenant or sub-tenant of the land[4];

(d)   state either[5]:

(i)   the claimant's interest in the land; or
(ii)   the basis of the claimant's right to possession; and

(e)   state the circumstances in which the land was occupied without licence or consent.[6]

---

[95] PD 55, para. 1.2.
[96] New Form N5.
[97] CPR Part 55.3(4).
[98] CPR Part 55.4.
[99] PD 55 para. 2.
[1] See CPR Part 22.
[2] PD 55 para. 2.1(1).
[3] PD 55, para. 2.1(2).
[4] This is a requirement for the claim to be against "trespassers".
[5] PD 55, para. 2.6.
[6] PD 55, para. 2.6.

The land which is the subject of the proceedings should be identified precisely. In the case of a building, or structure, identification is usually easily achieved by reference to the postal address. However, if part of a building only is wrongfully occupied, it will be necessary to identify that part: for example, by reference to a floor or room number(s) or (in more difficult cases) by reference to a plan.

In the case of land which does not wholly consist of buildings, *e.g.* open land unlawfully occupied by caravans, it is good practice (and essential in some cases) to annex a plan to the claim form which clearly delineates (by a red line or suitable marking) the area in question. The prospective claimant should take care to include all the land unlawfully occupied.

As a general rule, only the land which is shown to be occupied by trespassers can be the subject of proceedings. However, where the occupied premises form part of a wider area of land and the order is for possession of a smaller part, it is not unknown for the squatters to move to another part of the wider area of land. If that is the case, the possession order would not apply to the land then occupied[7] and fresh proceedings would have to be begun.[8] Accordingly, the prospective claimant should take care to include all necessary land in his proceedings: the court does have power to order possession even if the claim is drawn wider than the area in which the trespassers are currently located if there is convincing evidence (*e.g.* by proof of a threat that there is a real danger of trespass to the wider area).[9]

(ii) *Evidence* — Part 55 does not anticipate that written or oral evidence will be required in every possession claim; most of the relevant facts will be contained in the particulars of claim, duly verified and with any documentation attached, such as proof of title and relevant correspondence. Where a witness statement has been prepared, it must be filed with the claim form and particulars of claim.[10]

The claimant must provide a certificate of service at the hearing.[11] Any change of circumstances which takes place after issue and service of the claim form can also be set out in a witness statement if necessary.

(c) Service

Under the CPR, both the High Court and the county court may serve any document which the Court has issued or prepared.[12]

---

[7] See, *e.g. University of Essex v. Djemal* [1980] 1 W.L.R. 1301, CA, and *Ministry of Agriculture v. Heyman* (1989) 59 P. & C.R. 48.

[8] Cases of re-occupation of the subject land can be met by an application for leave to issue a claim for restitution: para. 4–075.

[9] Assuming that earlier authorities remain good law: see *University of Essex v. Djemal* [1980] 1 W.L.R. 1301, CA, and *Ministry of Agriculture v. Heyman* (1989) 59 P. & C.R. 48.

[10] CPR Part 55.8(5).

[11] CPR Part 55.8(6).

[12] CPR Part 6.3: no exception to this principle is expressly set out in Part 55. In accordance with CPR Part 6.3(b), the claimant may effect service if he wishes.

(i) *Time* — On issuing the claim, the court will fix a date for the claim to be heard.[13] While no time periods for claims against trespassers are indicated by Part 55 or its Practice Direction ("PD 55"), it is anticipated that the time between issue and hearing will be only a little longer than that required to serve the claim with the required notice period; in practice this will depend upon the availability of court time. The notice periods are[14]:

(1) in the case of residential property, not less than five days; and

(2) in the case of other land, not less than two days.

Where numbers of days are given, these are calculated as 'clear days' in accordance with the general provisions of the CPR, *i.e.* where a hearing has been fixed for Monday, June 14, service on trespassers occupying a residential property must take place on or before Friday, June 3.[15]

Acting under its general case management powers under CPR Part 3.1(2)(a), the court may extend or shorten the time for compliance with any rule.[16] PD 55 states at paras 3.1 and 3.2 that particular consideration will be given to the use of this discretion where the defendant has assaulted or threatened to assault the claimant or another resident in the locality, or where serious damage to property has occurred or is threatened. The court will also take these factors into account when listing any further hearing which may be required.

(ii) *Named Defendants* — Named defendants must be served by one of the usual methods set out in CPR Part 6.2. In practice, the usual methods of service will be personal service,[17] service by first class post or by leaving the documents at the defendant's place of service.[18]

(iii) *"Persons Unknown"* — Claims against trespassers who are "persons unknown" must be served by:

(1) attaching all documentation to the main door or some other part of the land so that it is clearly visible and, if practicable, inserting copies in a sealed transparent envelope addressed to "the occupiers" through the letterbox; or

---

[13] CPR Part 55.5(1).
[14] CPR Part 55.5(2).
[15] CPR Part 2.8.
[16] Note to CPR Part 55.5.
[17] See CPR Part 6.4.
[18] In accordance with CPR Part 6.5(4).

(2) placing stakes in the land in places where they are clearly visible to which are attached copies of the documentation in sealed transparent envelopes addressed to "the occupiers".

Where service is to be effected by the court, the claimant must supply sufficient stakes and transparent envelopes with its documentation when the claim is issued.[19] It is a common mistake, where "persons unknown" are involved, to address the documents required to be served on "the occupiers" to "persons unknown". Such a mistake amounts to a failure to comply with the requirements of the rules[20] and may have the result that service as a whole will be bad. Even given the overriding objective in CPR Part I, the use of "persons unknown" may be regarded as confusing and not clearly drawing to their attention the fact that the documents were meant for them.

(iv) *General* — A certificate of service should be provided at the hearing. Unlike the position under the old rules, the trespass procedure expressly requires this.[21]

If the proceedings involve both named defendants and "persons unknown," both methods of service prescribed by CPR Parts 6 and 55 must be used. Since the courts are likely to approach the construction and application of these rules with care, it is important to ensure that the precise requirements of the rules as to service are observed.[22]

In cases of difficulty, *e.g.* where there are large numbers of unlawful occupiers, or the nature of the land or occupation makes compliance with the rules impracticable, application can be made to the court for directions as to service. CPR Part 6.8 permits the court to direct other modes of service. Such an application can be made without notice with a witness statement in support which should explain the precise problem(s) experienced in effecting service in accordance with the rules. In order to avoid any difficulties which a defendant might raise at the hearing, it is advisable for the claimant to serve copies of any directions as to service together with those documents required to be served.

(d) Defendant's response

There is no requirement for a defendant to acknowledge service of a claim under Part 55, nor is judgment in default available to a claimant.[23] Where the claim has been issued against trespassers, no defence is required.[24]

---

[19] P.D. 55, para. 4.1
[20] See para. 4–074.
[21] CPR Part 55.8(6).
[22] Although see para. 4–074.
[23] CPR Part 55.7(1) & (4).
[24] CPR Part 55.7(2).

(e) Irregularities

4–074 It is not yet known whether the courts will apply the provisions of Part 55 as strictly as they did those under R.S.C. Ord. 113 and C.C.R. Ord. 24 Part I, which represented independent codes for dealing with trespassers. R.S.C. Order 113 and C.C.R., Order 24 constituted a special, independent procedural code, and the courts took a strict approach to their construction and application. In the period immediately following the introduction of the summary procedure a very strict approach was taken to irregularities, namely that the court had no discretion to waive any defect in compliance with the procedure,[25] but familiarity led the courts to relax this strictness. In *Burston Finance v. Wilkins and Persons Unknown*,[26] Oliver J. held that the court had a general discretion in accordance with Order 2, r. 1 to waive an irregularity in Order 113 proceedings, providing that no injustice was caused thereby. In *Westminster City Council v. Chapman*[27] the majority of the Court of Appeal held that the object of the rules was to ensure that, so far as is possible, people get to know of the application and are able to appear in court. It is particularly important to be procedurally correct in the case of unnamed occupiers since they will usually not have proceedings served on them individually.

Nevertheless, given the special nature of the summary jurisdiction, the courts scrutinised R.S.C. Order 113 applications with particular care[28] and were not particularly willing to assist a careless claimant. Similar care may be exercised under Part 55 with regard to the trespass procedure. One example of a common procedural error is referred to above, namely in serving proceedings addressed to "persons unknown" rather than "the occupiers", a possibility which also exists under in the new procedure. Of course, the Court should now observe the requirements of the overriding objective in CPR Part 1 when considering the effects of procedural errors. However, if the court is at all concerned on the facts of the specific case as to the justice of waiving defects in service, the likely result is the adjournment of the proceedings until proper service has been effected in part in order to give effect to the overriding objective. If the defect is more serious, the ultimate sanction of the court is to dismiss the application.

(f) Hearing

In a claim against trespassers, the hearing may take place as soon as enough time has been allowed for proper service of the claim documentation. At the hearing the court may:

---

[25] *Re 9 Orpen Road, Stoke Newington* [1971] 1 W.L.R. 166.
[26] *The Times*, July 17, 1975.
[27] [1975] 2 All E.R. 1103, CA.
[28] See, for example, *Wiltshire County Council v. Frazer* (1983) 47 P. & C.R. 69.

(1) Decide the claim;

(2) Give case management directions (including allocation of the claim); or

(3) Where a claim has been, in the court's opinion, wrongly started in the High Court, transfer it to the county court.

It is expected that most claims against trespassers will be dealt with at the first hearing. In cases where the claimant can show better title, and no questions of a lapsed tenancy or other bars to an immediate decision arise, the grant of an order for possession should be a formality.

Where a claim is genuinely disputed on grounds which appear to the court to be substantial, the court is more likely to give case management directions which will provide for a further hearing to take place at which full arguments on facts and law can be assessed.[29]

(i) *Small Claims Track* — Possession claims will only be allocated to the small claims track with the consent of all the parties.[30]

The parties are encouraged to allow the claim to be treated as a small claim by Part 55's suspension of the 'no costs' rules associated with all other small claims cases. Instead, the claim will be treated, for the purposes of costs, as though it were allocated to the fast track, except that trial costs shall be in the discretion of the court. Where the value of the claim is up to £3,000, the costs shall not exceed ordinary fixed fast track trial costs.[31]

Alternatively, where a claim has been allocated to the small claims track and all the parties agree, the court may order that the rules governing costs on the small claim track apply.[32] In practice this second option may not always prove popular: where a party considers its case to be stronger, it may wish to use the threat of recoverable trial costs as a weapon in the proceedings to encourage settlement. No costs are recoverable from "persons unknown".

Where a claim has been allocated to the small claims track, any fact may be proved by evidence in writing.[33]

(ii) *Fast Track and Multi-Track* — Claims allocated to the fast track or multi-track will follow the standard claims procedures set out in the remainder of the CPR, suitably tailored at the hearing. It is beyond the scope of this work to discuss all aspects of the procedures in detail.

---

[29] Part 55.8(2). Compare the approach which was taken when an arguable issue was raised under old RSC Order 113 and CCR Ord. 24 Part I: see *e.g. Henderson v. Law* (1984) 17 H.L.R. 237, CA.

[30] CPR. Part 55.9(2).

[31] CPR. Part 55.9(3).

[32] CPR. Part 55.9(4).

[33] CPR. Part 55.8(3).

(g) Execution of the order

4–075   The procedure for the enforcement of judgments and orders has not yet been completely revised by civil justice reform and, for the time being, have not affected the enforcement of possession orders.[34] In the High Court, under the surviving CPR Schedule 1 Ord. 113 r. 7, execution against trespassers is made by writ of possession in the prescribed form (No. 66A)[35] which is issued without the court's permission within a period of three months from the date of the order (contrary to normal practice under Schedule 1 Order 45, r. 3[36]). Following the expiry of that three month period, the court's permission is required[37]: this distinction is made in order to emphasise the urgent nature of an application for possession against trespassers. If the writ is not issued within the three month period, it will appear that the application was not urgent and the court will have an opportunity of considering the reasons for the delay (together with other circumstances which may have arisen since the making of the order) before granting permission.

The writ of possession authorises the sheriff to evict any persons found in occupation of the subject premises, notwithstanding that such persons were not named in the possession proceedings.[38] One advantage of execution of a writ of possession over a county court warrant is that the sheriff is entitled to require police assistance in executing a possession order.[39]

Although Schedule 1 Order 113, r. 7 makes no specific provision for a writ of restitution[40] to be issued in aid of execution, such a writ is in fact available: see *Wiltshire County Council v. Frazer (No. 2)*.[41] This is particularly useful in proceedings against trespassers as providing a swift remedy in circumstances where the squatters re-occupy the land after execution of the writ of possession. It is available:

"... only in those cases where there was a plain and sufficient nexus between the original recovery of possession and the need to effect further recovery of the same land."[42]

Execution in the county court is by warrant of possession under CPR Schedule 2 Ord. 24 r. 6. Permission is required if the warrant is issued after the expiry of three months from the date of the order. Rule 6(1) specifically

---

[34] New rules (CPR Parts 70–73) with regard to the enforcement of judgment debts come into force on 25 March 2002: see The Civil Procedure (Amendment No. 4) Rules 2001 S.I. No. 2792.

[35] Preserved by the CPR Part 4 *Practice Direction — Forms*, Table 2.

[36] CPR Sched. 1 Ord. 45, r. 3(2) was expressly disapplied by Ord. 113, r. 7(1).

[37] Which may be obtained without notice unless the court otherwise directs: CPR Sched. 1 Ord. 113, r.7(1).

[38] *R. v. Wandsworth County Court ex parte London Borough of Wandsworth* [1975] 1 W.L.R. 1314.

[39] Both under section 8(2) of the Sheriffs Act 1887 and at common law.

[40] Form 68, Part 4 *Practice Direction — Forms*, Table 2.

[41] [1986] 1 W.L.R. 109.

[42] *ibid.*, at 113.

provides that a warrant of restitution[43] may be issued in aid of the warrant of possession.

In the enforcement of a possession order, even if Convention rights are engaged by virtue of section 6 of the Human Rights Act 1998, no question with regard to Articles 6 or 8 arises separately from the decision to make the order in the first place. If Convention rights with regard to a fair trial, and to respect for the home etc., have been considered at the stage of making the order, they do not fall to be considered afresh when a warrant for possession is applied for and executed.[44a] Even if Convention rights were not properly given effect to at the hearing of the possession proceedings, it seems more appropriate that an application should be made to set aside the original order and to suspend the warrant for execution in the interim, rather than simply applying to set aside the warrant.

(h) Appeals

Appeals lie from District Judge to Circuit Judge, from Master or Circuit Judge to High Court Judge, and from High Court Judge to the Court of Appeal. For each level of appeal, permission to appeal must be obtained either from the appealed judge or from the judge or court appealed to. The appeals procedure, which is contained in CPR Part 52, is beyond the scope of this work.

Interim Possession Orders

(1) Introduction

The statutory basis for interim possession orders (IPOs) is found in sections 75 and 76 of the Criminal Justice and Public Order Act 1994 which were introduced to provide as a "quick and effective remedy against squatting"[44] in the case of both residential and business premises. The rules (and associated forms) setting out the procedure for obtaining IPOs followed the Lord Chancellor's Department Consultation Paper "New procedures to combat squatting in houses, shops and other buildings" (July 1994) and came into force on August 24, 1995. **4–076**

The interim procedure was introduced as a form of summary proceedings in the county court and the Rules amended CCR, Order 24 by introducing a new Part II to the Order and associated prescribed forms.[45] These rules are now found preserved in Schedule 2 to the CPR. No jurisdiction

---

[43] Form N50, Part 4 *Practice Direction — Forms*, Table 3.
[44] The Home Secretary's description when introducing the Bill: Hansard, H.C., cols. 29–30, January 11, 1994 and Home Office Press Release, August 24, 1995 (C.O.I. 9995). See also comments by A.T. Smith [1995] Crim.L.R. 19 especially at pp 25–26.
[44a] *See St Brice v. Southwark L.B.C.* [2002] 1 W.L.R. 1537, CA, especially at paras. 9–15 (Kennedy L.J.) and 20–27 (Chadwick L.J.).
[45] The forms are preserved by CPR Part 4 *Practice Direction — Forms*, Table 3.

is conferred on the High Court to make an IPO. It is likely that the general comments made above as to the nature of possession proceedings are applicable to the interim possession procedure although the more drastic nature of the IPO procedure almost ensures that the courts will approach it with caution — especially since it provides for orders to be enforceable by the police (not the county court bailiff), a prohibition on applying to set aside IPOs unless there has first been compliance with the order (*i.e.* the premises have been vacated) and a criminal sanction for non-compliance.

The many safeguards included in the interim procedural rules, including the serving of a notice of application and witness statement or affidavit in prescribed form, undertakings by the applicant landowner which exceed those normally given on an interim injunction and a hearing with notice in certain cases, strongly suggest the IPOs are not the speedy and effective remedy that the promoters of the legislation intended.[46] The principal aspects of the rules which might lead to a speedier recovery of possession are the criminal penalty for non-compliance and the requirement that the court fix a hearing date "as soon as possible".[47] However, there is cause to doubt that this ensures a speedier and more effective procedure and much depends on the court's ability to fix an early hearing. In appropriate cases, the courts are willing to fix speedy hearings for ordinary possession proceedings in any event. This, together with the requirement of notices of application in place of an application with or without notice (as in the draft rules), appear unlikely to make the IPO procedure significantly speedier than conventional possession applications — apart from the criminal sanction, which may speed up enforcement.

(2) *Availability of the IPO procedure*

4–077 The rules provide that an IPO application may be made if the following conditions are satisfied:

(1) the only claim is for the recovery of "premises"[48];

(2) the claim is made by a person who

    (a) has an immediate right to possession of the premises[49]; and

    (b) has had such a right throughout the period of unlawful occupation complained of[50];

---

[46] Indeed, the draft version of the rules set out in the Consultation Paper would have provided a potentially speedier procedure utilising without notice hearings and more circumscribed rights for respondents to contest IPOs, but these were substantially modified in the final rules.

[47] CPR Sch. 2 Ord. 24, r. 12(3).

[48] CPR Sch. 2 Ord. 24, r. 9(a). Ord. 24, r. 8(1)(c) defines "premises" as having the same meaning as in section 12 of the Criminal Law Act 1977. See Chap. 5, para. 5–024, below.

[49] See para. 4–061.

[50] CPR Sch. 2 Ord. 24, r. 9(b). Accordingly, IPOs will not be available if the squatting began prior to the expiry of an intermediate tenancy even though there is no doubt that the landlord subsequently becomes entitled to possession.

(3) the claim is made against a person (not being a tenant holding over after the termination of the tenancy) who entered the premises without the claimant's consent, and has not subsequently been granted such consent, but no application may be made against a person who entered the premises with the consent of the person who, at the time of entry, has an immediate right to possession of the premises[51]; and

(4) the claim is made within 28 days of the date which the claimant first knew, or ought reasonably to have known, that the defendant (or any of the defendants) was occupying the premises.[52]

The court is likely to consider with some care whether the claimant has complied with these requirements and also whether there is compliance with the procedural requirements referred to below. Since the application is heard in the absence of the respondent, unless he has filed a witness statement or affidavit, it is likely that county courts will, where the respondent is absent, require the high standard of disclosure of relevant facts and documents by the applicant as in the case of applications without notice for injunctions.

The principal incentive to proper conduct by applicants in IPO cases is provided by section 75 of the Criminal Justice and Public Order Act 1994. This imposes severe criminal penalties[53] for the making of materially "false or misleading" statements[54] for the purpose of obtaining an IPO. Equally severe penalties are imposed for making such statements for the purpose of resisting the making of an IPO[55] by defendants.

In the light of such criminal penalties, it is clearly essential for those advising witnesses in IPO proceedings to ensure the accuracy of the statements given in evidence. There is a particular need for care since there is prescribed form of witness statement or affidavit[56] in support of an application for an IPO. The deponent, who must make the witness statement or affidavit personally (unless a body corporate in which case the affidavit must be sworn by a duly authorised officer),[57] should not make such a witness statement or affidavit as a mere matter of form but should ensure that he is satisfied of the accuracy of the facts to be contained in the evidence. In the event that he is not so satisfied, careful consideration should be given as to whether the IPO procedure can be used at all. This will depend on whether the matters which cannot properly be deposed to are

---

[51] CPR Sch. 2 Ord. 24, r. 9(c).
[52] CPR Sch. 2 Ord. 24, r. 9(d).
[53] The offence is triable either way and, if tried on indictment, is punishable by up to two years' imprisonment and/or a fine and, if tried summarily, is punishable by up to six months' imprisonment and/or the statutory maximum fine. See s. 75(3) of the 1994 Act.
[54] Including the reckless making of such statements: s. 75(1)(b) of the 1994 Act.
[55] S. 75(2) of the 1994 Act.
[56] CPR Sch. 2 Ord. 24, r. 10(2)(b) and form N130 of the County Court Forms preserved by CPR Part 4 *Practice Direction — Forms*, Table 3.
[57] CPR Sch. 2 Ord. 24, r. 10(3).

central to the requirements of the IPO procedure or whether they are ancillary and not fundamental, and their absence is not likely to be fatal to the application.

(3) Procedure

4–078   As already noted, jurisdiction to make interim possession orders is conferred only on the county court although jurisdiction is given to district judges as well as to circuit judges.[58]

(a) Application to the court

(i) Form of application

4–079   The application is by a modified form of claim form for summary possession, together with a notice of application, supported by a witness statement or affidavit in prescribed form sworn by the applicant. The claim form seeks both a summary possession order and an interim possession order[59] since, once the interim order is made, the procedure continues with a view to a final order for possession being made. A certificate of service of the application and supporting witness statement or affidavit is also required.[60] The claimant must serve the notice of application and supporting witness statement or affidavit together with a blank form of defendant's affidavit[61] (attached to the notice of application) within 24 hours of the issue of the proceedings.[62] As mentioned above, paragraph 4–077, the claimant should ensure the truth and accuracy of the contents of his witness statement or affidavit in view of the criminal penalties for false and misleading statements.

(ii) Service of application

Service must be carried out by fixing a copy of the documents to the main door or other conspicuous part of the premises and, if practicable, inserting them through the letter-box in a sealed, transparent envelope addressed to "the occupiers".[63] Additionally, but not as an alternative, the application may be served by fixing similar sealed, transparent envelopes addressed to "the occupiers" to stakes placed in the ground at

---

[58] See para. 32 of the Consultation Paper — "This reflects the current experience of some district judges in this area and will make it easier to arrange urgent appointments as required by the procedure."

[59] CPR Sch. 2 Ord. 24, r. 10(2). The prescribed form is N130 (see *Practice Direction — Forms*, Table 3).

[60] CPR Sch. 2 Ord. 24, r. 11(4). The prescribed form is N132 of the County Court Forms (see *Practice Direction — Forms*, Table 3.

[61] Form N133 of the County Court Forms (see *Practice Direction — Forms*, Table 3).

[62] CPR Sch. 2 Ord. 24, r. 11(1).

[63] CPR Sch. 2 Ord. 24, r. 11(2).

conspicuous parts of the premises.[64] A certificate of service must be filed at or before the time fixed for the consideration of the application for the IPO.[65]

(iii) Hearing of the application

The court officer will, immediately upon the filing of the documents, fix **4–080** an appointment for the hearing of the application "as soon as possible"[66] after the documents have been filed but not less than three days after the date of issue of the application. The hearing, which may be held in chambers and in the absence of one or both of the parties,[67] is conducted in the absence of the respondent unless he has filed a witness statement or affidavit in opposition before the time fixed for the hearing.[68] The consideration of the application is on the witness statement or affidavit evidence and no oral evidence may be adduced except in response to questions put by the court.[69] The role of the parties at the hearing appears, on the face of r. 12, to be confined to answering the questions of the court on the evidence. It is unclear whether the court is required, or entitled, to hear submissions or permit cross-examination. The form of the rules makes it appear that the court is to direct the questioning and to conduct an almost inquisitorial form of hearing. This interpretation appears consistent with the intention that the procedure be speedy.

The court must make an IPO if[70]:

(1)   the claimant has filed the required affidavit of service;

(2)   the court is satisfied that

    (a)   the conditions in r. 9 are met; and

    (b)   the undertakings given by the applicant as a condition of making the order are "adequate."

The order is required to be in prescribed form[71] and must be to the effect that the defendant should vacate the subject premises within 24 hours of service of the order.

The court is required to "have regard to" whether the claimant has given or is prepared to give undertakings[72] in support of his application and, if so, whether they are "adequate". The undertakings are:

---

[64] CPR Sch. 2 Ord. 24, r. 11(3).
[65] CPR Sch. 2 Ord. 24, r. 11(4).
[66] CPR Sch. 2 Ord. 24, r. 11(3).
[67] CPR Sch. 2 Ord. 24, r. 12(3). This is a matter for the court to direct.
[68] CPR Sch. 2 Ord. 24, rr. 11(5) and 12(1).
[69] CPR Sch. 2 Ord. 24, r. 12(2).
[70] CPR Sch. 2 Ord. 24, r. 12(5). See also *City Photo Ltd v. The Occupiers* (unreported, February 10, 1997, CA).
[71] CPR Sch. 2 Ord. 24, r. 12(6) and form N134 of the County Court Forms.
[72] CPR Sch. 2 Ord. 24, r. 12(4).

(1) to reinstate the defendant if, after an IPO has been made, the court holds that the claimant was not entitled to the order;

(2) to pay damages if, after an IPO has been made, the court holds that the claimant was not entitled to the order;

(3) not to damage the premises pending final determination of the possession proceedings;

(4) not to grant a right of occupation to any other person pending final determination of the possession proceedings; and

(5) not to damage or dispose of any of the defendant's possessions pending final determination of the possession proceedings.

The prescribed form also contains the undertakings and, although the rules are not wholly explicit as to whether the court must always require such undertakings to be given, it seems reasonably clear that it is matter for the court in the circumstances of the case whether it requires some or all of the undertakings in order to safeguard the defendant.[73] However, the court is directed to consider whether any undertakings which it requires the applicant to give are "adequate"[74] which will require the court to assess, in some cases at least, the ability of the claimant to reinstate the defendant and to preserve the premises and possessions in the premises and also the means of the applicant. If the court requires an undertaking as to damages to be given, it is probable that it will wish to be satisfied of the ability of the claimant to meet any claim for damages in the event that it is ultimately determined that the claimant was not entitled to possession.

If the witness statements or affidavits, and the response to any of the court's questions, raise real issues which go to the entitlement of the claimant to an IPO there are two possible courses of action open to the court:

(1) adjourn the application, *e.g.* where the court considers the matter requires further investigation[75] but is not satisfied that it should simply reject the application for an IPO. There is no express power to adjourn contained in CPR Schedule 2 Order 24, Part II, but the court's general power to adjourn is not excluded. It is suggested

---

[73] The prescribed form N134 notes in the margin next to the undertakings "delete as appropriate".

[74] CPR Sch. 2 Ord. 24, r. 12(5)(b)(ii).

[75] See the *Consultation Paper*, para. 20: "It is possible that the court will require further information from the occupier as a result of reading the affidavit provided. In such a case, it will be open to the court to adjourn to a hearing with notice. However, we are concerned to ensure that this provision does not have the potential to deny the applicant the opportunity to gain an interim possession order, with the advantage of rapid enforcement and criminal sanctions." However, this comment was made in the context of draft rules which provided, initially, for an application without notice and its applicability is limited in the context of the final form of the rules.

that, given the urgent character of IPOs, the court should not follow this course of action unless it can deal with the matter more expeditiously than by refusing the IPO and allowing the application to continue as an ordinary summary possession application in accordance with r. 12(9); or

(2) refuse an IPO. In that case, the application proceeds as a possession application under Part 55[76] and

    (a) the proper officer must fix a return date for the originating application; and

    (b) the court may give directions for the future conduct of the proceedings.

The court might refuse to make an IPO (on the basis that the conditions of r. 9 are not satisfied) if it considers that there is an issue which, even on ordinary summary possession principles, would not justify the making of a possession order under CPR Part 55. The rules are not wholly clear as to the basis on which the court determines whether to make an IPO or not. On one view, the court is only concerned with whether the preconditions to entitlement in Order 24, r. 9 are met and the undertakings given by the applicant are adequate. However, the courts might take a similar approach to IPO applications to that taken under old RSC Order 113 and CCR Order 24 Part I summary proceedings, namely that if a dispute of fact becomes apparent the application will be refused if it cannot be easily resolved.[77] This might be considered as undesirable, and contrary to the overriding objective, in the context of what is meant to be a rapid and effective procedure, but it is suggested that such an approach would be justified given that IPO procedure is part of the possession rules (although not incorporated into Part 55), the draconian effects of making an order and the need to ensure that IPOs are only made in clear cases of an entitlement to possession. It should be noted, however, that (unlike the case of possession actions) the court will not have the option of holding a hearing with full oral evidence. Except in a case where a residential occupier has served an affidavit in opposition to the application, the county court is given no power in the new rules to permit the defendant to appear[78] and, even then, the evidence must be given by affidavit supplemented only by questions put by the court.[79]

---

[76] CPR Sch. 2 Ord. 24, r. 12(9). The provisions of Part 55 are not applied where the application simply continues since it began as "proceedings in which an application for an interim possession order is made"—r. 10(1). See Part 55.2.

[77] See *e.g. Henderson v. Law* (1984) 17 H.L.R. 237, CA.

[78] CPR Sch. 2 Ord. 24, r. 12(1) is not in precisely mandatory terms and it is possible that some courts will seek to allow an hearing with notice notwithstanding the absence of a respondent's affidavit. It is suggested that such an approach would be difficult to justify given that the inclusion of r. 12(1) appears to exclude the possibility of a hearing the respondent in other circumstances prior to the making of the IPO.

[79] CPR Sch. 2 Ord. 24, r. 12(2).

The court is also required, on making an IPO, to fix a return date which must be not less than seven days after the date on which the order is made.[80]

(b) Matters arising after making of IPO

(i) Service of the IPO

4–081 Where an IPO is made, the proper officer must submit a draft of the order "as soon as possible" to the judge or district judge by whom it was made for approval and when it has been approved, insert the time limit for service required by r. 13(1). The order must be served within 48 hours of the approval of the draft order by the judge or district judge. The prescribed form of application and the applicant's witness statement or affidavit must also be served. The mode of service is the same as that stipulated for service of the application[81]: see, above, paragraph 4–079.

The claimant must file a certificate of service of the claim form, the claimant's witness statement or affidavit and the IPO in the prescribed form before the return date. The court may not make a final order for possession unless such a witness statement or affidavit has been filed.[82]

(ii) The return date

The IPO expires automatically on the return date[83] unless the defendant has already successfully applied to set the IPO aside (see below). The court's powers on the return date are very wide and it may:

(1) make a final order for possession. This deals with the case where the court is satisfied of the entitlement of the claimant to the order. A final order for possession is an ordinary possession order under CPR Part 55 and is enforceable as such.[84] Such an order may not be made unless the claimant has filed an affidavit of service under r. 14(1)[85];

(2) dismiss the claim for possession.[86] This includes cases where the court does not consider that the claimant was entitled to possession or where it was clear that the case ought not to have been brought under Order 24 at all[87];

---

[80] CPR Sch. 2 Ord. 24, r. 12(7).
[81] CPR Sch. 2 Ord. 24, r. 13(2) and also r. 11(2) and (3) considered above.
[82] CPR Sch. 2 Ord. 24, r. 14(1).
[83] CPR Sch. 2 Ord. 24, r. 14(2).
[84] CPR Sch. 2 Ord. 24, r. 14(3)(a).
[85] See above and r. 13(2).
[86] CPR Sch. 2 Ord. 24, r. 14(3)(b).
[87] See *Henderson v. Law* (1984) 17 H.L.R. 237, CA at 241 considered at para. 1–172, above.

(3)   direct that the claimant may proceed under CPR Part 55, *i.e.* by ordinary possession procedure as if a claim for an IPO had not been made.[88] This order will be appropriate in cases where the Court is satisfied that, although IPO procedure is not appropriate, the case is fit for ordinary proceedings; or

(4)   make such other order "as appears appropriate". This, presumably, includes the power to direct that the proceedings continue as ordinary possession proceedings, *e.g.* where there is clearly a genuine issue to be tried on the facts as to the claimant's entitlement to possession.

As mentioned above, it is possible that the courts will consider whether or not there is a reason to give case management directions as in the case of proceedings under Part 55.

(c) Steps the respondent may take to resist an IPO

(i) Before an IPO is made

A defendant may appear at the hearing of the application for an IPO provided that he has first filed evidence in opposition. Indeed, if a defendant wishes to contest the application for an IPO he must swear a witness statement or affidavit since the rules do not permit him to appear to contest the application unless a witness statement or affidavit has been filed prior to the hearing.[89] In the event that evidence is filed, the defendant may attend to answer such questions as the court may put to him on either his own or the claimant's witness statement or affidavit. However, it appears that it is open to the court in any event to direct that the hearing should take place in the absence of the defendant.[90] It is important that respondents should appreciate the need to file evidence in order to attend since, if they do not and an IPO is made, they may not then apply to set aside the IPO prior to its automatic expiry on the return date[91] unless the order has been complied with (*i.e.* the premises have been vacated) and there are "grounds of urgency".[92] As in the case of a claimant's evidence, a defendant must ensure the truth and accuracy of the contents of his witness statement or affidavit given the criminal penalties for making false and misleading statements: see, above, paragraph 4–073.

4–082

---

[88] CPR Sch. 2 Ord. 24, r. 14(3)(c).
[89] CPR Sch. 2 Ord. 24, rr. 11(5) and 12(1).
[90] CPR Sch. 2 Ord. 24, r. 12(3). The drafting leaves the sub-rule open to the construction that the power of the court to direct only applies to whether the hearing is in chambers.
[91] CPR Sch. 2 Ord. 24, r. 14(2).
[92] CPR Sch. 2 Ord. 24, r. 15(1).

(ii) After an IPO is made

The court may hear an application to set aside an IPO before the return date (when it will expire in any event) "on grounds of urgency" provided that the defendant has complied with the terms of the order and vacated the premises. This means that the defendant cannot apply prior to the return date unless he has first given up possession — regardless of how strong his case may be. What circumstances amount to "grounds of urgency" are not defined, but left to the court to deal with on the facts of each case. Such grounds might include a case where the defendant was away at the time of the making of the IPO, has good grounds for setting aside the order and is being unjustifiably kept out of his home or place of business prior to the return date. The defendant's application to set aside must be supported by a witness statement or affidavit[93] and, once received by the court, will be subject to directions as to the date for the hearing[94] and the period, and form, of notice (if any) to be given to the claimant.

The court's powers, on an application to set aside where no notice is required to be given to the claimant, are confined to dealing with the issue whether the IPO should be set aside and all consequential matters, including the enforcement of the claimant's undertakings, are left to be dealt with on the return date.[95] If the court orders the IPO to be set aside without notice to the claimant, the court will serve a copy of the application to set aside and supporting evidence on the claimant.[96]

Where notice is directed to be given to the claimant, the court may treat the application as one to bring forward the return date in which case, presumably, it will then be able to deal with not only the order to be made (since the IPO will then expire automatically) but consequential matters such as the enforcement of the claimant's undertakings.[97] The rules are silent as to what should happen if the court directs that the claimant be notified but does not bring forward the return date: it appears that it may simply determine, in the light of the defendant's evidence, whether to set aside the IPO on the basis that it is no longer satisfied that the conditions in rule 9 are met. It is suggested that it will usually be preferable for the court to bring forward the return date on an application to set aside since, in that event, it will have full powers to give directions for the action to proceed, to make a final order for possession or dismiss the claim for possession and make any consequential orders.

---

[93] CPR Sch. 2 Ord. 24, r. 15(2).
[94] CPR Sch. 2 Ord. 24, r. 15(3).
[95] CPR Sch. 2 Ord. 24, r. 15(5) and 15(3)(b).
[96] CPR Sch. 2 Ord. 24, r. 15(6) and see below.
[97] CPR Sch. 2 Ord. 24, r. 15(7) then applies r. 14(2) to (8) apply as if the accelerated return date was the return date originally fixed by the court.

(iii) Enforcement of applicant's undertakings

Where the court holds that the claimant was not entitled to an IPO, the defendant may apply for the purpose of obtaining relief pursuant to the undertakings given by the claimant. As a result of the inability of a defendant to make an application unless he has first complied with the IPO, it is likely that if the defendant seeks to have the order set aside he will, if successful, have a claim against the claimant at least for compensation for being forced out of possession. This is likely to be greater in cases where the court sets aside the IPO and dismisses the claim for possession altogether than where the court simply directs that the proceedings continue under CPR Part 55. However, it does highlight the curious situation under the rules where a defendant cannot apply until he has complied with the order and vacated the premises.[98] Although the defendant has a certain measure of protection in the event of false statements being made by the applicant in the witness statement or affidavit in support of the IPO, this might be cold comfort if, in the meanwhile, he has had to vacate the premises.

(d) Enforcement

Unlike ordinary orders for possession (summary or otherwise) IPOs are not enforceable by warrants for possession but by the police.[99] The IPO must be served within 48 hours of the date on which it is approved by the court: see paragraph 4–081, above. Following compliance with the above requirements, enforcement is then wholly within the hands of the police. Accordingly, the efficacy of the procedure is wholly dependent upon the ability and willingness of the local police to respond quickly to the IPO.[1] There is no requirement that the local police be served with a copy of the IPO although the court may order that the IPO be served in such manner as it shall direct[2] which may be wide enough to include a direction to serve the police. In any event, since the rules do not directly involve the police, it will be for the claimant to prove service of the IPO. Indeed, if the criminal sanctions are to be invoked, the claimant must ensure that service can be proved in accordance with the criminal standard of proof. It will also be for the claimant to alert the police to the service of the IPO and any failure to comply with it.

4–083

---

[98] No doubt introduced in the interests of greater speed and efficacy. Whether the right balance between speed and fairness has been struck by the legislation and rules is open to question, particularly in the light of Art. 8 of the ECHR.

[99] CPR Sch. 2 Ord. 24, r. 13(3) (enforcement by warrant of possession is expressly excluded) and section 76 of the 1994 Act.

[1] In practice the police have proved reluctant to divert resources into what they consider to be "civil matters". This has led many practitioners to encourage potential applicants to use the slower, but more predictable, standard possession procedure.

[2] CPR Sch. 2 Ord. 24, r. 13(2). The draft rules did include such a requirement.

Section 75 of the 1994 Act makes it a criminal offence[3] to fail to comply with an IPO where the order had been made and served in accordance with the rules and the person subject to this order[4] (a) fails to leave the premises within 24 hours beginning with the time of service of the order or, (b) having left, re-enters (or attempts to re-enter) the premises as a trespasser within one year of the date of the service of the order. Any person on the premises as a trespasser at any time within one month after the service of the order is presumed to have been in occupation of the premises at the time of service unless he proves to the contrary.[5]

Where, on the return date, a final order for possession is made this is then enforceable as an ordinary possession order under CPR Part 55, *i.e.* by warrant for possession by the court bailiffs.[6]

Injunctions

General principles

(1) Types

4–084 A party may obtain an injunction,[7] which is an order of the court directing the party subject to it, either to restrain an unlawful act (a negative, or *prohibitory* injunction) or to require positive steps to be taken to remedy the effects of an unlawful act (a positive, or *mandatory* injunction), *e.g.* an order to remove items wrongfully brought onto land which may be obstructing it or otherwise causing harm. In exceptional circumstances an injunction may lie to prevent a threatened wrong (a *quia timet* injunction). Unlike the trespass possession procedure,[8] injunctive relief has the

---

[3] Punishable by a fine not exceeding level 5 on the standard scale and/or imprisonment for a term of not more than six months. The Home Secretary, introducing the Bill, described the provisions as providing a "quick and effective remedy against squatting": Hansard, H.C., cols. 29–30, January 11, 1994. Given the complexities of the procedure for interim possession orders, it is questionable whether IPO procedure is any quicker in practice than the use of ordinary procedure in a truly urgent case where an application can be made to shorten the time periods.

[4] Meaning a person in occupation of the premises at the time of service of the order: section 76(4). This will no doubt lead to arguments as to whether persons were still in "occupation" at the time of service, although the use of the term "occupation" appears to mean more than physically present so that a deliberate absence at the time of service is unlikely to provide a good defence.

[5] Section 76(4).

[6] CPR Sch. 2 Ord. 24, r. 14(8).

[7] A fuller account of the principles governing the grant of injunctions can be found, *e.g.*, in *Spry's Equitable Remedies* (5th ed.), Chapter 4, *Snell's Equity* (30th. ed.), Chapter 45 and the Supreme Court Practice 1999 (in the notes to RSC, Ord. 29, r. 1 to which reference back is made by current editions of the White Book). For current procedure, see CPR Parts 23 (applications) and 25.1 (interim remedies), and *Practice Direction — Interim Injunctions* (Feb. 2001).

[8] See paras. 4–065 and 4–075.

drawback that it cannot be obtained against "persons unknown",[9] *i.e.* it is of no assistance where the identity of the trespassers is unknown. An injunction may be sought as part of the final relief in proceedings for unlawful interference with land (a final, or permanent injunction), or to obtain an interim remedy prior to the final hearing of the action (an interim, or interlocutory injunction).[10]

Mandatory injunctions are regarded with more circumspection by the Courts than negative orders since they require the doing of a particular act or series of acts and this requires, to a certain degree, the supervision of the court. The general conditions for the grant of mandatory and *quia timet* injunctions were considered by the House of Lords in *Redland Bricks Ltd v. Morris*,[11] where Lord Upjohn stated[12]:

> "The grant of a mandatory injunction is, of course, entirely discretionary and unlike a negative injunction can never be 'as of course'. Every case must depend essentially upon its own particular circumstances. Any general principles for its application can only be laid down in the most general terms:
>
> (1)   A mandatory injunction can only be granted where the plaintiff shows a very strong probability upon the facts that grave damage will accrue to him in the future. As Lord Dunedin said in 1919 it is not sufficient to say 'timeo'. [*Attorney-General for the Dominion of Canada v. Ritchie Contracting and Supply Co.* [1919] A.C. 999, 1005, P.C.]. It is a jurisdiction to be exercised sparingly and with caution but in the proper case unhesitatingly.
>
> (2)   Damages will not be a sufficient or adequate remedy if such damage does happen. This is only the application of a general principle of equity; it has nothing to do with Lord Cairns' Act or *Shelfer's* case [1895] 1 Ch. 287.
>
> (3)   Unlike the case where a negative injunction is granted to prevent the continuance or recurrence of a wrongful act the question of the cost to the defendant to do works to prevent or lessen the likelihood of a future apprehended wrong must be an element to be taken into account;

---

[9] Except in the special circumstances (unconnected with the remedies which form the subject-matter of this book) provided for by s. 187B of the Town and Country Planning Act 1990 — see s. 187B (3)) and CPR Schedule 1 R.S.C. Ord. 110. See, further, *Friern Barnet U.D.C. v. Adams* [1927] 2 Ch. 25, CA and In re *Wykeham Terrace, Brighton, Sussex* [1971] 1 Ch. 204.

[10] This section is concerned with injunctions which protect on enforce substantive rights and not with special forms of injunctions (*i.e.* freezing (formerly referred to as "Mareva") injunctions and search (formerly "Anton Pillar") orders) which are not concerned with such matters but with execution and evidence.

[11] [1970] A.C. 652.

[12] *ibid.* at 665–666.

(a) Where the Defendant has acted without regard to his neighbour's rights, or has tried to steal a march on him or has tried to evade the jurisdiction of the Court or, to sum it up, has acted wantonly and quite unreasonably in relation to his neighbour he may be ordered to repair his wanton and unreasonable acts by doing positive work to restore the status quo even if the expense to him is out of all proportion to the advantage thereby accruing to the Plaintiff. As illustrative of this see *Woodhouse v. Newry Navigation Co.* [1898] 1 I.R. 161;

(b) But where the Defendant has acted reasonably, though in the event wrongly, the cost of remedying by a positive action his earlier activities is most important for two reasons. First, because no legal wrong has yet occurred (for which he has not been recompensed at law and in equity) and, in spite of gloomy expert opinion, may never occur or possibly only upon a much smaller scale than anticipated. Secondly, because if ultimately heavy damage does occur the Plaintiff is in no way prejudiced for he has his action at law and all his consequential remedies in equity.

So the amount to be expended under a mandatory order by the defendant must be balanced with these considerations in mind against the anticipated possible damage to the plaintiff and if, on such balance, it seems unreasonable to inflict such expenditure upon one who for this purpose is no more than a potential wrongdoer then the Court must exercise its jurisdiction accordingly. Of course, the Court does not have to order such works as upon the evidence before it will remedy the wrong but may think it proper to impose upon the defendant the obligation of doing certain works which may upon expert opinion merely lessen the likelihood of any further injury to the plaintiff's land . . .

(4) If in the exercise of its discretion the Court decides that it is a proper case to grant a mandatory injunction, then the Court must be careful to see that the Defendant knows exactly in fact what he has to do and this means not as a matter of law but as a matter of fact, so that in carrying out an order he can give his contractors the proper instructions.

This has been well settled for a long time but I regret that I cannot agree with Danckwerts L.J. ([1967] 1 W.L.R. 967, 974B), that the observations of Joyce J., in *Attorney-General v. Staffordshire County Council* [1905] 1 Ch. 326, 342 have not been followed in practice. My experience has been quite the opposite. There may be cases where, to revert to the simple illustration I gave earlier, the Defendant can be ordered "to restore the right of way to its former condition". This is so simple as to require no further elucidation in the Court order. But in anything more complicated the Court must in fairness to the Defendant tell him what he has to do, although it may well be by reference to plans prepared by some surveyor . . ."

A mandatory *interim* injunction[13] will only be granted in the most compelling circumstances since it requires the performance of some act by the defendant prior to trial which often will involve pre-empting certain decisions as to liability at trial, *e.g.* an order to demolish a structure built on the claimant's land without his consent. The applicant will have to demonstrate clearly why the injunction should be granted at an interim stage rather than awaiting trial.[14]

Quia timet injunctions are granted sparingly, as the above passage from the speech of Lord Upjohn in the *Redland Bricks* case demonstrates.[15] It is not enough for the claimant to show simply that he fears the commission of a wrong, or the causing of damage: there must be a very strong probability that harm will accrue to him in the future.

As Morison J. said in *Secretary of State for Transport & Ors. v. Morozzo & Others*[16]:

"In order to establish their claim to injunctive relief . . . they [the Plaintiffs] must show that there has been a wrongful interference with property belonging to the Plaintiffs, and a real fear that such interference will continue unless restrained by injunction, and that injunctive relief is otherwise the appropriate remedy. In each of the cases with which I am concerned, the Plaintiffs have supported their claims with voluminous evidence . . ."[17]

---

[13] See, *e.g. Bonner v. Great Western Railway* (1883) 24 Ch.D. 1, *Canadian Pacific Railway v. Gaud* [1949] 2 K.B. 239, CA, *Shepherd Homes Ltd v. Sandham* [1971] Ch. 340, *Astro Exito Navigacion S.A. v. Southland Enterprise Co. Ltd (No. 2)* [1982] Q.B. 1284, *Locabail International Finance Ltd v. Agroexport* [1986] 1 W.L.R. 657, CA, and below.

[14] As in *Daniel v. Ferguson* [1891] 2 Ch. 27, CA where the defendant had been served with a notice of motion seeking an injunction but had rushed ahead with his unlawful building operations before the hearing.

[15] See para. 4–090 below.

[16] Unreported, September 9, 1994. This was one of the cases against those protesting against the construction of the A12–M11 link road in north-east London in 1993/5 . Protests took the form of both trespass to land in the possession of the then Department of Transport and to the equipment used for the construction of the road.

[17] The evidence included photographic evidence and the transcripts of many hours of video taped activities of the defendants. The learned judge also granted a wide injunction to prevent trespass to goods also on a *quia timet* basis since he accepted that the protestors, once excluded from the land, would be likely to continue their protest campaign by interfering with the equipment belonging to the Department of Transport and its contractors when it was off the sites in the possession of the Department. He stated:

"I see no reason why, in the circumstances of this case, the court should wait to see if the tort is committed, and there are, in my judgment, real grounds for believing that, even after the court has made the trespass injunction, unlawful acts will be continued against the Plaintiffs' property . . ."

(2) Final or interim

(a) Final injunctions

4–085 Such injunctions are of permanent effect and are granted as final relief to a party to an action as opposed to an interim injunction which is intended to be of temporary effect pending the final determination of proceedings. There are a number of requirements which must generally be satisfied before a permanent injunction will be granted:

> (i)   the party claiming the injunction must do so in order to protect or enforce a legal or equitable right to which he is entitled. A *quia timet* injunction may also be sought to guard against a threatened injury to such a right (see para. 4–084 above);

> (ii)   the award of damages must not be an adequate remedy; and

> (iii) the party seeking the injunction must not himself be guilty of conduct such as would lead the court to refuse him relief.

4–086 *(i) Legal or equitable right* — It is not enough that some general complaint is made: in order to obtain an injunction a claimant must demonstrate that he has some specific right or interest in the subject matter of the injunction, *e.g.* in the property which is subject to trespass or nuisance or the benefit of the restrictive covenant which he seeks to enforce.

4–087 *(ii) Damages inadequate* — An injunction will generally be refused if damages will be an adequate remedy[18] such as where the party wronged can properly be compensated in damages[19] or where the wrong was unlikely to occur again. The position is quite different if the wrong is a continuing one[20] or one which requires a mandatory or restraining order. A party will not be subjected to a permanent order of the court (breach of which is a contempt of court) if there are sufficient means of dealing with the wrong which has occurred short of granting an injunction.

However, in the case of a trespass where the claimant's title is not disputed it is not generally necessary for the claimant to show he has suffered actual loss as a result of the trespass or that he will, in fact, suffer loss if the trespass is permitted to continue[21] (likewise, where there is an interference with an easement[22]). Further, in a case where the defendant has totally dispossessed the claimant by an unlawful encroachment on his land, a mandatory injunction is "inevitable."[23]

---

[18] *London and Blackwall Railway v. Cross* (1886) 31 Ch.D. 354 at 369.
[19] *e.g. Hodgson v. Duce* (1856) 2 Jur. (N.S.) 1014 (defendant too poor to make damages worthwhile).
[20] *e.g.* where there is a continuing trespass or nuisance.
[21] See *Woollerton & Wilson Ltd v. Richard Costain Ltd* [1970] 1 W.L.R. 411, *John Trenberth Ltd v. National Westminster Bank Ltd* (1979) 39 P. & C.R. 104, *Patel v. W.H. Smith (Eziot) Ltd* [1987] 1 W.L.R. 853, CA and *London Borough of Harrow v. Donohue* [1995] 1 E.G.L.R. 257, CA.
[22] See paras. 2–007 and 2–093.
[23] *London Borough of Harrow v. Donohue*, above.

(iii) Conduct of claimant — Since the grant of an injunction is an equitable **4–088** remedy, the court has a discretion whether or not to grant it and will be guided by familiar equitable principles in exercising that discretion.

A claimant may be refused an injunction if he has himself acted improperly[24] or has otherwise not come to equity "with clean hands".

Further, undue delay on the part of an applicant[25] for an injunction may defeat a claim for an injunction by reason of the delay itself[26] and also if the circumstances amount to acquiescence[27] by the applicant in the activity of the other party, *i.e.* a waiver of the applicant's right to seek an injunction.[28] In *Blue Town Investments Ltd v. Higgs and Hill plc,*[29] the Vice-Chancellor stated:

> "Standing by and watching a man proceeding on the basis that rights will not be enforced and then seeking to turn round and claim equitable relief based on such rights is conduct which par excellence disentitles the plaintiff from claiming equitable relief."

If a party wishes to obtain an interim injunction, it is important that he acts promptly in seeking such relief.[30]

(b) Interim injunctions

(i) Prohibitory interim injunctions — Although the court's discretion to **4–089** grant injunctions under section 37 of the Supreme Court Act 1981 is wide,[31] and this discretion is ultimately one for the court, negative interim injunctions are usually granted on the principles established by the House of Lords in *American Cyanamid v. Ethicon.*[32] Although injunctions are in

---

[24] *e.g.* by misleading the opposing party or the court (*Armstrong v. Sheppard v. Short Ltd* [1959] 2 Q.B. 384), acting in breach of statute (*Malone v. Metropolitan Police Commissioner* [1980] Q.B. 49), or in breach of contract (*General Billposting Co. Ltd v. Atkinson* [1909] A.C. 118).

[25] *Blue Town Investments Ltd v. Higgs and Hill plc* [1990] 1 W.L.R. 696.

[26] If the delay is such so as to cause prejudice to the other party: see *Snell's Equity* at 35–36.

[27] *Shaw v. Applegate* [1977] 1 W.L.R. 970. Mere delay itself does not amount to acquiescence: *Lamare v. Dixon* (1873) L.R. 6. H.L. 414.

[28] On waiver generally, see *Chitty on Contracts* (28th ed.) Vol. 1, paras. 3–076 to 3–079.

[29] [1990] 1 W.L.R. 696, at 701.

[30] *Sherwell v. Combined Incandescent Mantles Syndicate Ltd* [1907] W.N. 211 at 212.

[31] "Just and convenient . . ." See also CPR Part 25 and the *Practice Direction — Interim Injunctions* (Feb. 2001).

[32] [1975] A.C. 396, HL. See further *NWL Ltd v. Woods* [1979] 1 W.L.R. 1294, HL; *Cayne v. Global Resources Ltd* [1984] 1 All E.R. 225, *Locabail international Finance Ltd v. Agroexport* [1986] 1 W.L.R. 657, CA and *Lawrence David Ltd v. Ashton* [1991] 1 All E.R. 385, CA. These guidelines, although generally applicable, are not statutory requirements and there are cases where they have not been applied, *e.g.* where the issue is a simple matter of construction: see *Associated British Ports v. T.G.W.U.* [1989] 1 W.L.R. 939, HL at 979–980 and, further, *Hampstead & Suburban Properties Ltd v. Diomedous* [1969] 1 Ch. 248 at 259 ("a plain and uncontested breach of a clear covenant . . ."). The guidelines may also not be applied where there is no real prospect of trial: *NWL Ltd v. Woods*, above. Further, in *London Borough of Harrow v. Donohue* [1995] 1 E.G.L.R. 257 the Court of Appeal held that "in a situation . . . where the land owner has been totally dispossessed by the defendant's encroaching building" the court has a very limited discretion, namely whether to make

general sought and obtained with notice, they may be obtained *without notice* in cases of real urgency.[33]

The main principles, set out by Lord Diplock in *American Cyanamid*[34] may be summarised as follows:

(1) there must be a serious question to be tried. This does not require proof of the applicant's case, or even that there is necessarily a prima facie case. The applicant merely has to demonstrate that there is a serious issue — providing there is some prospect of success at trial.[35] The court will usually have to decide the claim to injunctive relief on the basis of affidavit evidence, but will not embark on a trial by affidavits or witness statements;

(2) if the applicant satisfies the court that there is a serious question to be tried, the court will then proceed to strike the balance of convenience:[36]

(a) if the applicant would be adequately compensated in damages at trial, and the defendant would be able to pay for them, an injunction will normally be refused;

(b) if an injunction is granted, the court must be satisfied that the defendant will be properly compensated in damages if the action proceeds to trial and the defendant succeeds. Providing that condition is met and the claimant would be able to pay the damages, then the strength of the defendant's case is generally immaterial to the grant of an injunction;[37]

(c) if the balance between the parties comes out reasonably even, then the court will seek to preserve the status quo existing prior to the issue of proceedings (or application for

---

an order for possession or a mandatory order to take down the offending building (*per* Waite L.J. at p. 259). This is, no doubt, subject to the usual equitable defences such as laches and acquiescence.

[33] See below, para. 4–093.

[34] [1975] A.C. 396, HL, at 407–9. Post-CPR and the Human Rights Act 1998, it appears that the *American Cyanamid* guidelines survive. They were applied as "a general rule which governs most cases in which a court is invited to grant an interim injunction restraining the defendant until the trial of the action from doing the things of which the claimant makes complaint" in *Douglas and others v. Hello! Ltd* [2001] 2 All E.R. 289, CA, at 302, para. 50 *per* Brooke L.J. In that case, the Court of Appeal considered how a human rights issue might be dealt with in the context of the guidelines. See also *Imutran Ltd v. Uncaged Campaigns Ltd* [2001] 2 All E.R. 385 at paras 15–19.

[35] *Cayne v. Global Natural Resources plc* [1984] 1 All E.R. 225, CA, at 230, Eveleigh L.J. stated "If I am in doubt and if the issue seems to be one that is not frivolous, in other words is one for which there is supporting material, then I would conclude that there is a triable issue." See also *Lawrence David Ltd v. Ashton* [1991] 1 All E.R. 385, CA, at 395–396. In *Series 5 Software Ltd v. Clarke* [1996] 1 All E.R. 853, Laddie J revisited the *American Cyanamid* guidelines, concluding that a judge could consider the overall merits of the case before him in deciding whether or not to grant an interim injunction.

[36] For an example of the court striking the balance, see *Rafique v. Trustees of the Walton Estate* (1992) 65 P. & C.R. 356.

[37] *Jennings v. Jennings* [1898] 1 Ch. 378 and *Lawrence David Ltd v. Ashton*, above.

injunction if significantly later). It should be noted that the preservation of the status quo is the last resort not the principal aim of an interim injunction;[38] and

(3)   the court will occasionally consider the relative strength of each party's case, but generally only if the injunction would dispose of an action which has run a large part of its course[39] or would be the equivalent of a final order.[40]

As is noted above, in the case of trespass to land a landowner is prima facie entitled to an injunction restraining the trespass even in the absence of damage. In such a case, the court is generally not concerned with the "balance of convenience" in determining whether to grant an interim injunction.[41] The court may depart from this prima facie rule, *e.g.* (on an interlocutory application) where the defendant establishes an arguable case that he is entitled to do that which is said to amount to a trespass.[42]

The court may, however, be reluctant to grant an injunction if it is drawn in too wide a form, such as an order "not to trespass" or "not to commit a nuisance" since this could cover a very wide range of issues unrelated to the specific complaint of the claimant and does not give the defendant a very clear warning as to what he should not do. However, it is always open to a claimant to seek a wider form of injunction in cases where the particular facts justify it.

(ii) Mandatory interim injunctions — The approach to interlocutory injunctions set out by Lord Diplock in *American Cyanamid* is applicable to negative injunctions only.[43] In the case of mandatory interim injunctions, a stricter approach is taken and the court must be satisfied that the claimant's case for relief is particularly strong.[44] In *Locabail International Finance Ltd v. Agroexport*[45] Mustill L.J. stated that:

4–090

"The matter before the court is not only an application for a mandatory injunction, but is an application for a mandatory interlocutory injunction which, if granted, would amount to the grant of a major part of the relief claimed in the action. Such an application should be approached with caution and the relief granted only in a clear case."

[38] *Hubbard v. Pitt* [1976] Q.B. 142, CA at 190 and *Garden Cottage Foods Ltd v. Milk Marketing Board* [1984] A.C. 130, HL, at 140.
[39] *Cayne v. Global Natural Resources plc* [1984] 1 All E.R. 225, and *Lawrence David Ltd v. Ashton*, above at 395–396.
[40] *Cambridge Nutrition Ltd v. BBC* [1990] 3 All E.R. 523, CA.
[41] *e.g. Patel v. W.H. Smith (Eziot) Ltd* [1987] 1 W.L.R. 853, CA and *London Borough of Harrow v. Donohue* [1995] 1 E.G.L.R. 257, CA.
[42] *Patel*, above, at 859 (applying the test in *American Cyanamid Co. v. Ethicon Ltd* [1975] A.C. 396).
[43] And only in a modified form in cases of trespass to land: see above and also *Redland Bricks Ltd v. Morris* [1970] A.C. 652, HL.
[44] See *Redland Bricks Ltd v. Morris ibid.* at 665–666 (the passage is quoted above, para. 4–084).
[45] [1986] 1 W.L.R. 657, at 664.

In the special case of a trespassing defendant whose encroachment totally dispossesses the lawful owner, a mandatory final injunction will be granted almost as a matter of course. It is likely that such an approach to final orders will make it easier to obtain similar interim orders in clear cases.[46]

In accordance with Lord Upjohn's approach in *Redland Bricks*,[47] the form of a mandatory order must be carefully drawn so that the defendant knows exactly what he must do to comply fully with the order. The court will refuse a mandatory order if it is difficult or impossible for the other party to comply[48] or where the continued supervision of the court is necessary.[49]

4–091 *(iii) The necessity for an undertaking in damages*[50] — Where interim injunctions are sought from the Court it is usual for the party seeking the injunction to give a cross-undertaking in damages,[51] to ensure that if it becomes clear that the injunction ought not to have been made,[52] the defendant can be compensated for any loss which has resulted from the making of the order providing it is not too remote.[53] The undertaking is given to the Court not to the other party,[54] unless it is made by agreement between the parties, *e.g.* in return from an undertaking in place of an injunction. Although in practice claimants are not always required to demonstrate that they have the means to meet any claim on the undertaking, the Court may consider evidence of the adequacy of the claimant's means and refuse to make the order if not satisfied as to means, or discharge an order already made if there has been material non-disclosure on the issue.[55] There are certain circumstances where an undertaking will not be required,[56] but in most cases if it is not given expressly it will be implied as a matter of course.[57]

---

[46] See *London Borough of Harrow v. Donohue* [1995] 1 E.G.L.R. 257, CA.

[47] See above, Lord Upjohn's general principle 4, para. 4–084.

[48] *Harold Stephen & Co. Ltd v. Post Office* [1977] 1 W.L.R. 1172.

[49] *e.g.* lengthy building works — *Attorney-General v. Staffordshire County Council* [1905] 1 Ch. 336 and *Kennard v. Corp Bros & Co. Ltd* [1922] 2 Ch. 1.

[50] See further, below, under Procedure at 4–093.

[51] See CPR Part 25 *Practice Direction — Interim Injunctions* para. 5.1(1).

[52] For example, because the Court had no power to order the injunction or the Claimant does not justify the application on the evidence. See *e.g. Griffith v. Blake* (1884) 27 Ch. D. 474.

[53] *Smith v. Day* (1882) 21 Ch. D. 421 at 424.

[54] If it is enforced, an inquiry as to the appropriate damages may be ordered: see *Lock International plc v. Beswick* [1989] 1 W.L.R. 1268 at 1285–6, where Hoffmann J. discharged an Anton Pillar ("freezing") order.

[55] *Lock International plc v. Beswick*, above, at 1278–9 and 1285 where the inadequacy of means and material noon-disclosure were among the grounds for discharge of the order.

[56] An undertaking is not required where the Crown seeks to enforce the law and no alternative means are available: *F. Hoffmann-La Roche A.G. v. Secretary of State for Trade and Industry* [1975] A.C. 295, HL. This does not apply where the Crown is simply seeking to protect its own property rights. See *Snell's Equity* (13th ed.) para. 45–46 p. 736 for other exceptions. If a public authority has other means available to it to enforce the law, but simply chooses to enforce by means of an injunction, then an undertaking is required: *Rochdale Borough Council v. Anders* [1988] 3 All E.R. 490 and *Kirklees Metropolitan Borough Council v. Wickes Building Supplies Ltd* [1991] 3 W.L.R. 985, CA.

[57] *Howard v. Press Printers Ltd* (1904) 74 L.J. Ch. 100 at 104–5.

(iv) Other terms — The Court may also impose other terms as a precondi- **4–092**
tion to making an injunction such as security for costs, or the payment of
money into Court[58].

(3) Jurisdiction and procedure

(a) High Court

The jurisdiction of the High Court is found in section 37 of the Supreme **4–093**
Court Act 1981 and is governed by CPR Part 25. Under section 37, the
High Court may by order (whether interim or final) grant an injunction in
all cases in which it appears to the court to be "just and convenient" to do
so. Any such order may be made either unconditionally or on such terms
and conditions as the court thinks just. An application for an interim
injunction may be made even though there is no claim for a final remedy
of that kind[59]. Applications may be made either in the Queen's Bench
Division (by application in chambers) or in the Chancery Division (by
application in open court) and are generally made on notice following the
issue of the claim form.[60] The current procedural requirements are set out
principally in CPR Part 25[61] and the associated *Practice Direction — Interim
Injunctions*[62] and require for applications on notice[63] that:

(1)   the application notice should set out the order sought and the
        date, time and place of the hearing;

(2)   the application notice and evidence in support must be served as
        soon as practicable after issue and in any event not less than three
        days before the court is due to hear the application[64];

(3)   "whenever possible" a draft of the order sought should be filed
        with the application notice and a disk containing the draft should
        also be available to the court[65]; and

(4)   generally evidence may be given by witness statement or, where
        verified by a statement of truth, in the statement of case or

---

[58] *Harman Pictures, N. V. v. Osborne* [1969] 1 W.L.R. 723 at 739.
[59] CPR Part 25, r. 25.4.
[60] CPR Part 25, r. 25.1. A defendant may apply for an interim order although he may be
      required to undertake to file and counterclaim or issue a writ as a term of the relief:
      Sargant v. Read (1876) 1 Ch.D. 600 and *Marcus Publishing plc v. Hutton-Wild Communications
      Ltd* [1990] R.P.C. 576, CA.
[61] See also the general rules for making applications in CPR Part 23 and for evidence in CPR
      Part 38.
[62] The current version at the time of going to press was February 2001.
[63] Sections 2 and 3 of the *Practice Direction*.
[64] Para. 2.3 provides that where the court is to serve, sufficient copies of the application
      notice and evidence in support for the court and for each respondent should be filed for
      issue and service.
[65] To speed up amendments and the preparation and sealing of the order by the Court
      Office: para. 2.4 of the *Practice Direction*.

application notice[66]. The evidence must set out the facts on which the applicant relies for the claim being made against the defendant, including all material facts of which the court should be made aware.

In cases of real urgency[67] an application can be made without notice to the other party:[68] this should usually be following the issue of the claim form and supported by a witness statement, but in appropriately urgent circumstances, interim injunctions can be sought and obtained in advance of the issue of the claim form[69] although conditions should normally be imposed including an undertaking to issue proceedings (or other directions as to the commencement of proceedings) and to serve them with the injunction[70].

In all cases where application is made without notice the application notice, evidence in support and a draft order should be filed with the court two hours before the hearing "wherever possible".[71] However, if an application is made before the application notice has been issued, a draft order should be provided at the hearing, and the application notice and evidence in support must be filed with the court on the same or next working day or as ordered by the court.[72] The evidence should explain why it was necessary to make the application without notice.[73] Unless secrecy is essential, informal steps should be taken to notify the defendant of the application.[74] Other terms may also be imposed, such as the notification of the order to the opposing party in a particular manner. Such terms imposed by the court are usually given in the form of undertakings by the applicant and should be strictly complied with, since failure to comply is a contempt.[75] An injunction without notice is often limited in effect to a number of days and a return date for a hearing with notice is fixed or it may be made "until further order" giving the defendant the right to apply to the court (usually on notice to the claimant) to discharge or vary the injunction.

---

[66] Para. 3.2 of the *Practice Direction*. Affidavits should be used where the Court directs or on applications for freezing or search orders: paras 3.1, 3.2.

[67] *Bates v. Lord Hailsham of St Marylebone* [1972] 1 W.L.R. 1373 at 1380 (*per* Megarry J. "ex parte injunctions are for cases of real urgency, where there has been a true impossibility of giving notice of motion."). The urgency may arise from the difficulty of obtaining a sufficiently speedy inter partes hearing: *Beese v. Woodhouse* [1970] 1 W.L.R. 586.

[68] Under the previous RSC it was possible to have an *ex parte* application made where the defendant is notified: *Pickwick International Inc. (G.B.) Ltd v. Multiple Sound Distributors Ltd* [1972] 1 W.L.R. 1213. Para. 4.3(3) of the *Practice Direction — Interim Injunctions* (Feb. 2001) under CPR Part 25 formalises the matter by requiring that "except in cases where secrecy is essential, the applicant should take steps to notify the respondent informally of the application."

[69] CPR Part 25.2 and *Practice Direction — Interim Injunctions*, Section 4.

[70] *Practice Direction — Interim Injunctions* para. 4.4.

[71] *Practice Direction — Interim Injunctions* para. 4.3 and 4.4(1).

[72] *ibid.* para. 4.3(2).

[73] *ibid.*, para. 3.4.

[74] *ibid.*, para. 4.3(3).

[75] *P.S. Refson & Co. Ltd v. Saggers* [1984] 1 W.L.R. 1025.

Further, since the grant of an injunction without notice is made in the absence of the opposing party, it is a strict requirement that the applicant disclose all material facts to the court — whether or not they support the application.[76] In the event that the applicant fails to make such disclosure, the court may discharge the injunction on the application of the defendant[77] although this will inevitably depend not only on the nature and materiality of the facts not disclosed but also on the explanation for the failure to disclose.[78]

The applicant for an interim injunction, as a condition of the grant of such an order, must generally give an undertaking[79] by his counsel that he will compensate the defendant in damages for any losses suffered as a result of the grant of the injunction in the event that it is determined that the order ought not to have been made. This applies even where the undertaking may be of little value, such as where the applicant is financially weak, or legally aided.[80]

(b) County Court

The county court has general ancillary jurisdiction to grant injunctions **4–094** under section 38 of the County Courts Act 1984[81] and "in any proceedings in a county court the court may make any order which could be made by the High Court if the proceedings were in the High Court".[82] This general power, introduced by the Courts and Legal Services Act 1990, substituted for the earlier more limited jurisdiction which was generally tied to the requirement that other relief be claimed in the proceedings. There is still provision, in section 38(4) for the limitation of the scope of the ancillary jurisdiction by regulation.[83]

Under the CPR the principles and procedure applying to, injunctions in the county court are generally the same as in the High Court.[84]

---

[76] See, *e.g. R. & Kensington Income Tax Commissioners* [1917] 1 K.B. 486 at 504, CA and *Tate Access Floors Inc. v. Boswell* [1991] 2 W.L.R. 304 at 319–321. The common law requirements are added to by the parallel requirement of para. 3.3 of the *Practice Direction — Interim Injunctions* to set out in the evidence in support of the application "all material facts of which the court should be made aware."

[77] An application to discharge may also be made without notice in appropriate cases: *London City Agency (J.C.D.) Ltd v. Lee* [1970] Ch. 597.

[78] See *Brink's Mat Ltd v. Elcombe* [1988] 1 W.L.R. 1350, *Behbehani v. Salem* (Note) [1989] 1 W.L.R. 723 and *Tate Access Floor Inc.* [1991] 2 W.L.R. 304.

[79] CPR Part 25 *Practice Direction — Interim Injunctions* para. 5.1(1) and *Fenner v. Wilson* [1893] 2 Ch. 656, although not where the Crown seeks to enforce the law and no alternative means are available: *F. Hoffmann-La Roche A.G. v. Secretary of State for Trade and Industry* [1975] A.C. 295, HL. See also para. 4–091 above.

[80] *Allen v. Jambo Holdings Ltd* [1980] 1 W.L.R. 1252, CA.

[81] As amended by the s. 3 of the Courts and Legal Services Act 1990.

[82] See *Burris v. Azadani* [1995] 1 W.L.R. 1372, CA, at 1376–7.

[83] See the County Court Remedies Regulations 1991 which prohibits the County Court from "prescribed relief" defined by r. 2 (including the removal of assets from the jurisdiction of the High Court or dealing with assets) except in limited cases.

[84] Although there are limitations on the ability to make freezing orders and search orders: see the County Court Remedies Regulations 1991, reg. 3.

(4) Wording of the order

(a) Generally

4–095　A number of the forms for injunction are prescribed by the CPR. The substantive terms of the order sought should be sufficiently well-drawn to make it as clear as possible to the party subject to it to know precisely what he may not do (or must do) both as a matter of law and in fact.[85] The severe consequences of a breach of injunction — *i.e.* for contempt of court — require the courts to scrutinise carefully the wording of any proposed injunction.

(b) Trespass cases

4–096　Since the term "trespass" (even when confined to real property interests) can cover a wide variety of wrongs, a court is likely to be reluctant simply to order a defendant "not to trespass" to, or on, the claimant's land. There may, however, be circumstances where a court is prepared to sanction a wide form of words, *e.g.* where the court is faced with a persistent trespasser who has trespassed in a number of different ways which make it impractical or ineffectual to limit the scope of the trespassing to be prohibited. An example can be found in one of the series of cases against those protesting against the construction of new roads, *Secretary of State for Transport v. Morozzo.*[86] There an injunction "not to trespass" granted by Morison J. with regard to land was coupled with an order to prevent trespass to goods,

> "... which are used whether actively or otherwise for the purposes of the construction of the link road as defined the Statement of Claim herein and which are situated on the land as defined in the Statement of Claim herein or going to or from the land or any part thereof for the purposes of the construction of the link road ..."

The applicant for an injunction must always consider carefully the form of the order sought and ensure not only that it is clear and precise, but that it actually covers the full extent of the relief required, *e.g.* it may not be sufficient to seek an order restraining a company acting through its officers[87] — but also to restrain it acting via its employees or agents.[88]

---

[85] See, *e.g. Hackett v. Baiss* (1875) L.R. 20 Eq. 494, *Parker v. First Avenue Hotel Co.* (1883) 24 Ch.D. 282 at 286, *Ellerman Lines Ltd v. Read* [1928] 2 K.B. 144 at 158, *Redland Bricks v. Morris* [1970] A.C. 652, HL at 666.

[86] Unreported, September 9, 1994. See para. 4–084.

[87] Although this is of questionable necessity (save as a means of clarifying what is meant) since the deeds of those acting on behalf of a company (or natural person) will be those of the principal.

[88] See *Marengo v. Daily Sketch and Sunday Graphic Ltd* [1948] 1 All E.R. 406 and *Attorney-General v. Newspaper Publishing plc* [1988] Ch. 333.

One form (for which there exist many variations) would be "to restrain XYZ Ltd whether acting by its officers, servants, agents or otherwise howsoever from . . ."

Lord Upjohn in the *Redland Bricks* case[89] noted the particular importance of drawing up the terms of the order clearly in the case of a mandatory injunction so that the party served "knows exactly in fact what he has to do" both as a matter of law and as a matter of fact.

(c) Nuisance cases

An injunction, as previously mentioned,[90] should be sufficiently well drawn to make it quite clear to the party subject to it to know precisely what he must or must not do both as a matter of law and as a matter of fact. However, in the context of nuisance the court will not shrink from granting a prohibitory injunction simply because the nature of the nuisance to be restrained is such that there will inevitably be some uncertainty in whether or not a nuisance is being committed in breach of the injunction. In *Hampstead and Suburban Properties Ltd v. Diomedous*[91] Megarry J. said:

4–097

> "The court is always slow to repose on the easy pillow of uncertainty; and there have been many instances of the grant of interlocutory injunctions to restrain the commission of nuisances, despite the difficulty that there often is in defining precisely what degree of smell or noise or vibration amounts to a nuisance . . . The fact that a defendant enjoined from committing a nuisance may have some difficulty in going as close as he can to the dividing line without crossing it is in my judgment no reason for not enjoining him in a case where it is plain that wherever the line ought to be drawn he is overstepping it by a wide margin."

Since nuisance is an unreasonable interference with the rights of a claimant to occupy his land it is important in drafting an order restraining the defendant's activities that those activities only be restrained to the extent to which they are unreasonable or constitute an actionable nuisance. Thus in *Kennaway v. Thompson*[92] the injunction granted in order to restrain the nuisance caused by the racing of motor boats did not prohibit that activity absolutely; motor-boat racing was permitted to continue but subject to restrictions as to the number and duration of events which could be held and as to the level of the noise of the boats using the lake at any other time. Such "qualified injunctions" are often a satisfactory way of establishing a *modus vivendi* between claimant and defendant where the

---

[89] [1970] A.C. 652 at 666–667.
[90] See paras. 4–095 and 4–096 above.
[91] [1969] 1 Ch. 248, 257G-258B.
[92] [1981] Q.B. 88.

defendant's activities can be limited according to time, extent or numbers: thus an injunction could be granted permitting a playground to be used only by children under 12 years old between 10 a.m. and 6.30 p.m.[93]; or restraining the use of an oil depot between 10 p.m. and 6 a.m.[94] Similarly in the case of nuisances caused by the noise of building operations an injunction will only prohibit the building operations to the extent that they cause a nuisance by reason of the unreasonable level of the noise or the unreasonable hours at which the building operations take place.[95]

4–098   Instead of specifying in detail what the defendant may or may not do, the court may grant him and his successors in title liberty to apply to the court for a modification or variation of the order to take account of changed circumstances or proposals by the defendant to carry out the prohibited activities without causing a nuisance.[96] In *Tetley v. Chitty*[97] in which the court granted an injunction prohibiting all go-karting on the defendant's land, the defendant had liberty to apply to the court to vary or discharge the injunction if he could produce an acceptable scheme.

(5) Suspended orders

4–099   An injunction is, by its nature, a discretionary remedy. The courts have used their discretion to suspend the operation of injunctions. For instance, this may be a proper course where the imposition of an injunction requiring immediate abatement of the nuisance by the defendant would have effects disproportionate to the nuisance prohibited. In *Stollmeyer v. Trinidad Lake Petroleum Co. Ltd*[98] the defendant had caused nuisance by polluting water, and the Privy Council held that the defendant could not "excuse or defend their wrong by showing how disproportionate is the loss which they will suffer" (compared to the benefit to the claimant in not suffering the nuisance). However, these "considerations may be relevant to the form of remedy, especially to the time and opportunities which should be given them for finding some way out of their difficulties."[99] In that case the Privy Council suspended the injunction for two years.[1] Where such suspension is sought by a defendant it may be appropriate that the defendant should undertake as a condition of the suspension

---

[93] *Dunton v. Dover District Council* (1978) 76 L.G.R. 87.
[94] *Halsey v. Esso Petroleum Co Ltd* [1961] 1 W.L.R. 683, 703.
[95] Compare *Andreae v. Selfridge & Co Ltd* [1938] Ch. 1. But see *Shoreham-By-Sea UDC v. Dolphin Canadian Proteins Ltd* (1972) 71 LGR 261, 268 *per* Donaldson J: "It is not for this court to adopt the role of technical adviser and say that particular measures have to be taken".
[96] *Pride of Derby and Derbyshire Angling Association v. British Celanese Ltd* [1953] 1 Ch. 149.
[97] [1986] 1 All E.R. 663, 675.
[98] [1918] A.C. 485.
[99] *ibid.*, at 494. See also *Jordan v. Norfolk CC* [1994] N.P.C. 69.
[1]   See also the *Pride of Derby* case [1953] Ch. 149 (defendant given two years to modify its sewerage works); *Hole v. Chard Union* [1894] 1 Ch. 293 (defendant given six months to modify sewerage works); *Manchester Corporation v. Farnworth* [1930] A.C. 171 (electricity generating works given one year's suspension); *Halsey v. Esso Petroleum Ltd* [1961] 2 All E.R. 145 (six weeks given to abate nuisance caused by oil depot).

to compensate the claimant for any loss or damage suffered during the period of suspension.[2]

(6) Damages in lieu of injunction

The power to award damages in lieu of an injunction[3] was first provided by section 2 of the Chancery Amendment Act 1858 (usually known as "Lord Cairns' Act")[4] and is currently found in section 50 of the Supreme Court Act 1981 which is in the following terms: **4–100**

> "Where the Court of Appeal or the High Court has jurisdiction to entertain an application for an injunction or specific performance, it may award damages in addition to, or in substitution for, an injunction or specific performance."

The County Court is given similar power by section 38 of the County Courts Act 1984.

(a) Jurisdiction

The statutory provisions confer on Courts the power to award damages where, in the absence of the power, they would have granted an injunction and also where they could have granted an injunction but would not have done so in the exercise of their discretion.[5] The court has, in effect,   **4–101**

---

[2] See *Stollmeyer v. Trinidad Lake Petroleum Co Ltd* [1918] A.C. 485, 497; *Manchester Corporation v. Farnworth* [1930] AC 171; the *Pride of Derby* case [1952] 1 All E.R. 1326, 1341 (first instance). See also *Frost v. King Edward VII Welsh etc Association* [1918] 2 Ch. 180, 195; *Reinhardt v. Mentasti* (1889) 42 Ch. D. 685, 690.

[3] For a fuller account see Spry's *Equitable Remedies* (5th ed.), Chap. 7. See also *Snell's Equity* (30th ed.), pp [45–25]–[45–29], Jolowicz [1975] C.L.J. 224, Pettit [1977] C.L.J. 369. For examples of cases in which the court awarded damages in lieu of an injunction in respect of trespass see *Kelsen v. Imperial Tobacco Company (of Great Britain and Ireland) Ltd* [1957] 2 Q.B. 334, *Bracewell v. Appleby* [1975] Ch. 408 and *Jaggard v. Sawyer* [1995] 1 W.L.R. 269.

[4] Lord Cairns' Act conferred the power on the Court of Chancery alone. Part of the function of the Act was simply to enable that court to award damages so that litigants who had started an action there but who were not entitled to an equitable remedy would not be obliged to start a new action at law. It was well established however that the Act also conferred power to award damages where a common law court could not (see below). As a result of s. 16 of the Judicature Act 1873 the power conferred by Lord Cairns' Act was vested in the High Court. Lord Cairns' Act was repealed by s. 5 of the Statute Law Revision and Civil Procedure Act 1883, but that section contained a proviso which preserved the jurisdiction established by Lord Cairns' Act, as did the Statute Law Revision Act 1893 which repealed s. 5; *Leeds Industrial Co-operative Society Limited v. Slack* [1924] A.C. 851, HL at 861–863.

[5] It is nowhere stated in terms that the court has jurisdiction to award damages in cases in which, before Lord Cairns Act, it would have had jurisdiction to grant an injunction but would have chosen not to do so. However, as well as being the most natural interpretation of the words of the statute, this view accords best with the authorities: see especially *Hooper v. Rogers* [1975] Ch. 43, CA, *per* Russell L.J. at 48 — "The case in this court therefore boils down to the question of whether it is one in which the judge could have (however unwisely in the context of the relationship of unremitting hostility between the parties) made a mandatory order . . ."

the option of substituting damages if the grant of an injunction would be too harsh on the defendant or if the refusal to grant any remedy would be unjust to the claimant.

An important feature of the power is that the court is able to award damages where it would not have been able to at common law (including circumstances where there has been a breach of a restrictive covenant enforceable only in equity[6]). Thus the court can award damages for the whole injury suffered where the damage or a proportion of the damage did not accrue until after the commencement of proceedings.[7] It can award damages in respect of injuries not yet suffered, *i.e.* in lieu of a *quia timet* injunction, and thus obviate the need for the claimant to bring repeated actions for damages.[8] Further, it can award damages in lieu of an injunction where such damages are not specifically pleaded by the claimant.[9]

It is also open to the court to award damages in lieu of an injunction where a situation giving rise to a discretion on the part of the court to grant an injunction existed at the time the action was commenced but has ceased to exist by the time of the hearing.[10]

(b) Exercise of the court's discretion

4–102   The most influential statement of the principles that should govern the exercise of the court's discretion to grant damages in lieu of an injunction has been that of A.L. Smith L.J. in *Shelfer v. City of London Electric Lighting Company*:[11]

> "Many judges have stated, and I emphatically agree with them, that a person by committing a wrongful act (whether it be a public company for public purposes or a private individual) is not thereby entitled to ask the Court to sanction his doing so by purchasing his neighbour's rights, by assessing damages in that behalf, leaving his

---

[6]   See . . .

[7]   See *Davenport v. Rylands* (1865) L.R. 1 Eq. 302, *Fritz v. Hobson* (1880) 14 Ch.D. 542.

[8]   *Leeds Industrial Co-operative Society Ltd v. Slack* [1924] A.C. 851, HL See also *Holland v. Worley* (1884) 26 Ch.D. 578, *Baxter v. Four Oaks Properties* [1965] Ch. 816, *Hooper v. Rogers* [1975] Ch. 43.

[9]   *Catton v. Wyld* (1863) 32 Beav. 266, 55 E.R. 105, *Betts v. Neilson* (1868) L.R. 3 Ch. 429, 441. See also *Marcic v. Thames Water Utilities Ltd (No. 2)* [2001] 4 All E.R. 326 upheld, in part, by the Court of Appeal [2002] 2 W.L.R. 932.

[10]   See, *e.g. Fritz v. Hobson* (1880) 14 Ch.D. 542. Here the claimant brought an action against the defendant in respect of the nuisance caused by the defendant's obstructing the access to the claimant's house. By the time of the hearing the nuisance had abated so that it was no longer possible to grant an injunction. The court nevertheless awarded damages in substitution for the injunction. See also *Davenport v. Rylands*, above.

[11]   [1895] 1 Ch.D. 287, CA at 322. The statement was, strictly, obiter. However, it has been applied as a general principle since: see, *e.g.*, *Jaggard v. Sawyer* [1995] 1 W.L.R. 269, CA. At p. 287 Millett L.J. noted that "A.L. Smith L.J.'s checklist has stood the test of time; but it needs to be remembered that it is only a working rule and does not purport to be an exhaustive statement of the circumstances in which damages may be awarded instead of an injunction."

neighbour with the nuisance, or his lights dimmed, as the case may be.

In such cases the well-known rule is not to accede to the application, but to grant the injunction sought, for the plaintiff's legal right has been invaded, and he is prima facie entitled to an injunction.

There are, however, cases in which this rule may be relaxed, and in which damages may be awarded in substitution for an injunction as authorized by this section.

In any instance in which a case for an injunction has been made out, if the plaintiff by his acts or laches[12] has disentitled himself to an injunction the Court may award damages in its place. So again, whether the case be for a mandatory injunction or to restrain a continuing nuisance, the appropriate remedy may be damages in lieu of an injunction, assuming a case for an injunction to be made out.

In my opinion, it may be stated as a good working rule that — if the injury to the Plaintiff's legal rights is small, and is one which is capable of being estimated in money,[13] and is one which can be adequately compensated by a small money payment, and the case is one in which it would be oppressive to the defendant to grant an injunction: then damages in substitution for an injunction may be given.

There may also be cases in which, though the four above-mentioned requirements exist, the defendant by his conduct, as, for instance, hurrying up his buildings so as if possible to avoid an injunction, or otherwise acting with a reckless disregard to the plaintiff's rights, has disentitled himself from asking that damages may be assessed in substitution for an injunction."

Cases in which it has been held that the grant of an injunction would be oppressive to the defendant are often those where the injunction sought was a mandatory one and would require the pulling down of a building already completed or near completion[14] or would otherwise

---

[12] The following are cases in which laches or acquiescence on the part of the claimant led the court to award damages rather than grant an injunction: *Eastwood v. Lever* (1863) 4 De G. J. & S. 114, *Senior v. Pawson* (1866) L.R. 3 Eq. 330, *Fishenden v. Higgs and Hill* (1935) 153 L.T. 128, *Bracewell v. Appleby* [1975] Ch. 408, *Shaw v. Applegate* [1977] 1 W.L.R. 970.

[13] In the following case the defendant's argument that damages should be awarded in substitution for an injunction were rejected by the court on the grounds that damages were impossible to assess: *Pennington v. Brinsop Hall Coal Company* (1877) 5 Ch.D. 769, *Wood v. Conway Corporation* [1914] 2 Ch. 47, *Pride of Derby and Derbyshire Angling Association Ltd v. British Celanese Ltd* [1953] Ch. 149.

[14] *Isenberg v. East India House Estate Co.* (1863) 3 De G. J. & S. 263, *National Provincial Glass Plate Insurance Company v. Prudential Insurance Company* (1877) 6 Ch.D. 757, *Holland v. Worley* (1884) 26 Ch.D. 578, *Colls v. Home and Colonial Stores Ltd* [1904] A.C. 179, *Leeds Industrial Co-operative Society v. Slack* [1924] A.C. 851, HL, *Price v. Hilditch* [1930] 1 Ch. 500, *Fishenden v. Higgs and Hill Ltd* (1935) 153 L.T. 128, *Wrotham Park Estates Co. Ltd v. Parkside Homes Ltd* [1974] 1 W.L.R. 798 and *Jaggard v. Sawyer* [1995] 1 W.L.R. 269, CA. The decision of the Court of Appeal in *Surrey County Council v. Bredero Homes Ltd* [1993] 1 W.L.R. 1361 was disapproved by the House of Lords in *Attorney-General v. Blake* [2001] 1 A.C. 268 and the approach in *Wrotham Park* and *Jaggard v. Sawyer* preferred.

involve the defendant in expenditure far exceeding the loss suffered by the claimant.[15]

In *Fishenden v. Higgs and Hill Ltd*[16] the Court of Appeal emphasised the discretionary nature of the power to grant damages in lieu of an injunction. Their lordships disapproved the practice of rigidly applying the four rules laid down by A.L. Smith L.J. in *Shelfer* and stated that the fact that one of the rules was not fulfilled did not necessarily entitle the court to grant an injunction. A.L. Smith L.J.'s rules have however been applied in the majority of cases since *Shelfer* in which there has been serious consideration of the principles governing the exercise of the power. The *Shelfer* approach was approved in *Kennaway v. Thompson*[17] and in *Jaggard v. Sawyer*.[18]

Other factors which have sometimes influenced the exercise of the discretion are: the fact that incidental benefits may accrue to the claimant as a result of the defendant being allowed to continue the wrong complained of;[19] the fact that the claimant has earlier shown himself willing to accept a pecuniary settlement;[20] the fact that the defendant was ignorant of the fact that he was infringing the claimant's rights;[21] the fact that the defendant has earlier affirmed his intention of carrying out his obligations and that the claimant has been prejudiced through reliance on this affirmation.[22]

---

[15] *Baxter v. Four Oaks Properties Ltd* [1965] Ch. 816; *Bracewell v. Appleby* [1975] Ch. 408; *Shaw v. Applegate* [1977] 1 W.L.R. 970. A principle often expressed in the cases (the converse of the dictum of A.L. Smith L.J. quoted above, that the defendant should not be permitted to buy the claimant's rights) is that the court should not, by granting an injunction to the claimant, enable the claimant to extort large sums from the defendant as the price of not enforcing the injunction: see, *e.g. Isenberg v. East India House Estate Co.* (1863) 3 De G.J. & S. 263, at 273, *Colls v. Home and Colonial Stores Ltd* [1904] A.C. 179, at 193, *Baxter v. Four Oaks Properties* above at 829 and *per* Sir Thomas Bingham M.R. in *Jaggard v. Sawyer*, above, at pp 282H-283A. Arguments to the effect that damages should be awarded in lieu of an injunction because the grant of an injunction would result in hardship to the defendant disproportionate to that suffered by the claimant were rejected in *Smith v. Smith* (1875) L.R. 20 Eq. 500, *Krehl v. Burrell* (1878) 7 Ch.D. 551, *Martin v. Price* [1894] 1 Ch. 276, *Cowper v. Laidler* [1903] 2 Ch. 337, *Achilli v. Tovell* [1927] 2 Ch. 243, *Morris v. Redland Bricks* [1967] 1 W.L.R. 967, CA, and *Kennaway v. Thompson* [1981] Q.B. 88, CA. Further, when the unlawful act leads to the total dispossession of the claimant the Court of Appeal has held that damages in lieu should not be awarded but that, in such a case, a mandatory injunction was "inevitable": *London Borough of Harrow v. Donohue* [1995] 1 E.G.L.R. 257, CA.

[16] (1935) 153 L.T. 128.

[17] [1981] Q.B. 88, CA.

[18] [1995] 1 W.L.R. 269, CA. *Jaggard* itself was approved by the House of Lords in *Attorney-General v. Blake* [2001] 1 A.C. 268.

[19] *National Provincial Glass Plate Insurance Co. v. Prudential Insurance Co.* (1877) 6 Ch.D. 757.

[20] *Senior v. Pawson* (1866) L.R. 3 Eq. 330. See also *Morris v. Redland Bricks* [1967] 1 W.L.R. 967 (in the Court of Appeal), 980 and 986.

[21] *Smith v. Smith* (1875) L.R. 20 Eq. 500, *Baxter v. Four Oaks Properties Ltd* [1965] Ch. 816, *Shaw v. Applegate* [1977] 1 W.L.R. 970.

[22] *Greenwood v. Hornsey* (1886) 33 Ch.D. 471.

(c) Measure of damages

Damages in lieu of an injunction must cover the whole area which would   **4–103**
have been covered by an injunction. It follows therefore that such damages must cover damage which accrues after the issue of the claim form[23]
and, when the injunction would have been *quia timet*, damage which has
yet to accrue.[24] In cases where the damage has been to the amenity of the
claimant's land (*e.g.* due to interference with easements of light) the measure has been the diminution in value of the claimant's land.[25] In *Bracewell
v. Appleby*[26] damages for trespass were assessed as the sum which the
claimants could reasonably have asked of the defendant for a licence to
use their private road.[27] In *Marcic v. Thames Water Utilities Ltd (No. 2)*[28] the
Court of Appeal, finding the Defendant liable in nuisance, held that:

> Where a sewerage undertaker in performance of its statutory duty
> and in the exercise of its statutory powers constructs a new system it
> will be liable if this results in a foreseeable nuisance unless this was
> inevitable . . . It will be no answer to show that disproportionate
> expenditure would have been needed to avoid the nuisance. That
> may, however, be a reason for the court to award damages in respect
> of the nuisance rather than a mandatory injunction to abate it.

The Court of Appeal did not go so far as the trial judge[29] to indicate that
damages should be awarded not only on the basis of past wrongdoing
but also in respect of future wrongs in order to afford the claimant "just
satisfaction" under the ECHR. However, the Court of Appeal did make
it clear that an award of damages in lieu may have to be modified by
considerations arising from Article 8 rights, although it disagreed with
the trial judge on the approach to proportionality. Lord Phillips M.R.
held[29a]:

> When considering Mr Marcic's claim under the Human Rights Act,
> the Judge proceeded on the premise that this required a fair balance
> to be struck between the competing interests of Mr Marcic and
> Thames' other customers. In this context he was prepared to

---

[23] See the cases cited in n. 14 above.

[24] See the cases cited at n. 14 above.

[25] *Isenberg v. East India House Estate Co.* (1863) 3 De G. J. & S. 263; *National Provincial Glass
Plate Insurance Co. v. Prudential Insurance Co.* (1877) 6 Ch.D. 757; *Leeds Industrial Co-opera-
tive Society v. Slack* [1924] A.C. 851; *Price v. Hilditch* [1930] 1 Ch. 500; *Fishenden v. Higgs and
Hill Ltd* (1935) 153 L.T. 128.

[26] [1975] Ch. 408.

[27] An analogous measure had been applied in the earlier case of *Wrotham Park Estates Co. Ltd
v. Parkside Homes* [1974] 1 W.L.R. 798. See also *Jaggard v. Sawyer*, discussed below.

[28] [2002] 2 W.L.R. 932, CA at para. 113 (Lord Phillips M.R., giving the judgment of the Court),
upholding in part the judgment at [2001] 4 All E.R. 326.

[29] [2001] 4 All E.R. 326 at para. 18.

[29a] Above at paras. 116–118.

contemplate that the system of priorities used by Thames might be "entirely fair", notwithstanding that this would result in nothing being done to remedy Mr Marcic's flooding in the foreseeable future. We doubt whether such a situation would be compatible with Mr Marcic's rights under Article 8. The decision of the Strasbourg Commission in *S. v France* (1990) 65 D & R 250 suggests to the contrary ... This suggests that where an authority carries on an undertaking in the interest of the community as a whole it may have to pay compensation to individuals whose rights are infringed by that undertaking in order to achieve a fair balance between the interests of the individual and the community.

The facts were extreme in that the statutory undertaker had repeatedly failed to take action to prevent repeated flooding to the claimant's property from overloaded drains[29b], which breached his rights under Article 8 of the ECHR, and the Court considered that the claimant should not be required to return to court repeatedly to enforce his rights.

The assessment of damages ordered in lieu of an injunction should be consistent with the general principle of *restitutio in integrum* discussed above at paragraphs 4–002 to 4–008. This is consistent with the approach of Lord Wilberforce in *Johnson v. Agnew*[30] (albeit in the context of a contract claim), where he stated:

> "The general principle for the assessment of damages is compensatory, *i.e.*, that the innocent party is to be placed, so far as money can do so, in the same position as if the contract had been performed, where the contract is one of sale, this principle normally leads to

---

[29b] See *Marcic v. Thames Water Utilities Ltd (No. 1)* [2001] 3 All E.R. 698.

[30] [1980] A.C. 367, HL, at 400G. This might appear to be inconsistent with the decision of Brightman J. in *Wrotham Park Estate Co. Ltd v. Parkside Homes Ltd*, above: see *Jaggard v. Sawyer*, above. However, in *Jaggard*, at pp 281–282, Sir Thomas Bingham M.R. did not accept that Brightman J.'s decision in *Wrotham Park* was —

> "based on other than compensatory principles. The defendants had committed a breach of covenant, the effects of which continued. The judge was not willing to order the defendants to undo the continuing effects of that breach. He had therefore to assess the damages necessary to compensate the plaintiffs for this continuing invasion of their right."

Such compensation was provided by a measure which represented the "obvious relationship" between the profits earned by the defendants and the sum which they would reasonably have been willing to pay to secure a release from the covenant. Millett L.J. considered the point at pp. 289–292 and also held that Brightman J.'s approach was consistent with purely compensatory principles since "the amount of the profit which the defendant expected to make was a relevant factor" in the assessment of what the claimant might have obtained as the price of giving consent. The difference of view between Millett L.J. in *Jaggard* and Steyn L.J. in *Surrey County Council v. Bredero Homes Ltd* [1993] 1 W.L.R. 1361, 1366–7, appears to be resolved by the disapproval of the *Bredero* case by the majority of the House of Lords in *Attorney-General v. Blake* [2001] 1 A.C. 268. Lord Steyn preferred to express no opinion on his own earlier judgment in *Bredero*, though noting that there had been "substantial academic debate" on the decision.

assessment of damages as at the date of the breach . . . But this is not an absolute rule: if to follow it would give rise to injustice, the court has power to fix such other date as may be appropriate in the circumstances".

In *Jaggard v. Sawyer*,[31] the Court of Appeal approached the assessment of damages where an interim injunction was refused for the breach of a restrictive covenant on a compensatory basis (applying *Shelfer*). Sir Thomas Bingham M.R., approving the decision of the county court, stated:

"The judge considered the value of the injury to the plaintiff's right as capable of being estimated in money. He based himself on the *Wrotham Park* approach. In my view he was justified. He valued the right at what a reasonable seller would sell it for. In situations of this kind a plaintiff should not be treated as eager to sell, which he very probably is not. But the court will not value the right at the ransom price which a very reluctant plaintiff might put on it. I see no error in the judge's approach to this aspect . . ."

Although the effect of this decision may appear to sanction an approach to compensatory damages which closely resembles the restitution of a sum by which a defendant has become unjustly enriched at the expense of a claimant, it is explicable as compensation:

(1) the aspect of compensation under consideration is (the claimant having been deprived by the court of his primary remedy of injunction) the value of the loss of the claimant's right to exact a price for giving consent to a breach of the covenant. In that exercise the defendant's profit would be relevant, presumably as a factor influencing the price which the claimant might reasonably have required;[32] and

(2) the Court did not assess such a price simply by reference to the value of the defendant's benefit to the defendant but what the claimant could reasonably have required. A seller in the market, bargaining for the relaxation of a restrictive covenant, would be unlikely (it is suggested) to be able to demand from a purchaser a price equivalent to the whole value which the purchaser would gain. There would be in most cases no point to a purchaser buying the right if he had to hand over the whole of his benefit to the seller.[33]

---

[31] Above.
[32] See *per* Millett L.J. at p. 291D-H.
[33] Although the Master of the Rolls' exclusion of ransom value (at pp. 282H-283A) is a little difficult to square with the above approach since it might be the case that the true value

4–104 *(6) Human Rights*

A discussion of the full range of possible applications of Convention rights under the Human Rights Act 1998 to injunctions lies beyond the scope of this work[34]. However, since the Court is expressly made a "public body" within section 6 of that Act[35] and it is "unlawful for a public authority to act in a way which is incompatible with a Convention right"[36] it appears that courts must act compatibly with Convention rights when exercising their discretion to make injunctive orders[37] and when ordering damages in lieu of an injunction[38]. There are a growing number of examples where Convention rights have been taken into account in the exercise of such discretion[39].

For example, in *Tandridge District Council v. Delaney*[40] the Deputy Judge considered the powers of local authorities to obtain injunctions restraining breaches of planning control in the light of the Convention. He applied the ECHR as relevant to the exercise of the Court's discretion and his consideration underlines the close link between the approach of the courts under domestic law and that of the ECHR under Article 8.

In *Ashdown v. Telegraph Group Ltd*,[41] Lord Phillips M.R. noted (in the context of a breach of copyright claim) that:

> "We would add that the implications of the Human Rights Act must always be considered where the discretionary relief of an injunction is sought . . ."

Specifically, under section 12 of the 1998 Act, where the court "is considering whether to grant any relief which, if granted, might affect the exercise of the Convention right to freedom of expression" specific provisions apply which are designed to protect freedom of expression. In such cases, the court must pay particular regard to the importance of the right to freedom of expression under the ECHR.[42]

---

of the claimant's right would include ransom value, namely where (on the evidence) the claimant would have only bargained away his right on such a basis.

[34] See *e.g.* Clayton & Tomlinson, *The Law of Human Rights* (OUP, 2000 and Grosz, Beatson & Duffy, *Human Rights* (Sweet & Maxwell, 2000).

[35] S. 6(3)(a).

[36] S. 6(1).

[37] On the question of the "horizontal effect" of the Convention: see Clayton & Tomlinson, *op. cit.*, paras. 5.80–5.99, 5.114 & 5.115 and Grosz, Beatson & Duffy, *op. cit.*, paras. 4–01, 4–15 to 4–17 and *Douglas & others v. Hello! Ltd* [2001] 2 W.L.R. 992 at 1025–6, para. 128 (Sedley L.J.).

[38] *Marcic v. Thames Water Utilities Ltd (No. 2)* [2002] EWCA Civ 64. See para. 4–103, above.

[39] See *Tandridge D.C. v. Delaney and Ashdown v. The Telegraph Group*, below, *Broadmoor Special Hospital Authority v. Robinson* [2000] 1 W.L.R. 1590 at 1601, *Douglas & others v. Hello! Ltd* [2001] 2 W.L.R. 992 and *South Bucks D.C. v. Porter* [2002] 1 All E.R. 425, CA.

[40] [2000] 1 P.L.R. 11.

[41] [2001] 4 All E.R. 666.

[42] See the *Ashdown* and *Douglas* cases, above, and *Reynolds v. Times Newspapers Ltd* [2001] 2 A.C. 127.

In *South Bucks D.C. v. Porter*[42a] in considering a challenge to decisions by local authorities to remove gipsy caravans from land occupied in breach of planning control, Simon Brown L.J. held:

"Proportionality requires not only that the injunction be appropriate and necessary for the attainment of the public interest objective sought — here the safeguarding of the environment — but also that it does not impose an excessive burden on the individual whose private interests — here the gipsy's private life and home and the retention of his ethnic identity — are at stake."

Self-help

Introduction

A right to self-help remedies may be available both where there is a trespass   **4–105**
to land or where there is a private nuisance. The victim of a tort, however, must be careful not to exceed such a right where it exists. To exceed such a right may itself amount to tortious conduct and may even result in a breach of the criminal law. The rights of self-help which we consider below must therefore be exercised cautiously (if they are to be exercised at all) both for that reason and because the Courts do not favour self-help.[43] That predisposition against self-help remedies appears to receive support from the Human Rights Act 1998, and the requirements of Article 6 of the ECHR, at least where that provision is applicable[44] and engaged. In any event, it should be noted that where a claimant has sought injunctive relief against a defendant in respect of a tortious interference with land and the injunction is refused, the claimant is not thereafter entitled to rely upon his right of self-redress.[45]

(1) Trespass

(1) Force

This is by far the most uncertain remedy available to a landowner against   **4–106**
a trespasser and must be exercised with the greatest caution: indeed, the best course would be to avoid forcible self-help altogether. Whilst a landowner may expel a trespasser himself, the use of excessive force (which is often a matter for fine judgment) will itself amount to a trespass against the trespasser and, in certain cases, amount to a criminal offence.

[42a] [2002] 1 All E.R. 425, CA, at para. 41.
[43] See generally *Burton v. Winters* [1993] 1 W.L.R. 1077, CA.
[44] See s. 6 of the 1998 Act and para. 1–139 *et seq.*
[45] *Ibid.*, at 1082.

A landowner may expel a trespasser who has entered his land — regardless of whether the trespasser had entered first or whether the claimant has already obtained a possession order from the court.[46] If the ejector is not the owner entitled to possession of the land, then self-help is not available unless that person has been authorised to eject the trespasser by the owner in possession.[47] The mere use of self-help by a person other than those already mentioned will itself be a trespass against the person of the original trespasser.

Further, the use of self-help is subject to the following restrictions:

(a) if the original wrongful entry was peaceful, the landowner must first require the trespasser to leave.[48] In the case of a violent entry by the trespasser, no such request is necessary[49]; and

(b) the owner must, in any event, only use such force against the trespasser as is reasonably necessary to eject him from the land.

Requirement (b) presents the greatest difficulty to the would-be ejector since what amounts to reasonable force is difficult to judge precisely, particularly in circumstances where a landowner is seeking to remove by physical force a person who may well be unwilling to be ejected. If excessive force is used, then the original trespasser himself may bring an action in trespass (in respect of his person) against the ejector.[50] Further, the use of force may amount to a criminal office if the provisions of the Criminal Law Act 1977 are infringed.[51]

4–107   In the case of trespass by encroachment, self-help should only be resorted to in the clearest and most simple cases, and certainly must not be attempted if an application to the Court for an injunction has failed. In *Burton v. Winters*[52], the claimant obtained a declaration that a neighbour's garage wall had trespassed over her boundary but had been refused a mandatory injunction to remove it. She then made repeated attempts to prevent access to the garage by building a wall and was herself the subject of an injunction. The Court of Appeal rejected the claimant's asserted entitlement to self-redress in the following terms[53]:

"In my opinion, this never was an appropriate case for self-redress, even if the plaintiff had acted promptly. There was no emergency. There were difficult questions of law and fact to be considered and

---

[46] *Aglionby v. Cohen* [1955] 1 Q.B. 558.

[47] *Monks v. Dykes* (1839) 4 M. & W. 567 and *Holmes v. Bagge* (1853) 1 E. & B. 782.

[48] *Scott v. Matthew Brown & Co. Ltd* (1884) 51 L.T. 746 and *Hemmings v. Stoke Poges Golf Club Ltd* [1920] 1 K.B. 720, CA.

[49] *Tullay v. Reed* (1823) 1 C. & P. 6 and *Polkinghorn v. Wright* (1845) 8 Q.B. 197.

[50] *Green v. Bartram* (1830) 4 C. & P. 308, *Oakes v. Wood* (1837) 2 M. & W. 791 and *Ball v. Axten* (1866) 4 F. & F. 1019.

[51] See below, Chapter 5, paras. 5–023 to 5–027.

[52] [1993] 1 W.L.R. 1077

[53] Above at 1082, *per* Lloyd L.J.

the remedy by way of self-redress, if it had resulted in the demolition of the garage wall, would have been out of all proportion to the damage suffered by the plaintiff ... Self-redress is a summary remedy, which is justified only in clear and simple cases, or in an emergency. Where a plaintiff has applied for a mandatory injunction and failed, the sole justification for a summary remedy has gone. The court has decided the very point in issue. This is so whether the complaint lies in trespass or nuisance."

(2) Peaceable re-entry

In the case of the lessor of premises, in certain circumstances that lessor may forfeit the lease and re-enter premises peaceably. However, such right to re-enter is now strictly controlled by statute:

4–108

(1) in the case of all residential premises except excluded tenancies and statutorily protected tenants,[54] by the Protection from Eviction Act 1977,[55] recovery of possession is forbidden except by legal process; and

(2) in the case of other premises, by the Criminal Law Act 1977[56] which forbids forcible entry.[57]

Following the amendments introduced by the Housing Act 1988, breach of the Protection from Eviction Act 1977 not only amounts to a criminal offence but now gives rise to a civil remedy in damages.[58]

Peaceable re-entry is relatively uncommon, although a revival in interest due to the possibility of defeating a claim for relief from forfeiture[59] lost its impetus as a result of the decision of the House of Lords in *Billson v. Residential Apartments Ltd.*[60]

In *Billson*,[61] Lord Templeman stated:

"A tenant may apply for relief after a landlord has forfeited by reentry without first obtaining a court order for that purpose but the court in deciding whether to grant relief will take into account all the

---

[54] See ss. 3, 3A and 8(1) of the 1977 Act (as amended) and below, paras. 5–006 to 5–017.
[55] See below, paras. 5–006 to 5–017.
[56] See below, paras. 5–023 to 5–027.
[57] It is open to dispute whether an entry in contravention of the Criminal Law Act 1977 is a valid re-entry for the purposes of forfeiture. It would be highly undesirable to allow such entries to be effective and would permit landlords to profit from their own wrongdoing.
[58] See below, paras. 5–019 to 5–022.
[59] *Billson & Others v. Residential Apartments Ltd* [1991] 3 W.L.R. 264, CA (now reversed by the House of Lords [1992] 1 A.C. 494) — following the difference of views expressed in *Smith v. Metropolitan City Properties* [1986] 1 E.G.L.R. 52, *Official Custodian for Charities v. Parway Estates Developments Ltd* [1985] Ch. 151 and *Abbey National Building Society v. Maybeech Ltd* [1985] Ch. 190.
[60] [1992] 1 A.C. 494.
[61] *ibid.* at p. 540.

circumstances, including delay, on the part of the tenant. Any past judicial observations which might suggest that a tenant is debarred from applying for relief after the landlord has re-entered without first obtaining a court order for that purpose are not to be so construed."

(3) Section 7 of the Animals Act 1971

4–109   This is considered briefly in Chapter 5,[62] below.

(4) Distress damage feasant

4–110   Distress damage feasant is a self-help remedy which allows a person to seize another's chattel found unlawfully on his land doing damage as a means of compelling the owner of the chattel to pay compensation for the wrong.[63] In *Watkinson v. Hollington*,[64] Scott L.J. stated:

> "The gist of the procedure was the right of the occupier to seize the cattle at the very moment of the damage, while they were doing it — 'damage feasant' — and to detain them. It was a remedy of distress which, differing from other forms of distress, could be exercised out of hand, at any time of the day or night."

Although, as the above passage indicates, this remedy was traditionally most used in the case of straying livestock causing damage (and has now been replaced in that context by statutory remedies in the Animals Act 1971[65]) it still remains as a remedy for other chattels causing damage to property, *e.g.* vehicles.[66] Although it has been suggested[67] that the power to distrain by way of distress damage feasant against animals other than "livestock" may be unaffected, this does not appear to be supported by the wording of section 7(1) of the Animals Act which abolishes the right "to seize and detain any animal".

4–111   The remedy may be exercised only where there has been an actionable trespass and by someone with sufficient interest to maintain an action in trespass.[68] Further, while the chattel is being retained pursuant to the right of distress, no action in damages for trespass will lie. The remedies of distress damage feasant and damages appear to be mutually exclusive — although it is open to the distrainor to restore the chattel to its owner and then sue in damages. If the retention of the chattel does not produce the desired response from its owner (which it might well not do in the case of a chattel of relatively low value causing substantial damage), then the

---

[62] See below, para. 5–038 *et seq.*
[63] See, *e.g. Watkinson v. Hollington* [1944] K.B. 16.
[64] *ibid.* at 20.
[65] See s. 7 of the 1971 Act and below, para. 5–038.
[66] *Ambergate Railway v. Midland Railway* (1853) 2 E. & B. 793 (locomotives).
[67] *Clerk & Lindsell, op. cit.,* para. 31–31, at p. 1684, n. 29.
[68] See *Burt v. Moore* (1793) 5 T.R. 329 and *Churchill v. Evans* (1809) 1 Taunt. 529.

injured party has no option but to abandon his attempt at self-help, return the chattel to its owner and bring an action to recover damages. If the chattel distrained is lost or destroyed without fault on the part of the distrainor, he may rely on his right of action in damages.

As the passage from *Watkinson v. Hollington* demonstrates, distress damage feasant can be levied at any time of the day:[69] however, the seizure must be made whilst the trespassing chattel remains on the land of the injured party[70] and it cannot be followed and seized once it has left that land (or been removed)[71] — even if the chattel is returned to the land on another occasion.[72] The property seized must be kept on the land where it was seized, or be impounded.[73]

The person who has seized the chattel in exercise of the right of distress damage feasant must return it to its owner if that owner pays proper compensation for the damage caused by the chattel. The owner should himself estimate the proper compensation and tender it to the distrainor in order to be able to demand the return of his chattel.[74] Distress damage feasant is only a means to an end and the distrainor must return the chattel seized if the compensation is tendered.

Unlike the provisions for straying livestock in the Animals Act 1971, or in the case of distress for rent (where statute has also intervened),[75] the common law right of distress carries no power of sale.[76]

Distress damage feasant had been mooted as an answer to the question **4–112** of the legality of private "wheel-clamping" on the footing that the clamping of the car amounted to a seizure. However, this approach was rejected by the Court of Appeal in *Arthur v. Anker & Another*,[77] where the claimant sued a wheel-clamper for trespass to goods in clamping his car, which was parked on private land at which signs had been erected to warn trespassers that clamping was in operation. The defence raised, and accepted at first instance, was that:

(a)   the claimant had consented to the clamping regime[78]; and

---

[69] See also Co. Litt. 142a.
[70] Although it is not clear whether it is necessary to seize the chattel whilst it is actually causing damage — although the passage quoted from *Watkinson v. Hollington* appears to suggest the contrary as does *Wormer v. Biggs* (1845) 2 C. & K. 31. The likelihood of further damage may be sufficient.
[71] *Clement v. Milner* (1800) 3 Esp. 95.
[72] *Vaspor v. Edwards* (1701) 12 Mod. 658.
[73] *ibid.* at 664.
[74] Even if the distrainor himself is making exorbitant demands: *Sorrell v. Paget* [1950] 1 K.B. 252, CA at 265.
[75] In the case of distress for rent, statute has provided a power to sell goods seized (although the common law rule was as in the case of distress damage feasant): see the Distress For Rent Acts 1689 and 1737 and s. 5 of the Landlord and Tenant Act 1730 and, further, *Hill & Redman's Landlord and Tenant*, A[5901]–A[5962].
[76] *Boden v. Roscoe*, above.
[77] [1997] Q.B. 564
[78] On the difficulties which consent arguments can give rise to, see *Vine v. Waltham Forest B.C.* [2000] 4 All E.R. 169, CA, where the clamping of a trespassing car was held to be a

    (b)   the defendant, as agent on behalf of the owners of the land, had merely been exercising the landowners' right to distrain the vehicle for damage feasant in trespass.

Dismissing the claimant's appeal on the first ground of defence, the Court of Appeal, by a majority, held that it was inappropriate to use a medieval remedy in context of vehicle clamping.[78a] Sir Thomas Bingham M.R., gave three reasons for refusing to allow this element of the defence:

    (1)   whereas distress damage feasant was developed to stop an existing trespass or to prevent future damage by a trespassing chattel, clamping is used as a deterrent, which is conceptually different;

    (2)   distress damage feasant requires some loss or damage to have occurred. This need not be actual damage to the land, but could take place through obstruction to the use of the land: mere trespass, however, is not enough, and it defies logic to allow the distrainor to rely on the cost of the distress alone to justify the distress;[79] and

    (3)   the fixed fine for the release of a clamped vehicle, regardless of the time of day and other facts surrounding the act of trespass, and which is paid to an agent who has suffered no damage, has no compensatory element.

Neill L.J. agreed, adding that the foundation of the common law doctrine had been weakened by legislation such as the Animals Act 1971 and that the courts should do nothing to encourage the use of clamping without notice. Where notice is given, the doctrine of consent is more appropriate.

(5) Human Rights

4–113   Reference has already been made to the protection of rights under the ECHR by the Human Rights Act 1998. As is set out above, the common law retains vestiges of the ability to recover possession by means of "self-help", and it may be that the 1998 Act impacts on such remedies at least where they are relied on by public authorities within the meaning of

---

trespass itself and that a particular notice was insufficient on the facts to draw the consequences of trespass to the car owner's attention such as to mean that the owner has willingly assumed the risk of clamping. Normally, however, notices which were posted where they were bound to be seen would lead to a finding that the trespassing driver had knowledge of and appreciated the warning.

[78a] Hirst L.J., dissenting, considered that because the tort of trespass was actionable *per se* no damage needed to be shown for distress damage feasant to be used, that the common law could usefully adapt the remedy for use in modern contexts and that a fixed fine was capable of amounting to proper compensation for the act of trespass.

[79] This latter approach was taken by the High Court of New Zealand in *Jamieson's Tow & Salvage Ltd. v. Murray* [1984] 2 N.Z.L.R. 144.

section 6. It must remain unlikely that the ECHR will apply where only private rights are in issue and the protagonist is not a public authority[80] since, in *X (Di Palma) v. UK*,[81] the European Commission rejected as inadmissible a claim that a tenant had been deprived of her possessions in breach of Article 1 of the First Protocol because it concerned only private contractual issues. The landlord had forfeited the lease and taken possession of the applicant's flat. The Court had no jurisdiction under the County Courts Act 1984, as it was then drafted, to grant relief from forfeiture and the applicant argued that the legislation was unjust in that it (a) permitted, or did not prevent, the landlord's repossession of the applicant's premises and forfeiture of the lease and (b) failed to provide a sufficient remedy in respect of the interference with her right to property. She argued that the rights under the convention on which she relied implied not only a negative obligation to abstain from acting but also in certain circumstances a positive duty and that the Government failed to legislate to protect the rights claimed by applicant. The Commission rejected the claim and concluded that:

> "... the relations between the applicant and the landlord were regulated by a private contract (the lease) which set out the mutual obligations of the parties. The terms of the lease were neither directly prescribed nor amended by legislation, although substantial quantities of legislation regulate the operation of leases in a general way, mainly with a view to protecting the position of tenants. Thus, for example, in order to gain possession of the flat, the landlord had to take proceedings before the courts to obtain a possession order, without which eviction of the applicant would have been unlawful. In view of the exclusively private law relationship between the parties to the lease the Commission considers that the respondent Government cannot be responsible by the mere fact that the landlord by its agents, who were private individuals, brought the applicant's lease to an end in accordance with the terms of that lease, which set out the agreement between the applicant and the company. The question arises whether any other aspect of the applicant's complaint under Prot. No. 1 Art.1 would give rise to a breach of the State's responsibility under the Convention. It is true that the landlord issued proceedings in the domestic courts in order to forfeit the applicant's lease. This fact alone is not however sufficient to engage State responsibility in respect of the applicant's rights to property, since the public authority in the shape of the County Court merely provided a

---

[80] Although at the time the matter comes before the Court, the Court's discretionary powers should be exercised consistently with Convention Rights since the Court is itself subject to the Act: see s. 6(3)(a).

[81] Reported as *Application No. 11949/86 v. UK* (1988) 10 E.H.R.R. 149 especially at para. 1 at p. 154. See *Di Palma v. Victoria Square Property Co. Ltd.* [1985] 2 All E.R. 669, CA, for the domestic proceedings. Note also the comments on the case by the Court of Appeal in *Michalak v. Wandsworth L.B.C.* [2001] EWCA Civ 271 at paras. 47 and 64.

forum for the determination of the civil right in dispute between the parties. In contending that State responsibility for an interference with rights protected by the Convention arises in respect of this complaint, the applicant seeks to demand that a State be subject to a positive obligation to protect the property rights of an individual in the context of his dispute with another private individual. It is not necessary for the purposes of the present decision to attempt an exhaustive description of the circumstances in which such an obligation may arise. In the present case the applicant and the landlord had entered into contractual arrangements set out in the lease which expressly provided for the applicant's tenancy to terminate if rent remained unpaid once demanded."

However, if the right is exercised by a public authority there is a question as to what extent such means can be regarded as surviving the right of the party against whom the remedy is enforced to have his or her civil rights (if engaged) determined by an impartial and independent tribunal under Article 6 of the Convention. For example, if possession is recovered by self-help (limited as those opportunities may be) the physical act causing dispossession not only determines the occupation but also achieves the recovery of possession, avoiding the need for legal proceedings. The European Court of Human Rights has, to an extent at least, recognised the protection of the Article 8 rights of even those who have set up home unlawfully.[82] Further, to a limited extent, the common law protects *de facto* possession[83] and to that extent civil rights may be engaged, as well as potential Convention rights under Article 8.

The question of consistency with Article 6 arises in that the rights to occupy and possession are determined by the act of the landowner and not by an independent and impartial tribunal. Proportionality may not be easily established given that appropriate court procedures exist for the recovery of possession including the ability to get a case before the courts at short notice in cases of urgency.[84] Whilst procedures for reinstatement and compensation in cases of unlawful eviction exist, it remains uncertain whether these suffice to ensure compliance with Article 6, since they only apply after the event, although they may provide an answer to a challenge under Article 1 of the First Protocol.

In *R. (Alconbury Developments Ltd and others) v. Secretary of State for the Environment, Transport and the Regions*[85] the House of Lords applied the "composite approach" to administrative action found in *Albert & Le Compte v. Belgium*[86] and *Bryan v. United Kingdom*,[87] and held that

---

[82] *Buckley v. United Kingdom* (1996) 23 E.H.R.R. 101, at paras 12 & 52–54 of the judgment, & *Chapman v. United Kingdom* (2001) B.H.R.C. 48 at para. 101 of the judgment. See above at para. 4–071.

[83] See Chapter 1, paras. 1–003 to 1–016.

[84] See, above, at para. 4–073.

[85] [2001] 2 W.L.R. 1389.

[86] (1983) 5 E.H.R.R. 533.

[87] (1995) 21 E.H.R.R. 342.

discretionary administrative action did not itself have to comply with Article 6 given the existence of judicial review which secured compliance. The context, however, was quite different and involved public law discretionary decision-making in the general area of planning and compulsory purchase. The discretion there lay not merely as to procedure (which is the area of concern here) but as to the substantive outcome. The fact that self-help determines rights rather than a discretionary decision taken in the wider public interest suggests that a more rigorous approach is required.[88] However, the jurisdiction of the civil courts to determine property rights is much wider than in judicial review and are courts of "full jurisdiction",[89] having power to determine both facts and law which should ensure Article 6 compliance.

Nonetheless, difficulties remain in that recourse to the court only occurs after the event, by which stage occupation may have been lost even if only for a limited period and there may have been violations of Article 8 rights to the home or private life. It seems unlikely that the use of self-help would necessarily be regarded as proportionate to the aims to be achieved unless there existed genuinely compelling circumstances for deciding to proceed otherwise than by legal action.

(2) Nuisance

Introduction: the law does not favour abatement

A person who suffers a private nuisance is entitled to abate it. He may remedy the nuisance by taking action on his own land: for instance, he may cut the branches or roots of a tree which encroach on his land.[90] He may also remedy the nuisance by entering on to his neighbour's land and taking appropriate action to abate it.[91] However, the law does not favour abatement by a private individual, because of the "disorders"[92] or the likelihood of a breach of the peace[93] that may result from an attempt at   4–114

---

[88] See *e.g.* Lord Hoffmann in *Alconbury*, above, at para. 74. *Kathro v. Rhondda Cynon Taff County Borough Council* [2001] Env. L.R. 402, *Friends Provident Life & Pensions Ltd v. Secretary of State* [2002] 1 W.L.R., *R (Cummins) v. Camden L.B.C.* [2001] EWHC 1116 (Admin), *Adlard v. Secretary of State* [2002] E.W.C.A Civ. 735 and *Bovis Homes Ltd v. New Forest D.C. & Secretary of State* [2002] EWHC 483 (Admin), and, further, Elvin & Maurici [2001] J.P.L. 883 at 885–9 & 894–898.

[89] To use the phrase employed in the Strasbourg cases: see *e.g. Le Compte v. Belgium* (1981) 4 EHRR 554 and *Ashingdane v. UK* (1985) 7 E.H.R.R. 528, para. 57.

[90] *Lemmon v. Webb* [1895] A.C. 1; *Butler v. Standard Telephones* [1940] 1 K.B. 399. But he may not appropriate what he has severed, and if he does so he is liable for conversion for their value: *Mills v. Brooks* [1919] 1 K.B. 555. See also, above, paras. 4–110 to 4–112, for the analogous remedy, distress damage feasant, in the case of trespass.

[91] *Baten's Case* (1610) 9 Rep. 54b; *R. v. Rosewell* (1699) 2 Salk. 459; *Raikes v. Townsend* (1804) 2 Smith 9; *Jones v. Williams* (1843) 11 M. & W. 176; *Perry v. Fitzhowe* (1845) 8 Q.B. 757, 775. See also Law Commission Working Paper No. 78, Rights of Access to Neighbouring Land (1980).

[92] Sir Matthew Hale, *De Portubus Mans*, Pt. 2, Chap. VII; and see generally *Burton v. Winters* [1993] 1 W.L.R. 1077, CA.

[93] Compare *R. v. Chief Constable of Devon and Cornwall* [1982] Q.B. 458, 473. See also paras. 4–105 to 4–107.

self-help; and the burden of proof is on the party abating the nuisance to show that he has not exceeded his right to abate.[94] A party wishing to abate a nuisance must, therefore, both be sure that the nuisance which he wishes to abate is actionable and be careful only to act within his rights. If the party wishing to abate exceeds his rights, he may be liable for any damage resulting.[95] However, in clear cases where the injury is apparent on the first view of the matter[96] and where the remedial steps necessary to abate the nuisance are plain, abatement is often a cheap and quick remedy and it has the advantage that it may avoid litigation.

Notice

4–115   Before a right of abatement is exercised notice should be given to the wrongdoer to remedy the nuisance, unless:

(a)   the nuisance can be removed without entry onto the wrongdoer's land[97]; or

(b)   if the nuisance can only be abated with entry onto the wrong-doer's land, in cases of emergency where there is a danger to persons or property and there is no reasonable opportunity to give notice.[98]

This appears to be settled by *Lemmon v. Webb*,[99] though there are earlier cases which indicate that no notice is needed to the party who has actually committed the nuisance[1] (as opposed to a wrongdoer who merely continues a nuisance[2]). It also appears to be clearly established that notice is required where the abatement would involve the demolition of a dwelling-house which is occupied.[3]

Right to abate must be exercised within a reasonable time and reasonably

The justification for the remedy of abatement is that some nuisances require immediate remedy. Thus Blackstone stated:[4]

---

[94] *Lagan Navigation Co. v. Lamberg Bleaching, Dyeing and Finishing Co.* [1927] A.C. 226 (cutting away banks to allow escape of flood water; held unjustifiable because abater failed to prove he had not caused unnecessary damage (even if there was a nuisance)).

[95] *ibid.*

[96] See *Kirby v. Sadgrove* (1797) 3 Anst. 892, 895–896, *per* Eyre C.J. (commoner's interference with plaintiff's trees was not a lawful abatement).

[97] *Lemmon v. Webb* [1894] 3 Ch. 1; [1895] A.C. 1.

[98] *Jones v. Williams* (1843) 11 M. & W. 176, 182; compare *Lemmon v. Webb* [1894] 3 Ch. 1, 13.

[99] [1894] 3 Ch. 1.

[1] *Earl of Lonsdale v. Nelson* (1832) 2 B. & C. 302, 311–312. See also *Job Edwards v. Birmingham Navigations* [1924] 1 K.B. 341, 355.

[2] *Penruddock's Case* (1597) 5 Co. Rep. 100(b); *Jones v. Williams* (1843) 11 M. & W. 176.

[3] *Perry v. Fitzhowe* (1846) 8 Q.B. 757.

[4] Comm Bk III Ch. 1.

"And the reason why the law allows this private and summary method of doing one's self justice, is because injuries of this kind, which obstruct or annoy such things as are of daily inconvenience and use, require immediate remedy; and cannot wait for the slow progress of the ordinary forms of justice."

In *Moffett v Brewer*[5] Greene J said:

"This summary method of redressing a grievance, by the act of an injured party, should be regarded with great jealousy, and authorised only in cases of particular emergency, requiring a more speedy remedy than can be had by the ordinary proceedings at law."

On the basis of these authorities it was held by the Court of Appeal in *Burton v. Winters*[6] that the claimant was not entitled to seek to abate an encroachment on her and by a wall which had been built in 1975 (more than 15 years before the claimant sought to abate the encroachment) the right not having been exercised within a reasonable time and there being no emergency: "self –redress would have been out of all proportion to the damage suffered by the plaintiff".[7] It is clear that in the circumstances of that case, for the removal of a wall to be reasonable, an emergency would be required before self-help could be justified as reasonable. However, in the case of abatement of encroachments by roots and branches, it seems clear that reliance upon self-help may be reasonable even if there is no urgency in requiring their removal.[8] The principle appears to be that if self-help is to be relied upon it must be carried out reasonably and proportionately.

Abatement must not be excessive

No more must be done than is necessary to abate the nuisance.[9] Thus in abating a private nuisance a party must take reasonable care that there should be no unnecessary damage to the wrongdoer's property. Where, for instance, part only of a house on a servient tenement causes an obstruction to a dominant owner's right of light, the dominant owner is entitled only to pull down so much of the house as obstructs the light.[10]

4–116

---

[5] (1848) Iowa 1 Greene 348, 350.
[6] [1993] 1 W.L.R. 1081.
[7] *ibid.*, at 1082.
[8] *Lemmon v. Webb* [1895] A.C. 1 and see para. 4–114 above.
[9] *Lagan Navigation Co. v. Lamberg Bleaching, etc., Co.* [1927] A.C. 226, 241, 246. Also *Greenslade v. Halliday* (1830) 6 Bing. 379; *Hill v. Cock* (1872) 26 L.T. 185.
[10] *Penruddock's Case* (1597) 5 Co. Rep. 100(b); *James v. Hayward* (1631) 1 (W.) Jones 221, 222; *Cooper v. Marshall* (1757) 1 Burr. at 268. See also *Cawkwell v. Russell* (1856) 26 L.J. Ex. 34 (entitlement to abate by wholly blocking drain where nuisance caused by sending sewage down drains, notwithstanding that wrongdoer had a right to use drains for sending water).

Further, if there are two ways of abating a nuisance, the abater must choose the least mischievous[11] but:

> "if by one of these alternative methods some wrong would be done to an innocent third party or to the public, then that method cannot be justified at all, although an interference with the wrongdoer himself might be justified. Therefore, when the alternative method involves such interference, it must not be adopted; and it may become necessary to abate the nuisance in a manner more onerous to the wrongdoer."[12]

Any unnecessary damage inflicted during an abatement of a nuisance may amount to an actionable trespass against the party committing the nuisance.[13]

Abatement before damage

4–117   Since a nuisance may in some circumstances occur before damage has accrued[14] it may in those circumstances be permissible to abate the nuisance before any damage is caused.[15] However, it is not possible to "abate" a nuisance before the nuisance itself has actually arisen. Thus, one cannot remove the scaffolding or fencing from a building which is not yet a nuisance but which would be a nuisance when completed[16] nor can one remove the foundation of a wall which will be a nuisance[17] nor can one cut the branches of a neighbour's tree which are likely to grow over one's land but which have not yet done so.[18] The only "pre-emptive" remedy to stop an apprehended nuisance which has not yet arisen is to seek a *quia timet* injunction from the Court.[19]

No breach of the peace

4–118   Blackstone said that a party aggrieved was only entitled to abate a nuisance "so as he commits no riot in the doing of it".[20] However, in some circumstances it may be that reasonable force may be used in order to abate a nuisance,[21] though perhaps it is only reasonable to use any force at all in the case of an emergency.

---

[11]   *Roberts v. Rose* (1865) L.R. 1 Ex. 82, 89, *per* Blackburn J.
[12]   *ibid.*
[13]   *Lagan Navigation Co. v. Lamberg Bleaching, etc., Co.* [1927] A.C. 226.
[14]   See above, para. 2–004.
[15]   *Penruddock's Case* (1597) 5 Co. Rep. 100(b). See *Smith v. Giddy* [1904] 2 K.B. 448; *Lemmon v. Webb* [1894] 3 Ch. 1, 11.
[16]   *Norrice v. Baker* (1613) 1 R.R. 393.
[17]   *ibid.*
[18]   *ibid.*
[19]   See above, para. 4–084 *et seq.*
[20]   3 Bl. Comm. Ch. 1, s. 4; *Colchester Corpn v. Brooke* (1845) 7 Q.B. 339, 377, *per* Lord Denman C.J.
[21]   See *McCurdy v. Norrie* (1912) 6 D.L.R. 134; compare *Lorraine v. Norrie* (1912) 6 D.L.R. 122.

Can abatement be "positive"?

It is clearly established that where a nuisance is caused by a withdrawal   **4–119**
of support due to the dilapidation of a neighbour's building, one may
abate the nuisance by entering on the neighbour's land and effecting the
necessary repairs.[22] Thus it does seem that one can take steps with a permanent and "positive" effect upon a wrongdoer's land in order to abate a
nuisance: one is not simply confined to taking steps with a "negative"
effect, such as the abatement of a nuisance caused by trees by the cutting
off of branches.

In the context of the law of highways, there does appear to be a limitation on the right of abatement to exclude acts with a positive or permanent effect such as the construction or reconstruction of bridges or
structures necessary for use of a way[23]. However, there seems little reason
to extend into the context of private nuisance this principle in the law of
highways and public nuisance, where there is usually a public body
charged with the duty of repairing the way and where chaos might ensue
if "every individual who was obstructed in his desire to cross would be
equally entitled to erect a permanent structure of his own design,
although the obligation to repair and the incidental right to determine the
method might be in other persons, who, moreover, might be reached" by
public law remedies.[24] Of course, any "positive" acts taken to abate a private nuisance must, as indicated above, be limited only to those acts
which are necessary for the abatement of the nuisance.

Nuisances by omission?

There are dicta which indicate that nuisances caused by omissions to act   **4–120**
or non-feasance will rarely give rise to a right to abate.[25] However, these
dicta again were made in the context of public nuisance under the law of
highways where there is usually a body charged with the maintenance of
the highway. Further, these dicta are hard to reconcile with the judgment
of Parke B. in *Jones v. Williams*[26] which assumed that abatement could be
justified even in cases where the owner of the land had merely been in
"default in not performing some obligation incumbent on him". In any
event, it is clear that abatement is available to remedy one of the commonest nuisances by "omission", namely a nuisance caused by doing

---

[22] *Bond v. Nottingham Corporation* [1940] Ch. 429, 438–439. Similarly, a dominant owner may
maintain the surface of a right of way. See also *Newcomer v. Coulson* (1877) 5 Ch.D. 133;
Jones v. Pritchard [1908] 1 Ch. 630, 638.

[23] *Campbell Davys v. Lloyd* [1901] 2 Ch. 518 (rebuilding of bridge on public right of way on
plaintiff's land was not a lawful abatement); *Earl of Lonsdale v. Nelson* (1823) 2 B. & C. 302
(rebuilding of structure for safe navigation of river was not a lawful abatement; see 311,
per Best J.).

[24] *Campbell Davys v. Lloyd* [1901] 2 Ch. 518, 523–524.

[25] *ibid.*

[26] (1843) 11 M. & W. 176.

nothing to prevent one's trees growing over one's neighbour's land.[27] In principle, there seems to be nothing to prevent the remedy of abatement being applicable to cases where the nuisance arises from an omission of the wrongdoer; though, until the matter is settled, a party suffering from such a nuisance (except in the case of nuisance caused by encroaching trees or, perhaps, in the case of emergency) would be best advised to rely upon his other remedies.

Effect of abatement

4–121 If a party abated a nuisance, the old action *quod permittat posternere*, by which abatement was claimed by order of the Court, would not lie.[28] It is still the law that an action through the Court will not lie for the abatement of a nuisance after the claimant has himself abated the nuisance.[29] However, abatement will probably not prevent a party who has abated the nuisance from bringing an action for damages which he has sustained prior to abatement.[30] It is hard to see why it should, since there seems to be nothing mutually inconsistent in an action for damages and the exercise of a right to abate (though there are statements which indicate that the effect of exercising the right to abate is to destroy the right to bring an action for damages in respect of the nuisance[31]). It should be noted that a person is not obliged to exercise his right of abatement: he will not lose his right to damages and an injunction will not be refused if he refrains from exercising his right to abate.[32]

Abatement after action

4–122 In *Lane v. Capsey*[33] a house, in the possession of the court's receiver, obstructed a right of way. The dominant owner sought a mandatory injunction which Chitty J. refused. However, Chitty J. gave leave to the dominant owner to pursue such lawful remedies as he might have, notwithstanding that the house was in the possession of the receiver. The question whether the right to abate still existed was expressly left open. The question was decided in *Burton v. Winter*[34]. In that case the claimant had brought an action for trespass and nuisance seeking an injunction for

---

[27] *Lemmon v. Webb* [1895] A.C. 1.

[28] *Baten's Case* (1610) 9 Co. Rep. 54(b), 5(a); Fitzherbert's *Natura Brevium*, 183, I(a).

[29] *Lane v. Capsey* [1891] 3 Ch. 411, 416.

[30] *Kendrick v. Bartland* (1679) 2 Mod. Rep. 253. See also *Lemmon v. Webb* [1894] 3 Ch. 1, 24; *Smith v. Giddy* [1904] 2 K.B. 448; *Job Edwards v. Birmingham Navigations* [1924] 1 K.B. 341, 356.

[31] Blackstone, (21st ed.) Vol. 3, pp 219–220; *Lagan Navigation Co. v. Lamberg Bleaching, etc., Co.* [1927] A.C. 226, 244, *per* Lord Atkinson. See also Salmond and Heuston, *Torts*, (21st ed.) pp. 574–575.

[32] *Lemmon v. Webb* [1894] 3 Ch. 1, 24; *Smith v. Giddy* [1904] 2 K.B. 448; *Job Edwards v. Birmingham Navigations* [1924] 1 K.B. 341, 356; *Leakey v. National Trust* [1980] 1 All E.R. 17, 34; *Bradburn v. Lindsay* [1983] 2 All E.R. 408, 413.

[33] [1891] 3 Ch. 411.

[34] [1993] 1 W.L.R. 1077, CA.

the removal of a wall built by the defendant's predecessors in title. The wall had been built in 1975 and proceedings were commenced in 1986. The judge had granted a declaration that the wall was built half on the claimant's land but refused an injunction. The claimant thereafter purported to exercise her rights of abatement or self-redress. The Court of Appeal held that:

> "Self-redress is a summary remedy, which is justified only in clear and simple cases, or in an emergency. Where a plaintiff has applied for a mandatory injunction and failed the sole justification for the summary remedy has gone. The court has decided the very point in issue. This is so whether the complaint lies in trespass or nuisance".[35]

[35] *ibid.*, at 1082.

Chapter Five

Statutory remedies for interference with land

People must not do things for fun. We are not here for fun. There is no reference to fun in any Act of Parliament.

[A.P. Herbert, Uncommon Law (1935)]

Introduction

There are a number of important statutory provisions which are rele- **5–001**
vant to unlawful interference with land. Some statutes, such as the original form of the Protection from Eviction Act 1977, provide no civil
remedy but merely a criminal penalty (although this has been remedied
in part by sections 27 and 28 of the Housing Act 1988). The Animals
Act 1971 provides a statutory scheme governing interference by animals
which includes the protection of interests in land. Further, general
changes have been introduced by the coming into force of the Human
Rights Act 1998 on October 2, 2000. It is not proposed to list here every
statutory provision or scheme which concerns unlawful interference
with land, but to consider some of the principal provisions which are
related to the common law categories considered elsewhere in this
book.

Effect of the European Convention on Human Rights

Before considering certain detailed schemes for the protection against **5–002**
interference of land, it is necessary to note that where interferences may
be sanctioned by statute or sanctioned subject to controls, the exercise of
the provisions and especially any discretions under them should be considered in the light of the provisions of the European Convention on
Human Rights ("ECHR") as applied by the Human Rights Act 1998.
Aspects of the application of the ECHR and the 1998 Act have already

been considered in Chapters 1 and 4.[1] Whilst the 1998 Act only applies to "public authorities", this includes Courts[2] and so, when powers fall to be exercised by the court they should be considered in the context of any rights under the ECHR which may be engaged. Indeed, as the Court of Appeal held in *R (McLellan) v. Bracknell Forest D.C. & Others*[3] Convention rights may fall to be considered at two levels:

(a)   the "macro" level, namely whether the statutory provision which applies is itself compatible with the ECHR; and

(b)   the "micro" level, namely in ensuring compatibility with the ECHR in the circumstances of the case where a statutory provision is applied.

Recent decisions have given some guidance on the "macro" and "micro" applications of Convention rights,[4] particularly in the context of Articles 6, 8 and Article 1 of the First Protocol which are the most frequently applicable ECHR provisions to land issues.[5] Sedley L.J. made it clear in *London Borough of Lambeth v. Howard*[6] that any attempt to evict a person from his or her home would engage at least Article 8 and require the appropriate assessment to be carried out in the context of the rights engaged. As is discussed in Chapter 1,[7] the rights under Article 8 are broadly interpreted and can include the protection of rights in the context of business premises if they are closely connected with the private lives of the persons affected.[8] Article 1 of the First Protocol applies generally to "possessions" and is not limited even to tangible property.[9]

---

[1]   See paras. 1–127 to 1–135 and 4–104 and 4–113. See Clayton & Tomlinson, *The Law of Human Rights* (OUP, 2000) and Grosz, Beatson & Duffy, *Human Rights* (Sweet & Maxwell, 2000).

[2]   S. 6(3)(a). "Public authorities" within s. 6 includes central and local government and extends more widely to other public bodies See *e.g. R. v. Panel on Takeover and Mergers ex p. Datafin* [1987] Q.B. 815, CA, and Grosz, Beatson & Duffy, *op. cit.*, at pp. 60–75.

[3]   [2002] 1 All E.R. 899, CA.

[4]   *Poplar Housing & Regeneration Community Association Ltd v. Donoghue* [2001] 3 W.L.R. 183, CA, *London Borough of Lambeth v. Howard* (2001) 33 H.L.R. 58, CA, and *R (McLellan) v. Bracknell Forest D.C. & Others*, above, CA. See also the decision of the European Court of Human Rights in *Gillow v. United Kingdom* (1989) 11 E.H.R.R. 335 and *Mellacher v. Austria* (1989) 12 E.H.R.R. 391.

[5]   It is, of course, possible that other rights under the ECHR might be engaged in particular cases. Article 14 was unsuccessfully raised in *R (McLellan) v. Bracknell Forest D.C.*, above, at para. 104.

[6]   Above, especially at paras. 30–32. See 1–128 to 1–131, above.

[7]   See paras. 1–128 to 1–130 and 1–135.

[8]   See paras. 1–128 and 1–129 and *Niemietz v. Germany* (1992) 16 E.H.R.R. 97, where a lawyer's office fell within the meaning of "home" given the close connection between his private life and his office.

[9]   See para. 1–135.

Wrongful failure to deliver up possession

Action for double value

Under section 1 of the Landlord and Tenant Act 1730,[10] where a tenant for a term of years,[11] or for life, wilfully holds over[12] in respect of any premises following the determination of his tenancy, or fails to deliver up possession in compliance with the requirements of a valid written notice[13] to deliver up possession (or quit[14]), without consent he may be held liable in damages assessed on the basis of double the annual value of the land he wrongfully occupies.

An action for double value[15] may be brought within six years[16] only by the landlord or the reversioner, either before or after possession is recovered. The action is not a claim for rent[17] and the sum due may not be distrained for.[18]

Since a tenant who remains in occupation pursuant to a statutory scheme of security, such as under the Rent Act 1977, is exercising a right granted to him by Parliament and is not acting wrongfully, it is highly unlikely that an action for double value could be maintained against such a person.

Action for double rent

In accordance with section 18 of the Distress for Rent Act 1737 any tenant[19] who gives a notice to quit, and then fails to deliver up possession at the time specified in the notice and remains in occupation as a trespasser and is treated by the landlord as such,[20] is liable to pay to the landlord double the rent which was payable under the tenancy for the remainder of his occupation. The liability can be ended by the tenant giving up possession

5–003

5–004

---

[10] A full account of this right is given in *Hill & Redman's Landlord and Tenant*, paras. A[9646]–A[9685].

[11] This includes a tenant from year to year but not a tenant for any lesser period: *Doe d. Hull v. Wood* (1840) 14 M. & W. 682 at 686 and *Wilkinson v. Hall* (1837) 3 Bing. N.C. 508.

[12] The holding over must be deliberate, not mistaken or accidental: see, *e.g. Swinfen v. Bacon* (1861) 6 H. & N. 846 and *Rawlinson v. Marriott* (1867) 16 L.T. 207.

[13] See *Plumber & John v. David* [1920] 1 K.B. 326. However, the notice may be given before or after the tenancy determines (provided that it does not demand possession before the time at which the tenant's interest determines): *Cutting v. Derby* (1776) 2 Wm. Bl. 1075 and *Cobb v. Stokes* (1807) 8 East 358.3

[14] A notice to quit or determine suffices for the purpose of an action for double value: *Messenger v. Armstrong* (1785) 1 Term Rep. 53.

[15] The value is determined at the date of termination of the tenancy or the date the notice was given, if later: *Soulsby v. Neving* (1808) 9 East 310.

[16] S. 19 of the Limitation Act 1980.

[17] S. 1 of the 1730 Act stipulates recovery "by action of debt".

[18] *Timmins v. Rowlinson* (1765) 1 Wm. Bl. 533 at 535.

[19] This includes weekly tenants.

[20] *Oliver Ashley (Holdings) Ltd. v. Ballard (Kent) Ltd.* [2000] Ch. 12, CA.

of the premises.[21] Unlike the entitlement to double value the liability for double rent can be enforced as rent in arrears.[22]

Interference with statutory security of tenure

5–005 Security of tenure is conferred on a number of types of occupier of land and, in general, the schemes conferring such security only permit termination of the interest of the occupier, or interference with such interest, in accordance with the provisions of the relevant statute. Residential occupiers are protected by a considerable body of legislation dealing not only with private sector[23] and public sector occupiers[24] but also with narrower categories such as agricultural employees[25] and the occupiers of caravans and mobile homes.[26] Business tenants[27] and occupiers of agricultural holdings[28] are also protected. The principal means of protection of such occupiers[29] is to place stringent[30] restrictions on the landlord's ability to terminate such interests and to recover possession: for example, statutory tenancies under the Rent Act 1977 and assured tenancies under the Housing Act 1988 cannot be terminated[31] except by order of the court.

Although few of these statutory schemes themselves provide any special remedy for interference,[32] occupiers protected in possession by statute have the protection of the law of trespass and nuisance to protect their interests while those interests continue. The protection afforded by statute creates a sufficient entitlement to possession for the protected occupier to use trespass or nuisance if his occupation is unlawfully disturbed[33]. Whilst the provisions of each of the statutes creating security of tenure[34] should be consulted in order to determine whether (and how)

[21] *Booth v. Macfarlane* (1831) 1 B. & Ad. 904.
[22] *Timmins v. Rowlinson* (1765) 1 Wm. 81. 533 and *Soulsby v. Neving* (1808) 9 East 310.
[23] Principally the Rent Act 1977 and the Housing Act 1988 (which, with exceptions, applies to residential tenancies created after January 15, 1989).
[24] Part IV of the Housing Act 1985.
[25] The Rent (Agriculture) Act 1976 and Part I, Chap. III of the Housing Act 1988 (generally applying from January 15, 1989).
[26] The Caravan Sites Act 1968 and the Mobile Homes Act 1983.
[27] Part II of the Landlord and Tenant Act 1954.
[28] The Agricultural Holdings Act 1986 replaced by the Agricultural Tenancies Act 1995 for new agricultural tenancies entered into from September 1, 1995 (with certain exceptions set out in s. 4).
[29] Who are not exclusively tenants, since certain licences are protected also by, *e.g.* the Housing Act 1985 and the Agricultural Holdings Act 1986.
[30] The stringency varying from scheme to scheme; for example, the protection conferred by the Caravan Sites Act 1968 is relatively minor when compared to that under the Rent Act 1977.
[31] Other than where the occupier voluntarily gives up possession. The stringency of the protection of residential occupiers has been ameliorated by the presumption that new tenancies entered into after 1991 are assured shorthold tenancies.
[32] S. 27(3) of the Housing Act 1988 is an exception: see below, paras. 5–020 to 5–022.
[33] *Pemberton v. Southwark London Borough Council* [2000] 1 W.L.R. 1672, CA, discussed at para. 1–014 under the heading "Tolerated Trespassers."
[34] And specialist works dealing with them in detail: *e.g. Megarry on the Rent Acts* (11th ed.), *Hill & Redman's Law of Landlord and Tenant* (18th ed.) and *Woodfall's Landlord and Tenant*.

such security can be terminated or circumscribed,[35] now reinforced by a need to consider any issues arising under the Human Rights Act 1998,[36] there are some provisions of more general application which are considered below.

The Protection from Eviction Act 1977

The Protection from Eviction Act 1977 provides statutory protection for residential occupiers by controlling the method by which possession of residential land can lawfully be obtained. The Act is the statutory successor to the Protection from Eviction Act 1964, which was itself consolidated into the Rent Act 1965. The original legislation was enacted following the recommendations in the Report of the Committee on Housing in Greater London,[37] which was itself a response to the use of intimidation and violence to secure vacant possession of tenanted properties.[38]

5–006

The protection provided by the Act is of two types, corresponding with the parts of the Act: Part I creates the offences of unlawful eviction and harassment and provides that, except in limited cases, possession cannot lawfully be recovered without a court order. Part II is concerned with the validity of notices to quit. The protection of Part I extends to all "residential occupiers".

Meaning of "residential occupier"

Generally

A "residential occupier" is widely defined by section 1 of the Act:

5–007

> "(1) In this section 'residential occupier', in relation to any premises, means a person occupying the premises as a residence, whether under a contract or by virtue of any enactment or rule of law giving him the right to remain in occupation or restricting the right of any other person to recover possession of the premises."

---

[35] Where there are restrictions on termination, any attempt to regain possession unlawfully may well amount to a trespass and/or breach of covenant, and harassment of tenants entitled to remain in occupation may be a nuisance, trespass and/or breach of covenant for quiet enjoyment.

[36] See, above, and *London Borough of Lambeth v. Howard* (2001) 33 H.L.R. 58, CA, and *R (McLellan) v. Bracknell Forest D.C. & Others* [2002] 1 All E.R. 899, CA.

[37] Also known as the Milner Holland Report: (1965) Cmnd. 2605. The original Act was modelled closely on a New York police statute, considered at pp. 176–7 of the Report. For further details on the background to the legislation, see *R. v. Burke* [1991] 1 A.C. 135, HL, at 145–7, per Lord Griffiths.

[38] Known as "Rachmanism" — named after Perec Rachman who allegedly employed threats and violence to intimidate his Rent Act protected tenants to give up their homes so that he could sell the vacant buildings for greater profit.

It is not necessary for a person to be present in person in the premises to be in occupation for the purposes of the Act. In *Schon v. London Borough of Camden*,[39] Glidewell L.J. held that the test of "occupation" under the Rent Act 1977[40] was equally applicable to the Protection from Eviction Act[41]:

> ". . . there is a long line of authority for the proposition that, under the Rent Acts, a person may occupy premises as his residence although he is physically absent from the premises, provided that, to put it broadly, the absence is not, and is not intended to be, permanent and either his spouse or some other member of his family is physically in occupation or, at the very least, furniture and belongings remain in the premises."

Whilst the court in *Schon* was considering "occupation" in the context of the offence of causing a residential occupier to give up occupation, it is likely that it will bear the same meaning elsewhere in the Act.

Contractual tenants and tenants occupying by virtue of security of tenure

The class of persons who fall into the category of "residential occupiers" is very wide. All contractual tenants, including service tenants and assignees, are protected during the duration of the contract. When the contractual term or period of the residential tenancy comes to an end, the former tenant may be protected in different ways. If one of the statutory schemes providing security of tenure applies to the contractual tenancy,[42] then the right to remain in occupation and the termination of that right depend on the provisions of the statutory scheme in question. If none of the various schemes conferring security of tenure applies, the former residential tenant who remains in occupation may be protected in a more limited sense under the terms of the Protection from Eviction Act 1977 itself. Section 3[43] stipulates that possession of residential premises cannot be regained until there has been a court order, unless the tenancy is an excluded tenancy under section 3A. The protection is of a more limited form and does not extend beyond the requirement that possession be recovered by proceedings, but this at least ensures that the landlord must bring his claim before a court and demonstrate his entitlement to possession. By section 2,[44] a former tenant whose contractual right to

---

[39] (1986) 18 H.L.R. 341, D.C.

[40] See Megarry on the Rent Acts (11th ed.), Vol. 1, pp. 235–249 and, *e.g. Skinner v. Geary* [1931] 2 K.B. 546, CA, *Brown v. Brash* [1948] 2 K.B. 247, CA, *Gofor Investments Ltd. v. Roberts* (1975) 29 P. & C.R. 366, CA and *Brickfield Properties v. Hughes* (1987) 20 H.L.R. 108, CA.

[41] (1986) 18 H.L.R. 341, CA. Schiemann J. agreed.

[42] *e.g.* the Rent (Agriculture) Act 1976, the Rent Act 1977 and the Housing Acts 1980–88. A full consideration of these statutes is beyond the scope of this work: for further consideration of these statutes, see generally *Woodfall, Hill & Redman* and *Megarry on the Rent Acts*.

[43] See below, para. 5–017.

[44] See below, para. 5–016.

remain has been forfeited but who remains in occupation is similarly protected.

Licensees

The quality of protection which the 1977 Act confers on a licensee depends upon the nature of the licence in question. A contractual licensee is a residential occupier (as defined by section 1(1)) during the existence of a contractual right to remain. When the contractual right has been determined, the former licensee becomes a trespasser.[45]

A bare licensee, who has no contractual rights, has a reasonable period in which to leave the premises once his licence has been determined.[46] At the determination of that reasonable period, he also becomes a trespasser.[47] Licensees are protected, as in the case of tenants, by the Act's controls over the recovery of possession of residential premises unless the licence is an excluded licence within section 3A.

Trespassers are also residential occupiers under the second limb of section 1(1): although they have no right to occupy premises, the Criminal Law Act 1977 restricts the rights of the owner to recover possession. Accordingly, a trespasser is protected because it is an offence to use violence to secure entry to the premises, save with lawful authority.[48]

A service tenancy is a form of tenancy and is protected as such by the Act. In the general law, there is a distinction between service occupiers and service tenants[49]: however, a service occupier may also be a "residential occupier" for the purposes of section 1(1). During the currency of his contract of employment, a service occupier falls within the definition because he has a contractual right to remain.[50] By section 8(2) of the Act any person who, under the terms of his employment, is granted exclusive possession of residential property is considered to be a tenant for the purposes of the Act.

The spouse of any person who is protected under the Act as a residential occupier is also protected, by means of the statutory right of occupation created by Part IV of the Family Law Act 1996.[51]

---

[45] *R. v. Blankley* [1979] Crim.L.R. 166 (Knightsbridge Crown Court).

[46] On the validity of notices to quit see the Protection from Eviction Act 1977, s. 5, discussed below, para. 5–018.

[47] On the need for reasonable notice see above, para. 4–062.

[48] Criminal Law Act 1977, s. 6(1). See below, para. 5–024.

[49] For a full analysis of the meaning of "service occupier" and "service tenant" see Woodfall para. 1.029 and Hill and Redman, paras. A [782]–[900].

[50] The contract of employment and contractual licence may be indivisible in law, but the licensor/employer may recover possession from the occupier/employee notwithstanding the fact that the latter is challenging the lawfulness of the termination of his employment and seeking reinstatement: *Ivory v. Palmer* [1975] I.C.R. 340, CA.

[51] See below, para. 5–036.

Excluded tenancies and licenses

5–008   Tenancies and licenses are excluded from the operation of the Act (apart from sections 1 and 2) if they fall into the categories defined by section 3A.[52] There are five categories of excluded tenancy and licence:

(1)   where the occupier shares part of the accommodation with his landlord or licensor[53] provided that:

(a)   the sharing is under the terms of the tenancy or licence[54]; and

(b)   the shared accommodation forms part or all of the premises which the landlord or licensor occupied as his only or principal home, both immediately before the tenancy or licence was granted and also at the time it came to an end[55];

(2)   where the occupier shares part of the accommodation with a member of his landlord or licensor's family.[56] As above, for the tenancy or licence to be excluded:

(a)   the sharing must be under the terms of the tenancy or licence[57] and

(b)   the shared accommodation must form part or all of the premises which the member of the landlord or licensor's family was occupying as his only or principal home, both immediately before the tenancy or licence was granted and also at the time it came to an end.[58]

In this case, there is an extra precondition to exclusion[59]:

(c)   the landlord or licensor[60] must also have his only or principle home in the same building as the shared accommodation, both immediately before the tenancy or licence was granted and also at the time it came to an end and the building must not be a purpose-built block of flats[61];

---

[52]   Inserted by s. 31 of the Housing Act 1988.

[53]   If more than one person is the landlord or licensor any reference to the landlord or licensor in s. 3A(2) and (3) should be construed as a reference to any one of those persons, *i.e.* there is no requirement that the accommodation should be shared with all of a number of joint landlords or licensors: s. 3A(4).

[54]   S. 3A(2)(a).

[55]   S. 3A(2)(b).

[56]   S. 3A(5) of the Act expressly applies the definition of "family" in s. 113 of the Housing Act 1985.

[57]   S. 3A(3)(a).

[58]   S. 3A(3)(b).

[59]   S. 3A(3)(c).

[60]   Or at least one of a number of joint landlords/licensors: s. 3A(4).

[61]   S. 3A(5)(c) of the Act incorporates the definition of "purpose-built block of flats" found in Part III of Sched. 1 to the Housing Act 1988.

(3) where the tenancy or licence was granted as a temporary expedient to any person who had entered either the premises in question, or any other premises, as a trespasser[62];

(4) where a tenancy or licence confers the right to occupy the premises for the purposes of a holiday[63]; and

(5) where a tenancy or licence is granted otherwise than for money or money's worth.[64]

There is an additional category of excluded licence:

(6) the licence is excluded if it confers rights of occupation in a hostel within the meaning of the Housing Act 1985[65] and such hostel is provided by certain bodies specified by section 3A(8)(a)-(h)[66] or by any person specified by the Secretary of State in a statutory instrument made under section 3A(8)(i).[67]

For the purposes of the Act, "accommodation" does not include areas used for storage or as a means of access.[68] Accommodation is shared with another person if the occupier has the use of it in common with that person (whether or not in common with others).[69]

Part I: the criminal offences of unlawful eviction and harassment

The protection of the residential occupier is further strengthened by the creation of a number of criminal offences by section 1 of the Act:

5–009

(1) unlawful eviction of a residential occupier;

---

[62] S. 3A(6). Such circumstances may be difficult to distinguish from cases where the circumstances do not give rise to an intention to create a tenancy: see, *e.g. Longrigg, Burrough & Trounson v. Smith* [1979] E.G.L.R. 42, CA, *Cardiothoracic Institute v. Shrewdcrest Ltd* [1986] 1 W.L.R. 368 and *Javad v. Aqil* [1991] 1 All E.R. 243, CA.

[63] S. 3A(7)(a). See also s. 9 of the Rent Act 1977 and para. 9 of Sched. 1 to the Housing Act 1988 (excluding holiday lettings in similar terms to s. 3A(7)(a)) and *Buchman v. May* [1978] 2 All E.R. 993, CA. In *Buchman* the Court of Appeal held that the dictionary definition of "holiday" as a "period of cessation of work or period of recreation" would suffice provided that "recreation" was not too narrowly construed.

[64] S. 3A(7)(b). This may include cases of "family" licences or acts of friendship: see, *e.g. Cobb v. Lane* [1952] 1 T.L.R. 1037, CA, *Facchini v. Bryson* [1952] 1 T.L.R. 1386, CA. at 1389–90, *Tanner v. Tanner* [1975] 3 All E.R. 776, CA. and *Chandler v. Kerley* [1978] 2 All E.R. 942, CA, *West Wiltshire District Council v. Snelgrove* (1997) 20 H.L.R. 57, CA. In *Snelgrove* the Court of Appeal held that payments of £10 per day in respect of food and services under an act of friendship did not amount to money or money's worth, and that the licence was thus excluded from the operation of the Act.

[65] S. 3A(8) defines "hostel" by reference to the Housing Act 1985, s. 622.

[66] *e.g.* local authorities, housing action trusts, the Housing Corporation or registered housing associations.

[67] Currently the London Hostels Association Ltd (under the Protection from Eviction (Excluded Licences) Order 1991 (S.I. 1991 No. 1943)) and The Shaftesbury Society (under the Protection from Eviction (Excluded Licences) (The Shaftesbury Society) Order 1999 (S.I. 1999 No. 1758))

[68] S. 3A(5)(a).

[69] S. 3A(4).

(2)   harassment of a residential occupier by any person[70]; and

(3)   harassment of a residential occupier by a landlord or his agent.[71]

Unlawful eviction

5–010   This offence is created by section 1(2) of the 1977 Act. Using the wording of the sub-section, the elements of that offence can be broken down as follows. An offence is committed if:

(1)   any person

(2)   unlawfully deprives

(3)   a residential occupier of

    (a)   any premises; or

    (b)   his occupation of the premises or any part thereof; or

    (c)   attempts to do (a) or (b).

It may be seen from the first element that the offence can be committed by any person and not simply a landlord. Where an offence is committed by a body corporate, section 1(6) provides that where the offence was committed with the consent or the connivance of any officer of the company (such as the director, manager or secretary), or an officer was neglectful in allowing the offence to be committed, that officer is also guilty of the offence.

The question of what constitutes "unlawful deprivation" has been considered by the courts on several occasions. In *R. v. Yuthiwattana*,[72] where the occupier was locked out overnight, the Court of Appeal rejected the suggestion made by Lord Evershed M.R. in *Commissioners of the Crown Lands v. Page*[73] that eviction "must be of a permanent character". In *Yuthiwattana* Kerr L.J. said[74]:

> "In our view, permanency goes too far. For instance, if the owner of the premises unlawfully tells the occupier that he must leave the premises for some period, it may be of months or weeks, and then excludes him from the premises, or does anything else with the result that the occupier effectively has to leave the premises and find other accommodation, then it would in our view be open to a jury to

---

[70] In *Schon v. London Borough of Camden* (1986) 18 H.L.R. 341 at 345, Glidewell L.J. held that s. 1(3)(a) and (b) constitute one offence of harassment with two alternative intentions: (a) intent to cause the occupier to give up the premises; and (b) intent to cause the occupier to refrain from exercising any right or pursuing any remedy in respect of the premises.

[71] It follows logically from *Schon's* case, above, that this subsection also comprises one offence with two alternative intentions.

[72] (1984) 16 H.L.R. 49, CA.

[73] [1960] 2 Q.B. 274 at 279, CA.

[74] Above at p. 53.

convict the owner under sub-section (2) on the ground that he had unlawfully deprived the occupier of his occupation. On the other hand, cases which are more properly described as 'locking out' or not admitting the occupier on one or even more isolated occasions, so that in effect he continues to be allowed to occupy the premises but is then unable to enter, seem to us to fall appropriately under sub-section (3)(a) or (b), which deals with acts of harassment."

Yuthiwattana was considered by the Divisional Court in *Costelloe v. London Borough of Camden*[75] where the occupier was excluded for an hour, until police intervention led to readmission. Although the landlord then offered to allow the occupier to stay for a night, the occupier declined the offer. On appeal by case stated, the Divisional Court held that the conviction under section 1(2) was safe only if there was evidence before the court that the landlord intended to exclude the occupier permanently. Woolf J. emphasised that it is the intention behind the exclusion that is crucial to the *Yuthiwattana* test. If a landlord excluded a residential occupier, unlawfully intending to evict the occupier permanently, an offence under section 1(1) would be committed even if the landlord relented and readmitted the occupier. Indeed, a subsequent (perhaps expedient) change of mind would not alter the existence of the earlier unlawful intention to evict permanently.

The meaning of "residential occupier" is discussed above.[76] "Premises" appears to have a wide meaning: in *Thurrock Urban District Council v. Shina*[77] a single room with a shared kitchen was held to be "premises" within the 1977 Act.

Defences

Criminal liability may be avoided in two ways. Firstly, it is a necessary element of the offence that the eviction must be unlawful, hence, once an order for possession has been granted, no offence under the Act is committed in regaining entry in pursuance of the order.[78] This is not truly a defence, as the burden of proof of all elements of the offence lies upon the prosecution. Secondly, it is a defence for the person accused to prove that he believed and had reasonable cause to believe, that the residential occupier had ceased to reside in the premises. Both limbs of the defence are questions of fact for the tribunal of fact: *R. v. Davidson-Acres.*[79]

---

[75] [1986] Crim.L.R. 249.
[76] See para. 5–007.
[77] (1972) 23 P. & C.R. 205, (a case on s. 30 of the Rent Act 1965).
[78] Nor under the Criminal Law Act 1977, s. 6. See further below, paras. 5–024 and 5–025.
[79] [1980] Crim. L.R. 50, CA.

Harassment

5–011   Sections 1(3) and (3A)[80] both create offences of harassment.

(1) Section 1 (3)

5–012   Following the wording of the sub-sections, the elements of the offence under section 1(3) can be broken down as follows. An offence is committed if:

(1)   any person[81]

(2)   with intent to cause

(3)   a residential occupier of any premises

(4)

   (a)   to give up the occupation of the premises or any part thereof; or

   (b)   to refrain from exercising any right or pursuing any remedy in respect of the whole or part of the premises; and

(5)

   (a)   does acts likely to interfere with the peace or comfort of the residential occupier or members of his household; or

   (b)   persistently withdraws or withholds services reasonably required for the occupation of the premises as a residence.

In *Schon v. London Borough of Camden*[82] Glidewell L.J. held that section 1(3) did not create two offences, but one offence whose commission may involve either of two intentions.[83] The actus reus is an act likely to interfere with the peace or comfort of the residential occupier. The mens rea is either an intention to cause the residential occupier to give up the occupation, or an intention to cause the residential occupier to refrain from exercising any right or pursuing any remedy.

In *Schon* an elderly Rent Act protected tenant refused to leave her flat while her landlord renovated a flat above. The Magistrates Court found that the landlord had spoken to the tenant in a manner which caused her anxiety and distress, intending to make her leave the premises while the works were carried out, and convicted the landlord under section 1(3)(a). Allowing the appeal, Glidewell L.J.[84] held that an intention to force an occupier to leave the premises for a limited period of time was not an intention to make the tenant give up occupation. The court applied, by

---

[80]   Added by s. 29 of the Housing Act 1988.
[81]   Note that the offence is not restricted to the landlord or licensor of the premises as is the case under s. 1(2): see above.
[82]   (1986) 18 H.L.R. 341, DC.
[83]   *ibid.* at 345.
[84]   *ibid.* at 347.

analogy with cases under the Rent Acts,[85] the concept that a tenant may be in occupation (even if physically absent) so long as there is both an intention to return and some token of occupation, such as keeping personal items or furniture in the demised premises. However, the landlord's intention to force the residential occupier to leave for a limited period amounted to an intention to cause the occupier to refrain from exercising the right to occupy the demised premises and it followed that the landlord should have been convicted of the offence under section 1(3)(b).

The requisite mens rea was further considered in *R. v. Phekoo*.[86] The landlord was convicted of an offence under section 1(3)(a) of the Act, having threatened two residential occupiers with violence. The defence had been that the landlord did not know the occupiers were actually subtenants, but thought that they were squatters. The Court of Appeal held that it was for the prosecution to prove that the landlord did not honestly believe that the occupiers were not residential occupiers. However, it was also for the landlord to show that he had reasonable grounds upon which an honest belief that the occupiers were not residential occupiers could have been based. It appears that the appeal was misconceived in any event since trespassers are protected by the Act.[87] In *West Wiltshire District Council v. Snelgrove*,[88] where the *Phekoo* defence was raised, Simon Brown L.J., referring to *Norton v. Knowles*[89] highlighted the distinction between a lack of knowledge of the facts and a lack of knowledge of the law. Having determined that the premises were "excluded premises", he concluded at page 63:

> "If, contrary to the view I have formed, the Laceys were properly to have been regarded in law as "residential occupiers", then, in my judgment, the respondents could not have successfully invoked the *Phekoo* defence. They knew full well all the relevant facts; indeed, it was their version of the facts which was accepted in its entirety. No doubt a mistaken belief as to whether or not they were contravening the statute would have been highly relevant by way of mitigation and thus on the issue of penalty. In my opinion, however, it could not have provided them with a defence to the informations."[90]

The actus reus of harassment can take two forms. Firstly, it can take the form of acts likely[91] to interfere with the peace and comfort of a residential occupier. A single act can constitute an offence under this

5–013

---

[85] *Brown v. Brash & Ambrose* [1948] 2 K.B. 247, CA. and the other authorities cited at n. 40 above.

[86] [1981] 1 W.L.R. 1117, CA.

[87] See above, paras. 5–007 and 5–025.

[88] (1997) 30 H.L.R. 57.

[89] [1969] 1 Q.B. 572.

[90] But see also his qualifications of this remark in *Wandsworth London Borough Council v. Osei-Bonsu* (1998) 31 H.L.R. 515.

[91] S. 1(3) originally referred to "acts calculated to interfere": "likely" was substituted for "calculated" by s. 29 of the Housing Act 1988 in respect of acts committed after

sub-section.[92] Nor do the acts complained of need to be civil wrongs — although the contrary was suggested by Ormrod L.J. in *McCall v. Abelesz*[93] the Court of Appeal in *R. v. Yuthiwattana*[94] declined to follow *McCall*, and held that an act[95] which was neither a breach of contract, nor a tort, was capable of being harassment within the meaning of the Act.

The point was further considered by the house of Lords in *R. v. Burke*[96] where the acts complained of comprised preventing the tenants from using some (but not all) of the toilets and bathrooms in the building and deliberately disconnecting the doorbells. The Appellant contended that *Yuthiwattana* was wrongly decided, and that the "acts" referred to in section 1(3) must be unlawful ones. The House of Lords rejected that submission. Lord Griffiths, having considered the Milner Holland Report,[97] held that Parliament had not intended to restrict the meaning of "acts" in such a manner. He continued[98]:

> "A further reason for rejecting the argument that the act must involve a civil wrong is that harassment is not confined to the landlord and tenant relationship. The protected class is 'the residential occupier' which as defined by section 1(1) is far wider than 'tenant'. Furthermore not only landlords but 'any person' may be guilty of harassment. Therefore there may be no contractual relationship of any kind between the victim and the harasser, an obvious example being fellow occupiers who have fallen out."

Omissions are not "acts" for the purpose of this limb of section 1(3) and the only "omissions" which can found an offence under this sub-section are the specific cases of withdrawing or withholding services reasonably required for the occupation of the premises.[99] In *R. v. Zafar Ahmad*,[1] a landlord started rebuilding works on the demised premises without the final consent of the tenant. The premises were rendered uninhabitable by removal of the bathroom fittings. When the tenant objected, the works were left unfinished for a period of 11 months. The jury evidently accepted that the landlord did not commence the works intending to harass the occupier, but convicted on the basis that the harassment lay in

---

January 15, 1989. The substitution means the prosecution no longer needs to prove ulterior motive, but needs merely to convince the tribunal of the fact that, objectively viewed, the acts complained of would have had the effect of causing discomfort, *etc.*

[92] See *R. v. Evangelos Polycarpou* (1983) 9 H.L.R. 129, CA (a case under the Rent Act 1965) and s. 6(c) of the Interpretation Act 1978.

[93] [1976] 1 Q.B. 585, CA at 597E.

[94] (1984) H.L.R. 49 at 60, CA.

[95] A continuing refusal to replace a key lost by the tenant.

[96] [1991] 1 A.C. 135, HL.

[97] See above, para. 5–006, n. 37.

[98] (1984) H.L.R. 49 at 147E, CA.

[99] From the wording of the latter part of s. 1(3) the withdrawing/withholding element is an alternative to "acts": see below.

[1] (1986) 18 H.L.R. 416, CA.

the failure to finish the works. The Court of Appeal quashed the conviction on the basis that the wording of the section made criminal "acts" but not omissions. However, in *Sampson v. Wilson*[2], in the context of a damages claim under sections 27 and 28 of the Housing Act 1988, His Honour Judge Roger Cooke (sitting as a Deputy Judge of the Chancery Division) described the leaving of landlord's works half-finished as "classic harassment" and awarded damages accordingly.[3]

The second limb of section 1(3) concerns the alternative actus reus of persistently withdrawing or withholding services. The requirement of "persistence" suggests that a trivial or "one-off" withholding of a service will not constitute an offence. In *R. v. Abrol*,[4] the Court of Appeal held that there must be, "an element of deliberate continuity in withholding the services". However, it would seem that a single act of withdrawing a service, such as disconnecting the supply of electricity, can amount to a persistent withholding of the supply: *Hooper v. Eaglestone*.[5] Indeed, a single, but continuing, withdrawal or withholding of a service appears capable of being regarded as "persistent" — particularly where that service is withheld over a significant period of time.

Ormrod L.J. suggested in *McCall v. Abelesz*[6] that the landlord could not be prosecuted for withholding or withdrawing a service he was not contractually obliged to provide. In light of the House of Lord's decision in *R. v. Burke*[7] it is suggested that this restriction does not represent the law, and the withholding of any service reasonably required for the occupation of the premises is capable of forming the actus reus of an offence.

(2) Section 1(3A)

The elements of the offence under section 1(3A) can be broken down as follows. The landlord of a residential occupier or an agent of the landlord will be guilty of an offence if: **5–014**

(1)

    (a)   he does acts likely to interfere with the peace or comfort of the residential occupier or members of his household; or

    (b)   he persistently withdraws or withholds services reasonably required for the occupation of the premises in question as a residence; and

---

[2] (1994) 26 H.L.R. 486, reversed on appeal, [1996] Ch. 39, but not on this point.
[3] See also *R. v. Burke* [1990] 2 All E.R. 385, HL.
[4] [1972] Crim.L.R. 318, CA. In *Westminster City Council v. Peart* the Divisional Court declined to decide the point, disposing of the case by considering the adequacy of the informations.
[5] (1977) 34 P. & C.R. 311. The case concerned s. 3(1)(c) of the Caravan Sites Act 1968 which is in all material aspects the same as s. 1(3) of the Act.
[6] [1976] 1 Q.B. 585, at 596H, CA.
[7] [1991] 1 A.C. 135, HL.

(2)   (in either case)

    (a)   he knows; or

    (b)   has reasonable cause to believe

(3)   that the conduct is likely to cause the residential occupier

    (a)   to give up the occupation of the whole or part of the premises; or

    (b)   to refrain from
        (i)   exercising any right; or
        (ii)   pursuing any remedy in respect of the whole or part of the premises.

Essentially, this subsection mirrors section 1(3), so only the differences are considered here. There are three principal differences between section 1(3) and section 1(3A):

(1)   the section 1(3) offence can be committed by any person, whereas the section 1(3A) offence can be committed only by "the landlord" or any agent of his;

(2)   the section 1(3) offence requires proof of intention, whereas the section 1(3A) offence requires no proof of intention, only that the offender subjectively knew, or alternatively objectively had reasonable cause to believe, that the acts would have the specified consequences; and

(3)   unlike the section 1(3) offence, there is a defence to the section 1(3A) offence if the landlord or agent can prove that he had reasonable grounds for so acting.[8]

"Landlord" is defined by section 1(3C) to include not only the reversioner who is prevented from occupying the premises by a right granted to the occupier but also one whose right to recover possession is restricted.[9] The definition also includes any superior landlord. It follows from section 1(3C)(b) that the relation between a rightful landowner and a squatter is treated for the purposes of these provisions as analogous to that of landlord and tenant since the Criminal Law Act 1977 places restrictions on the right to recover possession[10] even of premises occupied by squatters.

---

[8] S. 1(3B). As with the question of belief and reasonable cause under s. 1(2) (see above para. 5–007) this question would appear to be for the tribunal of fact.
[9] As in the case of the landlord of premises where there is a statutory tenancy under the Rent Act 1977 or an assured tenancy under the Housing Act 1988.
[10] See below, para. 5–024.

Penalties

Section 1(4) provides that, on summary conviction, the maximum penalty is either a fine not exceeding level 5 on the standard scale,[11] or six months imprisonment, or both. On indictment, the maximum penalty is an unlimited fine,[12] or two years imprisonment, or both. Both at summary trial and on indictment, the Court may also make a compensation order against a convicted offender.[13]

5–015

Restrictions on re-entry

Section 2 of the Act makes it unlawful to enforce a right of entry or forfeiture in respect of a dwelling-house, in which a person is lawfully residing, without first obtaining a court order. Entering the premises in an attempt to enforce such a right of re-entry without such an order would be an offence under section 1.

5–016

Restrictions on eviction

Section 3 of the Act makes it unlawful to recover possession from an occupier at the end of a tenancy, which is neither a statutorily protected tenancy[14] nor an excluded tenancy, under section 3A,[15] "otherwise than by proceedings in the court".[16] "Statutorily protected tenancy" is defined by section 8 of the Act and includes protected tenancies within the Rent Act 1977[17] and assured tenancies within Part I of the Housing Act 1988.[18] Any remaining Rent Act statutory tenancies[19] do not fall within the definition of "statutorily protected tenancy", and therefore come within the protection of section 3.[20] This means that when a statutory tenancy arises under section 2 of the Rent Act 1977 on the termination of the prior contractual tenancy section 3 of the Protection from Eviction Act 1977 will then apply.

5–017

---

[11] Currently £5,000: s. 17 of the Criminal Justice Act 1991 amending s. 32(9) of the Magistrates Court Act 1980.

[12] By s. 19 of the Criminal Justice Act 1992, the Crown Court must have regard to an offender's means when setting the level of a fine.

[13] Ss. 35–8 of the Powers of the Criminal Courts Act 1973, s. 40 of the Magistrates' Courts Act 1980 as amended by Sched. 4 of the Criminal Justice Act 1991.

[14] See s. 8(1) of the Act and *Haniff v. Robinson* [1993] Q.B. 419, CA.

[15] See above, para. 5–008.

[16] See *Haniff v. Robinson* [1993] Q.B. 419, CA. and the discussion below.

[17] S. 1 of the Rent Act 1977.

[18] In order to recover possession in these cases a court order is required by either s. 98 of the Rent Act 1977, s. 82 of the Housing Act 1985 or s. 5 of the Housing Act 1988.

[19] Which are increasingly rare given the phasing out of the 1977 Act protection from January 15, 1989.

[20] Whereas protected tenancies are excluded. Woolf L.J. in *Haniff v. Robinson* [1993] Q.B. 419 at 426 stated that the reason for this was that "there is a separate regime of protection provided for such tenants." Presumably this refers to the fact that a protected tenant would first have to be served with a notice to quit in accordance with s. 5.

If a possession order is obtained against a statutory tenant, or any person protected by the Protection from Eviction Act, it is unlawful for the landlord to attempt to eject the tenant otherwise than by means of a warrant for possession. In *Haniff v. Robinson*[21] the Court of Appeal held that where the 1977 Act applied it was not lawful for a landlord to use "self-help" to recover possession of premises even where an order for possession has already been made by the county court: execution of an order for possession of a dwelling-house must be by the court.[22]

Section 3 applies to an "occupier" of premises "let as a dwelling", not "a residential occupier" as such. An "occupier" is defined by section 3(2) as, "any person lawfully residing in the premises or any part of them at the termination of the former tenancy". Since January 15, 1988, the section has applied to licences also.[23] Transitional provisions give the same protection to licences created under restricted contracts after November 28, 1980.[24]

Since the Act relates to residential occupation, and the courts have indicated a willingness to apply analogous Rent Act tests,[25] it is considered that the Rent Act authorities which consider the requirement "let as a separate dwelling" in section 1 of the Rent Act[26] are of considerable assistance in construing "let as a dwelling" in section 3.[27] If the Rent Act cases are applicable (as they seem to be), then it is necessary to look at the purpose of the letting to determine whether the parties intended the letting to be a residential one. In *Wolf v. Hogan*,[28] Denning L.J. stated:

> ". . . it is necessary to look at the purpose of the letting. If the lease contains an express provision as to the purpose of the letting, it is not necessary to look further, but, if there is no express provision, it is open to the court to look at the circumstances of the letting. If the house is constructed for use as a dwelling, it is reasonable to infer that the purpose was to let as a dwelling, but if it is constructed for use as a lock up shop, the reasonable inference is that it was let for

[21] [1993] Q.B. 419, CA, distinguishing *Aglionby v. Cohen* [1955] 1 Q.B. 558 and disapproving a passage to contrary effect at pp. 386–87 of *Megarry on the Rent Acts*. See also *Kyriakou v. Pandeli* [1980] C.L.Y. 1648.

[22] See CCR Ord. 26, r. 17 and RSC, Ord. 43, r. 3.

[23] S. 3(2B). The date is that on which s. 30 of the Housing Act 1988 came into force. "Let" and "tenancy" in s. 3 are to be construed consistently with the application of the section to licences, *i.e.* should be read as including "licensed" and "licence."

[24] S. 3(2A). The date is that on which the s. 64 of the Housing Act 1980 came into force.

[25] *e.g.* "occupation" — *Schon v. London Borough of Camden* (1986) 18 H.L.R. 341, CA, discussed above, para. 5–007.

[26] See Hill and Redman, paras. C [308]–[320] and *e.g. Wolf v. Hogan* [1949] 2 K.B. 194, CA, *Horford Investments v. Lambert* [1976] Ch. 39, CA, *St Catherine's College v. Dorling* [1980] 1 W.L.R. 66, CA, and *Henry Smith's Charity Trustees v. Wagle* [1990] Q.B. 42, CA. There does not appear to be a requirement that the premises should be let solely for the purposes of a dwelling: *Vickery v. Martin* [1944] K.B. 679, CA. and *R v. Brighton and Area Rent Tribunal ex p. Slaughter* [1954] 1 Q.B. 446.

[27] Note the absence of the requirement of a separate dwelling from s. 3.

[28] [1949] 2 K.B. 194, at 205, CA.

business purposes. If the position were neutral, it would be proper to look at the actual use."

Since it is necessary to look at the purposes of the letting agreed, or implemented, by the parties at the time of the letting it is not open to one party unilaterally to change the use[29] and a tenant cannot simply begin residential occupation of business premises and thereby establish Rent Act or Housing Act security of tenure. If the landlord agrees to such a change either expressly, or by implication, then the premises can be regarded as having been "let as a dwelling"[30] and section 3 will then apply.

Section 3, however, does not apply to the temporary housing of the homeless by a public body pursuant to a statutory duty and "occupied as a dwelling under licence" does not include the occupation of bed and breakfast accommodation as a purely temporary arrangement.[31]

Section 4 contains special provisions applicable to agricultural employees: detailed consideration of these provisions lies outside the scope of this work.

Part II: notices to quit

Section 5 of the Act provides that a notice to quit[32] residential premises   **5–018**
served either by a landlord or a tenant, or by a periodic licensee or licensor,[33] is not valid unless it:

(1)   is in writing;

(2)   contains the information prescribed by statutory instrument;[34] and

(3)   is given not less than 4 weeks before it takes effect.[35]

The section does not apply to a licensee for a single period, such as a service licensee who occupies during the duration of his employment,[36] nor

---

[29]   *Wolf v. Hogan* above, and *Henry Smith's Charity Trustees v. Wagle*, above.
[30]   *Russell v. Booker* (1982) 263 E.G. 513, CA and *Henry Smith's Charity Trustees v. Wagle*, above.
[31]   *Mohammed v. Royal Borough of Kensington and Chelsea*, (1995) 27 H.L.R. 439
[32]   For the general law governing notices to quit see Hill and Redman paras. A [8127]–[8529] and above, Chap. 4, paras. 4–061 to 4–063.
[33]   S. 5(1B). The date is that on which s. 32 of the Housing Act 1988 came into force.
[34]   Currently, the Notices to Quit, *etc.*, (Prescribed Information) Regulations 1988, (S.I. 1988 No. 2201). Broadly, the information tells the occupier that the landlord/licensor must obtain an order for possession before he can lawfully be evicted and that an order cannot be applied for until the notice has expired. The information further advises the occupier to take legal advice and that he may be entitled to legal aid.
[35]   The four week period must run from the date of service of the notice and the time is calculated to include the first day and exclude the last day: *Schnabel v. Allard* [1967] 1 Q.B. 627, CA. The date of expiry should be at the end of a complete period of the tenancy: *Shnabel v. Allard*.
[36]   *Norris v. Checksfield* [1991] 1 W.L.R. 1241, CA at 1248A, *per* Woolf L.J.

does it apply to the termination by a licensor of a non-periodic licence prior to its expiry.[37] This appears to follow from the fact that, at common law, the function of a notice to quit is only to terminate a periodic tenancy.[38] Further, the provision does not apply to tenancies at will which are not periodic in nature and can be terminated at the will of the parties.[39]

It appears that the statutory requirement to provide the information prescribed does not mean that a notice to quit must be in the precise form prescribed to be valid, so long as all the information required is present and the tenant (or licensee) would not be misled by it.[40]

The tort of unlawful eviction

5–019   The Protection from Eviction Act 1977 and its statutory predecessors created criminal offences, but no civil liability, for unlawful eviction. In *McCall v. Abelesz*,[41] Lord Denning went so far as to suggest that there was no need to give a civil remedy for harassment, as existing remedies were already sufficient.[42] Parliament subsequently took a different view, and in sections 27 and 28 of the Housing Act 1988[43] created a statutory tort of unlawful eviction. Additional remedies for more general acts of harassment have also been provided by the Protection from Harassment Act 1997 — see below.

The Housing Act 1988, sections 27 and 28

5–020   The duty not to commit the tort lies on a "landlord" or any person acting on the landlord's behalf and is owed to a "residential occupier".[44] A landlord in breach is termed "the landlord in default" by sections 27(1) and (2).

---

[37] Assuming that the licensor may lawfully terminate it: see above, Chap. 4, paras. 4–061 to 4–063. If there were no right to terminate, s. 5 would still not apply but there might well be other remedies open to the licensee to prevent eviction, *e.g.* injunction or specific performance.

[38] See, *e.g. Doe d. Warner v. Browne* (1807) 8 East 165 and *Centaploy Ltd v. Matlodge Ltd* [1973] 2 All E.R. 720 at 728.

[39] *Crane v. Morris* [1965] 3 All E.R. 77, CA.

[40] *Beckerman v. Durling* (1981) 6 H.L.R. 87, CA and *Swansea City Council v. Hearn* (1990) 23 H.L.R. 284, CA. In both cases the argument that the notice must comply strictly with the prescribed form was rejected. Sufficiency is always a question of fact: in *Beckerman*, counsel conceded that there were no material differences between the forms prescribed under the 1975 and 1980 regulations. In *Swansea* Dillon L.J. suggested, at 292, that the notice would be valid if it was sufficiently close to the prescribed form so as not to confuse the recipient. Ralph Gibson L.J. was more explicit and stated that a notice will be valid if it is not misleading, gives the recipient sufficient information, and warns the recipient to seek legal advice.

[41] [1976] 1 Q.B. 585, CA at 594D.

[42] Lord Denning's comments on existing remedies were optimistic: he considered only contractual remedies as between landlord and tenant, such as breach of the covenant for quiet enjoyment. The Act covers more relationships than that of landlord and tenant.

[43] The section has effect from June 9, 1988: s. 27(1).

[44] S. 27(1) and (2).

Section 27(9)(a) expressly applies the definition of "residential occupier" found in section 1 of the Protection from Eviction Act 1977[45] to section 27.

The "landlord" is defined as the person who, but for the residential occupier's right to occupy, would be entitled to occupation of the premises, including a superior landlord.[46] The definition therefore includes a licensor under a non-excluded licence, or the rightful occupier of land occupied by squatters who has not complied with the restrictions on recovery of possession imposed by the Criminal Law Act 1977. A landlord's agent cannot be liable himself for damages under sections 27 and 28 since section 27(3) provides that it is the landlord who is liable to pay damages.[47]

The tort is committed when certain acts are carried out by a landlord or someone acting on his behalf. Some torts require the presence of a mental element, whereas others do not. The torts the commission of which do not require a mental element are:

(a) unlawfully depriving a residential occupier of his occupation of the whole of the residential premises;[48]

(b) unlawfully depriving a residential occupier of his occupation of part of the residential premises;[49]

(c) attempting unlawfully to deprive a residential occupier of his occupation of the whole of the residential premises;[50] and

(d) attempting unlawfully to deprive a residential occupier of his occupation of part of the residential premises.[51]

The acts which require a mental element in the commission of a tort are:

(a) any act likely to interfere with the peace or comfort of a residential occupier (or a member of his household), which results in the

---

[45] See above, para. 5–007.
[46] S. 27(9)(c): this is very similar to the definition appearing in s. 1(3C) of the Protection from Eviction Act 1977 which was introduced by s. 29 of the 1988 Act.
[47] *Sampson v. Wilson*, [1996] Ch. 39. The court held that the provisions were aimed at landlords, not agents, although a landlord could, of course, be liable for the acts of his agent. The court declined to follow the tentative views expressed on this issue in *Jones v. Miah* (1992) 24 H.L.R. 578, CA.
[48] S. 27(1).
[49] S. 27(1).
[50] S. 27(2)(a). The difference between the s. 27(1) and (2) torts was highlighted by the Court of Appeal in *Murray v. Aslam* (1995) 27 H.L.R. 285, esp. at 290–291 (per Sir Thomas Bingham M.R.)
[51] S. 27(2)(b). *Abbott v. Bayley* [1999] L. & T. Rev. 267 concerned the "constructive eviction" of a tenant by a combination of the landlord's acts. The landlord purported to determine the assured tenancy while the tenant was on holiday and re-let the property to two new tenants. The original tenant re-occupied his bedroom, but left after receiving threats from the landlord's father.

residential occupier giving up his right to occupy the premises as his residence;[52] and

(b) persistently withdrawing or withholding services reasonably required for the occupation of the premises as a dwelling, which results in the residential occupier giving up his right to occupy the premises as his residence.[53]

The requisite mental elements for the above acts are either:

(a) knowing that the act is likely to cause the residential occupier to give up the occupation of the premises or part thereof;[54] or

(b) having reasonable cause to believe that the act is likely to cause the residential occupier to give up occupation of the premises or part thereof;[55] or

(c) knowing that the act is likely to cause the residential occupier to refrain from exercising any right or pursuing any remedy in respect of the premises or part thereof;[56] or,

(d) having reasonable cause to believe that the act is likely to cause the residential occupier to refrain from exercising any right or pursuing any remedy in respect of the premises or part thereof.[57]

The statutory torts closely mirror the offences created by the Protection from Eviction Act 1977 with the exception of harassment which does not result in the occupier leaving the premises, which is only actionable under the Protection from Harassment Act 1997.[58]

The remedy provided by 27(3) to the former residential occupier[59] against the landlord in default is damages "in respect of his loss of the right to occupy the premises in question as his residence".

The liability under the statutory tort is additional to any other liability which may arise, "in tort, in contract or otherwise".[60] However damages cannot be awarded twice for the same loss.[61]

Defences

5–021   Several defences or partial defences are provided to avoid liability under section 27(3):

---

[52] S. 27(2)(b).
[53] S. 27(2)(b).
[54] S. 27(2)(b)(i).
[55] S. 27(2)(b)(i).
[56] S. 27(2)(b)(ii).
[57] S. 27(2)(b)(ii).
[58] It may also be a breach of covenant of quiet enjoyment (where there is a relationship of landlord and tenant). See above, Chap. 3, at paras. 3–024 to 3–041.
[59] Defined by s. 27(9)(d).
[60] S. 27(5).
[61] See *Kaur v. Gill, The Times,* June 15, 1995, CA.

(1) it is a defence for the landlord in default to reinstate the residential occupier in the residential premises at any time before the proceedings are finally disposed of[62] so that he again becomes the residential occupier in those premises.[63] The temporary reinstatement of the occupier in the subject premises may not be sufficient to amount to "reinstatement" within section 27(6)(a) if the return is only for a short period of time and is followed by a premature, but final, departure.[64] Proceedings are "disposed of" on the earliest date by which proceedings have been determined and when the time for an appeal has passed, or an appeal has been withdrawn or abandoned;[65]

(2) financial liability can be escaped if, at the request of the displaced occupier, the court makes an order as a result of which the residential occupier is reinstated in the premises so that he becomes again the residential occupier.[66] Clearly, if the court makes an order which does not lead to reinstatement, e.g. if the landlord fails to comply with it, liability will remain. It is not clear what the result is if an occupier obtains such an order but does not serve or otherwise seek to enforce it. It may be thought that in such a case, providing that it can be established that (had the tenant sought to enforce the order) the landlord would have reinstated the occupier, such an occupier should not be entitled to recover section 27(3) damages since his loss would result from the failure to enforce. The correctness of that approach must be in doubt: firstly, it would still involve permitting the landlord to profit from his own wrong-doing. Secondly, a similar argument could be applied to seek to deprive a tenant of section 27(3) damages in circumstances where it is argued that the displaced occupier failed to seek a reinstatement order which would, if obtained, have led to the landlord reinstating the occupier. There is nothing in section 27(6) to suggest that there is any duty on the former residential occupier to make a request to the court for an order[67] and it is difficult to see why a displaced occupier should be in a worse position if he has not obtained an order;

---

[62] See further, *Tagro v. Cafane* [1991] 1 W.L.R. 378, CA.
[63] S. 27(6)(b).
[64] See the suggestion to this effect in *Murray v. Aslam* (1995) 27 H.L.R. 284, CA, at 293 per Sir Ralph Gibson. Sir Thomas Bingham M.R. expressed himself in more equivocal terms at p. 291. It is suggested that Sir Ralph Gibson is correct in principle but that the courts are likely to scrutinise contentions to such effect with considerable care. However, if the temporary re-occupation is merely a stop-gap adopted by a desperate tenant who has no choice (in the Murray case the tenant was left in the street in the rain with a young child), but who does not wish to return permanently as the result of the landlord's behaviour, it is doubtful whether there has been "reinstatement."
[65] 34 s. 27(6).
[66] This follows from the final words of s. 27(6)(b); "as mentioned in paragraph (a) above."
[67] Following actionable conduct on the part of the landlord it may also be easy to understand why a tenant might not wish to be reinstated.
[68] S. 27(7)(b). See also *Murray v. Aslam*, above.

(3)   liability can be reduced if before the proceedings were begun the landlord in default offered to reinstate the residential occupier into the premises and the offer was unreasonably declined.[68] It appears that an offer motivated by the issue of proceedings will not avoid liability unless those proceedings lead to an order within section 27(6)(b).[69] If the residential occupier has found alternative accommodation before the offer is made, the court may reduce the damages if it would have been unreasonable for the residential occupier to have declined the offer of reinstatement had he not obtained the alternative accommodation;

(4)   the conduct of the residential occupier or any person residing with him may also justify the court in reducing the damages if that conduct was "such that it is reasonable to mitigate the damages".[70] Since the defence appears to involve proof of aggravating or provoking conduct by the occupier,[71] such conduct must have occurred prior to the event which gave rise to the landlord in default's to justify a reduction of liability, *i.e.* damages are not to be reduced if the former occupier conducts himself badly as a result of his eviction or harassment. Reductions in damages will depend on the conduct of the defendant, assessed in the context of the circumstances of the case;[72]

(5)   it is also a defence for the landlord in default to prove that at the time he deprived the residential occupier of the possession (as set out in section 27(1)) or at the time the acts were done, or attempts made, he had reasonable cause to believe that the residential occupier had ceased to reside at the premises and as a result had given up occupation of the premises;[73] and

(6)   if the tortious liability would arise only by the doing of acts or the withdrawal or withholding of services, it is a defence for the landlord in default to show he had reasonable grounds for such behaviour.[74]

---

[69] There would be nothing unusual in proceedings which sought both an injunction and damages. If the court is not able to determine whether, at the date of the hearing, s. 27(6)(b) will be satisfied the best course may be to grant the injunction and to adjourn the question of damages under s. 27(3). In most cases, it is likely that any injunction to reinstate will have been sought on an interim basis (frequently without notice) prior to trial and it will be known by the hearing whether s. 27(6)(b) is applicable.

[70] S. 27(7)(a): the wording appears somewhat circular.

[71] In *Tagro v. Cafane* [1991] 1 W.L.R. 378, CA at 384F, Lord Donaldson M.R. described the effect of this sub-section as "a contributory negligence concept." See, further, below.

[72] *Regalgrand Ltd. v. Dickerson & Wade* (1996) 29 H.L.R. 620.

[73] S. 27(8)(a). See *Wandsworth London Borough Council v. Osei-Bonsu* (1998) 31 H.L.R. 515.

[74] S. 27(8)(b).

Assessment of section 27(3) damages

Where the occupier has lost the right to occupy as a result of the acts of the landlord, the measure of damages is set out in detail in section 28 of the Housing Act 1988.[75] Such damages are not measured by the normal tortious measure of providing compensation to the tenant for the wrong caused,[76] but are designed to take away from the landlord any financial gain accruing as a result of the unlawful eviction. A valuation formula is provided[77] and an award is based on the difference between the value of the subject premises subject to the right of occupation of the residential occupier, and its value on the assumption that the occupier's right has ceased. The subject of the valuation is "the building" and its curtilage, which can be larger than the residential premises in question: the wide basis of the formula is clearly intended to deprive the landlord of any uplift in value which other premises of his may receive by reason of the vacant possession of the subject premises.[78] It is to be assumed that the landlord is selling the building in the open market to a willing buyer, that neither the residential occupier nor his family wish to purchase, and that the land in which the landlord has an interest cannot be substantially redeveloped[79] nor the building demolished. Valuations must take account of the actual position of the property, as in *Melville v. Bruton*[80] where valuers for both parties had been instructed to consider the value of the property with vacant possession which in fact contained two further tenants. Accordingly, the Court of Appeal substituted a lower value. The date for valuation stipulated by section 28 is the date immediately before the unlawful eviction.

5–022

Although the assessment of section 27 damages involves a more precise type of calculation than does the assessment of punitive damages, it resembles the latter to the extent that it is intended to deprive the landlord of the value of his advantage rather than compensate the occupier for his loss. This is to be contrasted with the common law measure of damages where the cost of alternative accommodation, or loss of rental income,[81] is recoverable by the displaced occupier in accordance with the decision in

---

[75] See also *Tagro v. Cafane* above, *Melville v. Bruton* (1996) 29 H.L.R. 319 and *King v. Jackson* (1997) 30 H.L.R. 541.

[76] See above, paras. 4–002 to 4–008. Contrast damages awarded to the harassed tenant for breach of covenant for quiet enjoyment: see *e.g. Perera v. Vandiyar* [1953] 1 W.L.R. 672, CA and *Owen v. Gadd* [1956] 2 Q.B. 99, CA and above, paras. 3–023 to 3–026.

[77] S. 28(3).

[78] *e.g.* the unlawful eviction may have been accomplished in order to complete the process of emptying a larger building which the landlord proposes to sell or refurbish and re-let on a more profitable basis. The penal nature of the award of damages is limited, since the valuation formula does not take into account the possibility of redevelopment.

[79] S. 28(6) defines "substantial development" as being other than that for which permission is granted by the General Development Order 1988 (now the Town and Country Planning (General Permitted Development) Order 1995 (S.I. 1995 No. 418), or a change of use of the building other than a change to residential use.

[80] (1996) 29 H.L.R. 319.

[81] Where the occupier owns other accommodation which he has to occupy by reason of the landlord's ousting him from possession.

Mira v. Aylmer Square Investments.[82] The aim of depriving the landlord of a gain unlawfully obtained is clearly restitutionary in character and appears to be a statutory form of recovery for unjust enrichment. To that extent, as considered in Chapter 4, paras. 4–017 to 4–022, there have been related developments in the common law since there are now elements of restitution of unlawfully obtained benefits in claims for mesne profits against trespassers.

In the first reported case on these provisions, *Tagro v. Cafane*,[83] the defendant landlord subjected the claimant tenant to what Lord Donaldson M.R. described as "war".[84] Rent was demanded at 2 a.m., the toilet door was kicked down while the tenant was using it, and eventually, the locks were changed while she was out, and the contents of her room wrecked. Some days later, the defendant offered a key, but the claimant was so frightened of him she could no longer sleep at the premises.

The Court of Appeal first considered liability and, specifically, whether the tenant had been reinstated by the offer of the key. Lord Donaldson considered that she had not, because the lock to which the key was proffered did not work, and the wrecking of the room made it reasonable for the tenant to decline to continue living there. It is for the tenant to choose whether or not to be reinstated.[85]

Lord Donaldson then considered quantum. Counsel for the defendant contended that, since his own lease contained absolute prohibitions against assignment and subletting, the lease had a nil value to any buyer, as the purchaser would face forfeiture proceedings from the freeholder. Lord Donaldson held that the valuation formula provided by the Act could override any such provision, in effect requiring the assumption that the landlord's interest is alienable.[86] Accordingly, the award of £31,000 damages was upheld.[87]

The award of damages under sections 27 and 29 does not exclude the award of damages at common law. In *Kaur v. Gill*[88] the Court of Appeal held that common law damages could be awarded against a landlord for breaches of covenant for quiet enjoyment in addition to statutory damages since the common law damages related to the tenant's complaints of harassment and not to her claim for statutory damages for unlawful eviction. Accordingly, the concession that common law damages were

---

[82] (1990) 22 H.L.R. 182, CA.

[83] [1991] 1 W.L.R. 378, CA.

[84] *ibid.* at 380G.

[85] See also para. 5–021 above on the question whether temporary re-occupation always amounts to "re-instatement" and *Murray v. Aslam* [1995] 27 H.L.R. 284, CA.

[86] Compare cases on other areas of assessment of compensation/valuation such as *IRC v. Crossman* [1937] A.C. 26, HL and *Lady Fox's Exors v. IRC* [1994] 2 E.G.L.R. 185, CA.

[87] Although it should be noted that the defendant had unwisely failed to adduce expert evidence of his own as to the quantum of damages and was unable to challenge effectively the plaintiff's evidence.

[88] *The Times*, June 15, 1995. *Mason v. Nwokorie* [1994] 1 E.G.L.R. 59, CA, was distinguished on the basis that *Mason* involved the award of general damages for loss of the right to occupy.

excluded by the 1988 Act made in *Tagro v. Cafane*[89] does not appear to have been correct. Further, since the statutory damages are, by section 27(3), expressly related to the loss of the right to occupy it is likely that other common law damages which do not provide compensation for such a loss can be awarded as well as statutory damages. In principle, common law exemplary damages should also be recoverable since they are not intended to provide compensation for the loss of the right to occupy: see Chapter 4, above, paragraphs 4–023 to 4–030. Further, damages recoverable at common law for the cost of having to seek alternative accommodation[90] are also likely to be recoverable in addition to statutory damages since they are consequential upon, although independent from, the loss of the right to occupy the subject premises. In any event, section 27(3) specifically restricts the Act to situations where the occupier has lost his rights to occupy and in other cases[91] the harassed tenant must rely upon common law compensatory and exemplary damages.

The Criminal Law Act 1977, Part II

Part II of the Criminal Law Act 1977[92] creates five offences relating to entering and remaining on property. The Act was intended to clarify criminal liability for trespass, particularly the squatting of residential premises, while leaving self-help remedies against such squatters lawful. The five offences replace the old offences of forcible entry and forcible detainer.[93]   5–023

Violence to secure entry

Section 6 creates the offence of using or threatening violence to secure entry to premises. The offence can only by committed if there is someone on the premises who is opposed to the entry which is being effected by violence or threats thereof, and the person so using or threatening the violence knows that to be the case. It is immaterial whether the violence is directed towards property or the person opposed to the entry[94] and the purpose of the entry is irrelevant.   5–024

---

[89] [1991] 1 W.L.R. 378, CA, at 379H-380A. The point was not argued since it does not appear that the respondents were called upon by the Court of Appeal to make submissions: see 384H.

[90] *Mira v. Aylmer Square Investments* (1990) 22 H.L.R. 182, CA.

[91] Especially where the tenant is reinstated.

[92] As amended by the Criminal Justice and Public Order Act 1994.

[93] S. 13(1). See the Forcible Entry Acts 1381, 1391, 1429, 1588 and 1623 summarised in 3 Bac. Abr. Tit. Forcible Entry and Detainer (7th ed.) p. 716. See *McPhail v. Persons Unknown* [1973] Ch. 447, CA.

[94] Compare *Henning v. Stoke Poges Golf Club* [1920] 1 K.B. 720, CA.

Meaning of "premises"

The definition of "premises" to which section 6 applies is found in section 12(1)(a) and is a wide one. Section 12(1)(a) provides an exclusive definition and contains four categories of "premises":

(1)   any building;

(2)   any part of a building under separate occupation[95];

(3)   any land ancillary to a building, which means land adjacent to that building and used (or intended for use) in connection with the occupation of that building or any part of it[96]; and

(4)   the site[97] comprising any building or buildings together with any land ancillary thereto.

"Building"

"Building" itself is partially defined by section 12(2) although it is an open-ended definition which is stated to "apply also" to the following (non-exclusive) categories:

(1)   any structure[98] other than a moveable one; and

(2)   any of the following provided they are designed or adapted[99] for use for residential purposes[1] —

(a)   any moveable structure;
(b)   any vehicle; or
(c)   any vessel.

Although the basic term "building" is not fully defined it is likely (apart from the extended meaning set out above) to be given its ordinary

---

[95] S. 12(2)(a).

[96] S. 12(2)(b).

[97] Note the use of site rather than the narrower "curtilage" which is often found used in connection with buildings: see *e.g. Methuen-Campbell v. Walters* [1979] Q.B. 525, CA, *Dyer v. Dorset County Council* [1989] 1 Q.B. 346, CA and s. 55(2)(d) of the Town and Country Planning Act 1990. This suggests that Parliament did not intend the concept of "site" to have the connotation of restricted size which attaches to "curtilage."

[98] See *e.g. Hobday v. Nichol* [1944] 1 All E.R. 302 at 304 ("anything which is constructed . . .") and *Perlman v. Harrow School Governors* [1979] 1 Q.B. 56, CA ("structural alteration or addition").

[99] It is not clear to what extent premises need to be "adapted" in order to satisfy this requirement. It may be that the mere installation of basic furniture, together with cooking and sanitary equipment will be sufficient: it is suggested that sufficient must be done in order to enable the premises to be used for residential purposes in a substantial sense.

[1] Note that the premises do not have to be in actual use for residential purposes provided they are designed or adapted for residential use.

meaning. It is suggested that "building" principally means[2] a reasonably substantial structure which is intended to last for a considerable period of time and which has both an interior and exterior.[3] Although decisions on the meaning of statutory provisions often only provide limited assistance, they can be helpful when they construe ordinary English words. In *Stevens v. Gourley*,[4] Byles J. considered the meaning of "building" in the Metropolitan Building Act, 18 & 19 Vict., c. 122:

> "What is a 'building'? Now the verb 'to build' is often used in a wider sense than the substantive 'building.' Thus, a ship or a barge builder is said to build a ship or barge, a coach-builder to build a carnage; so, birds are said to build nests; but neither of these when constructed can be a 'building.' It is a well-established rule, that the words of an Act of Parliament, like those of any other instrument, must if possible be construed according to their ordinary grammatical sense. The imperfection of the human language renders it not only difficult, but absolutely impossible, to define the word 'building' with any approach to accuracy. One may say of this or that structure, this or that is not a building; but no general definition can be given; and our lexicographers do not attempt it. Without, therefore, presuming to do what others have failed to do, I may venture to suggest, that, by 'a building' is usually understood to be a structure of considerable size, and intended to be permanent, or at least to endure for a considerable time. A church, whether constructed of iron or wood, undoubtedly is a building. So a 'cowhouse' or 'stable' has been held to be a building the occupation of which as tenant entitles the party to be registered as a voter . . . On the other hand, it is equally clear that a birdcage is not a building, neither is a wig-box, or a dog-kennel, or a hen-coop, — the very value of these things being their portability."

In *Brown v. Leicester Corporation*,[5] Pollock B. approach the question of "building" in a similar manner:

> "A small kennel for a lap dog could not be called a building. But it is a question of degree, and in this case we come to a structure 9 feet long, 7 feet high, 3 feet wide, erected some 30 feet in front of the line

---

[2] See, *e.g. Stevens v. Gourley* (1859) 7 C.B.N.S. 99; *Moir v. Williams* [1892] 1 Q.B. 264 at 270; *Long Eaton Recreation Grounds Co. v. Midland Railway Co.* [1902] 2 K.B. 574, CA.; *Nussey v. Provincial Bill Posting Co. and Eddison* [1909] 1 Ch. 738, CA.; *Buckingham County Council v. Callingham* [1951] 2 All E.R. 822, CA. at 738 and 742–3 (Fletcher Moulton L.J. dissenting) and *Cheshire County Council v. Woodward* [1962] 2 Q.B. 126. These cases all consider the meaning of "building" in a variety of contexts none of which are directly applicable but which may be of some assistance in interpreting the 1977 Act provisions.

[3] Otherwise an embankment might be a "building": see *Long Eaton Recreation Grounds Co. v. Midland Railway Co.* [1902] 2 K.B. 574. Note the extended meaning given to "building" which includes a "structure."

[4] (1859) 7 C.B.N.S. 99.

[5] (1892) 57 J.P. 70.

of the street, and roofed in and fastened securely to the ground, intended to be used by a person inside, and not easily carried away ... A structure like that may properly be called a building."

There are areas where the definition of "building" will cause difficulties: whilst a caravan, motorised mobile home, or houseboat may easily fall within the "moveable structure" category, a tent used for residential premises is unlikely to be considered a "structure".[6] Temporary structures constructed in trees by protestors[7] are unlikely to be regarded as "buildings" where they cannot be said to be designed or adapted for residential use. It is suggested that is unlikely that roughly constructed platforms can properly be said to be moveable structures "designed" or "adapted" for residential use[8] although it is possible that they might be regarded as "structures."

Defences

5–025   The offence cannot be committed if the person seeking to enter has lawful authority so to do: however, simply having an interest in the property, or a right to possess or occupy it does not constitute lawful authority.[9]

It is a defence for the person accused to show that at the time of the alleged offence he was, or was acting on behalf of, a "displaced residential occupier" or "protected intending occupier" of the premises in question.[10] It is for the accused to adduce evidence that he was such an occupier, or agent, but if he adduces "sufficient evidence" he is presumed to be, or be acting on behalf of, such an occupier unless the contrary is proved by the prosecution. This appears intended to create greater protection for "legitimate" occupiers by imposing only something in the nature of an evidential, or provisional, burden of proof on them to establish the defence and then shifting the burden to the prosecution to prove a negative, namely that they do not fall within such categories of person. This may be contrasted with the original form of section 6(3), now repealed and replaced by section 6(1A), which placed the burden squarely

---

[6] Unless, perhaps, it were an exceptionally substantial marquee with significant structural elements.

[7] See for example the instance on the M11–A12 Link Road protest in north-east London in November 1993 which centred on the Department of Transport's proposal to remove a tree on George Green, Wanstead. Although protestors sought to obtain an ex parte injunction to prevent disturbance of an alleged "treehouse" (relying on s. 6 of the 1977 Act) the issue was not resolved since the court subsequently abridged time for making a summary possession order under RSC, Order 113 (see Chap. 1) which was upheld by the Court of Appeal: *Secretary of State for Transport v. Thornton*, unreported, November 24, 1993.

[8] Rather, any nominal residential use simply disguises the real aim of design or adaptation to advance the protest.

[9] S. 6(2).

[10] S. 6(1A). The original version of the defences was contained in s. 6(3) which was repealed by s. 72(4) of the Criminal Justice and Public Order Act 1994. S. 6(1A) was introduced by s. 72(2) of that Act. See *R. v. Forest Justices ex p. Hartmann* [1991] Crim.L.R. 641.

on the accused to establish the defence on the balance of probabilities. The provision is unsatisfactory in that the concept of "sufficient" evidence to satisfy a provisional burden of proof which might be rebutted is not a clear one.

The "displaced residential occupier" appears to be related to the "residential occupier" of the Protection from Eviction Act 1977. Section 12(4) defines the "displaced residential occupier" as any person who was occupying any premises as a residence before they were excluded from the premises (or access to them) by a trespasser. Such a person remains a displaced occupier for as long as he is kept out of occupation by the trespasser, or any subsequent trespasser.[11] However, a trespasser who was occupying premises as his residence does not become a displaced residential occupier on removal.[12] The Act enlarges the common law definition of trespasser[13] by rendering anyone who enters property through a title or licence granted by a trespasser also a trespasser.[14] Further, a trespasser who is given time to leave the premises is still considered to be a trespasser, notwithstanding that he has been given an implied licence by being given time to leave.[15]

The concept of the "protected intending occupier" was originally found only in connection with the original version of section 7[16] but has been redefined by section 12A and applied to the amended forms of both sections 6 and 7. A "protected intending occupier" must be an individual which excludes corporate bodies.[17] There are 3 categories of "protected intending occupiers":

(1)   an occupier with a freehold interest, or leasehold interest with not less than two years of the term still to run, in the subject premises and —

     (a)   he requires those premises for his own occupation as a residence;

     (b)   he is excluded from occupation of the premises, or any access to them, by a person who entered them as a trespasser;

---

[11] S. 12(4).

[12] S. 12(4). The Act thus avoids clothing the ousted residential trespasser with the appearance of having a lawful claim to re-enter, and any displaced trespasser will not be able to rely on the defence of the displaced residential occupier if, having been ousted, he uses violence to secure re-entry in contravention of s. 6(1).

[13] On which see above, para. 1–001 and Chap. 1, generally.

[14] S. 12(6).

[15] S. 12(7).

[16] See the original forms of s. 7(2) and (4).

[17] S. 7(1)(b) and s. 12A(1) and (2). The language used in s. 12A(1) and (2) is not wholly clear, i.e. "an individual is a protected intending occupier . . ." but it appears likely that this will be construed as meaning that a protected intending occupier must be an individual although, if that were correct, the use of "individual" in s. 7(1)(b) would be redundant.

    (c)   he (or a person acting on his behalf) holds a written statement[18] which—

        (i)   specifies his interest in the premises;

        (ii) states that he requires the premises for occupation as a residence for himself;

        (iii) in respect of the statement[19] —

            (1) is signed by the person whose interest is specified in the statement in the presence of a justice of the peace or a commissioner for oaths; and

            (2) the justice or commissioner has subscribed his name as a witness to the signature.

(2)   the occupier has a tenancy of the subject premises (other than one falling within category (1), above, under section 12A(2)(a)) or a licence to occupy those premises granted by a person with a free-hold interest, or leasehold interest with not less than two years of the term still to run, in the premises[20] and —

    (a)   he requires those premises for his own occupation as a residence;

    (b)   he is excluded from occupation of the premises, or any access to them, by a person who entered them as a trespasser;

    (c)   he (or a person acting on his behalf) holds a written statement[21] which—

        (i)   states that he has been granted a tenancy of those premises or a licence to occupy those premises;

        (ii) specifies the interest in the premises of the person who granted that tenancy or licence to occupy;

        (iii) states that the occupier requires the premises for occupation as a residence for himself;

        (iv) in respect of the statement[22] —

            (1) it is signed by the landlord and by the tenant or licensee in the presence of a justice of the peace or a commissioner for oaths; and

            (2) the justice or commissioner has subscribed his name as a witness to the signatures.

(3)   the occupier has a tenancy of the subject premises (other than one falling in categories (1) and (2), above, under section 12A(2)(a) and (4)(a)) or a licence to occupy those premises granted by any body[23] mentioned in section 14 of the Rent Act 1977, the Housing Corpo-

---

[18] S. 12A(2)(d).
[19] S. 12A(2)(d) and (3).
[20] S. 12A(4).
[21] S. 12A(4)(d).
[22] S. 12A(4)(d)(iv) and 12A(5).
[23] S. 12A(6).

ration, Housing for Wales, or a registered housing association within the meaning of the Housing Associations Act 1985[24] and —

(a) he requires those premises for his own occupation as a residence;

(b) he is excluded from occupation of the premises, or any access to them, by a person who entered them as a trespasser;

(c) a certificate has been issued to the occupier by or on behalf of the authority referred to above[25] stating that —

   (i) he has been granted a tenancy of those premises or a licence to occupy those premises as a residence by that authority; and

   (ii) the authority which granted that tenancy or licence to occupy is one of those referred to above being of a description specified in the certificate.

The meaning of "premises" has already been considered in connection with the section 6 offences above.[26] "Access" is defined[27] as meaning in relation to any premises "any part of any site or building within which those premises are situated which constitutes an ordinary means of access to those premises (whether or not that is its sole or primary use)."

It is an offence to make a statement for the purposes of section 12A(2)(d) or (4)(d) which the maker knows to be false in a material particular or if he recklessly makes such a statement which is false in a material particular.[28]

Although section 12A(9) provides a defence in respect of a protected intending occupier arising from the failure to produce the statement of certificate referred to above this only applies to an offence under section 7 and not to section 6.[29]

Under section 7(2), such a person is the freeholder or a long lease-holder[30] who requires the premises for his own occupation as a residence, but is prevented from occupying or gaining access to those premises because of the occupation of the trespasser.

The offence can only be tried summarily. On conviction, the maximum penalty is either a fine not exceeding level 5 on the standard scale,[31] or six months imprisonment, or both. A compensation order may also be made against a convicted offender.[32]

---

[24] S. 12A(6)(a) and (7).

[25] S. 12(6)(d).

[26] S. 12(1)(a) and (2).

[27] S. 12(1)(b).

[28] S. 12A(8).

[29] Since the concept of the "protected intending occupier" is only used in s. 6 as part of a defence to an otherwise criminal entry.

[30] That is, the owner of a lease which has not less than 21 years to run.

[31] Currently £5,000. See s. 37(2) of the Criminal Justice Act 1982 as amended by s. 17 of the Criminal Justice Act 1991.

[32] Ss. 35–8 of the Powers of the Criminal Courts Act and s. 40 of the Magistrates' Courts Act 1980 (as amended by Sched. 4 to the Criminal Justice Act 1991.)

"Squatters' rights"

The term "squatters' rights" is often used in connection with this part of the Criminal Justice Act 1977 and is often misunderstood. In truth, the "rights" conferred by the Act are prohibitions on forcible entry (as set out above) and do not involve the conferring of any rights of occupation upon those trespassing. The Act does not prohibit all self-help remedies against trespassers but simply provides the forms of protection discussed above.

Adverse occupation of residential premises

5–026 Any person who is on premises as a trespasser after having entered as such is guilty of the offence created by section 7(1) if he fails to leave those premises when required to do so by either a "displaced residential occupier", an individual who is a "protected intending occupier", or someone acting on their behalf.[33] The maximum penalty for both the offences created by this section is either a fine not exceeding level 5 on the standard scale,[34] or six months imprisonment, or both.

The meaning of the terms "displaced residential occupier" and "protected intending occupier" have already been considered in connection with section 6, above.

There are a number of defences to liability under section 7 provided both by sections 7(3) and 12A(9):

(1) if the accused can prove that the premises are, or form part of, premises used mainly for non-residential purposes[35] and that he was not on any part of the premises used wholly or mainly for residential purposes;[36] or

(2) if the accused can prove that, although he requested to see the written statement under sections 12A(2)(d) or (4)(d), or (as the case may be) the certificate under section 12A(6)(d) at the time the accused was required to leave, the person claiming to be or acting on behalf of a "protected intending occupier" failed to produce the statement or certificate to the accused.[37] Note that any document purporting to be a certificate under section 12A(6)(d) should be received in evidence and be deemed to have been issued by or on behalf of the authority stated in the certificate

---

[33] S. 7(1) uses the phrase "by or on behalf of" which indicates the requirement to leave does not need to come directly from the occupier himself.

[34] S. 7(5).

[35] S. 7(3)(a).

[36] This corresponds to the defence formerly provided by the original provisions of s. 7(7) prior to amendment by the Criminal Justice and Public Order Act 1994.

[37] S. 12A(9)(a).

unless the contrary is proved.[38] This defence applies only to "protected intending occupiers."

Other offences

Section 8 of the Criminal Law Act 1977 also creates the offence of entering as a trespasser carrying a weapon of offence[39] without lawful excuse or authority. The maximum penalty for this offence is either a fine not exceeding level 5 on the standard scale,[40] or three months imprisonment, or both. Section 9 creates a further offence of trespassing on foreign diplomatic or consular premises, including such premises when closed, or the premises of certain international organisations. It is also an offence to trespass on the private residence of a diplomatic agent. It is a defence for the accused person to prove that he believed that premises were not premises to which the section applies.[41] This summary offence can only be prosecuted with the Attorney General's leave,[42] and the maximum penalty is either a fine not exceeding level 5 on the standard scale,[43] or six months imprisonment, or both.

5–027

Finally, section 10 makes it an offence to obstruct an officer of the court who is enforcing any judgment or order for the recovery of or the delivery up of land. The order must have been made under either of the procedures for recovery of land occupied solely by a person, other than a tenant holding over at the determination of a tenancy, who has entered into or remains in occupation of the premises without the consent or licence of the person claiming possession or his predecessors in title.[44] Liability can be avoided if the accused can prove that he believed the person he obstructed was not an officer of the court, and the maximum penalty is either a fine not exceeding level 5 on the standard scale,[45] or six months imprisonment, or both.

---

[38] S. 12A(9)(b), which corresponds to the defence formerly provided by the original provisions of s. 7(8) prior to amendment. Compare, *e.g.* the certificate provisions of para. 5(2) of Part IV of Sched. 15 to the Rent Act 1977 and para. 3(2) of Pt. II of Sched. 2 to the Housing Act 1988.

[39] S. 8(2) defines this as "any article made or adapted for use for causing injury to or incapacitating a person, or intended by the person having it with him for such use." This definition is the same as that in the s. 10(1)(b) of the Theft Act 1968.

[40] S. 32 of the Magistrates' Courts Act 1980 (as amended by s. 17 of the Criminal Justice Act 1991).

[41] S. 9(3).

[42] S. 9(6).

[43] Above.

[44] From October 1, 2001, the procedures set out in CPR 55 and 56 must be used. On these provisions see, further, above, Chap. 4, paras. 4–064 to 4–075.

[45] Above.

The Protection from Harassment Act 1997

The 1997 Act, while not relating specifically or exclusively to real property, provides direct remedies for landlords, tenants, licensors and licensees under both criminal and civil law. Two new criminal offences and a new sentencing power are created together with a civil entitlement for the claimant to an injunction and/or damages. The Act also extends the limitation period for bringing claims for personal injuries caused by acts of harassment from three years to six.[46] Section 32 of the Crime and Disorder Act 1998 increased sentencing powers for harassment offences found to have a racial motivation.

The offence and tort of harassment

Rather than attempting to suggest what will amount to harassment under the 1997 Act, the draughtsman defined the offence and tort by reference to its effect on the victim.[47] Section 1(1) states:

> "A person must not pursue a course of conduct—
> (a) which amounts to harassment of another, and
> (b) which he knows or ought to know amounts to harassment of the other."

A "course of conduct" involves at least two occasions[48] and "conduct" includes speech.[49] The mens rea may be assessed either subjectively or objectively, by reference to whether the reasonable person in possession of the same knowledge would have considered the defendant's course of conduct to amount to an act of harassment.[50] Section 1(3) sets out four courses of conduct to which s.1(1) does not apply:[51]

(a) those pursued for the purpose of preventing or detecting crime;[52]

(b) those pursued under any enactment or rule of law;[53]

---

[46] S. 6, amending the Limitation Act 1980.
[47] S. 7(2) states that harassment includes alarming a person or causing them distress.
[48] S. 7(3). In *Lau v. DPP* [2000] Crim. L.R. 580 and *Woolford v. DPP* (D.C.) May 9, 2000, CO/1072/00 it has been held that the further apart the incidents take place and the more indirect their means of delivery, the less likely it is that there has been a "course of conduct". The decision will be made on the facts of the case under consideration.
[49] S. 7(4), but not the giving of presents: *King v. DPP* (2000) *Independent*, July 31, 2000.
[50] S. 1(2).
[51] S. 12 also allows the Home Secretary to certify that specified persons on specified occasions were acting on behalf of the Crown in the interests of national security, *etc.*
[52] S. 1(3)(a).
[53] S. 1(3)(b).

(c)   those pursued to comply with any condition or requirement imposed by any person under any enactment;[54] and

(d)   those which are reasonable to pursue in the particular circumstances.[55]

The courts have so far been reluctant to interpret the Act widely, and have prevented its abuse where the alleged harassment has involved demonstration and protest on matters of public interest and was not deliberately provocative.[56]

The Offence

The offence is set out in section 2 of the Act but is framed entirely by reference to the elements and defences set out in section 1, above. The offence is summary only and is punishable by a fine not exceeding level 5 on the standard scale and/or six months imprisonment.

The court may also impose a restraining order on the defendant, prohibiting him, for a specific period or until a further order is made, from conduct which harasses the victim. The breach of a restraining order without reasonable excuse is itself an offence punishable on indictment by up to five years imprisonment, and/or a fine, or summarily by imprisonment for a term not exceeding six months and/or a fine not exceeding the statutory maximum.

The Tort

An actual or apprehended breach of section 1 may also be the subject of a claim for an injunction or damages, or both, under section 3 of the 1997 Act. The Act specifically allows damages for any anxiety and financial loss arising from the harassment.

The 1997 Act also provides a mechanism by which the victim of harassment is to police any breach of an injunction granted for his or her protection. The breach of an injunction without reasonable excuse constitutes a separate offence under the Act[57], which is not actionable in the usual way as a contempt of court[58]. In the event that this offence is committed, the victim may apply for a warrant for the arrest of the defendant[59], which

---

[54] S. 1(3)(b).
[55] S. 1(3)(c). In *DPP v. Selvanayagam* (1999) *The Times*, June 23, 1999, the appellant's co-defendants had been parties to an injunction attempting to prevent harassment in the course of protest at a Mink fur-farm. The Appellant knew of the injunction, but was unaware of its specific terms, and her conduct could therefore be considered reasonable.
[56] See *DPP v. Selvanayagam*, above, *Huntingdon Life Sciences Ltd v. Curtin* (1997) *The Times*, December 11, 1997 and *Redmond-Bate v. DPP* (1999) 163 J.P. 789.
[57] S. 3(6).
[58] S. 3(7). Where the defendant has already been punished for contempt of court, he cannot be convicted of the s. 3(6) offence.
[59] S. 3(3).

may only be issued if the application is substantiated on oath[60] and the judge has reasonable grounds for believing that the offence has been committed.[61]

The section 3(6) offence is punishable in the same way as the section 5(5) offence for the breach of a restraining order, as discussed above.

Putting people in fear of violence

The most serious offence under the 1997 Act is to pursue a course of conduct which puts another to fear, on at least two occasions,[62] that violence will be used against him.[63] The mens rea of the offence is identical to that for the offence of harassment, subject only to the changes to the actus reus.[64] Defences (a)–(c)[65] above are also identical, but the reasonableness defence (d) is only available where the course of conduct is reasonable for the protection of himself or another or for the protection of his or another's property.[66]

A convicted offender may be punished, on indictment, by up to five years imprisonment and/or by a fine, or summarily to up six months imprisonment and/or a fine not exceeding the statutory maximum.[67] A restraining order may also be imposed on an offender under section 4, any breach of which is a section 5(5) offence as set out above. Where a section 4 offence is tried on indictment, the jury may substitute a verdict that the defendant is guilty of harassment.[68]

The Caravan Sites Act 1968

5–028   Owners of caravans who station those caravans on sites belonging to others, or those who occupy caravans owned by others, do not enjoy the protection conferred by the Protection from Eviction Act 1977 but instead are specially protected by Part I of the Caravan Sites Act 1968.[69] Section 5(5) of the amended 1968 Act specifically excludes from the scope of the 1977 Act "any premises being a caravan stationed on a protected site". Part I of the 1968 Act introduced a similar, but separate, regime for protecting the occupiers of caravans stationed on "protected sites".

---

[60] S. 3(5)(a).
[61] S. 3(5)(b).
[62] The tautology is included in the framing of the section.
[63] S. 4(1).
[64] S. 4(1) and 4(2).
[65] S. 4(3)(a) and (b).
[66] S. 4(3)(c)
[67] S. 4(4).
[68] S. 4(5).
[69] Part I of the 1968 Act was not significantly affected by the amendments introduced by the Criminal Justice and Public Order Act 1994, below.

Scope of the Act

The scope of Part I of the Act is set out in section 1(1) which states that Part I applies to any licence or contract:[70] **5–029**

> "... under which a person is entitled to station a caravan on a protected site (as defined by sub-section (2) below) and occupy it as his residence, or to occupy as his residence a caravan stationed on any such site ..."

Part I applies not only to the person who occupies his own caravan on a protected site but also to the occupier[71] of a caravan stationed on a protected site and which belongs to the site owner.

Meaning of "protected sites"

"Protected site" is defined[72] as: **5–030**

> "... any land in respect of which a site licence is required under Part I of the Caravan Sites and Control of Development Act 1960 or would be so required if paragraph 11 of Schedule 1 to that Act (exemption of land occupied by local authorities) were omitted ..."

There is specifically excluded from the definition of "protected site" land where the relevant planning permission or site licence is expressed to be granted for holiday use only where there are terms which prohibit the stationing of a caravan on the land for human habitation for some times of the year.[73]

Part I of the Caravan Sites and Control of Development Act 1960, which sets out detailed provisions for licensing by local authorities,[74] prohibits an occupier of any land from causing or permitting any part of that land to be used as a caravan site unless he is the holder if a site licence then in force, *i.e.* a licence under Part I which authorises the use of the land as a caravan site.[75] The consequences of the absence of planning permission or a site licence on the application of Part I of the 1968 Act are considered below.

---

[70] Even if made before the passing of the Act.
[71] "Occupier" is defined by s. 1(3) as the person who, by virtue of an estate or interest in land held by him is entitled to possession of such land or would be so entitled but for the rights of any other person under licence granted in respect of that land.
[72] S. 1(2).
[73] S. 1(2)(a) and (b).
[74] S. 3–12 of that Act.
[75] S. 1(1). Contravention of this provision is a criminal offence: s. 1(2).

Meaning of "caravan"

5–031   For the purposes of the 1960 Act, "caravan" is defined as:

> ". . . any structure designed or adapted for human habitation which
> is capable of being moved from one place to another (whether by
> being towed, of being transported on a motor vehicle or trailer) and
> any motor vehicle so designed or adapted, but does not include —
> (a)   any railway rolling-stock which is for the time being on rails
> forming part of a railway system, or
> (b)   any tent . . ."

This definition is incorporated into the 1968 Act so that "caravan" has the
same meaning in both Acts.

Absence of site licence or planning permission

5–032   In cases where the site on which the caravan is stationed does not enjoy
the benefit of a current licence under the 1960 Act the question arises
whether such a site is a "protected site" within the 1968 Act. There are
strong arguments for the proposition that a site must enjoy a licence (and
have planning permission for use as a caravan site) in order to be a "protected site": these include the undesirability of granting security of tenure
to a caravan occupier in breach of planning and licensing law which regulates the use of land in the public interest. If the site were nonetheless a
"protected site", and did not need planning permission, enforcement
action could be taken against it by the local planning authority to require
the removal of the caravans, and yet the occupier would be protected
from eviction.[76]

Further, section 1(2) of the 1968 Act clearly contemplates the existence
of a planning permission and/or site licence — an argument that the
phrase "a site licence is required" did not mean that a licence had to
be in existence was decisively rejected by the Court of Appeal on two
occasions.[77] In *Balthasar v. Mullane*,[78] Glidewell L.J. said:

---

[76] This distinction would now seem particularly odd since the amended form of s. 178 of the
Town and Country Planning Act 1990 enables a local planning authority to enter land
specifically for the purposes of ensuring compliance with the provisions of an enforcement notice which includes the removal of caravans and the forced discontinuance of use
of the land as a caravan site. Further, an injunction may be obtained by a local planning
authority under s. 187B of that Act to achieve the same effect. Compare the previous position in *Doncaster BC v. Green* [1992] 2 P.L.R. 58, CA.

[77] *Balthasar v. Mullane* [1985] 2 E.G.L.R. 260, CA and *Adams v. Watkins* [1990] 2 E.G.L.R. 185,
CA. An earlier contrary decision of the Divisional Court in *Hooper v. Eaglestone* (1977) 34
P. & C.R. 311 was not cited in *Balthasar* and not followed in *Adams*. Only *Hooper* was a case
under the 1968 Act, whereas the others were concerned with the Mobile Homes Act 1983.
However, since the definition of "protected site" under s. 5 of the 1983 Act directly incorporates the 1968 Act, it appears that the reasoning in the later decisions should apply to
the 1968 Act.

[78] [1985] 2 E.G.L.R. 260, CA. at 263.

"I cannot believe that Parliament intended to bring about a situation in which the owners of land could be subjected to an enforcement notice requiring them to remove a caravan on the land and yet be unable to remove the caravan to comply with the notice, thus being at risk of committing a criminal offence because persons residing in the caravan had the protection of the Mobile Homes Act. In my judgment, the meaning of a protected site in section 1(2) of the Caravan Sites Act 1968 involves the site being one in respect of which planning permission has been granted for the stationing of one or more caravans. If planning permission has not been granted, then the site is not a protected site within the meaning of the Act . . ."

Although this decision may fail to protect the innocent caravan occupier from an unscrupulous land owner who lets or licenses pitches on caravan sites without the requisite site licence or planning permission, the public policy reasons set out by Glidewell L.J. in *Balthasar* are compelling.[79] Indeed, that reasoning was adopted and followed by the Court of Appeal in *Adams v. Watkins*[80] where Mustill L.J. stated:

". . . although it certainly does seem strange that an occupier is in a worse position as regards eviction if his landlord is law-abiding than if he is not, it is well possible that, as Sir Michael Kerr has suggested in argument, the Legislature has deliberately chosen to place the interests of the community ahead of those of the individual occupier — a view which is consonant with section 4(3) of the 1968 Act, to which I have already referred."

A more difficult situation arises where the occupier of the caravan has been allowed into occupation, or to station his caravan, on a site in respect of which a valid site licence and planning permission existed at the time the agreement was entered into but subsequently lapses. In the *Adams* case, the planning permission and the site licence were both subject to a condition that the use of the land as a caravan site should be discontinued in 1977: the Court of Appeal held that, notwithstanding the initial grant of permission and site licence, the site was not a "protected site". The conclusion of the Court is supported by section 4(6) which provides generally for the suspension of an order for possession but states that:

"Where a site licence in respect of the site is expressed to expire at the end of a specified period, the period for which the enforcement may be suspended by virtue of this section shall not extend beyond the expiration of the licence."

---

[79] Indeed, the previous inconsistent decision of the Divisional Court in *Hooper v. Eaglestone*, above, did not consider the planning enforcement aspects of site licensing.
[80] [1990] 2 E.G.L.R. 185, CA.

Preconditions to recovery of possession

5–033   Where Part I of the Act does apply, then a residential contract[81] is determinable by notice. In order to have effect that notice must be given[82] not less than four weeks before the date on which it is to take effect. As is generally the case with residential premises under the Protection from Eviction Act 1977 the landlord of a caravan site may only seek to recover possession by means of court[83] proceedings.[84] The term "recover possession" does not appear in section 3(1)(b). The expression actually used is "enforcement of any right to exclude the occupier from the protected site or from any such caravan[85] or to remove or exclude any such caravan from the site."

Where a court is asked to make a possession order following the expiration or determination of a residential contract, the court has general powers to postpone the operation or suspend the execution of a possession order provided that such a period does not exceed 12 months from the date of the making of the order.[86] Whether the court suspends or postpones the suspension order and the length of such suspension or postponement, depends on what the court considers to be reasonable.[87] If the court decides to postpone or suspend the order, it may impose such terms as it thinks reasonable including conditions as to the payment of rent or other periodical payments or of arrears.[88] Further, it has power subsequently to vary the terms of the order and any suspension, again providing that the suspension does not exceed the 12 months maximum period.[89]

Whereas the courts' discretion under the Rent Act 1977 is broad and general, the court is specifically directed by the 1968 Act as follows:[90]

---

[81]   *i.e.* such licence or contract as is referred to in s. 1(1).

[82]   It appears that a notice is "given" when it is received, *i.e.* the time runs from the time when the notice actually reaches the intended recipient: see *Sun Alliance and London Assurance Co. Ltd v. Hayman* [1975] 1 W.L.R. 177, CA, — on the meaning of "given" under s. 25 of the Landlord and Tenant Act 1954. *Crate v. Miller* [1947] K.B. 946, CA and *Schnabel v. Allard* [1967] 1 Q.B. 627, CA.

[83]   The "Court" for the purposes of Part I of the Act means the County Court: s. 5(1).

[84]   Otherwise he will be committing a criminal offence: see s. 3 of the 1968 Act.

[85]   *i.e.* one which the occupier is entitled by the contract to station and occupy, or to occupy, as his residence on the protected site: s. 3(1)(a). This accordingly includes exclusion from either the occupier's own caravan or from one which he has occupied by agreement with the site owner.

[86]   S. 4(1).

[87]   On the requirement of "reasonableness" in the context of s. 100 of the Rent Act 1977 see *Megarry on the Rent Acts* (11th ed.), Vol. 1, pp. 387–393 and *Rhodes v. Cornford* [1947] 2 All E.R. 601, CA. The general approach must be that the court should take into account all circumstances which are relevant at the date of the hearing and which affect the interests of the landlord and/or the tenant, acting in a judicial manner with regard to the scheme and purpose of the relevant legislation. These case specific considerations are reinforced by the requirements of the Human Rights Act 1998 and, in particular, Article 8 of the ECHR. See *London Borough of Lambeth v. Howard* (2001) 33 H.L.R. 58, CA, considered above at 1–127 to 1–135 and 5–002.

[88]   S. 4(2).

[89]   S. 4(3).

[90]   S. 4(4).

"In considering whether or how to exercise its powers under this section, the court shall have regard to all the circumstances, and in particular to the questions—

(a) whether the occupier of the caravan site has failed, whether before or after the expiration or determination of the relevant residential contract, to observe any terms or conditions of that contract, any conditions of the site licence, or any reasonable rules made by the owner for the management and conduct of the site or the maintenance of caravans thereon;

(b) whether the occupier has unreasonably refused an offer by the owner to renew the residential contract or make another such contract for a reasonable period and on reasonable terms;

(c) whether the occupier has failed to make reasonable efforts to obtain elsewhere other suitable accommodation for his caravan (or, as the case may be, another suitable caravan and accommodation for it)."

It is implicit in this that the court may well refuse to suspend the order for possession, or suspend it only for a short period, if the occupier has acted in breach of his residential contract or has breached any of the conditions of the site licence. Sub-paragraph (b) suggests that the owner of a protected site has some statutory support in terminating the residential contract with the aim of obtaining more favourable terms, or moving the occupier within the site, since the court is required to have regard to the question of whether the occupier has been offered alternative terms. Of course, the court is not obliged to have regard to such terms unless they are reasonable and have been unreasonably refused and even then the landlord is not automatically entitled to possession within a short time.

A further privilege is accorded to the occupier since, where the court suspends the enforcement of the possession order sought under the Act, the normal rule is that there should be no order for costs unless the court (having regard to the conduct of the owner or of the occupier) considers there are special reasons for making such a costs order.[91] The only situations where the court may not suspend an order are:

(1) for a period beyond a maximum period of 12 months from the date of the order;[92]

(2) where the proceedings are taken by a local authority within the meaning of section 24 of the 1960 Act;[93]

(3) where no site licence under Part I of the 1960 Act is in force in respect of the site;[94] and

[91] S. 4(5).
[92] S. 4(1).
[93] S. 4(6).
[94] S. 4(6)(b).

(4)   where the site licence in respect of the site is expressed to expire at the end of a specified period, beyond the date set for the expiration of the licence.[95]

Remedies

5–034   Apart from the criminal aspects of Part I, which are considered in the next section, the following remedies appear to be available to the unlawfully evicted or harassed occupier of a protected site:

(1)   an injunction which requires the owner to re-admit the occupier back into the caravan or to allow him to restation the caravan on the protected site;[96] and

(2)   in the event that the licence or contract has been breached by the site owner, damages for breach of agreement (including possibly aggravated or exemplary damages[97]).

While it seems unusual, as a matter of public policy, to exclude caravan owners from a right to damages under sections 27 & 28 of the Housing Act 1988, this is the logical consequence of the use of a definition of "residential occupier" in the 1988 Act which is taken from the 1977 Act but is not extended to include those tenants covered by the 1968 Act. See above, paragraph 5–007.

Offences

5–035   Section 3 of the Act creates a number of criminal offences to protect occupiers of caravans against unlawful eviction and harassment by the owners of "protected sites". It follows from the decisions in *Balthasar v. Mullane*[98] and *Adams v. Watkins*[99] that no offence is committed under section 3 where a person evicts an occupier, or harasses him, if the site is not a protected site. Further section 3 does not apply to the exercise by any person of a right to take possession of a caravan of which he is the owner (other than where the right is conferred by or arises on the expiration or determination of a residential contract) or to anything done pursuant to the order of any court.[1] The offences comprise the commission by "a person"[2] of the following:

---

[95]   S. 4(6).
[96]   Such an injunction could be sought either in support of the contractual right to occupy the caravan (from which the site owner has derogated) or in support of the statutory right in s. 3(1)(b) not to be evicted without court order.
[97]   See above, paras. 4–023 to 4–030.
[98]   [1985] 2 E.G.L.R. 260.
[99]   [1990] 2 E.G.L.R. 185.
[1]   S. 3(5).
[2]   S. 3(1). Note that the offences may be committed by persons other than the landowner: compare the offences under the Protection from Eviction Act 1977, above, paras. 5–011 to 5–017.

(1)   during the subsistence of the contract,[3] unlawfully depriving[4] the occupier of his occupation on the protected site of any caravan which the occupier is entitled by the contract to station and occupy, or to occupy, as his residence on that site;[5] or

(2)   the enforcement, otherwise than by court proceedings, of any right to exclude the occupier from the protected site or from any such caravan, or to remove or exclude any such caravan from the site;[6] or

(3)   during the subsistence of the contract or after its expiration or determination,[7] the doing of acts calculated to interfere with the peace or comfort of the occupier or persons residing with him, or the persistent[8] withdrawal or withholding of services or facilities reasonably required for the occupation of the caravan as a residence on the site. Such acts or omissions must have been carried out with intent to cause the occupier either —

   (a)   to abandon the occupation of the caravan or remove it from the site; or
   (b)   to refrain from exercising any right or pursuing any remedy in respect thereof.

A person guilty of an offence under section 3 is punishable summarily by fine not exceeding level 5 of the standard scale or by imprisonment for a term not exceeding six months, or both.

"Occupier" is defined widely[9] to include the person who was the occupier under a residential contract which has expired or been determined. Where the occupier has died (before or after the expiration or determination of the contract), the definition of "occupier" includes the surviving spouse[10] if residing with the occupier at the date of his death or (in default of the spouse having so resided) any member of the deceased occupier's family[11] if residing with the occupier at the date of his death.[12]

---

[3] Contrast the wording of s. 3(1)(c). It appears that there is no offence under s. 3(1)(a) if there is deprivation of occupation, *etc.*, after the expiry of the contract.
[4] See *R. v. Yuthiwattana* (1984) 16 H.L.R. 49, CA, *Costelloe v. London Borough of Camden* [1986] Crim.L.R. 249 and the discussion of the similar words in the Protection from Eviction Act 1977 above, para. 5–010.
[5] S. 3(1)(a).
[6] S. 3(1)(b).
[7] Contrast s. 3(1)(a), above.
[8] See *R. v. Abrol* [1972] Crim.L.R. 318, CA, *Hooper v. Eaglestone* (1977) 34 P. & C.R. 311, DC, and the discussion of "persistence" in connection with s. 1 of the Protection from Eviction Act 1977 above, para. 5–013.
[9] S. 3(2).
[10] S. 3(2)(a).
[11] This is not defined. See s. 5 of the Mobile Homes Act 1983 and, *e.g. Dyson Holdings Ltd. v. Fox* [1976] Q.B. 503 (a Rent Act case).
[12] S. 3(2)(b).

It is a defence to any of the offences under section 3 if the accused can prove that he believed, and had reasonable cause to believe, that the occupier of the caravan had ceased to reside on the site.[13]

The Family Law Act 1996

5–036   Part IV of the Family Law Act 1996 replaced and restructured the scope of protection given to spouses and former spouses under the Matrimonial Homes Act 1983. Spouses who have no property rights in the matrimonial home are given a statutory licence to remain there subject to a court order.[14] If one spouse has a beneficial interest in the property, the other spouse's rights of occupation take effect as a charge on the property, capable of protection under the Land Registration Act 1925, or the Land Charges Act 1972, as appropriate.[15]

The Access to Neighbouring Land Act 1992: section 6(2)

5–037   The terms of this Act are considered briefly in Chapter One.[16] If the applicant who has obtained an access order from the court contravenes the order or fails to comply with its terms and conditions, the court may "without prejudice to any other remedy available, make an order for the payment of damages." Liability rests with "any person" breaching the terms of the order and damages may be awarded in favour of "any other person affected" by the breach of the order who makes an application under section 6(2).

The terms of the court's jurisdiction appear not to exclude any common law remedy since the power to award damages is expressed to be without prejudice to other remedies. It appears that if the applicant or his associates act in contravention of the order, they have exceeded their right to enter the servient land and the ordinary principles of trespass will thereupon apply. Where there is a breach of the access order, the respondent (or other person affected) will be able to obtain an injunction if the ordinary preconditions for the grant of an injunction are met.

The basis of assessment of damages under section 6(2) is unclear: they could be restricted only to such damage or loss as flows from the contravention of the order, or they may be assessed simply on the ordinary basis of damages for trespass. To the extent that section 6(2) damages prove to be narrower than trespass damages, if the contravention of the order means that the applicant has become a trespasser, there appears no reason

---

[13] S. 3(4) and *R. v. Carr-Briant* [1943] K.B. 607. Compare s. 27(8)(a) of the Housing Act 1988.
[14] S. 30.
[15] S. 31, and see the Land Registration (Matrimonial Home Rights) Rules 1997 (S.I. 1997 No. 1964)
[16] See above, para. 1–090.

why the person affected should not also recover damages at common law — although there should not be double recovery for the same loss. Some basis for restricting damages under section 6(2) only to losses flowing directly from the breach of the order may be found in the fact that the court already has power to require the payment of consideration for the privilege of entry[17] and to impose a condition requiring the payment of compensation for disturbance[18] when making the order.

The Party Wall etc Act 1996

The Party Wall etc Act 1996 makes provision for the owner of a party wall to commence works on that wall with or without the consent of the adjoining landowner. The Act was designed to dovetail with the Access to Neighbouring Land Act 1992, and there is little overlap between them in practice. The Act gives a building owner whose land includes a party wall the right to gain access to and undertake works on that wall, and to recoup a share of the cost from the wall's co-owner. The Act also gives rights to the co-owner of the party wall affected. Three means of protection are provided by section 7:

(a)   The building owner must not cause his co-owner any "unnecessary inconvenience" in the exercise of his rights under the Act;[19]

(b)   The building owner must compensate his co-owner for any loss or damage resulting from the works executed;[20]

(c)   The building owner must afford protection to the building and security of the co-owner by erecting temporary structures if necessary;[21]

Other forms of protection for the co-owners of party walls are provided elsewhere in the Act:

(d)   Where a party wall has been laid open,[22] the building owner must pay a fair allowance to the co-owner in respect of any disturbance and inconvenience caused;[23]

(e)   Where a building owner is required to make good any damage caused by his works,[24] the co-owner can require the expenses be

[17] S. 2(5)–(8) of the Act.
[18] S. 2(4) of the Act.
[19] S. 7(1).
[20] S. 7(2).
[21] S. 7(3).
[22] Under s. 2(2) of the Act.
[23] S. 11(6).
[24] For certain works in s. 2(2).

assessed[25] and paid in lieu of payment for the works done to the party wall.[26]

Indirect forms of protection are provided by the Act, such as obligations that all works should comply with the provisions of other statutory requirements and in accordance with any agreed plans.[27] Any failure by the building owner to meet these conditions will be actionable as breaches of statutory duty. Where rights of entry are exceeded, these will be actionable under the law of trespass; likewise, careless work and other damages outside the scope of the provisions set out above will be actionable under the law of negligence.

The Animals Act 1971

5–038   The common law position with regard to trespassing animals is summarised in Chapter One, above.[28] The Act abolished some of the more ancient common law actions (such as cattle trespass) but certain common law liabilities still exist. Although a detailed commentary on the law of animals is outside the scope of this work,[29] the general scheme of the Act is as follows:

(1)   section 2(1) imposes a form of strict liability on the keeper of an animal which belongs to a "dangerous species"[30] if that animal causes damage;

(2)   section 2(2) also imposes strict liability on the keepers of animals of non-dangerous species if:

(a)   such an animal causes damage which is of the kind which the animal, unless restrained, was likely to cause or, if caused by that animal, was likely to be severe; and

(b)   the likelihood of the damage or of its being severe was due to characteristics of the animal which are not normally found in animals of the same species or are not normally to be found except at particular times or in particular circumstances;[31] and

(c)   those characteristics were known to the keeper or were at any time known to a person who at that time had charge of the animal as the keeper's servant or, where the keeper is the

---

[25] By procedures set out in s. 10.

[26] S. 11(8).

[27] S. 7(5).

[28] See above, paras. 1–053 to 1–054.

[29] See P.M. North, *The Modern Law of Animals* (1972), *Halsbury's Laws*, Vol. 2, paras. 429–438 and *Clerk & Lindsell on Torts* (18th ed.), Chap. 21.

[30] "Dangerous species" is defined by s. 5(2) and s. 11 of the 1971 Act.

[31] See *Cummings v. Grainger* [1977] Q.B. 397; *Wallace v. Newton* [19821 1 W.L.R. 375, *Curtis v. Betts* [1990] 1 W.L.R. 459 and *Flack v. Hudson* [2001] 2 W.L.R. 982.

head of a household, were known to another keeper of the animal who is a member of that household and under the age of 16;

(3) strict liability for the behaviour of dogs is imposed by section 3;

(4) section 4, which replaced the old action for cattle trespass now provides a form of strict liability for straying livestock generally. "Livestock" is defined by section 11 to include most animals in ordinary farm use including fowl and deer which are not in the wild state but does not include, for example, rabbits and bees.[32] An action under section 4 lies not only in favour of a person in possession of the land but also of owners or occupiers and makes recoverable not only damages for harm caused "to the land or any property on it"[33] but also the expenses of keeping the livestock while it cannot be restored to its owner or which is being detained under section 7;

(5) section 7 creates a procedure for the detention of animals which are found causing damage by a landowner on his land.[34] The animal may be detained for no more than 48 hours unless the landowner has given notice to the police and to the animal's owner if his identity is known. During the period of detention, the detaining landowner is obliged to feed and treat the animal with reasonable care.[35] If the animal's owner tenders sufficient compensation, or if none is due under section 4 and the animal is claimed by the person entitled to possession of it, the animal must be returned. If the animal is lawfully detained for 14 days, then the landowner detaining may sell it[36] by public auction or in a market and there is a requirement to account for the proceeds of sale;[37] and

(6) section 8 makes provision for animals straying onto the highway.

Defences

The 1971 Act creates a number of defences for the possessor of the offending livestock:

---

[32] Note that at common law, bees foraging for nectar are not to be regarded as trespassers: *Tutton v. A.D. Walter Ltd.* [1986] Q.B. 61.

[33] This appears to exclude the possibility of recovering damages for purely financial loss, *i.e.* to be recoverable losses must be consequent on physical damage to the land or property on it.

[34] The right to follow this procedure takes the place of the old right of distress damage feasant for animals, which has been abolished: s. 7(1).

[35] S. 7(6).

[36] S. 7(4).

[37] S. 7(5).

(a)   where the damage is wholly attributable to the fault of the person suffering it (applicable to sections 2 to 4),[38] subject to the failure to fence at (f) below;

(b)   where the person suffering the damage has voluntarily accepted the risk thereof (section 2 liability only);[39]

(c)   there is no liability for damage caused by an animal kept on any premises or structure to a person trespassing there provided that the animal was not kept there for the protection of the property or, if the animal were kept for the protection of persons or property, that the keeping for such purpose was not unreasonable (section 2 liability only);[40]

(d)   under section 3, where the dog belonged to the occupier or its presence was authorised by the occupier;[41]

(e)   where the presence of an animal straying from the highway was a lawful use of the highway (section 4 liability only);[42]

(f)   where the damage could have been prevented by fencing — although in determining whether liability is excluded under section 5(1) (see (a), above) the damage is not regarded as due to the fault of the person suffering damage by reason only of a failure to fence;[43] and

(g)   contributory negligence.[44]

Part III of the Environmental Protection Act 1990 — Statutory Nuisance

Introduction

5–039   By comparison with other areas of the common law, statute law has had relatively little impact on the law of nuisance. Parliament's greatest intervention has come with the concept of "statutory nuisance", which derives from the law of public health and housing[45]. For much of the post-war period, the controlling statute was the Public Health Act 1936, sections 91 to 100, later supplemented by the Public Health (Recurring Nuisances) Act 1969 and the Control of Pollution Act 1974, sections 58 to 59. Since January 1, 1991, those provisions have been replaced by the Environmental

---

[38] S. 5(1).
[39] S. 5(2).
[40] S. 5(3).
[41] S. 5(4).
[42] S. 5(5).
[43] S. 5(6).
[44] S. 10 which applies the Law Reform (Contributory Negligence) Act 1945.
[45] See, generally, McCracken, Jones, Pereira & Payne, *Statutory Nuisance* (2001).

Protection Act 1990, Part III,[46] as amended by the Noise and Statutory Nuisances Act 1993[47] and the Environment Act 1995. Local authority powers and duties under this legislation is also reinforced to some extent by the positive duty which may arise under Article 8 of the ECHR applied through sections 6 and 7 of the Human Rights Act 1998[48].

To be a "statutory nuisance" as defined by the Environmental Protection Act 1990, any given premises must be:

(1) in such a state as to be prejudicial to health or a nuisance;[49]

(2) emitting smoke, so as to be prejudicial to health or a nuisance;[50]

(3) emitting fumes or gas, so as to be prejudicial to health or a nuisance;[51]

(4) a source of dust, steam, smell or other effluvia arising on industrial, trade or business premises which are prejudicial to health or a nuisance;[52]

(5) upon which there is any accumulation or deposit which is prejudicial to health or is a nuisance;[53]

(6) upon which is kept any animal, in such a manner, or by reason of the nature of the premises, as is prejudicial to health or a nuisance;[54]

(7) emitting noise so as to be prejudicial to health or a nuisance,[55] including noise emitted from or caused by a vehicle, machinery or equipment in the street;[56] or

(8) in any other state as statute may declare to be a statutory nuisance.[57]

These categories are largely derived from section 91 of the Public Health Act 1936 and from sections 58 and 59 of the Control of Pollution Act 1974. Cases concerning these Acts remain useful guides to the construction of

---

[46] S. 164(2) of the Environmental Protection Act 1990. The Act came into force two months after it received the Royal Assent on November 1, 1990.

[47] Which came into force on January 5, 1994, two months after receiving the Royal Assent.

[48] See, generally, Grosz, Beatson & Duffy, *Human Rights* pp. 265–291 and Clayton & Tomlinson, *The Law of Human Rights*, Chapter 12, *Lopez Ostra v. Spain* (1994) 20 E.H.R.R. 277, *Guerra v. Italy* (1998) 26 E.H.R.R. 357, *R. (on the application of Vetterlien) v. Hampshire County Council* [2001] EWHC Admin. 560 and *Hatton v. United Kingdom*, (2002) 34 E.H.R.R. 1 2001 (which has been accepted for re-hearing by the Grand Chamber).

[49] S. 79(1)(a).

[50] S. 79(1)(b).

[51] S. 79(1)(c).

[52] S. 79(1)(d).

[53] S. 79(1)(e).

[54] S. 79(1)(f).

[55] S. 79(1)(g).

[56] S. 79(ga).

[57] S. 79(1)(h).

the current legislation, since many of the concepts have been carried through into the 1990 Act (although in modified form). Land which is in a "contaminated state" by reason of harmful or potentially harmful substances in or under land are not statutory nuisances within Part III.[58] Special provision for "contaminated land"[59] is now contained in Part IIA of the 1990 Act which contains it own procedures for remedial action and enforcement.

Scope of Part III

5–040   Section 79 of the 1990 Act is wide in scope. It applies to all land,[60] which by operation of the Interpretation Act 1980, includes buildings and other structures, land covered by water, any estate, interest, easement or servitude over land.[61] It also applies to any vessel, except one powered by steam reciprocating machinery.[62] "Premises" also includes caves,[63] ponds, pools, ditches, gutters or watercourses[64] and all tents, vans, sheds and similar structures used for human habitation.[65] Public sewers and sewage disposal works are not, however, within the scope of the Act.[66]

---

[58] S. 79(1A) and (1B), inserted by para. 89 of Sched. 22 to the Environment Act 1995. "Harm" and "substance" are defined by ss. 78A and 78B in Part IIA of the 1990 Act. Part IIA of the 1990 Act (which comprises ss. 78A to 78YC) was inserted by s. 57 of the Environment Act 1995.

[59] Defined by s. 78A(2) of the 1990 Act as land which appears to the appropriate local authority to be in such a condition (by reason of the substances in or under the land) that "(a) significant harm is being caused or there is a significant possibility of such harm being caused" or "(b) pollution of controlled waters is being, or is likely to be, caused . . ." The resolution of these issues is to be in accordance with s. 78A(5) and guidance issued by the Secretary of State for the Environment pursuant to s. 78YA. At the date of writing, no such guidance had been issued.

[60] S. 79(7).

[61] Interpretation Act 1980, s. 5 and Sched. 1.

[62] S. 79(7) and (12). See *West Mersea Urban District Council v. Fraser* [1950] 2 K.B. 119, under the Public Health Act 1936, for an example involving a houseboat.

[63] *Gardiner v. Sevenoaks District Council* [1950] W.N. 260. The case turned on whether a cave used to store cinema films were "premises" within the meaning of s. 1 of the Celluloid and Cinematograph Films Act 1922. The cave in question was sealed by a door: Lord Goddard C.J. observed, *obiter*, that an open cave might not be "premises".

[64] S. 259(1) of the Public Health Act 1936.

[65] S. 268 of the Public Health Act 1936, amended, but not repealed, by the Environmental Protection Act 1990.

[66] *R. v. Parlby* (1889) 22 Q.B.D. 520; *Fulham Vestry v. London County Council* [1897] 2 Q.B. 76. The basis of the former decision seems to be that, as sewage works were almost inevitably going to be a source of nuisance, yet at the same time were not only necessary but their provision was required by statute, Parliament could not have intended them to fall within the scope of the Act. This seems to be a precursor to the argument in *Allen v. Gulf Oil* [1981] A.C. 1001. The *Fulham Vestry* case turns on a jurisdictional point, namely that Parliament could not have intended "the construction of great public works" such as sewers built by a local authority to be subject to scrutiny by "magistrates sitting as petty sessions". It is submitted that this view is probably incorrect, unless a purported prosecution under the Act were to amount to judicial review of a statutory body's decision.

"Prejudicial to health or a nuisance"

This phrase is the key test for whether a statutory nuisance has arisen. The **5–041** test comprises two separate limbs: it is not necessary to show that premises are both in a state prejudicial to health and a nuisance. The effect of this distinction was clearly explained by Stephen J. in *Bishop Auckland Local Board v. Bishop Auckland Iron and Steel Co. Ltd*[67] a case on section 91 of the Public Health Act 1875. That section used the phrase "nuisance or injurious to health", but the following dicta of Stephen J. were expressly approved as applicable to the 1936 Act by Lord Wilberforce in *Salford City Council v. McNally*:[68]

> "... the words 'nuisance or injurious to health' do not mean 'nuisance injurious to health.' That is obviously not their natural meaning, and I object, unless compelled to give words a meaning which is different from their obvious natural one.
> ... The natural sense of the words seems to me the best one to apply in the present case, *i.e.* a nuisance either interfering with personal comfort or injurious to health; for instance, a man may catch typhoid fever or diphtheria without being exposed to a nuisance. On the other hand, many persons at one time believed that tanners' yards and other places where strong, disagreeable smells prevailed, were beneficial to health in some cases. I think the legislature intended to strike at those sorts of cases, *i.e.* at anything which would diminish the comfort of life though not injurious to health, and anything which would in fact injure health."

Accordingly, it is also unnecessary to prove that any given nuisance is prejudicial to health.[69]

To be "prejudicial to health", a situation must be "injurious or likely to cause injury to health".[70] Premises likely to attract vermin which might, in turn, cause or spread disease can be prejudicial to health.[71] An accumulation of inert material, such as builders' rubble, scrap iron and broken glass, which would not of itself be harmful unless walked upon by someone entering the land was not "prejudicial to health".[72] Inadequate sound

---

[67] (1882) 10 Q.B.D. 138, 141.
[68] [1976] A.C. 379, HL, at 389E.
[69] See also *Great Western Railway Co. v. Bishop* (1872) L.R. 7 Q.B. 550, also per Stephen J. That case concerned s. 8 of the Nuisances Removal Act 1855. The dicta of Cockburn C.J. in the *Great Western* case were applied to s. 91 of the Public Health Act 1936, in *Coventry City Council v. Cartwright* [1975] 1 W.L.R. 845, by Lord Widgery C.J. at p. 849B, semble in accordance with a concession by counsel.
[70] S. 79(7) of the Environmental Protection Act 1979. The test is objective: is the situation one which is prejudicial to health? See *Cunningham v. Birmingham City Council* [1998] Env. L.R. 1.
[71] *Coventry City Council v. Cartwright* [1975] 1 W.L.R. 845 (albeit strictly obiter).
[72] S. 79 aims to prevent the risk of ill health, not the risk of physical injury: *R. v. Bristol City Council ex parte Everett* [1999] Env. L.R. 587. The landowner might well be liable to

insulation of a dwelling-house near to road or rail traffic can also make premises "prejudicial to health",[73] as can penetration by damp from outside.[74] The layout of premises may, of itself, be "prejudicial to health".[75] There is a degree of overlap with the test for whether premises are, "unfit for human habitation", under the Housing Act 1985, section 189, but the two statutory codes are not to be treated as either complementary or coterminous.[76]

To be a "nuisance", premises must be in such a state as to constitute a nuisance at common law, either as a public or private nuisance.[77] This is in contrast to the earlier approach of the Courts, which was to give "nuisance" its widest sense, rather than its technical sense.[78] A detailed examination of the law of private nuisance has already been undertaken in Chapter 2, and need not be summarised here. It has been decided under the Public Health Act 1875 that the nuisance complained of must be one connected in some way to public health matters or possibly the permanent comfort of the complainant.[79] Although this decision has been approved, there is little modern authority expressly supporting this contention.[80] However, it should be noted that the following have been specifically decided as not constituting a "nuisance" within the meaning of the 1936 and 1990 Acts: defective windows and gutters causing discomfort to the occupier,[81] and dirty, stained and peeling walls in a

any person injured while on the premises by reason of the Occupiers' Liability Act 1957 and Occupiers' Liability Act 1984.

[73] *London Borough of Southwark v. Ince* (1989) 21 H.L.R. 504.
[74] *Pollway Nominees Ltd v. London Borough of Havering* (1989) 21 H.L.R. 462.
[75] *Oakley v. Birmingham City Council* [1998] 31 H.L.R. 1070.
[76] *Salford City Council v. McNally* [1976] A.C. 379, HL, on the predecessors of the relevant section Lord Wilberforce, at p. 389, gave directions as to how the 1936 Act was to be applied, "[Magistrates] should keep close to the wording of the Act and ask themselves, after they have found the condition of the premises, the questions (1) is the state of the premises such as to be injurious or likely to cause injury to health, or (2) is it a nuisance? To consider these questions in terms of fitness or unfitness for human habitation is undesirable and likely to confuse."
[77] *National Coal Board v. Thorn* [1976] 1 W.L.R. 543.
[78] See, for instance, *Betts v. Penge Urban District Council* [1942] 2 K.B. 154, where a landlord's removing of the front door of tenant's flat was held to be a "nuisance" within the meaning of the Public Health Act 1936. The case was expressly disapproved in *Salford City Council v. McNally* [1976] A.C. 379, HL. The *Betts* decision was probably influenced by the absence of any other protection for the tenant, such as is now afforded by the Protection from Eviction Act 1977: see above 5–003 to 5–014.
[79] *Bishop Auckland Local Board v. Bishop Auckland Iron Co.* (1882) 10 Q.B.D 138, *per* Stephen J. at p. 140.
[80] See *Coventry City Council v. Cartwright* [1975] 1 W.L.R. 845, where Lord Widgery C.J. approved the restriction to the context of public health, and referred to *Bishop Auckland*, *ibid.* However, a year later, in *National Coal Board v. Thorne* [1976] 1 W.L.R. 543, Watkins J. defined nuisance, in the context of the 1936 Act, without reference to the need for the nuisance complained of to be connected in some way with public health. Lord Widgery C.J. agreed. The *Bishop Auckland* case was cited but not expressly dealt with. However, in *Salford City Council v. McNally* [1976] A.C. 378, HL, Lord Wilberforce, at p. 389E, implicitly approved the additional restriction imposed by Stephen J. The better view, on the authorities and in principle, is that the nuisance complained of must be in some way referable to public health.
[81] *National Coal Board v. Thorne* [1976] 1 W.L.R. 521

dwelling-house, causing discomfort and inconvenience to the tenant.[82] Although there are suggestions that a lack of sound insulation which caused the sounds of everyday domestic activities to be audible in an adjacent flat was capable of being a noise nuisance[83] this must now be read in the light of the House of Lords' decision in *Southwark London Borough Council v. Mills*[84] that the audible activities must in themselves be a nuisance. "Everyday activities" which were an "ordinary and reasonable use" of the adjoining land, although audible, were not a nuisance.

Other specific forms of statutory nuisance

All other forms of statutory nuisance must also either be prejudicial to health or be a nuisance. The specific heads of statutory nuisance created by the Act can now be considered.   **5–042**

Section 79(1)(b): smoke

Section 79(1)(b) makes the emission of smoke a specific form of statutory nuisance. "Smoke" includes soot, ash, grit, and gritty particles emitted in smoke.[85] Smoke particles need not be visible to constitute a nuisance.[86] This category of statutory nuisance was not covered by the 1936 Act. The subsection does not apply to premises occupied by the Crown or visiting armed forces for the purposes of defence.[87] Nor does it apply to smoke from the chimney of a private dwelling, within a smoke control area, dark smoke from an industrial boiler or other industrial or trade premises, or from a steam railway locomotive.[88]   **5–043**

Section 79(1)(c): fumes and gases

Section 79(1)(c) deals with the emission of fumes and gases from private dwellings only. A "private dwelling" includes any building or part of a building used or intended to be used as a dwelling.[89] It also includes the   **5–044**

---

82 *Springett v. Harold* [1954] 1 W.L.R. 521.
83 *Network Housing Association Ltd v. Westminster City Council* [1994] E.G.C.S. 173 but see *Southwark London Borough Council v. Mills*, below. Although *Network Housing* was cited in argument in the *Southwark* case, it was not discussed by the House of Lords.
84 [1999] 3 W.L.R. 939, HL. This decision was made in the context of the covenant of quiet enjoyment but the principles expounded by Lord Hoffmann and Lord Millett, relating to nuisance, appear to be of general application.
85 S. 79(7).
86 *Griffiths v. Pembrokeshire County Council* [2000] 18 L.S. Gaz. R. 36.
87 S. 79(2). "Visiting Forces" are defined by reference to the Visiting Forces Act 1952.
88 These exceptions fall within the scope of (and are further defined in) ss. 1, 2, 18, 19, 43 and Schedule 1 of the Clean Air Act 1993.
89 S. 79(7). A "private dwelling" is not a dwelling occupied for business purposes: *GE Stevens (High Wycombe) Ltd v. High Wycombe Corporation* [1962] 2 Q.B. 547; *Segal Securities Ltd v. Thoseby* [1963] 1 Q.B. 887 (Sachs J). The latter case was concerned with construction of a covenant. A private dwelling must have someone dwelling in it at the relevant time: *Stott v. Hefferon* [1974] 1 W.L.R. 1270, a case under the National Insurance Act 1965.

garden attached to a dwelling-house.[90] "Fumes" includes any airborne solid matter smaller than dust; and "gases" include vapour and moisture which condenses from them.[91]

Section 79(1)(d): dust, steam, smell and other effluvia

5–045   Section 79(1)(d) deals with the emission of dust, steam, smell or other effluvia arising on industrial, trade or business premises." Industrial, trade or business premises" includes premises used for any treatment or processing, as well as manufacture, and any premises where matter is burnt in connection with any industrial, business or trade process.[92] "Dust" is defined not to include particles emitted from a chimney in smoke and "steam" does not include emissions from railway locomotives.[93] The word, "effluvia" has been accepted as being an unspecified combination of smells and fumes.[94] In *Bishop Auckland Local Board v. Bishop Auckland Iron and Steel Co. Ltd.* the Queen's Bench Divisional Court considered that, at least on the facts of the case, smells and effluvia were the same.[95]

Section 79(1)(e): accumulations and deposits

5–046   Section 79(1)(e) is concerned with "any accumulation or deposit". As has already been noted, an accumulation of inert material, which would only

---

[90] *Stevenage Borough Council v. Wilson* [1993] 1 Env. L.R. 214.

[91] The restriction on premises to which this subsection applies derives from s. 79(4): other premises fall within Part II of the Clean Air Act 1993. The definitions of "dust" and "fumes" are from s. 79(7).

[92] S. 79(7). There is no further definition of these terms in the Act, but the terms have been considered in other context. "Trade" means buying and selling, a calling or a class of skilled labour: *Skinner v. Jack Breach* [1927] 2 K.B. 220, 225–7, per Lord Hewart C.J.; also, organised seeking after profits: *Aviation & Shipping Co. v. Murray (Inspector of Taxes)* [1961] 1 W.L.R. 974, CA. "Industry" was considered to be identical to "trade" in *Skinner*. "Business" is an occupation, distinct from pleasure, *Rolls v. Miller* (1884) 27 Ch.D. 71, 88, CA, per Lindley L.J. : it is said to be wider than "trade": *Re: A Debtor (Number 490 of 1935)* [1936] Ch. 237, CA, per Lord Wright M.R. An isolated transaction, without an intention to repeat the transaction may not be a "business": *Re: Griffin* (1890) 60 L.J.Q.B. 235, CA, at p. 237, per Lord Esher M.R.

[93] S. 79(7), which also defines a "chimney" as any structure or opening through which smoke may be emitted. For a case on dust, see *Wivenhoe Port Ltd v. Colchester Borough Council* [1985] J.P.L. 175 (H.H.J. Butler, Colchester Crown Court); affirmed [1985] J.P.L. 396, CA.: the dust in that case was soya powder blowing from ships being unloaded.

[94] *Malton Board of Health v. Malton Manure Co.* (1879) 4 Ex.D. 302: the unspecified effluvia was blown from an artificial manure manufacturer's plant, in which animal bones were dissolved in sulphuric acid. There is no definition of "effluvia" in any of the statutes.

[95] [1882] 10 Q.B.D. 138. The case was decided under the Public Health Act 1875, which dealt only with an "accumulation or deposit". The word "effluvia" was used by Stephen J. in the course of his judgment to describe fumes arising from smouldering accumulations of ash and cinders from the Defendant's metal worksection Stephen and Field JJ. held that the smell of the smouldering, which found its way through the sewers of the locality and into the water closets of adjoining dwelling-houses was capable of being a nuisance, even though it was not "injurious to health. "

be harmful if walked upon is not an "accumulation or deposit prejudicial to health".[96]

Section 79(1)(f): the keeping of animals

Section 79(1)(f) covers any animal kept in such a place or manner as to be prejudicial to health or a nuisance. The health in question is human, not that of the animal. Although the Queen's Bench Divisional Court has held that the keeping of a large quantity of dogs, which cause disturbance by their barking, did not constitute a statutory nuisance, it seems that this decision was either wrong, or restricted to its own facts.[97] The House of Lords has subsequently accepted, without argument, that barking dogs could constitute a statutory nuisance.[98] The subsection is apt to cover the situation where a nuisance is caused by animals escaping from premises.[99]

5–047

Section 79(1)(g) and (ga): noise

Noise is dealt with by both section 79(1)(g) and (ga). Section 79(1)(g) controls noise emitted from premises[1]: the latter subsection was inserted by section 2 of the Noise and Statutory Nuisances Act 1993. If noise does not emanate from premises, but affects them such that there is a nuisance to or injuriousness to the health of the occupier, the affected premises may fall within the scope of section 79(1)(a).[2] Whether noise constitutes a legal nuisance is a matter of fact and degree, but the cause of the noise can be taken into account.[3] Section 79(1)(g) does not apply to noise made by aircraft, apart from model aircraft.[4]

5–048

Under sections 58 and 59 of the Control of Pollution Act 1974, it has been held that noise made in the street or a public place was not "emitted from premises".[5] However the new definition in section 79(7) of the 1990 Act, whereby "premises" includes "land", ought to be sufficient to cover noise made in the streets.[6] In any event, the problem has now been specifically addressed, at least in part, by subsection 79(1)(ga) of the amended

[96] *Coventry City Council v. Cartwright* [1975] 1 W.L.R. 845.
[97] *Galer v. Morrissey* [1955] 1 W.L.R. 110. Lord Goddard C.J.'s observation, *obiter*, that smelly dogs could constitute a statutory nuisance underlines the irrationality of holding noisy dogs could not. The decision has been doubted in *Coventry City Council v. Cartwright*, above, and *Wivenhoe Port Ltd v. Colchester Council* [1985] J.P.L. 175.
[98] *Aitken v. South Hams District Council* [1995] 1 A.C. 262, HL; the case was brought under the Control of Pollution Act 1974, s. 58.
[99] *R. v. Walden-Jones, ex p. Coton* [1963] Crim.L.R. 839.
[1] "Noise" includes vibrations: s. 79(7).
[2] *Southwark London Borough Council v. Ince* (1989) 21 H.L.R. 462.
[3] See *Gaunt v. Fynney* (1872) 8 Ch.App. 8, 42 L.J. Ch. 122, CA.
[4] S. 79(6). Aircraft noise and vibration are comprehensively dealt with by s. 77 of the Civil Aviation Act 1982.
[5] *Tower Hamlets London Borough Council v. Manzoni & Walder* (1984) J.P. 123.
[6] However, there may be logistical problems in actually enforcing against such a nuisance, unless it was recurring nuisance associated with a particular location, such as the taxi service-station in *Hammersmith LBC v. Magnum Automated Forecourts Ltd* [1978] 1 W.L.R. 50, CA.

1990 Act, and the Noise and Statutory Nuisance Act 1993.[7] Subsection 79(1)(ga) applies to noise emitted from or caused by a vehicle, machinery, or equipment[8] in a street.[9] It does not apply to noise caused by traffic, the armed forces of the Crown or visiting forces.[10]

Section 79(1)(h): other statutory nuisances

5–049　Lastly, section 79(1)(h) covers any other matter declared by other statutes to constitute a statutory nuisance.[11]

Enforcement

5–050　The duty to enforce against statutory nuisances is given to the relevant local authority.[12] Private prosecutions are also specifically provided for by the Act.[13] A local authority faced with a statutory nuisance has three concurrent, options, namely that it can:

(1)　bring a prosecution;

(2)　use its powers of entry to carry out the works itself; or

(3)　seek the remedies available to any person suffering a nuisance from the Court.[14]

The use of these remedies is both controlled and prescribed by the Act: see further below. It is the duty of every local authority to inspect its area for statutory nuisances which should be prosecuted and take such steps as are reasonably practicable to investigate any complaint received about a

---

[7]　The Act came into effect on January 5, 1994, two months after Royal Assent: s. 12(1).

[8]　"Equipment" includes a musical instrument: s. 79(7) of the 1990 Act (as amended).

[9]　"Street" means any highway or any road, footway, square, or court which is, for the time being, open to the public: s. 79(7) (as amended).

[10]　"Visiting Forces" are defined by reference to the Visiting Forces Act 1952.

[11]　For instance: s. 141 of the Public Health Act 1936 (insanitary wells, tanks cisterns and water-butts); s. 259(1) of the Public Health Act 1936 (any pond, pool, ditch, gutter or watercourse which is so foul as to be prejudicial to health or a nuisance); s. 268(2) of the Public Health Act 1936 (any tent, van, shed, or similar structure used for human habitation which is prejudicial to health or a nuisance); and s. 151(2) of the Mines and Quarries Act 1954 (unfenced abandoned mine-shafts or quarries). S. 92 of the Public Health Act 1936 covered nuisances in the workplace: this is now covered under the Health and Safety at Work Act 1974. Although dealt with by s. 5 and Sched. 3 of the Noise and Statutory Nuisances Act 1993, noise from audible intruder alarms has not been specifically made a statutory nuisance under this sub-section.

[12]　A local authority for these purposes is a district council, a London Borough Council, the Common Council of the City of London, and the Council of the Isles of Scilly: s. 79(7). Under the Public Health (Control of Disease) Act 1984, a Port Health Authority can be designated: by s. 79(8), it then acts as local authority for all statutory nuisance purposes, save those relating to noise under s. 79(1)(g). For the purposes of Part III of the 1990 Act, local authorities also have jurisdiction over all statutory nuisances caused in or on the territorial sea adjoining that authority's territory.

[13]　S. 82.

[14]　These include injunctions. A local authority has power to prosecute or defend legal proceedings under the Local Government Act 1972, s. 222.

statutory nuisance by a person living in its area.[15] A local authority has wide powers of entry under the Act, including, on obtaining a Justices' warrant, a power in a proper case to enter premises by force to carry out its functions under the Act.[16] A local authority also has wide powers to enter, open, remove or immobilise any vehicle, machinery or equipment causing a statutory noise nuisance.[17] A local authority can also take such samples from the premises as it deems fit. Obstructing the local authority in execution of its rights to enter or remove is a summary offence, punishable by a fine not exceeding level 2 on the standard scale.[18] Any officer or member of the local authority acting in good faith is immune from any action or claim arising from their performance or their duties under the 1990 Act.[19]

Abatement notices

Where a local authority is satisfied that a statutory nuisance exists, or is likely to occur or recur within its area,[20] it has a duty to serve an abatement notice.[21] An abatement notice can require any or all of the following: **5–051**

(1)   abatement of the nuisance;

(2)   prohibition of its occurrence;

(3)   prohibition of its recurrence;[22]

(4)   restriction of its occurrence;

(5)   restriction of its recurrence;

(6)   the execution of such works as may be necessary for the above purposes; and

---

[15] S. 79(1).

[16] Para. 2 of Sched. 3.

[17] Para. 2A of Sched. 3. The police must be informed before such action is taken, and the machinery secured when opened or entered. The police must also be informed of the location of removed machinery.

[18] Para. 3(1) of Sched. 3. See also s. 32 of the Magistrates' Courts Act 1980 (as amended by s. 17 of the Criminal Justice Act 1991).

[19] Para. 5 of Sched. 3.

[20] This includes nuisances suffered inside its area, but caused outside it, where the local authority may act as if the nuisance were within its area: s. 81(2). This includes taking action against another local authority: *R. v. Epping (Waltham Abbey) Justices ex p. Burlinson* [1948] 1 K.B. 79, an action under the 1936 Act.

[21] S. 80(1). Should the authority default on its responsibilities, Sched. 3, para. 4 contains provisions enabling the Secretary of State to take various corrective measures. However, in *Nottingham Corporation v. Newton* [1974] 1 W.L.R. 923 it was held, obiter, that the use of the word "shall" did not bind the local authority to serve an abatement notice, if other remedies were available to it. In that case, the local authority elected to use powers under the 1936 Act, not Housing Act 1957 powers. It is a practice of some authorities to serve "informal" notices, prior to service of a formal abatement notice, as a negotiating technique: the legality of such a device is less clear that its obvious usefulness.

[22] A notice served to prevent recurrence of a statutory nuisance remains in effect indefinitely: *R. v. Birmingham Justices ex p. Guppy* (1988) 152 J.P. 159.

(7)   the taking of such other steps as may be necessary for the above purposes.

The notice must also specify the time or times within which the requirements it contains must be complied with[23] and it should state what works are required to abate the nuisance.[24] An abatement notice served under the Control of Pollution Act 1974 (semble, also one served under the Public Health Acts) remains effective, and may form the basis of enforcement action, notwithstanding the repeal of those Acts and the absence of any transitional provisions.[25]

An abatement notice must, *prima facie*, be served on the person responsible for the nuisance,[26] namely the person to whose act, default or sufferance[27] the nuisance is attributable.[28] In the case of street noise within the meaning of section 79(7)(ga) of the 1990 Act, the "person responsible" in relation to a vehicle means the registered owner and any other person who is for the time being driving it. The "person responsible" for machinery or equipment is the person operating it for the time being.[29] If those persons cannot be found, the notice may be served by attaching it to the vehicle, machinery or equipment in question.[30] If the statutory nuisance arises from a structural defect, however, the notice should be served on the owner of the premises.[31] Likewise, where the person responsible cannot be found, or where the nuisance has not yet occurred, the notice should be served on the owner or the occupier of the premises.[32] For the

---

[23] S. 80(1). There is no prescribed form for the notice. What is a reasonable time is a question of fact, in all the circumstances: *Bristol Corporation v. Sinnot* [1918] 1 Ch. 62, CA, a case actually decided on similar provisions in the Public Health Act 1857; *Strathclyde Regional Council v. Tudhope* [1983] J.P.L. 536, a case on s. 58 of the Control of Pollution Act 1974.

[24] If positive action is needed to abate the nuisance, the required steps must be stated in the notice (*Kirklees Metropolitan Borough Council v. Field* [1998] Env. L.R. 337) unless the action (or choice of actions) is obvious: *Budd v. Colchester District Council* [1999] Env. L.R. 739. See also *R. v. Falmouth & Truro Port Health Authority ex parte South West Water Ltd* [2000] Env. L.R. 658 and *Sevenoaks District Council v. Brands Hatch Leisure Group Ltd* [2001] Env. L.R. 86. For further discussion of the development of the law relating to abatement see Malcolm [2000] J.P.L. 894 and Lewis [2000] J.P.L. 1011 and Garner, Environmental Law at IIB [82].

[25] *Aitken v. South Hams District Council* [1995] 1 A.C. 262, HL, applying s. 16(1)(b) of the Interpretation Act 1978.

[26] S. 80(2)(a).

[27] On "sufferance", see *Sedleigh-Denfield v. O'Callaghan* [1940] A.C. 880, HL. An occupier can remain liable for creating a nuisance even when he no longer occupies the premises, hence has no control over them: *Thompson v. Gibson* (1841) 7 M. & W. 456, per Parke B.

[28] S. 79(7).

[29] The definitions come from s. 79(7), as amended. The owner of the vehicle is defined by reference to the owner for the purposes of the Vehicles (Excise) Act 1971. It is to be regretted that Parliament did not think fit to give local authorities the option of enforcing against the owner of equipment or machinery, rather than simply the operator.

[30] S. 80A(2)(b). If the person responsible for the vehicle, machinery or equipment can be found within the hour, he must also be served: s. 80A(3). Removal of a notice, other than by the person responsible or his authorised agent is an offence punishable by a fine on scale 3 on the standard scale: s. 80A(6), (7).

[31] S. 80(2)(b).

[32] S. 80(2)(c). The owner is responsible for nuisances arising by reason of the structure of the premises, even if he is not responsible for the nuisance itself: *Pollway Nominees Ltd v. London Borough of Havering* (1989) 21 H.L.R. 462.

purposes of section 80(2), "owner" means the person receiving the rack rent of the premises, whether on his own account or as agent or trustee for another person.[33] If the conduct of more than one person renders them responsible for a nuisance, they must all be served, even though the actions of any one of them alone would not constitute a nuisance.[34] An abatement notice can be appealed to the magistrates' court within 21 days of service by any person served with one.[35]

Appeals against abatement notices

Appeals relating to abatement notices are governed by the Statutory Nuisance (Appeals) Regulations 1995.[36] Commencement of an appeal against an abatement notice does not, generally, suspend the operation of the notice. The only circumstances in which the notice is suspended are set out in the 1995 Regulations. The effect of a notice is only suspended if compliance would require expenditure on the carrying out of works or, in the case of noise nuisance,[37] the noise is caused by the appellant in performance of a duty imposed by law upon him.[38] However, the Regulations further provide that, even if the above preconditions to suspension are made out, the notice will not be suspended if the nuisance to which the notice relates is injurious to health, or is likely to be of such a short duration that suspension of the notice would rob it of any practical effect; or, where compliance with the notice would require expenditure, the cost of compliance would not be disproportionate to the public benefit to be expected from compliance.[39] The local authority serving the abatement notice is required to state on the face of the notice whether the exceptions to suspension apply and, if so, why.[40] Failure to do so disapplies the exceptions, therefore leading to the suspension of the effect of the notice if an appeal is made.[41]

5–052

The grounds upon which an abatement notice may be appealed are also set out in the 1995 Regulations. The defences are:[42]

5–053

(1)   the abatement is not justified under section 80 of the 1990 Act;

(2)   there has been some informality, defect, or error in, or in connection with the abatement notice;

---

[33] *Camden London Borough Council v. Gunby* [1999] 4 All E.R. 602, taking the definition from s. 64(1) Clean Air Act 1993, to include the managing agent of the property. The definition thus differs from that used in s. 81A, which excludes agents.

[34] S. 81(1).

[35] S. 80(3) and para. 1 of Sched. 3. Appeal from the Magistrates' Court lies to the Crown Court.

[36] S.I. 1995 No. 2644. The Regulations came into force on November 8, 1995.

[37] That is, a case within s. 79(1)(g) or (ga).

[38] Reg. 3(1)(b).

[39] Reg. 3(2).

[40] Reg. 3(3).

[41] Reg. 3(1)(c).

[42] Reg. 2(2).

(3)   the local authority has unreasonably refused to accept compliance with alternative requirements or the requirements imposed by the authority are either unnecessary or unreasonable in character or extent;

(4)   the time or times given for compliance with the notice are unreasonably short;

(5)   if the statutory nuisance falls within certain categories,[43] and arises from trade, industrial or business premises, or is caused by smoke emitted from a chimney,[44] then the "best practicable means"[45] were used to prevent or counteract the nuisance;

(6)   the abatement notice is more onerous than a notice, consent, or determination under the Control of Pollution Act 1974 which is already in force in respect of noise emitted from premises or under the Noise and Statutory Nuisance Act 1993 in respect of noise emitted from vehicles, machinery or equipment;

(7)   the abatement notice should have been served on another person;[46]

(8)   as between the owner and the occupier of the premises, the abatement notice could have been served on the other party, and it would have been more equitable to have done so; or

(9)   the abatement notice could have been served on another party and it would have been more equitable to have done so.

If the ground of appeal is that another person could or should have been served, the appellant must serve a copy of the notice of appeal on that person.[47] In any event, the appellant may serve a copy of his notice of appeal on any other person having an estate or interest in the premises to which the appeal relates.[48]

On hearing an appeal, the Court may quash or vary the notice or dismiss the appeal.[49] If the Court varies the notice, the notice as varied is final

---

[43]   The categories specified in reg. 2(2)(e)(i), with the corresponding section in the Act of 1990, are as follows: premises in such a state as to be prejudicial to health or a nuisance (s. 79(1)(a)); dust, steam, smell or other effluvia arising on industrial, trade or business premises which are prejudicial to health or a nuisance (s. 79(1)(d)); accumulations or deposits which are prejudicial to health or are a nuisance (s. 79(1)(e)); the keeping of any animal, in such a manner, or by reason of the nature of the premises, which is prejudicial to health or a nuisance (s. 79(1)(f)); and the emitting of noise so as to be prejudicial to health or a nuisance (s. 79(1)(g)).

[44]   See s. 79(1)(b) of the Act.

[45]   See below.

[46]   In *AMEC Building Limited v. London Borough of Camden* [1997] Env. L.R. 330 the notice was served on a sister company trading from the same address and came to the attention of the intended recipient; it was nonetheless held to have been invalidly served.

[47]   Reg. 2(4).

[48]   *ibid.*

[49]   Reg. 2(5).

but otherwise takes effect as if served by the local authority.[50] If the ground of appeal is that there has been some informality, defect, or error, in or in connection with the abatement notice, the Court must dismiss the appeal if it is satisfied that the informality, defect, or error was not material.[51] Further, the Court may make such order as it sees fit, to determine the contribution to the costs of the specified works to be made by any person who has been served with a copy of the notice of appeal.[52] Similarly, it may determine the proportions in which any costs of the local authority which have become recoverable under the Act should be paid by the appellant and any person who has been served with a copy of the notice of appeal.[53] As between owners and occupiers of premises, the Court must have regard to the terms of any tenancy between those parties.[54]

Prosecutions

Failure to comply with an abatement notice within the specified time is an offence.[55] General defences include proof of any of the grounds for appealing the Notice under the 1995 Regulations or showing that the notice has not been served. It is also a defence to show that the defendant is not the person by whose act, default or sufferance the nuisance arose or continued.[56] There are a number of specific defences.[57] There is a statutory defence of "reasonable excuse".[58] There is also a defence, available only to certain statutory nuisances, that the "best practicable means" of avoiding the nuisance or its consequences have been adopted.[59] Although there is no specific authority, all of the grounds for appealing the abatement notice under the Statutory Nuisance (Appeals) Regulations 1995 should be available although the appellant has not availed himself of the right to appeal the notice. However, this course of action is not advisable and the defences ought to be raised by way of appeal against the notice.

---

[50] *ibid.*

[51] reg. 2(3)

[52] reg. 2(6)(a), subject to the caveat in reg. 2(7)(b).

[53] reg. 2(6)(b), again subject to the caveat in reg. 2(7)(b).

[54] reg. 2(7)(a).

[55] S. 80(4).

[56] *Warner v. Lambeth London Borough Council* [1984] 15 H.L.R. 42, a case under the 1936 Act. *Carr v. Hackney London Borough Council* (1995) 28 H.L.R. 749 confirmed that the same defence is available under the 1990 Act.

[57] As opposed to general defences, such as denial of the actus reus.

[58] The test for the existence of "reasonable excuse" is whether there was some overwhelming or difficult situation which the defendant was not able to control, which led to the breach: *Wellingborough Borough Council v. Gordon* [1993] Env. L.R. 218, 221, *per* Taylor L.J., rejecting the submission that the defendant was not able to control revellers at his birthday party from playing over-amplified reggae music. Personal circumstances such as illness may amount to "reasonable excuse": see for example *Hope Butuyuyu v. London Borough of Hammersmith & Fulham* [1997] Env. L.R. D13. Once the defendant has established evidence of a reasonable excuse on the balance of probabilities, it is for the prosecution to prove beyond reasonable doubt that the excuse is not reasonable: *John Polychronakis v. Richard & Jerrom Ltd* [1998] Env. L.R. 346.

[59] See para. 5–054, below.

On conviction, the punishment is a fine not exceeding level 5 on the standard scale,[60] plus up to a further one-tenth of that level for each day[61] on which the failure to comply with the notice continues after conviction, save that, where the offence is committed on industrial, trade or business premises, the maximum fine is £20,000.[62]

If the local authority is of the opinion that the powers of the magistrates' courts are insufficient to secure the abatement, prohibition, or restriction of a statutory nuisance, it may commence proceedings in the High Court for such remedies as the High Court would afford any person seeking remedies against nuisance.[63] These remedies include interlocutory injunctions, which are available even where there are proceedings on foot in the magistrates' court.[64] The local authority need not pass a formal resolution that the magistrates' court proceedings would be inadequate, at least prior to any challenge of its decision.[65] The section only empowers local authorities to proceed against statutory nuisances.[66] The costs of the action and of any works carried out by the local authority to abate the statutory nuisance, including any accrued interest, can form a charge on the premises in question[67] if the local authority serves a notice specifying both the amount claimed and the interest rate to be applied.[68]

---

[60] See s. 32 of the Magistrates' Courts Act 1980 (as amended by s. 17 of the Criminal Justice Act 1991).

[61] *Canterbury City Council v. Ferris* [1997] Env. L.R. 14.

[62] S. 80(4). See n.83 above.

[63] S. 81(5), subject to defences arising under ss. 60–61 of the Control of Pollution Act 1974, incorporated by s. 81(6) of the 1990 Act.

[64] *Hammersmith London Borough Council v. Magnum Automated Forecourts Ltd* [1978] 1 W.L.R. 50, CA, a case under the Control of Pollution Act 1974, s. 58 [effectively the same as s. 81(5)], where an injunction was granted restraining the 24 hour operation of an automated taxi service centre, even though the abatement notice was under appeal in the magistrates' court.

[65] *Warwick Rural District Council v. Miller-Mead* [1962] Ch. 442, CA, under s. 100 of the Public Health Act 1936. In that case, the resolution to use the summary procedure was passed 3 days after the writ was issued: it was held (per Lord Evershed M.R. and Danckwerts L.J., Willmer L.J. dissenting) that when the effective steps in the action were taken, the Council had the necessary intention. The use of s. 81(5) was clarified in *Vale of the White Horse District Council v. Allen & Partners* [1997] Env. L.R. 212. Before issuing a claim form, the local authority must have formed the opinion that summary proceedings would be inadequate. No separate power to issue proceedings is given by s. 222 Local Government Act 1972. If no opinion is formed before issue, any claim made is liable to be struck out under CPR 3.4, or the Authority subject to judicial review.

[66] *Boyce v. Paddington Corporation* [1903] 1 Ch. 109, a case on similar provisions under the Disused Burial Grounds Act 1884.

[67] S. 81A. The local authority shall have such powers of enforcement as a mortgagee under the Law of Property Act 1925, s. 81A(8). The charge does not extend to a vessel: s. 81A(9).

[68] S. 81A(2), where other more detailed requirements are set out. There is a right of appeal within 21 days to the County Court: s. 81(4), (6). The Court can uphold, vary or dismiss the notice: s. 81A(7).

The defence of "best practicable means"

The statutory defence that the "best practicable means" were used to pre-   **5–054**
vent or counteract the effects of a nuisance, is available to some statutory
nuisances.[69] Unless the premises upon which the nuisance arises are
industrial, trade or business premises, the "best practicable means"
defence is not available to the following nuisances:

(1)   being in a state prejudicial to health or a nuisance;[70]

(2)   emitting such dust, steam, smell or other effluvia as to be
       prejudicial to health or a nuisance;[71]

(3)   accumulation or deposit which is prejudicial to health or is a
       nuisance;[72]

(4)   the keeping of any animal, in such a manner or, by reason of the
       nature of the premises, is prejudicial to health or a nuisance;[73]

(5)   emitting noise so as to be prejudicial to health or a nuisance;[74] and

(6)   noise emitted from or caused by a vehicle, machinery or
       equipment in the street.[75]

In any case, the defence is also not available where the nuisance is one of
the following:

(7)   emission of smoke, other than from a chimney;[76]

(8)   emitting fumes or gas, so as to be prejudicial to health or a
       nuisance;[77] and

(9)   in any other state as statute may declare to be a statutory
       nuisance.[78]

The onus of proving the defence lies upon the defendant. The defence of
"best practical means" is interpreted by reference to criteria laid down in
section 79(9). It requires only what is reasonably practicable, having
regard to local conditions and circumstances, the current state of technical

---

[69]   The defence is contained in s. 80(7) and further defined in s. 79(7).
[70]   S. 79(1)(a).
[71]   S. 79(1)(d).
[72]   S. 79(1)(e).
[73]   S. 79(1)(f).
[74]   S. 79(1)(g). In respect of noise nuisance, there are further statutory defences arising from
        the interaction of s. 80(9) of the 1990 Act and ss. 61, 65, 66 and 67 of the Control of
        Pollution Act 1974.
[75]   S. 79(ga).
[76]   S. 79(1)(b).
[77]   S. 79(1)(c).
[78]   S. 79(1)(h).

knowledge and financial implications.[79] However, the section does require the best practicable means: means which are accepted industry practice, but not best practice, will not afford a defence.[80] The means referred to include the design, installation, maintenance and manner and periods of operation of plant and machinery, or the design, construction and maintenance of buildings or structures.[81] The test is not to be applied so as to be incompatible with any other duty imposed by law, nor with requirements of safety and safe working conditions.[82] Exigencies, emergencies and the unforeseeable are excepted.[83] The defence need only be proved to the civil standard, on the balance of probabilities.[84]

Abatement

5–055   Where service of an abatement notice has not caused the abatement of a statutory nuisance, the local authority is empowered to abate the nuisance itself, taking whatever steps are necessary, irrespective of whether it seeks to bring a prosecution.[85] The wide powers to enter premises, already noted in the context of examining potential nuisances, are again available.[86] Any expenses incurred by the local authority may be recovered by registering a charge on the premises or by obtaining an order for payment by instalments.[87]

Private Prosecutions

5–056   Private prosecutions are specifically provided for by section 82: any person aggrieved may lay an information.[88] There is no requirement that the person aggrieved first serve an abatement notice, or otherwise warn the proposed defendant that an information will be laid, but the person aggrieved must give written notification to the proposed defendant that proceedings will be commenced and specifying the matters complained

---

[79]   In *Wivenhoe Port Limited v. Colchester Borough Council* [1985] J.P.L. 396, CA, it was held that increased expenditure, and even unprofitability, caused by more stringent controls is not, of itself, a defence. Compare the use of "BATNEEC" (best available techniques not entailing excessive cost) in Part I of the 1990 Act: see, for example, s. 7(4). The defence does not require a business which is being lawfully conducted from a particular place to relocate; the defence is made out when no further steps can be taken at the current premises: see *Manley v. New Forest District Council* [2000] Env. L.R. D11.

[80]   *Scholefield v. Schnuck* (1855) 19 J.P. 84; decided under a similar test contained in the Factories Act 1844.

[81]   S. 79(9)(b).

[82]   S. 79(9)(c) and (d).

[83]   S. 79(9)(d).

[84]   *Wivenhoe Port Limited v. Colchester Borough Council* [1985] J.P.L. 396, CA.

[85]   S. 81(3).

[86]   Para. 5–050, above.

[87]   S. 81A and 81B.

[88]   S. 82(1). Because the section is criminal in nature, the appropriate procedure is to lay an information: *R. v. Inner London Crown Court ex p. Bentham* [1989] 1 W.L.R. 408, CA, applying *Northern Ireland Trailers Ltd v. Preston Corporation* [1972] 1 W.L.R. 203, both cases under the equivalent provision of the 1936 Act, s. 99.

of.[89] There must be 21 days between the service of the notice and the laying of the information, save in cases of nuisance, where the period is three days.[90]

The private prosecution provisions closely follow the mechanism prescribed for local authority prosecutions, under sections 80 and 81. *Prima facie*, proceedings are to be brought against the person responsible for the statutory nuisance.[91] As before, this is the person to whose act, default or sufferance the nuisance is attributable.[92] If the statutory nuisance arises from a structural defect, however, the notice shall be served on the owner of the premises.[93] Where the person responsible cannot be found, or where the nuisance has not yet occurred, the notice shall be served on the owner or the occupier of the premises.[94] In the case of noise nuisance arising from a vehicle, equipment or machinery in the street, the notice may be served on the person responsible for the machinery but not on the machinery itself.[95] If the conduct of more than one person renders them responsible for a nuisance, they must all be served, even though the actions of any one of them alone would not constitute a nuisance.[96]

On the hearing of the information, the magistrates may find that the nuisance either exists or is abated but likely to recur.[97] If they so find, they may require abatement of the nuisance within a time they specify, which includes a power to order any necessary works, or may order the taking of steps to prevent the recurrence of the nuisance, again having power to order any works.[98] The magistrates have power to order works which go beyond any contractual or statutory repairing obligation.[99] Additionally, they may also prohibit the use of premises for human habitation until they are rendered fit for that purpose.[1] The magistrates may also impose a fine not exceeding level 5 on the standard scale.[2]

---

[89] S. 82(6), making good the deficiency in the equivalent section under the 1936 Act, noted in *Sandwell Borough Council v. Bujok* [1990] 1 W.L.R. 1350, HL. There is currently no reported case on how a breach of this requirement is to be dealt with: it is submitted that an information laid in such circumstances should be struck out, but it is possible that a suitable compensation might be made by awarding the costs against the complainant, even if successful: see the observations of Lord Griffiths (Lords Keith, Templeman, Ackner and Lowry, concurring) in the *Sandwell* case, above at p. 1359.

[90] S. 82(7).

[91] S. 82(4)(a).

[92] S. 82(4)(a). See para. 5–051, above.

[93] S. 82(4)(b). See para. 5–057, above.

[94] S. 80(2)(c). The owner is responsible for nuisances arising by reason of the structure of the premises, even if he is not responsible for the nuisance itself: *Pollway Nominees Ltd v. London Borough of Havering* (1989) 21 H.L.R. 462.

[95] S. 82(6), not amended by the 1993 Act: compare the new s. 80A.

[96] S. 82(5).

[97] S. 82(1).

[98] S. 82(2).

[99] *Birmingham District Council v. Kelly* (1985) 17 H.L.R. 572 and *R. v. Highbury Corner Magistrates' Court, ex p. Edwards* (1994) 26 H.L.R. 682.

[1] S. 82(3).

[2] See s. 32 of the Magistrates' Courts Act 1980 (as amended by s. 17 of the Criminal Justice Act 1991).

Failure to comply with an order from the magistrates within the specified time is, in the absence of a reasonable excuse,[3] an offence.[4] On conviction, the punishment is a fine not exceeding level 5 on the standard scale,[5] plus a further one-tenth of that level per day on which the failure to comply with the notice continues after conviction. The additional power available under section 80, to increase the fine to £20,000 where the offence is committed on industrial, trade or business premises, does not apply.[6] If the further offence of failure to comply with an order of the magistrates is committed, the magistrates may direct the local authority to take such steps to abate the nuisance, having given the authority an opportunity to be heard.[7] A similar power is available where the magistrates conclude that the person responsible for the nuisance, the owner and the occupier of the offending premises cannot be found.[8] The magistrates also have power to award the complainant compensation for the expenses of bringing the proceedings.[9] However, the Divisional Court has indicated that it does not consider it appropriate to use this mechanism for awarding "substantial" compensation: the correct forum for the award of compensation is a civil court.[10]

The "best practical means" defence applies to proceedings brought under this section as it does to a prosecution under section 80.[11] A person against whom proceedings have been brought may avoid liability by showing that he was not the person by whose act, default, or sufferance the nuisance arose or continued.[12]

The Crown

5–057   Although the Crown is bound by the Act, it may not be prosecuted: a declaration that the Crown's acts are unlawful is, however, available.[13]

---

[3] See note 58, above.
[4] S. 82(8).
[5] See above.
[6] Compare s. 80(4).
[7] S. 82(11).
[8] S. 82(13).
[9] See s. 82(12) and s. 130 of the Powers of the Criminal Courts Act 2000.
[10] *Herbert v. London Borough of Lambeth* (1991) 24 H.L.R. 299, per Woolf L.J., Pill J. agreeing. See also *British Waterways Board v. Norman* (1994) 26 H.L.R. 232, where the implications on costs of the criminal nature of the proceedings are considered in some depth. In *Davenport v. Walsall Metropolitan Borough Council* [1997] Env. L.R. 24 the Divisional Court upheld the decision of the magistrates not to award compensation for a statutory nuisance, as they considered the quantification exercise too difficult. This case underlines the desirability of using the civil courts to seek compensation in all but the most straightforward and insubstantial cases of nuisance.
[11] S. 82(9) and (1). For the substance of the defence, see para. 5–050, above.
[12] *Carr v. Hackney London Borough Council, The Times*, March 9, 1995.
[13] S. 159(2). The Sovereign is not affected in a personal capacity: s. 159(5).

Criminal penalties for trespass — the Criminal Justice and Public Order Act 1994

The formerly inaccurate statements on signs stating that "trespassers will be prosecuted" are now a much closer representation of the law following the enactment of the Criminal Justice and Public Order Act 1994. The Home Office's consultation paper "Squatting"[14] in 1991 also discussed the issue but did not put forward any fixed proposals or policy but described the problems which squatting creates (including "business" squatting) and concluded that the criminalisation of at least some aspects of squatting was justified in cases where the wider public interest was involved. This has, in part, occurred through the introduction of "interim possession orders" by the 1994 Act implemented by the addition of Part II to Order 24 of the County Court Rules[15] which have been preserved by the CPR notwithstanding the general revision to possession procedures.[16] Although it may be undesirable as a matter of principle to confuse civil and criminal liability thus, such confusion does appear elsewhere, *e.g.* in the overlap between the offences of harassment under the Protection from Eviction Act 1977 and the Protection from Harassment Act 1997 and remedies available to tenants for breach of covenant of quiet enjoyment and of the covenant not to derogate from grant. Further, the need to provide something more effective than purely civil remedies for those who find their homes occupied by squatters may be a good reason. There has also been concern expressed with regard to trespass by groups such as "new-age travellers" and those who occupy sites of public works as a means of protest or preventing the works from proceeding.[17]

Others aspects of squatting have taken on a serious aspect which may merit the intervention of criminal legislation, for example the squatting of vacant business premises,[18] and the Government also considered the criminalisation of unauthorised gipsy encampments: see D.O.E. Consultation Paper "Reform of the Caravan Sites Act 1968."[19] However, matters have not proceeded significantly further to this end following the 1994 Act and issues may arise in this respect under the Human Rights Act 1998.

The Criminal Justice and Public Order Act 1994[20] has introduced a number of criminal offences related to the use of land covering areas

---

[14] October 1991.

[15] See the Lord Chancellor's Department Consultation Paper "New procedures to combat squatting in houses, shops and other buildings", July 1994.

[16] See 4–076 to 4–083.

[17] *e.g.* the widespread action taken over the extension to the M3 motorway at Twyford Down near Winchester in 1993, over the A12–M11 Link Road in north-east London from 1993 to 1995 and over the Newbury By-pass in 1995–1997. See *e.g. Secretary of State v. Haughian* (1997) Env. L.R. 59, CA.

[18] See the Consultation Paper, paras. 31, 32, 61 and D.O.E. Circulars 1/94 and 18/94.

[19] August 8, 1992.

[20] See Smith [1995] Crim.L.R. 19 and Campbell [1995] Crim.L.R. 28 and *R. v. Lincolnshire C.C. ex p. Atkinson* (1995) 8 Admin. L.R. 529, Sedley J.

which are more traditionally dealt with by trespass and nuisance in private law. The many new offences created reflect much of the concern expressed by central government in recent papers on the issues referred to above. Amongst the legislative changes brought about by the 1994 Act are included the following:

(1) section 61 confers on the police power to direct persons to leave and remove vehicles if the senior officer on the scene reasonably believes that:

    (a) there are two or more persons trespassing;[21]

    (b) they are present there with the common purpose of residing there for any period;

    (c) reasonable steps have been taken by or on behalf of the occupier[22] to ask them to leave; and

any of the persons have caused damage to the land or to property on the land or have used threatening, abusive or insulting words or behaviour towards the occupier, a member of his family or his employee or agent or that the trespassers have between them six or more vehicles on the land.

Failure to leave the land "as soon as reasonably practicable"[23] amounts to a criminal offence[24] as does entering the land as a trespasser within three months of the giving of the direction. Defences to the above include the defence that the person was not trespassing or that he had reasonable excuse for failing to leave the land as soon as reasonably practicable or for re-entering as a trespasser;[25]

(2) section 63 confers power on the police to deal with "raves", *i.e.* gatherings on land in the open air of 100 or more persons (whether or not trespassers) at which amplified music[26] is played during the night (with or without intermissions) which by reason

---

[21] "Trespass" is defined by s. 61(9) as "trespass as against the occupier of the land" subject to certain extensions to the meaning given in s. 61(7).

[22] Defined by s. 61(7)(b) as including the local authority in the case of public common land and by s. 61(9) as the person entitled to possession of the land by virtue of an interest or estate held by him. This appears to exclude from the definition of "occupier" a long-term squatter in the course of acquiring title by adverse possession and who might have better relative title than the recent trespassers.

[23] *R. v. Krumpa and Anderson* [1989] Crim.L.R. 295.

[24] Punishable by a fine not exceeding level 4 on the standard scale and/or imprisonment for a term of not more than three months: s. 61(4).

[25] S. 61(6).

[26] "Music" is defined by s. 61(1)(b) as including "sounds wholly or predominantly characterised by the emission of a succession of repetitive beats." Clearly the draftsman had no confidence that everything played at raves amounted to music as generally understood.

of its loudness and duration and the time at which it is played is likely to cause serious distress to the inhabitants of the locality.[27] Powers are also conferred on the police to prevent the preparation of a rave,[28] to direct ten or more persons reasonably believed to be waiting for a rave to begin or attending a rave to leave,[29] to direct any person reasonably believed to be "on his way" to a rave not to proceed to the gathering[30] and to enter and seize vehicles and sound equipment.[31] Directions to leave as soon as reasonably practicable[32] are enforceable by criminal penalties as is re-entering the land within seven days of the giving of the direction.[33] It is a defence that a person had a reasonable excuse for failing to leave the land as soon as reasonably practicable or re-entering within seven days of the direction but since the powers are exercisable whether or not the persons on the land are trespassers there is no defence that the person was not trespassing. However, occupiers of the land, members of their family, employees or agents of his and any person whose home is situated on the land are exempt from the duty to comply with directions under section 63 and hence from the criminal offences;[34]

(3)   section 68 creates the offence[35] of "aggravated trespass"[36] in circumstances where a person —

(a)   trespasses on land[37] in the open air; and

(b)   does anything intended to have the effect of

---

[27] There is an exemption for gatherings authorised by an entertainments licence: s. 63(9).

[28] S. 63(2)(a).

[29] S. 63(2)(b) and (c).

[30] S. 65.

[31] S. 64. S. 66 confers various powers on the Court to forfeit sound equipment used in connection with raves.

[32] R. v. Krumpa [1989] Crim.L.R. 295.

[33] S. 63(6) — a fine not exceeding level 4 on the standard scale and/or imprisonment for a term of not more than three months.

[34] S. 63(5) and (10). The inclusion of "agent" creates an area of uncertainty which the organisers of raves may be able to exploit (particularly if they are the occupiers of the land or live on the land or have the co-operation of the occupier of the land) by seeking to appoint as agents some or all of those coming onto the land as "agents". It does not appear that the requirement of having a home on the land applies to employees or agents. Whilst such appointments may be blatant "shams", some may be genuine particularly with regard to persons assisting with the organisation of the rave. However, there is clearly room for confusion.

[35] Punishable by a fine not exceeding level 4 on the standard scale and/or imprisonment for a term of not more than three months: s. 68(3).

[36] Introduced, it appears, to deal with the more vigorous forms of protest from parties such as hunt saboteurs and animals rights activists. See the Home Secretary's speech introducing the Bill: Hansard, H.C., col. 29, January 11, 1994.

[37] Which excludes highways except those comprising a footpath, bridleway or byway under the Wildlife and Countryside Act 1981 or a cycle track: ss. 68(5)(a) and 61(9)(b)(i). See also Part II of the Countryside and Rights of Way Act 2000.

> (i) intimidating persons engaging in a lawful activity[38] on that land (or about to engage in such an activity) so as to deter any of them from engaging in that activity; or
>
> (ii) obstructing that activity; or
>
> (iii) disrupting that activity.[39]
>
> There exist police powers[40] to direct persons to leave the land who are reasonably believed to be committing aggravated trespass or who have committed it or intend to commit it.[41] It is an offence to fail to comply with such a direction as soon as reasonably practicable.[42] It is also an offence to re-enter the land as a trespasser within three months of the direction.[43] Defences to the above include the defence that the person was not trespassing or that he had reasonable excuse for failing to leave the land as soon as reasonably practicable or for re-entering as a trespasser;[44]

(4) new powers for the prohibition of "trespassory assemblies" are to be inserted into Part II of the Public Order Act 1986 by sections 70 and 71 of the 1994 Act;[45]

(5) sections 72–74 make extensive amendments to the Criminal Law Act 1977 (see paragraphs 5–020 to 5–024, above);

---

[38] It is "lawful" if the activity may be engaged in without committing an offence or trespassing on the land: s. 68(2). In *Hibberd v. Muddle* (1996, Unreported) the means of felling trees was in breach of the Health & Safety at Work etc Act 1974, but was nonetheless "lawful".

[39] Actual disruption need not take place; an intention to disrupt is enough: see *Winder v. DPP* (1996) 160 JP 713.

[40] S. 69(1).

[41] *Capon v. DPP* (1998) *The Independent*, March 23, 1998.

[42] *R. v. Krumpa* [1989] Crim.L.R. 295.

[43] S. 69(3)(b).

[44] S. 69(4).

[45] This part of the legislation has already been tested in *Director of Public Prosecutions v. McKeown* and *Director of Public Prosecutions v. Jones* [1999] 2 A.C. 540. In that case, a group of 21 protestors assembled on the verge of the A344 near Stonehenge to peacefully protest against the making of an order under the new s. 14A Public Order Act 1986 prohibiting trespassory assemblies within 4 miles of the monument for a set time period. The House of Lords held, by a 3:2 majority, that an assembly on a highway did not automatically amount to a trespass: the public have the right to enjoy a highway for any reasonable purpose, provided that they do not cause a nuisance or obstruct the right of others to pass and repass over the highway. Whether an assembly amounts to an unreasonable use of the highway (and is thus "trespassory") will depend on the facts of each individual case and is for the court hearing the matter to decide.

(6)   section 75 makes it a criminal offence[46] to fail to comply with an "interim possession order" in respect of any premises[47] made in summary proceedings.[48] Where the order had been made and served in accordance with the relevant rules of court, an offence is committed if the person subject to the order[49] either fails to leave the premises within 24 hours beginning with the time of service of the order or, having left, re-enters (or attempts to re-enter) the premises as a trespasser within one year of the date of the service of the order. Any person on the premises as a trespasser at any time within one month after the service of the order is presumed to have been in occupation of the premises at the time of service unless he proves to the contrary;[50] and

---

[46] Punishable by a fine not exceeding level 5 on the standard scale and/or imprisonment for a term of not more than six months. Parliament evidently viewed this offence as more serious than those created under ss. 63, 64 and 68 even though there might not be the disruptive element present in the case of "aggravated trespass" or "raves". The Home Secretary, introducing the Bill, described the provisions as providing a "quick and effective remedy against squatting": Hansard H.C., cols. 29–30, January 11, 1994. Given the complexities of the procedure now proposed for interim possession orders, it is questionable whether IPO is any quicker in practice than the use of ordinary summary procedure in a truly urgent case where application is made to abridge time.

[47] S. 75(4) defines "premises" as having the same meaning as in Pt. II of the Criminal Law Act 1977. In other words, the interim procedure will apply to "buildings" rather than to "land" and will provide no interim relief for those whose open land is squatted.

[48] S. 75(4) and 76(8) define such an order as an interim possession order made under rules of court for the bringing of summary proceedings for possession of premises which are occupied by trespassers. Such proceedings are distinct from ordinary summary possession proceedings and followed the Lord Chancellor's Department's consultations over the form of such rulesection. The consultation document was published in July 1994 ("New Procedures to Combat Squatting in Houses, Shops and Other Buildings"). The County Court (Amendment No. 2) Rules 1995 (S.I. 1995 No. 1582 and County Court (Forms) (Amendment No. 2) Rules 1995 (S.I. 1995 No. 1583) which came into force on August 24, 1995 amended Order 24 of the County Court Rules and the County Court 1995 (Forms) Rules 1982 (S.I. No. 586) to allow for an accelerated interim possession procedure to be available to persons with an immediate right to possession of "premises" (using the definition in s. 12 of the Criminal Law Act 1977) provided it is made within 28 days of the Applicant's first knowing of the unlawful occupation of the premises by the Respondent. No equivalent procedure was introduced into the old RSC 113 and even with the introduction of the new possession rules in CPR Part 55 the interim possession procedures are found in CPR Schedule 2 in what remains of Order 24. Accordingly they continue to apply to the County Court only. See, further, the commentary on the procedure in Chap. 4, paras. 4–076 to 4–083 and the Home Office Press Release, August 24, 1995 (C.O.I. 9995).

[49] Meaning a person in occupation of the premises at the time of service of the order: s. 76(4). This will no doubt lead to arguments as to whether persons were still in "occupation" at the time of service, although the use of the term "occupation" appears to mean more than physically present so that a deliberate absence at the time of service would not necessarily be a good defence.

[50] S. 76(4).

(7)   section 77 confers on local authorities power to direct a person[51] residing in a vehicle[52] or vehicles on land forming part of a highway, or on other land which is unoccupied land or on any occupied land without the consent of the owner[53] to leave that land and remove vehicles and property which they have with them. Failure to comply with the direction as soon as practicable or re-entering the land within three months of the giving of the direction is a criminal offence, punishable by a fine only not exceeding level 3 on the standard scale: section 77(3). The offence can only be committed by persons on the land when the direction was made: the *Lincolnshire C.C.* case, above. Section 77(2) operates in personam not in rem.[53a] Where there is contravention of a direction under section 77, on a complaint by a local authority magistrates courts have power[54] under section 78 to authorise that local authority to enter the land and remove any property or vehicles

---

[51] Referred to by the section heading as "unauthorised campers". This will not only cover so-called "new-age travellers" but also gipsies — in accordance with the proposal set out in the earlier White Paper (above). ss. 80, 168(3) and Sched. 11 repeal ss. 6–12 of the Caravan Sites Act 1968 (duty to provide accommodation for gipsies) substituting a new power in s. 24 of the Caravan Sites and Control of Development Act 1960 to provide working space and facilities in addition to accommodation for gipsy caravans. This provided the source of much debate during its passage through Parliament and, at the Report Stage (see Hansard HL, cols. 1529–1564, July 11, 1994), the Lords substantially amended the provisions (taking away most of their substance) only to have them reversed in the later stages of the Bill. Accordingly, the principal means has been removed for remedying the "affront to the national conscience" of the lack of proper accommodation for gipsies referred to by Henry J. in *R. v. the Secretary of State for the Environment & Others ex p. Smith, Hilden & Others* [1988] C.O.D. 3 and transcript for August 28, 1988. See also D.O.E. Circulars 1/94 and 18/94. and *R. v. Lincolnshire C.C. ex p. Atkinson*, (1995) 8 Admin L.R. 529. For the effect of Articles 8 and 14 of the ECHR on decision-making on gypsies see *e.g. Buckley v. U.K.* 23 E.H.R.R. 101 and *Chapman v. U.K.* (2001) BHRC 48. The Strasbourg authorities still leaves a wide margin of appreciation to the national authorities in weighing the public interest in taking action against the private rights of those affected. See *Chapman* at paras. 91 and 92 — "a margin of appreciation must, inevitably, be left to the national authorities, who by reason of their direct and continuous contact with the vital forces of their countries are in principle better placed than an international court to evaluate local needs and conditions. This margin will vary according to the nature of the Convention right in issue, its importance for the individual and the nature of the activities restricted, as well as the nature of the aim pursued by the restrictions ..." (para. 91).

[52] Defined by s. 77(6)(b) as including "caravans" (as they are defined in s. 29(1) of the Caravan Sites and Control of Development Act 1960).

[53] This power allows a local authority, in effect, to take direct action for trespass to land in private ownership (not in the sense of bringing civil proceedings for possession) although it might have no entitlement to possession. However, before taking action, a local authority must consider the effect of its proposed action on the individuals concerned — "considerations of common humanity" — per Sedley J. in the *Lincolnshire C.C.* case, above.

[53a] It is unclear whether Parliament intended that any significance be attached to the omission of "reasonably" which is present in many of the other provisions in this part of the 1994 Act relating to the giving of directions.

[54] This power does not include consideration of whether the local authority acted reasonably in giving a direction under s. 77, but only to whether the council complied with formalities under the Act. See *R . v. Wolverhampton Metropolitan Borough Council and Another ex parte Dunne and Another, The Times*, January 2, 1997 ([1995] T.L.R. 9).

and to take such steps to secure entry as might be specified in the order. Obstruction of the execution of such an order is also an offence under section 78(4). Defences include demonstrating that the failure to leave or remove vehicles or property as soon as practicable or his re-entry with a vehicle was due to illness, mechanical breakdown or other immediate emergency.[56]

The above legislation gave rise to considerable public debate and controversy both inside[57] and outside[58] Parliament and it is certainly true that the potentially severe nature of the penalties for the statutory interferences with the land provide a strong contrast with the civil remedies available: compare the normal order for possession available in civil summary proceedings and the possible six months' term of imprisonment under section 76 of the 1994 Act for failure to comply with an interim possession order within 24 hours of the service of the order. Whether the need to provide effective remedies for trespass, and for squatting in particular, has led to the provision of remedies which are too severe will only become apparent over a long period of time.[59] Taking action in such cases additionally falls to be balanced against potential Convention rights in accordance with sections 3 and 6 of the Human Rights Act 1998.[60]

---

[56] S. 77(5).

[57] See, *e.g.* Hansard, HL, July 7, 1994 and July 11, 1994 and [1995] Crim.L.R. 1 (Editorial), 19 (A.T. Smith) and 28 (S. Campbell). A.T. Smith appears to sum up the views of many in describing Part *v.* of the Act as "a mean-spirited, intolerant, ungenerous piece of work that may, if equally ungenerously implemented, lay trouble in store for years to come." In the *Lincolnshire C.C.* case, Sedley J. referred to "this new and in some ways draconic legislation".

[58] Including, in the Autumn of 1994, the occupation of the roof of the Houses of Parliament by protestors, a large demonstration on the site of the A12–M11 Link Road in north-east London and the invasion of the Home Secretary's own garden.

[59] A research paper on the use of the new provisions has been published by the Home Office: "Trespass and Protest", available from HMSO or from the Home Office website.

[60] See *e.g.* Clayton & Tomlinson, *The Law of Human Rights* (OUP, 2000).

Appendices

Appendix 1

Statutory Extracts

Landlord and Tenant Act 1730
c. 28)

An Act for the more effectual preventing Frauds committed by Tenants, and for the more easy Recovery of Rents, and Renewal of Leases.Former Provisions with regard to Rents, 32H. 8. c. 37, 8 Ann. c. 14. For securing to Lessors and Land Owners their just Rights, and to prevent Frauds frequently committed by Tenants. **A1–001**

1 Persons holding over Lands, etc., after Expiration of Leases, to pay double the yearly Value.

In case any Tenant or Tenants for any Term of Life, Lives or Years, or other Person or Persons, who are or shall come into Possession of any Lands, Tenements or Hereditaments, by, from or under, or by Collusion with such Tenant or Tenants, shall wilfully hold over any Lands, Tenements or Hereditaments, after the Determination of such Term or Terms, and after Demand made, and Notice in Writing given, for delivering the Possession thereof, by his or their Landlords or Lessors, or the Person or Persons to whom the Remainder or Reversion of such Lands, Tenements or Hereditaments shall belong, his or their Agent or Agents thereunto lawfully authorized; then and in such Case such Person or Persons so holding over, shall, for and during the Time he, she and they shall so hold over, or keep the Person or Persons intitled, out of Possession of the said Lands, Tenements, and Hereditaments, as aforesaid, pay to the Person or Persons so kept out of Possession, their Executors, Administrators or Assigns, at the Rate of double the yearly Value of the Lands, Tenements and Hereditaments so detained, for so long time as the same are detained, to be recovered in any of his Majesty's Courts of Record, by Action of Debt,[. . .][1]

[1] Words repealed by Statute Law Revision Act 1948 (c. 62), Sch. 1

5 Method of recovering Seck Rents, etc

And whereas the Remedy for recovering Rents Seck, Rents of Assize and chief Rents, are tedious and difficult,' from and after the twenty-fourth Day of **June** one thousand seven hundred and thirty-one, all and every Person or Persons, Bodies Politick and Corporate, shall and may have the like Remedy by Distress, and by impounding and selling the same, in cases of Rents Seck, Rents of Assize and chief Rents, which have been duly answered or paid for the Space of three Years, within the Space of twenty Years before the first Day of this present Session of Parliament, or shall be hereafter created, as in case of Rent reserved upon Lease; any Law or Usage to the contrary notwithstanding.

Distress for Rent Act 1737
c. 19)

An Act for the more effectual securing the Payment of Rents, and pre- venting Frauds by Tenants.Whereas the several laws heretofore made for the better security of rents, and to prevent frauds committed by tenants, have not proved sufficient to obtain the good ends and purposes designed thereby, but rather the fraudulent practices of tenants, and the mischief intended by the said Acts to be prevented have of late years increased, to the great loss and damage of their lessors or landlords:

A1–002

18   Tenants holding after the time they notify for quitting, to pay double rent.

And whereas great inconveniences have happened and may happen to landlords whose tenants have power to determine their leases, by giving notice to quit the premises by them holden, and yet refusing to deliver up the possession when the landlord hath agreed with another tenant for the same: from and after the said twenty fourth day of June one thousand seven hundred and thirty eight, in case any tenant or tenants shall give notice of his, her, or their intention to quit the premises by him, her, or them holden, at a time mentioned in such notice, and shall not accordingly deliver up the possession thereof at the time in such notice contained, that then the said tenant or tenants, his, her, or their executors or administrators, shall from thenceforward pay to the landlord or landlords, lessor or lessors, double the rent or sum which he, she, or they should otherwise have paid, to be levied, sued for, and recovered at the same times and in the same manner as the single rent or sum, before the giving such notice, could be levied, sued for, or recovered; and such double rent or sum shall continue to be paid during all the time such tenant or tenants shall continue in possession as aforesaid.

Criminal Law Act 1977

PART II

OFFENCES RELATING TO ENTERING AND REMAINING ON PROPERTY

6 Violence for securing entry.

A1–003   (1) Subject to the following provisions of this section, any person who, without lawful authority, uses or threatens violence for the purpose of securing entry into any premises for himself or for any other person is guilty of an offence, provided that —

> (a) here is someone present on those premises at the time who is opposed to the entry which the violence is intended to secure; and
>
> (b) the person using or threatening the violence knows that that is the case.

[(1A) Subsection (1) above does not apply to a person who is a displaced residential occupier or a protected intending occupier of the premises in question or who is acting on behalf of such an occupier; and if the accused adduces sufficient evidence that he was, or was acting on behalf of, such an occupier he shall be presumed to be, or to be acting on behalf of, such an occupier unless the contrary is proved by the prosecution.][1]

(2) [Subject to subsection (1A) above,][2]The fact that a person has any interest in or right to possession or occupation of any premises shall not for the purposes of subsection (1) above constitute lawful authority for the use or threat of violence by him or anyone else for the purpose of securing his entry into those premises.

(3) [. . .][3]

(4) It is immaterial for the purposes of this section —

> (a) whether the violence in question is directed against the person or against property; and
>
> (b) whether the entry which the violence is intended to secure is for the purpose of acquiring possession of the premises in question or for any other purpose.

(5) A person guilty of an offence under this section shall be liable on summary conviction to imprisonment for a term not exceeding six months or to a fine not exceeding [level 5 on the standard scale][4] or to both.

(6) A constable in uniform may arrest without warrant anyone who is, or whom he, with reasonable cause, suspects to be, guilty of an offence under this section.

(7) Section 12 below contains provisions which apply for determining

when any person is to be regarded for the purposes of this Part of this Act as a displaced residential occupier of any premises or of any access to any premises[and section 12A below contains provisions which apply for determining when any person is to be regarded for the purposes of this Part of this Act as a protected intending occupier of any premises or of any access to any premises][5].

1 added by Criminal Justice and Public Order Act 1994 c.33 Pt V s 72 (2)
2 words inserted by Criminal Justice and Public Order Act 1994 c.33 Pt V s 72 (3)
3 repealed by Criminal Justice and Public Order Act 1994 c.33 Pt V s 72 (4)
4 Words substituted by Criminal Justice Act 1982 (c.48), s. 46
5 words inserted by Criminal Justice and Public Order Act 1994 c.33 Pt V s 72 (5)

[7 Adverse occupation of residential premises.

(1) Subject to the following provisions of this section and to section 12A(9) below, any person who is on any premises as a trespasser after having entered as such is guilty of an offence if he fails to leave those premises on being required to do so by or on behalf of —

(a) a displaced residential occupier of the premises; or

(b) an individual who is a protected intending occupier of the premises.

(2) In any proceedings for an offence under this section it shall be a defence for the accused to prove that he believed that the person requiring him to leave the premises was not a displaced residential occupier or protected intending occupier of the premises or a person acting on behalf of a displaced residential occupier or protected intending occupier.

(3) In any proceedings for an offence under this section it shall be a defence for the accused to prove —

(a) that the premises in question are or form part of premises used mainly for non-residential purposes; and

(b) that he was not on any part of the premises used wholly or mainly for residential purposes.

(4) Any reference in the preceding provisions of this section to any premises includes a reference to any access to them, whether or not any such access itself constitutes premises, within the meaning of this Part of this Act.

(5) A person guilty of an offence under this section shall be liable on summary conviction to imprisonment for a term not exceeding six months or to a fine not exceeding level 5 on the standard scale or to both.

(6) A constable in uniform may arrest without warrant anyone who is, or whom he, with reasonable cause, suspects to be, guilty of an offence under this section.

(7) Section 12 below contains provisions which apply for determining when any person is to be regarded for the purposes of this Part of this Act as a displaced residential occupier of any premises or of any access to any

premises and section 12A below contains provisions which apply for determining when any person is to be regarded for the purposes of this Part of this Act as a protected intending occupier of any premises or of any access to any premises.][1]

[1] substituted by Criminal Justice and Public Order Act 1994 c.33 Pt V s 73

8 Trespassing with a weapon of offence.

(1) A person who is on any premises as a trespasser, after having entered as such, is guilty of an offence if, without lawful authority or reasonable excuse, he has with him on the premises any weapon of offence.

(2) In subsection (1) above "weapon of offence" means any article made or adapted for use for causing injury to or incapacitating a person, or intended by the person having it with him for such use.

(3) A person guilty of an offence under this section shall be liable on summary conviction to imprisonment for a term not exceeding three months or to a fine not exceeding [level 5 on the standard scale][1] or to both.

(4) A constable in uniform may arrest without warrant anyone who is, or whom he, with reasonable cause, suspects to be, in the act of committing an offence under this section.

[1] Words substituted by Criminal Justice Act 1982 (c.48), s. 46

9 Trespassing on premises of foreign missions, etc.

(1) Subject to subsection (3) below, a person who enters or is on any premises to which this section applies as a trespasser is guilty of an offence.

(2) This section applies to any premises which are or form part of —

(a) the premises of a diplomatic mission within the meaning of the definition in Article 1(i) of the Vienna Convention on Diplomatic Relations signed in 1961 as that Article has effect in the United Kingdom by virtue of section 2 of and Schedule 1 to the Diplomatic Privileges Act 1964;

[(aa) the premises of a closed diplomatic mission;][1]

(b) consular premises within the meaning of the definition in paragraph 1(j) of Article 1 of the Vienna Convention on Consular Relations signed in 1963 as that Article has effect in the United Kingdom by virtue of section 1 of and Schedule 1 to the Consular Relations Act 1968;

[(bb) the premises of a closed consular post;][2]

(c) any other premises in respect of which any organisation or body is entitled to inviolability by or under any enactment; and

(d) any premises which are the private residence of a diplomatic agent (within the meaning of Article 1(e) of the Convention mentioned in paragraph (a) above) or of any other person who is entitled to inviolability of residence by or under any enactment.

[(2A) In subsection (2) above —

"the premises of a closed diplomatic mission" means premises which fall within Article 45 of the Convention mentioned in subsection (2)(a) above (as that Article has effect in the United Kingdom by virtue of the section and Schedule mentioned in that paragraph); and

"the premises of a closed consular post" means premises which fall within Article 27 of the Convention mentioned in subsection (2)(b) above (as that Article has effect in the United Kingdom by virtue of the section and Schedule mentioned in that paragraph);][3]

(3) In any proceedings for an offence under this section it shall be a defence for the accused to prove that he believed that the premises in question were not premises to which this section applies.

(4) In any proceedings for an offence under this section a certificate issued by or under the authority of the Secretary of State stating that any premises were or formed part of premises of any description mentioned in paragraphs (a) to (d) of subsection (2) above at the time of the alleged offence shall be conclusive evidence that the premises were or formed part of premises of that description at that time.

(5) A person guilty of an offence under this section shall be liable on summary conviction to imprisonment for a term not exceeding six months or to a fine not exceeding [level 5 on the standard scale][4] or to both.

(6) Proceedings for an offence under this section shall not be instituted against any person except by or with the consent of the Attorney General.

(7) A constable in uniform may arrest without warrant any one who is, or whom he, with reasonable cause, suspects to be, in the act of committing an offence under this section.

[1] S. 9(2)(aa) inserted by Diplomatic and Consular Premises Act 1987 (c.46), s. 7(1)(a)
[2] S. 9(2)(bb) inserted by Diplomatic and Consular Premises Act 1987 (c.46), s. 7(1)(b)
[3] S. 9(2A) inserted by Diplomatic and Consular Premises Act 1987 (c.46), s. 7(2)
[4] Words substituted by Criminal Justice Act 1982 (c.48), s. 46

10 Obstruction of court officers executing process for possession against unauthorised occupiers.

(1) Without prejudice to section 8(2) of the Sheriffs Act 1887 but subject to the following provisions of this section, a person is guilty of an offence if he resists or intentionally obstructs any person who is in fact an officer of a court engaged in executing any process issued by the High Court or by any county court for the purpose of enforcing any judgment or order for the recovery of any premises or for the delivery of possession of any premises.

(2) Subsection (1) above does not apply unless the judgment or order in question was given or made in proceedings brought under any provisions of rules of court applicable only in circumstances where the person

claiming possession of any premises alleges that the premises in question are occupied solely by a person or persons (not being a tenant or tenants holding over after the termination of the tenancy) who entered into or remained in occupation of the premises without the licence or consent of the person claiming possession or any predecessor in title of his.

(3) In any proceedings for an offence under this section it shall be a defence for the accused to prove that he believed that the person he was resisting or obstructing was not an officer of a court.

(4) A person guilty of an offence under this section shall be liable on summary conviction to imprisonment for a term not exceeding six months or to a fine not exceeding [level 5 on the standard scale][1] or to both.

(5) A constable in uniform or any officer of a court may arrest without warrant anyone who is, or whom he, with reasonable cause, suspects to be, guilty of an offence under this section.

(6) In this section "officer of a court" means —

    (a) any sheriff, under sheriff, deputy sheriff, bailiff or officer of a sheriff; and

    (b) any bailiff or other person who is an officer of a county court within the meaning of the County Courts Act 1959.

[1] Words substituted by Criminal Justice Act 1982 (c.48), s. 46

11 [. . .][1]

[1] Repealed by Police and Criminal Evidence Act 1984 (c.60), s. 119(2), Sch. 7 Pt. I

12 Supplementary provisions.

(1) In this Part of this Act —

    (a) "premises" means any building, any part of a building under separate occupation, any land ancillary to a building, the site comprising any building or buildings together with any land ancillary thereto, and (for the purposes only of sections 10 and 11 above) any other place; and

    (b) "access" means , in relation to any premises, any part of any site or building within which those premises are situated which constitutes an ordinary means of access to those premises (whether or not that is its sole or primary use).

(2) References in this section to a building shall apply also to any structure other than a movable one, and to any movable structure, vehicle or vessel designed or adapted for use for residential purposes; and for the purposes of subsection (1) above —

    (a) part of a building is under separate occupation if anyone is in occupation or entitled to occupation of that part as distinct from the whole; and

(b) land is ancillary to a building if it is adjacent to it and used (or intended for use) in connection with the occupation of that building or any part of it.

(3) Subject to subsection (4) below, any person who was occupying any premises as a residence immediately before being excluded from occupation by anyone who entered those premises, or any access to those premises, as a trespasser is a displaced residential occupier of the premises for the purposes of this Part of this Act so long as he continues to be excluded from occupation of the premises by the original trespasser or by any subsequent trespasser.

(4) A person who was himself occupying the premises in question as a trespasser immediately before being excluded from occupation shall not by virtue of subsection (3) above be a displaced residential occupier of the premises for the purposes of this Part of this Act.

(5) A person who by virtue of subsection (3) above is a displaced residential occupier of any premises shall be regarded for the purposes of this Part of this Act as a displaced residential occupier also of any access to those premises.

(6) Anyone who enters or is on or in occupation of any premises by virtue of —

(a) any title derived from a trespasser; or
(b) any licence or consent given by a trespasser or by a person deriving title from a trespasser,

shall himself be treated as a trespasser for the purposes of this Part of this Act (without prejudice to whether or not he would be a trespasser apart from this provision); and references in this Part of this Act to a person's entering or being on or occupying any premises as a trespasser shall be construed accordingly.

(7) Anyone who is on any premises as a trespasser shall not cease to be a trespasser for the purposes of this Part of this Act by virtue of being allowed time to leave the premises, nor shall anyone cease to be a displaced residential occupier of any premises by virtue of any such allowance of time to a trespasser.

[(7A) Subsection (6) also applies to the Secretary of State if the tenancy or licence is granted by him under Part III of the Housing Associations Act 1985.][1]

(8) No rule of law ousting the jurisdiction of magistrates' courts to try offences where a dispute of title to property is involved shall preclude magistrates' courts from trying offences under this Part of this Act.

[1] added by Government of Wales Act 1998 c.38 Sch 16 Para 3 (3)

[12A Protected intending occupiers: supplementary provisions.

(1) For the purposes of this Part of this Act an individual is a protected intending occupier of any premises at any time if at that time he falls within subsection (2), (4) or (6) below.

(2) An individual is a protected intending occupier of any premises if —

    (a) he has in those premises a freehold interest or a leasehold interest with not less than two years still to run;

    (b) he requires the premises for his own occupation as a residence;

    (c) he is excluded from occupation of the premises by a person who entered them, or any access to them, as a trespasser; and

    (d) he or a person acting on his behalf holds a written statement —

        (i)   which specifies his interest in the premises;

        (ii) which states that he requires the premises for occupation as a residence for himself; and

        (iii) with respect to which the requirements in subsection (3) below are fulfilled.

(3) The requirements referred to in subsection (2)(d)(iii) above are —

    (a) that the statement is signed by the person whose interest is specified in it in the presence of a justice of the peace or commissioner for oaths; and

    (b) that the justice of the peace or commissioner for oaths has subscribed his name as a witness to the signature.

(4) An individual is also a protected intending occupier of any premises if —

    (a) he has a tenancy of those premises (other than a tenancy falling within subsection (2)(a) above or (6)(a) below) or a licence to occupy those premises granted by a person with a freehold interest or a leasehold interest with not less than two years still to run in the premises;

    (b) he requires the premises for his own occupation as a residence;

    (c) he is excluded from occupation of the premises by a person who entered them, or any access to them, as a trespasser; and

    (d) he or a person acting on his behalf holds a written statement —

        (i)   which states that he has been granted a tenancy of those premises or a licence to occupy those premises;

        (ii) which specifies the interest in the premises of the person who granted that tenancy or licence to occupy ("the landlord");

        (iii) which states that he requires the premises for occupation as a residence for himself; and

        (iv) with respect to which the requirements in subsection (5) below are fulfilled.

(5) The requirements referred to in subsection (4)(d)(iv) above are —

    (a) that the statement is signed by the landlord and by the tenant or licensee in the presence of a justice of the peace or commissioner for oaths;

(b) that the justice of the peace or commissioner for oaths has subscribed his name as a witness to the signatures.

(6) An individual is also a protected intending occupier of any premises if —

(a) he has a tenancy of those premises (other than a tenancy falling within subsection (2)(a) or (4)(a) above) or a licence to occupy those premises granted by an authority to which this subsection applies;

(b) he requires the premises for his own occupation as a residence;

(c) he is excluded from occupation of the premises by a person who entered the premises, or any access to them, as a trespasser; and

(d) there has been issued to him by or on behalf of the authority referred to in paragraph (a) above a certificate stating that —

(i) he has been granted a tenancy of those premises or a licence to occupy those premises as a residence by the authority; and

(ii) the authority which granted that tenancy or licence to occupy is one to which this subsection applies, being of a description specified in the certificate.

(7) Subsection (6) above applies to the following authorities —

(a) any body mentioned in section 14 of the Rent Act 1977 (landlord's interest belonging to local authority etc.);

(b) the Housing Corporation;[and]¹

(c) [. . .]¹

[(d) a registered social landlord within the meaning of the Housing Act 1985 (see section 5(4) and (5) of that Act).]²

(8) A person is guilty of an offence if he makes a statement for the purposes of subsection (2)(d) or (4)(d) above which he knows to be false in a material particular or if he recklessly makes such a statement which is false in a material particular.

(9) In any proceedings for an offence under section 7 of this Act where the accused was requested to leave the premises by a person claiming to be or to act on behalf of a protected intending occupier of the premises —

(a) it shall be a defence for the accused to prove that, although asked to do so by the accused at the time the accused was requested to leave, that person failed at that time to produce to the accused such a statement as is referred to in subsection (2)(d) or (4)(d) above or such a certificate as is referred to in subsection (6)(d) above; and

(b) any document purporting to be a certificate under subsection

(6)(d) above shall be received in evidence and, unless the contrary is proved, shall be deemed to have been issued by or on behalf of the authority stated in the certificate.

(10) A person guilty of an offence under subsection (8) above shall be liable on summary conviction to imprisonment for a term not exceeding six months or to a fine not exceeding level 5 on the standard scale or to both.

(11) A person who is a protected intending occupier of any premises shall be regarded for the purposes of this Part of this Act as a protected intending occupier also of any access to those premises.][3]

[1] words repealed by Government of Wales Act 1998 c.38 Sch 18 (VI) Para 1
[2] words substituted by SI 1996/2325 Sch 2 Para 8
[3] added by Criminal Justice and Public Order Act 1994 c.33 Pt V s 74

Housing Act 1988
CHAPTER 50

Part I

Rented Accommodation

Chapter IV

Protection from Eviction

27 Damages for unlawful eviction.

(1) This section applies if, at any time after 9th June 1988, a landlord (in this section referred to as "the landlord in default") or any person acting on behalf of the landlord in default unlawfully deprives the residential occupier of any premises of his occupation of the whole or part of the premises.

A1–004

(2) This section also applies if, at any time after 9th June 1988, a landlord (in this section referred to as "the landlord in default") or any person acting on behalf of the landlord in default —

(a) attempts unlawfully to deprive the residential occupier of any premises of his occupation of the whole or part of the premises, or

(b) knowing or having reasonable cause to believe that the conduct is likely to cause the residential occupier of any premises —

(i) to give up his occupation of the premises or any part thereof, or

(ii) to refrain from exercising any right or pursuing any remedy in respect of the premises or any part thereof,

does acts likely to interfere with the peace or comfort of the residential occupier or members of his household, or persistently withdraws or withholds services reasonably required for the occupation of the premises as a residence,

and, as a result, the residential occupier gives up his occupation of the premises as a residence.

(3) Subject to the following provisions of this section, where this section applies, the landlord in default shall, by virtue of this section, be liable to pay to the former residential occupier, in respect of his loss of the right to occupy the premises in question as his residence, damages assessed on the basis set out in section 28 below.

(4) Any liability arising by virtue of subsection (3) above —

(a) shall be in the nature of a liability in tort; and

(b) subject to subsection (5) below, shall be in addition to any liability arising apart from this section (whether in tort, contract or otherwise).

507

(5) Nothing in this section affects the right of a residential occupier to enforce any liability which arises apart from this section in respect of his loss of the right to occupy premises as his residence; but damages shall not be awarded both in respect of such a liability and in respect of a liability arising by virtue of this section on account of the same loss.

(6) No liability shall arise by virtue of subsection (3) above if —

(a) before the date on which proceedings to enforce the liability are finally disposed of, the former residential occupier is reinstated in the premises in question in such circumstances that he becomes again the residential occupier of them; or

(b) at the request of the former residential occupier, a court makes an order (whether in the nature of an injunction or otherwise) as a result of which he is reinstated as mentioned in paragraph (a) above;

and, for the purposes of paragraph (a) above, proceedings to enforce a liability are finally disposed of on the earliest date by which the proceedings (including any proceedings on or in consequence of an appeal) have been determined and any time for appealing or further appealing has expired, except that if any appeal is abandoned, the proceedings shall be taken to be disposed of on the date of the abandonment.

(7) If, in proceedings to enforce a liability arising by virtue of subsection (3) above, it appears to the court —

(a) that, prior to the event which gave rise to the liability, the conduct of the former residential occupier or any person living with him in the premises concerned was such that it is reasonable to mitigate the damages for which the landlord in default would otherwise be liable, or

(b) that, before the proceedings were begun, the landlord in default offered to reinstate the former residential occupier in the premises in question and either it was unreasonable of the former residential occupier to refuse that offer or, if he had obtained alternative accommodation before the offer was made, it would have been unreasonable of him to refuse that offer if he had not obtained that accommodation,

the court may reduce the amount of damages which would otherwise be payable to such amount as it thinks appropriate.

(8) In proceedings to enforce a liability arising by virtue of subsection (3) above, it shall be a defence for the defendant to prove that he believed, and had reasonable cause to believe —

(a) that the residential occupier had ceased to reside in the premises in question at the time when he was deprived of occupation as mentioned in subsection (1) above or, as the case may be, when the attempt was made or the acts were done as a result of which he gave up his occupation of those premises; or

(b) that, where the liability would otherwise arise by virtue only of the doing of acts or the withdrawal or withholding of services, he had reasonable grounds for doing the acts or withdrawing or withholding the services in question.

(9) In this section —

(a) "residential occupier", in relation to any premises, has the same meaning as in section 1 of the 1977 Act;

(b) "the right to occupy", in relation to a residential occupier, includes any restriction on the right of another person to recover possession of the premises in question;

(c) "landlord", in relation to a residential occupier, means the person who, but for the occupier's right to occupy, would be entitled to occupation of the premises and any superior landlord under whom that person derives title;

(d) "former residential occupier", in relation to any premises, means the person who was the residential occupier until he was deprived of or gave up his occupation as mentioned in subsection (1) or subsection (2) above (and, in relation to a former residential occupier, "the right to occupy" and "landlord" shall be construed accordingly).

28 The measure of damages.

(1) The basis for the assessment of damages referred to in section 27(3) above is the difference in value, determined as at the time immediately before the residential occupier ceased to occupy the premises in question as his residence, between —

(a) the value of the interest of the landlord in default determined on the assumption that the residential occupier continues to have the same right to occupy the premises as before that time; and

(b) the value of that interest determined on the assumption that the residential occupier has ceased to have that right.

(2) In relation to any premises, any reference in this section to the interest of the landlord in default is a reference to his interest in the building in which the premises in question are comprised (whether or not that building contains any other premises) together with its curtilage.

(3) For the purposes of the valuations referred to in subsection (1) above, it shall be assumed —

(a) that the landlord in default is selling his interest on the open market to a willing buyer;

(b) that neither the residential occupier nor any member of his family wishes to buy; and

(c) that it is unlawful to carry out any substantial development of any of the land in which the landlord's interest subsists or to demolish the whole or part of any building on that land.

(4) In this section "the landlord in default" has the same meaning as in section 27 above and subsection (9) of that section applies in relation to this section as it applies in relation to that.

(5) Section 113 of the Housing Act 1985 (meaning of "members of a person's family") applies for the purposes of subsection (3)(b) above.

(6) The reference in subsection (3)(c) above to substantial development of any of the land in which the landlord's interest subsists is a reference to any development other than —

(a) development for which planning permission is granted by a general development order for the time being in force and which is carried out so as to comply with any condition or limitation subject to which planning permission is so granted; or

(b) a change of use resulting in the building referred to in subsection (2) above or any part of it being used as, or as part of, one or more dwelling-houses;

and in this subsection "general development order" [has the meaning given in section 56(6) of the Town and Country Planning Act 1990][1] and other expressions have the same meaning as in that Act.

[1] Words substituted by Planning (Consequential Provisions) Act 1990 (c.11), s. 4, Sch. 2 para. 79(1)

33 Interpretation of Chapter IV and the 1977 Act.

(1) In this Chapter "the 1977 Act" means the Protection from Eviction Act 1977.

(2) In section 8 of the 1977 Act (interpretation) at the end of subsection (1) (statutory protected tenancy) there shall be inserted —

"(e) an assured tenancy or assured agricultural occupancy under Part I of the Housing Act 1988."

(3) At the end of that section there shall be added the following subsections —

"(4) In this Act "excluded tenancy" and "excluded licence" have the meaning assigned by section 3A of this Act.

(5) If, on or after the date on which the Housing Act 1988 came into force, the terms of an excluded tenancy or excluded licence entered into before that date are varied, then —

(a) if the variation affects the amount of the rent which is payable under the tenancy or licence, the tenancy or licence shall be treated for the purposes of sections 3(2C) and 5(1B) above as a new tenancy or licence entered into at the time of the variation; and

(b)   if the variation does not affect the amount of the rent which is so payable, nothing in this Act shall affect the determination of the question whether the variation is such as to give rise to a new tenancy or licence.

(6) Any reference in subsection (5) above to a variation affecting the amount of the rent which is payable under a tenancy or licence does not include a reference to —

(a)   a reduction or increase effected under Part III or Part VI of the Rent Act 1977 (rents under regulated tenancies and housing association tenancies), section 78 of that Act (power of rent tribunal in relation to restricted contracts) or sections 11 to 14 of the Rent (Agriculture) Act 1976; or

(b)   a variation which is made by the parties and has the effect of making the rent expressed to be payable under the tenancy or licence the same as a rent for the dwelling which is entered in the register under Part IV or section 79 of the Rent Act 1977."

Protection from Eviction Act 1977

PART I

UNLAWFUL EVICTION AND HARASSMENT

1 Unlawful eviction and harassment of occupier.

A1–005 (1) In this section "residential occupier", in relation to any premises, means a person occupying the premises as a residence, whether under a contract or by virtue of any enactment or rule of law giving him the right to remain in occupation or restricting the right of any other person to recover possession of the premises.

(2) If any person unlawfully deprives the residential occupier of any premises of his occupation of the premises or any part thereof, or attempts to do so, he shall be guilty of an offence unless he proves that he believed, and had reasonable cause to believe, that the residential occupier had ceased to reside in the premises.

(3) If any person with intent to cause the residential occupier of any premises —

(a) to give up the occupation of the premises or any part thereof; or
(b) to refrain from exercising any right or pursuing any remedy in respect of the premises or part thereof;

does acts [likely][1] to interfere with the peace or comfort of the residential occupier or members of his household, or persistently withdraws or withholds services reasonably required for the occupation of the premises as a residence, he shall be guilty of an offence.

[(3A) Subject to subsection (3B) below, the landlord of a residential occupier or an agent of the landlord shall be guilty of an offence if —

(a) he does acts likely to interfere with the peace or comfort of the residential occupier or members of his household, or
(b) he persistently withdraws or withholds services reasonably required for the occupation of the premises in question as a residence,

and (in either case) he knows, or has reasonable cause to believe, that conduct is likely to cause the residential occupier to give up the occupation of the whole or part of the premises or to refrain from exercising any right or pursuing any remedy in respect of the whole or part of the premises.

(3B) A person shall not be guilty of an offence under subsection (3A) above if he proves that he had reasonable grounds for doing the acts or withdrawing or withholding the services in question.

(3C) In subsection (3A) above "landlord", in relation to a residential occupier of any premises, means the person who, but for —

(a) the residential occupier's right to remain in occupation of the premises, or

(b) a restriction on the person's right to recover possession of the premises,

would be entitled to occupation of the premises and any superior landlord under whom that person derives title.][2]

(4) A person guilty of an offence under this section shall be liable —

(a) on summary conviction, to a fine not exceeding £400 or to imprisonment for a term not exceeding 6 months or to both;

(b) on conviction on indictment, to a fine or to imprisonment for a term not exceeding 2 years or to both.

(5) Nothing in this section shall be taken to prejudice any liability or remedy to which a person guilty of an offence thereunder may be subject in civil proceedings.

(6) Where an offence under this section committed by a body corporate is proved to have been committed with the consent or connivance of, or to be attributable to any neglect on the part of, any director, manager or secretary or other similar officer of the body corporate or any person who was purporting to act in any such capacity, he as well as the body corporate shall be guilty of that offence and shall be liable to be proceeded against and punished accordingly.

[1] Word substituted by Housing Act 1988 (c.50), s. 29(1) (read with s. 44(2)(b))
[2] S.1(3A)–(3C) inserted by Housing Act 1988 (c.50), ss. 29(2), 44(2)(b)

2 Restriction on re-entry without due process of law.

Where any premises are let as a dwelling on a lease which is subject to a right of re-entry or forfeiture it shall not be lawful to enforce that right otherwise than by proceedings in the court while any person is lawfully residing in the premises or part of them.

3 Prohibition of eviction without due process of law.

(1) Where any premises have been let as a dwelling under a tenancy which is [neither a statutorily protected tenancy nor an excluded tenancy][1] and —

(a) the tenancy (in this section referred to as the former tenancy) has come to an end, but

(b) the occupier continues to reside in the premises or part of them,

it shall not be lawful for the owner to enforce against the occupier, otherwise than by proceedings in the court, his right to recover possession of the premises.

(2) In this section "the occupier", in relation to any premises, means any

person lawfully residing in the premises or part of them at the termination of the former tenancy.

[(2A) Subsections (1) and (2) above apply in relation to any restricted contract (within the meaning of the Rent Act 1977) which —

(a) creates a licence; and

(b) is entered into after the commencement of section 69 of the Housing Act 1980;

as they apply in relation to a restricted contract which creates a tenancy.][2]

[(2B) Subsections (1) and (2) above apply in relation to any premises occupied as a dwelling under a licence, other than an excluded licence, as they apply in relation to premises let as a dwelling under a tenancy, and in those subsections the expressions "let" and "tenancy" shall be construed accordingly.

(2C) References in the preceding provisions of this section and section 4(2A) below to an excluded tenancy do not apply to —

(a) a tenancy entered into before the date on which the Housing Act 1988 came into force, or

(b) a tenancy entered into on or after that date but pursuant to a contract made before that date,

but, subject to that, "excluded tenancy" and "excluded licence" shall be construed in accordance with section 3A below.][3]

(3) This section shall, with the necessary modifications, apply where the owner's right to recover possession arises on the death of the tenant under a statutory tenancy within the meaning of the Rent Act 1977 or the Rent (Agriculture) Act 1976.

[1] Words substituted by Housing Act 1988 (c.50), ss. 30(1), 44(2)(b)
[2] S. 3(2A) inserted by Housing Act 1980 (c.51), s.69(1)
[3] S. (2B)-(2C) inserted by Housing Act 1988 (c.50), ss. 30(2), 44(2)(b)

[3A Excluded tenancies and licences.

(1) Any reference in this Act to an excluded tenancy or an excluded licence is a reference to a tenancy or licence which is excluded by virtue of any of the following provisions of this section.

(2) A tenancy or licence is excluded if —

(a) under its terms the occupier shares any accommodation with the landlord or licensor; and

(b) immediately before the tenancy or licence was granted and also at the time it comes to an end, the landlord or licensor occupied as his only or principal home premises of which the whole or part of the shared accommodation formed part.

(3) A tenancy or licence is also excluded if —

(a) under its terms the occupier shares any accommodation with a member of the family of the landlord or licensor;

(b) immediately before the tenancy or licence was granted and also at the time it comes to an end, the member of the family of the landlord or licensor occupied as his only or principal home premises of which the whole or part of the shared accommodation formed part; and

(c) immediately before the tenancy or licence was granted and also at the time it comes to an end, the landlord or licensor occupied as his only or principal home premises in the same building as the shared accommodation and that building is not a purpose-built block of flats.

(4) For the purposes of subsections (2) and (3) above, an occupier shares accommodation with another person if he has the use of it in common with that person (whether or not also in common with others) and any reference in those subsections to shared accommodation shall be construed accordingly, and if, in relation to any tenancy or licence, there is at any time more than one person who is the landlord or licensor, any reference in those subsections to the landlord or licensor shall be construed as a reference to any one of those persons.

(5) In subsections (2) to (4) above —

(a) "accommodation" includes neither an area used for storage nor a staircase, passage, corridor or other means of access;

(b) "occupier" means, in relation to a tenancy, the tenant and, in relation to a licence, the licensee; and

(c) "purpose-built block of flats" has the same meaning as in Part III of Schedule 1 to the Housing Act 1988;

and section 113 of the Housing Act 1985 shall apply to determine whether a person who is for the purposes of subsection (3) above a member of another's family as it applies for the purposes of Part IV of that Act.

(6) A tenancy or licence is excluded if it was granted as a temporary expedient to a person who entered the premises in question or any other premises as a trespasser (whether or not, before the beginning of that tenancy or licence, another tenancy or licence to occupy the premises or any other premises had been granted to him).

(7) A tenancy or licence is excluded if —

(a) it confers on the tenant or licensee the right to occupy the premises for a holiday only; or

(b) it is granted otherwise than for money or money's worth.

[(7A) A tenancy or licence is excluded if it is granted in order to provide accommodation under Part VI of the Immigration and Asylum Act 1999.][2]

(8) A licence is excluded if it confers rights of occupation in a hostel, within the meaning of the Housing Act 1985, which is provided by —

(a) the council of a county, [county borough,][3]district or London Borough, the Common Council of the City of London, the Council of the Isles of Scilly, the Inner London Education Authority, [the London Fire and Emergency Planning Authority,][4] a joint authority within the meaning of the Local Government Act 1985 or a residuary body within the meaning of that Act;

(b) a development corporation within the meaning of the New Towns Act 1981;

(c) the Commission for the New Towns;

(d) an urban development corporation established by an order under section 135 of the Local Government, Planning and Land Act 1980;

(e) a housing action trust established under Part III of the Housing Act 1988;

(f) [. . .][5]

(g) the Housing Corporation [. . .][6];

[(ga) the Secretary of State under section 89 of the Housing Associations Act 1985;][7]

[(h) a housing trust (within the meaning of the Housing Associations Act 1985) which is a charity or a registered social landlord (within the meaning of the Housing Act 1985); or][8]

(i) any other person who is, or who belongs to a class of person which is, specified in an order made by the Secretary of State.

(9) The power to make an order under subsection (8)(i) above shall be exercisable by statutory instrument which shall be subject to annulment in pursuance of a resolution of either House of Parliament.][1]

[1] S. 3A inserted by Housing Act 1988 (c.50), ss. 31, 44(2)(b)
[2] added by Immigration and Asylum Act 1999 c.33 Sch 14 Para 73
[3] words inserted by Local Government (Wales) Act 1994 c.19 Sch 8 Para 4 (1)
[4] words added by Greater London Authority Act 1999 c.29 Sch 29 (I) Para 27
[5] repealed by Government of Wales Act 1998 c.38 Sch 18 (IV) Para 1
[6] words repealed by Government of Wales Act 1998 c.38 Sch 16 Para 2 (a)
[7] added by Government of Wales Act 1998 c.38 Sch 16 Para 2 (b)
[8] paragraph substituted for word and paragraph by SI 1996/2325 Sch 2 Para 7

4 Special provisions for agricultural employees.

(1) This section shall apply where the tenant under the former tenancy (within the meaning of section 3 of this Act) occupied the premises under the terms of his employment as a person employed in agriculture, as defined in section 1 of the Rent (Agriculture) Act 1976, but is not a statutory tenant as defined in that Act.

(2) In this section "the occupier", in relation to any premises, means —

(a) the tenant under the former tenancy; or

(b) the widow or widower of the tenant under the former tenancy residing with him at his death or, if the former tenant leaves no such widow or widower, any member of his family residing with him at his death.

[(2A) In accordance with section 3(2B) above, any reference in subsections (1) and (2) above to the tenant under the former tenancy includes a reference to the licensee under a licence (other than an excluded licence) which has come to an end (being a licence to occupy premises as a dwelling); and in the following provisions of this section the expressions "tenancy" and "rent" and any other expressions referable to a tenancy shall be construed accordingly.][1]

(3) Without prejudice to any power of the court apart from this section to postpone the operation or suspend the execution of an order for possession, if in proceedings by the owner against the occupier the court makes an order for the possession of the premises the court may suspend the execution of the order on such terms and conditions, including conditions as to the payment by the occupier of arrears of rent, mesne profits and otherwise as the court thinks reasonable.

(4) Where the order for possession is made within the period of 6 months beginning with the date when the former tenancy came to an end, then, without prejudice to any powers of the court under the preceding provisions of this section or apart from this section to postpone the operation or suspend the execution of the order for a longer period, the court shall suspend the execution of the order for the remainder of the said period of 6 months unless the court —

(a) is satisfied either —
  (i) that other suitable accommodation is, or will within that period be made, available to the occupier; or
  (ii) that the efficient management of any agricultural land or the efficient carrying on of any agricultural operations would be seriously prejudiced unless the premises are available for occupation by a person employed or to be employed by the owner; or
  (iii) that greater hardship (being hardship in respect of matters other than the carrying on of such a business as aforesaid) would be caused by the suspension of the order until the end of that period than by its execution within that period; or
  (iv) that the occupier, or any person residing or lodging with the occupier, has been causing damage to the premises or has been guilty of conduct which is a nuisance or annoyance to persons occupying other premises; and

(b) considers that it would be reasonable not to suspend the execution of the order for the remainder of that period.

(5) Where the court suspends the execution of an order for possession under subsection (4) above it shall do so on such terms and conditions, including conditions as to the payment by the occupier of arrears of rent, mesne profits and otherwise as the court thinks reasonable.

(6) A decision of the court not to suspend the execution of the order under subsection (4) above shall not prejudice any other power of the court to postpone the operation or suspend the execution of the order for the whole or part of the period of 6 months mentioned in that subsection.

(7) Where the court has, under the preceding provisions of this section, suspended the execution of an order for possession, it may from time to time vary the period of suspension or terminate it and may vary any terms or conditions imposed by virtue of this section.

(8) In considering whether or how to exercise its powers under subsection (3) above, the court shall have regard to all the circumstances and, in particular, to —

(a) whether other suitable accommodation is or can be made available to the occupier;

(b) whether the efficient management of any agricultural land or the efficient carrying on of any agricultural operations would be seriously prejudiced unless the premises were available for occupation by a person employed or to be employed by the owner; and

(c) whether greater hardship would be caused by the suspension of the execution of the order than by its execution without suspension or further suspension.

(9) Where in proceedings for the recovery of possession of the premises the court makes an order for possession but suspends the execution of the order under this section, it shall make no order for costs, unless it appears to the court, having regard to the conduct of the owner or of the occupier, that there are special reasons for making such an order.

(10) Where, in the case of an order for possession of the premises to which subsection (4) above applies, the execution of the order is not suspended under that subsection or, the execution of the order having been so suspended, the suspension is terminated, then, if it is subsequently made to appear to the court that the failure to suspend the execution of the order or, as the case may be, the termination of the suspension was —

(a) attributable to the provisions of paragraph (a)(ii) of subsection (4), and

(b) due to misrepresentation or concealment of material facts by the owner of the premises,

the court may order the owner to pay to the occupier such sum as appears sufficient as compensation for damage or loss sustained by the occupier as a result of that failure or termination.

[1] S. 4(2A) inserted by Housing Act 1988 (c.50), ss. 30(3), 44(2)(b)

PART II

NOTICE TO QUIT

5 Validity of notices to quit.

(1) [Subject to subsection (1B) below][1] no notice by a landlord or a tenant to quit any premises let (whether before or after the commencement
of this Act) as a dwelling shall be valid unless —

    (a) it is in writing and contains such information as may be
prescribed, and

    (b) it is given not less than 4 weeks before the date on which it is to
take effect.

[(1A) Subject to subsection (1B) below, no notice by a licensor or a
licensee to determine a periodic licence to occupy premises as a dwelling
(whether the licence was granted before or after the passing of this Act)
shall be valid unless —

    (a) it is in writing and contains such information as may be
prescribed, and

    (b) it is given not less than 4 weeks before the date on which it is to
take effect.

(1B) Nothing in subsection (1) or subsection (1A) above applies to —

    (a) premises let on an excluded tenancy which is entered into on or
after the date on which the Housing Act 1988 came into force
unless it is entered into pursuant to a contract made before that
date; or

    (b) premises occupied under an excluded licence.][2]

(2) In this section "prescribed" means prescribed by regulations made
by the Secretary of State by statutory instrument, and a statutory instrument containing any such regulations shall be subject to annulment in
pursuance of a resolution of either House of Parliament.

(3) Regulations under this section may make different provision in
relation to different descriptions of lettings and different circumstances.

A1–006

[1] Words inserted by Housing Act 1988 (c.50), ss. 32(1), 44(2)(b)
[2] S. 5(1A)(1B) inserted by Housing Act 1988 (c.50), ss. 32(2), 44(2)(b)

Limitation Act 1980

PART I

ORDINARY TIME LIMITS FOR DIFFERENT CLASSES OF ACTION

Time limits under Part I subject to extension or exclusion under Part II

A1–006/1 **1 Time limits under Part I subject to extension or exclusion under Part II.**

(1) This Part of this Act gives the ordinary time limits for bringing actions of the various classes mentioned in the following provisions of this Part.

(2) The ordinary time limits given in this Part of this Act are subject to extension or exclusion in accordance with the provisions of Part II of this Act.

Actions founded on tort

2 Time limit for actions founded on tort.

An action founded on tort shall not be brought after the expiration of six years from the date on which the cause of action accrued.

Actions to recover land and rent

15 Time limit for actions to recover land.

(1) No action shall be brought by any person to recover any land after the expiration of twelve years from the date on which the right of action accrued to him or, if it first accrued to some person through whom he claims, to that person.

(2) Subject to the following provisions of this section, where —

    (a)   the estate or interest claimed was an estate or interest in reversion or remainder or any other future estate or interest and the right of action to recover the land accrued on the date on which the estate or interest fell into possession by the determination of the preceding estate or interest; and

    (b)   the person entitled to the preceding estate or interest (not being a term of years absolute) was not in possession of the land on that date;

no action shall be brought by the person entitled to the succeeding estate or interest after the expiration of twelve years from the date on which the right of action accrued to the person entitled to the preceding estate or interest or six years from the date on which the right of action accrued to the person entitled to the succeeding estate or interest, whichever period last expires.

(3) Subsection (2) above shall not apply to any estate or interest which falls into possession on the determination of an entailed interest and which might have been barred by the person entitled to the entailed interest.

(4) No person shall bring an action to recover any estate or interest in land under an assurance taking effect after the right of action to recover the land had accrued to the person by whom the assurance was made or some person through whom he claimed or some person entitled to a preceding estate or interest, unless the action is brought within the period during which the person by whom the assurance was made could have brought such an action.

(5) Where any person is entitled to any estate or interest in land in possession and, while so entitled, is also entitled to any future estate or interest in that land, and his right to recover the estate or interest in possession is barred under this Act, no action shall be brought by that person, or by any person claiming through him, in respect of the future estate or interest, unless in the meantime possession of the land has been recovered by a person entitled to an intermediate estate or interest.

(6) Part I of Schedule 1 to this Act contains provisions for determining the date of accrual of rights of action to recover land in the cases there mentioned.

(7) Part II of that Schedule contains provisions modifying the provisions of this section in their application to actions brought by, or by a person claiming through, the Crown or any spiritual or eleemosynary corporation sole.

16 Time limit for redemption actions.

When a mortgagee of land has been in possession of any of the mortgaged land for a period of twelve years, no action to redeem the land of which the mortgagee has been so in possession shall be brought after the end of that period by the mortgagor or any person claiming through him.

17 Extinction of title to land after expiration of time limit.

Subject to —

(a)   section 18 of this Act; and
(b)   section 75 of the Land Registration Act 1925;

at the expiration of the period prescribed by this Act for any person to bring an action to recover land (including a redemption action) the title of that person to the land shall be extinguished.

18 Settled land and land held on trust.

(1) Subject to section 21(1) and (2) of this Act, the provisions of this Act shall apply to equitable interests in land [. . .][1] as they apply to legal estates.

Accordingly a right of action to recover the land shall, for the purposes of this Act but not otherwise, be treated as accruing to a person entitled in possession to such an equitable interest in the like manner and circumstances, and on the same date, as it would accrue if his interest were a legal estate in the land (and any relevant provision of Part I of Schedule 1 to this Act shall apply in any such case accordingly).

(2) Where the period prescribed by this Act has expired for the bringing of an action to recover land by a tenant for life or a statutory owner of settled land —

- (a) his legal estate shall not be extinguished if and so long as the right of action to recover the land of any person entitled to a beneficial interest in the land either has not accrued or has not been barred by this Act; and

- (b) the legal estate shall accordingly remain vested in the tenant for life or statutory owner and shall devolve in accordance with the Settled Land Act 1925;

but if and when every such right of action has been barred by this Act, his legal estate shall be extinguished.

(3) Where any land is held upon trust [. . .][1] and the period prescribed by this Act has expired for the bringing of an action to recover the land by the trustees, the estate of the trustees shall not be extinguished if and so long as the right of action to recover the land of any person entitled to a beneficial interest in the land [. . .][1] either has not accrued or has not been barred by this Act; but if and when every such right of action has been so barred the estate of the trustees shall be extinguished.

(4) Where —

- (a) any settled land is vested in a statutory owner; or
- (b) any land is held upon trust [. . .][1];

an action to recover the land may be brought by the statutory owner or trustees on behalf of any person entitled to a beneficial interest in possession in the land [. . .][1] whose right of action has not been barred by this Act, notwithstanding that the right of action of the statutory owner or trustees would apart from this provision have been barred by this Act.

[1] Words repealed by Trusts of Land and Appointment of Trustees Act 1996 c.47 Sch 4 Para 1

19 Time limit for actions to recover rent.

No action shall be brought, or distress made, to recover arrears of rent, or damages in respect of arrears of rent, after the expiration of six years from the date on which the arrears became due.

Acknowledgment and part payment

29   Fresh accrual of action on acknowledgment or part payment.

(1) Subsections (2) and (3) below apply where any right of action (including a foreclosure action) to recover land or an advowson or any right of a mortgagee of personal property to bring a foreclosure action in respect of the property has accrued.

(2) If the person in possession of the land, benefice or personal property in question acknowledges the title of the person to whom the right of action has accrued —

- (a)   the right shall be treated as having accrued on and not before the date of the acknowledgment; and
- (b)   in the case of a right of action to recover land which has accrued to a person entitled to an estate or interest taking effect on the determination of an entailed interest against whom time is running under section 27 of this Act, section 27 shall thereupon cease to apply to the land.

(3) In the case of a foreclosure or other action by a mortgagee, if the person in possession of the land, benefice or personal property in question or the person liable for the mortgage debt makes any payment in respect of the debt (whether of principal or interest) the right shall be treated as having accrued on and not before the date of the payment.

(4) Where a mortgagee is by virtue of the mortgage in possession of any mortgaged land and either —

- (a)   receives any sum in respect of the principal or interest of the mortgage debt; or
- (b)   acknowledges the title of the mortgagor, or his equity of redemption;

an action to redeem the land in his possession may be brought at any time before the expiration of twelve years from the date of the payment or acknowledgment.

(5) Subject to subsection (6) below, where any right of action has accrued to recover —

- (a)   any debt or other liquidated pecuniary claim; or
- (b)   any claim to the personal estate of a deceased person or to any share or interest in any such estate;

and the person liable or accountable for the claim acknowledges the claim or makes any payment in respect of it the right shall be treated as having accrued on and not before the date of the acknowledgment or payment.

(6) A payment of a part of the rent or interest due at any time shall not extend the period for claiming the remainder then due, but any payment of interest shall be treated as a payment in respect of the principal debt.

(7) Subject to subsection (6) above, a current period of limitation may be repeatedly extended under this section by further acknowledgments or payments, but a right of action, once barred by this Act, shall not be revived by any subsequent acknowledgment or payment.

30 Formal provisions as to acknowledgments and part payments.

(1) To be effective for the purposes of section 29 of this Act, an acknowledgment must be in writing and signed by the person making it.

(2) For the purposes of section 29, any acknowledgment or payment —

(a) may be sent by the agent of the person by whom it is required to be made under that section; and

(b) shall be made to the person, or to an agent of the person, whose title or claim is being acknowledged or, as the case may be, in respect of whose claim the payment is being made.

31 Effect of acknowledgment or part payment on persons other than the maker or recipient.

(1) An acknowledgment of the title to any land, benefice, or mortgaged personality by any person in possession of it shall bind all other persons in possession during the ensuing period of limitation.

(2) A payment in respect of a mortgage debt by the mortgagor or any other person liable for the debt, or by any person in possession of the mortgaged property, shall, so far as any right of the mortgagee to foreclose or otherwise to recover the property is concerned, bind all other persons in possession of the mortgaged property during the ensuing period of limitation.

(3) Where two or more mortgagees are by virtue of the mortgage in possession of the mortgaged land, an acknowledgment of the mortgagor's title or of his equity of redemption by one of the mortgagees shall only bind him and his successors and shall not bind any other mortgagee or his successors.

(4) Where in a case within subsection (3) above the mortgagee by whom the acknowledgment is given is entitled to a part of the mortgaged land and not to any ascertained part of the mortgage debt the mortgagor shall be entitled to redeem that part of the land on payment, with interest, of the part of the mortgage debt which bears the same proportion to the whole of the debt as the value of the part of the land bears to the whole of the mortgaged land.

(5) Where there are two or more mortgagors, and the title or equity of redemption of one of the mortgagors is acknowledged as mentioned above in this section, the acknowledgment shall be treated as having been made to all the mortgagors.

(6) An acknowledgment of any debt or other liquidated pecuniary claim shall bind the acknowledger and his successors but not any other person.

(7) A payment made in respect of any debt or other liquidated pecuniary claim shall bind all persons liable in respect of the debt or claim.

(8) An acknowledgment by one of several personal representatives of any claim to the personal estate of a deceased person or to any share or interest in any such estate, or a payment by one of several personal representatives in respect of any such claim, shall bind the estate of the deceased person.

(9) In this section "successor", in relation to any mortgagee or person liable in respect of any debt or claim, means his personal representatives and any other person on whom the rights under the mortgage or, as the case may be, the liability in respect of the debt or claim devolve (whether on death or bankruptcy or the disposition of property or the determination of a limited estate or interest in settled property or otherwise).

Fraud, concealment and mistake

32 Postponement of limitation period in case of fraud, concealment or mistake.

(1) Subject to [subsection (3)][1] [subsections (3) and (4A)][2] below, where in the case of any action for which a period of limitation is prescribed by this Act, either —

(a) the action is based upon the fraud of the defendant; or
(b) any fact relevant to the plaintiff's right of action has been deliberately concealed from him by the defendant; or
(c) the action is for relief from the consequences of a mistake;

the period of limitation shall not begin to run until the plaintiff has discovered the fraud, concealment or mistake (as the case may be) or could with reasonable diligence have discovered it.
References in this subsection to the defendant include references to the defendant's agent and to any person through whom the defendant claims and his agent.

(2) For the purposes of subsection (1) above, deliberate commission of a breach of duty in circumstances in which it is unlikely to be discovered for some time amounts to deliberate concealment of the facts involved in that breach of duty.

(3) Nothing in this section shall enable any action —

(a) to recover, or recover the value of, any property; or
(b) to enforce any charge against, or set aside any transaction affecting, any property;

to be brought against the purchaser of the property or any person claiming through him in any case where the property has been purchased for valuable consideration by an innocent third party since the fraud or concealment or (as the case may be) the transaction in which the mistake was made took place.

(4) A purchaser is an innocent third party for the purposes of this section —

- (a) in the case of fraud or concealment of any fact relevant to the plaintiff's right of action, if he was not a party to the fraud or (as the case may be) to the concealment of that fact and did not at the time of the purchase know or have reason to believe that the fraud or concealment had taken place; and
- (b) in the case of mistake, if he did not at that time of the purchase know or have reason to believe that the mistake had been made.

[(4A) Subsection (1) above shall not apply in relation to the time limit prescribed by section 11A(3) of this Act or in relation to that time limit as applied by virtue of section 12(1) of this Act.][3]

[(5) Sections 14A and 14B of this Act shall not apply to any action to which subsection (1)(b) above applies (and accordingly the period of limitation referred to in that subsection, in any case to which either of those sections would otherwise apply, is the period applicable under section 2 of this Act).][4]

[1] Words "subsections (3) and (4A)" substituted (1.3.1988) for words "subsection (3)" by Consumer Protection Act 1987 (c. 43), ss. 6(6), 50(2), Sch. 1 para. 5(a)
[2] Words "subsections (3) and (4A)" substituted (1.3.1988) for words "subsection (3)" by Consumer Protection Act 1987 (c. 43), ss. 6(6), 50(2), Sch. 1 para. 5(a)
[3] S. 32(4A) inserted (1.3.1988) by Consumer Protection Act 1987 (c. 43), ss. 6(6), 50(2), Sch. 1 para. 5(b)
[4] S. 32(5) added with saving by Latent Damage Act 1986 (c. 37), ss. 2(2), 4(1)(2)

Discretionary exclusion of time limit for actions for defamation or malicious falsehood

[32A Discretionary exclusion of time limit for actions for defamation or malicious falsehood.

(1) If it appears to the court that it would be equitable to allow an action to proceed having regard to the degree to which —

- (a) the operation of section 4A of this Act prejudices the plaintiff or any person whom he represents, and
- (b) any decision of the court under this subsection would prejudice the defendant or any person whom he represents,

the court may direct that that section shall not apply to the action or shall not apply to any specified cause of, action to which the action relates.

(2) In acting under this section the court shall have regard to all the circumstances of the case and in particular to —

- (a) the length of, and the reasons for, the delay on the part of the plaintiff;
- (b) where the reason or one of the reasons for the delay was that all or any of the facts relevant to the cause of action did not

become known to the plaintiff until after the end of the period
mentioned in section 4A —

 (i) the date on which any such facts did become known to him,
 and

 (ii) the extent to which he acted promptly and reasonably once
 he knew whether or not the facts in question might be
 capable of giving rise to an action; and

 (c) the extent to which, having regard to the delay, relevant
 evidence is likely —

 (i) to be unavailable, or

 (ii) to be less cogent than if the action had been brought within
 the period mentioned in section 4A.

(3) In the case of an action for slander of title, slander of goods, or other
malicious falsehood brought by a personal representative —

 (a) the references in subsection (2) above to the plaintiff shall be
 construed as including the deceased person to whom the cause
 of action accrued and any previous personal representative of
 that person; and

 (b) nothing in section 28(3) of this Act shall be construed as affecting
 the court's discretion under this section.

(4) In this section "the court" means the court in which the action has
been brought.]¹

¹ substituted by Defamation Act 1996 c.31 s 5 (4)

*Discretionary exclusion of time limit for actions in respect of personal injuries
or death*

38 Interpretation.

(1) In this Act, unless the context otherwise requires —

 "action" includes any proceeding in a court of law, including an
 ecclesiastical court;

 "land" includes corporeal hereditaments, tithes and rent-charges and
 any legal or equitable estate or interest therein[. . .]¹ but except
 as provided above in this definition does not include any
 incorporeal hereditament;

 "personal estate" and "personal property" do not include chattels
 real;

 "personal injuries" includes any disease and any impairment of a
 person's physical or mental condition, and "injury" and cognate
 expressions shall be construed accordingly;

 "rent" includes a rentcharge and a rentservice;

 "rentcharge" means any annuity or periodical sum of money charged
 upon or payable out of land, except a rent service or interest on
 a mortgage on land;

"settled land", "statutory owner" and "tenant for life" have the same meanings respectively as in the Settled Land Act 1925;

"trust" and "trustee" have the same meanings respectively as in the Trustee Act 1925; and

[. . .][1]

(2) For the purposes of this Act a person shall be treated as under a disability while he is an infant, or of unsound mind.

(3) For the purposes of subsection (2) above a person is of unsound mind if he is a person who, by reason of mental disorder within the meaning of the [Mental Health Act 1983][2], is incapable of managing and administering his property and affairs.

(4) Without prejudice to the generality of subsection (3) above, a person shall be conclusively presumed for the purposes of subsection (2) above to be of unsound mind —

(a) while he is liable to be detained or subject to guardianship under [the Mental Health Act 1983 (otherwise than by virtue of section 35 or 89)][3]; and

[(b) while he is receiving treatment as an in-patient in any hospital within the meaning of the Mental Health Act1983 or mental nursing home within the meaning of the Nursing Homes Act 1975 without being liable to be detained under the said Act of 1983 (otherwise than by virtue of section 35 or 89), being treatment which follows without any interval a period during which he was liable to be detained or subject to guardianship under the Mental Health Act 1959, or the said Act of 1983 (otherwise than by virtue of section 35 or 89) or by virtue of any enactment repealed or excluded by the Mental Health Act 1983.][4]

(5) Subject to subsection (6) below, a person shall be treated as claiming through another person if he became entitled by, through, under, or by the act of that other person to the right claimed, and any person whose estate or interest might have been barred by a person entitled to an entailed interest in possession shall be treated as claiming through the person so entitled.

(6) A person becoming entitled to any estate or interest by virtue of a special power of appointment shall not be treated as claiming through the appointor.

(7) References in this Act to a right of action to recover land shall include references to a right to enter into possession of the land or, in the case of rentcharges and tithes, to distrain for arrears of rent or tithe, and references to the bringing of such an action shall include references to the making of such an entry or distress.

(8) References in this Act to the possession of land shall, in the case of tithes and rentcharges, be construed as references to the receipt of the tithe or rent, and references to the date of dispossession or discontinuance of possession of land shall, in the case of rent charges, be construed as references to the date of the last receipt of rent.

(9) References in Part II of this Act to a right of action shall include references to —

    (a) a cause of action;

    (b) a right to receive money secured by a mortgage or charge on any property;

    (c) a right to recover proceeds of the sale of land; and

    (d) a right to receive a share of interest in the personal estate of a deceased person.

(10) References in Part II to the date of the accrual of a right of action shall be construed —

    (a) in the case of an action upon a judgment, as references to the date on which the judgment became enforceable; and

    (b) in the case of an action to recover arrears of rent or interest, or damages in respect of arrears of rent or interest, as references to the date on which the rent or interest became due.

[1] Words repealed by Trusts of Land and Appointment of Trustees Act 1996 c.47 Sch 4 Para 1
[2] Words substituted by Mental Health Act 1983 (c. 20), s. 148, Sch. 4 para. 55(a)
[3] Words substituted by virtue of Mental Health Act 1983 (c. 20), s. 148, Sch. 4 para. 55(b)(i)
[4] S. 38(4)(b) substituted by Mental Health Act 1983 (c. 20), s. 148, Sch. 4 para. 55(b)(ii)

SCHEDULES

SCHEDULE 1

PROVISIONS WITH RESPECT TO ACTIONS TO RECOVER LAND

A1–007

Section 15(6), (7)

PART I

ACCRUAL OF RIGHTS OF ACTION TO RECOVER LAND

Accrual of right of action in case of present interests in land

1

Where the person bringing an action to recover land, or some person through whom he claims, has been in possession of the land, and has while entitled to the land been dispossessed or discontinued his possession, the right of action shall be treated as having accrued on the date of the dispossession or discontinuance.

2

Where any person brings an action to recover any land of a deceased person (whether under a will or on intestacy) and the deceased person —

    (a) was on the date of his death in possession of the land or, in the case of a rentcharge created by will or taking effect upon his death, in possession of the land charged; and

529

(b) was the last person entitled to the land to be in possession of it;

the right of action shall be treated as having accrued on the date of his death.

3

Where any person brings an action to recover land, being an estate or interest in possession assured otherwise than by will to him, or to some person through whom he claims, and —

(a) the person making the assurance was on the date when the assurance took effect in possession of the land or, in the case of a rentcharge created by the assurance, in possession of the land charged; and

(b) no person has been in possession of the land by virtue of the assurance;

the right of action shall be treated as having accrued on the date when the assurance took effect.

Accrual of right of action in case of future interests

4

The right of action to recover any land shall, in a case where —

(a) the estate or interest claimed was an estate or interest in reversion or remainder or any other future estate or interest; and

(b) no person has taken possession of the land by virtue of the estate or interest claimed;

be treated as having accrued on the date on which the estate or interest fell into possession by the determination of the preceding estate or interest.

5

(1) Subject to sub-paragraph (2) below, a tenancy from year to year or other period, without a lease in writing, shall for the purposes of this Act be treated as being determined at the expiration of the first year or other period; and accordingly the right of action of the person entitled to the land subject to the tenancy shall be treated as having accrued at the date on which in accordance with this sub-paragraph the tenancy is determined.

(2) Where any rent has subsequently been received in respect of the tenancy, the right of action shall be treated as having accrued on the date of the last receipt of rent.

6

(1) Where —

(a) any person is in possession of land by virtue of a lease in writing by which a rent of not less than ten pounds a year is reserved; and

(b) the rent is received by some person wrongfully claiming to be
     entitled to the land in reversion immediately expectant on the
     determination of the lease; and

(c) no rent is subsequently received by the person rightfully so
     entitled;

the right of action to recover the land of the person rightfully so entitled
shall be treated as having accrued on the date when the rent was first
received by the person wrongfully claiming to be so entitled and not on
the date of the determination of the lease.

(2) Sub-paragraph (1) above shall not apply to any lease granted by the
Crown.

Accrual of right of action in case of forfeiture or breach of condition

7

(1) Subject to sub-paragraph (2) below, a right of action to recover land
by virtue of a forfeiture or breach of condition shall be treated as having
accrued on the date on which the forfeiture was incurred or the condition
broken.

(2) If any such right has accrued to a person entitled to an estate or
interest in reversion or remainder and the land was not recovered by
virtue of that right, the right of action to recover the land shall not be
treated as having accrued to that person until his estate or interest fell
into possession, as if no such forfeiture or breach of condition had
occurred.

Right of action not to accrue or continue unless there is adverse possession

8

(1) No right of action to recover land shall be treated as accruing unless
the land is in the possession of some person in whose favour the period of
limitation can run (referred to below in this paragraph as "adverse possession"); and where under the preceding provisions of this Schedule any
such right of action is treated as accruing on a certain date and no person
is in adverse possession on that date, the right of action shall not be treated
as accruing unless and until adverse possession is taken of the land.

(2) Where a right of action to recover land has accrued and after its
accrual, before the right is barred, the land ceases to be in adverse possession, the right of action shall no longer be treated as having accrued and
no fresh right of action shall be treated as accruing unless and until the
land is again taken into adverse possession.

(3) For the purposes of this paragraph —

(a) possession of any land subject to a rentcharge by a person
     (other than the person entitled to the rentcharge) who does
     not pay the rent shall be treated as adverse possession of the
     rentcharge; and

531

(b)   receipt of rent under a lease by a person wrongfully claiming to be entitled to the land in reversion immediately expectant on the determination of the lease shall be treated as adverse possession of the land.

(4) For the purpose of determining whether a person occupying any land is in adverse possession of the land it shall not be assumed by implication of law that his occupation is by permission of the person entitled to the land merely by virtue of the fact that his occupation is not inconsistent with the latter's present or future enjoyment of the land.

This provision shall not be taken as prejudicing a finding to the effect that a person's occupation of any land is by implied permission of the person entitled to the land in any case where such a finding is justified on the actual facts of the case.

Possession of beneficiary not adverse to others interested in settled land or land held on trust for sale

9

Where any settled land or any land [. . .]¹[subject to a trust of land]¹ is in the possession of a person entitled to a beneficial interest in the land or in the proceeds of sale (not being a person solely or absolutely entitled to the land or the proceeds), no right of action to recover the land shall be treated for the purposes of this Act as accruing during that possession to any person in whom the land is vested as tenant for life, statutory owner or trustee, or to any other person entitled to a beneficial interest in the land or the proceeds of sale.

¹   Words repealed by Trusts of Land and Appointment of Trustees Act 1996 c.47 Sch 4 Para 1

PART II

A1–008

MODIFICATION OF SECTION 15 WHERE CROWN OR CERTAIN CORPORATIONS SOLE ARE INVOLVED

10

Subject to paragraph 11 below, section 15(1) of this Act shall apply to the bringing of an action to recover any land by the Crown or by any spiritual or eleemosynary corporation sole with the substitution for the reference to twelve years of a reference to thirty years.

11

(1) An action to recover foreshore may be brought by the Crown at any time before the expiration of sixty years from the date mentioned in section 15(1) of this Act.

(2) Where any right of action to recover land which has ceased to be foreshore but remains in the ownership of the Crown accrued when the land was foreshore, the action may be brought at any time before the expiration of —

(a) sixty years from the date of accrual of the right of action; or

(b) thirty years from the date when the land ceased to be foreshore;

whichever period first expires.

(3) In this paragraph "foreshore" means the shore and bed of the sea and of any tidal water, below the line of the medium high tide between the spring tides and the neap tides.

12

Notwithstanding section 15(1) of this Act, where in the case of any action brought by a person other than the Crown or a spiritual or eleemosynary corporation sole the right of action first accrued to the Crown or any such corporation sole through whom the person in question claims, the action may be brought at any time before the expiration of —

(a) the period during which the action could have been brought by the Crown or the corporation sole; or

(b) twelve years from the date on which the right of action accrued to some person other than the Crown or the corporation sole;

whichever period first expires.

13

Section 15(2) of this Act shall apply in any case where the Crown or a spiritual or eleemosynary corporation sole is entitled to the succeeding estate or interest with the substitution —

(a) for the reference to twelve years of a reference to thirty years; and

(b) for the reference to six years of a reference to twelve years.

Environmental Protection Act 1990

PART III

STATUTORY NUISANCES AND CLEAN AIR

Statutory nuisances

A1–009 **79 Statutory nuisances and inspections therefor.**

(1) [Subject to subsections (1A) to (6A) below][1], the following matters constitute "statutory nuisances" for the purposes of this Part, that is to say —

- (a) any premises in such a state as to be prejudicial to health or a nuisance;
- (b) smoke emitted from premises so as to be prejudicial to health or a nuisance;
- (c) fumes or gases emitted from premises so as to be prejudicial to health or a nuisance;
- (d) any dust, steam, smell or other effluvia arising on industrial, trade or business premises and being prejudicial to health or a nuisance;
- (e) any accumulation or deposit which is prejudicial to health or a nuisance;
- (f) any animal kept in such a place or manner as to be prejudicial to health or a nuisance;
- (g) noise emitted from premises so as to be prejudicial to health or a nuisance;
- [(ga) noise that is prejudicial to health or a nuisance and is emitted from or caused by a vehicle, machinery or equipment in a street [or in Scotland, road][2]; and][3]
- (h) any other matter declared by any enactment to be a statutory nuisance;

and it shall be the duty of every local authority to cause its area to be inspected from time to time to detect any statutory nuisances which ought to be dealt with under section 80 below [or sections 80 and 80A below][4] and, where a complaint of a statutory nuisance is made to it by a person living within its area, to take such steps as are reasonably practicable to investigate the complaint.

[(1A) No matter shall constitute a statutory nuisance to the extent that it consists of, or is caused by, any land being in a contaminated state.

(1B) Land is in a "contaminated state" for the purposes of subsection (1A) above if, and only if, it is in such a condition, by reason of substances in, on or under the land, that —

- (a) harm is being caused or there is a possibility of harm being caused; or

534

(b)   pollution of controlled waters is being, or is likely to be, caused;

and in this subsection "harm", "pollution of controlled waters" and "substance" have the same meaning as in Part IIA of this Act.][1]

(2) Subsection (1)(b) and (g) above do not apply in relation to premises —

(a)   occupied on behalf of the Crown for naval, military or air force purposes or for the purposes of the department of the Secretary of State having responsibility for defence, or

(b)   occupied by or for the purposes of a visiting force;

and "visiting force" means any such body, contingent or detachment of the forces of any country as is a visiting force for the purposes of any of the provisions of the Visiting Forces Act 1952.

(3) Subsection (1)(b) above does not apply to —

(i)   smoke emitted from a chimney of a private dwelling within a smoke control area,

(ii)   dark smoke emitted from a chimney of a building or a chimney serving the furnace of a boiler or industrial plant attached to a building or for the time being fixed to or installed on any land,

(iii)   smoke emitted from a railway locomotive steam engine, or

(iv)   dark smoke emitted otherwise than as mentioned above from industrial or trade premises.

(4) Subsection (1)(c) above does not apply in relation to premises other than private dwellings.

(5) Subsection (1)(d) above does not apply to steam emitted from a railway locomotive engine.

(6) Subsection (1)(g) above does not apply to noise caused by aircraft other than model aircraft.

[(6A) Subsection (1)(ga) above does not apply to noise made —

(a)   by traffic,

(b)   by any naval, military or air force of the Crown or by a visiting force (as defined in subsection (2) above), or

(c)   by a political demonstration or a demonstration supporting or opposing a cause or campaign.][5]

(7) In this Part —

"chimney" includes structures and openings of any kind from or through which smoke may be emitted;

"dust" does not include dust emitted from a chimney as an ingredient of smoke;

["equipment" includes a musical instrument;][6]

"fumes" means any airborne solid matter smaller than dust;

"gas" includes vapour and moisture precipitated from vapour;

"industrial, trade or business premises" means premises used for any industrial, trade or business purposes or premises not so used on which matter is burnt in connection with any industrial, trade or business process, and premises are used for industrial purposes where they are used for the purposes of any treatment or process as well as where they are used for the purposes of manufacturing;

"local authority" means, subject to subsection (8) below, —

- (a) in Greater London, a London borough council, the Common Council of the City of London and, as respects the Temples, the Sub-Treasurer of the Inner Temple and the Under-Treasurer of the Middle Temple respectively;
- (b) [in England]⁷outside Greater London, a district council; (ba) [. . .]⁸
- [(bb) in Wales, a county council or county borough council;]⁹
- (c) the Council of the Isles of Scilly; [and]¹⁰
- [(d) in Scotland, a district or islands council or a council constituted under section 2 of the Local Government etc (Scotland) Act 1994;]¹⁰

"noise" includes vibration;

["person responsible" —

- (a) in relation to a statutory nuisance, means the person to whose act, default or sufferance the nuisance is attributable;
- (b) in relation to a vehicle, includes the person in whose name the vehicle is for the time being registered under [the Vehicle Excise and Registration Act 1994]¹¹ and any other person who is for the time being the driver of the vehicle;
- (c) in relation to machinery or equipment, includes any person who is for the time being the operator of the machinery or equipment;

, and]¹²

"prejudicial to health" means injurious, or likely to cause injury, to health;

"premises" includes land and, subject to subsection (12) [and [, in relation to England and Wales,]¹³ section 81A(9)]¹⁴ below, any vessel;

"private dwelling" means any building, or part of a building, used or intended to be used, as a dwelling;

["road"has the same meaning as in Part IV of the New Roads and Street Works Act 1991;]¹⁵

"smoke" includes soot, ash, grit and gritty particles emitted in smoke;

["street" means a highway and any other road, footway, square or court that is for the time being open to the public;.]¹⁶

and any expressions used in this section and in [the Clean Air Act 1993][17] have the same meaning in this section as in that Act and [section 3 of the Clean Air Act 1993][18] shall apply for the interpretation of the expression "dark smoke" and the operation of this Part in relation to it.

(8) Where, by an order under section 2 of the Public Health (Control of Disease) Act 1984, a port health authority has been constituted for any port health district [or in Scotland where by an order under section 172 of the Public Health (Scotland) Act 1897 a port local authority or a joint port local authority has been constituted for the whole or part of a port][19], the port health authority[, port local authority or joint port local authority, as the case may be][20] shall have by virtue of this subsection, as respects its district, the functions conferred or imposed by this Part in relation to statutory nuisances other than a nuisance falling within paragraph (g) [or (ga)][21]of subsection (1) above and no such order shall be made assigning those functions; and "local authority" and "area" shall be construed accordingly.

(9) In this Part "best practicable means" is to be interpreted by reference to the following provisions —

(a) "practicable" means reasonably practicable having regard among other things to local conditions and circumstances, to the current state of technical knowledge and to the financial implications;

(b) the means to be employed include the design, installation, maintenance and manner and periods of operation of plant and machinery, and the design, construction and maintenance of buildings and structures;

(c) the test is to apply only so far as compatible with any duty imposed by law;

(d) the test is to apply only so far as compatible with safety and safe working conditions, and with the exigencies of any emergency or unforeseeable circumstances;

and, in circumstances where a code of practice under section 71 of the Control of Pollution Act 1974 (noise minimisation) is applicable, regard shall also be had to guidance given in it.

(10) A local authority shall not without the consent of the Secretary of State institute summary proceedings under this Part in respect of a nuisance falling within paragraph (b), (d) or (e) [and in relation to Scotland, paragraph (g) or (ga),][22]of subsection (1) above if proceedings in respect thereof might be instituted under Part I [or under regulations under section 2 of the Pollution Prevention and Control Act 1999][23][. . .][24].

(11) The area of a local authority which includes part of the seashore shall also include for the purposes of this Part the territorial sea lying seawards from that part of the shore; and subject to subsection (12) [and [, in

relation to England and Wales,][25]section 81A(9)][26]below, this Part shall have effect, in relation to any area included in the area of a local authority by virtue of this subsection —

(a) as if references to premises and the occupier of premises included respectively a vessel and the master of a vessel; and

(b) with such other modifications, if any, as are prescribed in regulations made by the Secretary of State.

(12) A vessel powered by steam reciprocating machinery is not a vessel to which this Part of this Act applies.[[[28][1][1][129][30]

1 substituted by Environment Act 1995 c.25 Sch 22 Para 89
2 words inserted by Environment Act 1995 c.25 Sch 17 Para 2 (a)
3 added by Noise and Statutory Nuisance Act 1993 c.40 s 2 (2) (b)
4 Words inserted by Noise and Statutory Nuisance Act 1993 c.40 s 2 (2) (c)
5 added by Noise and Statutory Nuisance Act 1993 c.40 s 2 (3)
6 definition added by Noise and Statutory Nuisance Act 1993 c.40 s 2 (4) (a)
7 words inserted by Local Government (Wales) Act 1994 c.19 Sch 9 Para 17 (5)
8 the word 'and' following paragraph (b) is repealed by Environment Act 1995 c.25 Sch 24 Para 1
9 added by Local Government (Wales) Act 1994 c.19 Sch 9 Para 17 (5)
10 paragraph (d) and the word "and" immediately preceding it are added by Environment Act 1995 c.25 Sch 17 Para 2 (b) (i)
11 words substituted by Vehicle Excise and Registration Act 1994 c.22 Sch 3 Para 27
12 definition substituted by Noise and Statutory Nuisance Act 1993 c.40 s 2 (4) (b)
13 words inserted by Environment Act 1995 c.25 Sch 17 Para 2 (b) (ii)
14 Words inserted by Noise and Statutory Nuisance Act 1993 c.40 s 10 (1)
15 added by Environment Act 1995 c.25 Sch 17 Para 2 (b) (iii)
16 Definition inserted by Noise and Statutory Nuisance Act 1993 c.40 s 2 (4) (c)
17 words substituted by Clean Air Act 1993 c.11 Sch 4 Para 4 (a)
18 words substituted by Clean Air Act 1993 c.11 Sch 4 Para 4 (b)
19 words inserted by Environment Act 1995 c.25 Sch 17 Para 2 (c) (i)
20 words inserted by Environment Act 1995 c.25 Sch 17 Para 2 (c) (ii)
21 Words added by Noise and Statutory Nuisance Act 1993 c.40 s 2 (5)
22 words inserted by Environment Act 1995 c.25 Sch 17 Para 2 (d)
23 words inserted by Pollution Prevention and Control Act 1999 c.24 Sch 2 Para 6
24 words repealed by Environmental Protection Act 1990 c.43 Sch 16 (I) Para 1
25 words inserted by Environment Act 1995 c.25 Sch 17 Para 2 (e)
26 Words added by Noise and Statutory Nuisance Act 1993 c.40 s 10 (1)
27 words substituted by SSI 2000/323 Sch 10 (1) Para 3 (6)
28 In relation to Scotland:
29 In relation to a London borough:
30 modified by London Local Authorities Act 1996 c.ix s 24 (1)

79 Statutory nuisances and inspections therefor.

(1) Subject to subsections (1A) to (6A) below, the following matters constitute "statutory nuisances" for the purposes of this Part, that is to say —

(a) any premises in such a state as to be prejudicial to health or a nuisance;

(b) smoke emitted from premises so as to be prejudicial to health or a nuisance;

(c) fumes or gases emitted from premises so as to be prejudicial to health or a nuisance;

   (d)   any dust, steam, smell or other effluvia arising on industrial, trade or business premises and being prejudicial to health or a nuisance;

   (e)   any accumulation or deposit which is prejudicial to health or a nuisance;

   (f)   any animal kept in such a place or manner as to be prejudicial to health or a nuisance;

   (g)   noise emitted from premises so as to be prejudicial to health or a nuisance;

  (ga) noise that is prejudicial to health or a nuisance and is emitted from or caused by a vehicle, machinery or equipment in a street or in Scotland, road; and

   (h)   any other matter declared by any enactment to be a statutory nuisance;

and it shall be the duty of every local authority to cause its area to be inspected from time to time to detect any statutory nuisances which ought to be dealt with under section 80 below or sections 80 and 80A below and, where a complaint of a statutory nuisance is made to it by a person living within its area, to take such steps as are reasonably practicable to investigate the complaint.

(1A) No matter shall constitute a statutory nuisance to the extent that it consists of, or is caused by, any land being in a contaminated state.

(1B) Land is in a "contaminated state" for the purposes of subsection (1A) above if, and only if, it is in such a condition, by reason of substances in, on or under the land, that —

   (a)   harm is being caused or there is a possibility of harm being caused; or

   (b)   pollution of controlled waters is being, or is likely to be, caused;

and in this subsection "harm", "pollution of controlled waters" and "substance" have the same meaning as in Part IIA of this Act.

(2) Subsection (1)(b) and (g) above do not apply in relation to premises —

   (a)   occupied on behalf of the Crown for naval, military or air force purposes or for the purposes of the department of the Secretary of State having responsibility for defence, or

   (b)   occupied by or for the purposes of a visiting force;

and "visiting force" means any such body, contingent or detachment of the forces of any country as is a visiting force for the purposes of any of the provisions of the Visiting Forces Act 1952.

(3) Subsection (1)(b) above does not apply to —

   (i)   smoke emitted from a chimney of a private dwelling within a smoke control area,

   (ii) dark smoke emitted from a chimney of a building or a

chimney serving the furnace of a boiler or industrial plant attached to a building or for the time being fixed to or installed on any land,

(iii) smoke emitted from a railway locomotive steam engine, or

(iv) dark smoke emitted otherwise than as mentioned above from industrial or trade premises.

(4) Subsection (1)(c) above does not apply in relation to premises other than private dwellings.

(5) Subsection (1)(d) above does not apply to steam emitted from a railway locomotive engine.

(6) Subsection (1)(g) above does not apply to noise caused by aircraft other than model aircraft.

(6A) Subsection (1)(ga) above does not apply to noise made —

(a) by traffic,

(b) by any naval, military or air force of the Crown or by a visiting force (as defined in subsection (2) above), or

(c) by a political demonstration or a demonstration supporting or opposing a cause or campaign.

(7) In this Part —

"chimney" includes structures and openings of any kind from or through which smoke may be emitted;

"dust" does not include dust emitted from a chimney as an ingredient of smoke;

"equipment" includes a musical instrument;

"fumes" means any airborne solid matter smaller than dust;

"gas" includes vapour and moisture precipitated from vapour;

"industrial, trade or business premises" means premises used for any industrial, trade or business purposes or premises not so used on which matter is burnt in connection with any industrial, trade or business process, and premises are used for industrial purposes where they are used for the purposes of any treatment or process as well as where they are used for the purposes of manufacturing;

"local authority" means, subject to subsection (8) below, —

(a) in Greater London, a London borough council, the Common Council of the City of London and, as respects the Temples, the Sub-Treasurer of the Inner Temple and the Under-Treasurer of the Middle Temple respectively;

(b) in England outside Greater London, a district council;

(bb) in Wales, a county council or county borough council;

(c) the Council of the Isles of Scilly; and

(d) in Scotland, a district or islands council or a council constituted under section 2 of the Local Government etc (Scotland) Act 1994;

"noise" includes vibration;

"person responsible" —

    (a) in relation to a statutory nuisance, means the person to whose act, default or sufferance the nuisance is attributable;

    (b) in relation to a vehicle, includes the person in whose name the vehicle is for the time being registered under the Vehicle Excise and Registration Act 1994 and any other person who is for the time being the driver of the vehicle;

    (c) in relation to machinery or equipment, includes any person who is for the time being the operator of the machinery or equipment;

, and

"prejudicial to health" means injurious, or likely to cause injury, to health;

"premises" includes land and, subject to subsection (12) and, in relation to England and Wales, section 81A(9) below, any vessel;

"private dwelling" means any building, or part of a building, used or intended to be used, as a dwelling;

"road"has the same meaning as in Part IV of the New Roads and Street Works Act 1991;

"smoke" includes soot, ash, grit and gritty particles emitted in smoke;

"street" means a highway and any other road, footway, square or court that is for the time being open to the public;.

and any expressions used in this section and in the Clean Air Act 1993 have the same meaning in this section as in that Act and section 3 of the Clean Air Act 1993 shall apply for the interpretation of the expression "dark smoke" and the operation of this Part in relation to it.

(8) Where, by an order under section 2 of the Public Health (Control of Disease) Act 1984, a port health authority has been constituted for any port health district or in Scotland where by an order under section 172 of the Public Health (Scotland) Act 1897 a port local authority or a joint port local authority has been constituted for the whole or part of a port, the port health authority, port local authority or joint port local authority, as the case may be shall have by virtue of this subsection, as respects its district, the functions conferred or imposed by this Part in relation to statutory nuisances other than a nuisance falling within paragraph (g) or (ga) of subsection (1) above and no such order shall be made assigning those functions; and "local authority" and "area" shall be construed accordingly.

(9) In this Part "best practicable means" is to be interpreted by reference to the following provisions —

    (a) "practicable" means reasonably practicable having regard among other things to local conditions and circumstances, to the current state of technical knowledge and to the financial implications;

(b)   the means to be employed include the design, installation, main-tenance and manner and periods of operation of plant and machinery, and the design, construction and maintenance of buildings and structures;

(c)   the test is to apply only so far as compatible with any duty imposed by law;

(d)   the test is to apply only so far as compatible with safety and safe working conditions, and with the exigencies of any emergency or unforeseeable circumstances;

and, in circumstances where a code of practice under section 71 of the Control of Pollution Act 1974 (noise minimisation) is applicable, regard shall also be had to guidance given in it.

(10) A local authority shall not without the consent of the Secretary of State institute summary proceedings under this Part in respect of a nuisance falling within paragraph (b), (d) [,(e) or (g)]^{27} and in relation to Scotland, [paragraph (ga)]^{27}, of subsection (1) above if proceedings in respect thereof might be instituted under Part I or under regulations under section 2 of the Pollution Prevention and Control Act 1999.

(11) The area of a local authority which includes part of the seashore shall also include for the purposes of this Part the territorial sea lying sea-wards from that part of the shore; and subject to subsection (12) and , in relation to England and Wales,section 81A(9) below, this Part shall have effect, in relation to any area included in the area of a local authority by virtue of this subsection —

(a)   as if references to premises and the occupier of premises included respectively a vessel and the master of a vessel; and

(b)   with such other modifications, if any, as are prescribed in regulations made by the Secretary of State.

(12) A vessel powered by steam reciprocating machinery is not a vessel to which this Part of this Act applies.

79   Statutory nuisances and inspections therefor.

(1) Subject to subsections (2) to (6A) below, the following matters constitute "statutory nuisances" for the purposes of this Part, that is to say —

(a)   any premises in such a state as to be prejudicial to health or a nuisance;

(b)   smoke emitted from premises so as to be prejudicial to health or a nuisance;

(c)   fumes or gases emitted from premises so as to be prejudicial to health or a nuisance;

(d) any dust, steam, smell or other effluvia arising on industrial, trade or business premises and being prejudicial to health or a nuisance;

(e) any accumulation or deposit which is prejudicial to health or a nuisance;

(f) any animal kept in such a place or manner as to be prejudicial to health or a nuisance;

(g) noise emitted from premises so as to be prejudicial to health or a nuisance;

(ga) noise that is prejudicial to health or a nuisance and is emitted from or caused by a vehicle, machinery or equipment in a street or in Scotland, road; and

(gb) smoke, fumes or gases emitted from any vehicle, machinery or equipment on a street so as to be prejudicial to health or a nuisance other than from any vehicle, machinery or equipment being used for fire brigade purposes;

(h) any other matter declared by any enactment to be a statutory nuisance;

and it shall be the duty of every local authority to cause its area to be inspected from time to time to detect any statutory nuisances which ought to be dealt with under section 80 below or sections 80 and 80A below and, where a complaint of a statutory nuisance is made to it by a person living within its area, to take such steps as are reasonably practicable to investigate the complaint.

(2) Subsection (1)(b) and (g) above do not apply in relation to premises —

(a) occupied on behalf of the Crown for naval, military or air force purposes or for the purposes of the department of the Secretary of State having responsibility for defence, or

(b) occupied by or for the purposes of a visiting force;

and "visiting force" means any such body, contingent or detachment of the forces of any country as is a visiting force for the purposes of any of the provisions of the Visiting Forces Act 1952.

(3) Subsection (1)(b) above does not apply to —

(i) smoke emitted from a chimney of a private dwelling within a smoke control area,

(ii) dark smoke emitted from a chimney of a building or a chimney serving the furnace of a boiler or industrial plant attached to a building or for the time being fixed to or installed on any land,

(iii) smoke emitted from a railway locomotive steam engine, or

(iv) dark smoke emitted otherwise than as mentioned above from industrial or trade premises.

(4) Subsection (1)(c) above does not apply in relation to premises other than private dwellings.

(5) Subsection (1)(d) above does not apply to steam emitted from a railway locomotive engine.

(6) Subsection (1)(g) above does not apply to noise caused by aircraft other than model aircraft.

(6A) Subsection (1)(ga) above does not apply to noise made —

(a) by traffic,

(b) by any naval, military or air force of the Crown or by a visiting force (as defined in subsection (2) above), or

(c) by a political demonstration or a demonstration supporting or opposing a cause or campaign.

(6B) Subsection (1)(gb) above does not apply in relation to smoke, fumes or gases emitted from the exhaust system of a vehicle.

(7) In this Part —

"chimney" includes structures and openings of any kind from or through which smoke may be emitted;

"dust" does not include dust emitted from a chimney as an ingredient of smoke;

"equipment" includes a musical instrument;

"fumes" means any airborne solid matter smaller than dust;

"gas" includes vapour and moisture precipitated from vapour;

"industrial, trade or business premises" means premises used for any industrial, trade or business purposes or premises not so used on which matter is burnt in connection with any industrial, trade or business process, and premises are used for industrial purposes where they are used for the purposes of any treatment or process as well as where they are used for the purposes of manufacturing;

"local authority" means, subject to subsection (8) below, —

(a) in Greater London, a London borough council, the Common Council of the City of London and, as respects the Temples, the Sub-Treasurer of the Inner Temple and the Under-Treasurer of the Middle Temple respectively;

(b) in England outside Greater London, a district council;

(bb) in Wales, a county council or county borough council;

(c) the Council of the Isles of Scilly; and

(d) in Scotland, a district or islands council or a council constituted under section 2 of the Local Government etc (Scotland) Act 1994;

"noise" includes vibration;

"person responsible" —

(a) in relation to a statutory nuisance, means the person to whose act, default or sufferance the nuisance is attributable;

(b)   in relation to a vehicle, includes the person in whose name the vehicle is for the time being registered under the Vehicle Excise and Registration Act 1994 and any other person who is for the time being the driver of the vehicle;

(c)   in relation to machinery or equipment, includes any person who is for the time being the operator of the machinery or equipment;

"prejudicial to health" means injurious, or likely to cause injury, to health;

"premises" includes land and, subject to subsection (12) and, in relation to England and Wales, section 81A(9) below, any vessel;

"private dwelling" means any building, or part of a building, used or intended to be used, as a dwelling;

"road"has the same meaning as in Part IV of the New Roads and Street Works Act 1991;

"smoke" includes soot, ash, grit and gritty particles emitted in smoke;

"street" means a highway and any other road, footway, square or court that is for the time being open to the public;

"vehicle" means a mechanically propelled vehicle intended or adapted for use on roads, whether or not it is in a fit state for such use, and includes any trailer intended or adapted for use as an attachment to such a vehicle, any chassis or body, with or without wheels, appearing to have formed a part of such a vehicle or trailer and anything attached to such a vehicle or trailer;

and any expressions used in this section and in the Clean Air Act 1993 have the same meaning in this section as in that Act and section 3 of the Clean Air Act 1993 shall apply for the interpretation of the expression "dark smoke" and the operation of this Part in relation to it.

(8) Where, by an order under section 2 of the Public Health (Control of Disease) Act 1984, a port health authority has been constituted for any port health district or in Scotland where by an order under section 172 of the Public Health (Scotland) Act 1897 a port local authority or a joint port local authority has been constituted for the whole or part of a port, the port health authority, port local authority or joint port local authority, as the case may be shall have by virtue of this subsection, as respects its district, the functions conferred or imposed by this Part in relation to statutory nuisances other than a nuisance falling within paragraph (g) or (ga) of subsection (1) above and no such order shall be made assigning those functions; and "local authority" and "area" shall be construed accordingly.

(9) In this Part "best practicable means" is to be interpreted by reference to the following provisions —

(a)   "practicable" means reasonably practicable having regard among other things to local conditions and circumstances, to the current state of technical knowledge and to the financial implications;

    (b) the means to be employed include the design, installation, maintenance and manner and periods of operation of plant and machinery, and the design, construction and maintenance of buildings and structures;

    (c) the test is to apply only so far as compatible with any duty imposed by law;

    (d) the test is to apply only so far as compatible with safety and safe working conditions, and with the exigencies of any emergency or unforeseeable circumstances;

and, in circumstances where a code of practice under section 71 of the Control of Pollution Act 1974 (noise minimisation) is applicable, regard shall also be had to guidance given in it.

(10) A local authority shall not without the consent of the Secretary of State institute summary proceedings under this Part in respect of a nuisance falling within paragraph (b), (d) or (e) and in relation to Scotland, paragraph (g) or (ga), of subsection (1) above if proceedings in respect thereof might be instituted under Part I [or under regulations under section 2 of the Pollution Prevention and Control Act 1999][23].

(11) The area of a local authority which includes part of the seashore shall also include for the purposes of this Part the territorial sea lying seawards from that part of the shore; and subject to subsection (12) and , in relation to England and Wales, section 81A(9) below, this Part shall have effect, in relation to any area included in the area of a local authority by virtue of this subsection —

    (a) as if references to premises and the occupier of premises included respectively a vessel and the master of a vessel; and

    (b) with such other modifications, if any, as are prescribed in regulations made by the Secretary of State.

(12) A vessel powered by steam reciprocating machinery is not a vessel to which this Part of this Act applies.

80 Summary proceedings for statutory nuisances.

(1) Where a local authority is satisfied that a statutory nuisance exists, or is likely to occur or recur, in the area of the authority, the local authority shall serve a notice ("an abatement notice") imposing all or any of the following requirements —

    (a) requiring the abatement of the nuisance or prohibiting or restricting its occurrence or recurrence;

    (b) requiring the execution of such works, and the taking of such other steps, as may be necessary for any of those purposes, and the notice shall specify the time or times within which the requirements of the notice are to be complied with.

(2) [Subject to section 80A(1) below, the abatement notice][1] shall be served —

(a) except in a case falling within paragraph (b) or (c) below, on the person responsible for the nuisance;

(b) where the nuisance arises from any defect of a structural character, on the owner of the premises;

(c) where the person responsible for the nuisance cannot be found or the nuisance has not yet occurred, on the owner or occupier of the premises.

(3) [A person served with an abatement notice][2] may appeal against the notice to a magistrates' court [or in Scotland, the sheriff][3]within the period of twenty-one days beginning with the date on which he was served with the notice.

(4) If a person on whom an abatement notice is served, without reasonable excuse, contravenes or fails to comply with any requirement or prohibition imposed by the notice, he shall be guilty of an offence.

(5) Except in a case falling within subsection (6) below, a person who commits an offence under subsection (4) above shall be liable on summary conviction to a fine not exceeding level 5 on the standard scale together with a further fine of an amount equal to one-tenth of that level for each day on which the offence continues after the conviction.

(6) A person who commits an offence under subsection (4) above on industrial, trade or business premises shall be liable on summary conviction to a fine not exceeding £20,000.

(7) Subject to subsection (8) below, in any proceedings for an offence under subsection (4) above in respect of a statutory nuisance it shall be a defence to prove that the best practicable means were used to prevent, or to counteract the effects of, the nuisance.

(8) The defence under subsection (7) above is not available —

(a) in the case of a nuisance falling within paragraph (a), (d), (e), (f) or (g) of section 79(1) above except where the nuisance arises on industrial, trade or business premises;

[(aa) in the case of a nuisance falling within paragraph (ga) of section 79(1) above except where the noise is emitted from or caused by a vehicle, machinery or equipment being used for industrial, trade or business purposes;][4]

(b) in the case of a nuisance falling within paragraph (b) of section 79(1) above except where the smoke is emitted from a chimney; and

(c) in the case of a nuisance falling within paragraph (c) or (h) of section 79(1) above.

(9) In proceedings for an offence under subsection (4) above in respect of a statutory nuisance falling within [paragraph (g) or (ga) of section 79(1)][5] above where the offence consists in contravening requirements imposed by virtue of subsection (1)(a) above it shall be a defence to prove —

(a) that the alleged offence was covered by a notice served under section 60 or a consent given under section 61 or 65 of the Control of Pollution Act 1974 (construction sites, etc); or

(b) §where the alleged offence was committed at a time when the premises were subject to a notice under section 66 of that Act (noise reduction notice), that the level of noise emitted from the premises at that time was not such as to a constitute a contravention of the notice under that section; or

(c) where the alleged offence was committed at a time when the premises were not subject to a notice under section 66 of that Act, and when a level fixed under section 67 of that Act (new buildings liable to abatement order) applied to the premises, that the level of noise emitted from the premises at that time did not exceed that level.

(10) Paragraphs (b) and (c) of subsection (9) above apply whether or not the relevant notice was subject to appeal at the time when the offence was alleged to have been committed.

[1] Words substituted by Noise and Statutory Nuisance Act 1993 c.40 s 3 (2)
[2] Words substituted by Noise and Statutory Nuisance Act 1993 c.40 s 3 (3)
[3] words inserted by Environment Act 1995 c.25 Sch 17 Para 3
[4] added by Noise and Statutory Nuisance Act 1993 c.40 s 3 (4)
[5] Words inserted by Noise and Statutory Nuisance Act 1993 c.40 s 3 (5)

[80A   Abatement notice in respect of noise in street.

(1) In the case of a statutory nuisance within section 79(1)(ga) above that —

(a) has not yet occurred, or

(b) arises from noise emitted from or caused by an unattended vehicle or unattended machinery or equipment,

the abatement notice shall be served in accordance with subsection (2) below.[1]]2

(2) The notice shall be served —

(a) where the person responsible for the vehicle, machinery or equipment can be found, on that person;

(b) where that person cannot be found or where the local authority determines that this paragraph should apply, by fixing the notice to the vehicle, machinery or equipment.

(3) Where —

(a) an abatement notice is served in accordance with subsection (2)(b) above by virtue of a determination of the local authority, and

(b) the person responsible for the vehicle, machinery or equipment can be found and served with a copy of the notice within an hour of the notice being fixed to the vehicle, machinery or equipment,

a copy of the notice shall be served on that person accordingly.

(4) Where an abatement notice is served in accordance with subsection (2)(b) above by virtue of a determination of the local authority, the notice shall state that, if a copy of the notice is subsequently served under sub-section (3) above, the time specified in the notice as the time within which its requirements are to be complied with is extended by such further period as is specified in the notice.

(5) Where an abatement notice is served in accordance with subsection (2)(b) above, the person responsible for the vehicle, machinery or equip-ment may appeal against the notice under section 80(3) above as if he had been served with the notice on the date on which it was fixed to the vehicle, machinery or equipment.

(6) Section 80(4) above shall apply in relation to a person on whom a copy of an abatement notice is served under subsection (3) above as if the copy were the notice itself.

(7) A person who removes or interferes with a notice fixed to a vehicle, machinery or equipment in accordance with subsection (2)(b) above shall be guilty of an offence, unless he is the person responsible for the vehicle, machinery or equipment or he does so with the authority of that person.

(8) A person who commits an offence under subsection (7) above shall be liable on summary conviction to a fine not exceeding level 3 on the standard scale.][3]

[1] In relation to a London borough:
(1) In the case of a statutory nuisance within section 79(1)(ga) or (gb) above that —
(a) has not yet occurred, or
(b) arises from noise emitted from or caused by an unattended vehicle or unattended machinery or equipment,
the abatement notice shall be served in accordance with subsection (2) below.
[2] words inserted by London Local Authorities Act 1996 c.ix s 24 (2)
[3] added by Noise and Statutory Nuisance Act 1993 c.40 s 3 (6)

81 Supplementary provisions.

(1) [Subject to subsection (1A) below, where][1] more than one person is responsible for a statutory nuisance section 80 above shall apply to each of those persons whether or not what any one of them is responsible for would by itself amount to a nuisance.

[(1A) In relation to a statutory nuisance within section 79(1)(ga) above for which more than one person is responsible (whether or not what any one of those persons is responsible for would by itself amount to such a nuisance), section 80(2)(a) above shall apply with the substitution of "any one of the persons" for "the person".

(1B) In relation to a statutory nuisance within section 79(1)(ga) above caused by noise emitted from or caused by an unattended vehicle or unattended machinery or equipment for which more than one person is responsible, section 80A above shall apply with the substitution —

(a) in subsection (2)(a), of "any of the persons" for "the person" and of "one such person" for "that person",

(b) in subsection (2)(b), of "such a person" for "that person",

(c) in subsection (3), of "any of the persons" for "the person" and of "one such person" for "that person",

(d) in subsection (5), of "any person" for "the person", and

(e) in subsection (7), of "a person" for "the person" and of "such a person" for "that person".][2]

(2) Where a statutory nuisance which exists or has occurred within the area of a local authority, or which has affected any part of that area, appears to the local authority to be wholly or partly caused by some act or default committed or taking place outside the area, the local authority may act under section 80 above as if the act or default were wholly within that area, except that any appeal shall be heard by a magistrates' court [or in Scotland, the sheriff][3]having jurisdiction where the act or default is alleged to have taken place.

(3) Where an abatement notice has not been complied with the local authority may, whether or not they take proceedings for an offence [or, in Scotland, whether or not proceedings have been taken for an offence,][4]under section 80(4) above, abate the nuisance and do whatever may be necessary in execution of the notice.

(4) Any expenses reasonably incurred by a local authority in abating, or preventing the recurrence of, a statutory nuisance under subsection (3) above may be recovered by them from the person by whose act or default the nuisance was caused and, if that person is the owner of the premises, from any person who is for the time being the owner thereof; and the court [or sheriff][5] may apportion the expenses between persons by whose acts or defaults the nuisance is caused in such manner as the court consider [or sheriff considers][5] fair and reasonable.

(5) If a local authority is of opinion that proceedings for an offence under section 80(4) above would afford an inadequate remedy in the case of any statutory nuisance, they may, subject to subsection (6) below, take proceedings in the High Court [or, in Scotland, in any court of competent jurisdiction,][6]for the purpose of securing the abatement, prohibition or restriction of the nuisance, and the proceedings shall be maintainable notwithstanding the local authority have suffered no damage from the nuisance.

(6) In any proceedings under subsection (5) above in respect of a nuisance falling within [paragraph (g) or (ga) of section 79(1)][7] above, it shall be a defence to prove that the noise was authorised by a notice under sec-

tion 60 or a consent under section 61 (construction sites) of the Control of Pollution Act 1974.

(7) The further supplementary provisions in Schedule 3 to this Act shall have effect.

1 Words substituted by Noise and Statutory Nuisance Act 1993 c.40 s 4 (2)
2 added by Noise and Statutory Nuisance Act 1993 c.40 s 4 (3)
3 words inserted by Environment Act 1995 c.25 Sch 17 Para 4 (a)
4 words inserted by Environment Act 1995 c.25 Sch 17 Para 4 (b)
5 words inserted by Environment Act 1995 c.25 Sch 17 Para 4 (c)
6 words inserted by Environment Act 1995 c.25 Sch 17 Para 4 (d)
7 Words added by Noise and Statutory Nuisance Act 1993 c.40 s 4 (4)

[81A Expenses recoverable from owner to be a charge on premises.

(1) Where any expenses are recoverable under section 81(4) above from a person who is the owner of the premises there mentioned and the local authority serves a notice on him under this section —

(a) the expenses shall carry interest, at such reasonable rate as the local authority may determine, from the date of service of the notice until the whole amount is paid, and

(b) subject to the following provisions of this section, the expenses and accrued interest shall be a charge on the premises.

(2) A notice served under this section shall —

(a) specify the amount of the expenses that the local authority claims is recoverable,

(b) state the effect of subsection (1) above and the rate of interest determined by the local authority under that subsection, and

(c) state the effect of subsections (4) to (6) below.

(3) On the date on which a local authority serves a notice on a person under this section the authority shall also serve a copy of the notice on every other person who, to the knowledge of the authority, has an interest in the premises capable of being affected by the charge.

(4) Subject to any order under subsection (7)(b) or (c) below, the amount of any expenses specified in a notice under this section and the accrued interest shall be a charge on the premises —

(a) as from the end of the period of twenty-one days beginning with the date of service of the notice, or

(b) where an appeal is brought under subsection (6) below, as from the final determination of the appeal,

until the expenses and interest are recovered.

(5) For the purposes of subsection (4) above, the withdrawal of an appeal has the same effect as a final determination of the appeal.

(6) A person served with a notice or copy of a notice under this section may appeal against the notice to the county court within the period of twenty-one days beginning with the date of service.

(7) On such an appeal the court may —

    (a)   confirm the notice without modification,

    (b)   order that the notice is to have effect with the substitution of a different amount for the amount originally specified in it, or

    (c)   order that the notice is to be of no effect.

(8) A local authority shall, for the purpose of enforcing a charge under this section, have all the same powers and remedies under the Law of Property Act 1925, and otherwise, as if it were a mortgagee by deed having powers of sale and lease, of accepting surrenders of leases and of appointing a receiver.

(9) In this section —

    "owner", in relation to any premises, means a person (other than a mortgagee not in possession) who, whether in his own right or as trustee for any other person, is entitled to receive the rack rent of the premises or, where the premises are not let at a rack rent, would be so entitled if they were so let, and

    "premises" does not include a vessel.

[(10) This section does not apply to Scotland.][1]][2]

[1]   words inserted by Environment Act 1995 c.25 Sch 17 Para 5
[2]   added by Noise and Statutory Nuisance Act 1993 c.40 s 10 (2)

[81B   Payment of expenses by instalments.

(1) Where any expenses are a charge on premises under section 81A above, the local authority may by order declare the expenses to be payable with interest by instalments within the specified period, until the whole amount is paid.

(2) In subsection (1) above —

    "interest" means interest at the rate determined by the authority under section 81A(1) above, and

    "the specified period" means such period of thirty years or less from the date of service of the notice under section 81A above as is specified in the order.

(3) Subject to subsection (5) below, the instalments and interest, or any part of them, may be recovered from the owner or occupier for the time being of the premises.

(4) Any sums recovered from an occupier may be deducted by him from the rent of the premises.

(5) An occupier shall not be required to pay at any one time any sum greater than the aggregate of —

    (a)   the amount that was due from him on account of rent at the date on which he was served with a demand from the local authority together with a notice requiring him not to pay rent to his landlord without deducting the sum demanded, and

(b) the amount that has become due from him on account of rent since that date.

[(6) This section does not apply to Scotland.]¹]²

¹ words inserted by Environment Act 1995 c.25 Sch 17 Para 5
² added by Noise and Statutory Nuisance Act 1993 c.40 s 10 (2)

82 Summary proceedings by persons aggrieved by statutory nuisances.

(1) A magistrates' court may act under this section on a complaint [or, in Scotland, the sheriff may act under this section on a summary application,]¹made by any person on the ground that he is aggrieved by the existence of a statutory nuisance.

(2) If the magistrates' court [or, in Scotland, the sheriff]² is satisfied that the alleged nuisance exists, or that although abated it is likely to recur on the same premises [or, in the case of a nuisance within section 79(1)(ga) above, in the same street]³[or, in Scotland, road]⁴, the court [or the sheriff]⁵shall make an order for either or both of the following purposes —

(a) requiring the defendant [or, in Scotland, defender]⁶ to abate the nuisance, within a time specified in the order, and to execute any works necessary for that purpose;

(b) prohibiting a recurrence of the nuisance, and requiring the defendant [or defender]⁷, within a time specified in the order, to execute any works necessary to prevent the recurrence;

and [, in England and Wales,]⁸may also impose on the defendant a fine not exceeding level 5 on the standard scale.

(3) If the magistrates' court [or the sheriff]⁹is satisfied that the alleged nuisance exists and is such as, in the opinion of the court[or of the sheriff]⁹, to render premises unfit for human habitation, an order under subsection (2) above may prohibit the use of the premises for human habitation until the premises are, to the satisfaction of the court[or of the sheriff]⁹, rendered fit for that purpose.

(4) Proceedings for an order under subsection (2) above shall be brought —

(a) except in a case falling within [paragraph (b), (c) or (d) below]¹⁰, against the person responsible for the nuisance;

(b) where the nuisance arises from any defect of a structural character, against the owner of the premises;

(c) where the person responsible for the nuisance cannot be found, against the owner or occupier of the premises.

[(d) in the case of a statutory nuisance within section 79(1)(ga) above caused by noise emitted from or caused by an unattended vehicle or unattended machinery or equipment, against the person responsible for the vehicle, machinery or equipment.]¹¹

(5) [Subject to subsection (5A) below, where][12] more than one person is responsible for a statutory nuisance, subsections (1) to (4) above shall apply to each of those persons whether or not what any one of them is responsible for would by itself amount to a nuisance.

[(5A) In relation to a statutory nuisance within section 79(1)(ga) above for which more than one person is responsible (whether or not what any one of those persons is responsible for would by itself amount to a nuisance), subsection (4)(a) above shall apply with the substitution of "each person responsible for the nuisance who can be found" for "the person responsible for the nuisance".

(5B) In relation to a statutory nuisance within section 79(1)(ga) above caused by noise emitted from or caused by an unattended vehicle or unattended machinery or equipment for which more than one person is responsible, subsection (4)(d) above shall apply with the substitution of "any person" for "the person".][13]

(6) Before instituting proceedings for an order under subsection (2) above against any person, the person aggrieved by the nuisance shall give to that person such notice in writing of his intention to bring the proceedings as is applicable to proceedings in respect of a nuisance of that description and the notice shall specify the matter complained of.

(7) The notice of the bringing of proceedings in respect of a statutory nuisance required by subsection (6) above which is applicable is —

(a)   in the case of a nuisance falling within [paragraph (g) or (ga) of section 79(1)][14] above, not less than three days' notice; and
(b)   in the case of a nuisance of any other description, not less than twenty-one days' notice;

but the Secretary of State may, by order, provide that this subsection shall have effect as if such period as is specified in the order were the minimum period of notice applicable to any description of statutory nuisance specified in the order.

(8) A person who, without reasonable excuse, contravenes any requirement or prohibition imposed by an order under subsection (2) above shall be guilty of an offence and liable on summary conviction to a fine not exceeding level 5 on the standard scale together with a further fine of an amount equal to one-tenth of that level for each day on which the offence continues after the conviction.

(9) Subject to subsection (10) below, in any proceedings for an offence under subsection (8) above in respect of a statutory nuisance it shall be a defence to prove that the best practicable means were used to prevent, or to counteract the effects of, the nuisance.

(10) The defence under subsection (9) above is not available —

(a)   in the case of a nuisance falling within paragraph (a), (d), (e), (f) or (g) of section 79(1) above except where the nuisance arises on industrial, trade or business premises;
[(aa) in the case of a nuisance falling within paragraph (ga) of section

79(1) above except where the noise is emitted from or caused by a vehicle, machinery or equipment being used for industrial, trade or business purposes;.][15]

(b) in the case of a nuisance falling within paragraph (b) of section 79(1) above except where the smoke is emitted from a chimney;

(c) in the case of a nuisance falling within paragraph (c) or (h) of section 79(1) above; and

(d) in the case of a nuisance which is such as to render the premises unfit for human habitation.

(11) If a person is convicted of an offence under subsection (8) above, a magistrates' court [or the sheriff][16]may, after giving the local authority in whose area the nuisance has occurred an opportunity of being heard, direct the authority to do anything which the person convicted was required to do by the order to which the conviction relates.

(12) Where on the hearing of proceedings for an order under subsection (2) above it is proved that the alleged nuisance existed at the date of the making of the complaint [or summary application][17], then, whether or not at the date of the hearing it still exists or is likely to recur, the court [or the sheriff][17]shall order the [defendant or defender (or defendants or defenders][18] in such proportions as appears fair and reasonable) to pay to the person bringing the proceedings such amount as the court [or the sheriff][17] considers reasonably sufficient to compensate him for any expenses properly incurred by him in the proceedings.

(13) If it appears to the magistrates' court [or to the sheriff][19] that neither the person responsible for the nuisance nor the owner or occupier of the premises [or (as the case may be) the person responsible for the vehicle, machinery or equipment][20] can be found the court [or the sheriff][19] may, after giving the local authority in whose area the nuisance has occurred an opportunity of being heard, direct the authority to do anything which the court [or the sheriff][19] would have ordered that person to do.

[1] words inserted by Environment Act 1995 c.25 Sch 17 Para 6 (a)
[2] words inserted by Environment Act 1995 c.25 Sch 17 Para 6 (b) (i)
[3] Words inserted by Noise and Statutory Nuisance Act 1993 c.40 s 5 (2)
[4] words inserted by Environment Act 1995 c.25 Sch 17 Para 6 (b) (ii)
[5] words inserted by Environment Act 1995 c.25 Sch 17 Para 6 (b) (iii)
[6] words inserted by Environment Act 1995 c.25 Sch 17 Para 6 (b) (iv)
[7] words inserted by Environment Act 1995 c.25 Sch 17 Para 6 (b) (v)
[8] words inserted by Environment Act 1995 c.25 Sch 17 Para 6 (b) (vi)
[9] words inserted by Environment Act 1995 c.25 Sch 17 Para 6 (c)
[10] Words substituted by Noise and Statutory Nuisance Act 1993 c.40 s 5 (3) (a)
[11] added by Noise and Statutory Nuisance Act 1993 c.40 s 5 (3) (b)
[12] Words substituted by Noise and Statutory Nuisance Act 1993 c.40 s 5 (4)
[13] added by Noise and Statutory Nuisance Act 1993 c.40 s 5 (5)
[14] Words inserted by Noise and Statutory Nuisance Act 1993 c.40 s 5 (6)
[15] added by Noise and Statutory Nuisance Act 1993 c.40 s 5 (7)
[16] words inserted by Environment Act 1995 c.25 Sch 17 Para 6 (d)
[17] words inserted by Environment Act 1995 c.25 Sch 17 Para 6 (e)
[18] words substituted by Environment Act 1995 c.25 Sch 17 Para 6 (e)
[19] words inserted by Environment Act 1995 c.25 Sch 17 Para 6 (f)
[20] Words inserted by Noise and Statutory Nuisance Act 1993 c.40 s 5 (8)

PART IX

GENERAL

159 Application to Crown.

A1–010   (1) Subject to the provisions of this section, the provisions of this Act and of regulations and orders made under it shall bind the Crown.

(2) No contravention by the Crown of any provision of this Act or of any regulations or order made under it shall make the Crown criminally liable; but the High Court or, in Scotland, the Court of Session may, on the application of any public or local authority charged with enforcing that provision, declare unlawful any act or omission of the Crown which constitutes such a contravention.

(3) Notwithstanding anything in subsection (2) above, the provisions of this Act and of regulations and orders made under it shall apply to persons in the public service of the Crown as they apply to other persons.

(4) If the Secretary of State certifies that it appears to him, as respects any Crown premises and any powers of entry exercisable in relation to them specified in the certificate that it is requisite or expedient that, in the interests of national security, the powers should not be exercisable in relation to the premises, those powers shall not be exercisable in relation to those premises; and in this subsection "Crown premises" means premises held or used by or on behalf of the Crown.

(5) Nothing in this section shall be taken as in any way affecting Her Majesty in her private capacity; and this subsection shall be construed as if section 38(3) of the Crown Proceedings Act 1947 (interpretation of references in that Act to Her Majesty in her private capacity) were contained in this Act.

(6) References in this section to regulations or orders are references to regulations or orders made by statutory instrument.

(7) For the purposes of this section in its application to Part II and Part IV the authority charged with enforcing the provisions of those Parts in its area is —

(a)   in the case of Part II, any waste regulation authority, and
(b)   in the case of Part IV, any principal litter authority.

SCHEDULES

SCHEDULE 3

STATUTORY NUISANCES: SUPPLEMENTARY PROVISIONS

Section 81

Appeals to magistrates' court

1

(1) This paragraph applies in relation to appeals under section 80(3) against an abatement notice to a magistrates' court.

(2) An appeal to which this paragraph applies shall be by way of complaint for an order and the Magistrates' Courts Act 1980 shall apply to the proceedings.

(3) An appeal against any decision of a magistrates' court in pursuance of an appeal to which this paragraph applies shall lie to the Crown Court at the instance of any party to the proceedings in which the decision was given.

(4) The Secretary of State may make regulations as to appeals to which this paragraph applies and the regulations may in particular —

    (a)   include provisions comparable to those in section 290 of the Public Health Act 1936 (appeals against notices requiring the execution of works);

    (b)   prescribe the cases in which an abatement notice is, or is not, to be suspended until the appeal is decided, or until some other stage in the proceedings;

    (c)   prescribe the cases in which the decision on appeal may in some respects be less favourable to the appellant than the decision from which he is appealing;

    (d)   prescribe the cases in which the appellant may claim that an abatement notice should have been served on some other person and prescribe the procedure to be followed in those cases.

A1–011

Appeals to Sheriff

[1A

(1) This paragraph applies in relation to appeals to the sheriff under section 80(3) against an abatement notice.

(2) An appeal to which this paragraph applies shall be by way of a summary application.

(3) The Secretary of State may make regulations as to appeals to which this paragraph applies and the regulations may in particular include or prescribe any of the matters referred to in sub-paragraphs (4)(a) to (d) of paragraph 1 above.]¹

¹ added by Environment Act 1995 c.25 Sch 17 Para 7 (a)

Powers of entry etc

2

(1) Subject to sub-paragraph (2) below, any person authorised by a local authority may, on production (if so required) of his authority, enter any premises at any reasonable time —

    (a) for the purpose of ascertaining whether or not a statutory nuisance exists; or

    (b) for the purpose of taking any action, or executing any work, authorised or required by Part III.

(2) Admission by virtue of sub-paragraph (1) above to any premises used wholly or mainly for residential purposes shall not except in an emergency be demanded as of right unless twenty-four hours notice of the intended entry has been given to the occupier.

(3) If it is shown to the satisfaction of a justice of the peace on sworn information in writing —

    (a) that admission to any premises has been refused, or that refusal is apprehended, or that the premises are unoccupied or the occupier is temporarily absent, or that the case is one of emergency, or that an application for admission would defeat the object of the entry; and

    (b) that there is reasonable ground for entry into the premises for the purpose for which entry is required,

the justice may by warrant under his hand authorise the local authority by any authorised person to enter the premises, if need be by force.

(4) An authorised person entering any premises by virtue of sub-paragraph (1) or a warrant under sub-paragraph (3) above may —

    (a) take with him such other persons and such equipment as may be necessary;

    (b) carry out such inspections, measurements and tests as he considers necessary for the discharge of any of the local authority's functions under Part III; and

    (c) take away such samples or articles as he considers necessary for that purpose.

(5) On leaving any unoccupied premises which he has entered by virtue of sub-paragraph (1) above or a warrant under sub-paragraph (3) above the authorised person shall leave them as effectually secured against trespassers as he found them.

(6) A warrant issued in pursuance of sub-paragraph (3) above shall continue in force until the purpose for which the entry is required has been satisfied.

(7) Any reference in this paragraph to an emergency is a reference to a case where the person requiring entry has reasonable cause to believe that circumstances exist which are likely to endanger life or health and

that immediate entry is necessary to verify the existence of those circumstances or to ascertain their cause and to effect a remedy.

[(8) In the application of this paragraph to Scotland, a reference to a justice of the peace or to a justice includes a reference to the sheriff.][1]

[1] added by Environment Act 1995 c.25 Sch 17 Para 7 (b)

[2A

(1) Any person authorised by a local authority may on production (if so required) of his authority —

(a)   enter or open a vehicle, machinery or equipment, if necessary by force, or

(b)   remove a vehicle, machinery or equipment from a street [or, in Scotland, road][1]to a secure place,

for the purpose of taking any action, or executing any work, authorised by or required under Part III in relation to a statutory nuisance within section 79(1)(ga) above caused by noise emitted from or caused by the vehicle, machinery or equipment.

(2) On leaving any unattended vehicle, machinery or equipment that he has entered or opened under sub-paragraph (1) above, the authorised person shall (subject to sub-paragraph (3) below) leave it secured against interference or theft in such manner and as effectually as he found it.

(3) If the authorised person is unable to comply with sub-paragraph (2) above, he shall for the purpose of securing the unattended vehicle, machinery or equipment either —

(a)   immobilise it by such means as he considers expedient, or

(b)   remove it from the street to a secure place.

(4) In carrying out any function under sub-paragraph (1), (2) or (3) above, the authorised person shall not cause more damage than is necessary.

(5) Before a vehicle, machinery or equipment is entered, opened or removed under sub-paragraph (1) above, the local authority shall notify the police of the intention to take action under that sub-paragraph.

(6) After a vehicle, machinery or equipment has been removed under sub-paragraph (1) or (3) above, the local authority shall notify the police of its removal and current location.

(7) Notification under sub-paragraph (5) or (6) above may be given to the police at any police station in the local authority's area or, in the case of the Temples, at any police station of the City of London Police.

(8) For the purposes of section 81(4) above, any expenses reasonably incurred by a local authority under sub-paragraph (2) or (3) above shall be treated as incurred by the authority under section 81(3) above in abating or preventing the recurrence of the statutory nuisance in question.][2]

[1]   words inserted by Environment Act 1995 c.25 Sch 17 Para 7 (c)
[2]   added by Noise and Statutory Nuisance Act 1993 c.40 s 4 (5)

Offences relating to entry

3

(1) A person who wilfully obstructs any person acting in the exercise of any powers conferred by paragraph 2 above shall be liable, on summary conviction, to a fine not exceeding level 3 on the standard scale.[1][2]

(2) If a person discloses any information relating to any trade secret obtained in the exercise of any powers conferred by paragraph 2 above he shall, unless the disclosure was made in the performance of his duty or with the consent of the person having the right to disclose the information, be liable, on summary conviction, to a fine not exceeding level 5 on the standard scale.

[1] In relation to England and Wales:
   (1) A person who wilfully obstructs any person acting in the exercise of any powers conferred by paragraph 2 or 2A above shall be liable, on summary conviction, to a fine not exceeding level 3 on the standard scale.
[2] In relation to England and Wales only words inserted by Noise and Statutory Nuisance Act 1993 c.40 s 4 (6)

Default powers

4

(1) This paragraph applies to the following function of a local authority, that is to say its duty under section 79 to cause its area to be inspected to detect any statutory nuisance which ought to be dealt with under section 80 and its powers under paragraph 2 above.[1][2]

(2) If the Secretary of State is satisfied that any local authority has failed, in any respect, to discharge the function to which this paragraph applies which it ought to have discharged, he may make an order declaring the authority to be in default.

(3) An order made under sub-paragraph (2) above which declares an authority to be in default may, for the purpose of remedying the default, direct the authority ("the defaulting authority") to perform the function specified in the order and may specify the manner in which and the time or times within which the function is to be performed by the authority.

(4) If the defaulting authority fails to comply with any direction contained in such an order the Secretary of State may, instead of enforcing the order by mandamus, make an order transferring to himself the function of the authority specified in the order.

(5) Where the function of a defaulting authority is transferred under sub-paragraph (4) above, the amount of any expenses which the Secretary of State certifies were incurred by him in performing the function shall on demand be paid to him by the defaulting authority.

(6) Any expenses required to be paid by a defaulting authority under sub-paragraph (5) above shall be defrayed by the authority in like manner, and shall be debited to the like account, as if the function had not been transferred and the expenses had been incurred by the authority in performing them.

(7) The Secretary of State may by order vary or revoke any order previously made by him under this paragraph.

(8) Any order under this paragraph may include such incidental, supplemental and transitional provisions as the Secretary of State considers appropriate.

[(9) This paragraph does not apply to Scotland.][3]

[1] In relation to England and Wales:
(1) This paragraph applies to the following function of a local authority, that is to say its duty under section 79 to cause its area to be inspected to detect any statutory nuisance which ought to be dealt with under section 80 or sections 80 and 80A and its powers under paragraph 2 or 2A above.
[2] In relation to England and Wales only words inserted by subsections (a) and (b) by Noise and Statutory Nuisance Act 1993 c.40 s 4 (7)
[3] added by Environment Act 1995 c.25 Sch 17 Para 7 (d)

Protection from personal liability

5

Nothing done by, or by a member of, a local authority or by any officer of or other person authorised by a local authority shall, if done in good faith for the purpose of executing Part III, subject them or any of them personally to any action, liability, claim or demand whatsoever (other than any liability under [section 17 or 18 of the Audit Commission Act 1998][1] (powers of district auditor and court)).

[1] words substituted by Audit Commission Act 1998 c.18 Sch 3 Para 21

Statement of right of appeal in notices

6

Where an appeal against a notice served by a local authority lies to a magistrates' court [or, in Scotland, the sheriff][1]by virtue of section 80, it shall be the duty of the authority to include in such a notice a statement indicating that such an appeal lies as aforesaid and specifying the time within which it must be brought.

[1] words inserted by Environment Act 1995 c.25 Sch 17 Para 7 (e)

Criminal Justice and Public Order Act 1994

PART V

PUBLIC ORDER: COLLECTIVE TRESPASS OR NUISANCE ON LAND

Powers to remove trespassers on land

61 Power to remove trespassers on land.

A1–012   (1) If the senior police officer present at the scene reasonably believes that two or more persons are trespassing on land and are present there with the common purpose of residing there for any period, that reasonable steps have been taken by or on behalf of the occupier to ask them to leave and —

    (a)   that any of those persons has caused damage to the land or to property on the land or used threatening, abusive or insulting words or behaviour towards the occupier, a member of his family or an employee or agent of his, or

    (b)   that those persons have between them six or more vehicles on the land,

he may direct those persons, or any of them, to leave the land and to remove any vehicles or other property they have with them on the land.

(2) Where the persons in question are reasonably believed by the senior police officer to be persons who were not originally trespassers but have become trespassers on the land, the officer must reasonably believe that the other conditions specified in subsection (1) are satisfied after those persons became trespassers before he can exercise the power conferred by that subsection.

(3) A direction under subsection (1) above, if not communicated to the persons referred to in subsection (1) by the police officer giving the direction, may be communicated to them by any constable at the scene.

(4) If a person knowing that a direction under subsection (1) above has been given which applies to him —

    (a)   fails to leave the land as soon as reasonably practicable, or

    (b)   having left again enters the land as a trespasser within the period of three months beginning with the day on which the direction was given,

he commits an offence and is liable on summary conviction to imprisonment for a term not exceeding three months or a fine not exceeding level 4 on the standard scale, or both.

(5) A constable in uniform who reasonably suspects that a person is committing an offence under this section may arrest him without a warrant.

(6) In proceedings for an offence under this section it is a defence for the accused to show —

(a) that he was not trespassing on the land, or

(b) that he had a reasonable excuse for failing to leave the land as soon as reasonably practicable or, as the case may be, for again entering the land as a trespasser.

(7) In its application in England and Wales to common land this section has effect as if in the preceding subsections of it —

(a) references to trespassing or trespassers were references to acts and persons doing acts which constitute either a trespass as against the occupier or an infringement of the commoners' rights; and

(b) references to "the occupier" included the commoners or any of them or, in the case of common land to which the public has access, the local authority as well as any commoner.

(8) Subsection (7) above does not —

(a) require action by more than one occupier; or

(b) constitute persons trespassers as against any commoner or the local authority if they are permitted to be there by the other occupier.

(9) In this section —

"common land" means common land as defined in section 22 of the Commons Registration Act 1965;

"commoner" means a person with rights of common as defined in section 22 of the Commons Registration Act 1965;

"land" does not include —

(a) buildings other than —

(i) agricultural buildings within the meaning of, in England and Wales, paragraphs 3 to 8 of Schedule 5 to the Local Government Finance Act 1988 or, in Scotland, section 7(2) of the Valuation and Rating (Scotland) Act 1956, or

(ii) scheduled monuments within the meaning of the Ancient Monuments and Archaeological Areas Act 1979;

(b) land forming part of —

(i) a highway unless it falls within the classifications in section 54 of the Wildlife and Countryside Act 1981 (footpath, bridleway or byway open to all traffic or road used as a public path) or is a cycle track under the Highways Act 1980 or the Cycle Tracks Act 1984; or

(ii) a road within the meaning of the Roads (Scotland) Act 1984 unless it falls within the definitions in section 151(2)(a)(ii) or (b) (footpaths and cycle tracks) of that Act or is a bridleway within the meaning of section 47 of the Countryside (Scotland) Act 1967;

"the local authority", in relation to common land, means any local authority which has powers in relation to the land under section 9 of the Commons Registration Act 1965;

"occupier" (and in subsection (8) "the other occupier") means —

(a)   in England and Wales, the person entitled to possession of the land by virtue of an estate or interest held by him; and

(b)   in Scotland, the person lawfully entitled to natural possession of the land;

"property", in relation to damage to property on land, means —

(a)   in England and Wales, property within the meaning of section 10(1) of the Criminal Damage Act 1971; and

(b)   in Scotland, either —

(i)   heritable property other than land; or
(ii)   corporeal movable property,

and

"damage" includes the deposit of any substance capable of polluting the land;

"trespass" means, in the application of this section —

(a)   in England and Wales, subject to the extensions effected by subsection (7) above, trespass as against the occupier of the land;

(b)   in Scotland, entering, or as the case may be remaining on, land without lawful authority and without the occupier's consent; and

"trespassing" and "trespasser" shall be construed accordingly;

"vehicle" includes —

(a)   any vehicle, whether or not it is in a fit state for use on roads, and includes any chassis or body, with or without wheels, appearing to have formed part of such a vehicle, and any load carried by, and anything attached to, such a vehicle; and

(b)   a caravan as defined in section 29(1) of the Caravan Sites and Control of Development Act 1960;

and a person may be regarded for the purposes of this section as having a purpose of residing in a place notwithstanding that he has a home elsewhere.

62 Supplementary powers of seizure.

(1) If a direction has been given under section 61 and a constable reasonably suspects that any person to whom the direction applies has, without reasonable excuse —

- (a) failed to remove any vehicle on the land which appears to the constable to belong to him or to be in his possession or under his control; or
- (b) entered the land as a trespasser with a vehicle within the period of three months beginning with the day on which the direction was given,

the constable may seize and remove that vehicle.

(2) In this section "trespasser" and "vehicle" have the same meaning as in section 61.

Retention and charges for seized property

67 Retention and charges for seized property.

(1) Any vehicles which have been seized and removed by a constable under section 62(1) or 64(4) may be retained in accordance with regulations made by the Secretary of State under subsection (3) below.

(2) Any sound equipment which has been seized and removed by a constable under section 64(4) may be retained until the conclusion of proceedings against the person from whom it was seized for an offence under section 63.

(3) The Secretary of State may make regulations —

- (a) regulating the retention and safe keeping and the disposal and the destruction in prescribed circumstances of vehicles; and
- (b) prescribing charges in respect of the removal, retention, disposal and destruction of vehicles.

(4) Any authority shall be entitled to recover from a person from whom a vehicle has been seized such charges as may be prescribed in respect of the removal, retention, disposal and destruction of the vehicle by the authority.

(5) Regulations under subsection (3) above may make different provisions for different classes of vehicles or for different circumstances.

(6) Any charges under subsection (4) above shall be recoverable as a simple contract debt.

(7) Any authority having custody of vehicles under regulations under subsection (3) above shall be entitled to retain custody until any charges under subsection (4) are paid.

(8) The power to make regulations under subsection (3) above shall be exercisable by statutory instrument which shall be subject to annulment in pursuance of a resolution of either House of Parliament.

(9) In this section —

"conclusion of proceedings" against a person means —

    (a)   his being sentenced or otherwise dealt with for the offence or his acquittal;

    (b)   the discontinuance of the proceedings; or

    (c)   the decision not to prosecute him,

whichever is the earlier;

"sound equipment" has the same meaning as in section 64, and "vehicle" has the same meaning as in section 61.

Disruptive trespassers

68 Offence of aggravated trespass.

(1) A person commits the offence of aggravated trespass if he trespasses on land in the open air and, in relation to any lawful activity which persons are engaging in or are about to engage in on that or adjoining land in the open air, does there anything which is intended by him to have the effect —

    (a)   of intimidating those persons or any of them so as to deter them or any of them from engaging in that activity,

    (b)   of obstructing that activity, or

    (c)   of disrupting that activity.

(2) Activity on any occasion on the part of a person or persons on land is "lawful" for the purposes of this section if he or they may engage in the activity on the land on that occasion without committing an offence or trespassing on the land.

(3) A person guilty of an offence under this section is liable on summary conviction to imprisonment for a term not exceeding three months or a fine not exceeding level 4 on the standard scale, or both.

(4) A constable in uniform who reasonably suspects that a person is committing an offence under this section may arrest him without a warrant.

(5) In this section "land" does not include —

    (a)   the highways and roads excluded from the application of section 61 by paragraph (b) of the definition of land in subsection (9) of that section; or

    (b)   a road within the meaning of the Roads (Northern Ireland) Order 1993.

Squatters

75 Interim possession orders: false or misleading statements.

(1) A person commits an offence if, for the purpose of obtaining an interim possession order, he —

(a) makes a statement which he knows to be false or misleading in a material particular; or

(b) recklessly makes a statement which is false or misleading in a material particular.

(2) A person commits an offence if, for the purpose of resisting the making of an interim possession order, he —

(a) makes a statement which he knows to be false or misleading in a material particular; or

(b) recklessly makes a statement which is false or misleading in a material particular.

(3) A person guilty of an offence under this section shall be liable —

(a) on conviction on indictment, to imprisonment for a term not exceeding two years or a fine or both;

(b) on summary conviction, to imprisonment for a term not exceeding six months or a fine not exceeding the statutory maximum or both.

(4) In this section —

"interim possession order" means an interim possession order (so entitled) made under rules of court for the bringing of summary proceedings for possession of premises which are occupied by trespassers;

"premises" has the same meaning as in Part II of the Criminal Law Act 1977 (offences relating to entering and remaining on property); and

"statement", in relation to an interim possession order, means any statement, in writing or oral and whether as to fact or belief, made in or for the purposes of the proceedings.

76 Interim possession orders: trespassing during currency of order.

(1) This section applies where an interim possession order has been made in respect of any premises and served in accordance with rules of court; and references to "the order" and "the premises" shall be construed accordingly.

(2) Subject to subsection (3), a person who is present on the premises as a trespasser at any time during the currency of the order commits an offence.

(3) No offence under subsection (2) is committed by a person if —

(a) he leaves the premises within 24 hours of the time of service of the order and does not return; or

(b) a copy of the order was not fixed to the premises in accordance with rules of court.

(4) A person who was in occupation of the premises at the time of service of the order but leaves them commits an offence if he re-enters

the premises as a trespasser or attempts to do so after the expiry of the order but within the period of one year beginning with the day on which it was served.

(5) A person guilty of an offence under this section shall be liable on summary conviction to imprisonment for a term not exceeding six months or a fine not exceeding level 5 on the standard scale or both.

(6) A person who is in occupation of the premises at the time of service of the order shall be treated for the purposes of this section as being present as a trespasser.

(7) A constable in uniform may arrest without a warrant anyone who is, or whom he reasonably suspects to be, guilty of an offence under this section.

(8) In this section —

"interim possession order" has the same meaning as in section 75 above and "rules of court" is to be construed accordingly; and
"premises" has the same meaning as in that section that is to say the same meaning as in Part II of the Criminal Law Act 1977 (offences relating to entering and remaining on property).

Powers to remove unauthorised campers

77 Power of local authority to direct unauthorised campers to leave land.

(1) If it appears to a local authority that persons are for the time being residing in a vehicle or vehicles within that authority's area —

    (a) on any land forming part of a highway;
    (b) on any other unoccupied land; or
    (c) on any occupied land without the consent of the occupier,

the authority may give a direction that those persons and any others with them are to leave the land and remove the vehicle or vehicles and any other property they have with them on the land.

(2) Notice of a direction under subsection (1) must be served on the persons to whom the direction applies, but it shall be sufficient for this purpose for the direction to specify the land and (except where the direction applies to only one person) to be addressed to all occupants of the vehicles on the land, without naming them.

(3) If a person knowing that a direction under subsection (1) above has been given which applies to him —

    (a) fails, as soon as practicable, to leave the land or remove from the land any vehicle or other property which is the subject of the direction, or
    (b) having removed any such vehicle or property again enters the land with a vehicle within the period of three months beginning with the day on which the direction was given,

he commits an offence and is liable on summary conviction to a fine not exceeding level 3 on the standard scale.

(4) A direction under subsection (1) operates to require persons who re-enter the land within the said period with vehicles or other property to leave and remove the vehicles or other property as it operates in relation to the persons and vehicles or other property on the land when the direction was given.

(5) In proceedings for an offence under this section it is a defence for the accused to show that his failure to leave or to remove the vehicle or other property as soon as practicable or his re-entry with a vehicle was due to illness, mechanical breakdown or other immediate emergency.

(6) In this section —

"land" means land in the open air;
"local authority" means —

    (a)   in Greater London, a London borough or the Common Council of the City of London;
    (b)   in England outside Greater London, a county council, a district council or the Council of the Isles of Scilly;
    (c)   in Wales, a county council or a county borough council;

"occupier" means the person entitled to possession of the land by virtue of an estate or interest held by him;
"vehicle" includes —

    (a)   any vehicle, whether or not it is in a fit state for use on roads, and includes any body, with or without wheels, appearing to have formed part of such a vehicle, and any load carried by, and anything attached to, such a vehicle; and
    (b)   a caravan as defined in section 29(1) of the Caravan Sites and Control of Development Act 1960;

and a person may be regarded for the purposes of this section as residing on any land notwithstanding that he has a home elsewhere.

(7) Until 1st April 1996, in this section "local authority" means, in Wales, a county council or a district council.

78 Orders for removal of persons and their vehicles unlawfully on land.

(1) A magistrates' court may, on a complaint made by a local authority, if satisfied that persons and vehicles in which they are residing are present on land within that authority's area in contravention of a direction given under section 77, make an order requiring the removal of any vehicle or other property which is so present on the land and any person residing in it.

(2) An order under this section may authorise the local authority to take such steps as are reasonably necessary to ensure that the order is complied with and, in particular, may authorise the authority, by its officers and servants —

    (a)   to enter upon the land specified in the order; and

    (b)   to take, in relation to any vehicle or property to be removed in pursuance of the order, such steps for securing entry and rendering it suitable for removal as may be so specified.

(3) The local authority shall not enter upon any occupied land unless they have given to the owner and occupier at least 24 hours notice of their intention to do so, or unless after reasonable inquiries they are unable to ascertain their names and addresses.

(4) A person who wilfully obstructs any person in the exercise of any power conferred on him by an order under this section commits an offence and is liable on summary conviction to a fine not exceeding level 3 on the standard scale.

(5) Where a complaint is made under this section, a summons issued by the court requiring the person or persons to whom it is directed to appear before the court to answer to the complaint may be directed —

    (a)   to the occupant of a particular vehicle on the land in question; or

    (b)   to all occupants of vehicles on the land in question, without naming him or them.

(6) Section 55(2) of the Magistrates' Courts Act 1980 (warrant for arrest of defendant failing to appear) does not apply to proceedings on a complaint made under this section.

(7) Section 77(6) of this Act applies also for the interpretation of this section.

79   Provisions as to directions under s. 77 and orders under s. 78.

(1) The following provisions apply in relation to the service of notice of a direction under section 77 and of a summons under section 78, referred to in those provisions as a "relevant document".

(2) Where it is impracticable to serve a relevant document on a person named in it, the document shall be treated as duly served on him if a copy of it is fixed in a prominent place to the vehicle concerned; and where a relevant document is directed to the unnamed occupants of vehicles, it shall be treated as duly served on those occupants if a copy of it is fixed in a prominent place to every vehicle on the land in question at the time when service is thus effected.

(3) A local authority shall take such steps as may be reasonably practicable to secure that a copy of any relevant document is displayed on the land in question (otherwise than by being fixed to a vehicle) in a manner designed to ensure that it is likely to be seen by any person camping on the land.

(4) Notice of any relevant document shall be given by the local authority to the owner of the land in question and to any occupier of that land unless, after reasonable inquiries, the authority is unable to ascertain the name and address of the owner or occupier; and the owner of any such land and any occupier of such land shall be entitled to appear and to be heard in the proceedings.

(5) Section 77(6) applies also for the interpretation of this section.

Land Registration Act 2002

PART 9

ADVERSE POSSESSION

96 Disapplication of periods of limitation

A1–014   (1) No period of limitation under section 15 of the Limitation Act 1980 (c. 58) (time limits in relation to recovery of land) shall run against any person, other than a chargee, in relation to an estate in land or rentcharge the title to which is registered.

(2) No period of limitation under section 16 of that Act (time limits in relation to redemption of land) shall run against any person in relation to such an estate in land or rentcharge.

(3) Accordingly, section 17 of that Act (extinction of title on expiry of time limit) does not operate to extinguish the title of any person where, by virtue of this section, a period of limitation does not run against him.

97 Registration of adverse possessor

Schedule 6 (which makes provision about the registration of an adverse possessor of an estate in land or rentcharge) has effect.

98 Defences

(1) A person has a defence to an action for possession of land if —

(a)   on the day immediately preceding that on which the action was brought he was entitled to make an application under paragraph 1 of Schedule 6 to be registered as the proprietor of an estate in the land, and

(b)   had he made such an application on that day, the condition in paragraph 5(4) of that Schedule would have been satisfied.

(2) A judgment for possession of land ceases to be enforceable at the end of the period of two years beginning with the date of the judgment if the proceedings in which the judgment is given were commenced against a person who was at that time entitled to make an application under paragraph 1 of Schedule 6.

(3) A person has a defence to an action for possession of land if on the day immediately preceding that on which the action was brought he was entitled to make an application under paragraph 6 of Schedule 6 to be registered as the proprietor of an estate in the land.

(4) A judgment for possession of land ceases to be enforceable at the end of the period of two years beginning with the date of the judgment if, at the end of that period, the person against whom the judgment was given

is entitled to make an application under paragraph 6 of Schedule 6 to be registered as the proprietor of an estate in the land.

(5) Where in any proceedings a court determines that —

(a) a person is entitled to a defence under this section, or

(b) a judgment for possession has ceased to be enforceable against a person by virtue of subsection (4),

the court must order the registrar to register him as the proprietor of the estate in relation to which he is entitled to make an application under Schedule 6.

(6) The defences under this section are additional to any other defences a person may have.

(7) Rules may make provision to prohibit the recovery of rent due under a rentcharge from a person who has been in adverse possession of the rentcharge.

PART 12

MISCELLANEOUS AND GENERAL

Supplementary

132 General interpretation

(1) In this Act —

A1–015

"charge" means any mortgage, charge or lien for securing money or money's worth;

"land" includes —

(a) buildings and other structures,

(b) land covered with water, and

(c) mines and minerals, whether or not held with the surface;

"legal estate" has the same meaning as in the Law of Property Act 1925 (c. 20);

"registered" means entered in the register;

"registered charge" means a charge the title to which is entered in the register;

"registered estate" means a legal estate the title to which is entered in the register, other than a registered charge;

"registered land" means a registered estate or registered charge;

SCHEDULE 6

REGISTRATION OF ADVERSE POSSESSOR

Section 97

Right to apply for registration

1

A1–016   (1) A person may apply to the registrar to be registered as the proprietor of a registered estate in land if he has been in adverse possession of the estate for the period of ten years ending on the date of the application.

(2) A person may also apply to the registrar to be registered as the proprietor of a registered estate in land if —

    (a) he has in the period of six months ending on the date of the application ceased to be in adverse possession of the estate because of eviction by the registered proprietor, or a person claiming under the registered proprietor,

    (b) on the day before his eviction he was entitled to make an application under sub-paragraph (1), and

    (c) the eviction was not pursuant to a judgment for possession.

(3) However, a person may not make an application under this paragraph if —

    (a) he is a defendant in proceedings which involve asserting a right to possession of the land, or

    (b) judgment for possession of the land has been given against him in the last two years.

(4) For the purposes of sub-paragraph (1), the estate need not have been registered throughout the period of adverse possession.

Notification of application

2

(1) The registrar must give notice of an application under paragraph 1 to —

    (a) the proprietor of the estate to which the application relates,

    (b) the proprietor of any registered charge on the estate,

    (c) where the estate is leasehold, the proprietor of any superior registered estate,

    (d) any person who is registered in accordance with rules as a person to be notified under this paragraph, and

    (e) such other persons as rules may provide.

(2) Notice under this paragraph shall include notice of the effect of paragraph 4.

Treatment of application

3

(1) A person given notice under paragraph 2 may require that the application to which the notice relates be dealt with under paragraph 5.

(2) The right under this paragraph is exercisable by notice to the registrar given before the end of such period as rules may provide.

4

If an application under paragraph 1 is not required to be dealt with under paragraph 5, the applicant is entitled to be entered in the register as the new proprietor of the estate.

5

(1) If an application under paragraph 1 is required to be dealt with under this paragraph, the applicant is only entitled to be registered as the new proprietor of the estate if any of the following conditions is met.

(2) The first condition is that —

(a) it would be unconscionable because of an equity by estoppel for the registered proprietor to seek to dispossess the applicant, and

(b) the circumstances are such that the applicant ought to be registered as the proprietor.

(3) The second condition is that the applicant is for some other reason entitled to be registered as the proprietor of the estate.

(4) The third condition is that —

(a) the land to which the application relates is adjacent to land belonging to the applicant,

(b) the exact line of the boundary between the two has not been determined under rules under section 60,

(c) for at least ten years of the period of adverse possession ending on the date of the application, the applicant (or any predecessor in title) reasonably believed that the land to which the application relates belonged to him, and

(d) the estate to which the application relates was registered more than one year prior to the date of the application.

(5) In relation to an application under paragraph 1(2), this paragraph has effect as if the reference in sub-paragraph (4)(c) to the date of the application were to the day before the date of the applicant's eviction.

Right to make further application for registration

6

(1) Where a person's application under paragraph 1 is rejected, he may make a further application to be registered as the proprietor of the estate

if he is in adverse possession of the estate from the date of the application until the last day of the period of two years beginning with the date of its rejection.

(2) However, a person may not make an application under this paragraph if —

(a)   he is a defendant in proceedings which involve asserting a right to possession of the land,

(b)   judgment for possession of the land has been given against him in the last two years, or

(c)   he has been evicted from the land pursuant to a judgment for possession.

7

If a person makes an application under paragraph 6, he is entitled to be entered in the register as the new proprietor of the estate.

Restriction on applications

8

(1) No one may apply under this Schedule to be registered as the proprietor of an estate in land during, or before the end of twelve months after the end of, any period in which the existing registered proprietor is for the purposes of the Limitation (Enemies and War Prisoners) Act 1945 (8 & 9 Geo. 6 c. 16) —

(a)   an enemy, or

(b)   detained in enemy territory.

(2) No-one may apply under this Schedule to be registered as the proprietor of an estate in land during any period in which the existing registered proprietor is —

(a)   unable because of mental disability to make decisions about issues of the kind to which such an application would give rise, or

(b)   unable to communicate such decisions because of mental disability or physical impairment.

(3) For the purposes of sub-paragraph (2), "mental disability" means a disability or disorder of the mind or brain, whether permanent or temporary, which results in an impairment or disturbance of mental functioning.

(4) Where it appears to the registrar that sub-paragraph (1) or (2) applies in relation to an estate in land, he may include a note to that effect in the register.

Effect of registration

9

(1) Where a person is registered as the proprietor of an estate in land in pursuance of an application under this Schedule, the title by virtue of adverse possession which he had at the time of the application is extinguished.

(2) Subject to sub-paragraph (3), the registration of a person under this Schedule as the proprietor of an estate in land does not affect the priority of any interest affecting the estate.

(3) Subject to sub-paragraph (4), where a person is registered under this Schedule as the proprietor of an estate, the estate is vested in him free of any registered charge affecting the estate immediately before his registration.

(4) Sub-paragraph (3) does not apply where registration as proprietor is in pursuance of an application determined by reference to whether any of the conditions in paragraph 5 applies.

Apportionment and discharge of charges

10

(1) Where —

   (a) a registered estate continues to be subject to a charge notwithstanding the registration of a person under this Schedule as the proprietor, and

   (b) the charge affects property other than the estate,

the proprietor of the estate may require the chargee to apportion the amount secured by the charge at that time between the estate and the other property on the basis of their respective values.

(2) The person requiring the apportionment is entitled to a discharge of his estate from the charge on payment of —

   (a) the amount apportioned to the estate, and

   (b) the costs incurred by the chargee as a result of the apportionment.

(3) On a discharge under this paragraph, the liability of the chargor to the chargee is reduced by the amount apportioned to the estate.

(4) Rules may make provision about apportionment under this paragraph, in particular, provision about —

   (a) procedure,

   (b) valuation,

   (c) calculation of costs payable under sub-paragraph (2)(b), and

   (d) payment of the costs of the chargor.

Meaning of "adverse possession"

11

(1) A person is in adverse possession of an estate in land for the purposes of this Schedule if, but for section 96, a period of limitation under section 15 of the Limitation Act 1980 (c. 58) would run in his favour in relation to the estate.

(2) A person is also to be regarded for those purposes as having been in adverse possession of an estate in land —

    (a) where he is the successor in title to an estate in the land, during any period of adverse possession by a predecessor in title to that estate, or

    (b) during any period of adverse possession by another person which comes between, and is continuous with, periods of adverse possession of his own.

(3) In determining whether for the purposes of this paragraph a period of limitation would run under section 15 of the Limitation Act 1980, there are to be disregarded —

    (a) the commencement of any legal proceedings, and

    (b) paragraph 6 of Schedule 1 to that Act.

Trusts

12

A person is not to be regarded as being in adverse possession of an estate for the purposes of this Schedule at any time when the estate is subject to a trust, unless the interest of each of the beneficiaries in the estate is an interest in possession.

Crown foreshore

13

(1) Where —

    (a) a person is in adverse possession of an estate in land,

    (b) the estate belongs to Her Majesty in right of the Crown or the Duchy of Lancaster or to the Duchy of Cornwall, and

    (c) the land consists of foreshore,

paragraph 1(1) is to have effect as if the reference to ten years were to sixty years.

(2) For the purposes of sub-paragraph (1), land is to be treated as foreshore if it has been foreshore at any time in the previous ten years.

(3) In this paragraph, "foreshore" means the shore and bed of the sea and of any tidal water, below the line of the medium high tide between the spring and neap tides.

Rentcharges

14

Rules must make provision to apply the preceding provisions of this Schedule to registered rentcharges, subject to such modifications and exceptions as the rules may provide.

Procedure

15

Rules may make provision about the procedure to be followed pursuant to an application under this Schedule.

Appendix 2

Rules of Court

The Civil Procedure Rules 1998

PART 55

POSSESSION CLAIMS

[55.1 Interpretation

In this Part —   A2–001

- (a) "a possession claim" means a claim for the recovery of possession of land (including buildings or parts of buildings);
- (b) "a possession claim against trespassers" means a claim for the recovery of land which the claimant alleges is occupied only by a person or persons who entered or remained on the land without the consent of a person entitled to possession of that land but does not include a claim against a tenant or sub-tenant whether his tenancy has been terminated or not;
- (c) "mortgage" includes a legal or equitable mortgage and a legal or equitable charge and "mortgagee" is to be interpreted accordingly; and
- (d) "the 1988 Act" means the Housing Act 1988.][1]

[1] added by SI 2001/256 Sch 1 Para 1

I — GENERAL RULES

[55.2 Scope

(1) The procedure set out in this Section of this Part must be used where the claim includes —

- (a) a possession claim brought by a —
  - (i) landlord (or former landlord);
  - (ii) mortgagee; or
  - (iii) licensor (or former licensor);

    (b)   a possession claim against trespassers; or

    (c)   a claim by a tenant seeking relief from forfeiture.

(2) This Section of this Part —

    (a)   is subject to any enactment or practice direction which sets out special provisions with regard to any particular category of claim; and

    (b)   does not apply where the claimant uses the procedure set out in Section II of this Part.

(CCR Order 24, Rule 10(1) provides that where an application for an interim possession order is made, unless otherwise provided, Part 55 does not apply)][1]

[1]   added by SI 2001/256 Sch 1 Para 1

[55.3   Starting the claim

(1) The claim must be started in the county court for the district in which the land is situated unless paragraph (2) applies or an enactment provides otherwise.

(2) The claim may be started in the High Court if the claimant files with his claim form a certificate stating the reasons for bringing the claim in that court verified by a statement of truth in accordance with Rule 22.1(1).

(3) The practice direction refers to circumstances which may justify starting the claim in the High Court.

(4) Where, in a possession claim against trespassers, the claimant does not know the name of a person in occupation or possession of the land, the claim must be brought against "persons unknown" in addition to any named defendants.

(5) The claim form and form of defence sent with it must be in the forms set out in the relevant practice direction.][1]

[1]   added by SI 2001/256 Sch 1 Para 1

[55.4   Particulars of claim

The particulars of claim must be filed and served with the claim form.

(The relevant practice direction and Part 16 provide details about the contents of the particulars of claim)][1]

[1]   added by SI 2001/256 Sch 1 Para 1

[55.5   Hearing date

(1) The court will fix a date for the hearing when it issues the claim form.

(2) In a possession claim against trespassers the defendant must be served with the claim form, particulars of claim and any witness statements —

   (a)   in the case of residential property, not less than 5 days; and

   (b)   in the case of other land, not less than 2 days, before the hearing date.

(3) In all other possession claims —

   (a)   the hearing date will be not less than 28 days from the date of issue of the claim form;

   (b)   the standard period between the issue of the claim form and the hearing will be not more than 8 weeks; and

   (c)   the defendant must be served with the claim form and particulars of claim not less than 21 days before the hearing date.

(Rule 3.1(2)(a) provides that the court may extend or shorten the time for compliance with any Rule)][1]

[1]   added by SI 2001/256 Sch 1 Para 1

[55.6 Service of claims against trespassers

Where, in a possession claim against trespassers, the claim has been issued against "persons unknown", the claim form, particulars of claim and any witness statements must be served on those persons by —

   (a)   (i)   attaching copies of the claim form, particulars of claim and any witness statements to the main door or some other part of the land so that they are clearly visible; and

        (ii)   if practicable, inserting copies of those documents in a sealed transparent envelope addressed to "the occupiers" through the letter box; or

   (b)   placing stakes in the land in places where they are clearly visible and attaching to each stake copies of the claim form, particulars of claim and any witness statements in a sealed transparent envelope addressed to "the occupiers".][1]

[1]   added by SI 2001/256 Sch 1 Para 1

[55.7 Defendant's response

(1) An acknowledgment of service is not required and Part 10 does not apply.

(2) In a possession claim against trespassers rule 15.2 does not apply and the defendant need not file a defence.

(3) Where, in any other possession claim, the defendant does not file a defence within the time specified in rule 15.4, he may take part in any hearing but the court may take his failure to do so into account when deciding what order to make about costs.

(4) Part 12 (default judgment) does not apply in a claim to which this Part applies.][1]

[1]   added by SI 2001/256 Sch 1 Para 1

[55.8 The hearing

(1) At the hearing fixed in accordance with rule 55.5(1) or at any adjournment of that hearing, the court may —

    (a) decide the claim; or

    (b) give case management directions.

(2) Where the claim is genuinely disputed on grounds which appear to be substantial, case management directions given under paragraph (1)(b) will include the allocation of the claim to a track or directions to enable it to be allocated.

(3) Except where —

    (a) the claim is allocated to the fast track or the multi-track; or

    (b) the court orders otherwise,

any fact that needs to be proved by the evidence of witnesses at a hearing referred to in paragraph (1) may be proved by evidence in writing.

(Rule 32.2(1) sets out the general rule about evidence. Rule 32.2(2) provides that rule 32.2 (1) is subject to any provision to the contrary)

(4) Subject to paragraph (5), all witness statements must be filed and served at least 2 days before the hearing.

(5) In a possession claim against trespassers all witness statements on which the claimant intends to rely must be filed and served with the claim form.

(6) Where the claimant serves the claim form and particulars of claim, he must produce at the hearing a certificate of service of those documents and rule 6.14(2)(a) does not apply.][1]

[1] added by SI 2001/256 Sch 1 Para 1

[55.9 Allocation

(1) When the court decides the track for a possession claim, the matters to which it shall have regard include —

    (a) the matters set out in rule 26.8 as modified by the relevant practice direction;

    (b) the amount of any arrears of rent or mortgage instalments;

    (c) the importance to the defendant of retaining possession of the land; and

    (d) the importance of vacant possession to the claimant.

(2) The court will only allocate possession claims to the small claims track if all the parties agree.

(3) Where a possession claim has been allocated to the small claims track the claim shall be treated, for the purposes of costs, as if it were proceeding on the fast track except that trial costs shall be in the discretion of the court and shall not exceed the amount that would be recoverable under rule 46.2 (amount of fast track costs) if the value of the claim were up to £3,000.

(4) Where all the parties agree the court may, when it allocates the claim, order that rule 27.14 (costs on the small claims track) applies and, where it does so, paragraph (3) does not apply.][1]

[1] added by SI 2001/256 Sch 1 Para 1

[55.10 Possession claims relating to mortgaged residential property

(1) This rule applies where a mortgagee seeks possession of land which consists of or includes residential property.

(2) Not less than 14 days before the hearing the claimant must send a notice to the property addressed to "the occupiers".

(3) The notice referred to in paragraph (2) must —

(a) state that a possession claim for the property has started;

(b) show the name and address of the claimant, the defendant and the court which issued the claim form; and

(c) give details of the hearing.

(4) The claimant must produce at the hearing —

(a) a copy of the notice; and

(b) evidence that he has served it.][1]

[1] added by SI 2001/256 Sch 1 Para 1

II — Accelerated Possesion Claims of Property Let on an Assured Shorthold Tenancy

[55.11 When this section may be used

(1) The claimant may bring a possession claim under this Section of this Part where —

(a) the claim is brought under section 21 of the 1988 Act[1] to recover possession of residential property let under an assured short-hold tenancy; and

(b) all the conditions listed in rule 55.12 are satisfied.

(2) The claim must be started in the county court for the district in which the property is situated.][2]

[1] 1988 c. 50; Section 21 was amended by the Local Government and Housing Act 1989 (c. 42), section 194(1) and Schedule 11, paragraph 103 and by the Housing Act 1996 (c. 52), sections 98 and 99.
[2] added by SI 2001/256 Sch 1 Para 1

[55.12 Conditions

The conditions referred to in rule 55.11(1)(b) are that —

(a) the tenancy and any agreement for the tenancy were entered into on or after 15 January 1989;

(b) the only purpose of the claim is to recover possession of the property and no other claim is made;

(c) the tenancy did not immediately follow an assured tenancy which was not an assured shorthold tenancy;

(d) the tenancy fulfilled the conditions provided by section 19A or 20(1)(a) to (c) of the 1988 Act[1];

(e) the tenancy —

    (i) was the subject of a written agreement;

    (ii) arises by virtue of section 5 of the 1988 Act but follows a tenancy that was the subject of a written agreement; or

    (iii) relates to the same or substantially the same property let to the same tenant and on the same terms (though not necessarily as to rent or duration) as a tenancy which was the subject of a written agreement; and

(f) a notice in accordance with sections 21(1) or 21(4) of the 1988 Act[2] was given to the tenant in writing.][3]

[1] 1988 c. 50; Section 19A was inserted by the Housing Act 1996 (c. 52), section 96(1); section 20(1) was amended by section 104 and Schedule 8, paragraph 2(3) of that Act.

[2] 1988 c. 50; Section 21(1) and 21(4) were amended by the Housing Act 1996 (c. 52), section 98.

[3] added by SI 2001/256 Sch 1 Para 1

[55.13 Claim form

(1) The claim form must —

(a) be in the form set out in the relevant practice direction; and

(b)

    (i) contain such information; and

    (ii) be accompanied by such documents, as are required by that form.

(2) All relevant sections of the form must be completed.

(3) The court will serve the claim form by first class post.][1]

[1] added by SI 2001/256 Sch 1 Para 1

[55.14 Defence

(1) A defendant who wishes to —

(a) oppose the claim; or

(b) seek a postponement of possession in accordance with rule 55.18, must file his defence within 14 days after service of the claim form.

(2) The defence should be in the form set out in the relevant practice direction.][1]

[1] added by SI 2001/256 Sch 1 Para 1

[55.15 Claim referred to judge

(1) On receipt of the defence the court will —

(a) send a copy to the claimant; and

    (b)   refer the claim and defence to a judge.

(2) Where the period set out in rule 55.14 has expired without the defendant filing a defence —

    (a)   the claimant may file a written request for an order for possession; and
    (b)   the court will refer that request to a judge.

(3) Where the defence is received after the period set out in rule 55.14 has expired but before a request is filed in accordance with paragraph (2), paragraph (1) will still apply.
(4) Where —

    (a)   the period set out in rule 55.14 has expired without the defendant filing a defence; and
    (b)   the claimant has not made a request for an order for possession under paragraph (2) within 3 months after the expiry of the period set out in rule 55.14,

the claim will be stayed.][1]

[1]   added by SI 2001/256 Sch 1 Para 1

[55.16   Consideration of the claim

(1) After considering the claim and any defence, the judge will —

    (a)   make an order for possession under rule 55.17;
    (b)   where he is not satisfied as to any of the matters set out in paragraph (2) —
        (i)   direct that a date be fixed for a hearing; and
        (ii) give any appropriate case management directions; or
    (c)   strike out the claim if the claim form discloses no reasonable grounds for bringing the claim.

(2) The matters referred to in paragraph (1)(b) are that —

    (a)   the claim form was served; and
    (b)   the claimant has established that he is entitled to recover possession under section 21 of the 1988 Act against the defendant.

(3) The court will give all parties not less than 14 days' notice of a hearing fixed under paragraph (1)(b)(i).
(4) Where a claim is struck out under paragraph (1)(c) —

    (a)   the court will serve its reasons for striking out the claim with the order; and
    (b)   the claimant may apply to restore the claim within 28 days after the date the order was served on him.][1]

[1]   added by SI 2001/256 Sch 1 Para 1

[55.17   Possession order

Except where rules 55.16(1)(b) or (c) apply, the judge will make an order for possession without requiring the attendance of the parties.][1]

[1]   added by SI 2001/256 Sch 1 Para 1

[55.18   Postponement of possession

(1) Where the defendant seeks postponement of possession on the ground of exceptional hardship under section 89 of the Housing Act 1980, the judge may direct a hearing of that issue.

(2) Where the judge directs a hearing under paragraph (1) —

(a)   the hearing must be held before the date on which possession is to be given up; and

(b)   the judge will direct how many days' notice the parties must be given of that hearing.

(3) Where the judge is satisfied, on a hearing directed under paragraph (1), that exceptional hardship would be caused by requiring possession to be given up by the date in the order of possession, he may vary the date on which possession must be given up.][1]

[1]   added by SI 2001/256 Sch 1 Para 1

[55.19 Application to set aside or vary

The court may —

(a)   on application by a party within 14 days of service of the order; or

(b)   of its own initiative,

set aside or vary any order made under rule 55.17.][1]

[1]   added by SI 2001/256 Sch 1 Para 1

SCHEDULE 1

Rule 50(3)

RSC ORDER 113

SUMMARY PROCEEDINGS FOR POSSESSION OF LAND

A2–002   **Rule 1 [. . .][1] to Rule 6 [. . .][1]**

[1]   repealed by SI 2001/256 Sch 3 Para 1

Rule 7   Writ of possession

(1) Order 45, rule 3(2) shall not apply in relation to an order for possession [in a possession claim against trespassers under Part 55][1] but no writ of possession to enforce such an order shall be issued after the expiry of three

months from the date of the order without the permission of the Court. An application for permission may be made without notice being served on any other party unless the Court otherwise directs.

(2) The writ of possession shall be in Form No. 66A.

[1] words substituted by SI 2001/256 r 25

Rule 8 [. . .][1]

[1] repealed by SI 2001/256 Sch 3 Para 1

Schedule 2
Rule 50(4)

CCR Order 24

Summary Proceedings for the Recovery of Land

Part I — Land

Rule 1 [. . .][1] to Rule 5 [. . .][1]

A2–003

[1] repealed by SI 2001/256 Sch 3 Para 1

Rule 6 Warrant of possession

(1) Subject to paragraphs (2) and (3), a warrant of possession to enforce an order for possession [in a possession claim against trespassers under Part 55][1] may be issued at any time after the making of the order and subject to the provisions of Order 26, rule 17, a warrant of restitution may be issued in aid of the warrant of possession.

(2) No warrant of possession shall be issued after the expiry of 3 months from the date of the order without the permission of the court, and an application for such permission may be made without notice being served on any other party unless the court otherwise directs.

(3) Nothing in this rule shall authorise the issue of a warrant of possession before the date on which possession is ordered to be given.

[1] words substituted by SI 2001/256 r 27 (a).

Rule 7 [. . .][1]

[1] repealed by SI 2001/256 Sch 3 Para 1

Part II — Interim Possession Orders

Rule 8 Definitions and interpretation

A2–004

(1) In this Part of this Order–

(a) "applicant" means a person who applies for an interim possession order;

(b) "premises" means premises within the meaning of section 12 of the Criminal Law Act 1977; and

(c) "respondent" means a person against whom an application for an interim possession order is made, whether or not that person is named in the application or order.

(2) Where a rule in this Part of this Order requires an act to be done within a specified number of hours, CPR rule 2.8(4) shall not apply to the calculation of the period of time within which the act must be done.

Rule 9 Conditions for interim possession order application

In [a possession claim against trespassers under Part 55][1], an application may be made for an interim possession order where the following conditions are satisfied–

(a) the only claim made in the proceedings is for the recovery of premises;

(b) the claim is made by a person who–

(i) has an immediate right to possession of the premises; and

(ii) has had such a right throughout the period of unlawful occupation complained of;

(c) the claim is made against a person (not being a tenant holding over after the termination of the tenancy) who entered the premises without the applicant's consent and has not subsequently been granted such consent, but no application for an interim possession order may be made against a person who entered the premises with the consent of the person who, at the time of entry, had an immediate right to possession of the premises; and

(d) the claim is made within 28 days of the date on which the applicant first knew, or ought reasonably to have known, that the respondent, or any of the respondents, was in occupation.

[1] words substituted by SI 2001/256 r 27 (b)

Rule 10 Issue of the applications

(1) In proceedings in which an application for an interim possession order is made, unless otherwise provided, [Part 55][1] shall not apply.

(2) The applicant shall file–

(a) a claim form;

(b) a witness statement or affidavit in support; and

(c) an application notice,

each of which shall be in the appropriate prescribed form, together with sufficient copies for service on the respondent.

(3) The witness statement or affidavit shall be sworn by the applicant personally or, where the application for an interim possession order is made by a body corporate, shall be sworn by an officer of the body corporate duly authorised to swear the witness statement or affidavit on its behalf.

(4) On the filing of the documents mentioned in paragraph (2), the court shall–

(a) issue the claim form and the application for an interim possession order;

(b) fix an appointment for the application to be considered; and

(c) insert the time of that appointment in the application notice filed under paragraph (2) and in the copy to be served on the respondent.

(5) The time fixed for consideration of the application for an interim possession order shall be as soon as possible after the documents have been filed, but not less than 3 days after the date on which the application for an interim possession order is issued.

[1] words substituted by SI 2001/256 r 27 (c)

Rule 11   Service of the notice of application

(1) Within 24 hours of the issue of the application for an interim possession order, the applicant shall serve the following documents on the respondents, namely–

(a) the application notice; and

(b) the prescribed form of respondent's witness statement or affidavit, which shall be attached to the application notice.

(2) The applicant shall serve the documents mentioned in paragraph (1) by fixing a copy of them to the main door or other conspicuous part of the premises and, if practicable, inserting through the letter-box at the premises a copy of the documents in a sealed, transparent envelope addressed to "the occupiers".

(3) Additionally (but not alternatively), the applicant may place stakes in the ground at conspicuous parts of the premises to each of which shall be fixed a sealed transparent envelope addressed to "the occupiers" and containing a copy of the documents.

(4) At or before the time fixed for consideration of the application for an interim possession order, the applicant shall file a witness statement or affidavit of service in the prescribed form in relation to the documents mentioned in paragraph (1).

(5) At any time before the time fixed for consideration of the application for an interim possession order the respondent may file a witness statement or affidavit in the prescribed form in response to the application.

Rule 12   Consideration of the application

(1) If the respondent has filed a witness statement or affidavit in accordance with rule 11(5), he may attend before the court when the application for an interim possession order is considered to answer such

591

questions on his witness statement or affidavit or on the applicant's witness statement or affidavit as the court may put to him.

(2) The parties' witness statements or affidavits shall be read in evidence and no oral evidence shall be adduced except in response to questions put by the court.

(3) If the court so directs, an application for an interim possession order may be dealt with in private and in the absence of one or both of the parties.

(4) In deciding whether to grant an interim possession order the court shall have regard to whether the applicant has given or is prepared to give undertakings in support of his application–

(a) to reinstate the respondent if, after an interim possession order has been made, the court holds that the applicant was not entitled to the order;

(b) to pay damages if, after an interim possession order has been made, the court holds that the applicant was not entitled to the order;

(c) not to damage the premises pending final determination of the possession proceedings;

(d) not to grant a right of occupation to any other person pending final determination of the possession proceedings; and

(e) not to damage or dispose of any of the respondent's possessions pending final determination of the possession proceedings.

(5) The court shall make an interim possession order if–

(a) the applicant has filed a witness statement or affidavit of service of the notice of application; and

(b) the court is satisfied that–

(i) the conditions specified in rule 9 are met; and

(ii) any undertakings given by the applicant as a condition of making the order are adequate.

(6) An interim possession order shall be in a prescribed form and shall be to the effect that the respondent vacate the premises specified in the claim form within 24 hours of service of the order.

(7) On the making of an interim possession order, the court shall fix a return date for the hearing of the claim which shall be not less than 7 days after the date on which the interim possession order is made.

(8) Where an interim possession order is made, the court officer shall submit a draft of the order as soon as possible to the judge or district judge by whom it was made for approval, and when the draft order has been approved the court shall insert in the order the time limit for service under rule 13(1).

(9) Where the court does not make an interim possession order–

(a) the court officer shall fix a return date for the hearing of the claim;

(b) the court may give directions for the further conduct of the matter; and

(c) subject to such directions, the matter shall proceed in accordance with [Part 55][1].

(10) When it has considered the application for an interim possession order, the court shall give a copy of the respondent's witness statement or affidavit (if any) to the applicant, if the applicant requests such a copy.

(11) The court shall serve any directions made under paragraph (9) on the parties and at the same time shall serve on the respondent a copy of the claim form and witness statement or affidavit in support.

[1] words substituted by SI 2001/256 r 27 (d)

Rule 13 Service and enforcement of the interim possession order

(1) An interim possession order must be served within 48 hours of the judge or district judge's approving the draft order under rule 12(8).

(2) The applicant shall serve copies of the claim form, the applicant's witness statement or affidavit and the interim possession order in accordance with rule 11(2) and (3) or in such other manner as the court may direct.

(3) Order 26, rule 17 (enforcement of warrant of possession) shall not apply to the enforcement of an interim possession order.

(4) If an interim possession order is not served within the time limit specified by this rule or by any order extending or abridging time, the applicant may apply to the court for directions for the application for possession to continue under [Part 55][1] as if it had not included a claim for an interim possession order.

[1] words substituted by SI 2001/256 r 27 (d)

Rule 14 Matters arising after making of an interim possession order

(1) Before the return date the applicant shall file a witness statement or affidavit of service in the prescribed form in relation to the documents specified in rule 13(2), and no final order for possession may be made unless such a witness statement or affidavit has been filed.

(2) The interim possession order shall expire on the return date.

(3) On the return date the court may make such order as appears appropriate and may in particular–

(a) make a final order for possession;
(b) dismiss the claim for possession;
(c) give directions for the application for possession to continue under [Part 55][1] as if it had not included a claim for an interim possession order.

(4) An order may be made on the return date in the absence of one or both of the parties.

(5) If the court holds that the applicant was not entitled to an interim possession order, the respondent may apply for relief pursuant to any undertakings given by the applicant.

(6) Unless it otherwise directs, the court shall serve a copy of any order or directions made under this rule on the parties.

(7) Unless the court otherwise directs, service on the respondent under paragraph (6) shall be in accordance with rule 11(2) and (3).

(8) Rule 6 (warrant of possession) shall apply to the enforcement of a final order for possession made under this rule.

[1] words substituted by SI 2001/256 r 27 (d)

Rule 15   Application to set aside an interim possession order

(1) If the respondent has vacated the premises, he may apply on grounds of urgency for the interim possession order to be set aside before the return date.

(2) An application under this rule shall be supported by a witness statement or affidavit.

(3) On receipt of an application to set aside, the judge or district judge shall give directions as to–

  (a)   the date for the hearing; and
  (b)   the period of notice, if any, to be given to the applicant and the mode of service of any such notice.

(4) No application to set aside an interim possession order may be made under CPR Part 39.3.

(5) Where no notice is required under paragraph (3)(b), the only matter to be dealt with at the hearing shall be whether the interim possession order should be set aside (and the consequent application of any undertaking given under rule 12(4)(a)) and all other matters shall be dealt with on the return date.

(6) The court shall serve on the applicant a copy of any order made under paragraph (5) and, where no notice is required under paragraph (3)(b), the court shall at the same time serve a copy of the respondent's application to set aside and the witness statement or affidavit in support.

(7) Where notice is required under paragraph (3)(b), the court may treat the application as an application to bring forward the return date, in which case rule 14(2) to (8) shall apply accordingly.

55PD.1

A2–005   **Practice Direction — Possession Claims**

This Practice Direction supplements Part 55

Section I

General Rules

55.3   Starting the claim

1.1   Except where the county court does not have jurisdiction, possession claims should normally be brought in the county court. Only exceptional circumstances justify starting a claim in the High Court.

1.2   If a claimant starts a claim in the High Court and the court decides that it should have been started in the county court, the court will normally either strike the claim out or transfer it to the county court on its own initiative. This is likely to result in delay and the court will normally disallow the costs of starting the claim in the High Court and any transfer.

1.3   Circumstances which may, in an appropriate case, justify starting a claim in the High Court are if -
    (1) there are complicated disputes of fact;
    (2) there are points of law of general importance; or
    (3) the claim is against trespassers and there is a substantial risk of public disturbance or of serious harm to persons or property which properly require immediate determination.

1.4   The value of the property and the amount of any financial claim may be relevant circumstances, but these factors alone will not normally justify starting the claim in the High Court.

1.5   The claimant must use the appropriate claim form and particulars of claim form set out in Table 1 to Part 4 Practice Direction. The defence must be in form *N11*, *N11B*, *N11M* or *N11R*, as appropriate.

1.6   High Court claims for the possession of land subject to a mortgage will be assigned to the Chancery Division.

55.4   Particulars of claim

2.1   In a possession claim the particulars of claim must:
    (1) identify the land to which the claim relates;
    (2) state whether the claim relates to residential property;
    (3) state the ground on which possession is claimed;
    (4) give full details about any mortgage or tenancy agreement; and
    (5) give details of every person who, to the best of the claimant's knowledge, is in possession of the property.

2.2   Residential property let on a tenancy

Paragraphs 2.3 and 2.4 apply if the claim relates to residential property let on a tenancy.

2.3   If the claim includes a claim for non-payment of rent the particulars of claim must set out:
    (1) the amount of due at the start of the proceedings;
    (2) in schedule form, the dates when the arrears of rent arose, all

amounts of rent due, the dates and amounts of all payments made and a running total of the arrears;

(3) the daily rate of any rent and interest;

(4) any previous steps taken to recover the arrears of rent with full details of any court proceedings; and

(5) any relevant information about the defendant's circumstances, in particular:

(a) whether the defendant is in receipt of social security benefits; and

(b) whether any payments are made on his behalf directly to the claimant under the Social Security Contributions and Benefits Act 1992.

2.4   If the claimant know of any person (including a mortgagee) entitled to claim relief against forfeiture as underlessee under *section 146(4)of the Law of Property Act 1925(or in accordance withsection 38of the Supreme Court Act 1981*, or *section 138(9C)of the County Courts Act 1984):*

(1) the particulars of claim must state the name and address of that person; and

(2) the claimant must file a copy of the particulars of claim for service on him.

2.5   Land subject to mortgage

If the claim is a possession claim by a mortgagee, the particulars of claim must also set out:

(1) if the claim relates to residential property whether:

(a) a land charge of Class F has been registered under section 2(7)of the Matrimonial Homes Act 1967;

(b) a notice registered under *section 2(8)or 8(3) of the Matrimonial Homes Act 1983* has been entered and on whose behalf; or

(c) a notice under *section 31(10) of the Family Law Act 1996* has been registered and on whose behalf; and

if so, that the claimant will serve notice of the claim on the persons on whose behalf the land charge is registered or the notice or caution entered.

(2) the state of the mortgage account by including:

(a) the amount of:

(i)   the advance;

(ii) any periodic repayment; and

(iii) any payment of interest required to be made;

(b) the amount which would have to be paid (after taking into account any adjustment for early settlement) in order to redeem the mortgage at a stated date not more than 14 days after the claim started specifying the amount of solicitor's costs and administration charges which would be payable;

    (c)   if the loan which is secured by the mortgage is a regulated consumer credit agreement, the total amount outstanding under the terms of the mortgage; and

    (d)   the rate of interest payable:

        (i)   at the commencement of the mortgage;

        (ii)   immediately before any arrears referred to in paragraph (3) accrued;

        (iii) at the commencement of the proceedings.

(3) if the claim is brought because of failure to pay the periodic payments when due:

    (a)   in schedule form, the dates when the arrears arose, all amounts due, the dates and amounts of all payments made and a running total of the arrears;

    (b)   give details of:

        (i)   any other payments required to be made as a term of the mortgage (such as for insurance premiums, legal costs, default interest, penalties, administrative or other charges);

        (ii)   any other sums claimed and stating the nature and amount of each such charge; and

        (iii) whether any of these payments is in arrears and whether or not it is included in the amount of any periodic payment.

(4) whether or not the loan which is secured by the mortgage is a regulated consumer credit agreement and, if so, specify the date on which any notice required by *sections 76 or 87 of the Consumer Credit Act 1974* was given;

(5) if appropriate details that show the property is not one to which *section 141 of the Consumer Credit Act 1974*applies;

(6) any relevant information about the defendant's circumstances, in particular;

    (a)   whether the defendant is in receipt of social security benefits; and

    (b)   whether any payments are made on his behalf directly to the claimant under the Social Security Contributions and Benefits Act 1992;

(7) give details of any tenancy entered into between the mortgagor and mortgagee (including any notices served); and

(8) state any previous steps which the claimant has taken to recover the money secured by the mortgage or the mortgaged property and, in the case of court proceedings, state:

    (a)   the dates when the claim started and concluded; and

    (b)   the dates and terms of any orders made.

Possession claim against trespassers

2.6   If the claim is a possession claim against trespassers, the particulars of claim must state the claimant's interest in the land or the basis of his right to claim possession and the circumstances in which it has been occupied without licence or consent.

55.5   Hearing date

3.1   Particular consideration should be given to the exercise of power if:
   (1) the defendant, or a person for whom the defendant is responsible, has assaulted or threatened to assault:

   (a)   the claimant;
   (b)   a member of the claimant's staff; and
   (c)   another resident in the locality;

   (2) there are reasonable grounds for fearing such an assault; or
   (3) the defendant, or a person for whom the defendant is responsible, has caused serious damage or threatened to cause serious damage to the property or to the home or property of another resident in the locality.

3.3   Where paragraph 2 applies but the case cannot be determined at the first hearing fixed under *rule 55.5*, the court will consider what steps are needed to finally determine the case as quickly as reasonably practicable.

55.6   Service in claims against trespassers

4.1   If the claim form is to be served by the court and in accordance with *rule 55.6(b)*the claimant must provide sufficient stakes and transparent envelopes.

55.8   Hearing

5.1   Attention is drawn to *rule 55.8(3)*. Each party should wherever possible include all the evidence he wishes to present in his statement of case, verified by a statement of truth.

5.2   If relevant the claimant's evidence should include the amount of any rent or mortgage arrears and interest on those arrears. These amounts should, if possible, be up to date of the hearing (if necessary by specifying a daily rate of arrears and interest). However, *rule 55.8(4)*does not prevent such evidence being brought up to date orally or in writing on the day of the hearing if necessary.

5.3   If relevant the defendant should give evidence of:
   (1) the amount of any outstanding social security or housing benefit payments relevant to rent or mortgage arrears; and

(2) the status of:

   (a)   any claims for social security or housing benefit about which a decision has not yet been made; and

   (b)   any applications to appeal or review a social security or housing benefit decision where that appeal or review has not yet concluded.

5.4   If:

(1) the maker of a witness statement does not attend the hearing; and

(2) the other party disputed material evidence contained in his statement,

 the court will normally adjourn the hearing so that oral evidence can be given.

5.5   Evidence in mortgage possession claim

Attention is drawn to *section 113 of the Land Registration Act 1925*which provides that office copies of the register and of documents filed in the Land Registry, including original charges, are admissible in evidence to the same extent as the originals.

55.9   Allocation

6.1   The financial value of the property will not necessarily be the most important factor in deciding the track for a possession claim and the court may direct a possession claim to be allocated to the fast track even though the value of the property is in excess of £15,000.

Consumer credit act claims relating to the recovery of land

7.1   Any application by the defendant for a time order under *section 129of the Consumer Credit Act 1974* may be made:

(1) in his defence; or

(2) by application notice in the proceedings.

[section 11 omitted]

Index

(References are to paragraph numbers)